Handbook of Research on Teaching Strategies for Culturally and Linguistically Diverse International Students

Clayton Smith
University of Windsor, Canada

George Zhou
University of Windsor, Canada

A volume in the Advances in Educational
Technologies and Instructional Design (AETID)
Book Series

Published in the United States of America by
IGI Global
Information Science Reference (an imprint of IGI Global)
701 E. Chocolate Avenue
Hershey PA, USA 17033
Tel: 717-533-8845
Fax: 717-533-8661
E-mail: cust@igi-global.com
Web site: http://www.igi-global.com

Library of Congress Cataloging-in-Publication Data

Names: Smith, Clayton, 1959- editor. | Zhou, George, 1967- editor.
Title: Handbook of research on teaching strategies for culturally and linguistically
    diverse international students / Clayton Smith and George Zhou, Editor.
Description: Hershey, PA : Information Science Reference, [2022] | Includes
    bibliographical references and index. | Summary: "This book explores the
    promising practices for teaching linguistically and culturally diverse
    international students within post-secondary educational institutions"--
    Provided by publisher.
Identifiers: LCCN 2021051179 (print) | LCCN 2021051180 (ebook) | ISBN
    9781799889212 (hardcover) | ISBN 9781799889236 (ebook)
Subjects: LCSH: Teacher effectiveness. | Multicultural education. | Foreign
    students--Social conditions.
Classification: LCC LB1025.3 .S853 2022 (print) | LCC LB1025.3 (ebook) |
    DDC 371.102--dc23/eng/20211104
LC record available at https://lccn.loc.gov/2021051179
LC ebook record available at https://lccn.loc.gov/2021051180

This book is published in the IGI Global book series Advances in Educational Technologies and Instructional Design (AE-
TID) (ISSN: 2326-8905; eISSN: 2326-8913)

British Cataloguing in Publication Data
A Cataloguing in Publication record for this book is available from the British Library.

All work contributed to this book is new, previously-unpublished material. The views expressed in this book are those of the
authors, but not necessarily of the publisher.

For electronic access to this publication, please contact: eresources@igi-global.com.

Advances in Educational Technologies and Instructional Design (AETID) Book Series

Lawrence A. Tomei
Robert Morris University, USA

ISSN:2326-8905
EISSN:2326-8913

MISSION

Education has undergone, and continues to undergo, immense changes in the way it is enacted and distributed to both child and adult learners. In modern education, the traditional classroom learning experience has evolved to include technological resources and to provide online classroom opportunities to students of all ages regardless of their geographical locations. From distance education, Massive-Open-Online-Courses (MOOCs), and electronic tablets in the classroom, technology is now an integral part of learning and is also affecting the way educators communicate information to students.

The **Advances in Educational Technologies & Instructional Design (AETID) Book Series** explores new research and theories for facilitating learning and improving educational performance utilizing technological processes and resources. The series examines technologies that can be integrated into K-12 classrooms to improve skills and learning abilities in all subjects including STEM education and language learning. Additionally, it studies the emergence of fully online classrooms for young and adult learners alike, and the communication and accountability challenges that can arise. Trending topics that are covered include adaptive learning, game-based learning, virtual school environments, and social media effects. School administrators, educators, academicians, researchers, and students will find this series to be an excellent resource for the effective design and implementation of learning technologies in their classes.

COVERAGE

- Virtual School Environments
- Instructional Design
- Instructional Design Models
- Classroom Response Systems
- E-Learning
- Higher Education Technologies
- Collaboration Tools
- Web 2.0 and Education
- Educational Telecommunications
- Online Media in Classrooms

IGI Global is currently accepting manuscripts for publication within this series. To submit a proposal for a volume in this series, please contact our Acquisition Editors at Acquisitions@igi-global.com or visit: http://www.igi-global.com/publish/.

The Advances in Educational Technologies and Instructional Design (AETID) Book Series (ISSN 2326-8905) is published by IGI Global, 701 E. Chocolate Avenue, Hershey, PA 17033-1240, USA, www.igi-global.com. This series is composed of titles available for purchase individually; each title is edited to be contextually exclusive from any other title within the series. For pricing and ordering information please visit http://www.igi-global.com/book-series/advances-educational-technologies-instructional-design/73678. Postmaster: Send all address changes to above address. © © 2022 IGI Global. All rights, including translation in other languages reserved by the publisher. No part of this series may be reproduced or used in any form or by any means – graphics, electronic, or mechanical, including photocopying, recording, taping, or information and retrieval systems – without written permission from the publisher, except for non commercial, educational use, including classroom teaching purposes. The views expressed in this series are those of the authors, but not necessarily of IGI Global.

Titles in this Series

For a list of additional titles in this series, please visit: www.igi-global.com/book-series

701 East Chocolate Avenue, Hershey, PA 17033, USA
Tel: 717-533-8845 x100 • Fax: 717-533-8661
E-Mail: cust@igi-global.com • www.igi-global.com

List of Contributors

Table of Contents

Section 5
Online Teaching and Learning

Detailed Table of Contents

Section 1
Introduction

Chapter 1
    Clayton Smith, University of Windsor, Canada
    George Zhou, University of Windsor, Canada

This chapter describes three studies that explore promising teaching practices for teaching linguistically
and culturally-diverse international students by identifying teaching practices that have high levels of
international student satisfaction and student perceptions of learning. The first study, using a mixed-
methods approach, found eight teaching practice areas that resonated with students. The second study,
using a qualitative approach, identified similarities and dissimilarities between STEM and non-STEM
students. The third study, using a qualitative approach, uncovered student preferences for online teaching
practices. Recommendations for professional practice are discussed, along with potential areas for further
research.

Section 2
Promising Practices for Teaching International Students

Chapter 2
    Rahul Kumar, Brock University, Canada
    Clinton Kewley, Brock University, Canada

Pre-pandemic Canadian universities relied on international student enrolment to generate revenue and
instill beneficial internationalization on Canadian campuses. As the pandemic disrupted established
pedagogical practices and international students' on-campus participation, how international programs
are delivered has been re-envisioned and recalibrated. Initially, changes in teaching and learning were
reactionary and predicated on available resources, often laden with problems identified in OCUFA
findings. Upon careful examination and reflection of current practices in Ontario universities, the authors
developed a framework derived from policy literature that examines international program delivery from

pedagogical, technological, and operational standpoints. The proposed framework can be applied in planning and evaluating universities' international program activities, near or far, mediated by technology or not, and applicable beyond the pandemic.

Chapter 3

Gideon Boadu, Excelsia College, Australia
Peninah Kansiime, Excelsia College, Australia
Sarah Eyaa, Alphacrucis University College, Australia
Shannon Said, Excelsia College, Australia

As higher education providers (HEPs) across the globe continue to recruit international students to improve their financial and diversity profiles, it is critical that sufficient effort is made to integrate cultural responsiveness across institutional systems with the goal of creating a good experience for these students. This critical collaborative reflection study is positioned within Fook's critical reflection framework. The authors story their experiences as international students in Australia and reflect on how such experiences have influenced their work as academics. The stories weave together to identify critical issues such as positive relationships, empathetic understanding, and sensitive pedagogies that are relevant in the pursuit of culturally responsive education in higher education institutions.

Chapter 4

James Alan Oloo, University of Windsor, Canada

Canada is among the top four most popular destinations for international students. Using narrative inquiry, this chapter explores lived experiences of two international students. The study is guided by three broad questions: 1) What are the main positive experiences of international students in Canada? 2) What are some of the challenges faced by international students during their studies in Canada? and 3) What should be done to enhance academic success of international students? Data were collected using semi-structured interviews as conversations. Data analysis reveals three main themes: mismatch between the students' academic expectations and reality, challenges relating to language, and self-efficacy and resilience. Recommendations are presented. These include working with international students to help identify factors that are likely to enhance the success of international students as identified by the students so that universities can create campus environments that allow for success.

Chapter 5

George Kofi Amoako, Ghana Communication Technology University, Ghana

The purpose of this research is to find out how teaching philosophy and curriculum design can affect graduates' employability skills. In the same way, university survival also depends on how well graduates perform in the workplace. Teaching philosophy affects curriculum design which in turn could affect employability. Higher education teachers and administrators' awareness of these variables and how they interplay could enhance student employability skills. Qualitative methodology was used in this research to investigate the relationship between teaching philosophy, curriculum design, and employability skills. The data for the study were sampled from both public and private universities in Ghana. The population size for the study was 12 respondents.

Chapter 6

Hangyu Zhang, University of Melbourne, Australia
Chenyang Zhang, University of Melbourne, Australia
Hanshu Wang, Monash University, Australia

This chapter aims to investigate teaching strategies aimed at enhancing Chinese international students' effective verbal communication in Australian universities. To do so, this study applies collective autoethnography to give the chance to the three authors (who are themselves Chinese students) to narrate their stories. Based on their experiences, this study builds a conceptual framework based on Bandura's triadic reciprocal determinism to explore the triadic reciprocal interaction between verbal communication, self-realization, and teaching and learning environment. Then, thematic analysis is applied to explore the diversities and similarities of their experiences in terms of the three elements/themes. By analyzing and examining each theme, this chapter uncovers the dynamic and reciprocal interrelationships between them on the basis of the three authors' voices, providing suggestions for further improvement on teaching strategies for international students' verbal communication.

Chapter 7

Cezar Scarlat, University "Politehnica" of Bucharest, Romania

This chapter shares the author's experience of teaching Project Management to diverse international students at three European universities. Besides didactic and technical challenges, there also were cultural and linguistic diversity challenges to be addressed. Working in small teams was a solution to better understand differences, encouraging intercultural communication. Specifically, the chapter is focused on particular aspects of the educational process: a single course (Project Management) and a single instrument used as teaching aid: proverbs as illustrative examples while teaching the abstract principles of project management. Although the use of proverbs for moral education is old and universal, their use while teaching abstract concepts of scientific management—as project management principles—is a premiere. The lessons learnt as result of the author's teaching experience and studies on the management meaning of proverbs, in different cultural and linguistic environments, open research avenues for further comparative, cross-, and inter-cultural studies.

Chapter 8

Syed Ali Nasir Zaidi, St. Clair College for AA&T, Canada

Although most Canadian university and college professors assume that international testing credentials such as IELTS, TOEFL, and CELPIP are suitable yardsticks to measure international students' language skills, the study presented in this chapter that adopted critical discourse analysis of international students' technical assignments suggests otherwise. Technical communication is different from cultural English, whereby the former measures students' technical skills in communicating highly scientific materials and cultural English may be used for interpersonal skills. The study used secondary data for data analysis and employed Bernstein's theoretical lens of elaborated code and restricted code. Findings revealed that 21st-century knowledge production, distribution, and its adequate reproduction are in the hands of well-rounded knowledge consumers in knowledge societies, and if the knowledge consumers are not well cognizant of their instrumental role in the knowledge economy owing to weak English language constructions, social inequalities will increase exponentially.

Section 3
Teaching About Academic Integrity

Chapter 9

Lilach Marom, Kwantlen Polytechnic University, Canada

This chapter focuses on the concept of plagiarism through a case study of Punjabi international students (PS) in Canadian higher education. While plagiarism by international students is often seen as a sign of deficiency and a lack of academic abilities, this chapter aims to conceptualize and contextualize the phenomenon of plagiarism. The quick association of international students with cases of plagiarism overlooks structural and academic barriers that push some students to commit plagiarism. This chapter also distinguishes between unintentional and intentional plagiarism; while the first is often rooted in academic and language barriers, the second reflects wider structural barriers. Understanding the factors underlying plagiarism can help institutions provide relevant support for international students rather than invest in increased surveillance mechanisms.

Chapter 10

Phoebe Eunkyung Kang, Ontario Institute for Studies in Education, Canada & University of Toronto, Canada

This chapter discusses academic integrity issues affecting East Asian international students in Canadian higher education contexts and further highlights the importance of addressing academic integrity issues to improve the inclusion of East Asian international students. The student body has shifted with the increasing number of international students in Canadian higher education contexts and the number of East Asian international students plays a significant role with the shift. East Asian international students bring in their unique cultural backgrounds to the teaching and learning environments in the Canadian higher education landscape. This chapter draws on the autoethnographic approach to discuss the persistence of the academic integrity issues East Asian international students have been facing. The chapter further makes practical and future research recommendations from a transnational educator's perspective.

Section 4
Student Development and Support

Chapter 11

To smoothly transition to the educational platforms and integrate into the new country, especially after the heinous impact of the COVID-19 pandemic, international students need adequate support from the leaders of educational institutions. Leaders not only refer to the administrative leaders but also include the teachers who lead these students in their regular classes. Leaders may also refer to their peers and even the students themselves, who make decisions about their own lives and lead themselves. The toolkit of emotional intelligence (EQ) is valuable for all leaders because it is a multifaceted ability that helps individuals apply the power of emotions as a source of trust, communication, and influence. This chapter focuses on an account of the learning experience of one international doctoral student's transition within a new cultural context. Self-reflection on the hurdles experienced and the importance of respectful communication during the evolution to becoming an international doctoral student in Ontario informs the analysis.

Chapter 12

This research offers a critical understanding of Western-dominant student engagement in terms of rethinking the sense of belonging of Chinese international graduate student populations. The Western perspective on student engagement in Canadian higher education fails to recognize the broader social and cultural inclusivity and diversities of student sense of belonging. Specifically, this research explores the challenges faced by Chinese international students engaging in Canadian graduate schools towards their sense of belonging. This study offers inclusive ways of rethinking Chinese international students' sense of belonging and engagement by deconstructing Western ideology on student experiences in Canadian higher education. Faculties, institutions, and university communities need to redefine the desired content of student engagement based on social justice values in terms of empowering democratic, inclusive, and diverse student experiences and strengthening their sense of belonging with the landscape of internationalization.

Chapter 13

Challenges that Chinese international students with low academic English proficiency encounter in academic reading and writing were exacerbated by remote learning during the COVID-19 pandemic. Qualitative and quantitative data were collected and analyzed from an online reading-writing support program at a Canadian university to examine Chinese students' challenges, perceptions of learning, as well as the impact of culturally responsive pedagogy (CRP) used in the program. The study indicates the benefits of CRP in improving language proficiency and critical thinking, facilitating student experience and satisfaction, constructing identities, promoting learner agency, and enhancing transformative inclusivity. The study also provides insights into effective online teaching pedagogies to help instructors better support low-proficiency international students in coping with academic challenges. In addition, the study suggests teaching practices for empowering international students studying remotely from various global locations, with potential applicability to different teaching contexts.

Chapter 14

Alfred Mupenzi, Western Sydney University, Australia

The chapter highlights students' initial contacts with the Australian formal education system, the deficit logic that underpins underachievement, and provides a discourse around what can be done to make the Australian education landscape more inclusive and accommodating to refugees and new arrivals. The author employs a storytelling/narrative approach that focuses on three research participants to explore factors that enable students to successfully navigate the Australian education system. The discussion explores themes drawn from the narratives of participants and are supported by scholarly research. In addition to the participants' narratives, the author provides an insider's narrative with a strong emphasis on the view that 'no one can tell the lived experience of refugees and new arrivals in Australia more accurately than themselves'. Narratives about lived experiences of refugees have frequently been told in the third person because many of the studies that were carried out used methodologies that kept participants passive rather than active.

Section 5
Online Teaching and Learning

Chapter 15

Shikha Gupta, Shaheed Sukhdev College of Business Studies, University of Delhi, India
Samarth Gupta, Shiv Nadar University, India

Multimedia technology and the internet have revolutionized the delivery and the reach of education through massive open online courses (MOOCs). Starting in 2011 when professors from Stanford University took a lead in starting such courses, teaching/learning through MOOCs has become a revolution of sorts with the professors and the higher education institutions (HEIs) realizing the benefits of several thousand students registering for an online course. Today, more than 11000 MOOCs are available from various countries spanning diverse cultures and languages, disrupting the teaching/learning models in the HEIs. This chapter outlines the history of MOOCs. It also suggests research questions towards the use of MOOCs in promoting international/intercultural communication. A critical assessment of the impact of online learning and MOOCs in the COVID-19 era is also presented.

This chapter reports on the project 'Blending MOOCs (Massive Open Online Courses) into English Language Teaching (ELT) Education with Telecollaboration (BMELTET)'. BMELTET aims to foster reflection on ELT with a COIL (Collaborative Online International Learning) MOOC blend. It promotes the engagement of international students based in the UK and studying on a Master's degree in ELT, with students and staff based in universities in Brazil, China, and Spain and with the participants on the MOOC from all over the world. BMELTET aims to debunk the myth of the 'native speaker' as the ideal teacher of English language, thus decolonising ELT through dialogic online intercultural exchanges in a safe 'third space'. Data were collected via two online surveys, the analysis of the 'live' Zoom exchanges, and focus groups with self-selected groups of students. This chapter reports on the impact that BMELTET had on the international students involved in it.

In 2020, the COVID-19 pandemic turned the world upside down and forced a redesign of the work models of most organizations, including educational institutions that urgently needed to adapt their teaching practices. This chapter reports the CBBC project, an event organized by six European universities with the objective to solve a real business challenge, in international teams, via a 360° communication campaign, analyzing the student's satisfaction and discusses it in light of a unique multi-cultural, online project. The findings contribute to support the validity of the online assessment model and some insights can help education managers and marketing academics to better understand the students learning perceptions in a multi-cultural/multi-national online environment. Also, as proposed by Stallings, it is of utmost importance to identify the aspects that students feel are important in their online learning environment, so the conclusions will enhance the knowledge about how educational tools can be improved to increase overall student satisfaction.

The COVID-19 pandemic posed challenges, including travel restrictions that limited opportunities for student exchange. One solution to promote intercultural learning amongst students in different countries was COIL. This chapter presents a collaborative online international learning (COIL) case study that engaged students from Canada and Spain in an intercultural learning experience. Professors worked collaboratively to design a five-week program of co-instruction within their higher education course schedules. Using technology and a combination of asynchronous and synchronous opportunities, students engaged in the course content and learned about their unique cultural applications and perspectives in relation to the content as they engaged in activities via cross-cultural teams. Administrators, students, and faculty found the benefits far outweigh the improvements needed. This chapter shares the details of this experience from administrative, faculty, and student perspectives.

Teaching international students can be challenging, either online or face-to-face. However, it can also be fruitful if one knows how to engage with international students in the learning and teaching environments, especially online. In Australia, traditional delivery of teaching was still going on for schools and higher education institutions until the end of March 2020, but this changed within weeks to remote or online methods due to the COVID-19 pandemic. At La Trobe University, Australia, teaching was paused for a week to cope with the learning and teaching 'shock' – that is to re-orientate teaching from face-to-face to completely offering courses remotely to international and domestic students. The symbiotic relationship between learning and teaching, as well as between students and teachers, must go on although through online medium. This chapter illustrates the journey of reflections of an early-career international academic unpacking the online practices of teaching and engaging international students in online learning environment at La Trobe University, Australia.

In response to COVID-19, universities have increasingly adopted online teaching to expand students' access to education. Integrating technology into online teaching is considered one of the best teaching practices since it provides international students with multiple benefits. Through a systematic review, this chapter goes through a critical analysis and synthesis process to explore the benefits technology brings to international students, leading to a more comprehensive understanding of how technology works best and what students' preferences truly are in an online context. Drawing on 20 selected articles, the review finds that there are five main benefits of online learning. It also provides conceptual work by identifying a taxonomy of three crucial values of technology integration to teaching international learners in an online environment. Implications are made with regards to the best teaching practices to reshape policies and curriculum designs. The study calls for further studies pertaining to featured factors of teachers and student and stakeholder focuses.

Preface

As the world moves toward an integrated global society, it is essential for teachers to understand the potential cultural and linguistic differences present in students. Many classrooms have accidentally made themselves exclusionary through rigid instruction. Teaching strategies must be flexible to cater to a diverse range of students. By catering to a wider range of students, the education system grows more inclusive, producing a higher volume of educated citizens.

Handbook of Research on Teaching Strategies for Culturally and Linguistically Diverse International Students explores the promising practices for teaching linguistically and culturally diverse international students within post-secondary educational institutions. This book presents the student voice as it relates to student satisfaction and student perceptions of learning, covering topics such as learning technology integration, student engagement, and instruction planning. It is an essential resource for faculty in higher education, university administration, preservice teachers, academicians, and researchers.

THE IMPORTANCE OF EACH CHAPTER

Each chapter of this edited volume displays a significant contribution to the field of teaching international students in post-secondary educational institutions. The authors focus on five distinct areas, including identification of the promising practices for teaching international students, teaching about academic integrity, student development and support, and online teaching and learning.

Clayton Smith and George Zhou, the book's editors, introduce the book in their chapter on "Teaching Culturally and Linguistically Diverse International Students: Connections Between Promising Teaching Practices and Student Satisfaction." This chapter describes three studies that explore promising teaching practices for teaching linguistically and culturally diverse international students by identifying teaching practices that have high levels of international student satisfaction and student perceptions of learning. Studies focus on identifying the key teaching practices, comparing the perspectives of STEM and non-STEM students, and uncovering student preferences for online teaching practices.

Promising Practices for Teaching International Students

In Chapter 2, Rahul Kumar and Clinton Kewley, with the title "Towards a Framework for Planning International Student Instruction," examine and reflect on current international student program practices in Ontario universities. They developed a framework derived from the policy literature that examines international program delivery from pedagogical, technological, and operational standpoints. The proposed framework can be applied in planning and evaluating universities' international program activities, near or far, mediated by technology or not, and applicable beyond the pandemic.

In Chapter 3, Gideon Boadu, Peninah Kanslime, Sara Eyaa, and Said Shannon, with the title "Culturally Responsive Education: Reflections and Insights for Enhancing International Student Experience in Higher Education," share their experiences as international students in Australia and reflect on how these experiences have influenced their work as academics. The stories weave together to identify critical issues, such as positive relationships, empathetic understanding, and sensitive pedagogies that are relevant in the pursuit of culturally responsive education in higher educational institutions.

In Chapter 4, James Oloo, with the title "Understanding and Enhancing Academic Experiences of Culturally and Linguistically Diverse International Students in Canada," explores the lived experiences of three culturally and linguistically diverse international students in Canada. His study revealed three main themes, including a mismatch between the students' academic expectations and reality, challenges relating to language, and self-efficacy and resilience.

In Chapter 5, George Kofi Amoako, with the title "Enhancing Employability Skills in Marketing Graduates Through Teaching Philosophy and Curriculum Design: A Ghanian Perspective," investigates the importance of teaching philosophy and curriculum design in higher educational institutions and its effect on the employability skills of its graduates. He also explores how best learning practices can be engaged in the classroom to enhance the employable skills acquired by the graduates.

In Chapter 6, Hangyu Zhang, Chenyang Zhang, and Hanshu Wang, with the title "Teaching Strategies for International Students' Effective Verbal Communication in Australia: A Collective Autoethnography of Chinese Students," investigates teaching strategies aimed at enhancing Chinese international students' effective communication in Australian universities. The study applies collective autoethnography to allow the three authors to narrate their stories. They build a conceptual framework to explore the triadic reciprocal interaction between verbal communication, self-realization, and teaching and learning environment, and provide suggestions for improvement of teaching strategies for international students' verbal communication.

In Chapter 7, Cezar Scarlat, with the title "Teaching Project Management Principles by Proverbs in Culturally and Linguistically Diverse Environments: Ten Years of Experience With International Students," shares the author's experience of teaching project management to diverse international students at three European universities. It specifically focuses on a single course (project management) and a single instrument used as a teaching aid (proverbs) to teach abstract principles. Lessons learned, while teaching in different cultural and linguistic environments, open research avenues for further comparative, cross- and inter-cultural studies.

In Chapter 8, Syed Ali Zaidi, with the title "Pedagogizing International Students' Technical Knowledge Consumption," argues that international students' English language skills are not technically appropriate, making them face hardships both academically and professionally. He also argues that international testing systems have some structural problems. The study used secondary data for data analysis and employed Bernstein's (1964) theoretical lens of elaborated code and restricted code.

Teaching About Academic Integrity

In Chapter 9, Lilach Marom, with the title "Putting Plagiarism under Scrutiny: Punjabi International Students and Barriers Within Canadian Higher Education," conceptualizes and contextualizes the phenomenon of plagiarism through a case study of Punjabi international students in Canadian higher education. The chapter distinguishes between unintentional and intentional plagiarism and makes a case for increasing relevant support for international students rather than investing in enhanced surveillance mechanisms.

In Chapter 10, Phoebe Eunkyung Kang, with the title "East Asian International Students and Academic Integrity in Higher Education: Cultural, Linguistic, Pedagogical, and Policy Implications," explores how academic integrity policy and praxis are understood and experienced by East Asian international students. It also discusses how institutional academic integrity policy impacts East Asian international students' perceptions, experiences and challenges in a Canadian higher education curriculum by drawing on the auto-ethnographic approach.

Student Development and Support

In Chapter 11, Rakha Zabin, with the title "Developing Fruitful Communication: How to Lead Culturally and Linguistically Diverse International Students With Emotional Intelligence," focuses on an account of the learning experience of one international doctoral student's transition within a new cultural context. Self-reflection on the hurdles experienced and the importance of respectful communication, during the evolution, to becoming an international doctoral student in Ontario (Canada) informs the analysis. The toolkit of emotional intelligence is presented as valuable for educational leaders due to its multifaceted ability to help individuals apply the power of emotions as a source of trust, communication, and influence.

In Chapter 12, Meng Xiao, with the title "Sense of Belonging: Rethinking Chinese International Student Engagement in Canadian Higher Education," offers a critical view of western dominant student engagement in terms of rethinking the sense of belonging of Chinese international graduate student populations. Specifically, it reports on research that explores the challenges faced by Chinese international students engaged in Canadian graduate schools regarding their sense of belonging, thus calling on institutions to redefine the content of student engagement based on social justice values in terms of empowering democratic, inclusive, and diverse student experiences.

In Chapter 13, Xiangying Huo, with the title "Effective Teaching Strategies for Chinese International Students at a Canadian University: An Online Reading-Writing Support Program," describes the challenges that Chinese international students with low academic English proficiency encountered in academic reading and writing during the COVID-19 remote learning. Reported study results found the benefits of culturally responsive pedagogy in improving language proficiency and critical thinking, facilitating student experience and satisfaction, constructing identities, promoting learner agency, and enhancing transformative inclusivity. Findings also provide insights into effective online teaching pedagogies to help instructors better support low-proficiency international students in coping with academic challenges.

In Chapter 14, Alfred Mupenzi, with the title "Navigating the Australian Education System: Refugees and New Arrivals – An Insider's View," highlights students' initial contacts with the Australian formal education system, the deficit logic that underpins underachievement, and provides a discourse around what can be done to make the Australian education landscape more inclusive and accommodating to refugees and new arrivals.

Online Teaching and Learning

In Chapter 15, Shikha Gupta and Samarth Gupta, with the title "Massive Open Online Courses: Promoting Intercultural Communication," outlines the history of Massive Open Online Courses (MOOCs) and how they have disrupted the teaching/learning models in higher educational institutions. They also present a critical assessment of the impact of online learning and MOOCs in the COVID-19 era.

In Chapter 16, Mariana Orsini-Jones, Abraham Cerveró-Carrascosa, and Kyria Finardi, with the title "A 'Glocal' Community of Practice to Support International ELT (International Language Teaching) Students in the UK: Project BMELTET," reports on project BMELTET 2020-2021 (Blending MOOCs-Massive Open Online Courses-for English Language Teacher Education with Telecollaboration) in its September-December cycle. The project repurposed the FutureLearn MOOC Understanding Language: Learning and Teaching (designed by the University of Southampton in collaboration with the British Council) by incorporating it into existing teacher education curricula. The integration of COIL/telecollaboration into the curriculum addressed the need to develop new approaches to teaching and learning that include the internationalization of the curriculum.

In Chapter 17, Alexandre Duarte and Kirstie Riedl, with the title "Perceived Learning Effectiveness and Student Satisfaction: Lessons Learned From an Online Multinational Intensive Program," report on the Cross Border Brand Communications project, an event organized by six European universities with the objective to solve a real business challenge, in international teams, via a 360° communication campaign, analyzing the students' satisfaction and discusses it within the context of a unique multicultural online project. Findings support the validity of the online assessment model and provide insights that can help education managers and marketing academics better understand students' learning perceptions in a multicultural/multinational online environment.

In Chapter 18, Jody-Lynn Rebec, Victor del Corte Lora, and Eunjung Riauka, with the title "Collaborative Online Intercultural Learning (COIL) Case Study: Canadian and Spanish Classes Develop Intercultural Competencies," presents a case study that investigated the COIL experience and evaluated how students and faculty experienced COIL and cultural competency development. Findings suggest that COIL improves intercultural competence.

In Chapter 19, Thi Kim Thu Le and Khanh Pham, with the title "A Systematic Review of Online Learning in the Context of International Students," explores the benefits online technology brings to international students, leading to a more comprehensive understanding of how technology works best and what students' preferences are in an online context. Drawing on twenty selected articles, their review finds five main benefits of online learning. It also identifies a taxonomy of three crucial values of technology integration to teaching international learners in an online environment.

In Chapter 20, Jasvir Kaur Nachatar Singh, with the title "Best Practices of Teaching and Engaging International Students in Online Learning: An Australian Perspective," describes, using autoethnography, the journey of reflections of an early-career international academic unpacking the online practices of teaching and engaging international students in an online learning environment at an Australian university. Reflections focus on the author's personal practices of online teaching and engaging international students in a synchronous online learning environment.

THE IMPACT OF THIS BOOK

This book introduces some of the most promising practices for teaching culturally and linguistically diverse international students within the context of international students' satisfaction and perceptions of learning. These include identification of the promising practices for teaching international students, teaching about academic integrity, student development and support, and online teaching and learning.

Our intention was to increase the international student voice in the continuing discussion of how best to enhance the international student learning experience in post-secondary educational institutions.

While satisfaction among international students is high, there is no denying the fact that international students face all kinds of challenges on both academic and non-academic levels. These include language barriers, exclusion from discussions, culturally related learning differences, academic support issues, cultural adjustment, social issues, and finances (Smith, 2016). There are also student satisfaction differences between international students in such areas as country of origin, study level, program, study stage, study time, and age (i-graduate International Insight, 2017). All of this suggests that instructors should analyze their teaching practices and consider implementing new and more effective teaching strategies to facilitate international student learning experiences for students with diverse language and cultural backgrounds.

As we move through and beyond the COVID-19 pandemic, we will likely see an increasing number of international students join our campus communities. While they will add to our multicultural diversity and reinforce a global perspective and exchange of ideas, it is essential that we fulfill our promise to deliver high-quality and impactful learning to those who have come so far from home to study and learn with us. Robin Metros Helms, assistant vice president for programs and global initiatives at the American Council on Education, said it well when she commented "We need to be paying attention to making sure that faculty are engaged in and central to internationalization efforts." (Redden, 2017). There is no better way to engage faculty than to support their continuing learning and experimentation with the promising practices for teaching international students that connect with student satisfaction and perceptions of learning.

REFERENCES

i-graduate International Insight. (2017). *Data regarding the 2016 international student barometer autumn wave*. i-graduate International Insight.

Redden, E. (2017, June 14). The state of campus internationalization. *Insider Higher Ed*. https://www.insidehighered.com/news/2017/06/14/survey-more-1100-us-colleges-looks-state-internationalization-efforts

Smith, C. (2016). Promoting international student success. In American Association of Collegiate Registrars and Admissions Officers (Ed.), The AACRAO international guide: A resource for international education professionals (pp. 105-115). American Association of Collegiate Registrars and Admissions Officers.

Acknowledgment

The editors would like to acknowledge the help of all the people involved in this project and, more specifically, the authors and reviewers that took part in the review process. Without their support, this book would not have become a reality.

First, the editors would like to thank each one of the authors for their contributions. Our sincere gratitude goes to the chapter's authors who contributed their time and expertise to this book.

Second, the editors wish to acknowledge the valuable contributions of the reviewers regarding the improvement of quality, coherence, and content presentation of chapters. Most of the authors also served as referees; we highly appreciate their double task.

Clayton Smith
University of Windsor, Canada

George Zhou
University of Windsor, Canada

Section 1
Introduction

Chapter 1
Teaching Culturally and Linguistically–Diverse International Students:
Connections Between Promising Teaching Practices and Student Satisfaction

Clayton Smith
https://orcid.org/0000-0002-7611-9193
University of Windsor, Canada

George Zhou
University of Windsor, Canada

ABSTRACT

This chapter describes three studies that explore promising teaching practices for teaching linguistically and culturally-diverse international students by identifying teaching practices that have high levels of international student satisfaction and student perceptions of learning. The first study, using a mixed-methods approach, found eight teaching practice areas that resonated with students. The second study, using a qualitative approach, identified similarities and dissimilarities between STEM and non-STEM students. The third study, using a qualitative approach, uncovered student preferences for online teaching practices. Recommendations for professional practice are discussed, along with potential areas for further research.

INTRODUCTION AND BACKGROUND

Partially due to the increasing enrolment of international students, colleges and universities in the U.S. and Canada are becoming more culturally and linguistically diverse. According to the Canadian Bureau of International Education (CBIE) and the Institute of International Education (IIE), more than 1.6 million

DOI: 10.4018/978-1-7998-8921-2.ch001

international students chose to study at Canadian and American post-secondary educational institutions in 2020 (CBIE, 2021; IIE, 2021).

Despite this trend, international students may face many problems when they arrive in their new host city. Culture shock, socialization, language barriers, changes in eating practices, and accommodations are all challenges they will need to confront. From the academic perspective, they will not only deal with new teaching methods and a new language used by their instructors, but they will also have to alter their learning strategies and preferences to a new learning environment (Lin & Yi, 1997; Rao, 2017; Smith et al., 2019). Unfortunately, though, few instructors have received training for teaching international students (Paige & Goode, 2009; Tran, 2020), which results in a less than optimal environment for intercultural learning.

Since 2020 and the outbreak of COVID-19, most students have experienced a change in the way instruction is delivered to them. It is estimated that approximately 90% of learning was online during the COVID-19 timespan (Radcliff et al., 2020). In fact, a rise has been seen in the popularity of North American online education in recent years, even before the pandemic. It seems that online learning is increasingly being favoured by a growing range of students of various ages and diverse backgrounds, including international students (Best Colleges, 2019). However, several gaps have been found in online teaching, including challenges faced by first-time online students, the impact of various course-loads, and learning effectiveness for additional-language students.

As a result, to achieve higher-student satisfaction and perceptions of learning, instructors must analyze their roles, and implement new teaching strategies to facilitate international students' learning experiences. With the aim of enhancing their academic performances, both offline and online, it is imperative for educators to apply more promising teaching practices that include measurable results, and report successful outcomes for students with diverse language and cultural backgrounds. This chapter provides insights from three distinct studies regarding the promising teaching practices. The first research study identified teaching practices that have high levels of student satisfaction and student perceptions of learning. A second study was conducted to explore the different teaching and learning preferences of international students, with emphasis on the differences between STEM (science, technology, engineering and mathematics) and non-STEM students' preferences. A third study was carried out to evaluate international online students' degrees of satisfaction regarding their instructors' teaching strategies and individual instructor characteristics. The research participants were unique to each study.

This chapter will explore three research questions:

1. What promising teaching practices have high levels of international student satisfaction and perceptions of learning?
2. What are the perceptional differences between international students enrolled in STEM and non-STEM academic programs, regarding the promising teaching practices for teaching international students?
3. How satisfied are international students with the online-teaching strategies they experienced, and what are their perceptions of learning with these strategies?

THEORETICAL FRAMEWORK

The studies presented in this chapter are based on the belief that the most effective teaching practices are where promising teaching practices, international student satisfaction, and student perceptions of learning meet (see Figure 1). It is guided by four theories. The primary theory used is Tinto's (1993) student integration model, which stated that students must integrate into both social and academic settings, formally and informally, to create a connection with their academic institution. Once a connection is made, commitment to careers and educational goals is established. The researchers also relied on the work of Darby and Lang (2019), which suggested that the personality of the instructor can affect learning; Tran's (2020) framework for teaching and learning for international students, that introduces the importance of connecting with academic and social experiences; and the research conducted by Smith et al. (2019) that identified a connection between promising practices for teaching international students with student satisfaction and perceptions of learning.

Figure 1. Identifying effective teaching practices

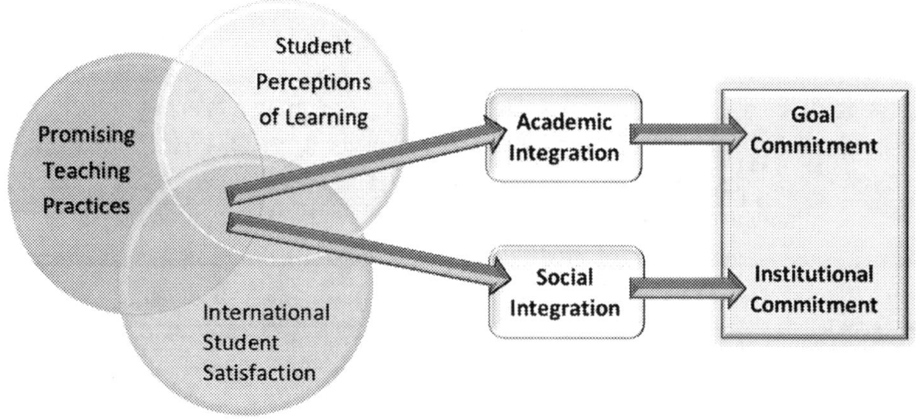

PROMISING PRACTICES FOR TEACHING INTERNATIONAL STUDENTS

Presently, campus internationalization initiatives focus primarily on external areas, including education abroad and student exchange, recruiting international students, and institutional partnerships (Helms et al., 2017). However, this is expected to change, as more institutions are developing academically-related internationalization initiatives. A growing number of institutions are increasing faculty engagement of internationalization efforts (Helms et al., 2017). To do this, faculty will need to critically examine their roles in campus internationalization, and implement teaching strategies that improve international students' academic performances. However, few instructors have received formal training for intercultural learning or inclusive education (Paige & Goode, 2009; Tran, 2020).

Satisfaction among international students studying at Canadian and U.S. colleges and universities is high. A survey (2018) reported that 96% of international students studying at Canadian institutions are either very satisfied, or satisfied, with their educational experiences, and recommend Canada as a study destination (CBIE International Student Survey, 2018). International Student Barometer findings (i-graduate International Insight, 2017) also suggested that international students are largely satisfied with their academic experiences at Canadian and American colleges and universities. Little variance in international student satisfaction of learning experiences was found for gender, while country of origin, study level, program, study stage, study time, and age were where the differences lie.

While their satisfaction with learning experiences is generally high, there is no denying the fact that international students must face all kinds of challenges on both academic and non-academic levels. Academic challenges include language barriers, exclusion from discussions, culturally-related learning differences, and academic support issues. Cultural adjustment, social issues, and finances are non-academic challenges which also factor into international students' lives (Smith, 2016).

To deal with these challenges, faculty must pursue a wide variety of teaching practices. Existing literature listed many promising teaching practices that can be added to their repertoire, which may help improve the teaching of international students, and result in high levels of student learning. Creating an inclusive teaching environment is an important element. Also, it is essential to put culturally-responsive teaching into practice in the classroom, including strategies like developing diverse cultural knowledge bases, designing culturally-relevant curriculum, building learning communities, and engaging in cross-cultural communication (Gay, 2010). Faculty should use differentiated instruction when teaching international students from different language backgrounds, which can help foster collective thinking to create a learning-centred context for students. Moreover, the role of faculty goes beyond the classroom. The academic supervisory relationship between instructors and students can impact students' academic success (Curtin et al., 2013), so instructors should support students in a broader way, by giving advice on academic programs, or providing them with employment information.

This mixed-methods' study identified the promising teaching practices to teach international students from different language and cultural backgrounds, by evaluating the rate of student-satisfaction levels and perceptions of learning. It is based on the belief that the most effective teaching practices are combined with high levels of student satisfaction and perceptions of learning. The researchers used a mixed-methods' research design that included an online-survey questionnaire, focus-group discussions, and individual interviews. Research participants were international students who study at a mid-sized, comprehensive, public university in Canada. The sample size is 3,467 international students from a wide array of countries of origin, study levels, academic programs, study stages, and ages.

The responses from the participants were in line with what was found by the Canadian Bureau of International Education. Most (93.9%) reported being satisfied, with their learning experiences at a Canadian university. Some (16.64%) of this group feel very satisfied, others (48.29%) feel satisfied, and many (28.97%) reported being somewhat satisfied.

Promising teaching practices received from respondents, that were reported as satisfied or very satisfied, varied from 49.7% to 82.9%. The teaching practices with the highest respondent satisfaction percentages (greater than 70%) fell into these areas: academic integrity, assessment, assignments, clarifying expectations, communicating outside of the classroom, lecture design and delivery, verbal communications, and visual communications.

Interestingly, all the promising teaching practices identified as having high levels of student satisfaction also have medium or high student perception levels of learning. While 13 teaching-practice areas received medium or high student perceptions of learning levels, some did not receive satisfied student responses. Table 1 shows student satisfaction and student perceptions of learning for teaching practices, as well as the correlation between student satisfaction and perceptions of learning for each teaching practice.

Table 1. Student satisfaction and student perceptions of learning for promising teaching practices

Promising Teaching Practices	Student Satisfaction (Satisfied/Very Satisfied)	Student Perceptions of Learning (Medium/High)	Correlation (r)
Academic Integrity			
Integrates information about academic honesty in instruction to prevent plagiarism	82.90%	95.60%	0.445*
Communicates what constitutes cheating and the consequences of academic dishonesty	77.80%	94.40%	0.482*
Makes use of librarians to teach about academic integrity	65.70%	88%	0.594*
Assessment			
Designs assessments that recognize and validate cultural differences in writing and communication styles	58.30%	84.10%	0.686*
Explains assessment criteria to students so that they know how they will be evaluated	71.40%	91.40%	0.582*
Uses fair assessment practices	70.80%	92.40%	0.595*
Assignments			
Assigns quick writing assignments, such as a "one minute paper" at the end of class, asking students to list anything needing further clarification	55.10%	81.60%	0.730*
Collects written questions about the lecture at the end of class	49.70%	77.50%	0.718*
Words instructions for assignments clearly	71.30%	92.40%	0.543*
Breaks up deadlines for large projects into phases so that students can brainstorm, draft, solicit feedback, revise, and edit throughout the semester	73.60%	92.30%	0.596*
Provides step-by-step instructions for assigned tasks	67.70%	92.20%	0.633*
Posts assignments and readings ahead of time	76.30%	92.20%	0.549*
Asks students to come to class with a written response to an assigned reading	59.80%	86.60%	0.678*
Clarifying Expectations			
Collects and makes available examples of recently completed, outstanding student work, so that students can see the format and standard of work expected	63.50%	84.60%	0.708*
Provides students with rules for discussion, participation, and group work	67.60%	90.10%	0.570*
Models how to ask questions, think critically, write good essays/reports, or read analytically by demonstrating these skills in class	63.10%	88.50%	0.648*
Provides clarity on course objectives and expectations, and major concepts to be covered	72.50%	92.70%	0.614*
Communicating Outside of the Classroom			
Sets up online discussion boards where students can pose questions, and use email or other communication technologies	64%	85.40%	0.664*

continues on following page

Table 1. Continued

Promising Teaching Practices	Student Satisfaction (Satisfied/Very Satisfied)	Student Perceptions of Learning (Medium/High)	Correlation (r)
Provides alternative ways for students and the instructor to communicate outside of the classroom	66.70%	88.80%	0.600*
Actively invites students to come to faculty office hours	71.10%	90%	0.574*
Takes every opportunity to enhance student-teacher dialogue outside of the classroom	66.90%	84.90%	0.680*
Lecture Design and Delivery			
Tells students what topics will be covered that day and how the lecture relates to information presented in previous lectures	73%	92.70%	0.587*
Uses interesting examples, real-life examples, and case studies	70.50%	92.40%	0.646*
Distributes electronically lecture notes/slides and handouts with explanations of key concepts and ideas	73%	94.10%	0.577*
Uses examples to illustrate and reinforce key concepts and ideas	72.20%	93.10%	0.617*
Verbal Communications			
Speaks clearly and at a normal rate, emphasizes key ideas and words, and provides enough pauses to allow time for questions and note-taking	69.70%	90.10%	0.569*
Asks for clarification when student responses are not clear	72.40%	94.10%	0.605*
Encourages students to ask questions	74.20%	93.90%	0.548*
Visual Communication			
Uses visuals (e.g., diagrams, charts, pictures, overheads) to aid comprehension	73.80%	95.10%	0.539*
Ensures that notes written on the board or on flip charts are legible from the furthest seat in the room	70.40%	93.30%	0.601*
Uses print rather than cursive writing	69.20%	93.30%	0.601*

* Significant at the 0.01 level.

In the focus group and interviews, students' responses were mainly positive. Most of them identified instructors as a key factor in the learning experience. Some characteristics, like humour, encouragement and support, and value of diverse cultures were welcomed by students. Many practices were endorsed by students of all educational levels, including a student-centred approach, use of interactive teaching methods, specific and prompt feedback, use of practical experiences, pleasant learning environment, and methods to support additional language learners. Undergraduate participants were interested in academic support, updated curricula, and partially filled slides in advance of class. They also emphasized the importance of experiential and applied learning, and close interaction with instructors. Graduate students spoke of the importance of a free learning environment, multi-modality teaching strategies, use of digital and visual materials, and emotional, physical, and non-judgmental support from their supervisors. Teaching methods that led to students becoming bored and having heavy workloads, such as too grammar-intensive teaching, and use of the repeating-listening pattern of teaching and learning, along with a lack of encouragement, received dissatisfaction from students.

There were some differences between course-based and research-based graduate student responses. Course-based graduate students commented on their course instructors and teaching methods, while research-based graduate students mostly commented on their relationship with supervisors. Table 2 compared the satisfying and dissatisfying teaching strategies reported by these two groups of students.

Table 2. Satisfying and dissatisfying teaching practices of course-based students and research-based graduate students

Groups	Satisfying Teaching Practices	Dissatisfying Teaching Practices
Course-Based Program Students	Free learning atmosphere Multi-modality and experiential teaching strategies Up-to-date course content and multiple teaching resources Instructor attitudes and experience in the field Approachable instructors Prompt feedback No phone policy Use of real-world examples	Failed to engage international students in class discussions Not open enough to the views of students Did not define terminology in advance of using it in class Use of student in-class presentations Lack of explanations Lack of class content Insufficient formative feedback
Research-Based Students	Good relationship with supervisor Desirable assignments Simultaneous engagement in their own research and joint research	Lack of supervision Failure to understand students' cultural backgrounds Insufficient non-academic support services and course options.

This study identified teaching practices that result in both student satisfaction and student perceptions of learning. Many students called for a multi-modal teaching style that combined traditional lectures and interactive methods. They also described some instructor characteristics as important factors in the student experience.

PROMISING PRACTICES FOR TEACHING STEM AND NON-STEM INTERNATIONAL STUDENTS

This qualitative study focused on exploring the promising teaching practices that have high levels of international satisfaction of learning. The findings indicate that instructors using these teaching practices will create a more accessible learning environment for international students. In addition, student characteristics (e.g., country of origin, field of study, level of study) will impact their preferred teaching practices. The researchers revealed 22 promising teaching practices where there is a significant difference between STEM and non-STEM students, regarding student satisfaction and perceptions of learning.

Due to the cultural differences, it is important to consider that international students prefer the teaching practices and approaches that they are accustomed to in their home countries (McKinnon, 2013). For example, the Asian-educational system mainly follows Confucianism values, which gives instructors the authority to be the holders of knowledge, and students maintain silence for most of the class (Le Ha

& Li, 2012). The learning styles and preferences of Chinese students may also be affected by the exam culture, with their learning strategies being more related to memorization (Lee, 1996). Also, learning styles and preferences may vary according to the student's field of study (Kulturel-Konak et al., 2011). Relevant former studies reported statistical differences in learning styles of students enrolled in different areas of study. For example, education and information technology students were more active learners, while law and science students were more reflective learners (Alumran, 2008). Engineering students preferred more active and concrete learning styles, while mathematics students were more intuitive (Harvey et al., 2010).

Corresponding to students' learning preferences, teaching practices applied in different subjects differ from each other. Literature corroborates that it is essential to match the learning preferences of students with corresponding teaching practice, but this does not always play out in real life (Vincent-Lancrin et al., 2019). Debdi et al. (2016) concluded that the teaching practices used by instructors in engineering and computer science courses were unaligned with students' learning preferences.

The data of this study was collected through a qualitative research design that included focus groups and individual interviews conducted at a mid-sized Canadian, comprehensive university. Most research participants were graduate students in thesis-based or course-based, master's degree programs. A total of 28 students (14 STEM students, and 14 non-STEM students) participated in the study.

Table 3. STEM and Non-STEM student responses on overall topics

Topics	STEM Respondents	Non-STEM Respondents
Overall Impression of Teaching Received	"Teachers are very good and [are] always open to questions." "Industrial experience is key. I am satisfied, due to practical applications."	"The depth of the program is well thought of." "One of the teachers was the best teacher I have ever had."
Most Enjoyable Memory	"They do this peer review thing." "[I] like two-way communication, where there is not just a slide-read." "Use of interactive technology, such as Kahoot"	"Well-structured class" "Discussion-based and presentations that include diversity" "Professors paid attention to students."
Teaching Practices Most Preferred	"Using visualizing tools, because some concepts are difficult to understand" "The storytelling method" "The seating arrangement where everyone can see each other"	"Able to crack a joke" "Use a lot of teamwork" "Use of rubrics" "Classes that have different structures" "Reviewed one chapter each class"
Teaching Practices Least Preferred	"Courses are heavily memorization-based." "Lectures that do not fully cover the content" "Professor's accent" "Presentation of lecture slides without full explanations"	"Didn't cover the book at all" "No feedback" "Lectures that are only theory-based" "Where there is little opportunity for engagement" "The main thing is having to know it is, because that is how it is."
Recommended Changes to Teaching Practices	"Provide lecture notes in addition to slides" "More concentration on the technical stuff" "Professors should be available during the last 15 minutes for questions." "Professor should be clearer and articulate properly." "Focus more on theory in class" "Reduce class size."	"Standardize how the grading goes, less differences between different classes" "Would want my professors to use more discussions, and to be more engaged" "Communicating outside of the classroom and having a place to talk to professors" "Having more international connections [and] socializing, in the university, in general"

Some overall topic findings regarding the impressions of the teaching received, the most enjoyable memory, the teaching practices most preferred, the teaching practices least preferred, and the recommended teaching practice changes are presented in Table 3. In general, the student responses were positive.

There is some variance between the two groups of students. STEM students mentioned that the most preferred teaching practices involved the interactions and engagement with teachers, face-to-face seating arrangements, the use of visualization tools, and the use of the story-telling method of lectures. The least preferred were the ones that required a large amount of memorization, and written assignments, because of the concern for cheating, and vague lecture slides. For non-STEM students, they preferred it when instructors managed time well and used the full lecture time available, used humour to connect with students, included teamwork and group projects in the course, used rubrics to provide feedback, and used a wide range of class instruction. Non-STEM students did not appreciate when instructors strayed from the textbook too much, and did not provide enough feedback. These students also voiced dissatisfaction with lectures that were too theory-based, and overly student-centred courses that lacked the guidance of instructors. Some non-STEM students preferred culturally-responsive teaching, and diversity and inclusion, while STEM students felt they were less important.

Findings of the study echoed several of the literature findings above. The field of study appears to be an important factor in understanding both the learning styles and teaching preferences of international students, so there is a need to use different teaching practices when teaching STEM and non-STEM students (Kulturel-Konak et al., 2011). Also, there are teaching practices used by non-STEM instructors that, if used by STEM instructors, could result in deeper and more efficient content learning (Harvey et al., 2010).

Students' responses on the teaching practices were mostly positive. They reported satisfaction with their instructors' use of teaching methods that shift the focus of instruction from the teacher to the student to enhance classroom learning. STEM and non-STEM students gave similar answers on the most preferred and least preferred teaching practices, and recommended teaching practices' changes. There are also some practices preferred by both groups, including the use of two-way communications, formative feedback, sharing lecture slides in advance, matching lecture topics with textbook topics, course organization, student engagement, managing speed of lecturing, and opportunities for applied or hands-on learning. Differences can be seen on the extent of specific teaching practices that should be used. For instance, non-STEM respondents wanted to see more use of discussion and group presentations, but while STEM students also liked this approach, they preferred knowledge transmission from the instructor.

PROMISING ONLINE TEACHING PRACTICES

With COVID-19 forcing post-secondary educational institutions to shift to open and online learning, it is imperative for educators to pay more attention to international students' needs. Finding strategies for teaching international students from diverse backgrounds in online settings is essential to ensure successful course completion. Gaps in academic performance between international and domestic students are evident (Grayson, 2008; He & Banham, 2011; Hechanova-Alampay et al., 2002; Kim et al., 2015), partly due to the language difficulties, culturally-related learning differences, academic support issues, and adjustment to a new educational system (Smith, 2016). This leads to international students being less satisfied with the student experience, and less engaged in the classroom, than their domestic peers (Kim et al., 2015).

The existing pre-COVID-19 literature mainly focused on two primary themes. The first is the importance of making clear what students are expected to do in an online class. The second is ensuring that instruction is student-centred and focused on diverse student needs. Darby & Lang (2019) emphasized the importance of clear communication within online learning, as it helps build community and socialization between teachers and students. Before forming any groups, it is important to discuss intercultural communications and cooperation (Walton, 2010) to ensure effective digital collaboration. Instructors are supposed to keep an open mind regarding cultural differences (Wang, 2006) and lessen the chance of misunderstandings during intercultural interactions (Chen & Starosta, 1998). Some other factors regarding communication should also be considered, such as language proficiency (Bossio & Bylyna, 2006), and form of lecture presentations (Guo & Jamal, 2012). Student-centered learning is also crucial for international online learners. This can be accomplished by introducing students to western educational practices (Smith et al., 2019), taking time to understand individual student needs (Kinsella, 1997), and by assessing students' comfort with technology (Woodley et al., 2017). However, research involving challenges that first-time online students face, and how they differ from what experienced online learners encounter, is lacking. The effectiveness of strategies for supporting online students, like differing course loads and making vague academic expectations, remain unclear.

This study employed a qualitative methodology, which included 15 individual interviews. Interview participants were international students who are representative of the international student population at a mid-sized, comprehensive university in Ontario, Canada. Graduate students made up 53% of the participants. Seven participants were in non-STEM programs, and the remaining students were in STEM programs. The courses (some asynchronous and others synchronous) students participated in were pivoted because of the COVID-19 pandemic.

Students' attitudes toward online learning were mixed. Three factors most of the students noticed about how online education differed from traditional learning that were less satisfying included ineffective communication, decreased sense of belonging, and varying assessment practices. Table 4 presents a summary of the interviewee responses to the questions relating to these three factors.

The lack of communication in online learning, especially during lectures, with assignment instruction and poor communication with feedback, brings about many challenges. Students noted that it was difficult starting conversations in the digital world, which hindered their ability to connect with students and teachers. Almost all participants noted that they did not feel a sense of community. They were lonely, and not sure who to turn to for help. Some instructors did try to increase the sense of belonging, by calling on students' names, or assigning group work. These efforts were much appreciated by students. Assessment practices changed drastically when education shifted to online. Many students felt grading was unfair, and pointed out that instructors and teaching assistants were not prepared for the online world. From these results, the negative effects of online learning were detrimental to the learning of culturally and linguistically diverse students.

Some other notable differences, related by the students, are also worth mentioning. Some instructors did not incorporate culturally-responsive teaching in their courses. Many students noted the lack of differentiated instruction, which led them to drop the course. Group work did not receive enough positive feedback from students, because of the inadequate effort made by some of the group members. In addition, internet connectivity was an issue, at times.

Table 4. Summary of responses regarding primary factors associated with online education

Factor	Summary of Responses
Communication	Communication outside of the classroom shifted from in-person discussions to digital conversations, with most instructors still offering virtual face-to-face office hours for students. Verbal communication during lectures was a concern for some students. There were mixed opinions on the communication received on assignment feedback. Most students were satisfied with the communication received about classroom expectations.
Sense of Belonging	Almost all participants agreed that there was a lack of community in the online learning environment. Students felt that most of their connection was through discussion boards, but not all professors utilized this feature in the online platform. Some students noted the communities built outside of the classroom, such as for group projects or assignments, but the community and sense of belonging within the classroom was limited. Online learning was very isolated, and students felt they had to learn everything on their own. Questions and interactions were encouraged during class. Students thought that the online learning environment was stressful. Students did not feel any discrimination; in fact, many students said there was respect within the classroom, which helped with the overall comfort levels. There was just a lack of connection and community. Students enjoyed it when they had group projects, because it allowed them to get to know their classmates.
Assessment Practices	Many instructors made online assessments in such a way that students cannot go back once they have submitted an answer. Drastic differences in grades between group members of the same project were noticed. Not enough variety: most courses just did multiple-choice assessments Grades were falling, because of the lack of participation. This can be an issue for students who do not feel comfortable speaking out loud. Marking done by GA's was unfair and unorganized. Some students believed the grading was fair and that instructors were very understanding.
Other Notable Differences	There was a lack of culturally responsive teaching, although some students believed it would not add to their learning. There was a lack of differentiated instruction. There was dissatisfaction with group members' input in projects. Peer-review forms were appreciated. Online learning is tiring if students do not get a break. Most students prefer synchronous learning, although there are some benefits to asynchronous learning. Online platforms are easy to use, although some students believe instructors need more training. The Internet is unreliable at times. Almost all the students appreciated the student-centred teaching implemented by instructors.

RECOMMENDATIONS

To improve students' academic performance and experiences, instructors are encouraged to take both satisfaction and student perceptions of learning into consideration. The following areas should be the focus, when applying a teaching method, including academic integrity, assessment, assignments, clarification of expectations, communication outside of the classroom, lecture design and delivery, verbal communications, and visual communications. Instructors should use a multi-modal teaching style that combines traditional lectures and interactive methods, which is also preferred by many students. Instructor characteristics are also an important factor in the student experience. Humour and jokes, identification of diverse cultures, patient and responsive support, as well as close interaction with peers are all methods that should not be underestimated.

When teaching students majoring in different academic areas, instructors need to use differentiated teaching strategies. As for STEM students, instructors should consider reducing class sizes, adding terminology explanations, playing up industrial experiences, using interactive technology and visualization tools, sharing lecture notes, and enhancing out-of-class learning opportunities. As for non-STEM students, instructors should consider ensuring program depth, engaging in discussion-based and team-work activities, focusing on diversity topics, using humour, enhancing opportunities to engage with students outside of the classroom, and increasing opportunities for students to socialize with other students from beyond their home country. Faculty who teach both STEM and non-STEM students should use student-centred teaching methods, two-way communications, engage in formative feedback, share lecture slides in advance, match lecture topics with textbook topics, ensure solid course organization, promote student engagement, manage lecture-delivery speed, and increase opportunities for applied or hands-on learning.

With the increasing demand of online education, digital teaching strategies must improve to foster student learning. Educators who have international students in their online classrooms should continue to use the following teaching practices, as they created increased satisfaction, and increased perceptions of learning: clarification of classroom expectations, diversity and inclusion, and student-centred teaching.

LIMITATIONS AND FUTURE RESEARCH

Inevitably, the studies have some limitations. For instance, the research data was collected based on one semester, rather than a full academic year, and the perceptions of student learning data was self-reported, which may affect the accuracy of association between the practices studied, and the diversity of students' responses. Furthermore, in the first study, the respondent rates of the online survey of participants, from different levels, were discordant, with graduate students making up to over two-thirds of the total. The underrepresented data of undergraduate students limited what can be said about international undergraduate students' experiences. In the second and third studies, participant quantity and the diversity of student course programs were not considerably varied. Also, responses failed to include teaching contexts.

All in all, international student learning is a topic that needs to be discussed constantly to ensure the success of these learners. Research on this topic has come a long way, but there is still so much more to explore. What are the other teaching practices that can be implemented to enhance learning? How can STEM and non-STEM students be further serviced to ensure that the appropriate teaching style is provided? What can be done to create community in online classrooms? What teaching practices should be used for specific student types? What can be done to help student development and support? These are only a fraction of the questions that still need answering before an impact can truly be made. By sharing the works in this book, it is hoped that there is movement one step closer to the finish line.

CONCLUSION

Findings of the three studies provided a deeper insight into international students' learning. The first study found that the most promising teaching practices identified as having high levels of student satisfaction also have medium/high student perceptions of learning. In the second study, the researchers examined different preferences of STEM and non-STEM international students on 22 promising teaching practices. Little difference was found in the two groups regarding their most, and least, preferred teaching practices, or recommended teaching practices' changes. The major differences lied in some specific areas, like knowledge transmission and culturally-responsive teaching. The last study explored the connection between the promising practices for teaching online international students with international student satisfaction and perceptions of learning. It found that many teaching practices, such as communication, sense of belonging, and marking schemes are essential factors to meet students' needs. Also, there are individual instructor characteristics preferred by online international students, including calling on students by name, and the use of humour and jokes.

The findings illustrated above are imperative for today's teaching reality, as it provides a blueprint about how to improve international student learning. International students come to western institutions expecting a high-quality education from a reputable school (Best Colleges, 2019). It is important that institutions work to continue to provide such education for these individuals, by following and building on the best teaching practices shown to enhance learning.

In the following chapters, there is further exploration on the teaching of international students, teaching about academic integrity, teaching unique types of international students, student development support, and online teaching and learning.

ACKNOWLEDGMENT

This research received no specific grant from any funding agency in the public, commercial, or not-for-profit sectors. In-kind support was provided by the University of Windsor.

REFERENCES

Alumran, J. (2008). Learning styles in relation to gender, field of study, and academic achievement for Bahraini University students. *Individual Differences Research*, *6*(4), 303–316.

Best Colleges. (2019). *2019 Online Education Trends Report*. https://res.cloudinary.com/highereducation/image/upload/v1556050834/BestColleges.com/edutrends/2019-Online-Trends-in-Education-Report-BestColleges.pdf

Bossio, E., & Bylyna, C. (2006). *Semester 2: Benchmarks report: Community worker outreach and development*. Unpublished manuscript, Colleges Integrating Immigrants to Employment, Ontario Ministry of Citizenship and Immigration, Toronto, Ontario, Canada.

Canadian Bureau of International Education. (2021). *The student's voice: National results of the 2018 CBIE international student survey*. https://cbie.ca/survey/

Chen, G.-M., & Starosta, W. J. (1998). A review of the concept of intercultural awareness. *Human Communication*, *2*, 27–54.

Curtin, N., Stewart, A. J., & Ostrove, J. M. (2013). Fostering academic self-concept: Advisor support and sense of belonging among international and domestic graduate students. *American Educational Research Journal*, *50*(1), 108–137. doi:10.3102/0002831212446662

Darby, F., & Lang, J. (2019). *Small teaching online*. John Wiley & Sons.

Debdi, O., Paredes-Velasco, M., & Velázquez-Iturbide, J. Á. (2016). Influence of pedagogic approaches and learning styles on motivation and educational efficiency of computer science students. *IEEE Revista Iberoamericana de Tecnologias del Aprendizaje, 11*(3), 213–218. doi:10.1109/RITA.2016.2590638

Gay, G. (2010). *Culturally responsive teaching: Theory, research, and practice.* Teachers College Press.

Grayson, J. P. (2008). The experiences and outcomes of domestic and international students at four Canadian universities. *Higher Education Research & Development, 27*(3), 215–230. doi:10.1080/07294360802183788

Guo, S., & Jamal, Z. (2012). *Cultural diversity and inclusive teaching.* Society for Teaching and Learning in Higher Education.

Harvey, D., Ling, C., & Shehab, R. (2010). Comparison of student's learning style in STEM disciplines. *IIE Annual Conference Proceedings,* 1-6.

He, Y., & Banhan, H. C. (2011). International student academic performance: Some statistical evidence and its implications. *American Journal of Business Education, 2*(5), 89–100. doi:10.19030/ajbe.v2i5.4073

Hechanova-Alampay, R., Beehr, T. A., Christiansen, N. D., & Van Horn, R. (2002). Adjustment and strain among domestic and international student sojourners: A longitudinal study. *School Psychology International, 23*(4), 458–474. doi:10.1177/0143034302234007

Helms, R. M., Brajkovic, L., & Struthers, S. (2017). *Mapping internationalization on U.S. campuses: 2017 edition.* https://cbie.ca/wp-content/uploads/2018/08/Student_Voice_Report-ENG.pdf

i-graduate International Insight. (2017). *Data regarding the 2016 international student barometer autumn wave.* i-graduate International Insight.

Institute of International Education. (2021). *Open doors 2021.* https://opendoorsdata.org/data/international-students/enrollment-trends/

Kim, Y. K., Edens, D., Iorio, M. F., Curtis, C. J., & Romero, E. (2015). Cognitive skills development among international students at research universities in the United States. *Journal of International Students, 5*(4), 526–540.

Kinsella, K. (1997). Creating an enabling learning environment for non-native speakers of English. In A. I. Morey & M. K. Kitano (Eds.), *Multicultural course transformation in higher education: A broader truth* (pp. 104–125). Allyn and Bacon.

Kulturel-Konak, S., D'Allegro, M. L., & Dickinson, S. (2011). Review of gender differences in learning styles: Suggestions for STEM education. *Contemporary Issues in Education Research, 4*(3), 9–18. https://doi.org/10.19030/cier.v4i3.4116

Le Ha, P., & Li, B. (2012). Silence as right, choice, resistance and strategy among Chinese 'Me Generation' students: Implications for pedagogy. *Discourse, 35*(2), 233–248. 306.2012.745733 doi:10.1080/01596

Lee, W. O. (1996). The cultural context for Chinese learners: conceptions of learning in the Confucian tradition. In D. Watkins & J. Biggs (Eds.), *The Chinese learner: Cultural, psychological and contextual influences* (pp. 25–41). The Comparative Education Research Centre, Faculty of Education, University of Hong Kong.

Lin, J.-C. G., & Yi, J. K. (1997). Asian international students' adjustment: Issues and program suggestions. *College Student Journal, 31*(4), 473–479.

McKinnon, S. (2013). A mismatch of expectations? An exploration of international students' perceptions of employability skills and work-related learning. In J. Ryan (Ed.), *Cross-cultural teaching and learning for home and international students: Internationalisation of pedagogy and curriculum in higher education* (pp. 211–224). Routledge.

Paige, R. M., & Goode, M. L. (2009). Intercultural competence in international education administration- cultural mentoring: International education professionals and the development of intercultural competence. In D. Deardorff (Ed.), *The SAGE handbook of intercultural competence* (pp. 333–349). SAGE Publications.

Radcliff, J., Aaron, D., Sterle, J. G., von Keyserlingk, M., Irlbeck, N., Maquivar, M., Wulster-Radcliffe, M., & Jones, C. (2020). Moving online: Roadmap and long-term forecast. *Animal Frontiers, 10*(3), 36-45. doi:10.1093/af/vfaa027

Rao, P. (2017). Learning challenges and preferred pedagogies of international students: A perspective from the United States. *International Journal of Educational Management, 31*(7), 1000–1016. doi:10.1108/

Smith, C. (2016). Promoting international student success. In American Association of Collegiate Registrars and Admissions Officers (Ed.), The AACRAO international guide: A resource for international education professionals (pp. 105-115). American Association of Collegiate Registrars and Admissions Officers.

Smith, C., Zhou, G., Potter, M., & Wang, D. (2019). Connecting best practices for teaching linguistically and culturally diverse international students with international student satisfaction and student perceptions of student learning. *Advances in Global Education and Research, 3*, 252-265.

Smith, C., Zhou, G., Potter, M., Wang, D., Pecoraro, M., & Paulino, R. (2019). Variability by individual student characteristics of student satisfaction with promising international student teaching practices. *Literacy Information and Computer Education Journal, 10*(2), 3160–3169.

Tinto, V. (1993). *Leaving college: Rethinking the causes and cures of student attrition.* University of Chicago Press.

Tran, L. T. (2020). Teaching and engaging international students: People-to-people connections and people-to-people empathy. *Journal of International Students, 10*(3), xii–xvii. https://doi.org/10.32674/jis.v10i3.2005

Vincent-Lancrin, S., Urgel, J., Kar, S., & Jacobin, G. (2019). *Measuring innovation in education 2019: What has changed in the classroom?* Educational Research and Innovation, OECD Publishing. doi:10.1787/9789264311671-en

Walton, J. (2010). Examining a transformative approach to communication education: A teacher-research study. *College Student Journal, 44*(1), 157–177.

Wang, H. (2006). Teaching Asian students online: What matters and why? *PAACE Journal of Lifelong Learning, 15*, 69–84.

Woodley, X., Hernandez, C., Parra, J., & Negash, B. (2017). Celebrating difference: Best practice in culturally responsive teaching online. *TechTrends*, *6*(5), 470–478. https://doi.org/10.1007/s11528-017-0207-z

KEY TERMS AND DEFINITIONS

Active Learning: Activities that students do to construct knowledge and understanding.

International Students: Students enrolled in post-secondary educational institutions, located in a country other than their home country.

Non-STEM Students: Students enrolled in a post-secondary educational institution in an academic program other than science, technology, engineering, or mathematics.

Online Learning: Education that takes place using the internet.

Promising Teaching Practices: Teaching practices that have been, or are being, evaluated, and for which strong quantitative and/or qualitative data shows positive learning outcomes.

STEM Students: Students enrolled in a post-secondary educational institution in science, technology, engineering, or mathematics academic program.

Student Engagement: Meaningful student involvement throughout the learning environment that results in students making a psychological investment in their learning.

Student Perceptions of Learning: Students' perceptions of the quantity and quality of learning they have acquired while enrolled in a post-secondary educational institution.

Student Satisfaction: Students' subjective evaluation of the outcomes and experiences associated with post-secondary education.

Section 2
Promising Practices for Teaching International Students

Chapter 2
Towards a Framework for Planning International Student Instruction

Rahul Kumar
ⓘ https://orcid.org/0000-0002-4247-6045
Brock University, Canada

Clinton Kewley
Brock University, Canada

ABSTRACT

Pre-pandemic Canadian universities relied on international student enrolment to generate revenue and instill beneficial internationalization on Canadian campuses. As the pandemic disrupted established pedagogical practices and international students' on-campus participation, how international programs are delivered has been re-envisioned and recalibrated. Initially, changes in teaching and learning were reactionary and predicated on available resources, often laden with problems identified in OCUFA findings. Upon careful examination and reflection of current practices in Ontario universities, the authors developed a framework derived from policy literature that examines international program delivery from pedagogical, technological, and operational standpoints. The proposed framework can be applied in planning and evaluating universities' international program activities, near or far, mediated by technology or not, and applicable beyond the pandemic.

INTRODUCTION

The COVID-19 pandemic's impact on higher education and student mobility has been immense worldwide. The choices and changes in modality of pre-pandemic teaching and learning have been disrupted profoundly since the pandemic changed pedagogical practices beginning in March 2020. New insights related to how courses are planned and delivered—and how students access them—have also emerged. This chapter examines the specific context of online course delivery that emerged as a result of the

DOI: 10.4018/978-1-7998-8921-2.ch002

pandemic and the lessons that stakeholders learned at various institutions in Ontario. Based on the lessons learned, the authors propose a framework that could be applied while deliberating online course delivery to international students. Although having emerged from reflections of practices adopted during the COVID-19 pandemic, the lessons learned will apply beyond the pandemic. Consequently, this chapter should appeal to higher education organization decision-makers and administrators as well as international students who opt to enroll in online courses.

The changed context resulting from the pandemic revealed that course delivery requires a different level of decision-making and planning. Researchers have identified numerous concerns needing attention (Gudiño Paredes et al., 2021; Liu & Shirley, 2021; Octaberlina & Muslimin, 2020). While these issues and the resulting deliberations are helpful, they seem to demand attention and resolution from program planners to each unique challenge separately. This stratagem is onerous, daunting, and seemingly unending. A more efficient and effective way may be to classify the issues into larger categories to form a framework. While the framework can be applied to any set of students, the discussion here focuses on international students' experiences because the importance of international students in Canadian postsecondary institutions and the issues they face are also unique (Calder et al., 2016; De Moissac et al., 2020). The purpose of this chapter is to introduce a framework that sheds light on the complexities associated with programs at the postsecondary level for international students.

The are many beneficial reasons for educating international students in Ontario universities and colleges, ranging from the internationalization of campuses (Knight, 2003; McGregor & Hunter, 2021); the exchange and integration of intercultural ideas and experiences into the curriculum and local culture (McGregor & Hunter, 2021; Taskoh, 2020); the socialization, training, and vetting of future high-skilled immigrants (Scott et al., 2015; Statistics Canada, 2020); the buttressing of declining domestic student enrolments (McGregor & Hunter, 2021); the cross-pollination of ideas between international and domestic students (Belkhodja & Esses, 2013; Knight, 1999); and augmenting the financial sustainability of postsecondary programs and campuses (Lu & Hou, 2019; Statistics Canada, 2020; Taskoh, 2020; Trilokekar & El Masri, 2019). These rationales can be classified as ideological, educational, and instrumental as per Stier's (2004) analysis. Regardless of the reasons, it is evident that Canadian universities and colleges are actively recruiting students from other countries. Moreover, the number of students attending postsecondary institutions in Canada in general and Ontario, in particular, is increasing. Figure 1 illustrates the steady rise in the number of international students at Ontario universities over a 5-year span.

Figure 1. Rise in international students in Ontario universities (Statistics Canada, 2021a)

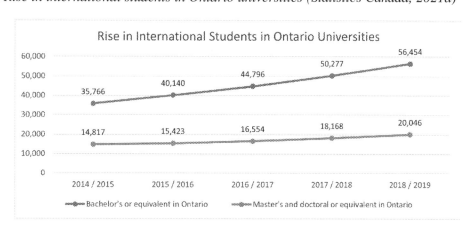

An increase in the number of international students has also been seen at Ontario colleges, as shown in Figure 2.

Figure 2. Rise in international students in Ontario colleges (Statistics Canada, 2021a)

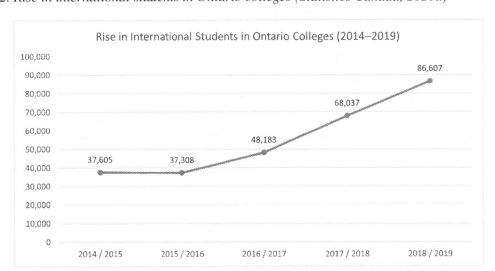

The reasons international students pursue higher education in Ontario universities and colleges vary considerably and stem partly from the context in which the students find themselves in their home countries—that is, the push factors (Cebolla-Boado et al., 2018; Li et al., 2021; Wu, 2014; Zhang & Noels, 2021). Universities and colleges primarily solicit international students in response to steady declines in government funding (Altbach & Knight, 2007; Macrander, 2016; Zhang & Noels, 2021) and a decrease in the domestic student population (Statistics Canada, 2020). Between 1984 and 2014, operating grants per full-time equivalent students decreased dramatically: Ontario universities experienced a 28% decrease in funding, while funding to Ontario colleges declined 37% (Canadian Federation of Students–Ontario, 2015). Revenue received from the federal and provincial governments continue its freefall decline. In 2019, government grants to Ontario universities and colleges comprised 24% of total university revenues, revealing a marked decline from 1982, when total government revenues received by universities represented 87% of their total operating revenues (Smith-Carrier, 2020). The quality of teaching in Ontario continues to pull students from elsewhere in the world, but that pull factor has remained a constant (Canadian Bureau of International Education [CBIE], 2018).

Ontario universities and colleges have adopted multiple strategies to offset such revenue reductions; however, one approach that has become most palatable is to buttress operating revenues by increasing international student enrolments (Cantwell, 2015; Choudaha, 2017; Smith-Carrier 2020; Zhang & Noels, 2021). Fees levied on international students comprise tuition fees, ancillary fees, and other per-use charges. Postsecondary international student fees in Ontario are unregulated, leading some to refer to these students as cash cows (Cantwell, 2015; Choudaha, 2017). Karram (2013) extends the notion of international students as objects of economic interest between nations and identifies a discursive positioning of international students as commodities to be secured via international trade practices, rather than as stakeholders in the international study-abroad dynamic.

Because international tuition fees remain unregulated in Ontario, universities and colleges are free to assign fees as they deem fit. Statistics Canada's pre-pandemic projections for Ontario universities' revenues for 2020–2021 estimated that 21% of total operating revenues would be generated via international student tuition fees, compared to a modest 23% originating from government transfers (Matias et al., 2021). As shown in Figures 3 and 4, the steep rise in international students' fees indicates an economic incentive for Ontario colleges and universities to recruit greater numbers of international students. Frenette et al. (2020) conclude that Canadian universities relied heavily on international students attending Canadian universities before the pandemic and anticipate this trend will continue, with the trajectory of international student fees continuing to increase.

Figure 3. Undergraduate fee comparison of Canadian and international students (Statistics Canada, 2021b)

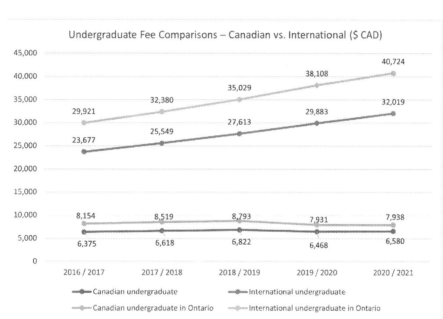

PANDEMIC-RELATED CHANGES TO DELIVERY OF COURSES AND PROGRAMS

Before the COVID-19 pandemic, most international students' instruction occurred alongside their Canadian counterparts in face-to-face settings. The pandemic changed all that. Due to various travelling, gathering, and interacting restrictions, the pandemic disrupted international students' in-person participation on Ontario university campuses. Moreover, the absence of international students' tuition payments translated into significant revenue losses for the institutions. Indeed, a reliance on international students has necessitated re-envisioning and recalibrating how programs are delivered. Initially, the alterations in teaching and learning practices brought about early in 2020 were reactionary, unimaginative, and based chiefly on readily available tools and resources (Dwivedi et al., 2020; Hodges et al., 2020; Openo, 2020). Although we acknowledge that other forms of blended, asynchronous, and synchronous teaching

Figure 4. Graduate fee comparison of Canadian and international students (Statistics Canada, 2021b)

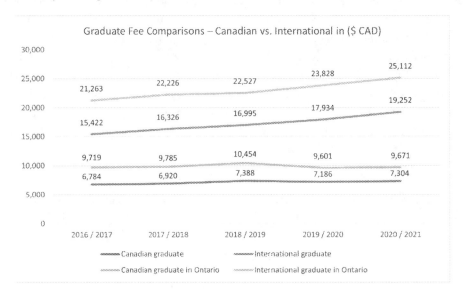

occurred before the pandemic, such courses and programs were carefully planned, and enrollment into the courses was delimited to students who had adequate skill sets, predilection for distance or online learning, and access to technology. All students, not just a select few who would have succeeded, were moved to technology-assisted delivery during the pandemic.

Faculty and student survey responses further reveal that the pivot to online learning was laden with problems (OCUFA, 2020). Subsequent planning and delivery of postsecondary programs (both under-graduate and graduate programs for 2020−2021 academic term) improved but continue to encounter challenges. Previously held assumptions, traditions, and practices were disrupted, and online course and program delivery displaced previous face-to-face modalities. Shifting from face-to-face delivery to an exclusively online format in pre-COVID times had been identified as a significant challenge (Davey et al., 2019). Thus, when a shift in teaching modality was thrust upon universities and colleges in little more than a weekend, it was not surprising to watch students' and instructors' anxiety levels heighten across North American campuses (Jamieson, 2020). A lack of preparedness for the pivot to online de-livery by the Ontario postsecondary sector similarly comes as no surprise; prior to the pandemic, only a small proportion of university and college instructors demonstrated interest in teaching online (Hodges et al., 2020).

While it may have been difficult for universities and colleges to pivot quickly to predominantly online instruction, it was harder still for international students (Firang, 2020). Most of the challenges facing students emerged because of online program delivery and had not been present during pre-pandemic face-to-face delivery of the same programs in host countries. The challenges included inadequate internet facilities, inaccessible teaching resources and other class materials, asynchronous time-zone sessions, absence of lab resources for instruction and experimentation, limited or no student interaction, and support accessibility issues. Of course, the list of grievances is much longer, varies considerably, and much has been written about it (Davey et al., 2019; Firang, 2020; Liu & Shirley, 2021; Openo, 2020). These challenges interfered with pre-pandemic, conventional models of teaching and learning. Each is-sue requires a solution specific to the problem. To understand the nature of the challenges, the authors present a framework to tackle and understand the complexity and interrelationship of issues currently faced by international students.

TOWARDS A NEW FRAMEWORK

The plethora of issues that emerged due to the rapid move to online delivery revealed three major components or aspects of course delivery: *pedagogical*, *technological*, and *operational*. The following section explains each of these components within the context of the proposed framework, followed by a discussion of their intricate interrelationships. The authors intentionally have left the definitions of these terms broad so that future researchers and scholars can tailor them to suit their intended purposes.

Pedagogical

The issues pertaining to teaching, learning, and assessment in relation to international students at the postsecondary level constitute the pedagogical component of the proposed framework. The way these elements are decided and negotiated is often a disciplinary matter and a choice of the faculty member delivering the course. There are, however, ample variances in the way things work in one university or program compared to another.

As individuals or collectively as a program, university faculty members typically retain control over the elements that comprise pedagogical decision-making. Sometimes their degrees of freedom with respect to decisions are limited by administrators of the program, department, or faculty. But often these restrictions are more explicitly (and sometimes intentionally) exerted on part-time, adjunct, or non-tenured faculty members (Finn, 2020).

The hallmark of university teaching in Ontario (and the Western world in general) is often different from the formalized structured lectures that many students are accustomed to in their home countries (Lin & Scherz, 2014; Zhu & Flaitz, 2005)—especially when students hail from places where class sizes are large, the method of teaching relies on lecturing to students, and the teacher's authority is not to be challenged (Lin & Scherz, 2014). Such differences in teaching style are witnessed in face-to-face classroom activities in the form of small and large group discussions, debates, and critiquing published articles. During the pandemic, the technology has been both important and a common denominator for higher education. Consequently, in the online environment, teaching activities were carried out both synchronously as well as asynchronously because available technologies afforded both these functions. The choice exclusively remained in the hands of the instructor of the course.

The distinction between synchronous and asynchronous modes of delivery was significant here. If instructors retained the choice of how the course was to be delivered, they could adjust such delivery based on whether the students had requisite technological availability and capability of participating in the course. If the format was prescribed (i.e., not at the behest of the instructor), one was limited in the kinds of accommodations that could be made for students' particular needs. For instance, if the delivery was prescribed to be synchronous, then issues faced by a student located in a different time zone could not be accommodated without altering the pedagogical decisions made at the outset of the course (as in foregoing that element of instruction, participation, or assessment). The instructor's adjustments to make accommodations are further hampered to adopt an asynchronous mode if a student suffers from low bandwidth accessibility issues.

The importance of a practical component in various disciplines has been recognized as vital by many scholars over the years (see Jolly & MacDonald, 1989; Kahn, 1990). These criteria in traditional face-to-face delivery of the program are accomplished by supplementing theoretical components with labs, site visits, and the like. In an online delivery mode, virtual laboratories sometimes provide a pale simulacrum of these components. The authors refer to them as pale substitutes because skills such as dissection in biology are not accomplished by the kinds of virtual reality technologies available at all universities (Dyrberg et al., 2017). Naturally, the necessity of these components is determined by discipline-specific, academic review committees that monitor quality, and to some extent the individual(s) teaching the course.

Another point of distinction between Western postsecondary education and the parts of the world where our international students come from is the way assessment is used. After all, assessment is inextricably linked to teaching and learning (Gore et al., 2009). While the prominence of *assessment of learning* is high in many international students' home countries, the notions of *assessment for learning* and *assessment as learning* are not as prevalent (Birenbaum et al., 2015). For instance, group-work papers and presentations, take-home exams, and other assessment methods may be unfamiliar to international students who had experienced educational systems that prioritize individual assessments via standardized testing. Consequently, the attitudes of students towards assessment, which is often viewed exclusively as assessment of learning, leads to adoption of practices that contravene academic integrity. The International Center for Academic Integrity (2021) indicates that almost 30% of students admit to cheating in some form. Instances of cheating in an online format—whether synchronous or asynchronous—are at best likely to remain the same or worsen. Should different technological tools such as Proctorio, ProctorTrack, and Respondus Lockdown be employed to overcome the emergent challenges? The repercussions of these are numerous and discussed elsewhere (see Kumar, 2020).

In sum, the pedagogical matters correspond to how the course is delivered, the elements (if any) that are applicable for practical work, and how it is be assessed, all within boundaries that are at times determined externally or left to the discretion of the instructor. The more degrees of freedom afforded to the instructors, the more they can accommodate the particularities and oddities that students in the course encounter. Of course, these pedagogical components, it is argued, should drive the technology and other elements that facilitate online instruction.

Technological

The issues that emerge related to the use of digital and internet communication technologies (ICTs) to deliver courses and programs to international students at the postsecondary level constitute the technological component of the framework. Jamieson (2020) advocated that the technology and ICT used needs to be adaptive in this online instructional environment; otherwise, students and instructors alike encounter a myriad of challenges.

ICT plays an integral role in facilitating a positive learning outcome for international students studying online and remotely (Davey et al., 2019). Therefore, the selection of a correct set of technologies is a must. Whether the required functionalities exist in available technologies is a separate matter. Take the example of Microsoft Teams, which was adopted soon after the pivot to online occurred. Initially, the software did not have the features that were considered essential for good pedagogical practices. Microsoft's competitors in video conferencing (like Zoom and LifeSize) also lacked functionality that good/decent pedagogy demanded.

Some elements of course delivery are under the direct control of the universities and colleges, including the choice of learning management systems and various digital tools and software. In circumstances where these technologies are internally housed, the degree of control increases as well, although the management and upkeep of those technologies increases their costs. The trend everywhere, therefore, is to adopt a commercial package. Students manage other elements at the receiving end. These components include student computer(s), cameras and audio equipment, the internet bandwidth provided by the local internet service provider (ISP), which is required to avail the course content (Octaberlina & Muslimin, 2020), and other specialized equipment, if needed. In addition to these two ends, there is also the infrastructure in the middle that neither end can control. This infrastructure makes it possible to deliver content from the university's end and access it at the student's location. In most circumstances, this middle layer is robust and reliable, and its existence never emerges in any substantive deliberations, while selecting the right technologies that map as per pedagogy necessitates. In practice, however, this arrangement puts the onus on students to acquire adequate technological tools (e.g., computers with adequate CPU and storage capability, internet bandwidth, and software compatibility) in order to enrol and have a positive educative experience in the program. An example during the pandemic is instructive here.

During the COVID-19 pandemic disruptions, international students accessed courses primarily from their home countries. In this context, many instructors were hostage to the reliability of this middle layer. As Octaberlina and Muslimin's (2020) research also highlighted, power outages in the students' communities mean students cannot participate in any synchronous course components with the rest of the class. Students affected by ongoing power disruptions could not effectively join in, even though the synchronous expectations were part of the assessments in the course. Even if the students had access to power generators at their end, they could not overcome the challenge of widespread power outages that not only affect the students' residences but also disable local ISP businesses. As a result, the students had no access to the necessary communication networks to participate in online remote learning. Individual students had little if any recourse to rectify regional power disruptions. Here, internet access was impossible. Prompt and creative solutions were needed to accommodate students who lost access through no fault of their own. The course instructors' solutions varied. One instructor altered assessment requirements (Pedagogical), another arranged for certain students to connect using their mobile phones (Technological), and in a third instance, student group members took it upon themselves to meet at alternative times (Operational) for group assignments and to share course information. These three solutions resolved the immediate technological problems students experienced by approaching the issues using pedagogy (P), technology (T), and operational (O) strategies.

Awareness of the technological component allows stakeholders to recognize that accommodations made in other spheres are temporary at best. Understanding that the gap in technology access has resulted in higher education experiments in some remote areas being severely curtailed (McKeown et al., 2021). Long-lasting solutions will be had if strategies emerge within the realm of technology. The primary concern is to ensure that both the deliverer and recipient have the right set of technologies. The next piece to address is the infrastructure in the middle. The service providers' infrastructure must be robust enough to allow students to access course materials. This middleware requirement often separates students in urban (often infrastructurally robust) areas from rural (often infrastructurally lacking) areas (McKeown et al., 2021). Also, if the adjustments required at the receiver's end are too extensive, the cost may be prohibitive for these students.

In summary, online instruction during the pandemic has made technology vital. It also has exposed the inequities between the so-called haves and have-nots of the world, not because students cannot afford the tuition or the requisite technology but rather because they live in areas where technological infrastructure is subpar, thus limiting their participation. Because technology undergirds the teaching and learning of the international students, its availability, accessibility, and distribution across various parts of the world also affects the technological dimension of the framework.

Operational

The operational elements that influence international students' remote online participation consist of a diverse set of issues. The operational component includes logistical matters at both the delivery and receiving ends of the teaching-learning dynamic that affect international students' participation in the course or the program. Examples of operational issues include the coordination of synchronous classes across multiple time zones, student study environments that are filled with constant distractions (vehicle-horns, children, other extraneous noises), academic integrity with remote invigilation, varied levels of language proficiency amongst students, access to university-provided supports, and artificial restrictions such as collective agreements that regulate (restrict) faculty members' scheduled availability. Although not an exhaustive list, it reveals the complexities arising from a purely operational perspective.

Attempts to bring students together in an online environment were a challenge even before the pandemic disrupted face-to-face classes (Davey et al., 2019). In online classes, course instructors have struggled to engage students due to the instructors' competencies with the higher levels of technological skills needed to sustain students' interests in online contexts (Gillett-Swan, 2017). Academic staff need to be appropriately trained to be comfortable and more competent with the technology necessary to facilitate an engaging and meaningful educational experience for online students. Demanding specific levels of technological competencies from instructors for online teaching would be another duty added to faculty members' existing contractual workloads (Gillett-Swan, 2017), and represents an example of an operational issue intersecting with technological and pedagogical elements. However, any sustainable, long-term solution to this operational challenge must originate from the Operational sector.

Students enrolled in pre-pandemic online courses differ from those currently in online courses. Previously, students made a conscious decision to register in an online course, a decision likely informed by whether the student had access to the technological components discussed earlier. Failure to acquire the necessary technology would have discouraged the student from registering in the course. Even the logistical issue of different time zones is something international students would have considered prior to registration; that is, the students were aware of the expectations required for full and productive participation in an online course. With the abrupt pivot ushered in by pandemic lockdowns and safety protocols, the choice was taken away from students. In the initial stages of the first wave of COVID-19 in Ontario, students had to decide mid-term if they would transition to complete their courses online. There was little opportunity for choice; rather, the only alternative to online study was to withdraw from one's classes. Withdrawal from studies was not a viable option for many students as it was academically unsatisfactory, financially expensive, and in short, a waste of time. International students faced even greater pressure to continue online when compared to their domestic counterparts because of the cost, time, and academic investment. Also, international students at the university had to retain their full-time student status to meet the requirements of their study permits and subsequent work permits. Dropping courses would have meant violating the conditions of a study permit and would jeopardize students' immigration status.

Still, studying remotely online can have benefits for students. Lane (2021) reports that international students appreciate some of these benefits, the biggest being the financial savings: International students are spared additional moving and living expenses when studying remotely from home. Culturally too, the challenges associated with acclimatization to a new culture are minimized if not eliminated. Time is also saved by avoiding unnecessary travel from residence to the site of one's classes.

It is imperative to note that operational issues, although not directly related to pedagogy or technology, are as potent as the other two components. On matters of legality, convenience, and cost, they exert sufficient pressure to demand alteration in either of the two dimensions. For instance, the collective agreements between faculty unions and the university stipulate the times when the courses can be offered. Although that may be understandable when the instruction occurs face-to-face, what is convenient here does not make it conducive for the international students who reside in different time zones. Yet, to overcome the predicament one either must make change to the mode of delivery (say, asynchronous instead of synchronous; pedagogical adjustment), or record the session (technological adjustment, but that still deprives the student of a live session with other students). In other words, depending on the issue, a different component prevails and trumps the other two.

PEDAGOGY, TECHNOLOGY, OPERATION (PTO) FRAMEWORK

The preceding section described each of the dimensions and components of the PTO framework separately. In reality, these elements operate in concert simultaneously, yet in different proportions. One way to visualize this framework is to imagine it as three geometric axes that determine the extent to which an issue has pedagogical, technological, and operational components (Figure 5).

Figure 5. PTO framework representation

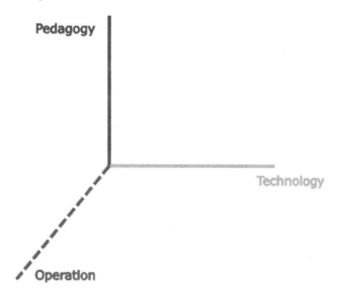

In this space, each issue encountered is plotted as P, T, O. The values of P, T, and O vary for each issue. The authors present two examples that will illustrate the conceptualization and the interconnectedness of the axes.

Issue 1

The issue of offering online synchronous courses to international students in different time zones in a remote area has elements of pedagogy (presumably, the decision to deliver the course synchronously), technology (the availability of the internet bandwidth from source to destination; students' ability to access the stream), and operation (discounting time-zone differences between where the instructor is and where the student is). This example has all three elements of P, T, and O. One of the solutions, in this case, could result in the course being offered asynchronously. This strategy would diffuse the operational concern of time-zone differences but may not fully resolve the technological issues if the delivery of the content does not conform to the Universal Design for Learning (UDL) Guidelines' Checkpoint 5 (CAST, 2018). The UDL principles apply to good teaching and learning practices regardless of where they occur. Still, in the pivot to online delivery, the limitations on the pedagogical side of things were exposed. To fully resolve these issues, considerable work needs to happen at the pedagogical end. For example, one approach could involve creating lessons that are accessible in various formats—visual, text, audio, video, illustrations. However, the requirement to deliver the content in multi-modal forms that adhere to UDL principles would require the university's operational support. The instructor might be a content expert but might lack the ability to create multi-modal lessons. This example illustrates how a comprehensive solution requires attention to P, T, and O simultaneously. It also reveals that the costs rise to resolve these issues.

Issue 2

The second issue corresponds to synchronous courses offered during a time that is inconducive for students. Courses offered during the regular working hours in Ontario, often between 8:00 a.m. and 10:00 p.m., while convenient locally, cause significant disruption for students accessing these courses during the middle of the night in different time zones. Even when a student accesses these courses during non-regular hours, their cognitive acuity may be impaired. At the university end, course offerings are often constrained by collective agreements between faculty unions in the respective universities and by the universities themselves. These terms are often negotiated for face-to-face offerings and as such do not account for access in different time zones. Indeed, this requirement is exacerbated in a synchronous course delivery model, which is a pedagogical issue, but the accommodations are constrained because of the operational matters of the collective agreements. Technological resolution to situations such as these is expensive, awkward, and clumsy. A pedagogical solution of changing the course to an asynchronous modality is possible, but that too is often limited by operational issues. That is, when contingent part-time faculty members deliver courses, they have little to no say in the mode of delivery of courses, which are often decided by the program committees and departments. By default, the best solution resides in the sphere of the operational matters. A student requesting (or demanding) a change to a course's scheduled time, designed around the lives of domestic students, cannot be resolved by the course instructor. Knowledge of the issue and where it predominantly lies in the framework offers a better chance for proponents of change to target the right authorities.

Both these issues are plotted on the framework axes in Figure 6. The illustration also shows the comparison of Issues 1 and 2, the former having more of a pedagogical and technological component, and the latter having more of an operational component.

Figure 6. Plotted issues to demonstrate the interconnections of PTO model

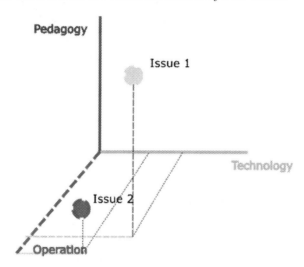

Both the issues presented here show that expansive solutions are also more expensive solutions, involving more than just the student and the teacher. Therefore, the shortcut of resolving emerging issues pedagogically is the modus operandi. As seen through the application of the PTO framework, the solutions that emerge are short term, seldom fully effective, and potentially compromise the quality of technologically mediated education for the international students who are accessing it from afar. This is not only problematic but also raises more questions about the sustainability and ethics of the international education enterprise. When universities charge more and want more international students, is it not in their best interest to offer high-quality programs that meet the students' needs? The worry, therefore, is that these issues may become concealed once again when universities revert to face-to-face delivery models. That is, these issues have emerged and became public/transparent due to the large-scale online delivery that commenced during the pandemic.

CONCLUSION

The embedded complexities of the interconnections between pedagogy, technology, and operations in the online delivery of higher education programs to international students are revealed by using the PTO framework. Although, post-pandemic educational practices and planning for them were the source of our reflection and proposal of the PTO framework, they extend beyond the current context, which is undoubtedly going to pass. In keeping with Weiner's (1976) now generally accepted advice to not "waste a crisis" (p. 227), we have seized the opportunity to plan a framework that will work beyond the current pandemic. The interplay of pedagogy, technology, and operation matters are applicable under what we consider a new *normal*, which is likely to resemble, in part, the *previous* normal because the pull and push factors of the host and recipient country are likely to persist.

The complexities, are further complicated by issues that are totally outside the purview of the course-delivering university and/or the student accessing the course. A new set of complexities arise because of the geo-political and environmental elements. The authors envision the PTO framework (the axes) encompassed within a sphere, with the sphere representing the geo-political relationships between the host country (in the authors' case Ontario, Canada) and the recipient's end (where the international student is accessing the course). Consequently, a class would have multiple spheres denoting the geo-political realities between the host and the recipient countries. Each sphere would encompass the particularities of each cluster of international students in their respective country of access.

The PTO framework provides a new way to conceptualize and view the problem faced by the universities when delivering programs to international students. The application of PTO works for future courses and can reveal the strengths and shortcomings of existing blended course offerings. It also provides a framework for analyzing past practices. We concede that neither this work nor the framework generates a list of best practices to be applied in various situations. We resisted the temptation to draft such a list because we contend that the PTO framework provides a robust tool to analyze and plan for delivery of courses and programs to all students—international or domestic, near or far, using technology or not—during and post-pandemic. The application of the framework to better plan and understand course and program delivery demands that the planners think of the contexts carefully and isolate the P, T, and O elements. As planners, the authors have experienced the benefits of using the PTO framework in their university while planning international student program delivery. The authors invite further investigation into the applicability of the PTO framework and encourage researchers to empirically test the model.

REFERENCES

Altbach, P., & Knight, J. (2007). The internationalization of higher education: Motivations and realities. *Journal of Studies in International Education, 11*(3–4), 290–305. doi:10.1177/1028315307303542

Belkhodja, C., & Esses, V. (2013). *Knowledge synthesis: Improving the assessment of international students' contribution to Canadian society*. Pathways to Prosperity. http://p2pcanada.ca/library/knowledge-synthesis-improving-the-assessment-of-international-students-contribution-to-canadian-society/

Birenbaum, M., DeLuca, C., Earl, L., Heritage, M., Klenowski, V., Looney, A., Smith, K., Timperley, H., Volante, L., & Wyatt-Smith, C. (2015). International trends in the implementation of assessment for learning: Implications for policy and practice. *Policy Futures in Education, 13*(1), 117–140. doi:10.1177/1478210314566733

Calder, M., Richter, S., Mao, Y., Kovacs-Burns, K., Mogale, R., & Danko, M. (2016). International students attending Canadian universities: Their experiences with housing, finances, and other issues. *Canadian Journal of Higher Education, 46*(2), 92–110. doi:10.47678/cjhe.v46i2.184585

Canadian Bureau of International Education. (2018, August). *The student's voice: National results of the 2018 CBIE international student survey* (CBIE Research in Brief No. 9). https://cbie.ca/wp-content/uploads/2018/08/Student_Voice_Report-ENG.pdf

Canadian Federation of Students–Ontario. (2015, July). *The impact of government underfunding on students.* https://cfsontario.ca/wp-content/uploads/2017/07/Factsheet-Underfunding.pdf

Cantwell, B. (2015). Are international students cash cows? Examining the relationship between new international undergraduate enrollments and institutional revenue at public colleges and universities in the US. *Journal of International Students, 5*(4), 512–525. doi:10.32674/jis.v5i4.412

CAST. (2018). *Checkpoint 5.1: Use multiple media for communication.* https://udlguidelines.cast.org/action-expression/expression-communication/use-multimedia

Cebolla-Boado, H., Hu, Y., & Soysal, Y. N. (2018). Why study abroad? Sorting of Chinese students across British universities. *British Journal of Sociology of Education, 39*(3), 365–380. doi:10.1080/01425692.2017.1349649

Choudaha, R. (2017). Three waves of international student mobility (1999–2020). *Studies in Higher Education, 42*(5), 825–832. doi:10.1080/03075079.2017.1293872

Davey, B., Elliott, K., & Bora, M. (2019). Negotiating pedagogical challenges in the shift from face-to-face to fully online learning: A case study of collaborative design solutions by learning designers and subject matter experts. *Journal of University Teaching & Learning Practice, 16*(1), 3. doi:10.53761/1.16.1.3

De Moissac, D., Graham, J., Prada, K., Gueye, N., & Rocque, R. (2020). Mental health status and help-seeking strategies of international students in Canada. *Canadian Journal of Higher Education, 50*(4), 52–71. doi:10.47678/cjhe.vi0.188815

Dwivedi, Y., Hughes, D., Coombs, C., Constantiou, I., Duan, Y., Edwards, J. S., Gupta, B., Lal, B., Misra, S., Prashant, P., Raman, R., Rana, N. P., Sharma, S. K., & Upadhyay, N. (2020). Impact of COVID-19 pandemic on information management research and practice: Transforming education, work and life. *International Journal of Information Management, 55*, 102211. Advance online publication. doi:10.1016/j.ijinfomgt.2020.102211

Dyrberg, N. R., Treusch, A. H., & Wiegand, C. (2017). Virtual laboratories in science education: Students' motivation and experiences in two tertiary biology courses. *Journal of Biological Education, 51*(4), 358–374. doi:10.1080/00219266.2016.1257498

Finn, S. (2020). Academic freedom and the choice of teaching methods. *Teaching in Higher Education, 25*(1), 116–123. doi:10.1080/13562517.2019.1672149

Firang, D. (2020). The impact of COVID-19 pandemic on international students in Canada. *International Social Work, 63*(6), 820–824. doi:10.1177/0020872820940030

Frenette, M., Choi, Y., & Doreleyers, A. (2020). International student enrolment in post-secondary education programs prior to COVID-19. *Economic Insights*, 105. https://www150.statcan.gc.ca/n1/pub/11-626-x/11-626-x2020003-eng.htm

Gillett-Swan, J. (2017). The challenges of online learning supporting and engaging the isolated learner. *Journal of Learning Design, 10*(1), 20–30. doi:10.5204/jld.v9i3.293

Gore, J., Ladwig, J., Elsworth, W., Ellis, H., Parkes, R., & Griffiths, T. (2009). *Quality assessment: Linking assessment tasks and teaching outcomes in the social sciences.* Australian Learning and Teaching Council. https://ltr.edu.au/vufind/Record/365398

Gudiño Paredes, S., de Jesús Jasso Peña, F., & de La Fuente Alcazar, J. (2021). Remote proctored exams: Integrity assurance in online education? *Distance Education, 42*(2), 200–218. doi:10.1080/01587919.2021.1910495

Hodges, C., Moore, S., Lockee, B., Trust, T., & Bond, A. (2020, March 27). The difference between emergency remote teaching and online learning. *EDUCAUSE Review.* https://er.educause.edu/articles/2020/3/the-difference-between-emergency-remote-teaching-and-online-learning

International Center for Academic Integrity. (2020). *Facts and statistics.* https://academicintegrity.org/resources/facts-and-statistics

Jamieson, M. (2020). Keeping a learning community and academic integrity intact after a mid-term shift to online learning in chemical engineering design during the COVID-19 pandemic. *Journal of Chemical Education, 97*(9), 2768–2772. doi:10.1021/acs.jchemed.0c00785

Jolly, B. C., & MacDonald, M. M. (1989). Education for experience: The role of practical experience in undergraduate and general clinical training. *Medical Education, 23*(2), 189–195. doi:10.1111/j.1365-2923.1989.tb00885.x PMID:2716558

Kahn, M. (1990). Paradigm lost: The importance of practical work in school science from a developing country perspective. *Studies in Science Education, 18*(1), 127–136. doi:10.1080/03057269008559984

Karram, G. L. (2013). International students as lucrative markets or vulnerable populations: A critical discourse analysis of national and institutional events in four nations. *Comparative and International Education, 42*(1), 6. Advance online publication. doi:10.5206/cie-eci.v42i1.9223

Knight, J. (1997). A shared vision? Stakeholders' perspectives on the internationalization of higher education in Canada. *Journal of Studies in International Education, 44*(1), 27–31. doi:10.1177/102831539700100105

Knight, J. (1999). Internationalisation of higher education. In H. de Wit & J. Knight (Eds.), Quality and internationalisation in higher education (pp. 13–28). Organisation for Economic Co-operation and Development (OECD). doi:10.1787/9789264173361-en

Knight, J. (2003). Updated internationalization definition. *Industry and Higher Education, 33*, 2–3. doi:10.6017/ihe.2003.33.7391

Kumar, R. (2020). Assessing higher education in the COVID-19 era. *Brock Education Journal, 29*(2), 37–41. doi:10.26522/brocked.v29i2.841

Lane, C. (2021, August 6). *How has online learning impacted international students?* https://www.topuniversities.com/student-info/studying-abroad-articles/how-has-online-learning-impacted-international-students

Li, L., Shen, W., & Xie, A. (2021). Why students leave Chinese elite universities for doctoral studies abroad: Institutional habitus, career script and college graduates' decision to study abroad. *International Journal of Educational Development, 84*, 102408. Advance online publication. doi:10.1016/j.ijedudev.2021.102408

Lin, S., & Scherz, S. (2014). Challenges facing Asian international graduate students in the US: Pedagogical considerations in higher education. *Journal of International Students, 4*(1), 16–33. doi:10.32674/jis.v4i1.494

Liu, Y., & Shirley, T. (2021). Without crossing a border: Exploring the impact of shifting study abroad online on students' learning and intercultural competence development during the COVID-19 pandemic. *Online Learning, 25*(1), 182–194. doi:10.24059/olj.v25i1.2471

Lu, Y., & Hou, F. (2019). Student transitions: Earnings of former international students in Canada's labour market. In A. H. Kim & M. Kwak (Eds.), *Outward and upward mobilities: International students in Canada, their families, and structuring institutions* (pp. 219–245). University of Toronto Press. doi:10.3138/9781487530563-014

Macrander, A. (2016). An international solution to a national crisis: Trends in student mobility to the United States post 2008. *International Journal of Educational Research, 8*(2), 1–20. doi:10.1016/j.ijer.2016.12.003

Massey, J., & Burrow, J. (2012). Coming to Canada to study: Factors that influence student's decisions to participate in international exchange. *Journal of Student Affairs Research and Practice, 49*(1), 83–100. doi:10.1515/jsarp-2012-6177

Matias, C., Popovic, A., & Lebel, A. (2021, August 18). *Projected financial impact of the COVID-19 pandemic on Canadian universities for the 2020/21 academic year* (Statistics Canada catalogue no. 81-595-M). https://www150.statcan.gc.ca/n1/en/pub/81-595-m/81-595-m2021002-eng.pdf?st=ZjCI26HC

McGregor, A., & Hunter, W. (2021). Internationalization in Ontario colleges: Patterns and policies. *Journal of Educational Informatics, 2*(1), 1–32. https://orcid.org/0000-0001-7346-4277. doi:10.51357/jei.v2i1.134

McKeown, J. S., Bista, K., & Chan, R. Y. (2021). COVID-19 and higher education: Challenges and successes during the global pandemic. In J. S. McKeown, K. Bista, & R. Y. Chan (Eds.), *Global higher education during COVID-19: Policy, society, and technology* (pp. 1–8). STAR Scholars.

Octaberlina, L., & Muslimin, A. (2020). EFL students perspective towards online learning barriers and alternatives using Moodle/Google Classroom during COVID-19 pandemic. *International Journal of Education, 9*(6), 1–9. doi:10.5430/ijhe.v9n6p1

OCUFA. (2020, November). *OCUFA 2020 study: COVID-19 and the impact on university life and education.* https://ocufa.on.ca/assets/OCUFA-2020-Faculty-Student-Survey-opt.pdf

Openo, J. (2020). Education's response to the COVID-19 pandemic reveals online education's three enduring challenges. *Canadian Journal of Learning and Technology, 46*(2), 1–12. doi:10.21432/cjlt27981

Scott, C., Safdar, S., Trilokekar, R., & El Masri, A. (2015). International students as "ideal immigrants" in Canada: A disconnect between policy makers' assumptions and the lived experiences of international students. *Comparative and International Education, 43*(3), 5. Advance online publication. doi:10.5206/cie-eci.v43i3.9261

Smith-Carrier, T. (2020, October 20). Low funding for universities puts students at risk for cycles of poverty, especially in the wake of COVID-19. *Academic Matters.* https://academicmatters.ca/low-funding-for-universities-puts-students-at-risk-for-cycles-of-poverty-especially-in-the-wake-of-covid-19/

Statistics Canada. (2020, November 25). International students accounted for all of the growth in postsecondary enrolments in 2018/2019. *The Daily.* https://www150.statcan.gc.ca/n1/daily-quotidien/201125/dq201125e-eng.htm

Statistics Canada. (2021a). *Post-secondary enrolments, by international standard classification of education, institution type, classification of instructional programs, STEM and BHASE groupings, status of student in Canada, age group and gender* (Table 37-10-0163-01). doi:10.25318/3710016301-eng

Statistics Canada. (2021b). *Canadian and international tuition fees by level of study* (Table 37-10-0045-01). doi:10.25318/3710004501-eng

Stier, J. (2004). Taking a critical stance toward internationalization ideologies in higher education: Idealism, instrumentalism and educationalism. *Globalisation, Societies and Education, 2*(1), 83–97. doi:10.1080/1476772042000177069

Taskoh, A. K. (2020). Internationalization in Canadian higher education institutions: Ontario. *Higher Education for the Future, 7*(2), 97–117. doi:10.1177/2347631120930538

Trilokekar, R., & El Masri, A. (2019). "International students are … golden": Canada's changing policy contexts, approaches, and national peculiarities in attracting international students and future immigrants. In A. H. Kim & M. Kwak (Eds.), *Outward and upward mobilities: International students in Canada, their families, and structuring institutions* (pp. 25–55). University of Toronto Press. doi:10.3138/9781487530563-005

Weiner, M. F. (1976). Don't waste a crisis—Your patient's or your own. *Medical Economics, 53*(5), 227.

Wu, Q. (2014). Motivations and decision-making processes of mainland Chinese students for undertaking master's programs abroad. *Journal of Studies in International Education, 18*(5), 426–444. doi:10.1177/1028315313519823

Zhang, Y. S. D., & Noels, K. (2021). The frequency and importance of accurate heritage name pronunciation for post-secondary international students in Canada. *Journal of International Students, 11*(3), 608–627. doi:10.32674/jis.v11i3.2232

Zhu, W., & Flaitz, J. (2005). Using focus group methodology to understand international students' academic language needs: A comparison of perspectives. *Teaching English as a Second or Foreign Language, 8*(4), 1–11. http://tesl-ej.org/ej32/a3.html

ADDITIONAL READING

Adnan, M., & Anwar, K. (2020). Online learning amid the COVID-19 pandemic: Students' perspectives. *Journal of Pedagogical Sociology and Psychology, 2*(1), 45–51. doi:10.33902/JPSP.2020261309

Association of Universities and Colleges of Canada. (2007, August). *Canadian universities and international student mobility.* http://www.cneec.org/cneec/articles/AUCCstudent_mobility_2007_e.pdf

El Masri, A., Choubak, M., & Litchmore, R. (2015). *The global competition for international students as future immigrants: The role of Ontario universities in translating government policy into institutional practice.* Higher Education Quality Council of Ontario. https://heqco.ca/wp-content/uploads/2020/03/Global-Competition-for-IS-ENG.pdf

Knight, J. (2019). Understanding international program and provider mobility in the changing landscape of international academic mobility: (Interviewed by Laura Baumvol). *SFU Educational Review, 12*(3), 41–47. doi:10.21810fuer.v12i3.1037

Smith, C., Zhou, G., Potter, M., & Wang, D. (2019). Connecting best practices for teaching linguistically and culturally diverse international students with international student satisfaction and student perceptions of student learning. In W. B. James & C. Cobonoglu (Eds.), *Advances in global education and research* (Vol. 3, pp. 252–265). USF M3 Publishing. https://scholar.uwindsor.ca/educationpub/24/

Statistics Canada. (2021). *Canadian and international tuition fees by level of study* (Table 37-10-0045-01). doi:10.25318/3710004501-eng

Watermeyer, R., Crick, T., Knight, C., & Goodall, J. (2021). COVID-19 and digital disruption in UK universities: Afflictions and affordances of emergency online migration. *Higher Education, 81*(3), 623–641. doi:10.100710734-020-00561-y PMID:32836334

Williams, K., Williams, G., Arbuckle, A., Walton-Roberts, M., & Hennebry, J. (2015). *International students in Ontario's postsecondary education system, 2000-2012: An evaluation of changing policies, populations and labour market entry processes.* Higher Education Council of Ontario. https://heqco.ca/wp-content/uploads/2020/03/International-Students-in-Ontario-ENG.pdf

Zimmerman, J. (2020, March 10). Coronavirus and the great online-learning experiment. *The Chronicle of Higher Education.* https://www.chronicle.com/article/coronavirus-and-the-great-online-learning-experiment/

KEY TERMS AND DEFINITIONS

Framework: A framework is a basic structure that undergirds the complexities of teaching and learning and reveals subtle but important interconnections amongst its constituent components. Within the context of this chapter, the framework is the conceptual structure proposed to categorize and cluster issues and provide clarity affecting international students at the postsecondary level.

Instructional Modality: Defines the methods employed in delivering a course and is closely related to the expectations that can be placed on students. Examples of instructional modality include synchronous, asynchronous, and hybrid modes of online delivery, in addition to the conventional face-to-face in-person delivery.

International Education: Within the context of this chapter, international education refers to international students accessing postsecondary courses offered in Ontario colleges and universities. This definition of international education is a hybrid between accepted terminology of international student and scholar mobility (ISSM) and international program and provider mobility (IPPM) coined by Knight (2019).

Operational Issues: Operational issues are defined as the operational decisions affecting when and how the courses and programs are delivered. These decisions and constraints significantly affect courses' accessibility and are magnified in the online environment.

Pedagogical Issues: Defines all elements of teaching that are typically decided by the instructor or the governing body of the program. Pedagogical issues include how to teach, what to assess, and the forms of assessments. The degree of freedom afforded to instructors teaching the course differs in colleges and universities and from discipline to discipline.

Technological Issues: Within the context of this chapter and framework, technological issues are the digital communication technologies used to deliver courses to the international students spread across the globe. Technological components include hardware and software at both the hosting and recipient end and infrastructural elements between the host and recipient.

Chapter 3
Culturally Responsive Education:
Reflections and Insights for Enhancing International Student Experience in Higher Education

Gideon Boadu
Excelsia College, Australia

Peninah Kansiime
Excelsia College, Australia

Sarah Eyaa
https://orcid.org/0000-0002-3330-1374
Alphacrucis University College, Australia

Shannon Said
Excelsia College, Australia

ABSTRACT

As higher education providers (HEPs) across the globe continue to recruit international students to improve their financial and diversity profiles, it is critical that sufficient effort is made to integrate cultural responsiveness across institutional systems with the goal of creating a good experience for these students. This critical collaborative reflection study is positioned within Fook's critical reflection framework. The authors story their experiences as international students in Australia and reflect on how such experiences have influenced their work as academics. The stories weave together to identify critical issues such as positive relationships, empathetic understanding, and sensitive pedagogies that are relevant in the pursuit of culturally responsive education in higher education institutions.

DOI: 10.4018/978-1-7998-8921-2.ch003

INTRODUCTION AND BACKGROUND LITERATURE

Many higher education institutions around the world have consistently sought opportunities to enhance their international presence by looking beyond their national and cultural borders and recruiting students from diverse national backgrounds. In Australia, about 400,000 international students are documented to have studied on student visas between 2008 and 2011 (Lawson, 2012). This trend has continued to grow and has only been interrupted by the current COVID-19 pandemic that oversaw the closure of international borders across the globe, including Australia (Hurley, 2020). The increased admission of international students has greatly changed population demographics in higher education institutions. Beyond the financial and economic benefits that international students bring to higher education providers and the host country, the number of international students that higher education providers enroll is one of the benchmarks considered in international university rankings. For instance, popular University ranking organisations such as Times Higher Education (THE) and Quacquarelli Symonds (QS) include international students as a metric in their rankings. In consequence, competition among higher education providers for international students has become more intense as many providers promise scholarship packages, world-class teaching and faculty, and positive student support culture in their recruitment advertisements (Adams, Leventhal & Connelly, 2012).

Within the highly competitive higher education environment, prospective international students are confronted with the difficulty of making important decisions regarding a destination country and higher education provider (Nafari, Arab & Ghaffari, 2017). While the projected international outlook of higher education providers could serve as a point of attraction to international students, several reasons account for why students choose to pursue international education. Phang (2013) found that students' choice of study destinations was informed by a range of factors including quality of communication between applicants and universities; attractiveness of the destination including university reputation, safety of the destination, language spoken and openness to diverse cultures; and social factors including network with friends and family, former lecturers and student testimonials. Similar studies revealed that the most important push and pull factors in destination choices were opportunities for personal growth (including acquisition of new skills and knowledge, opportunity to learn a new language) and the image as well as the reputation of the university (Eder, Smith & Pitts, 2010). Particularly, opportunities for personal and professional growth were deemed as giving students a professional competitive advantage over their peers. These were interrelated with critical factors such as social acceptance and culture of the people and how that shapes interaction with professors and other university staff. Other latent factors such as visa conditions, security, and cost of education were either facilitators or barriers (Eder et al., 2010; Nicholls, 2018). For other students, funding opportunities through aid and scholarships and conditions of the home country compared to conditions abroad were important considerations in provider choice (Mpinganjira, 2009; Nafari et al., 2017). It is evident that international students do not only seek quality academic programs but also rich academic experience and cultural acceptance.

Over the years, therefore, there has been an increased patronage of higher education by international students in several countries. Also, between January and July 2021, international student enrolments stood at 643484, of which 342,656 (53%) were for instance, data from Australian Department of Education, Skills and Employment shows that between January and December 2020, there were 882,482 international student enrolments of which 418,168 (47%) were in the higher education sector. In 2020, 59% of all international enrolments originated from five countries: China, India, Nepal, Vietnam and Brazil (Department of Education, Skills and Employment, 2020, 2021). The diverse cultural backgrounds of international students require higher education providers to develop and implement culturally and linguistically responsive pedagogies to meet the needs of their internationally and culturally diverse students. As Gatwiri and Ife (2021) note, "teaching is more than just a transfer of knowledge and skills: it is an act of love and a practice in vulnerability" (p. 1). Like school teachers, higher education faculty require a broad understanding of different races, socio-economic backgrounds, geographic regions, gender, sexuality, and religion (Kennedy, Henderson & Marsh, 2022) as these shape the personal and educational outlook of international students. It further requires higher education faculty to check their biases and assumptions about other cultures, develop appropriate instructional material and be committed to enhancing the learning experiences of students from minority cultures (Hutchinson & McAlister-Shields, 2020). Culturally responsive teaching in higher education could prepare students to develop and apply cultural competence in their future careers.

However, achieving culturally responsive teaching in higher education is not simplistic. Traditionally, the mode of instruction in higher education has been a lecture-style, yet this approach is grounded in Western ideology (Larke, 2013) and might not benefit culturally diverse students. The application of technology to higher education instruction has seen some success but there is no one-size-fits-all approach to instructional success. Researchers report that educators have difficulty understanding culturally responsive pedagogies, experience challenges with building relationships with diverse students, and have limited professional opportunities for developing cultural competence (Han et al., 2014). Further, international students report being culturally alienated, socially isolated, and academically disengaged with their teachers, other students and other higher education staff (Wu, Garza, & Guzman, 2015). Larke (2013) therefore argues that even though the idea of multicultural education has been widely applied to pre-tertiary education, its potential for higher education has not been fully explored.

Understanding international students' experiences is critical to supporting them socially, culturally, and academically. To achieve this, attention needs to be given to exploring avenues for improving the international student experience. Many universities have international student offices and departments who assist international students with housing, chaplaincy support, access to information, language, financial aid and other interventions from their admission until completion of their studies (Qadeer at el., 2021). These services serve as critical support systems for international students but more work needs to be done in this area to streamline the services to student expectations (Roberts & Dunworth, 2012). A recent survey of over 21,000 international students from 34 Australian universities by Ammigan & Langton (2018) showed that while many international students were satisfied with academic work, they were least satisfied with living conditions including accommodation, cultural integration, and social activities. The study also reported that arrival and support services did not influence the overall student satisfaction rating (Ammigan & Langton, 2018). Similarly, research by Ammigan and Jones (2018) found that international student satisfaction was greatly linked to the learning experience, though the research did not address whether the educational experience was culturally responsive. These findings suggest that other support services available to international students need to be enhanced through joint effort from academic units and student services departments in universities. In the academic space, teaching strategies that respond to international student cohorts, especially those from culturally and linguistically diverse backgrounds need to be integrated into instruction to provide equitable opportunities for success. Hutchinson and McAlister-Shields (2020) concluded that culturally responsive practices should be foundational in the higher education sector. While this is a commendable suggestion, gaps exist as to how higher education faculty navigate the implementation of culturally responsive education with the view to enhancing the education experience of culturally diverse international students.

More so, in the wake of the COVID-19 pandemic and the limited international student arrivals which has impacted the financial situation of many higher education providers (Hurley, 2020), countries like Australia have come to realise how some sectors of their economies were reliant on income from international student recruitment. This does not only have implications for marketing of academic courses but also raises the need for higher education providers to be innovative in integrating cultural dimensions into courses and course delivery.

STUDENT DIVERSITY AND CULTURALLY RESPONSIVE EDUCATION

Diversity as a concept in education refers to the differences that characterise students or groups of students including but not limited to identity and experience, nationality, culture and value systems, sexuality, socio-economic factors, age, and learning ability. The concept also embraces educator persona, background and beliefs about teaching (Sanger, 2020). Student diversity is a huge strength of many universities but also presents a challenge in several areas. The strength is that universities that boast of student and staff diversity are likely to do well in university rankings and could attract more international students. The challenge, as Alfred (2009) states, is that universities may not be able to meet all the needs of diverse students in a culturally meaningful manner. In Australia it is widely acknowledged that school-age students are increasingly diverse (Kennedy et al., 2022). Such diversity is also evident in the higher education sector as universities attract students from across the world. Many international students come to into the higher education environment with a diverse range of experiences and cultures from their home countries. It is expected that these cultures and experiences are central to their educational experiences in a new country and chosen higher education provider. Gay (2015) uses the analogy of products and services and argues that businesses become more productive when the design and distribution of services and products are informed by consumer needs, cultural values and behaviours. Similarly, higher education providers must not focus on content alone but must be open to different cultures and people in their classrooms and tailor their physical, curricular and pedagogical approaches toward cultural diversity in order to remain relevant and position students for success (Gleason, 2020).

Gay (2010) defines culturally responsive education as using heritage, experiences and ideologies of diverse racial groups to effectively teach students who are members of those same groups. In this context, cultures of diverse students become a filter for teaching specified content and building personal, cultural and social competencies. This definition is however limited because it restricts the concept to students' own cultures without recognising how cross-cultural comparisons and explanations could offer students an opportunity to learn about other cultures beside their own and thus gain a more complete academic experience. Using a socio-cultural approach, Alfred (2009, p. 143) conceptualises culturally responsive education as the recognition and utilisation of student "cultures, histories, and identities to plan and deliver instruction." Rychly and Graves (2012) propose a definition that highlights differences among students and between teachers and students. According to them, culturally responsive education embraces instructional practices that address cultural characteristics that differentiate students from each other and the teacher. On their part, Richards, Brown and Forde (2007) surmise that culturally responsive education has three dimensions: an institutional dimension, which focus on administrative procedures and values; a personal dimension, which reflects teacher beliefs and cultural orientation; and the instructional dimension, which encompasses resources, methods and strategies for teaching. The pedagogical dimension is of interest in this paper even though, as we shall see later, all dimensions connect intricately to inform teacher practice. Culturally responsive education contributes to inclusive education. Conway and Walker (2017) explain that inclusive education is underpinned by a social justice philosophy – that students, regardless of their experiences and cultures, have a right for their learning needs to be met.

Sanger (2020) argues that diversity in the areas of pedagogy, curricula and student demographics are beneficial for developing communication, critical thinking and problem-solving skills that prepare students for an increasingly globalized professional contexts. Gay (2015) also is emphatic that culturally responsive teaching challenges traditional teaching methods that seem to project superiority of dominant cultures and classes and instead highlights the place of minority and marginalised cultures in a pluralistic world. According to Gay (2015), the goal of culturally responsive education is to achieve equity, excellence and justice for students from diverse cultures and ethnicities. Gay (2015) goes further to highlight four ideological premises of culturally responsive education: educators' perceptions about cultural diversity influence their instructional decisions and actions; cultures exerting major influence on how and what children learn and how teachers teach; the demographic complexity of cultural groups and changing immigration trends warrant a dynamic approach to culturally responsive education; and culturally responsive education is more than differentiating subject content. These ideological premises provide a solid foundation for the implementation of culturally responsive education and encourages educators to constantly check their perspectives and practices and reflect on student diversity in order to implement culturally meaningful practices.

There is the need for deliberate preparation and incorporation of student diversity into course design and delivery. Also, educators should recognise and use student diversity to expand thinking and learning. Ignoring diverse backgrounds and identities and making diverse students feel invisible in the classroom does harm to students, albeit unintentional (Sanger, 2020). This raises the need for universities to develop cultural awareness and provide inclusive learning environments. Educators need to cultivate the knowledge base and skills for implementing pedagogies and curricula that are culturally responsive. As Gay (2015, p. 133) succinctly states, "multicultural competency is imperative to meeting these needs of diverse students." Further, given that there is no one perfect approach to teaching, educators need to employ a range of culturally diverse teaching methods to achieve desirable student outcomes (Gay, 2015). Gay (2015) states that culturally responsive education should happen occasionally but should be integrated into all aspects of teaching at all times. Nevertheless, it is important to recognise while it may not be possible to include all groups at all times, educators should have a commitment to culturally responsive practices. Recent research suggests that integrating culturally meaningful material into instruction and collaborative teaching methods could help achieve inclusion (Awang-Hashim, Kaur & Valdez, 2019).

The institutional positioning and responsiveness of universities to cultural issues is critical in any effort toward achieving culturally responsive education for international students. In light of this, Gleason (2020) makes a call for strategic academic leadership towards achieving inclusion and life-long learning in higher education. While culturally responsive education could create more productive educational experiences for international students, higher education providers and educators need to make practical consideration of their local settings and student demographics in order to ensure effective implementation.

CONCEPTUALISING THE STUDY

Reflection is critical to culturally responsive education. Educators reflect on their own practices and beliefs about other cultures (Rychly & Graves, 2012) as teacher perceptions and perspectives inform instructional practice (Gay, 2015). This study uses a reflective approach to explicate the authors' own experiences as international students and how they draw from those experiences to inform their teaching practices. All four authors are faculty members at private higher education institutions with a large international student cohort. Three of the four authors come from an international background, having previously been international students in Australia and other countries, and the other author is Australian born with migrant heritage, and has worked in cross-cultural community and educational settings for the past 15 years. As such, the aim of this chapter is twofold. Firstly, the three authors who were previously international students reflect on their personal learning experiences and share their insights around study satisfaction and perceptions of learning, and how these experiences now impact their own teaching and learning practices as educators. Secondly, drawing on Fook's (2015) critical stance to reflective practice, we analyse these reflections and draw implications for higher education pedagogies for engaging with international students. The study provides a critical exposition of the strategies and challenges of implementing culturally responsive practices, drawing from first-hand experience with linguistically and culturally diverse international students at an Australian higher education institution. This chapter will contribute to an international understanding of culturally responsive pedagogies in higher education institutions from those who were once international students and are now tertiary educators, offer significant insights to institutions and faculty about catering for diversity, and broaden the theoretical base for future research in multicultural education.

ANALYTIC FRAMEWORK: FOOK'S REFLECTIVE PRACTICE AND CRITICAL REFLECTION

Fook (2015) advocates for the use of reflective practice and critical reflection that seeks "to make professional practice more accountable through ongoing scrutiny of the principles upon which it is based" (p. 440). Fook extrapolates three concepts that have bearing upon these practices: reflective practice, reflection, and critical reflection. Drawing from the work of Donald Schön (1983, 1987, cited in Fook, 2015, p. 441), Fook (2015) explains that reflective practice seeks to discover the theory that underpins practice, rather than treating theory as that which is only verbally communicated – observation in *practice*, rather than through abstract instruction or words alone. Reflection is understood as a wider concept that encapsulates the approaches that one takes in their "life and actions" (Fook, 2015, p. 441), considering the role of ethics and moral dilemmas, amongst others. Critical reflection involves the apprehension of one's "very deeply held or fundamental assumptions" (Mezirow 1991, cited in ibid), with a willingness to change these to improve and diversify practice, where critical is understood as the ability to "be transformative" (ibid) rather than only to critique one's approaches and behaviours. Coupled with ascertaining these assumptions and how they impact on practice, critical reflection is also concerned with how power operates in various settings.

Fook (2015) proports a range of critical reflection questions for practitioners in her field of social work, though these are more broadly applicable to any form of professional practice that works directly with a range of diverse people. There are opportunities to utilise this framework to develop more critical, nuanced and perhaps more compassionate teaching approaches, that underscore the lived experiences and learning styles of international students in ways that promote their epistemological and ontological realities being heard and celebrated within the classroom. Similarly, Gatwiri and Ife (2021) expound upon the importance of working from a place of vulnerability and love that may be costly for the teacher, yet deeply impacting for teacher and student alike. Such an approach recognises the need for an "exchange of co-sharing knowledge in the classroom [that] promotes trust" (ibid, p. 1), is aware of and carefully manages "with deep discernment...the power dynamics that exist between students and teachers" (ibid) and fosters a learning environment that "produces a co-learning opportunity and dialogic process that allows students and teachers to engage in deep learning" (ibid, p. 3).

The following questions may promote a deeper investigation of the classrooms that host international students, and encourage more diverse responses and approaches to practice, with each categorised according to their philosophical basis, and reworked to be relevant to a tertiary educational environment (from Fook, 2015, p. 447):

Reflective Practice

- What assumptions am I making?
- What beliefs do I hold about power (others', my institution's, my own?)

Reflexivity Questions

- How do I influence this situation?
- How do my preconceptions impact student learning, and impact my interpretation of events and discussions?
- How does my presence make a difference in the classroom and in learning?
- What power do I have in the classroom, and how is this utilized when I engage with students?
- What do I believe about power, and how does this impact my interpretations of the experience of teaching?

Postmodern / Deconstruction-Based Questions

- What language or word patterns have I used?
- Have I created binary opposites, and if so, why? What is the impact of this, and does this exclude other perspectives?
- How do my beliefs of power relate to the mainstream or dominant perspectives?
- How have I constructed myself in relation to my students, other people, and power?

In answering these questions, Fook proposes that the following questions could be asked from a "critical stance" (2015, p. 447):

- How has my thinking changed, and what might I do differently now?
- How do I see my own power?
- Can I use my power differently?
- Do I need to change my ideas about myself or the situations in which I work?

Providing answers to such questions has the ability to apprehend worldviews and their impacts within the classroom, and can foster environments of curiosity and exploration that seek to be more inclusive in practice, especially where the majority of students within the room are from an international background.

AUTHOR REFLECTIONS

In this section we reflect on our own experiences as international students and as educators and show how these experiences have influenced our teaching practices as well as interactions with international students. It is worth noting that authors A, B and C were enrolled in different programs and their individual experiences were significantly personal and primed on their existing cultural experiences and expectations from their respective countries. Therefore, even though the reflections and subsequent analysis presented in this chapter are not broadly generalisable to all international students, it finds resonance with, and highlights the individualised nature of student experiences, the often untold stories, and the commitment universities must show to students from diverse cultures. The tone of these reflections is more personal in nature to reflect each author's experience and classroom practice.

This kind of narrative approach, called by various names by different cultures around the world, promotes the telling of stories that "are an important part of social change because they have the power to shape the way people think and feel about their worlds and how they interact within them" (Prasetyo, 2017, p. 1). The below narratives are therefore not simply the opinions of the authors, but instead highlight potentially common experiences for other international students that, when heard and reflected upon, can reveal current practices that impact upon international students' experiences of the classroom. Sharing experiences through the narrative form can teach us "how to deal with different individual situations by improvising alternative futures" (ibid). Alongside Fook's (2015) critically reflective questions, we hope that these stories find resonance with other students' experiences, to advocate for approaches that further support the wellbeing and flourishing of students from all backgrounds. We agree with Prasetyo's (2017, p.1) perspective:

The act of listening to a story told by another person creates a suspension of disbelief and displacement of perspective that helps people see through new eyes into a different world of truth.

Reflection by Author A

I am from Uganda and I came to Australia as an international student in 2012 to pursue a Doctor of Philosophy (PhD), having been awarded a scholarship by a university in New South Wales. Author A traveled to Australia with her three-year-old son and husband. We did not know anyone in Australia and my mother connected me to an old friend that she had last been in contact with about 30 years ago (Khanal & Gaulee, 2019). Miraculously for us, she lived in the same town as the university that I was going to study at. My mother's friend and her family hosted us for three weeks, helped us find a house close to the university and showed us around town to help us settle in. The support from our host family made settling into Australia so easy for us and helped us avoid some of the numerous challenges faced by international students. Seeing how helpful this was, we made a decision to always support international students, especially those from our country in whatever way we could so that the process of settling in would be easier for them (Prasetyo, 2017). This experience also made me more empathetic to international students because they encounter so many challenges (Khanal & Gaulee, 2019). I believe that our empathy and understanding attitude contribute to making their journey a little easier (Fook, 2015).

One of the first things I struggled with was settling in a new country that was significantly different from my home country. Much as there was information and guidelines on several aspects such as finding a house, preschool for children or finding a job, it was difficult to understand some of the terminologies and sometimes I needed someone to explain the finer details to me (Khanal and Gaulee, 2019). I also found that whenever I asked a question, I was directed to a website or given an information pack so that I could read and understand (Hsieh, 2007). This was not easy for me at the start but became easier as time went along. This opened my eyes to the issues that international students face, and, in my classes, I do devote 5 – 10 minutes to ask my students how they are doing and check if they have any challenges or issues, and clarify if they do not understand something regarding aspects of settling in. I will usually listen and give my experience where applicable or direct them to relevant resources or departments for help. Given that some international students usually struggle with seeking clarification when they do not understand, I explain to them the importance of asking when they do not understand and letting them know that it is okay (Mahmud, Amat, Rahman & Ishak, 2010). I point out to the students the importance of the student services department in helping them settle in their host country.

My second observation relates to the use of examples in class. During classes that I attended, I noticed that all examples given or case studies were based on Australia, Europe, China, or America, with hardly any drawn from the home countries of the international students. This made it hard for students to identify the application of concepts being taught in the context of their home countries (Alfred, 2009). In my teaching, I am conscious of using examples that are relevant to the home countries of international students and I do this by asking them to give examples of how the concepts being taught are applied in their countries (Fook, 2015). This allows them to understand the concepts better and gives them the confidence to evaluate the concepts within their national context. However, the application of the concept in Australia and other continents is not completely ignored; it is also integrated in the discussion by asking students to analyse the concepts from their perspective within the Australian context.

My third observation relates to group formation, especially during tutorials. Whenever students were required to form discussion groups, I observed that students preferred to form groups based on the countries they were from as it made interaction easier. While this was a convenient strategy for students because cross-cultural skills are not required when groups comprise people from the same country, it hinders the formation of relationships across diverse groups, thus limiting the social, academic, and cultural experience of students. As a student, I would have been interested in interacting with students from other countries or continents to build my interpersonal, communication and cross-cultural skills. Whenever I teach a class that has a mix of domestic and international students and group formation is required, I encourage students to form groups that comprise members from different countries (Fook, 2015; Gay, 2015). In the first group discussion, I ask them to learn one or two things about each other's cultures or countries and share. It is always interesting to listen to what they have learnt following the first discussion session. I find that this approach makes it easy for students to settle into the class because it enhances confidence (Larke, 2013).

Reflection by Author B

Leaving my home country for the first time for doctoral study came with mixed feelings of excitement and anxiety. I was excited at the prospect of experiencing a new culture, meeting new people, forming new networks, and completing my studies within the expected time. I was anxious of the unknown – I had no friends or family in Australia, I did not know if I would fit in, I did not know if I would successfully complete my studies. These fears and anxiety are shared by many international students, as research indicates (Forbes-Mewett & Sawyer, 2016; Alkandari, 2020). Despite these uncertainties, I had no reason to fail because family and friends back home had already started calling me doctor when I had barely commenced my studies. I was quite unsettled in the initial stages of my study as I felt little was being done by the university to help me settle in. I phoned the international student unit to discuss my concerns and they apologised and explained that research students are managed by the graduate research office and not the international office. I was completely unaware of this arrangement as I thought the international office was designed to support the educational and cultural transition of all international students (Ammigan, 2019). The graduate research office organised a meet and greet session but it involved only myself, two other students and a staff member, hence falling short of the support I expected.

As a doctoral student, I had an opportunity to undertake one coursework unit, for which I had missed three weeks due to delayed arrival. My first time in the lecture hall brought a weird feeling. Though it was a small class of about 10 students, I felt socially isolated as I could not approach nor was approached by anyone for a conversation. I did not understand my first lesson because the approach was different from what I was used to. Things improved in subsequent weeks regarding my grasp of content, but I yearned for some social connection as that was what I was accustomed to. I did not achieve this as everyone seemed to rush out of the lecture room after lecture. In my home country, students will usually hang around for a discussion about the lecture. I also had my own study group for each subject I took which doubled as a social group. The higher education I was used to was characterised by open communication, communality, and shared thinking among students. I quickly realised the stark difference in study culture as the one I was experiencing appeared to be more individualistic and isolationist. I managed to complete the course with a decent grade but no social connections. I felt the stress and strain of being alone in a country that was far away from home. As studies report, this state of anxiety and stress affects the mental health of many international students (Forbes-Mewett & Sawyer, 2016).

The next big phase of my studies was my research. I found the higher degree by research even more lonely and isolating. My two supervisors were my points of contact and connection, but there were some shocks along the way. These were linked to my own past approach to study and associated expectations. I had gone into the doctoral program with an ambitious expectation to complete my thesis and be awarded my degree in three years. As diligent as I was, I worked hard on my research and quickly produced drafts, expecting my supervisors to comment on my drafts and return them quickly. I expected positive comments and often became unsettled when my expected *timelines* for feedback were not met and when drafts were returned with critical comments. This pointed to a further cultural misalignment with my home country. In my home country, critical comments were framed with a generous, positive outlook. Relationships between staff and students seemed more friendly and social. As an international student I had to learn to cope and operate within a very strict professional context. At several points in my studies, I felt like quitting and returning to my home country as the entire experience of undertaking a difficult research project without social support and network was consuming. The tendency for students to drop out of university due to stress and exhaustion is high (Kehm et al., 2019) but this is even higher among research students as 1 in 5 students are reported to be likely to disengage from study in the face of difficulties (Johnson et al., 2020; Zhou, 2015).

However, my experience was not all doom and gloom. I had massive support from my supervisors who became very supportive and interested in my life outside of university. One of them would usually invite me for coffee, and we would talk about happenings in my home country, my culture, and family, food, life after PhD and a range of other interesting topics. She would talk about her own experience in a foreign country and suggest coping strategies. She encouraged me to take up tutoring positions, and join social groups on and off campus. Her presence and willingness to hear my story, learn about my culture and tell me how great I was doing was a major source of encouragement. I completed my doctoral studies in 3.5 years, six months later than I initially planned but the journey which seemed to have had a rocky start ended happily. Both supervisors, now colleagues, are still very supportive of my career and offer great advice whenever I reach out.

The above reflection demonstrates that a sense of connection is a key ingredient in one's success as an international student. Living in a foreign land away from family, friends and home culture is a difficult undertaking. This coupled with the stress and pressures that naturally come with studies warrant pedagogical innovation. Now, as a lecturer who teaches mostly international students, I have become culturally considerate in my lectures. I acknowledge that some of my international students may not have any social connections outside of the classroom, so I adopt culturally responsive approaches to make them feel engaged and encouraged.

My first approach is self-identification. This involves sharing my international background with students including some of my personal struggles as an international student and some coping strategies. I then encourage them to feel welcome in my class as I understand their experience and am better positioned to provide them with the needed support to succeed in their studies. I learn a few words in their home language such as *welcome* and *how are you?* in my quest to identify with them. Also, with many of my students having Indian and Nepalese backgrounds, I have learnt about the history and culture of their countries. I connect the material to their culture as much as possible and give them an opportunity to interpret the material from their cultural perspective, drawing on relevant examples from their home countries. With concepts that students find difficult to understand, I invite them to explain them in their home language and get it translated into English by students with higher expressive ability in the same class. Further, as many of my students like to communicate in their home language during group activities, I allow them that freedom but also expect them to communicate their group findings to the whole class in English. By this approach, I acknowledge their culture and also emphasise the English language requirement of their course (Fook, 2015). I join students to celebrate cultural weeks on campus where we wear our traditional clothing, perform cultural dances, and eat traditional food. Drawing from my own experience with assignment feedback, I adopt a strengths-based approach whereby I keep comments constructive and emphasise the positives while drawing attention to areas of improvement.

These pedagogical approaches are possible because my international students come from a homogenous cultural background and speak mutually intelligible home languages. This makes it more practicable to connect to their experiences, respect and integrate their cultures and religions while maintaining high academic standards to ensure success in their course. Challenges may, however, arise if students originate from diverse international backgrounds. Nevertheless, educators should still show commitment to their students and implement strategies that would make them feel supported in their learning.

Reflection by Author C

Contrary to the travel experiences shared by Author B above, my story is different, and it underscores the importance of relations and social networks for international students. In their research about social capital and international students in Australia, Neri and Ville (2008) have acknowledged the loss of social capital for international students requires them to form new ones because it helps them navigate the education system, and bears implications on their academic performance and welfare. Prior to travelling to Australia to commence my PhD journey, I reconnected with Author A through a friend living in Melbourne. Author A was studying at the same university that I was set to join. Author A was instrumental in orienting me about what to expect, including the things I should carry along with me to Australia.

As a single parent of a then five-year-old boy, Author A and her family welcomed us with open arms, sheltered us, introduced us into their social networks until we were ready to stand on our feet. Any international student would understand the value of having such contact in a foreign land. Unfortunately, my case is the exception rather than the rule. My experience at the academic level was also good and provided a sensitive and empathetic environment for me to complete my studies. My supervisors were both first generation migrants to Australia from South Africa and Norway. I believe that their background, coupled with decades of teaching and supervising international students, greatly enriched my experience as an international student. In Australia's education sector that is increasingly influenced by managerial and neo-liberalistic ideologies (Gatwiri & Ife, 2021), I did not feel like a commodity or just any other statistic to boost the university's rankings. I felt loved and supported, as my supervisors' interest in my success extended beyond academic circles into my wellbeing and that of my son.

My supervisors offered feedback in a timely and thought-provoking manner. They could tell when I had trouble understanding certain concepts, or when I was unable to find some literature relevant to the ideas I was developing. Not only did they show me how to do it, they suggested areas where I could search and also stepped in when I reached my wits end. It was not unusual for me to be up at 2am working on my thesis only to realise that one of my supervisors was also up that late working on the changes that I had incorporated and giving me feedback. At times I would go to bed at 4am, having submitted a draft, only for me to check my email at 7am with feedback. I did not realize how privileged I was until I shared my experiences with other students who unfortunately could not relate with this kind of empathetic relationship that I had with my supervisors. Education is indeed a relationship (Gatwiri & Ife, 2021), and the quality of that relationship determines our learning outcomes. The good relationship that I had with my supervisors taught me a lot that I now share with my students. Additionally, I shared a higher degree research room with other international students from Uganda (my home country), Zimbabwe, Egypt, Thailand, Zambia, Nepal, The Philippines, Sri Lanka, England, Jamaica, New Zealand and Australia. They were all very helpful and instrumental in helping me settle in and complete my studies. This group formed the core of my academic social capital and had a profound influence on my academic success (Neri & Ville, 2008). My principal supervisor brought us together very often to share our academic journeys. These meetings, usually out at a café, helped us to bond and form bonds outside of the confines of the university's four walls, bonds which we hold to date. We celebrated each other's success and did everything possible to support each other in the face of challenges that threatened our academic progress.

Students that I have taught across various institutions in Australia are mostly international students. Having been one, I can understand and empathise with their experiences and struggles. Having been taught well, I use my position to pay it forward by engaging in a relational teacher-student engagement in order for them to achieve their academic goals. This also stems from my professional background as a social worker because our profession is hinged on relationships with our clients. Those relationships can make or break our clients given the amount of professional power that we hold.

My timing in social work academia is also a bonus, given the fact that the profession is actively seeking to decolonise theory, research and practice (Nipperess & Williams, 2019). My students are mostly from Nepal, Brazil, India, Nigeria, Kenya and Pakistan. The first lecture is spent on creating rapport and trimming my powers as a lecturer by recognising their strengths and assuring them that I look forward to learning from them as I believe they bring a vast amount of knowledge from their diverse cultural experiences. I use an intersectional approach (Cho, Crenshaw, & McCall, 2013), to get to know them better, and quickly identify anything that may complicate their academic journey. My relationship with them is intentional, going beyond the greeting formalities at the start of the lecture to actually inquire if they are okay and if they need help with anything. The current COVID-19 lockdowns in Sydney have taken a toll on everyone, especially international students that have experienced job losses, isolation and various mental health challenges (Nguyen & Balakrishnan, 2020). Therefore, it is imperative that students are given an open door by lecturers to share their struggles and fears so that they are able to overcome them. Some of my students have experienced adverse life circumstances that gave them the resolve to quit school as they could not cope. However, the empathetic responses that we offer our students have made them stay and persist. I have had many students tell me how grateful they are for the help rendered. One of them said, "I have engaged with many Christian institutions and for them, Christianity is just a label. You and your colleague are different. You people really care and I don't know how I would have managed without your help. Thank you so much." This display of gratitude also makes me recognise that my identity as a Christian requires me to treat everyone with love, empathy and respect, that greatly influences my teaching practice. Coupled with this is my upbringing that was shaped by the Ubuntu philosophy that taught me that my humanity is dependent on others and therefore I should treat everyone with dignity and respect (Tusasiirwe et al., 2021).

In my teaching, I create an environment where cultural reflections are part of the learning journey to allow the expression of those cultural aspects that foster cohesion in the classroom and enrich students' learning journeys. Students are allowed to hold group discussions in their mother tongues and provide examples from their home countries. The recognition of students' unique cultural experiences and the opportunity given to share them provides a realistic learning environment that facilitates a respectful exchange of knowledge. It allows them to own their learning journeys and avoid the assumptive 'teacher knows it all' belief that has permeated formal education for centuries. Gatwiri and Ife (2021) write that "however much as we may plan, or specify 'learning outcomes' or class processes, the classroom is a social location, with all the unpredicted interaction, magic, passion, emotion, rage, hostility and vulnerability of any social situation, as social workers should know only too well" (p. 13). As a lecturer in a profession working with people that are experiencing various life challenges, my teaching pedagogy embraces the concept of vulnerability (Gatwiri & Ife, 2021) in the classroom in order to create a realistic environment that does not only foster individual growth but sets us all on a journey of lifelong learning.

REFLECTION ON OUR REFLECTION

The reflections above show how similar but different international student experiences can be. Higher education providers and educators should be aware of and take into consideration the different international student experiences and factor these into their pedagogies in order to achieve culturally responsive pedagogies. In this section we analyse the reflections above using Fook's (2015) critical questions as a guiding framework.

- How has our thinking changed, and what might we do differently now?
- How do we see our own power?
- Can we use our power differently?
- Do we need to change our ideas about ourselves or the situations in which we work?

How Has Our Thinking Changed, and What Might We Do Differently Now?

The reflections demonstrate how our ideas have changed since our days as international students and now as faculty members. It has changed from seeing ourselves as a minority group struggling to settle within a new country to people who advocate for the active inclusion of international students in higher education pedagogies. Now that we are faculty members, our experiences have demonstrated how ideas can change over time as a result of acquisition of different experiences and exposure to multiple cultures and situations. As international students many of us felt that systems and structures were either not useful or did not work in our favour (Roberts & Dunworth, 2012). For Author B particularly, it was difficult for them to settle in a new country with its own culture, laws, regulations, and unique educational structure (Neri & Ville, 2008). As members of the education system, we are committed to supporting international students to have a better experience than we had as international students. Our experiences teach us about the importance of being adaptive in a culture in order to achieve one's ultimate goals. What we can ask international students to do differently is to allow themselves time to settle into a new environment. We now understand that good relationships form a core part of one's success as an international student as shown in prior studies (Neri & Ville, 2008). With this understanding, we give opportunities both in class and outside of class for our students to initiate, build and sustain relationships. We are open and more accustomed to the idea of interculturality, that is the fusion of one's culture into the culture of the new country. Ultimately, we see and approach things from a different perspective and can now combine our own experiences as an international student and our experiences as faculty members to support students achieve the best possible outcomes. As noted in the reflections above, many international students may not have any social network beyond the classroom, and so our experiences have enabled us to be present in students' lives. This highlights the important role educators have in the lives of students and how pertinent it is to be open and approachable to students from different cultures.

How Do We See Our Own Power?

The relationship between international students and educators is obviously power-driven. Many international students come from cultures where optimal respect is accorded to elderly people and persons in authority as such educators. It is notable that many of our international students do not feel comfortable asking questions or requesting academic support as a result of their cultural experiences or cultural upbringing. Owing to this, many of our students naturally assume a submissive posture, creating power imbalance between them and educators. As educators, we aim to not exploit this power imbalance but to rather create an atmosphere for students to feel welcome to approach us with issues affecting their studies and life in Australia as a whole. We seek opportunities to share this power with students to empower them to develop the confidence to succeed. As shown in the above reflections, we bridge the power gap through the open relationship we have with students – identifying with student cultures, building rapport and celebrating cultural events with them. We also share our own experiences as international students to create a shared identity and a sense of presence in their lives. We understand that respecting students' cultures and not imposing our own powers on them creates an environment that is enabling and conducive for students to feel welcome and accepted. As Russell (2020) argues, equal power breeds social justice which is of critical value in a settler country like Australia to address racism and white privilege. While we understand that we retain much of the power in relation to content and pedagogy, we deconstruct this power in our relationship with them by connecting with students on both intellectual and personal levels, engaging in shared knowledge and thinking. This creates an atmosphere where students have a strong sense of belonging and are not intimidated by our presence, knowledge or skills. Such power balance removes the potential barriers which affect student performance and wellbeing. Consequently, we understand that for us to support international students to succeed in their studies, we need to deconstruct power to allow for maximal student participation and self-regulation. The locus of control therefore lies between students and educators and orientates toward an egalitarian power-sharing approach built on strong relational capacities and cultural awareness (Porter, 2007).

Can We Use Our Power Differently?

As explained above and demonstrated in our reflections, power can be used to maximise student learning. Rather than impose our authority and power on students, we use this power to create a socially just atmosphere in which students feel culturally attached and academically supported. We argue that the power an educator holds should be reflected in how their students succeed in their learning. With students originating from diverse cultures who often experience the reality of cultural misalignment with their home cultures, a balanced power approach could create opportunities for ongoing success (Porter, 2007). The use of a balanced power approach positions students not only to develop intellectual competencies, but also to maintain their own cultural identities and learn from other cultures. Therefore, if there is any difference in how w power could be used, this should be evident in the difference our pedagogies make to support student learning.

Do We Need to Change Our Ideas About Ourselves or the Situations in Which We Work?

Education is about people, culture and context specific factors. As such, educators should maintain increasing awareness of the context in which they work and the potential cultural implications for student engagement. As it is common for academics to move to different universities, it is important that they align their ideas about student engagement and support with the ideals and expectations of their new environment and the students they support. That is, educators must embody the policies and structures of their institutions and negotiate their approach to performing their roles within the boundaries of institutional structures (Russell, 2020). The reflections provided in this chapter demonstrate how our ideas have changed from being students to being educators. Openness to new ideas and approaches is important to ensure consistent and ongoing improvement in what we do as educators. Further, given the highly fluid nature of international student demographics, it is pertinent that educators maintain a reflexive pedagogical approach in order to purposefully meet the cultural needs of our students and support them achieve their goals. Not only must educators change their ideas about what they do and how they do it, but they must also consider changing ideas about themselves in order to better understand students and the best ways to engage them. This involves educators being aware of their own biases and suspending such biases as much as possible when engaging with students from diverse cultures. This principle of *epoché* (Langdridge, 2007) could help educators to bracket preconceived beliefs and assumptions in order to understand the real essence of their engagement with international students. Ongoing critical reflective practice could also enable educators to develop cultural competence to respond to the cultural needs of our students. As Russell (2020) notes, reflecting on our way of being, values, and approaches is foundational to developing cultural competence. This cultural competence should be visible in our practice in the ways we design our courses and organise teaching to maximise student cultural participation.

THEMES FROM THE REFLECTIONS AND ITS IMPLICATIONS FOR CULTURALLY RESPONSIVE PEDAGOGY

In this section, we analyse our reflections based on themes that reflect culturally responsive pedagogies for international students. Our analysis yielded three key themes below. While not all the themes relate to classroom pedagogy, we are of the view that the international student experience is not limited to teaching strategies alone, but that other co-instructional experiences contribute to the overall educational experience.

- Positive relationships
- Empathetic understanding
- Culturally sensitive pedagogies

Positive Relationships

The idea of relationships permeates our reflections as international students and our experience as educators. Having left our home countries for further study in a foreign country, we needed some networking and social support to succeed in our quest to obtaining higher education (Khanal & Gaulee, 2019). The reflections show that such networking and support systems are necessary even prior to the commencement of study. This is particularly evident in the cases of Author A and Author C who received some social support upon their arrival in Australia, making their settlement process easier. In the case of author B, such support and networking did not exist. Many international students find themselves in the situation of Author B as they leave their countries of origin without any form of social connection or relationship in their destination countries. Starting a new life in a foreign country without such support is obviously difficult for international students (Akanwa, 2015). Many higher education institutions in Australia make provision for international student accommodation. It is worth mentioning that many administrative units dedicated to handling international student affairs are doing their best to support international students but more needs to be done to create increased awareness about available services and how students can access such services, especially among postgraduate research students who are often managed by research divisions and not the mainstream international office in universities. Furthermore, international student departments need to recruit more staff who have completed studies as international students, because they have an experienced-based understanding of the dynamics of international student life (Madden-Dent, Wood & Roskina, 2019). Thus, they are able to provide advice and support from a practical and not theoretical point of view. Robert and Dunworth's (2012) research shows that students possessed some awareness of available services but did not understand how to access or use those services. While our focus in this chapter is not to ascertain the effectiveness of university housing units and other support systems, we are of the view that providing more awareness and efficient social support for students to find their preferred accommodation on and off campus could make a huge difference in the initial struggles of international students (Madden-Dent et al., 2019). We are also cognizant of the fact that many smaller high education providers may not have their own accommodation facilities.

In this case, specific advice about where to find off-campus accommodation that suits student needs could be provided prior to their arrival. Higher education providers could also institute an international student support system whereby new arrivals are buddied with existing students or alumni members from identical countries to orient them to university life. Our own experience as international students has enabled us to appreciate the level of support international students need to settle into their new study environment. Author A for instance highlights how the support she received upon arrival in Australia has encouraged her to provide similar support to international students from her home country, of which Author C is a direct beneficiary.

The theme of relationships was much more prominent in our formal and informal engagement with students. All three authors expressed the critical importance of open and supportive relationships with international students. Our reflections demonstrate that the classroom is an important place for students to establish a strong sense of belonging (Hsieh, 2007). A collaborative classroom atmosphere that is characterised by effective relationships is one that could support student engagement (Russell, 2020). Critical to this relationship in the classroom is the idea of self-identification. The reflections demonstrate that in predominantly international classrooms, recognising and identifying with students' cultures and sharing information about our own international experience create an atmosphere that is welcoming and supportive of students. Such open relationships also foster social justice and reduce the power imbalance that often shifts in favour of educators (Russell, 2020). The lesson from our experience is that international students are inclined to be submissive as a result of the impact of cultural factors and the lack of confidence to stand up for themselves. Identifying with student cultures and seeking to create an even playing field builds trust and provides students with the confidence to approach their educators and have genuine conversations about their studies. Further, creating opportunities for students to work in groups and engage with each other in their home language create feelings of acceptance and empowerment. As author C states, educators do not know it all. Also, as author B mentions, listening to students' stories and affirming their cultural identities is a morale booster. Our experience confirms the belief that shared thinking and understanding and reciprocal relationships dissipate the expert/novice ideology that characterise behaviourist approaches to teaching. Our practices have been informed by our own experiences as international students and the various forms of support our supervisors and peers provided to us during the course of our studies. The implication is that high quality, non-judgemental relationships are central to culturally responsive pedagogies for international students. Educators need strong cultural awareness, professional and interpersonal skills to initiate and maintain positive relationships with international students. This can help students cope with the demands and experience of being an international student (Wu, Garza, & Guzman, 2015).

Empathetic Understanding

Many international students experience culture shock, which often puts them in a precarious situation (Belford, 2017; Newsome & Cooper, 2016). The experiences of authors A and B highlight the potential impacts of such culture shock on the education and experiences of international students. Author B particularly recounts how the culture shock nearly made them quit their studies and return to their home country. Author C further underscores the adverse life circumstances international students face that make them vulnerable. In the face of such vulnerabilities, educators need to engage international students with a healthy dose of empathy and respect. Empathy develops from effective relationships, as discussed in the previous section. Our experience as international students has positioned us to be more empathic towards the needs and experiences of international students. We are able to see things from their perspective and appreciate the weight of the challenges they grapple with. Our understanding of the difficulties that international students face enable us to take the initiative to inquire about happenings in their lives and the support that they need to succeed in their studies. Empathy and respect are exhibited in our day-to-day relationships, and rapport building with students includes our understanding of how critical their culture is to their individual identities. We appreciate that it is not expected of students to leave their cultures and identities behind and assume a foreign culture in order to succeed. Therefore, as our reflections indicate, we are cognizant of the significance of connecting our pedagogies, examples and practices to the culturally relevant aspects of students' backgrounds. Author B, for instance, mentions how they frame feedback in a manner that emphasises the strength and potential of students. While this empathetic understanding derives from our personal experience as international students and educators, higher education providers and faculty members can similarly develop empathy towards international students by recognising cultural differences and providing adequate support, in turn making the cultural gaps and associated challenges less impacting on international students (Gatwiri & Ife, 2021). Demonstrating cultural empathy toward international students could contribute to student satisfaction and retention that many higher education providers are seeking to achieve (Belford, 2017). Author C highlights how such an approach has enabled students to complete their studies and ultimately succeed. Higher education pedagogies should recognise and appreciate vulnerability (Gatwiri & Ife, 2021) particularly for international students as it makes a big difference in their education experience.

Culturally Sensitive Pedagogies

The above reflections demonstrate that sensitivity to student cultures is an important determinant of any successful culturally responsive education. As Eckersley (2008) argues, culture is one of the key means for establishing a sense of identity and direction. In light of this, our practices embrace 1) establishment of cultural connections 2) cultural bonding among students, and 3) intercultural understanding. First, we explore cultural connection when teaching the contents. This occurs through the use of culturally relevant examples and offering opportunities for students to apply the content to their national contexts. As many students return to their home countries after their studies, this approach enables students to recognise not only the significance of the subject matter to their culture but also how respective concepts apply to the practical contexts in their home countries. Establishing explicit connections between student cultures and the subject content enables students to make meaning of the material and understand it from their cultural perspectives (Fook, 2015). Language is a critical aspect of culture. Like authors A, B and C, we acknowledge that many students come from countries where English is not their first language. Inviting students to explain certain concepts in their home language presents opportunities for students to develop confidence and contributes to peer-based understanding (Prasetyo, 2017). The rich learning experience that such cultural connections create enhances student understanding and fosters an appreciation of their cultures.

Cultural bonding and intercultural understanding among students occur within the context of classroom instruction and educators with an experience or an awareness of the complexities of being an international student can effectively facilitate that process (Hendrickson, Rosen & Aune, 2011). Here, we create collaborative learning opportunities through small group discussions involving all the cultures represented in the classroom. This affords an important opportunity for students to learn from each other's culture and obtain authentic intercultural understanding. Further, celebrating cultural weeks on campus strengthens respect and appreciation for all the cultures which communicates acceptance and satisfaction. The culturally sensitive nature of our practices aligns with research which demonstrates that students appreciate learning when the material has strong connections with their cultural identities and traditions (Boadu, 2021). Our pedagogies reflect the social justice principle that students regardless of their cultural background have a right to quality higher education (Gay, 2015; Conway & Walker, 2017). When teaching international students, educators in higher education should find interesting ways to present the content in culturally meaningful ways. While this may be challenging in highly technical disciplines, effort should be made toward creating higher education learning environments where diverse cultures of international students can be celebrated. Many higher education providers have international student departments which could advocate for culturally responsive university practices to support international student wellbeing and experience.

Further, in the prevailing covid-19 situation and the increased use of online teaching environments, there is still potential to incorporate culturally responsive pedagogies into online instruction. Educators could celebrate student cultures in an online environment through the use of online cultural rooms, teasing out the cultural elements in topics, providing opportunities for student self-expression and communication of culturally relevant information. Emerging research in this area suggests that learning management systems could play a key role in achieving culturally responsive teaching. Aydin and Kayabas (2018) argue that cultural sensitivity in an online teaching interface such as MOOC contributes to effective teaching and learning and to student satisfaction. Meri-Yilan's (2020) research and several studies (e.g. Gameel & Wlikins, 2019; Jacobsen, 2019; McLoughlin, 2001) also support the view that online environments could be used to foster social inclusion and reduce cultural limitations. The implication is that course designers and educators should rethink their systems and pedagogies and create more inclusive learning environments within which cultural diversity and pedagogic variety could be accommodated.

CONCLUSION

International education has become highly competitive as higher education providers strive to attract high quality students from overseas. To achieve this, higher education providers often make the promise of providing learning environments that foster cultural diversity and student engagement. The extent to which this promise is achieved is however not empirically established. In recognition that many international students have untold stories and experiences that affect their study experience, this chapter adopts Fook's (2015) reflective approach to muse on the authors' own experiences as international students to furnish an understanding of how culturally responsive education in higher education can promote international student wellbeing and enhance their educational experience. The study reveals that culturally responsive education thrives on respectful relationships, empathetic understanding and self-identification. Further, culturally responsive pedagogical approaches embrace establishing cultural connections, shared cultural understanding and interculturality. Our reflections demonstrate that culturally responsive education has a place in higher education, despite being considered as more suited to pre-tertiary education (Larke, 2013). Like Hutchinson and McAlister-Shields (2020), we argue that the approach should underpin higher education. Given that international students contribute to institutional growth and financial stability, it is pertinent that effort and attention is dedicated to providing culturally relevant experiences to inform student satisfaction and retention.

Engaging students in culturally responsive ways requires skill and capacity. Providers need to forge strong partnerships with various cultural groups in the community to improve their knowledge of diverse cultures and develop shared practices and understanding of cultural expectations. Ongoing professional development of staff is critical to the effective navigation of the complex terrain of student cultures. It is imperative for educators to be culturally aware of student backgrounds and implement respectful and responsive methods of engagement. As Gleason (2020) rightly observes, the continuing impact of higher education providers is not limited to the delivery of content but depends on how institutions continuously adapt to changing student demographics and implement curricular and pedagogical innovations to attract and maintain international students. To this end, the institutional, personal and instructional dimensions of culturally responsive education, as described by Richards et al. (2007), warrant attention.

While this study highlights the important place of culturally responsive education in higher education, it has some limitations. First, the study reflects on and analyses our own experience as international students and educators. Findings cannot be generalised to educators in other higher education providers. Also, we acknowledge the dynamics and homogeneity of our international student population. We do not assume that the strategies and practices outlined in this study will be effective when used for a different student population. Further, we acknowledge that university academics and administrative departments might view the topic of international student support differently. While tensions between these two divisions in universities exist, it is important for universities to adopt a cohesive, homogenous approach to international student support whereby the effort from academic departments and student support units culminate in positive international student experience. Exploring collaboration between admissions offices, student associations and alumni relations offices could also be a strategic way to include the voices of international students in recruitment efforts (Ammigan, 2019). Future research could examine if international students experience culturally responsive education in higher education institutions.

REFERENCES

Adams, T., Leventhal, M., & Connelly, S. (2012). International student recruitment in Australia and the United States: approaches and attitudes. In D. K. Deardorff, H. d. Wit, & J. D. Heyl (Eds.), *The SAGE handbook of international higher education* (pp. 399-416). SAGE Publications, Inc. https://www.doi.org/10.4135/9781452218397.n22

Akanwa, E. E. (2015). International students in western developed countries: History, challenges, and prospects. *Journal of International Students*, *5*(3), 271–284. doi:10.32674/jis.v5i3.421

Alfred, M. V. (2009). Nonwestern immigrants in continuing higher education: A sociocultural approach to culturally responsive pedagogy. *The Journal of Continuing Higher Education*, *57*(3), 137–148. doi:10.1080/07377360903262168

Alkandari, N. Y. (2021). Students anxiety experiences in higher education institutions. In V. V. Kalinin, C. Hocaoglu, & S. Mohamed (Eds.), *Anxiety disorders: The new achievements* (pp. 1–11). IntechOpen. doi:10.5772/intechopen.92079

Ammigan, R. (2019). Institutional satisfaction and recommendation: What really matters to International students? *Journal of International Students*, *9*(1), 262–281. doi:10.32674/jis.v9i1.260

Ammigan, R., & Jones, E. (2018). Improving the student experience: Learning from a comparative study of international student satisfaction. *Journal of Studies in International Education, 22*(4), 283–301. doi:10.1177/1028315318773137

Ammigan, R., & Langton, D. (2018). *The International student experience in Australia: Implications for administrators and student support staff.* International Education Association of Australia.

Awang-Hashim, R., Kaur, A., & Valdez, N. P. (2019). Strategising inclusivity in teaching diverse learners in higher education. *Malaysian Journal of Learning and Instruction, 16*(1), 105–128. doi:10.32890/mjli2019.16.1.5

Aydin, C. H., & Kayabas, B. K. (2018). Designing culturally sensitive massive open online courses: Learning culture and MOOCs in Turkey. In E. Toprak & E. Kumtepe (Eds.), *Supporting multiculturalism in open and distance learning spaces* (pp. 208–221). IGI Global. doi:10.4018/978-1-5225-3076-3.ch011

Belford, N. (2017). International Students from Melbourne Describing Their Cross- Cultural Transitions Experiences: Culture Shock, Social Interaction, and Friendship Development. *Journal of International Students, 7*(3), 499–521. doi:10.32674/jis.v7i3.206

Boadu, G. (2020). Historical significance and the challenges of African historiography. *Pedagogy, Culture & Society.* Advance online publication. doi:10.1080/14681366.2020.1843070

Cho, S., Crenshaw, K. W., & McCall, L. (2013). Toward a Field of Intersectionality Studies: Theory, Applications, and Praxis. *Signs (Chicago, Ill.), 38*(4), 785–810. doi:10.1086/669608

Conway, R., & Walker, P. (2017). Curriculum, learning, teaching and assessment adjustments. In P. Foreman & M. Arthur-Kelly. Inclusion in action (5th ed., pp.134-196). Cengage.

Department of Education, Skills and Employment. (2021). *International student data: Monthly summary.* https://internationaleducation.gov.au/research/international-student-data/Documents/MONTHLY%20SUMMARIES/2021/Jul%202021%20MonthlyInfographic.pdf

Department of Education, Skills and Employment (2020). *International student data: Monthly summary.* https://internationaleducation.gov.au/research/international-student-data/Documents/MONTHLY%20SUMMARIES/2020/Dec%202020%20MonthlyInfographic.pdf

Eckersley, R. (2008). Values and vision: Youth and the failure of modern western culture. *Youth Studies Australia, 27*, 10–19.

Eder, J., Smith, W. W., & Pitts, R. E. (2010). Exploring factors influencing student study abroad destination choice. *Journal of Teaching in Travel & Tourism, 10*(3), 232–250. doi:10.1080/15313220.2010.503534

Fook, J. (2015). Reflective practice and critical reflection. In J. Lishman (Ed.), *Handbook for practice learning in social work and social care: Knowledge and theory* (3rd ed., pp. 440–454). Jessica Kingsley Publishers.

Forbes-Mewett, H., & Sawyer, A. (2016). International students and mental health. *Journal of International Students, 6*(3), 661–677. doi:10.32674/jis.v6i3.348

Gameel, B. G., & Wilkins, K. G. (2019). When it comes to MOOCs, where you are from makes a difference. *Computers & Education, 136*, 49–60. doi:10.1016/j.compedu.2019.02.014

Gatwiri, K., & Ife, J. (2021). Teaching about vulnerability and love in social work: Lessons and reflections from two academics. *Social Work Education*, 1–16. doi:10.1080/02615479.2021.1972962

Gay, G. (2010). *Culturally responsive teaching: Theory, research, and practice* (2nd ed.). Teachers College Press.

Gay, G. (2015). The what, why, and how of culturally responsive teaching: International mandates, challenges, and opportunities. *Multicultural Education Review, 7*(3), 123–139. doi:10.1080/200561 5X.2015.1072079

Gleason, N. (2020). Strategic leadership for diversity and inclusion in higher education. In S. S. Sanger & N. W. Gleason (Eds.), Diversity and inclusion in global higher education (pp. 285-304). Palgrave Macmillan. doi:10.1007/978-981-15-1628-3_11

Han, H. S., Vomvoridi-Ivanović, E., Jacobs, J., Karanxha, Z., Lypka, A., Topdemir, C., & Feldman, A. (2014). Culturally responsive pedagogy in higher education: A collaborative self-study. *Studying Teacher Education, 10*(3), 290–312. doi:10.1080/17425964.2014.958072

Hendrickson, B., Rosen, D., & Aune, R. K. (2011). An analysis of friendship networks, social connectedness, homesickness, and satisfaction levels of international students. *International Journal of Intercultural Relations, 35*(3), 281–295. doi:10.1016/j.ijintrel.2010.08.001

Hsieh, M. H. (2007). Challenges for international students in higher education: One student's narrated story of invisibility and struggle. *College Student Journal, 41*(2), 379–391.

Hurley, P. (2020). *Coronavirus and international students.* Mitchell Institute, Victoria University.

Hutchinson, L., & McAlister-Shields, L. (2020). Culturally responsive teaching: Its application in higher education environments. *Education Sciences, 10*(124), 124. Advance online publication. doi:10.3390/educsci10050124

Jacobsen, J. (2019). Diversity and difference in the online environment. *Journal of Teaching in Social Work, 39*(4-5), 387–401. doi:10.1080/08841233.2019.1654589

Johnson, R. L., Coleman, R. A., Batten, N. H., Hallsworth, D., & Spencer, E. E. (2020). The quiet crisis of PhDs and COVID-19: Reaching the financial tipping point. doi:10.21203/rs.3.rs-36330/v2

Kehm, B. M., Larsen, M. R., & Sommersel, H. B. (2019). Student dropout from universities in Europe: A review of empirical literature. *Hungarian Educational Research Journal, 9*(2), 147–164. doi:10.1556/063.9.2019.1.18

Kennedy, K., Henderson, H., & Marsh, M. (2022). *Becoming a teacher* (7th ed.). Pearson.

Khanal, J., & Gaulee, U. (2019). Challenges of international students from pre-departure to post-study: A literature review. *Journal of International Students, 9*(2), 560–581. doi:10.32674/jis.v9i2.673

Langdridge, D. (2007). *Phenomenological psychology: Theory, research and method.* Pearson Education.

Larke, P. (2013). Culturally responsive teaching in higher education: What professors need to know. In S. Mayo & P. Larke (Eds.), *Integrating multiculturalism into the curriculum* (pp. 38–50). Peter Lang.

Lawson, C. (2012). *Student voices: Enhancing the experience of international students in Australia.* Australian Education International.

Newsome, L. K., & Cooper, P. (2016). International students' cultural and social experiences in a British university: "Such a hard life [it] is here. *Journal of International Students, 6*(1), 195–215. doi:10.32674/jis.v6i1.488

Madden-Dent, T., Wood, D., & Roskina, K. (2019). An inventory of international student services at 200 US universities and colleges: Descriptive data of pre-departure and post-arrival supports. *Journal of International Students, 9*(4), 993–1008. doi:10.32674/jis.v9i4.346

Mahmud, Z., Amat, S., Rahman, S., & Ishak, N. M. (2010). Challenges for international students in Malaysia: Culture, climate and care. *Procedia: Social and Behavioral Sciences, 7*, 289–293. doi:10.1016/j.sbspro.2010.10.040

McLoughlin, C. (2001). Inclusivity and alignment: Principles of pedagogy, task and assessment design for effective cross-cultural online learning. *Distance Education, 22*(1), 7–29. doi:10.1080/0158791010220102

Mpinganjira, M. (2009). Comparative analysis of factors influencing the decision to study abroad. *African Journal of Business Management, 3*(8), 358–365.

Nafari, J., Arab, A., & Ghaffari, S. (2017). Through the looking glass: Analysis of factors influencing Iranian student's study abroad motivations and destination choice. *SAGE Open, 7*(2), 1–19. doi:10.1177/2158244017716711

Neri, F., & Ville, S. (2008). Social capital renewal and the academic performance of international students in Australia. *Journal of Socio-Economics, 37*(4), 1515–1538. doi:10.1016/j.socec.2007.03.010

Nguyen, O. T. K., & Balakrishnan, V. D. (2020). International students in Australia - during and after COVID-19. *Higher Education Research & Development, 39*(7), 1372–1376. doi:10.1080/07294360.2020.1825346

Nicholls, S. (2018). Influences of international student choice of study destination: Evidence from the United States. *Journal of International Students, 8*(2), 597–622. doi:10.32674/jis.v8i2.94

Nipperess, S., & Williams, C. (2019). *Critical multicultural practice in social work: New perspectives and practices.* Allen & Unwin.

Phang, S. L. (2013). *Factors influencing international students' study destination decision abroad.* University of Gothenburg.

Porter, L. (2007). *Student behaviour: Theory and practice for teachers* (3rd ed.). Allen & Unwin.

Prasetyo, Y. E. (2017). From Storytelling to Social Change: The Power of Story in the Community Building. SSRN *Electronic Journal.* doi:10.2139/ssrn.3094947

Qadeer, T., Javed, M. K., Manzoor, A., Wu, M., & Zaman, S. I. (2021). The experience of international students and institutional recommendations: A comparison between the students from the developing and developed regions. *Frontiers in Psychology, 12*, 667230. doi:10.3389/fpsyg.2021.667230 PMID:34484030

Richards, H. V., Brown, A. F., & Forde, T. B. (2007). Addressing diversity in schools: Culturally responsive pedagogy. *Teaching Exceptional Children, 39*(3), 64–68. doi:10.1177/004005990703900310

Roberts, P., & Dunworth, K. (2012). Staff and student perceptions of support services for international students in higher education: A case study. *Journal of Higher Education Policy and Management, 34*(5), 517–528. doi:10.1080/1360080X.2012.716000

Russell, G. (2020). Reflecting on a way of being: Anchor principles of cultural competence. In J. Frawley J., G. Russell, & J. Sherwood (Eds), Cultural competence and the higher education sector (pp. 31-42). Springer.

Rychly, L., & Graves, E. (2012). Teacher characteristics for culturally responsive pedagogy. *Multicultural Perspectives, 14*(1), 44–49. doi:10.1080/15210960.2012.646853

Sanger, C. S. (2020). Diversity, inclusion, and context in Asian higher education. In S. S. Sanger & N. W. Gleason (Eds.), Diversity and inclusion in global higher education (pp. 1-30). Palgrave Macmillan. doi:10.1007/978-981-15-1628-3_1

Tusasiirwe, S., Kansiime, P., Eyaa, S., Namisango, F., & Bulamu, N. (2021). Living and revitalizing Ubuntu: Challenges of passing on Ubuntu values to the younger generation and attempted strategies to overcome them. In *Understanding ubuntu for enhancing intercultural communications* (pp. 85–101). IGI Global. doi:10.4018/978-1-7998-7947-3.ch008

Wu, H., Garza, E., & Guzman, N. (2015). International student's challenge and adjustment to college. *Education Research International, 2015*, 1–9. Advance online publication. doi:10.1155/2015/202753

Zhou, J. (2015, May). International students' motivation to pursue and complete a Ph.D. in the U.S. *Higher Education, 69*(5), 719–733. doi:10.100710734-014-9802-5

KEY TERMS AND DEFINITIONS

Culturally Responsive Education: A form of education that attends to the cultural needs of students.
Culture: The totality of an individual's background, heritage, and way of life.
Empathy: An informed emotional and physical drive to think of and respond to the needs and well-being of another.
Higher Education: Post-secondary education that usually occurs at universities and colleges.
International Student: A student studying in a country other their home countries.
Pedagogy: An approach to teaching students and engaging them on a subject or topic.
Reflective Practice: A form of personal introspection on past experiences and current practices.

Chapter 4
Understanding and Enhancing Academic Experiences of Culturally and Linguistically– Diverse International Students in Canada

James Alan Oloo
University of Windsor, Canada

ABSTRACT

Canada is among the top four most popular destinations for international students. Using narrative inquiry, this chapter explores lived experiences of two international students. The study is guided by three broad questions: 1) What are the main positive experiences of international students in Canada? 2) What are some of the challenges faced by international students during their studies in Canada? and 3) What should be done to enhance academic success of international students? Data were collected using semi-structured interviews as conversations. Data analysis reveals three main themes: mismatch between the students' academic expectations and reality, challenges relating to language, and self-efficacy and resilience. Recommendations are presented. These include working with international students to help identify factors that are likely to enhance the success of international students as identified by the students so that universities can create campus environments that allow for success.

INTRODUCTION

Canada is among the top destinations for international students from across the world. In 2020, 530,540 international students from over 200 countries were enrolled in various educational programs in Canada – a 135 percent increase from 2010 (Global Affairs Canada, 2020). While international students are unevenly distributed across the country, ranging from a low of less than one percent in Yukon Territory to a high of 46 percent in Ontario, there were international students in all Canadian provinces and ter-

DOI: 10.4018/978-1-7998-8921-2.ch004

ritories in 2020. Top source countries include India (34% of international students in Canada), China (22%), Vietnam (4%), South Korea (3%), and Iran (3%), accounting for close to seven out of 10 (or 66%) international students in Canada. A great majority of students from these countries could be described as coming from culturally and linguistically diverse backgrounds, often speaking at least two languages, including mother tongue that is neither English nor French – Canada's official languages. A survey of international students by the Canadian Bureau for International Education (2018) found that the number one reason for choosing Canada was because of "The quality of the Canadian education system" (p. 2).

The rise in the numbers of culturally and linguistically diverse international students presents opportunities and challenges for the students and the institutions where they study. International students bring several funds of knowledge, including social and cultural experiences and resources, with them that they draw upon to attain success (Kiramba & Oloo, 2019). However, as Macgregor and Folinazzo (2018), in their study of experiences of international students at a Canadian college, noted, "international students [often] face distinct challenges that arise from language issues as well as ones of a personal and social nature, all of which can lead to frustration and failure" (p. 299). Yet, not much systematic research has been conducted to examine academic experiences of culturally and linguistically diverse international students from a strength-based perspective as narrated by the students themselves.

The goal of this study is to explore experiences of culturally and linguistically diverse international students in Canada. The study contributes to research by disrupting deficit-centred discourse around international student experiences while amplifying the voices of three culturally and linguistically diverse international students and validating their strengths. This study is based on experiences of three international students in Canada and is not intended to make a general conclusion about experiences of international students.

Researcher Positionality

As a researcher, the author brings his identity and experience to this study. He is a Black Kenyan-Canadian educator who came to Canada as an international student and is currently working as an assistant professor in Ontario. His students include those from outside Canada and of culturally and linguistically diverse backgrounds. The author adopted relational ontology in his interaction with the study participants because it privileges their experiences and positions them as experts while helping reshape the author's role regarding who he is and is becoming in relation to this research, namely, a learner.

LITERATURE REVIEW

In 2018, international students in Canada contributed an estimated $21.6 billion to the country's economy (Global Affairs Canada, 2020). Other than the economic advantages that result from increasing the numbers of international students, there is also benefit in knowledge sharing, engagement with individuals from across the world, and preparation for a globalized world. International students do "enrich the Canadian post-secondary landscape [by] providing meaningful opportunities for multilateral dialogue in various intellectual and cultural spheres, thus enriching all students' knowledge of global history and issues" (De Moissac et al., 2020). Such dialogue can potentially "assist emerging adults seeking to develop cross-cultural competencies, invaluable in our globalized world" (p. 53).

Shadowen et al. (2019) highlight the important role played by international students in adding diversity and enhancing "educational value to the academic environment on campus by bringing to the classroom different cultural backgrounds, experiences, and worldviews and acting as 'cultural ambassadors' for their home country" (p. 130). Domestic students also benefit from the diverse student cohort through increased cultural awareness.

The increasing international student enrolment does not mean that experiences of such students are always positive. Many students experience challenges while transitioning to post-secondary education. For international students, these challenges may be compounded by the fact that they are adjusting to a new culture, environment, and life in a new country. As noted below, challenges faced by international students, whether academic in nature or not tend to impact their academic experiences.

Literature on international student experience often mentions the role of language, especially English proficiency, on the student experience (Brazill, 2021; Gatwiri, 2015; Kiramba & Oloo, 2019). Most Canadian post-secondary institutions require international students to successfully take English language proficiency tests such as the International English Language Testing System (IELTS) and the Test of English as a Foreign Language (TOEFL) as a condition for admission. Despite meeting such a requirement, many international students, including those from English-speaking countries, do experience challenges relating to English language fluency. Gatwiri (2015), in her study that examines the impact of language difficulties on the wellbeing of international students, points out that language fluency is not only a key determinant of successful integration and acculturation in a new culture, but is also "the most critical issue facing international students today" (p. 1).

International students are not a homogenous group, and their educational experience is often influenced by a variety of factors, including race and ethnicity, country of origin, and immigration status, among others. They are, however, some of "the most quiet, invisible, [and] underserved groups" (Mori, 2000, p. 143). This could help explain why many universities have an international students' services office that provides students with resources and supports. In general, this is premised on the fact that to varying degrees, "all students beginning studies require some support as they transition to university ... and acculturate to the new university context" (Mitchell et al., 2017, p. 17). "Acculturation of international students," Mitchell et al. write, is the process of "adopting beliefs and adapting behaviours of the new education culture in order to progress and succeed in their education program" (p. 17). The authors suggest that as a matter of equity, international students would benefit from "extra support" by academic staff. Similarly, Shadowen et al. (2019) reported that more support was associated with lower levels of depression among international students.

In their study that examined the mental health of international students in Manitoba, De Moissac et al. (2020) found that international students were at a higher risk of experiencing mental health distress compared to their domestic peers. They attributed this to such factors as "anxiety resulting from the unknown, strained personal relationships, loneliness, isolation ... and discrimination" (p. 53). Acculturative stress and limited English proficiency have also been linked to higher levels of depressive symptoms (Mitchell et al., 2017). Despite being more susceptible to exhibiting mental health problems including depression, international students are "more likely to report excellent mental health, score higher on the mental health scale, and report higher life satisfaction, higher self-esteem, and more positive body image than domestic respondents" (De Moissac et al., 2020, p. 52). Further, international students are less likely to talk about the challenges they may be experiencing. De Moissac et al. (2020) attribute this to a general preference by international students for self-reliance, lack of awareness of availability of healthcare and other support resources, and a cultural stigma around mental illness.

Marom (2021), in a study of experiences of Punjabi international students in Canada, found that many of the challenges faced by international students can be attributed to "the construction of higher education as a competitive market" (p. 2). As she puts it,

[Many international students] go through a recruitment and admission process that is mediated by agents, which often leads to problems in registration and programme selection. They are also vulnerable to high and unregulated tuition fees and face academic challenges as an outcome of a lack of academic and institutional support. (p. 2)

With respect to commercialization of higher education, evidence from Canada seems to support Marom's (2021) assertions. For example, in 2017/2018, international students paid approximately $4.0 billion, representing about 40 percent of all tuition fees paid to universities across Canada (Global Affairs Canada, 2020). Universities were also investing in international student recruitment.

In summary, studies show that culturally and linguistically diverse international students often experience challenges, such as, language difficulties, cultural differences and a lack of cultural responsiveness from their university, and social isolation, among others. These challenges tend to impact their academic and social wellbeing. Despite the challenges, increasing numbers of international students are enrolling in Canadian post-secondary institutions. For example, at the University of Windsor (in the province of Ontario), Memorial University of Newfoundland (Newfoundland and Labrador), University of Regina (Saskatchewan), and the University of Alberta (Alberta), at least four out of every ten graduate students are international students (Dwyer, 2017). International student persistence and success could be attributed, at least in part, to the support system in place at the institutions where they study and to their own cultural capital (Yosso, 2005).

THEORETICAL FRAMEWORK: COMMUNITY CULTURAL WEALTH

As stated above, about seven in ten international students in Canada come from South East Asia and the Middle East. Research on domestic students from similar backgrounds tends to highlight individual factors (e.g., family background, immigration status) and structural factors (e.g., education system, school environment, scholarships) in shaping post-secondary educational experience the of visible minority students (see for example, Kiramba & Oloo, 2019). On the other hand, research on experiences of international students has often highlighted the barriers and challenges they face and how the students need to adapt to their new environment (Gatwiri, 2015; Marom, 2021). This study contributes to research on international education by adopting a critical approach to understanding experiences of international students in Canada. It does this by disrupting deficit-centred discourse around international students while embracing strength-based perspective, namely the Community Cultural Wealth (Yosso, 2005) theoretical framework.

Yosso's (2005) Community Cultural Wealth (CCW) identifies six forms of cultural capital (that is, strengths, talents, experiences, etc.) that students of colour possess and draw upon. While they may overlap, the six forms of cultural capital include: aspirational, linguistic, social, familial, navigational, and resistance. *Aspirational capital* refers to the ability of the study participants, who in this case are international students of colour from culturally and linguistically diverse backgrounds, to maintain hopes and dreams for the future despite the present challenges that they may be experiencing. *Linguistic capital* includes intellectual and social skills attained through language resources that the study participants have access to. For linguistically diverse international students, linguistic capital encompasses native languages and dialects, as well as the colonial language, namely, English or French, in the new host country of Canada. *Social* and *Familial capitals* refer to the knowledge, skills, and understanding acquired and passed on through relationships with friends and family members, respectively. *Navigational capital* refers to the students' ability to maneuver within unfamiliar social institutions, while *Resistant capital* includes the knowledge and skills used to challenge inequality and enhance social justice.

While CCW theoretical framework (Yosso, 2005) has mostly been employed in research that explore experiences of socially marginalized and racialized minority groups (Kiramba & Oloo, 2019; Miller, et al., 2020; Winterer, et al., 2020), it has also been applied in studies with international students, especially those conducted in the United States (Anandavalli, 2021; Brazill, 2021; Lu, et al., 2015). This is due to a general recognition of parallel between the two categories of students. Anandavalli (2021), for example, argues that like other (domestic) students of colour, international students of colour do face "multiple interpersonal (e.g., isolation), and systemic barriers (e.g., biased national policies) due to their intersectional racial and immigrant [sic] identities" and that some of these barriers are unique to racialized students "as a result of their marginalized identities" (p. 111). Thus, the CCW's strengths-based approach enables researchers to leverage the strengths possessed by international students. Five of the six cultural capital (Yosso, 2005) identified above were especially relevant for unfolding and understanding the lived experiences of the study participants as they navigated their personal, social, and academic landscapes as international students in Canada. These include aspirational, familial, social, linguistic, and navigational capital.

METHODOLOGY: NARRATIVE INQUIRY

Using narrative inquiry (Clandinin, 2013), the chapter explores lived experiences of three international students in Canada who identify as coming from culturally and linguistically diverse backgrounds. The study is guided by three broad questions: 1) What are the main positive experiences of international students in Canada? 2) What are some of the challenges faced by international students during their studies in Canada? And 3) What should be done to enhance academic success of international students?

As humans, we make sense of our lived experiences through narratives (Oloo & Relland, 2021). Narrative inquiry is "a way of honoring lived experience as a source of important knowledge and understanding" (Clandinin, 2013, p. 42). Stories people live and tell "are a result of the confluence of social influences on a person's inner life, social influences on their environment, and their unique personal history" (Clandinin & Rosiek, 2007, p. 41). Unlike many other forms of qualitative research, narrative inquiry is "sensitive to the subtle textures of thought and feeling" (Webster & Mertova, 2007, p. 7) around the telling and retelling of lived experiences and enables the study participants to talk about events that are of most significance to them. Thus, stories of international students from culturally and linguistically diverse backgrounds are shaped by societal influence including sociocultural and historical situations where their experiences occur and continue to unfold. These include the issues of language, acculturation, as well as how international students navigate and adapt to their new university and home in Canada.

Setting and Participants

Participants in this study included three international students who are enrolled in undergraduate programs in Canada. The participants, two males and one female, were recruited through a call for participants on Facebook using purposeful and criteria-based sampling (Oloo & Relland, 2021). The criteria included those who had been in Canada on valid international student permit while attending a post-secondary institution for at least one year and self-identified as coming from culturally and linguistically diverse backgrounds. Five individuals responded to the call for participants. Of these, three participated in the study. They included (pseudonyms used for their names): Owino – a 22 year old male from Tanzania who speaks three languages and is a first generation international student in third year of Bachelor of Science. Owino developed an interest in studying in Canada after attending an education fair with his parents when he was in high school. Ali is a 21 year old male in his second year of Bachelor of Nursing. He is bilingual and his father was an international student in Saudi Arabia. Ali, who is from Oman, stated that it was always expected in his family that he would attend university in North America. Kaiya is a 21 year old female and first generation international student from Vietnam. A second year Bachelor of Social Work student, Kaiya learned about university education in Canada from a family friend.

Data Collection

Following research ethics approval by the author's institution and consent from the participants, we used semi-structured interview as conversations (Oloo & Relland, 2021) guided by open-ended research questions to explore experiences of the three participants. We entered into the research relationship with the participants with the view of "tap(ping) into the tacit knowledge available to the insiders and to learn from them rather than to study them" (Berger, 2016, p. 476). We engaged with each participant in two sessions of one-on-one dialogic conversations via video (Microsoft Teams) that lasted between 60 to 90 minutes. There were follow-up conversations over the phone to help clarify and expand on points in the participant stories. Data collection occurred in 2021.

Data Analysis and Interpretation

We transcribed the recorded interviews and employed paradigmatic analysis which allowed for the use of inductive conceptualizations to identify common themes across study participants' stories (Oloo & Relland, 2021). This enabled us to utilize "deductive processes to explore how well data fits with predetermined concepts, usually those reflected in an existing theoretical framework" (Sharp, Bye, & Cusick, 2018, p. 9), namely aspirational, familial, social, linguistic, and navigational capital – five of the six forms of social capital in Yosso's (2005) CCW.

FINDINGS

Data analysis revealed three main common themes, namely, a mismatch between the students' academic expectations and reality; issues relating to language; and self-efficacy and resilience. These are discussed below.

Mismatch between Academic Expectations and Realities

All the participants talked about the academic expectation-reality mismatch involving workload, grades, and extracurricular activities. As one study participant, Owino (pseudonym), stated,

I was a top student at my high school. I know I am a good student. However, I have struggled with the new way of learning in Canada. This semester, I am taking seven courses; everyone in my class has a similar course load. It is too much work. The readings are difficult too. This is not what I expected because everyone I know from my country that go for further studies overseas do come back with advanced degrees. I did not know it was this challenging.

Another participant, Kaiya, described the expectations she had based on her "investigations" and conversation with an education agent who she consulted to help prepare for studying in Canada. She knew that time management was going to be important and so she estimated amount of time she would spend on studies, employment, extra-curricular activities, and "getting to know Canada." Kaiya noted that:

My expectations of time allocation and commitment were way off from the reality during my first year. Academic work took more time than I had anticipated even though I would get away without reading some of the required or recommended texts. It was so busy at the university that year, I had to quit working after holding a part time job for just three weeks. I also reduced extra-curricular activities to going to the gym or jogging from four days to three days a week.

Kaiya continued,

Things improved after the first year. My original expectations of time management were, in general, much closer to the reality. I got a part time job, went to the gym five days a week, and attended sporting events when my university team was playing while maintaining good grades. Actually, my GPA improved. It was still stressful at times, but it has been getting better.

The participants spoke about the gap between their expectations and reality as it relates to their academic, extracurricular, and life in general. While this was created barriers and challenges that impacted their academic experience, the situation improved with time because they adopted new strategies or navigational capital (Yosso, 2005) that enabled them to more effectively navigate their way around their social and institutional environment.

Issues Relating to Language

All the three study participants spoke at least two languages, including English, which they had learned as a second or additional language in their home countries. To the participants, their language proficiency was a both a source of strength and a challenge. All the three said that they regularly spoke in their first language with friends in Canada and over the phone with friends and families at home. Kaiya and Ali noted that they each belonged to study groups where they often spoke in their first languages (Vietnamese and Arabic, respectively). Kaiya noted:

Vietnamese students here are very supportive. We encourage one another, do social things together, and study together. If you are having a bad day, you can speak with someone. We also check on each other to see if everyone is alright. It feels a little like home speaking in your language and surrounded by care and familiarity. Plus, you can ask classmates and senior students questions about assignments. You know, we are free to ask deep questions of each other and learn better.

Owino noted that he always looks forward to meeting with other Swahili speakers at church because it makes him feel at home and shift his focus from studies.

A participant, Ali, described how the language-related difficulties he faced impacted his academic and social life:

In [my country], people have always commented on how I speak English well. However, I have been struggling here because of my English. It is a different kind of English. Then, being in social work [program], we do a lot of reading and assignments that involve reflective writing and practice. I have not done as well as I know I am able to due to the pressures of writing in English. Also, some professors speak fast and pronounce things differently. Usually, I attend all the classes then review all class recordings later to help me understand the lesson and what was discussed. It is time consuming, but it is the only way for me to understand because of the Canadian English.

Ali added, "[Language difficulties] affects your confidence and well-being. You know, it makes it a bit harder to make friends and hang out with Canadians. We [international students] mainly interact with each other. We understand each other." As he put it,

One of the cool things about our study group that is made up of four of us is that we are in the same program and we are able to discuss assignments and academic work in our language and in English. We practice academic English while also thinking in our mother tongue. We all find [the strategy] useful. Rather than feel like we can't hang out with our Canadian classmates, we actually find discussing school work among ourselves very good.

Another participant, Owino, highlighted the dilemma of difficulty in socializing with domestic students due to language difficulties and finding acceptance among international students who may sometime resort to speaking their native languages and so do not embrace the opportunity to improve on their English language skills. Despite the difficulties associated with English language proficiency, the participants employed their linguistic capital (Yosso, 2005) to their advantage. Speaking their native languages and versions of English that were considered different, perhaps inferior to the 'Canadian English,' not only brought them a sense of familiarity and comfort, but also enhanced their academic and social experience.

Self-Efficacy and Resilience

Self-efficacy of international students is a significant predictor of their resilience (Sabouripour et al., 2021). While the former relates to a student's perception of their capabilities (Bandura, 1997), resilience refers to an individual's competence in the face of adversity. Thus, as Sabouripour et al (2021) write, "resilience characteristics are essential to effectively cope with change, and the best predictor of adjustment to the new environment among international students" (p. 5).

While international students face challenges in their new environments as described above, they also encounter opportunities for growth. Çankaya, Dong, and Liew (2017) highlight the importance of "student factors that predict benefits, growth or resilience for international students through their … transitioning experience" (p. 88). A common theme across the narratives of the three international students who participated in this study is that they tapped into their aspirational and navigational capital by developing and nurturing self-efficacy and resilience.

"I know that I have what it takes to succeed," one of the study participants, Owino, aptly stated. "It doesn't mean that I won't fall down. It's not about the fall, we all do; it is about rising back up. I have come this far … I have to attain success." Another participant, Kaiya, said:

I know people from my country who went overseas for further studies. I spoke with a few of them before coming to Canada and learned that life as an international student is not always easy. I got to think about this a lot before my flight [to Canada]. I made up my mind that no matter what challenges come my way, I was going to not only enjoy my time in Canada, but also earn my degree, and go for my master's [degree after graduating]. I know people who did it, and I can do it too.

Kaiya added that there were challenges that she had not prepared for:

Suddenly, you realize that the culture is different. This takes time to get used to especially coming from a society with different social norms. English is not good enough, or you talk too fast. You call the professor by their first name and if you do not communicate much with them, then that is not right. The way they teach at the university is different, and when it comes to grading, this prof was marking our assignments and not giving marks. I had never seen anything like that. How do you find your way around the library; who do you ask questions without appearing like you are stupid? You miss family events back home. It can get lonely too especially during winter. I know this guy in my class who got into depression. But you know, family and friends will support and give you encouragement, however, you have to have it within you to want to succeed. Do you know what I am saying? You need to encourage yourself, push yourself to win.

The study participants were more willing to seek help especially after their first year of studies. Ali, for example, stated,

In my culture, we generally try to figure things out by ourselves before we ask for help. I knew about resources at the university and professors always encourage us to contact them if we have questions. It was hard for me to admit that I was struggling or needed help. It is different now. I seek help if and when I need it, and also encourage other international students to do so. There is no wisdom is suffering in silence. Take the initiative, swallow your pride, [and] ask questions; help is often available.

Ali added,

Regarding your studies, you have to be strategic. My first year, I took like six courses each semester. It was too much, I did not perform well and was always anxious and stressed out. Now I know better.

I take summer school and this means that in fall and spring semesters, I take a manageable number of courses... I'm in nursing, but I have always liked humanities. I choose humanities as electives and this helps boost my GPA. You have to know how to survive.

From the participant stories, it was clear what they did to "attain success" or "win." These included acting from a conviction that they "had what it takes to succeed," "needed to encourage themselves," "had to be strategic" and had to "know how to survive." They then drew on various forms of capitals that they possessed, including navigational capital (seeking help when they needed it, or taking advantage of the resources that were available to them); social capital (reaching out to other international students for friendships, support, encouragement, and to share tips regarding assignments and non-academic activities), as well as aspirational capital (encouraging oneself).

DISCUSSION

The study examined experiences of three international students in Canada. It was guided by three broad questions: 1) What are the main positive experiences of international students in Canada? 2) What are some of the challenges faced by international students during their studies in Canada? And 3) What should be done to enhance academic success of international students? The participants identified several unique positive experiences that included those relating to transition and acculturalization, life in Canada, and their education. The participants talked about their own growth and maturation as individuals who were living away from home for the first time. They appreciated the opportunity for personal connections/friendships and positive cross-cultural experiences that different educational environment and the new society presented. They all mentioned their academic experience, freedom and safety, clean environment, and ability to have part-time employment while attending school as things that were useful to them. All the three indicated a desire to pursue graduate studies in Canada and/or remain in the country after finishing their studies.

The participants also reported that they have faced several challenges including those relating to language and a mismatch between their academic expectations and realities. The latter can sometimes be expected during transitions, such as to a university in a foreign country. However, they can impact the motivation and academic performance for international students. "University life," as Maloshonok and Terentev (2017) remind us, "requires first-year students to demonstrate greater levels of independence, self-regulation, and initiative compared to high school" (p. 356). This, as the current study shows, is not limited to domestic students but rather applies to international students as well. Maloshonok and Terentev (2017) suggest that,

[T]his transition is a period when expectations about 'what a university is like' and 'how students should behave at a university' are formed. The mismatch between these expectations and actual experience can lead to difficulties in adaptation to university life, dissatisfaction with study, and, finally, to withdrawal. (p. 356)

Stern (1966) uses the term "freshman myth" to describe the mismatch between educational expectations and realities among first year university students. As he puts it, the student "brings with him [sic] to college a naive, enthusiastic, and boundless idealism" (p. 411) and expectations that rarely meet reality" since "university experience in most cases is more challenging than was anticipated" (Maloshonok & Terentev, 2017, p. 3).

If this is the case for domestic students who are transitioning from high school to university in the same country, province, or even city, then the mismatch is likely more pronounced for international students. This is in spite of the fact that two of the participants, Ali and Kayla, stated that they "did their homework" regarding life and education in a foreign country before they came to Canada. Ali's father had been an international student in Saudi Arabia while Kayla sought advice of friends in her country of Vietnam. Both were convinced that they had an idea of what to expect. The two, together with Owino, noted that they were among the top students in their respective high schools in their home countries. So, the mismatched was not much about their academic ability. As well, it is worth noting that the participants did not regard themselves as being helpless in the face of the mismatch between their educational expectations and realities. Rather, they were intentional in employing various types of capital that was available to them (Yosso, 2005) to enable them to overcome some of the challenges. It is, thus, important that international students be involved in any strategies put in place by universities to help address the challenge.

One of the key points that stood out in this study was the determination by the study participants to succeed in their studies. When asked what kept them going during their challenging times, Kaiya said: "My family has a lot of hopes in me. I have to finish [the degree program] well and go for my master's [degree]." Similarly, Owino stated, "There is other way around it, I am going to graduate around the top of the class." Ali said, "I'm not in self-denial, challenges are real. But, I am well-able to succeed [in my studies]."

Self-determined motivation is closely linked to aspirational capital, which refers to an individual's ability to remain hopeful about the future, despite barriers that may be present (Yosso, 2005). Chirkov et al (2008) examined the link between self-determined motivation that international students have for studying abroad and how well the international student adapt to their new environment in the host country. They concluded that:

[International] students who feel that they initiated their decision to study abroad and stood behind it will be happier, less distressed and more successful in adjusting to a new country in comparison to those who feel they were pressured by other people or circumstances to move abroad. (p. 428)

As Çankaya, Dong, and Liew (2017) found, social self-efficacy is a predictor of personal growth initiative amongst international students. Yet, too often, studies on experiences of international students from culturally and linguistically diverse backgrounds tend to focus on challenges and difficulties while ignoring the fact that international students, such as those who participated in this study, do navigate the difficulties, and attain academic success as well as personal and social growth.

CONCLUSION

This study employed narrative inquiry methodology to examine the lived experiences of three international students from diverse linguistic and cultural backgrounds who are enrolled in Canadian universities. Because of the small number of the participants, it is not intended to make generalizable claims. The study is grounded on the CCW (Yosso, 2005) aspirational capital, linguistic capital, and navigational capital. By drawing on their aspirational capital, the study participants were able to stay motivated, adaptable, and hopeful about the future despite the challenges that they faced. They were able to employ their individual and collective agency to navigate their academic landscape. This included making friendships among themselves, and supporting and encouraging each other academically and socially. The international students also drew on their linguistic capital by, for example, discussing their assignments and academic projects in their native languages and in English in order to increase their understanding.

Canada has recorded a growth in international student enrolment over the past years and many universities in the country have developed strategies to attract international students. In some university programs in Ontario, for example, international students account for at least one half of registered students. That is, international students, including those from diverse cultural and linguistic backgrounds, are becoming increasingly important as a proportion of our student population, source of revenue, and diverse and thriving campuses.

As global competition for international students increases (Canadian Bureau for International Education, 2018), Canadian universities must position themselves as more than just places to get degrees. There is need for creating welcoming and dynamic campus environments that prepare students for success beyond university years. To do that effectively, critical spaces must be created for the voices of international students to be heard. They must be involved in decisions around how their experiences can be enhanced. As this study has indicated, many of the students were among the best in their countries and they met English language proficiency requirements before getting admission to Canadian universities. Yet, language related challenges were a common theme across participant stories. It is important to not only provide the students with the supports and resources that they need, but also to know from the students themselves how those resources should look like. This will make it possible to identify factors that are likely to enhance the success of international students as identified by the students so that universities can create campus environments that allow for success.

FUNDING

This research received no specific grant from any funding agency in the public, commercial, or not-for-profit sectors.

REFERENCES

Brazill, S. (2021). Narrative inquiry into Chinese international doctoral students' journey: A strength-based perspective. *International Journal of Doctoral Studies, 16*, 395–428. doi:10.28945/4785

Canadian Bureau for International Education. (2018). *The student's voice: National results of the 2018 CBIE international student survey.* CBIE Research in Brief Number 9. Retrieved December 21, 2021, from https://cbie.ca/wpcontent/uploads/2018/08/Student_Voice_Report-ENG.pdf

Çankaya, E. M., Dong, X., & Liew, J. (2017). An examination of the relationship between social self-efficacy and personal growth initiative in international context. *International Journal of Intercultural Relations, 61*, 88–96. doi:10.1016/j.ijintrel.2017.10.001

Chirkov, V. I., Safdar, S., de Guzman, D. J., & Playford, K. (2008). Further examining the role motivation to study abroad plays in the adaptation of international students in Canada. *International Journal of Intercultural Relations, 32*(5), 427–440. doi:10.1016/j.ijintrel.2007.12.001

Clandinin, D. J. (2013). *Engaging in narrative inquiry.* Left Coast Press.

Clandinin, D. J., & Rosiek, J. (2007). Mapping a landscape of narrative inquiry: Borderland spaces and tensions. In D. J. Clandinin (Ed.), *Handbook of narrative inquiry: Mapping a methodology* (pp. 35–75). Sage. doi:10.4135/9781452226552.n2

De Moissac, D., Graham, J. M., Prada, K., Gueye, N. R., & Rocque, R. (2020). Mental health status and help-seeking strategies of international students in Canada. *Canadian Journal of Higher Education, 50*(4), 52–71. doi:10.47678/cjhe.vi0.188815

Dwyer, M. (2017). *These Canadian universities have the most international students.* https://www.macleans.ca/education/which-canadian-universities-have-the-most-international-students/

Gatwiri, G. (2015). The influence of language difficulties on the wellbeing of international students: An interpretive phenomenological analysis. *Inquiries Journal/Student Pulse, 7*(5). http://www.inquiriesjournal.com/a?id=1042

Global Affairs Canada. (2020). *Assessing the economic impact of international students in Canada.* International Education Division. Retrieved February 23, 2022, from https://www.international.gc.ca/education/report-rapport/impact-2017/sec-3.aspx?lang=eng

Kiramba, L. K., & Oloo, J. A. (2019). "It's OK. She doesn't even speak English": Narratives of language, culture, and identity negotiation by immigrant high school students. *Urban Education.* Advance online publication. doi:10.1177/0042085919873696

Macgregor, A., & Folinazzo, G. (2018). Best practices in teaching international students in higher education: Issues and strategies. *TESOL Journal, 9*(2), 299–329. doi:10.1002/tesj.324

Maloshonok, N., & Terentev, E. (2017). The mismatch between student educational expectations and realities: Prevalence, causes, and consequences. *European Journal of Higher Education, 7*(4), 356–372. doi:10.1080/21568235.2017.1348238

Marom, L. (2021). Outsiders-insiders-in between: Punjabi international students in Canada navigating identity amid intraethnic tensions. *Globalisation, Societies and Education,* ●●●, 1–15. doi:10.1080/14767724.2021.1882291

Miller, R. A., Vaccaro, A., Kimball, E. W., & Forester, R. (2020). "'It's dude culture": Students with minoritized identities of sexuality and/or gender navigating STEM majors'. *Journal of Diversity in Higher Education.* Advance online publication. doi:10.1037/dhe0000171

Mitchell, C., Del Fabbro, L., & Shaw, J. (2017). The acculturation, language and learning experiences of international nursing students: Implications for nursing education. *Nurse Education Today, 56,* 16–22. doi:10.1016/j.nedt.2017.05.019 PMID:28623678

Mori, S. C. (2000). Addressing the mental health concerns of international students. *Journal of Counseling and Development, 78*(2), 137–144. doi:10.1002/j.1556-6676.2000.tb02571.x

Oloo, J. A., & Relland, M. (2021). "I think of my classroom as a place of healing": Experiences of indigenous students in a community-based master of education program in Saskatchewan. *Canadian Journal of Educational Administration and Policy*, (197), 94–107. doi:10.7202/1083335ar

Sabouripour, F., Roslan, S., Ghiami, Z., & Memon, M. A. (2021). Mediating role of self-efficacy in the relationship between optimism, psychological well-being, and resilience among Iranian students. *Frontiers in Psychology*, *12*, 675645. Advance online publication. doi:10.3389/fpsyg.2021.675645 PMID:34194372

Shadowen, N. L., Williamson, A. A., Guerra, N. G., Ammigan, R., & Drexler, M. L. (2019). Prevalence and correlates of depressive symptoms among international students: Implications for university support offices. *Journal of International Students*, *9*(1), 129–149. doi:10.32674/jis.v9i1.277

Webster, L., & Mertova, P. (2007). *Using narrative inquiry as a research method*. Routledge. doi:10.4324/9780203946268

Chapter 5
Enhancing Employability Skills in Marketing Graduates Through Teaching Philosophy and Curriculum Design:
A Ghanaian Perspective

George Kofi Amoako
Ghana Communication Technology University, Ghana

ABSTRACT

The purpose of this research is to find out how teaching philosophy and curriculum design can affect graduates' employability skills. In the same way, university survival also depends on how well graduates perform in the workplace. Teaching philosophy affects curriculum design which in turn could affect employability. Higher education teachers and administrators' awareness of these variables and how they interplay could enhance student employability skills. Qualitative methodology was used in this research to investigate the relationship between teaching philosophy, curriculum design, and employability skills. The data for the study were sampled from both public and private universities in Ghana. The population size for the study was 12 respondents.

INTRODUCTION

Employability of graduates has become a big issue among employers, higher education providers and policy makers in recent years (Huang, Turner & Chen, 2014; Wickramasinghe & Perera, 2010). Many employers are much more interested in recruiting graduates with employable skills than just the possession of university qualifications (Yorke, 2006). The International Labour Organisation (ILO) (2013) argues that employability skills, knowledge and competencies enhances one's ability to secure and retain a job, progress in the job and secure another job if he/she so desires. Perceived employability is a factor that influence students' satisfaction with a university(Trulla, et al 2018). For instance, in Ghana, the National

DOI: 10.4018/978-1-7998-8921-2.ch005

Accreditation Board (NAB), has directed that institutions seeking accreditation must provide the following in their course programs: objectives, content, competence-based training component, problem-based learning component and practical training, industrial attachment and internship. This has set the need to enhance higher learning education in the county. Another critical factor that the NAB considers before accreditation is tracer studies, which is the ability of the institution to know where its graduates are and what their employees say about their performance.

Researchers (Ahmad and Shah, 2018) have observed the increasingly desire of students to further their studies abroad and universities in Ghana have been receiving students from other countries who have or are obtaining their education in Ghana. A study conducted by Mahmoud et al (2020) posit that students population in both public and private universities in Ghana is well over 400,000, of which approximately 2% (15,185) are foreign students. Mahmoud et al (2020) observed that most of the students are from the West African sub region with Nigeria (84%) dominating the list of foreign students in Ghana. In a similar studies conducted by Adu-Gyamfi (n.d) the results of their findings shows that foreign students in Ghana was dominated by West African countries with Nigerians topping the list with (44%), followed by Togolese (20.2%), Liberians (16.1%) then Ivorians (13%). The remaining African countries and other advanced countries form less than 2% of the international student population in Ghana. These studies reveals that Ghana also attract students from other parts of the world which makes our students cultural diverse by learning from these foreign students.

The Government of Ghana and the National Accreditation Board (NAB) have realized the need for graduates to possess employability skills to enable them to thrive in their various field or career. The ex-deputy executive secretary and head of the accreditation department of NAB described employability skills as "those basic skills necessary for getting, keeping, and doing well on a job and enabling workers to get along with fellow workers and supervisors to make sound and critical decisions" (Adjei, 2018, p11; Accreditation News January-June 2018, Issue 001). The issue of graduate employability in the Ghanaian context is very often associated with how quickly a graduate can find employment after graduating from school. However, graduates complete their education and realise that either there are no jobs or limited jobs available competing for so many graduates who are churned out from our universities yearly. Also, not peculiar to Ghana is the issue of how scholars (e.g. Römgens, Scoupe, and Beausaert 2020; Peeters et al. 2019), employers and policymakers are concerned about how there is a mismatch between the skills required by the corporate world and the skills graduates acquire in the course of their studies. The situation puts pressure on higher education leaders from governments, educational advocates, etc to pay attention to graduate employability and make it a strategic issue at various universities in the country.

This research seeks to investigate the importance of teaching philosophy and curriculum design in higher educational institutions and its effect on graduates' employability skills. The study also investigates how best learning practices can be engaged in the classroom to enhance the employable skills acquired by the graduates. Giroux (2010) is of the view that the higher educational practice in the world is shifting from neoliberal forces and is aligning with the goals of business, government and the education systems. This has caused a debate globally about the role of higher educational institutions in producing employable graduates to occupy various positions in the emerging knowledge-based markets. Producing employable graduates requires that universities can tailor their curricula in line with what industries demand. There is evident in the extant literature (see, for example, Mahmoud et al (2020, and Ahmad and Shah, 2018) which indicates that the skills acquired by graduates are not able to meet the expectations of the corporate wold, hence the need for universities to re-examine their curriculum to cater for the needs of the corporate world. This position was reinforced by Yorke (2004) who posits that the situation of mismatch between graduate employability and the expectations of the corporate could be addressed through bridging the gap between curriculum teaching and assessment. This lack of curriculum activities that enhance employable skills can be linked to poor teaching philosophies that do not consider the employability skills demanded of the graduate.

Marketing Graduates and the World-of-Work

Success in the marketing research course depends largely on a student's ability to apply data analysis techniques to practical business applications. Usually, earlier courses such as business statistics teach these skills, however, many instructors are of the view that students do not retain an understanding of statistics that can be transferred to marketing and other functional areas (Nonis & Hudson, 1999). This means that a look at the curriculum design can help students to appreciate marketing research better. Moreover, in Ghana, much of the teaching of marketing is done in the class room with little practical marketing application. Marketing graduates may therefore lack the practical knowledge that is necessary to fully appreciate the application of marketing concepts in real work situations. Schlee and Harich (2010) posit that the employers have problems with the level of transferable skills that young marketing graduates who come to the field possess even though they have appreciable knowledge content of marketing.

Employers squarely blame the overall approach to education and learning as causing the incompetence in marketing and management graduates. Wilkins (2000) pointed out that, from a business perspective, employers seek marketing professionals who have developed the ability to identify problems, analyze and interpret data, and make relevant decisions – simply put, solve real-world problems. Scott and Frontczak (1996) argue that a gap exists between employer expectations of new marketing graduates and the skills these graduates bring to the workplace. This, however, could vary depending on the country and context. For this reason, educational institutions need to incorporate employability skills in the development of the course curriculum. This will prepare students wholly for the working environment. This paper investigates how teaching philosophy influences curriculum design and eventually employability of marketing graduates.

LITERATURE REVIEW

The educational institutions are responsible for training and shaping the manpower or the human capital for the business world. It has become the case that these graduates are developed and shaped to suit the market or problems relating to the business world, to enable them to offer solutions to the problems.

Employability and National Development

Employability has become of utmost importance to governments across the world and are therefore tasking the higher institutions with training and equipping graduates with employment related curriculum. According to Yorke (2004), employability is made up of a set of achievements - skills, knowledge, understandings and personal attributes - that make graduates more likely to get employment and be successful in their occupations, which benefits themselves, the organization, the community and the economy. It encompasses all skills that the graduate acquires while studying. Most institutions are embedding in the curriculum the forms of skills that encourages employability (Knight & Yorke 2004). University of Exeter defined employability (using Lee, 2000) as 'the establishment of clear mechanisms by which students can develop their abilities to use and deploy a wide range of skills and opportunities to enhance their own academic learning and enable them to become more employable'.

A review of current literature on the trends of development in the world reveals that the inadequate preparation of graduates in generic employability skills leads to the gap between the graduates and their ability to be gainfully employed. For example, Greatbatch and Lewis (2007) underscored that generic employable skills have become integral in a nation's education agenda and training for students in primary, secondary, further and higher education and their development is a priority for the UK government. They further pointed out that generic employability skills are essential because of how intensely competitive the labour market has become, thereby influencing employers in the private, public and the third sectors to seek employees who are flexible, take the initiative and have the ability to undertake multiple tasks in different environments. Therefore, employability skills have generally become more 'service oriented' unlike the narrow definition in the past, making information and social skills increasingly vital. This finding implies that the development of curriculum (for example, the teaching of the marketing discipline) should not only focus on only the marketing discipline but should also factor in other areas that will enhance the generic employability skills of the marketing graduate. From the employers' expectations, graduate's achievements in related subjects or disciplines are not only necessary but should be comprehensive enough for them to be employed. Sometimes the employers view the actual subjects studied as relatively unimportant. However, academic achievements that transcend the boundaries of the discipline such as the development of soft skills, are generally considered to be important in the recruitment of graduates.

The effective and rapid development of any nation depends on the type of graduates it has and, accordingly, this forms the bedrock of that nation. If the graduates possess the required skills for the market, then the issue of employability will not be a challenge for the governments in these countries.

Under the human capital concept or theory that Mincer introduced in 1958, one's income is proportionate to one's level of education and experience and, therefore, important for people to pay attention to schooling. Drawing from the insight of this theory is essential for governments to foster a conducive atmosphere that encourages growth in the stock of human capital since it is considered crucial to the performance of knowledge-based economies in the world. A report by Her Majesty's Treasury (HM) (2000) states that "Human capital directly increases productivity by raising the productive potential of employee. Improving skills and human capital is important in promoting growth, both as an input to production and by aiding technological progress. This has been recognized both in endogenous growth theory and also in empirical studies comparing growth in different countries". Furthermore, according to a former Secretary of State for Education and Employment, the failure to develop people has contributed to the UK's "productivity shortfall". He explained that "in part the shortfall reflects lower investment in physical capital. In another part, it also reflects less investment in human capital - a less swell-educated, less well-trained workforce" (Blunkett, 2001).

Concerning the types of employability skills, Harvey *et al.* (1997) identify that "most employers are looking for graduates who are proactive, can use higher level skills including analysis, critique, synthesis and multi layered communication to facilitate innovative teamwork in catalyzing the transformation of their organization". Precision Consultancy (2007) listed the following eight employability skills as necessary for all graduates to acquire before seeking employment: communication, teamwork, self-motivation, problem solving, planning and organizing, technology, initiative and enterprise and life-long learning.

Melanie Curtin (2017) indicated that The World Economic Forum on Future of Jobs Report compared ten critical skills desired by **global employers in 2015 and 2020 as shown in Figure 1 following.**

Some of the employability skills that have been identified to be lacking in young graduates are briefly discussed below:

Figure 1.

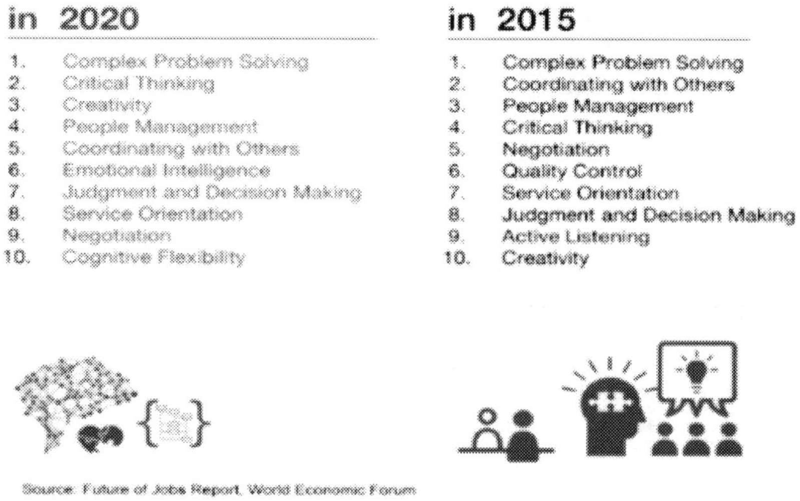

Source: Future of Jobs Report, World Economic Forum

Communication Skills

Over 86% of employers consider good communication skills to be important, yet many graduates cannot express themselves effectively (Archer & Davidson, 2008). Employers want graduates who are able to communicate effectively in all situations they find themselves during the discharge of their duties. A study conducted by Direito, Pereira, and de Oliveira Duarte (2012) observed that employees value graduates with oral and written communication than graduates who do not possess these communication skills. Also, similar studies was conducted by Pitan and Adedeji (2012) produced similar outcome. Looking at the importance of communication skills to employers, the researcher in teaching Marketing Fundamentals and Marketing Essentials in Ghana, engages students to summarize and analyze materials and do individual and group presentations to enhance their communication skills.

Interpersonal Skills

Employers regard the ability to work in teams as one of the most desirable graduate attributes (Hall & Buzwell, 201It is a vital skills needed to enable the graduate to interact and build positive relationships with people in the work place since the graduate will be working with different people in the same department or other departments. For instance, Husain et al. (2010) examined the interpersonal skills among Malaysians. They discovered that employers place importance to students' interpersonal skills, which is also consistent with studies conducted by Pitan and Adedeji (2012). Learning from these previous outcomes on interpersonal skills, the curriculum for marketing research, which this author teaches in Ghana has student group work as a major assessment component. This helps to build good interpersonal skills.

Personal Skills

Personal skills deals with looking after one's own wellbeing that is both the body and the mind and is considered one of the important skills that the graduate should have. Weligamage (2009) asserted that personal skills are necessary for employment. Personal skills are the basis upon which the other skills sit to function properly. Examples include: setting personal priorities, time management, self-esteem, and emotional intelligence. Research has found that personal image and personal branding attributes of sales executives in the insurance industry in Ghana affect the level of sales performance (Amoako & Okpattah, 2018). I inculcate personal skills development to students during the tutorial sessions for marketing research by encouraging them to manage their time well, giving them assignments and supervising them to complete within stipulated times.

Teaching Philosophy and Embedding Employability Skills in Curriculum Design

The higher learning institutions are considered as the best place for the student to acquire and develop the employability skills for the work environment after graduating. Curriculum philosophy provides educators with the insight into how students learn and what teaching methods would yield the best results, as well as the idea that learners' philosophies may evolve along with personal growth and experiences (Omstein, Pajak & Omstein, 2011). Thus, introducing soft skills that deal with students' communication and people skills into the curriculum would provide a holistic educational experience for students. Jackson (2014) indicated that factors influencing competence in employable skills include engagement with a skills agenda and quality of skills development in the learning program. This means that setting an employability agenda in the curriculum design and development influences graduate employability skills outcome. Some universities require teaching philosophy statements to be included as part of any application for recruitment. For example, in the USA, Cornell University's website (Cornell University, n.d.) states that the applicant's teaching philosophy is required in the faculty employment application process. Schönwetter, Friesen and Taylor (2002) indicated that a review of the literature demonstrates that a teaching philosophy statement has many purposes. These include: encouraging the dissemination of effective teaching clarifying what good teaching is; providing a rationale for teaching; promoting personal and professional development; guiding teaching behaviours; and organizing the evaluation of teaching.

Embedding the teaching of philosophy at the higher institution has become necessary to help teachers develop the thinking ability of the graduate in all areas of their lives especially their employability skills, which is important to the employers. Below are the various types of teaching philosophy developed by Cohen (1999) and Shaw (1995). According Raymond et al (2006) some sales job recruiters place importance on potential sales representatives having a broad knowledge of issues in the world .It is therefore suggested that marketing educators might attempt curriculum changes such as addressing current events as an ongoing component of normal class work and instruction. Assigning a student or small group of students the responsibility for a "topic of the day," could be very important in this situation and leading a *short* discussion on the implications of that for future business environment dynamics.

Essentialism

This approach to education has existed throughout history. It started with the Greek philosophers and has continued through the history of educational systems. With this approach, educators teach the basic skills of math, natural science, history etc. (Cohen, 1999; Shaw, 1995). The onus lies on the teacher/lecturer to instill moral values that will help students become successful in their fields. The students under this type of teaching philosophy are taught factual information and not vocational lessons. Students are also assessed academically through the test system. The shortcoming of this approach is that it does not allow students to think creatively. In an essentialist setting, students are taught cultural literature that is to acquire knowledge about the happenings of the environment. This approach is essentially endorsed by Ghanaian and African culture. The author tries to depart from this by encouraging students to be bold and assertive but respectful to all in the communication of their views.

Perennialism

This type of teaching philosophy believes that all students should be exposed to the same information and then the lecturer initiates discussions to enable students to question the authenticity of the topics introduced to them and asking thought provoking questions. The idea of this is that the students are taught "everlasting" information (Cohen, 1999; Shaw, 1995). Like essentialism, the instructor is the center of the discussions. The objective of this system is to open the minds of the students to scientific reasoning, and that factual information can be proven wrong. However, a major difference between the two is that, in perennialism, the student's contribution is necessary: this helps the student to become a critical thinker. Perennialists aim to help students discover those ideas that are insightful and give a timeless understanding of the human condition. Thus, the study of philosophy plays a vital part of the perennialist curriculum. The author uses this approach to urge students to think critically outside the box and to provide better alternative solutions.

Progressivism

This is the first philosophical approach that takes into account all the three learning types (auditory, visual and kinesthetic learners) of students. In the setup of this teaching method, the students are exposed to thought provoking games, books, manipulative objects, experimentation and social interaction between the students (Cohen, 1999; Shaw, 1995). Using this approach to design a curriculum considers the abilities of the students and suitable for diversity of students. This approach proposes a five-step method for solving problem, which are: 1) become aware of the problem; 2) define the problem; 3) propose various hypothesis to solve it; 4) examine the consequences of each hypotheses in the light of previous experience; and 5) test the most likely solution. This approach is essentially what many marketing lecturers in Ghana use in teaching marketing.

Curriculum Design and Student Employability

Tanner (1980) explains curriculum design as the planned and guided learning experiences and intended learning outcomes, formulated through the construction and reconstruction of experiences and knowledge, under the guidance of the institutions, for the learners' continual and willful growth in personal and social competence. Thus, it is a careful thought to the content in the curriculum to be used to train and prepare the graduate to be able to deal well with industry related issues. Pedagogically, situation learning theory suggests that people would learn better in situations that may give meaning to them. Because of this, the embedment of soft skills in the students' study programs or relevant contexts has continued to become the focus in the development of soft skills in higher education institutes (Hassan & Maharoff, 2014). For example, marketers with good soft skills like emotional intelligence are better able to connect with customers, and they know what moves consumers to buy, share, and promote a product or service (O'Donnell, 2015). The contents of the curriculum can be used as an educational strategy to develop out of the academia subjects embedded into the academic system for a comprehensive student skill development process to feed the industry and economy at large. An educator's orientation plays an important role in student learning, even if the educator is not aware of what his or her perspectives are (Danhoff, 2012). A teaching philosophy can simply be described as an educator's belief on how effective teaching should be done. A teaching philosophy establishes how educators see themselves engaging and interacting with students as learning proceeds (Owens, Miller & Grise-Owens, 2014). There are many approaches to teaching philosophy classifications. In my opinion, one of the simplest classification is the one that was proposed by Tanner. Tanner (1990) identifies three (3) different types of curriculum design as subject, learner and problem centered. According to Hopkins et al (2011) educators should also encourage students to be open-minded, creative, and explore opportunities including internships and positions that may not be their current career choice.This will help them to open minded and give them a broad view of the world. The study further suggested that educators can collaborate with other departments and develop engaging activities that focuses on the importance of reading, writing, and arithmetic and use learning control points and multiple deadlines to help students understand the importance of critical skills and topics and how to take advantage of opportunities within and outside of class. Knight and Yorke (2002, 2004) endorse the USEM model to help the higher institutions develop the right curriculum for their students. The U in the model stands for the level of understanding of the subjects being thought. The S is stands for the skills acquired by the graduates while in school. The E is stands for the efficacy, believes, personal qualities the graduate possess after graduation; and M stands for metacognition, which means the higher thinking ability of the graduates..

Subject-Centered

The subject-centered design corresponds normally to the textbook written for the specific subject. Tanner (1990) states that the curriculum can be built or organized around a subject matter by focusing on certain processes and strategies relating to the life of the individual. This approach is essentially what is being practiced by the author. Here, the life of the student should be considered to include his or her employability after graduating. Marketing research practitioners are brought to the classroom to share their experience with students. For example, marketing research executives from Millward Brown and PZ Ghana Limited have shared their experience with students.

Learner-Centered Curriculum

This type of module is centered on the learners themselves. It usually explores the learners' life, family, history or local environment. It is also anchored in the needs and interest of the learner. Tanner (1990) states that "the learner is not considered as a passive individual but as one who engages with his environment, thereby learning in the process". The learner-centered curriculum is not as strict as the subject-centered curriculum design. It usually gives the graduate the option to choose assignments and learning activities that will enable them to design their soft skills. It enables the student to become experts and to know what they need to know before they are employed. Many universities in Ghana are yet to fully adopt this approach.

Problem-Centered Curriculum

This is the third type of curriculum as stated by Tanner (1990). The problem-centered curriculum or problem based learning usually organizes subject matter around a problem, hypothetical or real, that must to be solved. It is inherently intensive and original because the students have a real purpose to their inquiry - that is, solving the problem.

From the literature review, it is evident that the type of teaching philosophy adopted by lecturers influence curriculum design and learning activities that, in turn, determine graduate employability skills outcomes. Further, curriculum design can influence teaching philosophy and graduate employability: skills outcome can likewise influence both curriculum design and teaching philosophy.

Figure 2.

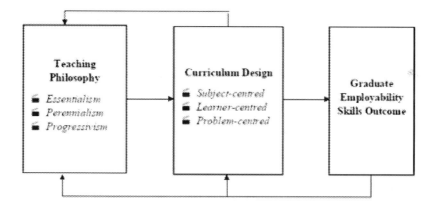

METHODOLOGY

Research Design

This study employed explorative qualitative design to understand the issues of graduate employability and curriculum issues among Ghanaian universities in Accra, Ghana. The choice of using a qualitative approach is informed by the researcher's view of the understanding depth and not the breath of the issues concerning graduate employability and curriculum issues, and this approach is also consistent with past studies (see, for example, Saab et al., 2021)

Qualitative Approach

Sampling

The data for the study was sampled from both public and private universities in Ghana. The population size for the study was 12 respondents. Business faculty members were asked if they were willing to answer the questions. Six questions were asked per faculty. They were assured that their response would be confidential. This sample size was based on the "information power" concept as suggested Malterud, Siersma and Guassora (2016) who argues that "information power indicates that the more information the sample holds relevant for the actual study, the lower amount of participants is needed". The sampling method was purposive so as to get the right information from the right people. Respondents were approached and asked if they were willing to be interviewed. Interviews were conducted for an average of twenty minutes per person. Appointments were booked in advance where necessary and those available were interviewed on scheduled dates.

Coding and Analysis of Data

Data collected was further coded and analysed. Data coding was employed in the collection process. Themes were generated from the coded data and thematic analysis was employed to arrive at findings made by the researcher.

Figure 3.

Institution	Position of Interviewee	Sector	Gender
University	Senior Lecturer	Public	Male
University	Lecturer	Public	Female
University	Lecturer	Private	Female
University	Lecturer	Private	Female
University	Lecturer	Private	Female
University	Lecturer	Private	Female
University	Senior Lecturer	Private	Male
University	Senior Lecturer	Private	Male
University	Lecturer	Private	Male
University	Lecturer	Private	Male
University	Lecturer	Private	Male
University	Lecturer	Private	Male
University	Lecturer	Private	Male

The table 1 shows the profile of respondents. In all, seven (7) respondents were males and five (5) were females. All respondents were lecturers in a university. Ten (10) respondents were lecturers in the private sector and two (2) in the public sector.

DISCUSSION OF FINDINGS

Academia and Industry

Bridging the Gap (Role of Accreditation Bodies)

From the findings, most of the respondents were of the view that accrediting agencies must facilitate the collaboration of academia and industry and insist on curricula that is inclusive of practical industry experience.

...By facilitating curriculum development in academic institutions (required to grant accreditation for business programs) in line with industry requirements and changes...

...Ensuring that curricula are designed to produce graduates who can start and/or grow or better still lead businesses. By producing graduates that are well grounded and well prepared in their chosen fields. Curricula that are practically oriented. Random surveys should be done to test its adherence and effects.

...They periodically review courses and programmes to ensure these courses that are taught in various institutions meet the needs of industry. They also encourage universities to partner with industry in designing programmes that are of mutual benefit. They sometimes suggest industry to bring their problems to higher educational institutions so they can assist them find solution to these problems through research.

Scott and Frontczak (1996) argue that some gaps exists between employer expectations of new marketing graduates and the skills that marketing graduates bring to the workplace. This could vary though from country to country and contexts. For this reason, educational institutions need to integrate employability skills in the development of the curriculum for the students.

Employability Skills (Role of NAB)

The majority of respondents indicated that the NAB should insist on internship and mentorship programmes as well as skills enhancement programmes as part of business education curricula.

...NAB as a regulator should ensure that business schools as part of their curriculum emphasize internships, business trips as well as establish close collaboration between industry and academia. For example, for approval of a business programme, the school must show proof of collaboration with the relevant professional bodies to ensure that such programmes are relevant to industry.

...Develop a template of likely careers every decade, and the sets of skills that graduates must possess. Also limit the intake of students into courses that are oversubscribed and therefore likely to result in

graduate unemployment. Finally, set up mentorship or attachment programs policies as part of university required curricula.

Employability has become an issue of concern for universities, policy makers and employers everywhere (Plewa, Galán-Muros & Davey, 2015). All stakeholders must come together to address critical issues in graduate employment. Whilst trying to recognize higher learning institution's ability to contribute to economic growth, it is important to differentiate between the development of subject base learning and the promotion of other soft skills that industry requires for graduate success. Curriculum design must therefore be intentional to achieve the desired goals.

Industry Practice (Role of Business Education and Research)

Almost all respondents emphatically stated that the relevance of business education and research in industry practice cannot be overemphasised. They noted, however, that the collaborative approach is very low in Ghana.

…I think that business education and research are important to industry. However, in Ghana because there is no proper collaboration between business institutions and industry, the benefits are not seen. For instance, if effective collaboration was in place, industry-funded research from the business institutions could be targeted at resolving specific industry challenges which would then promote effective and efficient running of businesses which would in turn, drive business productivity and growth.

…Very important. But at the moment, it only seems so much goes on in industry and academia separately. The efforts are not coordinated in both domains. Research often is either purely academic, or businesses operates mainly on intuition and not backed by theory and research.

Role of Employers to Business Education

The view of almost all of the respondents was that employers must partner with academia to engage students in practical and industry-relevant programmes that prepares students for the job market. Some were also of the view that industry experts could be made to deliver guest lectures to help prepare graduates for the career world.

…I think that employers should liaise with academia (especially business-oriented institutions) to ensure that relevant knowledge development information goes into the development of curricula. Secondly, employers should be willing to offer internship/attachment opportunity to business students for them to experience the practical relevance of what is taught in the lecture halls.

…by letting educators know what the job market demands so they can train people to fit in.

…By engaging with business schools on the calibre of graduates needed and would need in the future. They should partner with business schools and give guest lectures, offer opportunities for internship and provide periodic feedback on students' performance. Lecturers should also be given the opportunity

to undertake some discussions and insights into the workings of businesses to have a very good idea of current business trends etc.

There are many stakeholders involved in graduate employment. Every stakeholder involved with the graduate program believes that employability skills are necessary for the graduate to survive in the work environment (Tymon, 2013).

Teaching Philosophy

Relevance of Teaching Philosophy

Even though about 15% of respondents indicated that teaching philosophy was not too needful, the majority of the respondents were of a different view. The latter group asserted that it would help to at least know what to expect from new recruits.

…Yes. I think they are a good starting point for knowing what to expect from new recruit.

…It is necessary because every person teaches with an orientation and philosophy of how learning should happen, and therefore the role faculty has to play. If this is at variance with that of the school he works for or Accreditation board standards, it can create problems for the faculty member.

Impact of Teaching Philosophy Statement on Curriculum Design

About 85% of respondents answered 'yes' to this question. Most of them were of the view that curriculum design could reflect the teaching philosophy statement of the instructor and it is a good way to investigate the extent to which a lecturer would model a programme for tuition, which will, in effect, assist authorities to be certain if such models fall within the institution's policy.

…By and large I think teaching philosophy statement should affect curriculum design and activities because it may determine the content you want to deliver and how you want to deliver it for effective impact on your students.

…Yes. The approach for a course will vary across different faculty. This will largely influence the curriculum and the methods of teaching including the activities. The teaching philosophy is the teacher's approach to teaching and hence the foundation for teaching activities.

…To a large extent it can because if your teaching philosophy is, for example, teacher centred then you will design curricula and teach in that direction. If, on the other hand, it is student centred, then you will design curricula in that direction and that is how you will teach.

It is not enough for marketing graduates to come out with employability skills: the curricular should be designed to enable them to acquire these skills, as our findings indicate. Employability has become an urgent issue for discussion between employers and the government. While trying to recognize higher learning institution's ability to contribute to the economic growth, it is important to differentiate between the developments of subject base learning and the promotion of other soft skills. The work industry has been appreciative of the level of disciplinary understanding and skills exhibited by graduates as a result of higher learning. However, they have not been impressive enough considering their inability to exhibit other generic skills such as time management, problems solving abilities and communication.

This paper sought to explain the importance of teaching philosophy as part of the curriculum in schools. Knight and Yorke (2002, 2004) endorse the USEM model to help the higher institutions develop the right curriculum for their students. Most of the faculty interviewed were of the opinion that teaching philosophy affects curriculum design

THEORETICAL CONTRIBUTION

The findings can fill some important contextual gaps in the literature in that the study focused on the Ghanaian context where teachers and higher education managers as well as industry players are stakeholders in graduate employability development. Involving all stakeholders in skills development for marketing graduate is very critical. Although previous studies have discussed the challenges in employability of graduate, most of the literature is based on developed market perspective mostly in Europe and other advanced economies. Moreover most of the studies did not link teaching philosophy to curriculum development and employability .There has remained a surprising lack of research into business graduate employability in the African context particularly in Ghana. The conceptual model developed in this research can be useful for further research

MANAGERIAL IMPLICATIONS

The study provide useful and practical prompts for policy makers, teachers and higher education managers and administrators, and well the general public. Significant findings from this study is the impact that teaching philosophy can have on curriculum design and employability of graduate in Ghana. Many higher education managers can be guided by this findings in their design and implementations of higher education teacher training programs. They should also do more training to raise the level of awareness of teaching philosophy and curriculum design and and its consequences on employability skills development in Ghana.

LIMITATIONS AND DIRECTION FOR FUTURE RESEARCH

The research brought to light a number of interesting findings, however a few limitations have to be considered when interpreting and generalizing the results. Firstly, the study methodology qualitative which has inherent generalizability limitations. Moreover, though 'information power' concept was used in determining the sample size, bigger sample size could still have improved on outcomes of the study. Quantitative method can be employed in future studies to make research findings more generalizable. Also, our respondents were mainly business faculty. Involving more stakeholders like employers and students will make it more interesting and could enhance research outcomes and give a different perspective of the issues on the ground. Moreover extending research to other non -business graduates will be interesting. Using quanitative approach will help in the generalization of study findings to the greater population. Moreover the data collection was essentially cross section. Doing a longitudinal study will be helpful in establishing findings. This study can be done in other African countries and results compared.

CONCLUSION AND RECOMMENDATIONS

In conclusion, the main contribution made by this study is to explain the relationships amongst teaching philosophy, curriculum development and employability skills of graduates .Graduates with employable skills tend to have a higher chance of being employed than those who have no employable skills. This paper dealt with the current issues of graduates needing the employability skills for employment in the job market. Most stakeholders are of the view that employability skills of the graduate should be considered seriously and the necessary curriculum designed for the students. Types of teaching philosophy adopted can influence the employability skills developed in graduates. Faculty teaching marketing and other disciplines should be encouraged to adopt teaching philosophies that encourage the embedding of employability skills in their curriculum designs. In concluding this piece I want to refer to a statement Professor Peter Downes, Convener of Universities Scotland, made on taking pride in the job, which I think is very suitable and revealing. He said that, 'Universities have many responsibilities but none can be as important or evoke as much pride and satisfaction as the job of producing talented, skilled and highly motivated graduates who have confidence in themselves and their ability to forge a successful and rewarding career – whatever shape that takes" (Downes, 2009).

Higher education institutions should identify employability skills that industry and employers are looking for and design curriculum that helps students to acquire these skills. The formal approach to overcome the problem of embedding soft skills can be achieved by blending soft skills competencies into the design and development of curriculum of a program (Schulz, 2008). Institutions of higher learning are expected to train and develop the employable skills of the students in their various institutions. The views expressed in this paper are in agreement with the perspective of embedding soft skill by Bowden *et al.* (2000) and Jones (2000). It is clear from the findings of this study that employability of graduates can be influenced by teaching philosophy adapted by teachers.It is also came out that curriculum design can affect employability of graduates .Moreover the study revealed that teaching philosophy affects curriculum design and employability. It is important that the higher learning institutions adopt teaching philosophies that encourage the embedding of employability skills development activities in the curriculum for students and make it as learner-centered as possible. Faculty should be encouraged and exposed to employability skills related teaching philosophies. Author think that there are good insights from this study that may help marketing faculty and students engage in teaching and learning activities to better prepare graduates for an increasingly competitive employment market. The study also reveals that policy makers can engage faculty so they can be deliberate about employability skills development with their curriculum design

DISCLOSURE STATEMENT

No potential conflict of interest was disclosed by the author.

REFERENCES

Adjei, R (2018). Accreditation and Development of Employable Skills in Graduates. *Accreditation News*, (1).

Adu-Gyamfi, A. B. (n.d.). Graduate Unemployability in Ghana: Views of Unemployed Graduates. *Patrick Darkwa Department of Management Studies University of Cape Coast Ghana.*

Archer, W., & Davison, J. (2008). *Graduate employability.* The Council for Industry and Higher Education.

Amoako, G. K., & Okpattah, B. K. (2018). Unleashing salesforce performance: The impacts of personal branding and technology in an emerging market. *Technology in Society*, *54*, 20–26. doi:10.1016/j.techsoc.2018.01.013

Blunkett, D. (2001). *Education into employability: The role of the DfEE in the economy.* Speech at the Institute of Economic Affairs, London, UK.

Cornell University. (n.d.). Retrieved from https://gradschool.cornell.edu/academic-progress/pathways-to-success/prepare-for-your-career/take-action/teaching-philosophy-statement

Cohen, L. (1999). *Philosophical perspectives in education.* Retrieved June 14, 2005 from http://oregonstate.edu/instruct/ed416/pp3.html

Curtin, M. (2017). *World Economic Forum Future of Jobs Report 2015.* https://www.inc.com/melanie-curtin/the-10-top-skills-that-will-land-you-high-paying-jobs-by-2020-according-to-world-economic-forum.html

Danhoff, K. L. (2012). *A survey of graduate social work educators: Teaching perspectives and classroom environments* (Doctoral dissertation). Colorado State University Libraries.

Direito, I., Pereira, A., & de Oliveira Duarte, A. M. (2012). Engineering undergraduates' perceptions of soft skills: Relations with self-efficacy and learning styles. *Procedia: Social and Behavioral Sciences*, *55*, 843–851. doi:10.1016/j.sbspro.2012.09.571

Downes, P. (2009, April 13). *Universities Scotland.* Retrieved from https://www.universities-scotland.ac.uk/publications/taking-pride-in-the-job

Giroux, H. A. (2010). Bare pedagogy and the scourge of neoliberalism: Rethinking higher education as a democratic public sphere. *The Educational Forum*, *74*(3), 184–196. doi:10.1080/00131725.2010.483897

Greatbatch, D., & Lewis, P. (2007). *Generic Employability Skills II.* Retrieved from http://www.swslim.org.uk/ges/documents/GES_II-FULL_REPORT_06.03.07.pdf

Hall, D., & Buzwell, S. (2013). The problem of free-riding in group projects: Looking beyond social loafing as reason for non-contribution. *Active Learning in Higher Education*, *14*(1), 37–49. doi:10.1177/1469787412467123

Hassan, A., & Maharoff, M. (2014). The understanding of curriculum philosophy among trainee teachers in regards to soft skills embedment. *International Education Studies*, *7*(12), 84. doi:10.5539/ies.v7n12p84

Harvey, L., Moon, S., & Geall, V. (1997). *Graduates' Work: Organizational change and students' attributes*. Centre for Research into Quality. doi:10.1177/095042229701100504

Hopkins, C. D., Raymond, M. A., & Carlson, L. (2011). Educating students to give them a sustainable competitive advantage. *Journal of Marketing Education*, *33*(3), 337–347. doi:10.1177/0273475311420241

Husain, M. Y., Mokhtar, S. B., Ahmad, A. A., & Mustapha, R. (2010). Importance of employability skills from employers' perspective. *Procedia: Social and Behavioral Sciences*, *7*, 430–438. doi:10.1016/j.sbspro.2010.10.059

Huang, R., Turner, R., & Chen, Q. (2014). Chinese international students' perspective and strategies in preparing for their future employability. *Journal of Vocational Education and Training*, *66*(2), 175–193. doi:10.1080/13636820.2014.894933

Jackson, D. (2014). Testing a model of undergraduate competence in employability skills and its implications for stakeholders. *Journal of Education and Work*, *27*(2), 220–242. doi:10.1080/13639080.2012.718750

Lees, D. (2002). *Information for Academic Staff on Employability*. http://www. palatine.ac.uk/ files/ emp/1233.pdf

Mahmoud, M. A., Oppong, E., Twimasie, D., Husseini, M. M., Kastner, A. N. A., & Oppong, M. (2020). Culture and country choice of international students: Evidence from Ghana. *Journal of Marketing for Higher Education*, *30*(1), 105–124. doi:10.1080/08841241.2019.1688444

Malterud, K., Siersma, V. D., & Guassora, A. D. (2016). Sample size in qualitative interview studies: Guided by information power. *Qualitative Health Research*, *26*(13), 1753–1760. doi:10.1177/1049732315617444 PMID:26613970

Nonis, S. A., & Hudson, G. I. (1999). The second course in business statistics and it's role in undergraduate marketing education. *Journal of Marketing Education*, *21*(3), 232–241. doi:10.1177/0273475399213008

Ornstein, A. C., Pajak, E. F., & Ornstein, S. B. (2011). *Contemporary Issues in Curriculum* (5th ed.). Allyn & Bacon.

O'Donnell, K. R. (2015). *Six hard and six soft skills to look for when hiring your next marketing employee*. Retrieved from www.marketingprofs.com/articles/2015/28393

Owens, L. W., Miller, J. J., & Grise-Owens, E. (2014). Activating a teaching philosophy in social work education: Articulation, implementation, and evaluation. *Journal of Teaching in Social Work*, *34*(3), 332–345. doi:10.1080/08841233.2014.907597

Peeters, E., Nelissen, J., De Cuyper, N., Forrier, A., Verbruggen, M., & De Witte, H. (2019). Employability capital: A conceptual framework tested through expert analysis. *Journal of Career Development*, *46*(2), 79–93. doi:10.1177/0894845317731865

Pitan, O. S., & Adedeji, S. O. (2012). *Skills Mismatch among University Graduates in the Nigeria Labor Market*. Online Submission.

Plewa, C., Galán-Muros, V., & Davey, T. (2015). Engaging business in curriculum design and delivery: A higher education institution perspective. *Higher Education*, *70*(1), 35–53. doi:10.100710734-014-9822-1

Precision Consult. (2007). *Graduate Employment Skills*. Business Industry and Higher Education Collaboration Council.

Raymond, M. A., Carlson, L., & Hopkins, C. D. (2006). Do perceptions of hiring criteria differ for sales managers and sales representatives? Implications for marketing education. *Journal of Marketing Education*, *28*(1), 43–55. doi:10.1177/0273475305284640

Römgens, I., Scoupe, R., & Beausaert, S. (2020). Unraveling the concept of employability, bringing together research on employability in higher education and the workplace. *Studies in Higher Education*, *45*(12), 2588–2603. doi:10.1080/03075079.2019.1623770

Saab, M. M., Hegarty, J., Murphy, D., & Landers, M. (2021). Incorporating virtual reality in nurse education: A qualitative study of nursing students' perspectives. *Nurse Education Today*, *105*, 105045. doi:10.1016/j.nedt.2021.105045 PMID:34245956

Schulz, B. (2008). The importance of soft skills: Education beyond academic knowledge. *NAWA Journal of Language and Communication*, 146-154.

Schlee, R. P., & Harich, K. R. (2010). Knowledge and skill requirements for marketing jobs in the 21st century. *Journal of Marketing Education*, *32*(3), 341–352. doi:10.1177/0273475310380881

Scott, J. D., & Frontczak, N. T. (1996). Ad executives grade new grads: The final exam that counts. *Journal of Advertising Research*, *36*(2), 40–47.

Shaw, L. (1995). *Humanistic and social aspects of teaching*. Retrieved June 14, 2005 from http://edweb.sdsu.edu/LShaw/f95syll/ philos/phbehav.html

Schönwetter, D. J., Sokal, L., Friesen, M., & Taylor, K. L. (2002). Teaching philosophies reconsidered: A conceptual model for the development and evaluation of teaching philosophy statements. *The International Journal for Academic Development*, *7*(1), 83–97. doi:10.1080/13601440210156501

Tanner, D., & Tanner, L. N. (1990). *History of the school curriculum*. Macmillan Publisher Co.

Te Wiata, I. (2001). A big ask: To what extent can universities develop useful generic skills? In C. K. F. Bevan (Ed.), *Knowledge Demands for the New Economy* (pp. 290–297). Australian Academic Press.

Tobbell, J., & O'Donnell, V. L. (2013). Transition to postgraduate study: Postgraduate ecological systems and identity. *Cambridge Journal of Education*, *43*(1), 123–138. doi:10.1080/0305764X.2012.749215

Treasury, H. M. (2000). *Productivity in the UK: The evidence and the Government's approach*. UK Treasury.

Trullas, I., Simo, P., Fusalba, O. R., Fito, A., & Sallan, J. M. (2018). Student-perceived organizational support and perceived employability in the marketing of higher education. *Journal of Marketing for Higher Education*, *28*(2), 1–16. doi:10.1080/08841241.2018.1488334

Tymon, A. (2013). The student perspective on employability. *Studies in Higher Education*, *38*(6), 841–856. doi:10.1080/03075079.2011.604408

Visser, J. (2008). Constructive Interaction with Change: Implications for Learners and the Environment in which They Learn. In J. V. Visser-Valfrey (Ed.), *Learners in a Changing Learning Landscape: Reflection from a Dialogue on New Roles and Expectations* (Vol. 12, pp. 11–35). Springer. doi:10.1007/978-1-4020-8299-3_2

Weligamage, S. S. (2009). *Graduates' employability skills: Evidence from literature review*. University of Kelaniya.

Wickramasinghe, V., & Perera, L. (2010). Graduates', university lecturers' and employers' perceptions towards employability skills. *Education + Training*, *52*(3), 226–244. doi:10.1108/00400911011037355

Wilkins, J. L. M. (2000). Preparing for the 21st Century: The status of quantitative literacy in the United States. *School Science and Mathematics*, *100*(8), 405–418. doi:10.1111/j.1949-8594.2000.tb17329.x

Wilson, L. O. (1990). *Curriculum course packets ED 721 & 726* (Unpublished). School Curriculum-Hidden Curriculum-Messages, Students, Schools, Political, Example, and Public.

Yorke, M. (2004). *Employability in higher education: what it is - what it is not*. Retrieved 13 July, 2018. https://www.skillsyouneed.com/general/graduate-employability-skills.html

Yorke, M. (2006). Employability in higher education: what it is – what it is not. Learning and Employability. Series 1. The Higher Education Academy

ADDITIONAL READING

Chism, N. V. N. (1998). Developing a philosophy of teaching statement. *Essays on Teaching Excellence*, *9*(3), 1–2.

Finch, D., Nadeau, J., & O'Reilly, N. (2013). The future of marketing education: A practitioner's perspective. *Journal of Marketing Education*, *35*(1), 54–67. doi:10.1177/0273475312465091

Gray, D. M., Peltier, J. W., & Schibrowsky, J. A. (2012). The journal of marketing education: Past, present, and future. *Journal of Marketing Education*, *34*(3), 217–237. doi:10.1177/0273475312458676

Hopkins, C. D., Raymond, M. A., & Carlson, L. (2011). Educating students to give them a sustainable competitive advantage. *Journal of Marketing Education*, *33*(3), 337–347. doi:10.1177/0273475311420241

Kearns, K. D., & Sullivan, C. S. (2011). Resources and practices to help graduate students and postdoctoral fellows write statements of teaching philosophy. *Advances in Physiology Education*, *35*(2), 136–145. doi:10.1152/advan.00123.2010 PMID:21652498

Owens, L. W., Miller, J. J., & Grise-Owens, E. (2014). Activating a teaching philosophy in social work education: Articulation, implementation, and evaluation. *Journal of Teaching in Social Work*, *34*(3), 332–345. doi:10.1080/08841233.2014.907597

KEY TERMS AND DEFINITIONS

Curriculum: The term curriculum refers to the lessons and academic content taught in a school or in a specific course or program. Curriculum is a standards-based sequence of planned experiences where students practice and achieve proficiency in content and applied learning skills. In education, a curriculum is broadly defined as the totality of student experiences that occur in the educational experience and journey.

Employability: The skills and abilities that allow you to be employed. The quality of a person for being suitable for paid work. It can also be said to be a set of achievements – skills, understandings and personal attributes – that makes graduates more likely to gain employment and be successful in their chosen. It is also the acquisition of attributes (knowledge, skills, and abilities) that make graduates more likely to be successful in their chosen occupation.

Employability Skills: Employability Skills can be defined as the transferable skills needed by an individual to make them 'employable'. Along with good technical understanding and subject knowledge, employers often outline a set of skills that they want from an employee.

Marketing Graduate: A graduate who has specialize in marketing, mostly as the main focus of studies. A marketing major studies the branding and promotion of products and services to the public, which is targeted through specific demographics. Marketing touches many areas of study, so students will be well-versed in advertising, communications, consumer behavior, public relations, and marketing strategy and research.

Teaching Philosophy: Philosophy of teaching refers to fundamental philosophical analysis of pedagogical and personal approaches to teaching and learning. A person's teaching (philosophy) statement is a purposeful and reflective essay about the person's teaching beliefs and practices.

Chapter 6
Teaching Strategies for International Students' Effective Verbal Communication in Australia:
A Collective Autoethnography of Chinese Students

Hangyu Zhang
https://orcid.org/0000-0002-5981-2412
University of Melbourne, Australia

Chenyang Zhang
University of Melbourne, Australia

Hanshu Wang
Monash University, Australia

ABSTRACT

This chapter aims to investigate teaching strategies aimed at enhancing Chinese international students' effective verbal communication in Australian universities. To do so, this study applies collective auto-ethnography to give the chance to the three authors (who are themselves Chinese students) to narrate their stories. Based on their experiences, this study builds a conceptual framework based on Bandura's triadic reciprocal determinism to explore the triadic reciprocal interaction between verbal communication, self-realization, and teaching and learning environment. Then, thematic analysis is applied to explore the diversities and similarities of their experiences in terms of the three elements/themes. By analyzing and examining each theme, this chapter uncovers the dynamic and reciprocal interrelationships between them on the basis of the three authors' voices, providing suggestions for further improvement on teaching strategies for international students' verbal communication.

DOI: 10.4018/978-1-7998-8921-2.ch006

INTRODUCTION

Australia has the most significant proportion of international students in higher education (Hinton, 2020). According to YTD March 2021 international student data released by the Australian government (Australian Trade and Investment Commission, 2021), despite the decrease of total international enrolments due to Covid-19 restrictions, China, India, and Nepal accounted for more than half of all enrolments. Chinese international students have traditionally made up the most significant share of international students in Australian universities (Martin, 2020).

As reported by Briguglio and Smith (2012), Chinese international students in Australia could encounter various challenges and problems, such as culture shock, language-related problems, and verbal interactions in social life. In terms of Chinese students' academic experience, there are salient pedagogical differences between Chinese education and Western teaching styles (Jackson & Chen, 2018). For example, most participants argued that classroom discussion in their home country (China) was characterized by abundant teacher talk, while in their host countries (e.g., the UK, Australia, USA) students were encouraged to talk more (see Jackson & Chen, 2018). More importantly, Chinese students, as EFL learners, may struggle to communicate with culturally diverse people (Hall, 2013); it might be arduous for them to employ the same language tool (English) to share ideas and construct mutual understandings (Hall, 2013). All this may lead to Chinese international students being more likely to experience negative feelings than local students in Australia (Redfern, 2016). Furthermore, the differences between Chinese and Australian pedagogies (e.g., Briguglio & Smith, 2012; Jackson & Chen, 2018) may aggravate the language-related problems encountered by Chinese students. For example, in Australian universities there is a habit of "more talk in class" (Briguglio & Smith, 2012, p. 23), which means students are encouraged to engage in communicative activities. Teachers in Australian universities are also likely to adopt more discussion activities in their pedagogical design (Jackson & Chen, 2018). Given the above reasons, previous literature has portrayed some Chinese students as silent and passive in the U.S. universities, as found by Zheng (2010), and some Chinese students tend to be reluctant to express opposite views or critical opinions in the classroom (Wang et al., 2015). Therefore, the ability to communicate thoughts and perceptions in English is essential for Chinese international students in Australian universities.

In spite of its importance in Chinese students' learning experience in Australia, there are factors hindering effective verbal communication with teachers and other students. One main challenge is centered around culture differences. For example, the culture deriving from home country can formulate a unique way for Chinese students to organize language knowledge and share their opinions (see Hui, 2005), which sometimes exerts adverse effects on their interaction with others (Xiao & Petraki, 2007). In the meanwhile, other factors, such as individual language skills, personal emotional status, and social environment, also play a role on verbal communication.

With the aim to facilitate international students' verbal communication, previous studies have examined the effects of teaching strategies on international students' communication and experiences from the perspective of educators (e.g., Jackson & Oguro, 2017; Xue, 2013). In addition, Zheng (2010) confirmed the importance for Chinese international students to participate in student-centered classroom when studying in English-speaking countries. However, little attention has been paid to Chinese international students' voices about how they feel about verbal communication and what their expectation on future teaching strategies are. Probing into the inner thoughts and perceptions of Chinese students who have been studying in Australian universities provides a pertinent perspective for the research. Hence, this research seeks to explore teaching strategies for Chinese international students' effective verbal communication in Australian universities based on students' voices.

LITERATURE REVIEW

Communication – or the way people share their ideas and information – includes both verbal and nonverbal cues (Phutela, 2015). In general, verbal communication stands for the particular use of language to communicate with others and includes spoken and written language. Therefore, verbal communication is a central concern for the scientific study of communication and language (Rocci & de Saussure, 2016).

In linguistics research, the dichotomy between competence and performance proposed by Chomsky (1965) and further developed by Hymes (1972) separates abstract language knowledge and language production in actual utterances, with linguistics researchers attempting to explore the actual use of language in communication. Hymes (1974) made a remarkable contribution by developing his ethnography of communication based on both formal linguistics and social behaviors, highlighting the critical role of speech situation, speech event, and speech act in actual communication contexts. These paradigms foregrounded the construct of a model of communicative competence in language learning (Canale & Swain, 1980), including linguistic, discourse, pragmatic, and strategic competence. To achieve effective verbal communication, communicators are supposed to have an awareness of the key aspects of communicative competence.

In the following decades, the "pragmatic turn" in linguistic research underpinned the connection between language study and communication study (Rocci & de Saussure, 2016). Sperber and Wilson (1986) proposed a "code model" of communication. On the basis of the model, communication contains procedures of encoding, transmission, and decoding. In detail, the speaker first generates the content to communicate in mind and then encodes the content in sentences, following appropriate linguistic forms. After that, the hearer decodes the linguistic sentences to interpret and understand the content.

Verbal communication can be of varying quality; there are three possible outcomes, including understanding correctly, misunderstanding, and complete failure to understand (Hirst et al., 1994, p. 215; Weigand, 1999, p. 769). To achieve successful and effective verbal communication, the communicators are required to be understanding each other correctly. Founded on the code model (Sperber & Wilson, 1986), misunderstanding or complete failure to understand can occur as a results of a) lack of a shared code; b) noise in the channel so that the message is not transmitted accurately; or c) an error in encoding or decoding (Allote, 2016, p. 490).

Some researchers have focused on the verbal meaning in human language communication in social situations with approaches like discourse analysis (Brown et al., 1983) and conversation analysis (Kasper, 2009; Sacks, 1984), while some research is oriented towards the cognitive aspects of language and verbal communication (Rocci & de Saussure, 2016). In summary, social factors influencing verbal communication, including various contextual elements, and the cognitive processes that underpin it are all essential issues in verbal communication research.

A considerable amount of literature focuses on international students' experiences of verbal communication while studying abroad (e.g., Cox & Yamaguchi, 2010; Roy, 2019; Yeh & Inose, 2003). Due to language and culture barriers, academic differences, interpersonal problems, and some potential mental issues, international students are vulnerable (Yeh & Inose, 2003). Sherry et al. (2010) investigated international students' experiences in an American university and found that these students emphasized spoken language barriers far more than written language problems. More recently, in the same country, Roy (2019) focused on Asian students to identify the barriers they faced during study abroad and highlighted various aspects concerning verbal communication: for example, Asian students sometimes are unable to communicate their thoughts and concerns fluently (Roy, 2019). Similar results were also reported by Cox and Yamaguchi (2010). Asian students also tend to feel uncomfortable in open-ended discussion activities (Roy, 2019). What should be recognized is that although international students are required to pass an authentic English language test confirming their language proficiency before starting their study abroad, they may still encounter challenges to use English during academic learning for the disjuncture between language exams and the demands of various disciplinary discourses (Schmitt, 2005).

There are also studies concerning Chinese international students in universities abroad, especially in English-speaking countries. Previous literature has reported salient pedagogical differences between Chinese and Western institutions (Briguglio & Smith, 2012; Jackson & Chen, 2018). Jackson and Chen (2018) explored the perceptions and experiences of Chinese learners who had studied in Western countries, like Australia and America. Based on their findings, Western universities are more likely than Chinese universities to adopt discussion-based pedagogies in the classroom, which is consonant with Briguglio and Smith (2012)'s finding. Briguglio and Smith (2012) looked at Chinese students' experiences in Australia with regard to adaptation, language, and social interactions. This longitudinal study utilized qualitative data to compare participants' perceptions before and after their learning experiences in Australia. Its findings revealed prominent pedagogical differences between Chinese and Australian universities. Among the differences, the "more talk in class" (Briguglio & Smith, 2012, p. 23) approach, which means students are encouraged to engage in more communication activities, is a significant one. In this regard, ineffective verbal communication can profoundly influence Chinese international students' performance and experiences in Western universities. Pan et al. (2008) identified five major difficulties that Chinese students encounter abroad: the main one concerns language, which hampers Chinese students in participating in classroom discussion and intercultural communication. The ability to communicate with students from other backgrounds is also one of the most important skills that Chinese students want to learn whilst studying abroad (Yang et al., 2011). Overall, like other international students, Chinese international students are more likely to encounter various learning problems and negative feelings in association with their communication experiences whilst studying abroad (Hui, 2005; Redfern, 2016; Wang et al., 2015).

Given that verbal communication is a noteworthy issue in the field of international education, it raises questions about whether teachers can contribute to international students' verbal communication and what the prospective strategies can be. Lee (1997) summarized five difficulties that international students can have and discussed teachers' actions to address them. The five issues – listening ability, differences in cultural background, oral communication skills, vocabulary, and writing (Lee, 1997, p. 94) – are all related to verbal communication. From the teachers' perspective, Lee (1997) put forward useful pedagogical suggestions to help international students in the above five aspects, which are also effective strategies for verbal communication. For example, teachers may give more time to international students to reflect because sometimes they cannot think aloud like native speakers, create an atmosphere conducive to questions in the classroom, and try to avoid idiomatic language and slang that international students may not understand (Lee, 1997).

Instead of providing comprehensive teaching guides with international students, some researchers aimed at enhancing international students' communication skills in particular. Roy (2019) recommended several principles, such as self-awareness and empathy, for lecturers in the US to facilitate Asian students' learning experiences and improve their communication skills. Valentine and Cheney (2001) proposed several strategies for lecturers to promote the mutual benefits of structured interaction between international and local students. In the context of Australian higher education, Arkoudis et al. (2013) developed a framework for teachers to promote communication and interaction between international and domestic students. Their research project had a focus on teachers' curriculum design and adopted a video-analysis methodology. From a different angle, Ryan and Viete (2009) argued that Australian teachers needed to keep an open mind about what they might learn from international students and should create conditions for respectful interactions to occur.

Collectively, the previous literature has provided evidence that international students are more likely to encounter multifaceted challenges in verbal communication, and teachers can play a vital role in facilitating it. Therefore, effective teaching strategies are required to increase the effectiveness of international students' verbal communication and ensure a quality learning experience. However, few studies have delved specifically into Chinese students' verbal communication experiences in Australian universities and relevant teaching strategies from the students' perspectives; the current study hopes to address this literature gap.

CONCEPTUAL FRAMEWORK

The theoretical foundation of this study employs Bandura's Triadic Reciprocal Determinism (TRD). TRD, as a central concept of Bandura's social learning theory, claims that a learner's behaviors will both affect and be affected by personal characteristics and social environments (Bandura, 1977, 1978). In the TRD, there is a dynamic and reciprocal interrelationship between three components: person, behavior, and environment. According to Bandura (1977, 1989), personal factors reflect individual characteristics such as feelings, emotions, beliefs, attitudes and cognitive abilities; behavioral factors refer to anything that humans do, including motor and verbal actions; and environmental factors indicate the situational influences, which could derive from the social and family relationships that the person maintains and the physical surroundings of the individual.

Bandura's TRD model can be applied to represent a triadic reciprocal interaction between the three elements – verbal communication (verbal actions), self-realization, and teaching and learning environment. Based on this model, Chinese international students' verbal communication will both influence and be influenced by their personality traits and environmental stimuli. Thus, based on our research purpose and applying Bandura's TRD theory, the conceptual map in Figure 1 has been developed.

In this framework, verbal communication refers to thoughts and feelings expressed in spoken English; these speaking behaviors can occur in two main contexts: academic life and in social life. Chinese international students' self-realization refers to the emotions and attitudes that are generated whilst speaking English. Environmental stimuli refer to the teaching and learning environments that international students experience. This study will analyze how these three elements interact with each other based on Chinese international students' accounts.

Figure 1. Conceptual framework

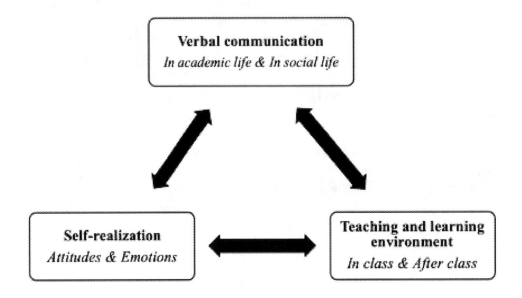

METHODOLOGY

The objective of this research project is to make sense of the three authors' experiences of teaching communication strategies to Chinese international students in Australian universities. The research paradigm suggests that the explored social reality and its potential meanings rely on social participants, rather than being separate from them. This paradigm is in conformity with constructivist ontology, which claims that "social phenomena and their meanings are continually being accomplished by social actors" (Bryman, 2016, p. 33). Following a constructivist view of the world, this research intends to inquire about the three authors' stories and their own perspectives. In this respect, the knowledge-generating process is navigated by means of an interpretivist epistemology to investigate the subjective meaning of social action (Grix, 2002).

The epistemological position – interpretivism – steers our research towards a qualitative methodology (Kamberelis & Dimitriadis, 2005). Meanwhile, in relation to our study's purpose, collective autoethnography is selected as a suitable research approach to investigate our three narratives. As a methodology, autoethnography seeks to provide the channel for researchers to awaken and re-awaken their memory, concentrating on particular topics, and thus helping them to gain insights into their stories during analysis (see Ellis et al., 2011; Ellis & Bochner, 2000; Chang et al., 2016; Guyotte & Sochacka, 2016). Thus, this methodology can provide a platform for us, as international students, to voice and critically reflect on our experiences together, and analyze these stories based on the conceptual framework and relevant literature.

Participants

The three authors, as introduced in Table 1, served as both participants and researchers in this collective autoethnographic inquiry. The three participant-researchers are Chinese international students enrolled in the Faculty of Education in an Australian university. Hangyu and Chenyang began their master course in

2019, experiencing both online and face-to-face classes, while due to the outbreak of Covid-19, Hanshu had to start her master course in 2020, only relying on distance education due to the travel ban. We built connections since we have similar research interests – foreign languages teaching and learning. Thus, this reflective project offered a platform for us to work together, explore our common interest of education issues, narrate our own stories, and provide different angles to achieve a deep analysis about the effects of teaching strategies on international students' verbal communication.

Table 1. Participant-researchers

Name	Gender	Age	Major	Experience (Years)
Hangyu Zhang	Female	25	Master of TESOL	2
Chenyang Zhang	Female	25	Master of TESOL	2
Hanshu Wang	Female	28	Master of Education	1.5

Data Collection

There are three stages in the gathering of data (the collective-investigation process) and two main tasks in the self-reflection process, as presented in Figure 2. Due to the influence of Covid-19, all discussions were conducted online by Zoom. In Stage I, we discussed our research issue and explored similar experiences to develop a set of questions for each other. These questions were intended to guide every author to evoke their experiences about teaching strategies in Australian universities. Then, we transitioned to Stage II, in which we applied cross-examination to help us compare the differences that existed in our experiences so as to understand each one's uniqueness. After that, the second task for each author was to write their own stories and share them on Google Drive, thereby trying to understand other authors' experiences. Last, we moved to Stage III, in which each author generated questions about the others' accounts to help them clarify their stories and attitudes.

Data Analysis

The data analysis addressed the narrative content of our written stories to study our experiences, thoughts and feelings. Thematic analysis was deemed an appropriate way to approach the collected data. This is because it can be used to analyze various forms of qualitative data sets, such as archival documents and interview transcripts (Nowell et al., 2017). Thematic analysis emphasizes 'what is told' (the content of participants' stories) instead of the structure of narratives (Riessman, 2008) – that is, how narratives are constructed in order to convey meaning (Wells, 2011). Applying thematic analysis aims to identify the main 'themes' in our narratives and provide a foundation for a theoretical understanding of the gathered data, which might make a theoretical contribution to the literature in our research area (Bryman, 2016).

Based on the framework of Braun and Clarke (2006), we followed a six-step guide. First, the collected data before analyzing it was familiarized. This involved reading the full written text and taking initial notes. After familiarizing ourselves with the data set, the initial codes were generated to identify emerging features of the data (e.g., using a phrase to describe semantic or latent content) through comparing

Figure 2. The process of data collection

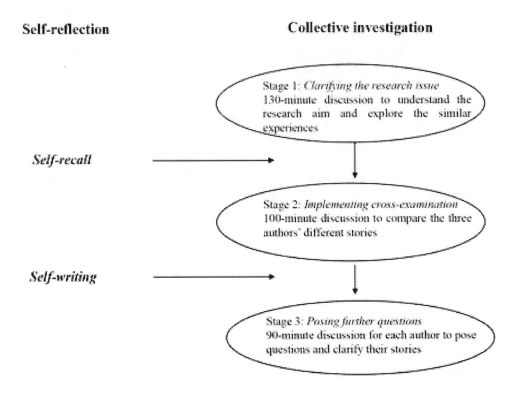

the differences and similarities between the three authors' narratives. The codes were designed to group data based on meaning, which could gain an overview of the main points about the whole dataset. Then, different codes were sorted into potential themes. Subsequently whether these themes that had emerged were related to the codes that had been extracted and the entire data set was checked in order to generate an accurate thematic map to represent, interpret and analyze data to address the research purpose. After that, each theme was clearly defined and named. Lastly, the final analysis of every theme was conducted to produce a scholarly report, with compelling extracted examples as evidence to respond to our research question.

Ethical Considerations

In social studies, ethical issues arising at various phases must be taken into account, since they directly relate to research integrity (Bryman, 2016). In collective autoethnographies, the ethics procedures relating to the researchers-participants should be carefully considered. While the authors of this autoethnographical study waived their anonymity, to maintain confidentiality, pseudonyms were used in the narratives when other people were mentioned in the researchers' stories, so that they could not be identified when the findings were reported.

FINDINGS AND DISCUSSION

In this section, we presented and analyzed the key issues that emerge from our individual narratives (Appendix 1) and follow-up verbal discussions to uncover the major concerns with respect to verbal communication and relevant teaching strategies during our study in Australia. With the application of thematic analysis, we are seeking to draw parallels between our experiences and perceptions. The three primary themes synthesized from our data include verbal communication, self-realization, and teaching and learning environment. For each theme, we summarized two different directions for further discussion.

Verbal Communication

In our narrative stories and collective discussions, we developed a consensus that verbal communication was an indispensable part of our life in Australia, incredibly important for the progress of learning. Unlike Hanshu, who conducted her international study online from China due to the epidemic restriction, Hangyu and Chenyang also acknowledged the vital role of verbal communication in social interactions. Intentionally or unintentionally, we were engaged in communicative actions frequently as international students in Australia. There were successful episodes or experiences of verbal communication in our stories. However, all of us, experienced frustrating communication breakdowns in various situations, as illustrated below.

In Academic Life at University

As the main topic addressed in our research is teaching strategies and learning experience, most of the communicative situations embedded in our narrative stories were pertinent to our academic life. Although we shared various academic learning situations consisting of in-class, after-class, online, and offline learning activities, we all mentioned our "inefficient" language understanding in verbal communication as L2 English speakers. As Schmitt (2005) argues, international students, whose first language is not English, may lack the ability to conduct academic learning in English due to the disjuncture between the language exams and the demands of various disciplinary discourses. According to our data, although the three of us had achieved good results in the language exams, we encountered difficulties in academic study. For example, Chenyang found it difficult to organize her words within a limited period of time when the teacher tried to initiate a one-on-one discussion with her. This is consistent with the finding reported by Rajendram et al. (2019) that international students found a disconnect between the content of their standard language tests and learning experience abroad. To facilitate fluent and understandable communication, we all used some strategies during verbal communication such as organizing the words before uttering in a discussion and translating the utterance from Chinese to English in advance.

Hanshu was one of the "special" international students only attending online classes in their home country because of Covid-19, while Hangyu and Chenyang also experienced online learning, but in Australia. In reference to our experience of communication through online learning, some lingering problems frequently addressed by previous scholars (e.g., Hui, 2005; Redfern, 2016; Wang et al., 2015) just became intensified. Hangyu described in her narrative story:

When I attended the workshop in my last term, which was a highly professional unit concerning research, there was a time I was allocated to a group with two Australian male students, native English speak-

ers. They had deep voices and spoke fast. More importantly, they shared common topics and cultural backgrounds. Consequently, it was actually difficult for me to follow their words and understand their punchlines (Appendix I).

Unlike offline tutorials or workshops, the communicative activities we were exposed to during online learning were limited. On most occasions, local teachers and tutors in Australian universities (who value communicative and discussion-based activities; Briguglio & Smith, 2012; Jackson & Chen, 2018) would split the whole class into several groups for free discussion, but they could not pay attention to each group simultaneously. Therefore, the communication within each group was actually not satisfying as we expected. Therefore, the communication within each group did not provide the level of scaffolding that Chinese students could have benefited from.

Despite the challenges and frustrations, we also had effective verbal communication sometimes. For example, Hanshu was appreciated for her experience in the English corner:

Gradually, my oral expression improved. I also made a good friend, Laura; she is from Saudi Arabia, also a non-native speaker, and we often chat via WhatsApp and practice our verbal communication skills together (Appendix I).

We acknowledge that studying as international students has been conducive to the development of our verbal communication skills in English. However, in this learning journey, we yearn for more assistance integrated into the teaching process to solve our problems that can have adverse effects on our learning experience in Australia.

In Social Life

For international students studying in Australia, verbal communication also intersects with our social interactions. To live and study in Australia, we are required to utilize English to communicate with others. As Hangyu voiced, academic content was not the only thing that we would talk about in after-class discussion activities. Beyond exchanging ideas for academic reasons, we sought to build a rapport with other students from various upbringings and cultural backgrounds through social interactions. Chenyang recalled her experience in a random group discussion:

The progress happened when I joined in group discussion, we built a good relationship with each other. Then, we chatted with each other through WhatsApp and Facebook about our assignment criteria and daily interesting things.

This quote shows that once we have common interests within a group of people and possess relevant knowledge of the topic, we can have successful social communication with others. In other situations, we may experience difficulties. Hangyu added in the verbal discussion:

Yes, usually there is no problem occurring in my daily communication, except for visiting the chemist or the vet. Although I have a good command of English, medical words are not included. When I need to buy a certain kind of medicine that I only know its Chinese name, I always show a picture to the staff at the chemist's because I cannot accurately verbalize my requirement in English.

The above experience is indicative of the challenges Chinese international students may encounter in social verbal communication, especially when it involves specialized words and expressions belonging to various disciplines.

Self-Realization

When we communicate verbally with other students or teachers in English, our experiences are closely related to our attitudes towards the action of communicating in English as well as our emotions during the process (e.g., He, 2013, 2017; Shao et al., 2013). According to our narratives and personal perceptions, our self-realization influences our behaviors and feelings in verbal communication.

Attitudes

As international students studying at an Australian university, we have the same attitude towards English communication. We all want to improve our verbal communication in English and to become acculturated into the education or life in Australia through effective communication. As Chenyang stated in her narrative:

In this learning journey, I thought a lot about what I wanted to learn, and what I actually achieved. My major was TESOL, since I wanted to be an English teacher in China at the beginning of my learning journey. However, one main challenge for me was the weakness in spoken English. In order to improve it, I sought to find ways to speak English either in class or after class (Appendix I).

Likewise, Hangyu had high expectations for herself in terms of verbal communication and had overall confidence in her English communicative competence. Such a positive attitude towards English communication echoes the finding reported by Yang, Webster, and Prosser (2011) that the ability to communicate with students from other backgrounds is what Chinese students want to improve during study abroad. With this attitude, we invested time and energy into improving our verbal communication, such as preparing some ideas in relation to the topic in advance, emailing teachers for assistance, and joining English corners.

In brief, we attached great importance to our verbal communication in English during our studies Australia, regarding it as indispensable for the effectiveness of our international academic journey. Despite recognizing our weaknesses and challenges, we believe verbal communication can be enhanced through appropriate teaching and learning strategies.

Emotions

In the initial stage of our study in Australia, our emotions were different. Hangyu was excited about her confidence in English speaking, whereas Chenyang felt fear and anxiety about her "weakness in spoken English". In contrast, Hanshu's negative emotions at the beginning of her online classes were on account of the challenges she encountered in understanding the teacher's words. She documented the situation:

I could only understand about 40% of what the teacher said in the online course, and I still could only capture the key words; understanding full sentences was impossible for me. This led to my poor under-

standing of the learning content, not to mention difficulties in communicating with teachers or even asking questions. Therefore, in the first year of my master's degree, I was silent in class for nearly two weeks (Appendix I).

When we first embarked on a new journey in an Australian university embracing a mixed identity of international students and non-native English speakers, on the one hand, we looked forward to improving our communication skills and becoming acculturated into the local education system; on the other hand, we felt nervous, embarrassed, or even frustrated at communicative challenges or failures and hesitated to take immediate action to remedy the situation. In our stories, we showed different ways to grapple with this predicament and negative emotions.

After being a silent learner for a period of time, Hanshu emailed the teacher for guidance and voiced her concern. Fortunately, Chenyang's teacher noticed her silence and spontaneously adopted impromptu strategies to help her address her issues. The negative emotions would be assuaged after the adoption of certain strategies, and we would feel more confident and grateful after overcoming the "silent phase". In this regard, external assistance or interference greatly influences our emotions and verbal communication, which alludes to the following overarching theme.

Teaching and Learning Environment

Our experiences of communicating in Australia and different emotions indicate that in our experience the teaching and learning environment had a profound impact on the development of our verbal communication. According to our narratives, there were several instances of conflicting communication experiences with respect to different classroom atmospheres, teaching activities, group organization, learning backgrounds, etc. A more detailed discussion will be presented below from two perspectives, in class and after class. This discussion corroborates how appropriate teaching strategies play a vital role in creating an external environment conducive to verbal communication.

In Class

As Chinese students studying at an Australian university, we have experienced salient differences between in-class teaching styles in China and Australia. As illustrated by Jackson and Chen (2018), Western teachers are inclined to adopt more discussion-based activities in teaching; according to our stories, group discussions seemed to be an indispensable component our classes. Our verbal communication experiences in group discussion were partly dependent upon the speaking environment, which was closely associated with teaching strategies. For instance, Hangyu described her discussion experiences in two different groups. In the first class, where the majority of students were from China, the tutor ensured that there was at least one non-Chinese student in each group. Hangyu appreciated the tutor's efforts:

She utilized this strategy to prevent the majority of Chinese students from communicating in their native language during group activities. How clever and thoughtful was she! Personally, I wanted to improve my English communication competence during my study in Australia, but I may have automatically used my native language while communicating with Chinese students (Appendix I).

In contrast to her successful experience in this class, she encountered a problem in another group discussion activity as the only non-native English speaker among the group members. We seek opportunities to communicate with native speakers as it benefits our English competence and fulfills our study abroad journey. However, sometimes, we might feel embarrassed or anxious as the only non-native speaker, because of an invisible barrier resulting from differences of values and cultures, language levels, or even stereotype preconceptions. The first tutor that Hangyu met utilized an effective teaching strategy to create an environment with cultural and linguistic diversity to facilitate international students' verbal communication in English, while the second teacher failed to realize the potential challenges or difficulties that Hangyu might encounter as the only "outsider" in her group. It is likely that given the complexity of that class, the teacher may not have been aware of the potential language or cultural barriers during students' communication. They paid little attention to the group allocations, which could influence the communicative environment for international students.

In light of the teacher's awareness of international students' unique needs in verbal communication, Chenyang benefited from her teachers' dedicated attention and corresponding strategies. She documented how her teacher, Tom, assisted her with her verbal communication when she felt nervous talking in the whole-class environment:

He was very patient to ask my opinions one-on-one during free discussion. This was really challenging for me since I could not organize my words in a limited time. Even though the sentences that I spoke were full of grammar mistakes, Tom was so patient and used some keywords to help me express my ideas. When I still felt it was hard to understand his meaning, he would explain it again in an easy way. Sometimes, I only spoke a little, but I still received lots of positive comments from Tom, which cheered me up (Appendix I).

Likewise, Hanshu also found assistance from her teachers incredibly helpful after demonstrating her difficulties during in-class communication and learning:

He said that he understood very well, and in later classes I was selected to read the content of the slides, which to some extent increased my confidence. In addition, he also set up a discussion group where he would slow down his speech to communicate with us and chose some simple and easy-to-understand vocabulary to explain as much as possible (Appendix I).

When we talk about teaching and learning environment, we refer to this multifaceted environment in a broad sense. With this in mind, our experiences suggest that teachers can create a better communicative environment for international students by applying more meticulous strategies in their teaching process (Jin & Cortazzi, 1997). During in-class discussion activities, teachers are supposed to maintain a balance of group allocation, controlling the proportion of local students and international students. This strategy is conducive to a facilitating environment for verbal communication whilst accommodating diversity. In the meanwhile, dedicated attention is required for quiet international students who may need extra help and proper encouragement. We have found that effective strategies include the use of simplified structures and easy-to-understand vocabulary to communicate with international students, slowing down speech, showing patience, and organizing ad-hoc discussion activities. In brief, dedicated attention should be complemented by strategies underpinned by a thorough understanding of the factors hindering international students' verbal communication such as lack of belonging, a sense of being an outsider, insufficient language resources, lack of practice, and so on (e.g., Pan et al., 2008, Redfern, 2016; Wang et al., 2015, Yao, 2016).

After Class

While discussing our previous experiences, there was a noteworthy point proposed by Hanshu that as an international student who could not come to Australia due to the epidemic restrictions, she lacked an authentic English communicative environment after class. Since the other two authors live in Australia as international students, there are opportunities to use English in daily communication and social interactions, which has helped their communicative competence and language proficiency. In contrast, Hanshu voiced her concern:

Although we have two classes a week, when we turn off the computer, we return to our native language environment. So there still exist barriers for online students to achieve effective verbal communication (Appendix I).

In this instance, only attending the two scheduled classes a week was not enough for Hanshu to adapt herself to an English communicative environment so as to acculturate herself into the education of an Australian university. Therefore, it is critical to consider what the faculty can do to provide online international students with more opportunities to immerse themselves in a communicative learning environment. From Hanshu's description, she found some communicative activities on her own to supplement her "study abroad" experience and achieve better verbal communication by increasing her personal skills. Nevertheless, her experience indicates the necessity of relevant workshops or communicative activities where international students in their home country can communicate with local students.

Hangyu mentioned that her group discussions were not limited to in-class activities, but the group members also met after class each week for certain collaborative homework. On the one hand, it can be an effective strategy for teachers to extend in-class learning activities to after-class meetings arranged by students themselves; on the other hand, it would be more effective if the teacher could arrange a series of online activities to build a rapport between remote international students and local students regularly. These strategies would not only provide us with more chances to practice verbal communication but would also relieve the stress about communicating with English speakers or other students from different cultures.

The Relationship between the Three Themes

According to the above analysis, the relationship between the three elements can be represented as shown in Figure 3. The diagram suggests that verbal communication, self-realization, and teaching and learning environment are inextricably linked. For verbal communication, both academic and social life require an environment that gives students the opportunity to express themselves. For example, in class, students' academic communication requires teachers to assign groups or set up breakout rooms to provide an opportunity for expression and discussion. After class, students' social skills also need to be enhanced, and English corners (as mentioned before) or other non-academic after class activities can provide opportunities for their daily communication. Conversely, the teaching and learning environment exists to enable verbal communication. If no communication activity takes place, then it will be meaningless.

Figure 3. The triadic reciprocal interaction between the three themes

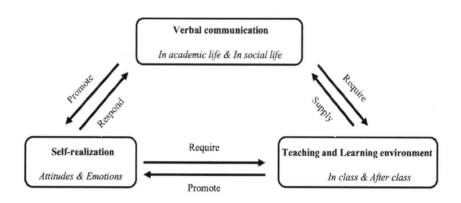

Effective verbal communication can facilitate positive attitudes and emotions in self-realization. Conversely, students' poor verbal communication can affect self-realization and can breed negative emotions. As the three authors mentioned, they all experienced frustration at one time or another due to their lack of verbal fluency. However, attitudes and emotions in self-realization will also respond to effective verbal communication. In our experience, if the teacher could provide help and encouragement, and the self-realization emotion becomes positive, then the students' verbal communication skills are likely to gradually improve. On the other hand, negative emotions will directly reflect a decline in verbal communication skills or even avoidance, resulting in students being afraid to speak and express themselves, thus forming a vicious circle in the long run.

In addition, self-realization also requires a teaching and learning environment that provides opportunities for students to experience an atmosphere conducive to learning and a sense of belonging. As mentioned earlier, international students have had to undertake online learning due to Covid-19; when they are deprived of an authentic learning environment and communication can only take place online, their emotions and attitudes are inevitably affected. This effect is not only reflected in their reduced enthusiasm for expressing themselves in English but may also lead to a sense of isolation. Thus, self-realization is inseparable from the teaching environment, and in the case of the teaching and learning environment, it can contribute to students' self-realization. Before Covid-19, authentic teaching situations allowed students to experience a learning atmosphere and provided chances to communicate with each other. The rapport can be improved between students and teachers. During Covid-19, the online teaching and learning scenario may have prevented a sense of belonging among the students; however, it can also ensure a certain degree of positive attitudes and emotions if the connection is as strong as possible online.

CONCLUSION

In this chapter, the relationships between international students' verbal communication, self-realization, and teaching and learning environment have been elucidated. Based on their interactions, six teaching strategies are proposed: 1. Resolving the contradiction between students' desire to improve their English and their speaking uneasiness; 2. Implementing simple communicative activities in class and gradually increasing speaking complexity to encourage international students' participation; 3. Designing group discussion but avoiding the gathering of students with the same mother tongue in the same group;4. Providing prompts to relieve international students' tension and anxiety when they respond to questions in class; 5. Offering channels to collect students' feedback about teaching content or approaches to tailor their teaching methods; 6. Organizing online and offline joint activities to make students feel free to communicate about their different cultures, academic difficulties, and emotional issues through Zoom. However, given the nature of the research approach (collective autoethnography), this study lacks generalizable conclusions. Thus, future research can be designed by applying mixed methods to enrich the dataset and thus improve the generalizability of results.

REFERENCES

Allote, N. (2016). Misunderstanding in verbal communication. In A. Rocci & L. de Saussure (Eds.), *Verbal communication* (Vol. 3, pp. 487–507). Walter de Gruyter GmbH & Co KG. doi:10.1515/9783110255478-025

Arkoudis, S., Watty, K., Baik, C., Yu, X., Borland, H., Chang, S., Lang, I., Lang, J., & Pearce, A. (2013). Finding common ground: Enhancing interaction between domestic and international students in higher education. *Teaching in Higher Education, 18*(3), 222–235. doi:10.1080/13562517.2012.719156

Australian Trade and Investment Commission. (2021). *YTD March 2021 international student data released.* https://www.austrade.gov.au/australian/education/news/data/ytd-march-2021-international-student-data-released

Bandura, A. (1977). *Social learning theory*. Prentice-Hall.

Bandura, A. (1978). The self system in reciprocal determinism. *The American Psychologist, 33*(4), 344–358. doi:10.1037/0003-066X.33.4.344

Bandura, A. (1989). Human agency in social cognitive theory. *The American Psychologist, 44*(9), 1175–1184. doi:10.1037/0003-066X.44.9.1175 PMID:2782727

Braun, V., & Clarke, V. (2006). 2006/01/01). Using thematic analysis in psychology. *Qualitative Research in Psychology, 3*(2), 77–101. doi:10.1191/1478088706qp063oa

Briguglio, C., & Smith, R. (2012). Perceptions of Chinese students in an Australian university: Are we meeting their needs? *Asia Pacific Journal of Education, 32*(1), 17–33. doi:10.1080/02188791.2012.655237

Brown, G., Brown, G. D., Brown, G. R., Gillian, B., & Yule, G. (1983). *Discourse analysis*. Cambridge University Press. doi:10.1017/CBO9780511805226

Bryman, A. (2016). *Social research methods* (5th ed.). Oxford University Press.

Canale, M., & Swain, M. (1980). Theoretical bases of communicative approaches to second language teaching and testing. *Applied Linguistics, 1*(1), 1–47. doi:10.1093/applin/1.1.1

Chang, H., Ngunjiri, F., & Hernandez, K.-A. C. (2016). *Collaborative autoethnography*. Routledge. doi:10.4324/9781315432137

Chomsky, N. (1965). *Aspects of the theory of syntax*. MIT Press.

Cox, K., & Yamaguchi, S. (2010). Japanese graduate nursing students' perceptions of the teaching performance of an intercultural teacher. *Nursing Education Perspectives, 31*(3), 156–159. PMID:20635619

Ellis, C., Adams, T. E., & Bochner, A. P. (2011). Autoethnography: An overview. *Historical Social Research. Historische Sozialforschung, 36*(4), 273–290. https://www.jstor.org/stable/23032294

Ellis, C., & Bochner, A. (2000). Autoethnography, personal narrative, reflexivity: Researcher as subject. In N. K. Denzin & Y. S. Lincoln (Eds.), Handbook of qualitative research (pp. 733–768). Sage.

Grix, J. (2002). Introducing students to the generic terminology of social research. *Politics, 22*(3), 175–186. doi:10.1111/1467-9256.00173

Guyotte, K. W., & Sochacka, N. W. (2016). Is This Research? Productive Tensions in Living the (Collaborative) Autoethnographic Process. *International Journal of Qualitative Methods, 15*(1). doi:10.1177/1609406916631758

Hall, S. (2013). Introduction. In S. Hall (Ed.), *Representation: Cultural representations and signifying practices* (pp. 1–11). Sage.

He, D. (2013). What makes learners anxious while speaking English: A comparative study of the perceptions held by university students and teachers in China. *Educational Studies, 39*(3), 338–350. doi:10.1080/03055698.2013.764819

He, D. (2017). How to cope with foreign language speaking anxiety effectively? The case of university students in China. *Electronic Journal of Foreign Language Teaching, 14*(2), 159-174. https://e-flt.nus.edu.sg/wp-content/uploads/2020/09/he.pdf

Henze, J., & Zhu, J. (2012). Current research on Chinese students studying abroad. *Research in Comparative and International Education, 7*(1), 90–104. doi:10.2304/rcie.2012.7.1.90

Hinton, T. (2020). *Number of Chinese student enrolments in Australia from 2010 to 2019, by education sector (in 1,000s)*. Retrieved from https://www.statista.com/statistics/430276/number-of-chinese-students-in-australia-by-education-sector/

Hirst, G., Susan, M., Peter, H., Philip, E., & Diane, H. (1994). Repairing conversational misunderstandings and non-understandings. *Speech Communication, 15*(3-4), 213–229. doi:10.1016/0167-6393(94)90073-6

Huang, J., & Rinaldo, V. (2009). Factors affecting Chinese graduate students' cross-cultural learning. *International Journal of Applied Educational Studies, 4*(1), 1–13.

Hui, L. (2005). Chinese cultural schema of education: Implications for communication between Chinese students and Australian educators. *Issues in Educational Research, 15*(1), 17–36.

Hymes, D. H. (1972). On Communicative Competence. In J. B. Pride & J. Holmes (Eds.), *Sociolinguistics: Selected Readings* (pp. 269–293). Penguin.

Hymes, D. H. (1974). *Foundations in sociolinguistics: An ethnographic approach.* University of Pennsylvania Press.

Jackson, J., & Chen, X. (2018). Discussion-based pedagogy through the eyes of Chinese international exchange students. *Pedagogies, 13*(4), 289–307. doi:10.1080/1554480X.2017.1411263

Jackson, J., & Oguro, S. (2017). Introduction: Enhancing and extending study abroad learning through intercultural interventions. In Intercultural interventions in study abroad (pp. 1-17). Routledge.

Jin, L., & Cortazzi, M. (1997). Expectations and questions in intercultural classrooms. *Intercultural Communication Studies, 7*(2), 37–62. https://www-s3-live.kent.edu/s3fs-root/s3fs-public/file/04-Lixian-Jin-Martin-Cortazzi.pdf

Kamberelis, G., & Dimitriadis, G. (2005). Into the fray: A practiced and practical set of analytical strata. In G. Kamberelis & G. Dimitriadis (Eds.), *On qualitative inquiry* (pp. 13–23). Teachers College Press.

Kasper, G. (2009). Locating cognition in second language interaction and learning: Inside the skull or in public view? *IRAL – International Review of Applied Linguistics in Language Teaching, 47*(1), 11–36. doi:10.1515/iral.2009.002

Lee, D. S. (1997). What Teachers Can Do To Relieve Problems Identified by International Students. *New Directions for Teaching and Learning, 70*(70), 93–100. doi:10.1002/tl.7011

Martin, F. (2020). *Chinese International Students' Wellbeing in Australia: The Road to Recovery.* The University of Melbourne. Retrieved from http://hdl.handle.net/11343/240399

Nowell, L. S., Norris, J. M., White, D. E., & Moules, N. J. (2017). Thematic Analysis:Striving to Meet the Trustworthiness Criteria. *International Journal of Qualitative Methods, 16*(1), 1609406917733847. doi:10.1177/1609406917733847

Pan, J.-Y., Wong, D. F. K., Joubert, L., & Chan, C. L. W. (2008). The Protective Function of Meaning of Life on Life Satisfaction Among Chinese Students in Australia and Hong Kong: A cross-cultural comparative study. *Journal of American College Health, 57*(2), 221–231. doi:10.3200/JACH.57.2.221-232 PMID:18809539

Patton, M. Q. (2002). *Qualitative research and evaluation methods* (3rd ed.). Sage Publications.

Phutela, D. (2015). The importance of non-verbal communication. *The IUP Journal of Soft Skills, 9*(4), 43.

Rajendram, S., Larson, E., & Sinclair, J. (2019). International graduate students' perspectives on high-stakes English tests and the language demands of Higher Education. *Language and Literature, 21*(4), 68–92.

Redfern, K. (2016). An empirical investigation of the incidence of negative psychological symptoms among Chinese international students at an Australian university. *Australian Journal of Psychology, 68*(4), 281–289. doi:10.1111/ajpy.12106

Riessman, C. K. (2008). Narrative methods for the human sciences. *Sage (Atlanta, Ga.).*

Rocci, A., & de Saussure, L. (2016). *Verbal communication* (Vol. 3). Walter de Gruyter GmbH & Co KG. doi:10.1515/9783110255478

Roy, S. R. (2019). Educating Chinese, Japanese, and Korean international students: Recommendations to American professors. *Journal of International Students, 3*(1), 10.

Ryan, J., & Viete, R. (2009). Respectful interactions: Learning with international students in the English-speaking academy. *Teaching in Higher Education, 14*(3), 303–314. doi:10.1080/13562510902898866

Sacks, H. (1984). Notes on methodology. In J. M. Atkinson & J. Heritage (Eds.), *Structures of Social Action: Studies in Conversation Analysis*. Cambridge University Press.

Schmitt, D. (2005). Writing in the international classroom. In Teaching international students: Improving learning for all. London: Routledge.

Shao, K., Yu, W., & Ji, Z. (2013). An exploration of Chinese EFL students' emotional intelligence and foreign language anxiety. *Modern Language Journal, 97*(4), 917–929. doi:10.1111/j.1540-4781.2013.12042.x

Sherry, M., Thomas, P., & Chui, W. H. (2010). International students: A vulnerable student population. *Higher Education, 60*(1), 33–46. doi:10.100710734-009-9284-z

Sperber, D., & Wilson, D. (1986). *Relevance: Communication and Cognition*. Blackwell.

Tran, L. T. (2009). Making visible 'hidden' intentions and potential choices: International students in intercultural communication. *Language and Intercultural Communication, 9*(4), 271–284. doi:10.1080/14708470902807693

Valentine, D., & Cheney, R. S. (2001). Intercultural business communication, international students, and experiential learning. *Business Communication Quarterly, 64*(4), 90–104. doi:10.1177/108056990106400410

Wang, C. C., Andre, K., & Greenwood, K. M. (2015). Chinese students studying at Australian universities with specific reference to nursing students: A narrative literature review. *Nurse Education Today, 35*(4), 609–619. doi:10.1016/j.nedt.2014.12.005 PMID:25537169

Webster, L., & Mertova, P. (2007). *Using narrative inquiry as a research method: An introduction to using critical event narrative analysis in research on learning and teaching*. Routledge. doi:10.4324/9780203946268

Weigand, E. (1999). Misunderstanding: The standard case. *Journal of Pragmatics, 31*(6), 763–785. doi:10.1016/S0378-2166(98)00068-X

Wells, K. (2011). *Narrative inquiry*. Oxford University Press. doi:10.1093/acprof:oso/9780195385793.001.0001

Xiao, H., & Petraki, E. (2007). An investigation of Chinese students' difficulties in intercultural communication and its role in ELT. *Journal of Intercultural Communication, 13*(6), 1–17.

Xu, S., & Connelly, F. M. (2009). Narrative inquiry for teacher education and development: Focus on English as a foreign language in China. *Teaching and Teacher Education, 25*(2), 219–227. .tate.2008.10.006 doi:10.1016/j

Xue, M. (2013). Effects of group work on English communicative competence of Chinese international graduates in United States institutions of higher education. *Qualitative Report, 18*, 14.

Yang, M., Webster, B., & Prosser, M. (2011). Travelling a thousand miles: Hong Kong Chinese students' study abroad experience. *International Journal of Intercultural Relations, 35*(1), 69–78. doi:10.1016/j.ijintrel.2010.09.010

Yao, C. W. (2016). Better English is the Better Mind: Influence of Language Skills on Sense of Belonging in Chinese International Students. *The Journal of College and University Student Housing, 43*(1).

Yeh, C. J., & Inose, M. (2003). International students' reported English fluency, social support satisfaction, and social connectedness as predictors of acculturative stress. *Counselling Psychology Quarterly, 16*(1), 15–28. doi:10.1080/0951507031000114058

Zheng, X. (2010). Re-interpreting Silence: Chinese International Students' Verbal Participation in US Universities. *International Journal of Learning, 17*(5), 451–464. doi:10.18848/1447-9494/CGP/v17i05/47068

APPENDIX 1: COLLECTIVE NARRATIVES

Hangyu

It was in August 2019 that I attended my first tutorial in Australia. Looking around the well-equipped classroom, I found that almost 80% of my classmates had a Chinese appearance. The tutor was a typical Western teacher who was dedicated to warming up the class and encouraged her students to express themselves freely. Feeling confident about my English communicative competence, I was somehow excited to express myself, and I tended to set quite high expectations for myself, which made me nervous in communication. To be honest, it's been a long time, so I cannot recall the specific teaching activities and contents of my very first tutorial. However, there was an episode that left a deep impression.

The tutor formed us into several groups and emphasized that she would guarantee that in each group there was a non-Chinese student. She utilized this strategy to prevent the majority of Chinese students from communicating in their native language during group activities. How clever and thoughtful was she! Personally, I wanted to improve my English communication competence during my study in Australia, but I may have automatically used my native language while communicating with Chinese students.

The group remained unchanged during the whole term, and we regularly had a group discussion from one to two hours each week. During the discussion, everyone used English to communicate, from academic readings to some personal experiences. Honestly, I was actually looking forward to the group discussion every week because it was the only time when I would communicate in English extensively. Due to my high expectations for myself, I would prepare some ideas in relation to the topic to be discussed in advance before our meetings to make sure I could express myself clearly. In the middle of our discussion, sometimes an idea occurred in my mind; then, I would automatically organize my words silently before cutting in. However, sometimes I could directly express myself fluently without silent preparation if the idea was not too complicated. It was really embarrassing when I failed to find a proper expression in the middle of my speech. But I have found myself better and better at dealing with such situations as I live in Melbourne. On the one hand, I am really grateful that the first tutor I met could apply that small strategy during the whole term, which helped me adapt to communication in English.

Obviously, problems arose during my study in Australia. When I attended the workshop in my last term, which was a highly professional unit concerning research, there was a time I was allocated to a group with two Australian male students, native English speakers. They had deep voices and spoke fast. More importantly, they shared common topics and cultural backgrounds. Consequently, it was actually difficult for me to follow their words and understand their punchlines. The half an hour seemed to be a whole day for me because I could not cut in, feeling embarrassed and anxious. Then I talked with my friend about the situation. Surprisingly, the same thing happened to him when he was the only non-native English speaker in the group. That's kind of frustrating! Personally speaking, I think diversity is good for my communication during study abroad, but I do not want to be the only outsider.

Chenyang

I, as an international student, have lived in Australia for nearly two years. Recently, I just finished all my master courses and graduated successfully. In this learning journey, I thought a lot about what I wanted to learn, and what I actually achieved. My major was TESOL, since I wanted to be an English teacher in China at the beginning of my learning journey. However, one main challenge for me was the weakness in spoken English. In order to improve it, I sought to find ways to speak English either in class or after class. Despite this learning goal, I always felt a strong feeling of anxiety and fear when speaking English in class. One teacher (Tom) might have realized that some students, including me, were silent in class. He was very patient to ask my opinions one-on-one during free discussion. This was really challenging for me since I could not organize my words in a limited time. Even though the sentences that I spoke were full of grammar mistakes, Tom was so patient and used some keywords to help me express my ideas. When I still felt it was hard to understand his meaning, he would explain it again in an easy way. Sometimes, I only spoke a little, but I still received lots of positive comments from Tom, which cheered me up. Moreover, Tom also provided me with many English-speaking practice programs, such as BBC six-minutes English and BBC learning English. He also suggested to me how to use these resources and encouraged me to practice for more than six months. When I did as he said, I realized the improvement in my spoken English, which increased my confidence to continue.

The other thing I also remembered clearly was how my other teacher (Vicky) encouraged students to express their ideas. I remember there were about 26 students in our class. Vicky divided us into 5 groups randomly. She suggested that each group mate should have opportunities to be the group leader. Thus, in our group, we decided that everyone would take turns to be the team leader every week. At the beginning, I did not realize this method could benefit my spoken English. The progress happened when I joined in group discussion, we built a good relationship with each other. Then, we chatted with each other through WhatsApp and Facebook about our assignment criteria and daily interesting things. These small things were really powerful to make me less afraid to speak. I remembered when it was my turn to be the team leader, I became confident to organize our group mates together to cooperate to finish a group assignment. This responsibility of being a leader pushed me to question others' ideas and share my opinions with others. In this process, I also learned how to propose a different argument in a positive way that would not make my friend feel uncomfortable. When I re-evoked these memories, I realized these small things are meaningful.

Hanshu

As a "special" international student, I have been studying in Australia for three semesters. However, I have never been to Australia due to the impact of Covid-19 and the government's border policy, which means that my courses for three semesters have all been online. Therefore, during this special learning journey, I experienced different ways of verbal communication. My major is a master's degree in education. I had had five years of experience as a teacher before enrolling in this master's degree, so I naively thought that I was very familiar with learning methods.

However, in the first semester of my master's degree, I encountered challenges. Since all our courses were conducted online, and my English was not very proficient at the time, I could only understand about 40% of what the teacher said in the online course, and I still could only capture the key words; understanding full sentences was impossible for me. This led to my poor understanding of the learning content, not to mention difficulties in communicating with teachers or even asking questions. Therefore, in the first year of my master's degree, I was silent in class for nearly two weeks. Although I always turned on the camera to make eye contact with the teacher, oral English created an invisible barrier to the communication between me and the teacher. Especially in group discussions, if the group was made up of all Chinese students, then everyone would "tacitly" turn off the camera and microphone, there would be no communication during the whole process, and no one would break the silence. If there were native speakers in the group discussion, then I would pluck up the courage to talk to them, but I would still translate the sentence to be spoken from Chinese to English in advance and then read it to them. Therefore, such communication was still inefficient.

This situation improved later, because I emailed my tutor (Harry) and told him of my concerns. He said that he understood very well, and in later classes I was selected to read the content of the slides, which to some extent increased my confidence. In addition, he also set up a discussion group where he would slow down his speech to communicate with us and chose some simple and easy-to-understand vocabulary to explain as much as possible. I also took the initiative to join the Faculty's English corner to chat about Australian slang, living habits and cultural styles with native-speaking students. Gradually, my oral expression improved. I also made a good friend, Laura; she is from Saudi Arabia, also a non-native speaker, and we often chat via WhatsApp and practice our verbal communication skills together.

As a special online international student, I think the biggest challenge for us is the lack of a language environment. Although we have two classes a week, when we turn off the computer, we return to our native language environment. So there still exist barriers for online students to achieve effective verbal communication.

Chapter 7

Teaching Project Management Principles by Proverbs in Culturally and Linguistically Diverse Environments:
Ten Years of Experience With International Students

Cezar Scarlat

University "Politehnica" of Bucharest, Romania

ABSTRACT

This chapter shares the author's experience of teaching Project Management to diverse international students at three European universities. Besides didactic and technical challenges, there also were cultural and linguistic diversity challenges to be addressed. Working in small teams was a solution to better understand differences, encouraging intercultural communication. Specifically, the chapter is focused on particular aspects of the educational process: a single course (Project Management) and a single instrument used as teaching aid: proverbs as illustrative examples while teaching the abstract principles of project management. Although the use of proverbs for moral education is old and universal, their use while teaching abstract concepts of scientific management—as project management principles—is a premiere. The lessons learnt as result of the author's teaching experience and studies on the management meaning of proverbs, in different cultural and linguistic environments, open research avenues for further comparative, cross-, and inter-cultural studies.

DOI: 10.4018/978-1-7998-8921-2.ch007

INTRODUCTION

This chapter aims to share a significant part of the author's experience of teaching management subjects internationally – both at undergraduate and master level – for about fifteen years (since 2006) – out of which the last decade (since 2010) includes almost exclusively teaching *Project Management* to international students.

The Project Management courses were taught to culturally and linguistically diverse international students (English as the teaching language) at three universities: University of Applied Sciences, Mikkeli, Finland (currently, since 2017, South-Eastern Finland University of Applied Sciences); Karel de Grote University College, Antwerp, Belgium; and University "Politehnica" of Bucharest, Romania.

Considering the overall number of students taught at these three universities over a decade, the international environment counted about eight hundred students, from more than thirty countries (and almost the same number of different cultural and linguistic environments) from five continents. Sharing the experiences of teaching in such a culturally and linguistically diverse, international environment is the scope of this work.

However, *the focus* of this chapter is on sharing one particular aspect of this teaching experience: using *proverbs as a teaching aid, an instrument for teaching and learning the principles of project management*, while teaching that specific section of the Project Management course.

It is noteworthy that many principles of modern scientific management – just one hundred years old, born with the seminal works of Taylor (1911), Gantt (1916) and Fayol (1917) among others – were identified and transmitted from generation to generation in the form of proverbs, even before humans invented the writing and then printed books (the proverbs mentioned in the writings of the philosophers from ancient Greece are the best evidence). The analysis of the proverbs' endurance over centuries reveals *four theses* regarding the proverbs' resilience and continuity, and *five paradoxes* regarding the proverbs' dynamics (Scarlat, 2015; 2019).

The habitual use of proverbs for moral education is old and universal. However, *the use of proverbs as illustrations of abstract concepts and principles of scientific management and entrepreneurship (in general) and project management (in particular) is a premiere.*

Project-based education is becoming common at all education levels (Boronat *et al.*, 2021); however, working in the international environment stimulates intercultural and inter-linguistic exchange – mainly in higher education and high level research. Unfortunately, the multicultural diversity possibly comes with inter-cultural clashes as well (Lewis, 1996; 2006; Hofstede, 2001).

On the other hand, conversely, the literature on teaching project management (in particular) is not so diverse. Therefore, this chapter deals with a particular, less discussed topic – the issue of *teaching project management (specifically its abstract principles)*, using *proverbs as teaching aid.*

Consequently, the remaining of this chapter is structured as follows: challenges of teaching international students (for both students and professors); teaching environment (presentation of universities, students, and teaching subject – project management); an original approach to proverbs' dynamics, their functions and educational role; presentation of three practical ways of using proverbs while teaching project management principles; lessons learnt; limitations and further research avenues, and conclusion.

CHALLENGES OF TEACHING INTERNATIONAL STUDENTS

An educational programme designed for international students is, by itself, challenging. As it involves teachers and students equally, the challenges are significant for both sides; however, the standpoint is different.

Challenges of Learning in a Different Country as International Student

For many students, the experience of travelling abroad for studies – regardless of regular or exchange students – is novel; then not only exciting but also challenging.

The author's own observations collected during fifteen years of teaching internationally (out of which about a decade dedicated to project management), and interactions with international students show that, among challenges the international students have to face, there are a few most common ones (common even in that sense that all are stressful – at least the first time, at the very beginning).

- Logistics challenges (accommodation, local food, transportation, insurance, financial issues).
- Challenges of new education environment at the host university (teaching language, grading system, structure of the degree programme, administrative regulations, university constitution).
- Challenges of new socio-cultural environment (different language, culture, social habits).
- Legal, political, environmental and other challenges.

Some of the logistic challenges (as insurance and additional financial support) could be solved in advance by students and their families, and a good part of the challenges of new education environment (*i.e.* didactic issues as grading system, structure of the degree programme, administrative regulations, university constitution, etc) are covered by mutual agreements between universities (as in the European Union Erasmus-type agreements). The host universities that organize study programmes in foreign languages open to international students also provide brochures containing guidelines for cultural immersion. Symmetrically, many counterpart universities have developed policies and strategies to support their students to develop intercultural competence. Along these lines, "as the number of Chinese students studying abroad has increased dramatically in recent years, most studies have focused on Chinese students' study abroad experiences and how these students adapt to different cultures" (Liao, 2020, p. 203); in this respect the case of the immersion program of Sichuan University is presented.

In most cases, as the teaching language is English, one of the eligibility criteria is a certain level of English proficiency (Kwao *et al.*, 2021) – thus the teaching language should not be an issue. This is in agreement with the author's own observations that most of the Germans, Finns or Dutch students as well as students from Anglophone countries do not look as having any English language problem. However, there always are a few students in a cohort for whom the communication seems to be an obstacle.

Learning abroad, in a different country, as an international student – as compared to the experience of studying abroad, immersed in a single cultural environment – is more complex and challenging, in terms of cultural and linguistic diversity. On the other hand, the paradox is that this diversity helps break the obstacles because "I am like the others" argument is stronger than student's natural introversion or cultural reticence. The author has learnt this argument in several instances, while discussing with international students.

It is significant to mention that amid its longer academic tradition, the business education in Europe seems to emulate the 'American model', at least in terms of the students' cultural and linguistic diversity. While in the United Stated having a certain degree of diversity is the norm for many decades, in the particular case of business studies taught in the European universities, this is a relatively more recent trend. The enlarged European Union has created the legal environment and many EU universities that tailored international business education programmes report a higher proportion of international students – resulting in a larger cultural and linguistic diversity. A good indicator of success is that top European MBA programmes successfully compete with the top North American ones: the Economist 2021 ranking includes in its 'top 10' five US universities and five EU universities (Economist, 2021).

The challenges for the international students are often mixed and intertwined, or such are the reasons behind. As an example, observed by the author, many students coming from the former Eastern European communist bloc are inclined to pay excessive attention to grades, as opposed to the most Western European students – mostly interested in acquiring knowledge and practical tools to master.

A few other non-EU students are interested in accessing the European Union labour market, while a minority are just looking to pass the exam/s.

A softer issue that transcends for some groups of international students, despite internationalization trends and globalization, is their native cultural print (*e.g.* the Extreme Oriental smiles and the Finns are shy).

Professor's Challenges of Teaching International Students

Subjectively speaking, teaching international students abroad was exciting and a source of professional satisfaction.

Some challenges of the international environment faced by professors are similar to the students' challenges. As for the students, the professors' immersion in a foreign culture, and working with colleagues in "international environment" are mitigating factors to soften the differences.

However, two challenges that look different have a common source.

The first notable challenge is dealing with uneven entry-levels of international students – a problem with several facets (at least five): different background undergrad-studies (in case of master-level students – from engineers to artists); different working experiences; different levels of mastering the English language; different cultural background, and different native languages. Some differences are just natural (as the first category and the last two), while others come from specific profiles of both outgoing and incoming universities.

The second and most recent challenge is facing the corona-crisis which brought about compulsory *online teaching*. The author's teaching experience during the last three semesters (spring and autumn 2020, spring 2021) of online teaching reveals a certain degree of dissatisfaction – as many colleagues and, surprisingly, students frankly declared that they lack and miss direct social interaction in the traditional "brick-and-mortar" classroom setup and environment. In principle, mixed challenges – cross-cultural teaching-learning (Bauler, 2019) in an international environment (Appiah-Kubi & Annan, 2020) – make teaching online more complex.

TEACHING ENVIRONMENT

The teaching environment is depicted from the author's perspective, shortly presenting: the host universities, the students and the subject that were taught. Author's direct experience of actively teaching abroad extends little more than a decade: it started and ended in Belgium between 2005-2006 and 2015-2016. The period under scrutiny – which corresponds to the period of teaching similar courses of *Project management* to international students at three universities from three European Union countries (Belgium, Finland and Romania) – also covers more than a decade: between 2008-2009 and 2020-2021.

The Universities

During the above mentioned period, courses in *Project management* were taught at these universities:

- Mikkeli University of Applied Sciences (MAMK), Finland (5,000 students);
- Karel de Grote (KdG) University College, Antwerp, Belgium (13,000 students);
- University "Politehnica" of Bucharest, Romania (25,000 students).

The author's direct experience within these universities and teaching visits in all seasons have revealed all kinds of changes in all of them – from infrastructure to organizational charts, from funding systems to restructuring the study programmes and curricula, from students to faculty members profiles. These universities have developed programmes of business studies, currently open to international students.

The international dimension is essential for the dynamic entrepreneurial culture of the university, as Clark (1998) studied the entrepreneurial dynamic universities, their transformation and progress to higher performance. Referring to the size of the entrepreneurial university as number of students, Clark's studies mention "small to middle size universities – 6,000 to approximately 13,000" (p. 142).

The Students

During the described timeline, the total number of international students taught was more than eight hundred, with an average of around 35 registered students per cohort. The proportion of international students largely varied across universities, and varied from year to year (Table 1). KdG reported the highest proportion of international students and MAMK had international students from most countries.

Table 1 indicates that *smaller universities* (*i.e.* MAMK with 5,000 students and Karel de Grote with 13,000 students) display higher attractiveness for international students, which is in-line with Clark's conclusion about the size of the *more dynamic and entrepreneurial* universities.

The free education system in Finland is an important reason for students from all over the world to travel to Finland to study. In addition, the Russian students see the travel's convenience and low cost as an advantage – which explains why their proportion is the largest among international students. In contrast, the international students in Belgium are explained on the grounds that many (most) natives travel abroad and a lot of spaces for international students open up as a result. Most of the international students come from many European nations and Turkey.

The restrictions brought by the corona-virus pandemic affected education sector seriously, and forcefully turned the teaching online quicker than expected, in many countries. In these cases the pandemic just functioned as technology accelerator (Scarlat, 2021; Scarlat & Stănciulescu, 2021; Scarlat *et al.*, 2021).

Table 1. Proportion of the international students, by universities

No	Indicators	Universities		
		MAMK **(2008 – 2014)**	**Karel de Grote** **(2013 – 2016)**	**"Politehnica"** **(2012 – 2021)**
1	Proportion of international students per cohort: limits (min – max) [%]	70% – 89%	76% – 97%	12% – 32%
2	Average proportion of international students per cohort [%]	82%	88%	25%
3	Number of countries / number of continents	27 counties 5 continents	19 countries 4 continents	16 counties 3 continents
4	Most international students were from:	Russia (more than local Finns)	Spain, Turkey, Netherlands	Spain, Portugal, Nigeria

Source: Author

The Teaching Subject: Project Management

The *Project Management* discipline encompasses a variety of issues (Lock, 2013) and the course delivery methods are even more varied (Haynes, 2019); in addition, each method of teaching should be adapted to the students' needs and characteristics.

The courses taught between the university years 2008-2009 and 2020-2021 were designed for the master-level, tailored per requirements and profile of each university. According to the course feedback, the current course content and/or methods were updated yearly. The subjects were as follows:

- *Project Management Skills* at Mikkeli University of Applied Sciences, Finland (2008 – 2014);
- *Project Management* at Karel de Grote University College, Antwerp, Belgium (2013 – 2016);
- *Project Management,* at University "Politehnica" of Bucharest, Romania (2012 – 2021).

The theoretical part of the course is centred on the project management principles (Scarlat, 2013; 2014; 2016). While the practical part of the course is easier to be understood by students (using cases and/or working on small projects), the abstract principles of the project management prove to be more difficult to tackle.

The Click: Proverbs!

Facing multiple challenges, coming from both sides of the classroom, the idea of using *proverbs* as teaching aid (Scarlat, 2007; 2008b) first occured while teaching Entrepreneurship, Business management, and Project management courses to undergraduate students at University "Politehnica" of Bucharest. Hence, teaching Entrepreneurship and Management disciplines using proverbs as a teaching aid, that started in early 2000s is, in all probability, a premiere (Scarlat, 2007; 2008a; 2008b). This exercise has continued (Scarlat, 2020) and extended to master and international students.

The role of proverbs in education, underlying their *power to communicate the sense of the concrete* was championed by Lauand (1995; 1998). Mieder (1983; 2003; 2008) claims that *proverbs speak louder than words* – of course, metaphorically.

PROVERBS: THEIR RESILIENCE, DYNAMICS AND FUNCTIONS

There are different non-conventional styles to teach – by music (Fleck & Kakouris, 2019) or culture (McAlister-Shields *et al.*, 2019) – even when teaching non-cultural, abstract science subjects. Therefore, teaching project management by a culture component as proverbs is a novelty but not entirely surprising.

Four Theses about the Proverbs' Resilience

The role of universities in education is undeniable. However, in spite of their venerable millennial age – cathedral or monastic schools were active in the 6th century (Riché, 1978) – universities are very young as compared to the 70 millennia history of *cognitive homo sapiens*, and it makes sense to wonder what was even before the precursors of universities (Scarlat, 2019; 2020).

According to Marrou (1948), the first schools in antiquity were in Mesopotamia (by religious temples, to train the priests and scribes), China (the 3rd millennium BC), and Egypt (by the pharaoh court). The access to these schools was limited – for ruling families and religious elite (Lyons, 2013); thus most of the population was illiterate. The knowledge was transmitted by repeating and memorization, from *magister* to disciples, and hand-written and copied books (most of them religious) were rare. It is very likely that, amid a scarcity of books, *magister was using proverbs as teaching aids* – Aristotle mentioning already old proverbs in his writings.

The religious commands and lessons of life frequently have merged: one of the oldest books, the *Bible* (religious *per se*), includes a chapter of lessons of life and civic education: *Proverbs* (Clements, 2003). Alter (2010) argues that the source of proverbs is even older: a collection of old Egyptian proverbs (the 2nd millennium BC) – that inspired the 'Book of Proverbs' *via* a translation in the Aramaic (Ruffle, 1995).

Besides wisdom literature (Crenshaw, 2000; Smoothers, 2000; Tate, Ballard & Tucker, 2000), the *proverbs played an important educative role* – not as an alternative but as subtle yet solid and continuous, particular kind to educate – *before the invention of printing and even writing*.

Table 2. The Four Theses on proverbs' resilience and durability – related to communication revolutions

No	Communication revolutions	The Theses
1	*Language revolution*: the emergence of articulate speaking (language)	*The first thesis*: The proverbs (anonymous and collective life experience lessons transmitted *orally*) preceded writing – *as primary education means for early humans.*
2	*Writing revolution*: the invention of writing	*The second thesis*: The proverbs continued to be transmitted orally and used as such even after the invention of writing. For example, the *written books of proverbs. Proverbs were initially used for the education of royal and religious elites only.*
3	*Printing revolution*: the invention of printing	*The third thesis*: The proverbs continued to be used even after the invention of printing – mostly for the basic education of an increasingly larger population (books with proverbs included). *The printed books made possible the development of modern universities.*
4	*E-communication revolution (ICT)*: mass communication using new e-technologies for data generation, transmission, processing, & storing	*The fourth thesis*: The proverbs continue to be used even after the emergence of newer information and communication technologies – which facilitate mass access and accelerate their transmission. *Proverbs are transmitted by all means and forms and continue to fulfil their educative role.*

Source: Scarlat (2019, pp. 53-55; 2020, pp. 268-269)

Therefore, the *collective and anonymous author* of these pieces of folk-art, orally transmitted along generations (Al Fahim, 1995; 2013) – *as universal and immortal educator* – should be praised. In this respect, Scarlat (2019, pp. 53-55) enounces *four theses related to the proverbs' resilience, durability and continuity* (Table 2).

The internet-supported *development of the social networks amplifies and accelerates* the effect of collective and anonymous transmission of proverbs. Many scholars (Chang & Wu, 2021; Wang *et al.*, 2021) currently study the growing and important role of social networks in online global communication.

Five Paradoxes about the Proverbs' Dynamics

While the four theses refer to how proverbs – communication means by excellence – have evolved through the history of communication revolutions, the five paradoxes that follow illustrate the evolution of proverbs in terms of their purpose: for what reason they were originally generated, and how they were used. Yet both standpoints show and strive to explain the resilience of the proverbs along their millennia-long history, in other words their dynamics.

Concerned by the resilience of proverbs along centuries and millennia, Scarlat (2015; 2019) had a deeper look at the way proverbs were generated and used, and proposed for analysis a bi-dimensional matrix model. The two dimensions for analysis are the proverbs' "generators" or initiators, and the proverbs' "users". Therefore, this matrix is called GU model – where G stands for *generators* and U symbolizes the *users* of proverbs. Figure 1 depicts the GU matrix model of *the proverbs' dynamics*, displaying a chronological evolution, in spite of the fact that the "time" dimension is not represented.

Figure 1. The GU matrix for analysing the proverbs' dynamics and illustrating the proverbs' paradoxes. Adapted: Scarlat (2015, pp. 39-44; 2019, pp. 55-62)

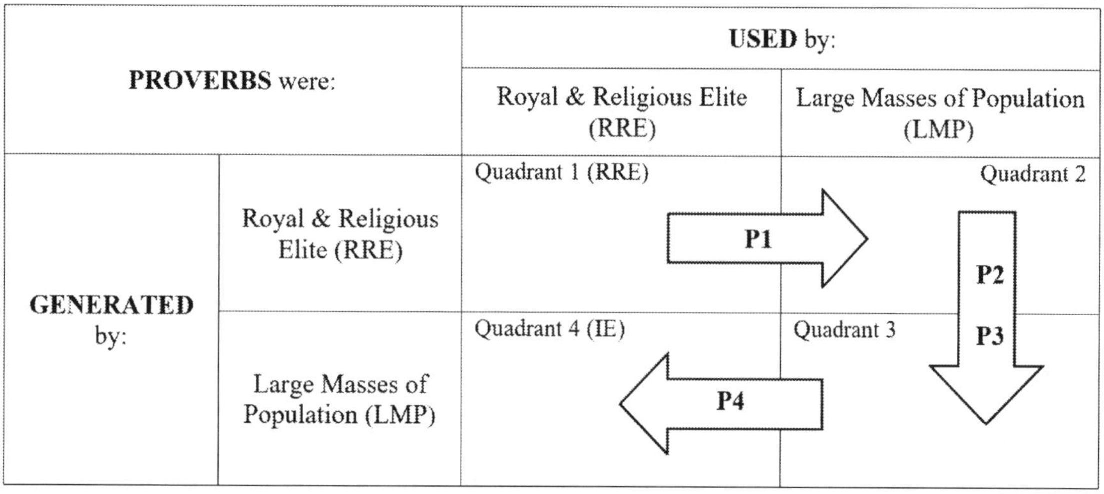

PROVERBS were:		**USED** by:	
		Royal & Religious Elite (RRE)	Large Masses of Population (LMP)
GENERATED by:	Royal & Religious Elite (RRE)	Quadrant 1 (RRE) P1	Quadrant 2 P2
	Large Masses of Population (LMP)	Quadrant 4 (IE) P4	Quadrant 3 P3

In time, the proverbs symbolically go along their millennial way from the quadrant 1 – which means that proverbs were {created by: *the royal and religious elite;* to be used by: *their own use*} (Tucker,

2000), in order, to the quadrants 2, 3 and 4 – which reads proverbs were {created by: *masses*; to be used by: *elite*}. The elites from quadrant 4 are not necessarily religious anymore, but intellectual elites (IE).

The analysis of the documented description of the proverbs' path along quadrants – symbolically represented in Table 3 – resulted in a set of five paradoxes (Scarlat, 2015; 2019).

- *Paradox of the proverbs' diffusion and dissemination* (P1): Although the royal and religious elite created the proverbs as a *corpus* of rules for good governance and healthy life (body of knowledge) for their own use, *the proverbs have diffused in time to the use of all population.*
- *Paradox of the proverbs' secularization* (P2): Although the royal and religious elites created the proverbs as a *corpus* of rules for good governance and healthy life for their own use (religious initially), the proverbs have diffused in time to the use of all population and *became instruments for their secular education.*
- *Paradox of the proverbs' enrichment* (P3): Although the proverbs conceived by the royal and religious elites as a *corpus* of rules for good governance and healthy life for their own use, the proverbs have diffused in time to the use of all population *and they have enriched in time, becoming richer and richer as a result of anonymous and collective contribution of masses.*
- *Paradox of proverbs' use by the intellectual elite* (P4): Although the proverbs largely became a rich anonymous and collective creation of large masses of people for their own use (education), the *proverbs started to be valued and used by the intellectual elites to produce cultured literature.*
- *Paradox of the proverbs' value* (P5): Although the proverbs seem to be of low value (because of their popular format and mass dissemination), they are *bearers of moral principles and high intellectual value.*

Freyha (1974) had explained the confusion between format and essence by the disparity between richness and intellectual value. The current tendency of the proverbs' vulgarisation is signalled by Lopez (2001).

Functions of Proverbs

Besides the traditional core- functions of proverbs:

- *Proverbs as wisdom treasure*
- *Proverbs as means of education*
- *Proverbs as means of trans-generational transmission of life experience (knowledge transfer),*

Paremiology scholars and their studies are revealing more functions as:

- *Expressions of 'imaginative thinking'* (Cauvin, 1976; Bonnet, 1982)
- *Source of information and research tool* (Benedict, 1943; Benedict & Mead, 1972; Scarlat, 2015)
- *Intercultural bridges in business management* (Salicrú i Lluch, 2008; Scarlat & Afendras, 2007)
- *Metaphors in professional and business communication* (Tannen, 1981; Adler, 1991; Gibson, 2001; Cacciaguidi-Fahy & Cunningham, 2007; Wei & Mayouf, 2009; Lee & Wu, 2021)
- *Mediator of inter-cultural management conflicts* (Adler, 1991; Cacciaguidi-Fahy & Cunningham, 2007; Zhou, 2021) and even intra-cultural conflicts (Salamone, 1976)

- *Standard models for decision making* (Scarlat, 2007)
- *Proverbs as teaching aids.*

The last listed function of proverbs is not the least in importance – because "proverbs as teaching aids" is integrated in "means of education". In addition, the five theses related to the proverbs' resilience show that proverbs always served for education; and, chronologically-wise – as the first paradox shows – the original purpose of the proverbs was education. Nevertheless, the use of proverbs as teaching aids while teaching subjects in the area of business studies (Scarlat, 2007; 2008b; 2020) – as entrepreneurship, business and project management (the project management principles, in particular) – is a novel approach.

PROVERBS REINVENTED: USING THE PROVERBS AS TEACHING AID

Regardless of the new technologies used in educational process (Lee & Nuatomue, 2021; Maganello *et al.*, 2021; Ramos *et al.*, 2021; Veryaeva & Solovyeva, 2021; Podder & Samanta, 2022), proverbs continue (in the author's opinion) to fulfil their educational function at all levels – even in the higher education – because, as shown in the previous section (theses and paradoxes), the *use of proverbs is not a matter of technology or education level, but an issue of basic inter-humans communication.*

In principle, the proverbs may be used in two different instances: (i) as teaching instruments, illustrating the principles of *Project Management* – which are abstract concepts by definition; (ii) as learning means, by assigning individual and/or small working group assignments centred on proverbs.

The author has used the proverbs while teaching the *Project Management* course in several ways – as it is shown below.

- Illustrative examples while presenting abstract concepts (as project management principles).
- Topic for classroom debates (while discussing project management principles).
- Support for home assignments (as optional, bonus assignments; they do not replace the compulsory assignments).

All these ways are discussed and exemplified in the following sections. None of them could replace own professor's teaching technologies, methods and techniques; the proverbs just complement, enhance and strengthen them.

Proverbs as Illustrative Examples While Teaching Project Management Principles

The principles section is one of the abstract topics to be taught in the Project management course; then, concrete examples should be provided.

The principles are essential because without them even otherwise well trained people make mistakes in project management and then fail. Two examples noted by the author during his consulting practice are provided in this respect: (i) a manager who successfully implemented several local development projects funded by EU programmes had made costly mistakes when managing an educational project without the knowledge of these principles; and (ii) a successful civil engineer who failed when was assigned a research project to manage. The examples of failed cases illustrate what happens when future project managers are taught to do things 'like that' without paying attention to principles: reasoning '*why*' the things should be done.

Therefore, the teaching of project management principles should be done interactively, providing cases and examples, making sure that students understand the concepts and can solve project problems. This is accomplished when students learn by doing, apply the appropriate principles, and do so independently.

An advantage of using proverbs – as short, metaphorical sentences – is to support decisions in unclear instances in which abstract concepts operate. Lack of experience and/or proper expertise may lead to confusion with costly consequences. Such instances occur when two concepts (project monitoring and project evaluation) are mixed up in theory and, even worse, in practice.

While visiting company headquarters, the author has seen, not only once, door signs labelling the department behind as 'Project Monitoring and Evaluation' – which eventually raised the following question: Are the people working in that department monitors *and* evaluators?

The discussions that followed with the persons in charge (officers and department managers) about specific issues of the job descriptions of the people working in these departments have revealed, in several cases, a certain degree of confusion.

While in most cases it is correctly understood that *monitoring and evaluation are different concepts* and, therefore, they require different sets of qualifications, skills and other relevant features, in a few cases the confusion made that same person is tagged as 'Monitor and Evaluator'. Even this uncommon situation is not necessarily a mistake – as long as the respective person has the required qualifications for both positions (monitor and evaluator) *and s/he is never asked to perform both roles in the same project*. Unfortunately, in a couple of cases the confusion observed was complete: both the office worker and his supervisor have considered monitoring and evaluation as equivalent and acted as such. And negative consequences regarding the quality of projects were reported. Regrettably, both cases were identified within higher education institutions. Similar cases were also identified in a few service companies; however, their analysis goes beyond the space allocated to this chapter.

These instances demonstrate that it is important to understand project management and associated concepts and principles (like project monitoring and project evaluation). Therefore, any educational means that may have a contribution in this respect should be considered.

In this line of thinking, while teaching courses of project management, providing proverbs-based examples to understand the project management principles is beneficial: the proverbs are effective (easy to understand), efficient (do not need much time), and, additionally, they are funny. In other words, the proverbs are easy to use and inexpensive teaching aids.

There are three types of evaluation (*ex-ante* evaluation, intermediary / mid-term evaluation, and *ex-post* evaluation) – besides self-evaluation and evaluation proper.

Table 3 depicts major differences between project monitoring and evaluation – by essential criteria and selected proverbs – in case of *ex-post evaluation* (the final evaluation, after the project implementation). The examples provided in Table 3 demonstrate the neat differences between the two principles and the slight differences between proverbs coming from different cultures.

The author has used this type of examples (Table 3) while teaching the Project Management course to international students; they come with genuine examples from their own regional communities, and provide new perspectives on the same general principle of project evaluation or monitoring – *e.g.* about the age of proverbs (they may refer to occupations non-existent nowadays); about different occupations country-specific; different seasons and climate; even local clothing and customs.

Table 3. Project monitoring vs. project evaluation: Essential differences and illustrations by proverbs

Differentiation criteria	Project monitoring	Project *ex-post* evaluation
What (the purpose)	Monitoring the implementation – in order to reach the project objective	Evaluate the effects and impact of reaching the objective – as planned
Who (is in charge to do)	The project manager	Independent, objective evaluator/s (not involved and/or interested in the project)
When (should be done)	During the project implementation stage	After the implementation stage (project is completed)
How (should be done)	Continuously	One-time exercise
Examples of illustrative proverbs	*Ochiul stăpânului îngraşă vita* (Romanian) [*The master's eye fattens the cow*] (Appendix 1) *Ciobanul bun păzeşte turma şi noaptea* (Romanian) [*The good shepherd guards the flock day and night*] *Not riposa colui che ha careo d'altrui* (Italian) [*The person in charge does not rest*] *A fi cu ochii în patru* (Romanian) [*To watch with four eyes*]	*Toamna se numără bobocii* (Romanian) [*In autumn the ducklings are counted*] (Appendix 1) *Don't count the chicken before they are out of the egg* (English) *Nu lăuda ziua înainte de asfinţit* (Romanian) [*Don't praise the day before the sunset*]

Source: Adapted (Scarlat, 2014, 2015, 2019)

Adding the different background training to the international students' cultural and linguistic differences, the discussions on the same proverb may lead to different standpoints. As an example, the metaphor of "the master's eye that fattens the cow" might generate discussions about 'master' and 'eye': are they symbolizing the same individual (the project manager) or, more subtle, they symbolize two different entities: the 'eye' is the project manager and the 'master' is the project sponsor (funding body, *etc.*). Ultimately, the diverse international students (enjoying diverse cultural backgrounds) uncover the diversity of proverb metaphors that reflect cultural situatedness. Thus, the grasp of abstract concepts deepens, and students better understand the practical implications (how the project management principles apply).

Proverbs as Topic for Classroom Debates on Project Management Principles

The situation described above about different interpretations of a certain proverb (the 'master's eye' in this instance) is considered normal because proverbs themselves bear encoded messages, under the metaphor format. Decoding the core-message is not always easy and/or unique. Therefore, the teaching of project management principles should be done intensively in an interactive manner, providing cases and examples, asking for feedback – to make sure that students understand the concepts and can solve project problems and manage similar situations in both near future (assignments, projects, exams) and distant future (their jobs, careers, and real business life).

Along the project lifecycle (Lock, 2013; Scarlat, 2013; 2014; 2016), the exercise of *self-evaluation* is also important. It is not an evaluation proper – as it is an internal evaluation; it is exercised with the methods and instruments of evaluation but conducted by the project manager. And this might be the reason behind the confusion between monitoring and evaluation, but not an excuse or a reason to not pay attention to the right understanding of project management principles and concepts.

The self-evaluation is an important resource of knowledge by the *lessons learnt*. There are many proverbs in this respect – just three examples:

- *Nimeni nu e născut învățat* (Romanian) [*Nobody is born learned*]
- *Ei kukaan ole seppä syntyessänsä* (Finnish) [*Nobody is born blacksmith*]
- *La experiencia es la madre de la ciencia* (Spanish) [*The experience is the mother of science*]

While teaching the project management principles to international students, these proverbs and others alike were used during classroom debates centred on the evaluation principle (specifically, self-evaluation); the students understood the importance of self-evaluation as an opportunity for lessons to be learnt. It also was on opportunity for intercultural and inter-linguistic exchange: the students from different countries came with similar examples from their own country, in their own maternal language.

The proverbs can be used as illustrative examples or – and this is the typical situation while teaching international students – as a starting point for argument-based discussions and debates. In turn, this type of exercise has two lines of discussions, following the embedded cultural and linguistic pattern of proverbs' character, as well as their meaning.

The first line of discussion is based on the fact that there are very similar proverbs in several cultural areas (*e.g.* Latin, Germanic, Slavic languages – to look at most populous in Europe only) and their similarity is explained mainly by this shared cultural heritage. Another explanation is even simpler, considering the natural environment: similar circumstances have induced in humans' minds similar reflections (Scarlat, 2015, p. 54).

Such reflections are mostly cause-effect trivial statements like "after night, a day will come" or "after rain, the sun will shine". Such universal natural cyclic phenomena are the reasons behind finding pretty similar proverbs in more languages.

The second line of discussion is more challenging. It involves asking international students to identify proverbs from their own cultural and linguistic environments *with similar meanings.* In this case, small working groups are built on cultural and linguistic similarity, with the task to explore and find proverbs in their own language to illustrate certain specific *Project Management* principles. Classroom discussions follow to compare and eventually identify similarities – and differences, among meanings of different proverbs (yet illustrating the same principle) coming from different linguistic environments.

To summarize, the classroom discussions and debates can be initiated – after presenting all principles (with or without providing proverb illustrations) – by proposing a new example of proverb and then inviting students to elaborate on the meaning of this proverb, and ultimately matching specific principle/s. The discussion is always educative and entertaining.

Proverbs as Bonus Assignments During the Course of Project Management

Bonus assignments are optional home works associated with the course of Project management. They do not replace the compulsory assignments but complement them – offering students the chance to improve their scores at no risk. Usually, the proverb-based home assignments follow the teaching session in which the previous two types of proverb use (illustrative examples while presenting the project management principles; and classroom debates – while discussing project management principles) were applied.

As a methodology, all three types of use are mixed and inter-linked. For example, when the professor's feedback on home assignments is given, a new session of classroom discussions may follow. The purpose of this exercise is to stimulate the intercultural and inter-linguistic exchange and mutual understanding among international students.

Table 4 depicts a basic typology of home assignments related to proverbs in teaching and learning project management principles. In principle, their complexity and difficulty increase from top to bottom.

Any real assignments may well be a combination of the basic types.

This type of assignment works well both as individual or teamwork, with slight advantage for the individual work. However, individuals gain more from it because of the effort required in understanding and then finding an appropriate proverb.

Table 4. A typology of home assignments of project management

No	Given Input (by Professor)	Asked Output (from students) To identify – in their own cultural environment – and provide	
		Project management principle	Proverb/s
1	**A project management principle** (after being explained and illustrated by a suitable proverb)	–	Other proverb/s with: - Similar wording and/or pattern as the given proverb - Telling different story, still good illustration for the given principle
2	**A project management principle** (after being explained but no proverb exemplification provided)	–	Proverb/s suitable as illustration/s for the given project management principle
3	**A single proverb** (after all project management principles were explained and corresponding suitable proverbs presented)	Identify the appropriate project management principle	Other proverb/s with: - Similar wording and/or pattern as the given proverb - Telling different story, still good illustration for the given principle

Source: Author

Ideally, the work by country teams would be more effective; however, multicultural, mixed teams have their own advantage because of stimulating the inter-cultural exchanges and networking that ensues.

A set of eight Romanian proverbs is presented in Appendix 1, corresponding to eight principles of project management (Scarlat, 2014; 2015; 2019): uniqueness of the project purpose; uniqueness of the project manager; project team principle; principle of the project hierarchy (simply known as Work Breakdown Structure – WBS); design (planning) *versus* implementation; 'stage-gate' principle; project monitoring; project evaluation. Each Romanian version of the proverb is associated with its corresponding English word-for-word translated versions and meaning in both quotidian language and project management terminology. This set is not exhaustive; however, it proved to be valid in various types of projects and industries, different circumstances and cultural environments. Arguably, it might be improved and expanded.

Appendix 2 displays a summarized collection of similar proverbs in several languages for the most illustrated project management principles.

Appendix 3 displays a collection of international project teams of different sizes (3-to-6 members – photos 1 ...4), while working on their team assignments in the classroom. The size of the inter-cultural team depends on the assignment type and the classroom size (photo 5 shows a class of forty students).

The professor's evaluation of the use of proverbs as teaching aids associated with the course of project management (project management principles, specifically) is overall positive – considering: higher efficiency in terms of the time needed to teach; slight improvement of the average grade per similar cohort of students; increased subjective spiritual satisfaction by the end of the course (as result of more relaxed professor-student interaction, and better intercultural communication).

From the students' perspective, the course evaluations show an increased satisfaction for using proverbs as teaching aids for two reasons. First, students find the exercise less intense and culturally validating thereby the classroom atmosphere. And second, is more pragmatic because it affords improving their mark through the bonus home assignments. In addition, the chance to better know each other and understand the cultural differences, while working in multi-cultural teams on their team assignments, was appreciated as well.

LESSONS LEARNT AND RECOMMENDATIONS

Most lessons learnt are linked to the circumstances in which the proverbs were used.

The first obstacle is also the first lesson for the professor: proverbs should be chosen carefully, because even in native language proverbs could have more than one meaning. And the English translation may well add more confusion. Therefore: (i) the selected proverbs should have no ambiguity; (ii) it is preferable to choose directly English language proverbs (or in the language of teaching).

The association of the right proverb with a certain principle of project management is not straightforward. Take as an example the Russian (although a beautiful metaphor of love) proverb: *Cannot hold two loves in one heart* ['*В одном сердце две любви не уместишь*']. Literally, the message is clear; there is no confusion about the sentiment. However, it is difficult to determine if the suitable project management principle is the uniqueness of the project purpose or the uniqueness of the project manager. In other words, the dilemma stands in the question: Is the heart symbolizing 'the purpose' or 'the manager'? A challenging discussion may follow; unfortunately, it will be time-consuming, and leave the matter unresolved.

Consequently, pick the proverb-examples carefully. When it is needed, the double-meaning or multiple-meaning proverbs may be chosen on purpose only (*e.g.* for debates).

In case of proverb-meaning-based debates, the teacher (the session moderator, in general) should carefully moderate the debating session – both as time and conflicts management (avoiding the conflict escalation). The lesson learned is that in order to avoid the possible development of debates on sensitive issues (mostly in case of strong personalities), care and caution should be exercised.

The entrepreneurial and basic management education may start at younger age, in high-school and even in primary school – when funny proverbs are a lot easier to illustrate abstract concepts.

LIMITATIONS AND FUTURE RESEARCH DIRECTIONS

When the teaching environment is highly diverse (culturally and linguistically), the discussions on the specific proverb's meanings in local culture might develop, spiralling to arguments and counter-arguments and, therefore, consuming more time; then the relatively short time allocated is a physical limitation.

A natural limitation is related to proverbs: some cultures and languages use proverbs more than others. From a communication standpoint, this issue is solved by using English. However, students' English language proficiency and fluency matter a great deal.

One surmountable limitation is the professor's available set of proverbs. Ideally, use of more proverbs, in more languages, from more cultural environments, would work better. This issue is continually worked on by completing comparative, inter-cultural studies (Scarlat & Kasim, 2008; Scarlat & Taatila, 2009; Scarlat & Albuquerque, 2009; Scarlat & Pavan, 2011) and multi-language studies (Scarlat & Afendras, 2007). These comparative inter-cultural studies on the proverbs' entrepreneurial and management meaning (project management included) extended the studies pioneered in the Romanian culture (Scarlat, 2008a), the Balkans (Scarlat & Afendras, 2007) and Balkans *versus* Arab world (Scarlat & Afendras, 2008). The studies on proverbs in different cultural/linguistic environments are promising for further comparative, cross- and inter-cultural studies (in both entrepreneurship–management and paremiology areas of knowledge).

The current plan is to engage in deeper and/or multi-language studies, and explore new languages and cultures. Diachronic studies on the proverbs (with management-related meaning in particular) could provide information about evolution of management in time, while synchronic studies of proverbs (with management significance) across culturally and linguistically diverse geographic areas could lead to identifying cultural prints on management practices. Combined studies might be considered as well.

The proposed *theses and paradoxes* related to the proverbs' dynamics are not only paremiology contributions but they also are able to generate further discussions, debates as well as deeper studies.

In addition, the management meaning of proverbs evolves itself: for example, the proverbs' meaning in the area of *sustainable development and environmental management* (Scarlat & Petrişor, 2021) – which is probably a premiere. The path for further studies is also open.

The current corona-virus pandemic is definitely another physical limitation by restrictions imposed to travel, mostly international travel. However, the pandemic accelerated digitalisation (Scarlat & Stănciulescu, 2021; Scarlat, Panduru & Stănciulescu, 2021) and stimulated the development of online teaching (Scarlat, 2021, 272-273). As long as pandemic continues, the online education process is an open, real-scale, research laboratory.

CONCLUSION

The influence of using proverbs as a teaching aid on the students' performance is difficult to assess, as there are many impacting factors such as use of other teaching aids, methods, and technologies. However, there are indicators that demonstrate a positive effect, besides the professor's own subjective satisfaction: increased class activity and interaction; a slight but positive trend of the students' grades; positive feedback from students about the use of proverbs.

The author's decade-long activity of teaching internationally (and ten years of teaching *Project Management* to international students, in particular) was paralleled by the corresponding research on proverbs with managerial meaning. Amid habitual use of proverbs for moral education, *the focused use of proverbs as a teaching aid in order to illustrate abstract concepts of management and entrepreneurship (in general) and the project management principles (in particular) is probably a premiere* (Scarlat, 2007; 2008b; 2014).

Surprisingly, the novelty is not the result of newer computerized technologies, but the result of looking back to the old wisdom, embedded in any cultural treasure, to be found in any language: the proverbs.

The proverbs were used in three different ways, individually or as a mix. Sets of proverbs, in different languages, illustrating project management principles are presented and their slight differences are discussed (and always new perspectives are revealed in the light of diverse cultural background). Intercultural exchange generates not only enriched knowledge but also better mutual understanding and higher degree of satisfaction (for both students and professor).

The use of proverbs as teaching aid does not replace or alter the use of other teaching methods and/ or instruments, own professor's teaching methodologies, style and manner of teaching; the proverbs just complement, enhance and strengthen them. The use of proverbs is just an additional, complementary instrument while teaching in higher education.

More than a decade of teaching and research internationally was an opportunity to confirm the theory of entrepreneurial university (Clark, 1998) in that respect of internationalization component as well as flexibility and entrepreneurial behaviour of the small to mid-sized universities (6,000 to 13,000 students).

Summarizing:

- *Proverbs* are as old as human articulate speaking; and they have evolved – as rhythmic and rhymed, collective and anonymous creations of the people, reflecting their life experience – within human communities and society up to-date, proving extraordinary resilience;
- *Proverbs with managerial meaning* are older than principles of the modern management science; and they have evolved along centuries, reflecting the people's work and trade, administration and business experiences;
- Collections of proverbs were originally used for royal and religious elites' education; and they have continuously evolved along centuries, maintaining their *educative role*, in its largest accept;
- Sets of proverbs with managerial meaning, maintaining their educative role, can be used as *teaching aids* (as metaphoric illustrative examples) while *teaching management subjects* – as project management, specifically *project management principles*;
- *Proverbs with managerial meaning exist in any language and culture*; and they can be used as universal means of communication and mutual understanding at high intellectual level, as teaching aids, while teaching abstract concepts of management and entrepreneurship – as project management, specifically project management principles – which is *the ultimate conclusion* of this work.

ACKNOWLEDGMENT

This research received no specific grant from any funding agency in the public, commercial, or not-for-profit sectors.

The author is grateful to all, so diverse international students who actively participated in the *Project Management* courses – at *Karel de Grote University College* in Antwerp, Belgium; *Mikkeli University of Applied Sciences* (currently South-Eastern Finland University of Applied Sciences), from Mikkeli, Finland; and *University "Politehnica" of Bucharest*, Romania – along more than ten years of wonderful intercultural teaching experience and cross-cultural exchange.

REFERENCES

Adler, N. (1991). *International Dimensions of Organizational Behaviour* (2nd ed.). PWS-Kent Publishing Company.

Al Fahim, M. A. J. (2013). *From Rags to Riches. A Story of Abu Dhabi.* Makarem LLC.

Alter, R. (2010). *The Wisdom Books: Job, Proverbs, and Ecclesiastes. A translation with commentary.* W.W. Norton & Company.

Appiah-Kubi, P., Annan, E. (2020). A Review of Collaborative Online International Learning. *International Journal of Engineering Pedagogy, 10*(1), 109-124. doi:10.3991/ijep.v10i1.11678

Bauler, C. (2019). Speech Acts and Cross-Cultural Pragmatics. In N. Erdogan & M. Wei (Eds.), *Applied Linguistics for Teachers of Culturally and Linguistically Diverse Learners* (pp. 223–238). IGI Global. doi:10.4018/978-1-5225-8467-4.ch009

Benedict, R. (1943). *Rumanian culture and behavior.* Institute for International Studies.

Benedict, R., & Mead, M. (1972). Rumanian culture and behavior. Colorado State University.

Bonnet, D. (1982). Le proverbe chez les Mossi du Yatenga (Haute Volta). Société d'études linguistiques et anthropologiques de France – SELAF.

Boronat, T., Quiles-Carrillo, O. F., Ivorra-Martinez, J., & Montanes, N. (2021). Do You Study or Work? Project based learning as an enriching experience in education. In M. Carmo (Ed.), Education Applications & Developments, Advances in Education and Educational Trends Series (pp. 159-166). InScience Press. doi:10.36315/2021ead13

Cacciaguidi-Fahy, S., & Cunningham, J. (2007). The Use of Strategic Metaphors in Intercultural Business Communication. *Managing Global Transitions International Research Journal, 5*(2), 133–155.

Cauvin, J. (1976). Les proverbes comme expression privilégiée de la pensée imageante. *Afrique et langage, 6,* 5-34.

Chang, C. L., & Wu, S. (2021). Using Online Social Networks to Globalize and Popularize Product Brands in Different Cultural Areas: A Relational Network Model. *Journal of Global Information Management, 29*(6), 1–30. doi:10.4018/JGIM.20211101.oa38

Clark, B. R. (1998). *Creating Entrepreneurial Universities: Organizational Pathways of Transformation.* Emerald Group Publishing Limited.

Clements, R. E. (2003). Proverbs. In J. D. G. Dunn & J. W. Rogerson (Eds.), *Eerdemans Commentary on the Bible.* Eerdemans Publishing Company.

Crenshaw, J. (2000). Unresolved Issues in the Wisdom Literature. In M. E. Tate, H. W. Ballard, & D. W. Tucker (Eds.), *An Introduction to Wisdom Literature and the Psalms.* Mercer University Press.

Economist. (2021). *Full-time MBA Ranking 2021.* http://whichmba.economist.com/ranking/full-time-mba

Fayol, H. (1917). *Administration industrielle et générale; prévoyance, organisation, commandement, coordination, controle.* H. Dunod et E. Pinat.

Fleck, E., & Kakouris, A. (2019, September). *Implementing Experiential Teaching Innovations to Encourage Entrepreneurial Activity* [Paper presentation]. Pre-Conference Workshop, the 14th European Conference on Innovation and Entrepreneurship (ECIE 2019), University of Peloponnese, Kalamata, Greece. https://www.academic-conferences.org/conferences/ecie/ecie-workshops/

Freyha, A. (1974). *A Dictionary of Modern Lebanese Proverbs.* Librairie du Liban.

Gantt, H. L. (1916). *Industrial Leadership.* Yale University Press.

Gibson, C. B., & Zellmer-Bruhn, M. E. (2001). Metaphors and meaning: An intercultural analysis of the concept of teamwork. *Administrative Quarterly Science, 46*(2), 274–306. doi:10.2307/2667088

Haynes, A. S. (2019). Reaching Diverse Learners by Offering Different Course Delivery Methods. In R. Jeffries (Ed.), *Diversity, Equity, and Inclusivity in Contemporary Higher Education* (pp. 34–55). IGI Global. doi:10.4018/978-1-5225-5724-1.ch003

Hofstede, G. (2001). *Culture's consequences: Comparing values, behaviours, institutions and organizations across nations.* Sage.

Kwao, A., Torto, G., Ackah-Jnr, F. R., & John, A. (2021). Speak English, Don't Speak Vernacular. Language Culture and Practice, and Policy Implications in Schools. *Advances in Social Sciences Research Journal, 8*(5), 617–629. doi:10.14738/assrj.85.10202

Lauand, L. J. (1995, December). *Anthropology and Education: Two Speeches - Memory & Education / Proverbs and the Sense of Concrete. Part I – Memory and Education* [Paper presentation]. Graduation Ceremony at Faculdade de Educação da Universidade de São Paulo, Brazil. http://hottopos.com/harvard1/memory.htm

Lauand, L. J. (1998, April). *Anthropology and Education: Two Speeches – Memory & Education / Proverbs and the Sense of Concrete. Part II – Proverbs and the Sense of the Concrete: the Basis of the Arab Education* [Paper presentation]. Universidad Autónoma de Madrid, Spain. http://hottopos.com/harvard1/memory.htm

Lee, S., & Wu, C.-H. (2021). Determinants of Consumption Behaviors of Korean Pop Culture in Taiwan. *International Journal of Asian Business and Information Management, 12*(3), 1–22. doi:10.4018/IJABIM.20210701.oa28

Lee, S. J., & Nuatomue, J. N. (2021). Students' Perceived Difficulty and Satisfaction in Face-to-Face vs. Online Sections of a Technology-Intensive Course. *International Journal of Distance Education Technologies, 19*(3), 1–13. doi:10.4018/IJDET.2021070101

Lewis, R. D. (1996). When Cultures Collide: Leading across cultures. Nicholas Brealey International.

Liao, X. (2020). Developing domestic students' intercultural competence – a case study: Immersion program of Sichuan University, China. In M. Carmo (Ed.), *Proceedings of the International Conference Education and New Developments – END 2020* (pp. 203-207). InScience Press. 10.36315/2020end044

Lock, D. (2013). *Project Management* (10th ed.). Gower.

Lopez, L. (2001). *Moglie e buoi... Escursione di uno storico nel mondo dei proverbi*. Rivista Abruzzese.

Lyons, M. (2013). *Books. A Living History*. Thames & Hudson.

Maganello, F., Pozzi, F., Passarelli, M., Persico, D., & Dagnino, F. M. (2021). A Dashboard to Monitor Self-Regulated Learning Behaviours in Online Professional Development. *International Journal of Distance Education Technologies*, *19*(1), 18–34. doi:10.4018/IJDET.2021010102

Marou, H. I. (1948). *Histoire de l'Education dans l'Antiquité*. Editions du Seuil.

Mawr, E. B. (1885). *Analogous proverbs in Ten Languages*. Paternoster.

McAlister-Shields, L., Hutchison, L., & Jones, B. E. (2019). Teaching Through Culture: The Case for Culturally Responsive Teaching in American Higher Education Institutions. In R. Jeffries (Ed.), *Diversity, Equity, and Inclusivity in Contemporary Higher Education* (pp. 88–107). IGI Global. doi:10.4018/978-1-5225-5724-1.ch006

Mieder, W. (1983). *Proverbs Are Never Out of Season: Popular Wisdom in the Modern Age*. Oxford University Press.

Mieder, W. (2003). *Proverbs and Social Sciences: An Annotated International Bibliography*. Schneider Verlag Hohengehren.

Mieder, W. (2008). "Proverbs Speak Louder than Words". Folk Wisdom in Art, Culture, Folklore, History, Literature, and Mass Media. Peter Lang. doi:10.3726/978-1-4539-0386-5

Podder, S. K., & Samanta, D. (2022). Green Computing Practice in ICT-Based Methods: Innovation in Web-Based Learning and Teaching Technologies. *International Journal of Web-Based Learning and Teaching Technologies*, *17*(4), 1–20. doi:10.4018/IJWLTT.285568

Ramos, D. B., Monteverde Martins Ramos, I., Gasparini, I., & Harada Teixeira de Oliveira, E. (2021). A New Learning Path Model for E-Learning Systems. *International Journal of Distance Education Technologies*, *19*(2), 34–54. doi:10.4018/IJDET.20210401.oa2

Riché, P. (1978). *Education and culture in the Barbarian West: From the Sixth through the Eighth Century*. University of South Carolina Press.

Ruffle, J. (1995). The Teaching of Amenemope and its Connection with the Book of Proverbs. In R. B. Zuck (Ed.), *Learning from Sages: Studies on the Book of Proverbs* (pp. 293–331). Baker Books.

Salamone, F. A. (1976). The arrow and the bird: Proverbs in the solution of Hausa conjugal conflicts. *Journal of Anthropological Research*, *32*(4), 358–371. doi:10.1086/jar.32.4.3630022

Salicrú i Lluch, R. (2008). Crossing Boundaries in Late Medieval Mediterranean Iberia: Historical Glimpses of Christian-Islamic Intercultural Dialogue. *International Journal of Euro-Mediterranean Studies*, *1*(1).

Scarlat, C. (2007). Teaching decision-making process through proverb cases: 12 Romanian proverbs. In *Proceedings of the Eighth International Conference on Operational & Quantitative Management (ICOQM-8): "Emerging Perspectives of Decision Making in a New Globalized World: Theory, Practice and Future Directions"* (pp. 400-406). Academic Press.

Scarlat, C. (2008a). Entrepreneurship and management in Romanians' proverbs. *UPB Scientific Bulletin, Series D, 70*(1), 13–22.

Scarlat, C. (2008b). Learning Business, Management, and Entrepreneurship by Proverb Cases: 21 Romanian Proverbs. *SPACE Journal Advances in Higher Education, 1*(1), 77–88.

Scarlat, C. (2013). Project Management Skills. Lecture notes. 2008 – 2014. Mikkeli University of Applied Sciences.

Scarlat, C. (2014). Proverbele: sinteză a experienţei de viaţă şi lecţiilor învăţate din managementul proiectelor [Proverbs: a synthesis of life-experience and lessons learnt on project management. In Managementul Proiectelor [Project Management] (pp. 135-160). Ed. Printech.

Scarlat, C. (2015). *Cartea cu proverbe de management* [The Book with Management Proverbs]. Ed. Printech.

Scarlat, C. (2016). Project Management. Lecture notes. 2013 – 2016. Karel de Grote University College.

Scarlat, C. (2019). *O sută de proverbe ale Românilor pentru 100 de ani de management modern* [One hundred Romanians' proverbs for 100 years of modern management]. Ed. Niculescu.

Scarlat, C. (2020). Communication Revolutions that Marked the History of Education. Proverbs in Education – Theses and Paradoxes. In M. Carmo (Ed.), *Proceedings of the International Conference Education and New Developments – END 2020* (pp. 266-270). InScience Press.

Scarlat, C. (2021). Today's Higher Education at a Crossroads. The Critical Point and Paradigm Shift in the Educator's Role. In M. Carmo (Ed.), Education Applications & Developments, Advances in Education and Educational Trends Series (pp. 265-277). InScience Press.

Scarlat, C., & Afendras, E. (2007, October). *Precursors to 21st Century 'Global' Business Management: Proverbial expressions from the Balkans* [Paper presentation]. Twelfth Annual AUSACE International Conference: "Communication at the Crossroad of Globalization", Dubai, UAE.

Scarlat, C., & Afendras, E. (2008, November). *Proverb Culture in Balkans – Communication Bridge between the Arabic Wisdom and Western Modern Management* [Paper presentation]. Thirteenth Annual AUSACE International Conference "Best Communication Practices in an Interconnected World", Richmond, VA, United States.

Scarlat, C., & Albuquerque, A. (2009). Business, management and entrepreneurship in Romanian and Portuguese proverbs. *SPACE Journal Advances in Higher Education, 2*(1), 121–134.

Scarlat, C., & Kasim, A. (2008, December). *Bridging the gap between Asian and European cultures through common proverb metaphors – in order to facilitate the business communication and international business* [Paper presentation]. The International Conference on International Studies (ICIS): "The Asia Pacific Region: Contemporary Trends and Challenges", Kuala Lumpur, Malaysia.

Scarlat, C., Panduru, D. A., & Stănciulescu, G. D. (2021). COVID-19 Pandemic: Threat, Opportunity or Accelerator? From Strategy Accelerator to Digital Acceleration. In *Proceedings of the 38th IBIMA (International Business Information Management Association) International Conference*. IBIMA Publishing. https://www.ibimapublishing.com

Scarlat, C., & Pavan, E. (2011). Is It the Same Old Story? It Is the Modern Business Management! In C. Jayachandran & S. Seshadri (Eds.), *Proceedings of the Twelfth International Conference of the Society for Global Business & Economic Development SGBED 2011: "Building Capabilities for Sustainable Global Business: Balancing Corporate Success & Social Good"* (pp. 830-839). Academic Press.

Scarlat, C., & Petrişor, A.-I. (2021). Old Proverbs for a Future Sustainable Development: An environmental management perspective. *Present Environment and Sustainable Development Journal, 15*(1), 93–107. doi:10.15551/pesd2021151008

Scarlat, C., & Stănciulescu, G. D. (2021). Covid-19 Pandemic: Threat or Accelerator? The Case of Romanian Book Publishing Industry. In M. Al Haziazi, A. Al Hajri, K. P. Subramanian, & S. Muthuraman (Eds.), Co-creating the Post COVID-19 World: Exploring Sustainable Paths (pp. 83-98). Arab Open University.

Scarlat, C., & Taatila, V. (2009, February). *Transcending the geographical borders through business management and entrepreneurship metaphors: Romanian and Finnish proverbs* [Paper presentation]. The Third International Conference on "Transcending Horizons through Innovative Practices", Indore, India.

Sharma, S., & Bumb, A. (2021). The Challenge Faced in Technology-Driven Classes during COVID-19. *International Journal of Distance Education Technologies, 19*(1), 66–88. doi:10.4018/IJDET.20210101.oa2

Smothers, T. (2000). Biblical Wisdom in its Ancient Middle Eastern Context. In M. E. Tate, H. W. Ballard, & D. W. Tucker (Eds.), *An Introduction to Wisdom Literature and the Psalms*. Mercer University Press.

Tannen, D. (1981). Health to Our Mouths: Formulaic Expressions in Turkish and Greek. In F. Coulmas (Ed.), *Conversational Routine* (pp. 37–54). Mouton. doi:10.1515/9783110809145.37

Tate, M. E., Ballard, H. W., & Tucker, D. W. (Eds.). (2000). *An Introduction to Wisdom Literature and the Psalms*. Mercer University Press.

Taylor, F. W. (1911). *The Principles of Scientific Management*. Harper and Brothers.

Tucker, W. D. (2000). Literary Forms in the Wisdom Literature. In M. E. Tate, H. W. Ballard, & D. W. Tucker (Eds.), *An Introduction to Wisdom Literature and the Psalms*. Mercer University Press.

Veryaeva, K., & Solovyeva, O. (2021). The Influence of Gamification and Platform Affordances on User Engagement in Online Learning. *International Journal of Distance Education Technologies, 19*(1), 1–17. doi:10.4018/IJDET.2021010101

Wang, X. W., Riaz, M., Haider, S., Alam, K. M., & Yang, M. (2021). Information Sharing on Social Media by Multicultural Individuals: Experiential, Motivational, and Network Factors. *Journal of Global Information Management, 29*(6), 1–25. doi:10.4018/JGIM.20211101.oa22

Wei, L., & Mayouf, M. A. (2009). The effects of the social status of the elderly in Libya on the way they institutionally interact and communicate with younger physicians. *Journal of Pragmatics*, *41*(1), 136–146. doi:10.1016/j.pragma.2008.09.001

Zhou, Y. (2021). How Chinese Multinational Corporations Solve Cross-cultural Conflicts in Internationalization - A Case Study of SAIC's Merging of Ssangyong Motor. *Advances in Social Sciences Research Journal*, *8*(5), 137–156. doi:10.14738/assrj.85.10181

ADDITIONAL READING

Erdogan, N., & Wei, M. (Eds.). (2019). *Applied Linguistics for Teachers of Culturally and Linguistically Diverse Learners*. IGI Global. doi:10.4018/978-1-5225-8467-4

Jeffries, R. (Ed.). (2019). *Diversity, Equity, and Inclusivity in Contemporary Higher Education*. IGI Global. doi:10.4018/978-1-5225-5724-1

Mieder, W. (1993). *International Proverb Scholarship: An Annotated Bibliography, with supplements*. Garland Publishing.

Mieder, W. (2009). *International Bibliography of Paremiology and Phraseology* (Vols. 1–2). Walter de Gruyter.

Mieder, W., & Litovkina, A. T. (1999). *Twisted Wisdom: Modern Anti-Proverbs*. The University of Vermont.

KEY TERMS AND DEFINITIONS

Ex Ante **Project Evaluation:** A phase of the project lifecycle, and a type of project evaluation, which consists of assessing the quality of the project planning *before* the implementation phase. See also: *Project Lifecycle*.

Ex Post **Project Evaluation:** A phase of the project lifecycle, and a type of project evaluation, which consists of assessing the quality of the project implementation *after* the implementation phase. See also: *Project Lifecycle*.

Paremiology: The study of proverbs and collections of proverbs. *Paremiology* should not be confused with *Paremiography* which is collecting proverbs and writing about them.

Project Implementation: A phase of the project lifecycle consisting of fulfilling the planned activities in order to accomplish the project purpose. See also: *Project Lifecycle*.

Project Lifecycle: The time elapsed from the moment a need is identified and intended to be addressed and solved (call this need 'problem') until the moment this problem is completely solved – which is the project purpose. The project lifecycle is composed of several phases: problem identification and definition; feasibility phase; project planning; *ex ante* evaluation; implementation; *ex post* evaluation. Another name for 'project lifecycle' is 'project life span'.

Project Monitoring: A principle of project management consisting of continuously controlling the process of project implementation; it is the responsibility of the project manager. See also: *Project Implementation.*

Stage-Gate: A principle of project management that refers to applying the technique of *stages* and corresponding *gates* during the phase of project planning (project design); this technique is to divide the process of planning in suitable stages, in order to check the quality of the work done in each stage, by gates; a gate is a checking and decision point (usually scientific committee, in which stakeholders are represented).

Teaching by Proverbs: The systematic style and manner of teaching abstract concepts using the proverbs as a teaching aid under the form of illustrative examples – still metaphoric but in common language. The use of proverbs does not replace or compete with other educational methods and/or technologies.

APPENDIX 1

Table 5 displays eight Romanian proverbs with large circulation, written in their current Romanian orthography – that illustrate the respective principles of managing projects. They are translated both word-by-word as well as meaning.

Table 5. Romanian proverbs which illustrate the project management principles, respectively

No.	Project management principles	Illustrative Romanian proverb	Word-for-word translation	Free translation of the proverb's meaning
1	**One Project Objective** (Uniqueness of the project purpose/ objective)	*Nu poţi ţine doi pepeni într-o mână*	*Can't hold two watermelons in one hand*	Cannot hold two; if try, both fail and break, as watermelons do! One withstands. [*i.e.*] One objective only (the project purpose). If try several, the project fails.
2	**One Project Manager** (Uniqueness of the project manager)	*Nu poţi sluji la doi stăpâni deodată*	*Can't serve two masters at once*	Having two masters simultaneously means confusion: which one to obey? [*i.e.*] Any project should have a project manager and only one – to report to.
3	**Project Team**	*Nu poţi aplauda cu o singură mână*	*Can't applaud with just one hand*	Applauding is, by definition, involving both hands, moving coherently together. [*i.e.*] Working in a project means coherently working together as team/s.
4	**Project Hierarchy**	*Orice naş îşi are naşul*	*Any godfather has his/her godfather*	A network of godfathers' godfathers (and so on) generates a hierarchy; The Godfather sits on top of this hierarchy. [*i.e.*] Project hierarchy means that each person involved has a unique direct supervisor; and this one reports to hers/ his; and so on, up to the Project Manager.
5	**Design (planning) *versus* Implementation**	*Judecă şi apoi vorbeşte*	*Judge and then speak*	It is rational and wise behaviour to speak (decide and act) only after judging (analyzing) all possible options. [*i.e.*] Concrete, practical implementation of the project can start only after completing the design (planning) phase.
6	**'Stage-Gate' Principle**	*Graba strică treaba*	*Hurry spoils the job*	When in a hurry for doing things, it is possible to make costly mistakes. [*i.e.*] Design of the project has 'gates' after each 'stage' – to identify possible flaws and fix them; otherwise, the design flaws lead to project failure ultimately.
7	**Project Monitoring**	*Ochiul stăpânului îngraşă vita*	*The master's eye fattens the cow*	To raise healthy livestock involves master's continuous supervision. [*i.e.*] A good project management involves controlling (monitoring).
8	**Project Evaluation**	*Toamna se numără bobocii*	*In autumn the ducklings are counted*	The result of farming (raising) ducks should be counted by autumn only – by the time ducklings become adult ducks. [*i.e.*] Project results should be evaluated after the project is fully implemented.

Source: (Scarlat, 2014; 2015; 2019)

APPENDIX 2

Table 6 displays examples of proverbs in several languages – with similar meaning – that illustrate three principles of project management. An explorative study indicates that these principles, along monitoring and evaluation, have the largest representation in popular representation. They are translated both word-by-word as well as meaning.

Table 6. Examples of similar proverbs in more languages – illustrating project management principles

Principles of project management	Illustrative proverb	Native language	Translation
One Project Objective (Uniqueness of the project purpose/ objective)	*Man kann nicht zwei Fliegen mit einer Klapper schlagen*	German	Can't catch two flies in one try
	Ba yek dast nemishe dota hendoone bardasht	Persian	Can't hold two watermelons in one hand
	Nu poţi ţine doi pepeni într-o mână	Romanian	Can't hold two watermelons in one hand
	За много дел не берись, а в одном отличись	Russian	Don't start doing several things at once; just a single one and excel
	一心不能二用	Mandarin Chinese	Don't even try do two different things at once
		Armenian	Can't crack two walnuts with a stone
		Arabic	The dog barking at two doors starves
One Project Manager (Uniqueness of the project manager)	*Two legs do not fit in a boot*	English	
		Turkish	Two helmsmen sink the boat
	사공이 많으면 배가 산으로 간다	Korean	Many helmsmen end the boat up on the rocks
	Viele Köche verderben den Brei	German	Many chefs spoil the soup
	Когда пастухов много, барана волк съест	Russian	When there are too many shepherds, sheep will be eaten by the wolf
	Nu încap două săbii într-o teacă şi nici doi domni într-o ţară săracă	Romanian	There is no room for two swords in a sheath, or two rulers in a poor country
	一山不能藏二虎	Chinese (HK)	There is no room for two tigers on a single mountain
'Stage-Gate' Principle	*Mai bine să întrebi, decât să te rătăceşti*	Romanian	Better ask for directions, rather than get lost
	Besser zweimal fragen, als einmal irregehen	German	Better ask for directions twice, rather than take the wrong way just once
	三思而後行	Chinese (HK)	Think three times before starting
	Трипут мери, једном сеци *Triput meri, jednom seci*	Serbian	Measure three times and cut once
	Три пъти мери, веднъж режи	Bulgarian	Measure three times, and cut once
	Yot ankam chaphi mi ankam ktri / Յոթ անգամ չափիր մի անգամ կտրիր	Armenian	Measure seven times before cutting once
		Turkish	Measure thousand times and cut once

Source: (Scarlat, 2014; 2015)

APPENDIX 3

Set of photos of multicultural project teams of variable size, working on assignments associated to the Project Management course, at *Karel de Grote University College, Antwerp, Belgium* (Figure 2: teams of three, November 2013; Figure 3: teams of four, November 2014) & *Mikkeli University of Applied Sciences*, Finland (Figure 4: teams of five, September 2010; Figure 5: teams of six, September 2011).

Figure 2.

Figure 3.

Figure 4.

Figure 5.

Figure 6. Class of international students by the end of the Project Management Skills course, at University of Applied Sciences, Mikkeli, Finland, September 2011
Source: All photos are from Author's own collection

Chapter 8
Pedagogizing International Students' Technical Knowledge Consumption

Syed Ali Nasir Zaidi
St. Clair College for AA&T, Canada

ABSTRACT

Although most Canadian university and college professors assume that international testing credentials such as IELTS, TOEFL, and CELPIP are suitable yardsticks to measure international students' language skills, the study presented in this chapter that adopted critical discourse analysis of international students' technical assignments suggests otherwise. Technical communication is different from cultural English, whereby the former measures students' technical skills in communicating highly scientific materials and cultural English may be used for interpersonal skills. The study used secondary data for data analysis and employed Bernstein's theoretical lens of elaborated code and restricted code. Findings revealed that 21st-century knowledge production, distribution, and its adequate reproduction are in the hands of well-rounded knowledge consumers in knowledge societies, and if the knowledge consumers are not well cognizant of their instrumental role in the knowledge economy owing to weak English language constructions, social inequalities will increase exponentially.

INTRODUCTION

International students have garnered much attention from educators, policy makers, and administrators of higher education institutions (Andrade, 2006), let alone the broader Canadian education community (Zhang & Zhou, 2010). Most international students arrive in Canada with well-established skill sets in their respective fields, and they are an important source of revenue for the Canadian education sector. For example, the Toronto—Waterloo corridor alone generated nearly 80,000 high-tech employment opportunities owing to the sheer dedication, innovative approaches, and technological prowess of highly dedicated international students (Wachsmuth & Kilfoil, 2021). However, the same international students became a

DOI: 10.4018/978-1-7998-8921-2.ch008

serious policy issue among policy makers, educators, and federal, provincial, and local politicians when such students are not accommodated professionally (Gopal, 2016; Sá & Sabzalieva, 2018). Some critics point to international students' poor communication skills as the cause of such policy disjunction, while others blame Canadian higher education systems. This chapter argues that some international students have poor technical communication skills because language-testing bodies such as the British Council, the American Cultural Center, and Immigration Canada evaluate only cultural English (Aina et al., 2013) even though English-speaking countries' higher education systems have become highly technical and industrialized (Andrade, 2006; Martinez, 2006). The most common language credentialing systems used by international students stem from International English Language Testing System (IELTS), Duolingo, the Canadian English Language Proficiency Index Program (CELPIP), and the Test of English as a Foreign Language (TOEFL). Although these gatekeeping language credentialing systems do provide thorough standardization, they do not facilitate the English-speaking language requirements nor address highly technical market trends (Martinez, 2006) needed by international students and more specifically a highly technical workforce. Most of these students are beleaguered because they bring poor language skills to their respective institutions of higher education (Zhou et al., 2021), resulting in an existential dilemma because of inappropriate language skills evaluated by language credentialing organizations (Hune-Brown, 2021) to meet highly demanding professional needs.

Almost all the language-testing credentialing administered by IELTS, TOFEL, and Duolingo revolves around cultural English needed to negotiate day-to-day social transactions (Freimuth, 2013). But the technical communication embedded in academic English and needed for survival in the highly tech-driven Canadian job market is diametrically opposite to what these international students expect from higher education institutions in Canada. On the one hand, it is highly technical and discipline specific; on the other hand, it demands very solid prior knowledge of the subject matter at hand. Technical language skills needed to survive, to innovate, and to thrive at any given workplace become crucial if these students lack technical knowledge (Caissie, 1978).

Similarly, international students' employment prospects are dependent on successful assimilation and integration of technical knowledge into highly demanding work environments (Sageev & Romanowski, 2001), which can be impacted significantly if the workforce of any given structure is not highly technical in its operational transactions and capacity (Mirel & Spilka, 2002). While most international students believe that successfully obtaining standardized language credentials from organizations such as IELTS, TOEFL, CELPIP, and Duolingo is sufficient, they do not understand the increasing and changing needs and demands of technical English in the Canadian labour market (Reave, 2004). For example, while digital sociology may have been unheard of 20 years ago, today it is an academically recognized phenomenon in an era of rapid digitization in academia. The same holds true for professions such as data analytics, machine learning, artificial intelligence, cryptocurrency, cyberspace, cybercrime cyber security, digital or computational social science, as well as epidemiology, with each discipline requiring high technical knowledge groundings not only in written but also in oral English communication (Harrison, 2011; National Academies of Sciences, Engineering, and Medicine, 2018).

Canadian higher education institutions accumulate annually exponential dividends by incorporating international students in the student body (Immigration, Refugees and Citizenship Canada, 2020; Rashed, 2017). Although international students can enter the workforce soon after graduation (Canadian Bureau for International Education, 2020; Choi et al., 2021), they are not likely to start their desired jobs beyond their work permits when they are on the verge of being deported (Hune-Brown, 2021). Herein lies the critical issue when international students' poor communication skills force them to do jobs other than their desired field of study—a loss to both Canada and the research-based knowledge economy. Students from China, India, Iran, and many other international destinations (Lewington, 2019; Scott et al., 2015) have joined graduate programs and obtained college diplomas, graduate certificates, and have completed English language programs but at the cost of innovation and research, which is a must for a knowledge economy like Canada (Goldring et al., 2009). Despite international students' advanced field-specific skills and competencies amassed in their home countries, they are unable to capitalize on the Canadian tech-driven market. Again, this chapter argues that the root cause of this issue is the technical communication gap and faculty members' assumptions that the students had properly acquired communication skills from language testing organizations. On the one hand, students are considered to be fluent in their field of studies due to their language assessment from International English Language Testing System (IELTS), Test of English as a Foreign Language, Canadian Language Benchmarks Placement (CLBPT), and Duolingo; on the other hand, they are opposite to what the myriad of international language assessment bodies such as IELTS, TOEFL, CLBPT, and Duolingo have evaluated (Willems & Gonzalez-DeHass, 2012).

RESEARCH PROBLEM

Too many international students are unable to integrate successfully in Canada's highly technical workplaces due to their poor technical communication skills. According to Martinez (2006), the world is going to be highly technical and Canada is no exception. Despite so many authentic English language testing bodies such as IELTS, TOEFL, CLBPT, and Duolingo and their rigorous gatekeeping credentialing, international students are seriously struggling (Hune-Brown, 2021) for better job opportunities in Canada. Here, this chapter argues that international students' English language skills are not technically appropriate, making them face hardships both academically and professionally. The author also argues that international testing systems have some structural problems (Willems & Gonzalez-DeHass, 2012). Moreover, complex ways of learning such as HyFlex, synchronous or asynchronous, flipped classrooms, or blended models have made even harder the lives of international students who have poor technical communication skills, which leave them unable to adopt innovative ways to understand the knowledge dissemination.

RESEARCH QUESTIONS

1. How do international students write, speak, read, and listen to the technical communication in the context of English?
2. How can faculty members address linguistically challenged students' concerns with regards to workplace success?
3. What language patterns do these international students use in the context of the sociology of education?
4. What are the implications of these behaviours on higher education?

LITERATURE REVIEW

The importance of the English language can not be denied in an age of globalization (Sawir, 2005). The global education migration industry is tapping the unprepared international students who turn to international education providers in hopes of finding better opportunities (Hune-Brown, 2021; Jackman et al. 2021). In this regard, internationalization of higher education is in a full swing and has become an integral part of institutional growth in Canada (Canadian Bureau for International Education, 2020; Qiang, 2003). For example, many Canadian institutions of higher education are completely dependent on internationalization projects to a point where annual institutional revenues are related directly to corporate success philosophy.

Similarly, international students arrived in Canada with English language testing scores in their hands. The following English testing systems evaluate international students: International English Language Testing System (IELTS), Duolingo, the Test of English as a Foreign Language (TOEFL), and the Canadian Language Benchmark Placement Test (CLBPT). International students assume that they have reached an apex in their language skills without knowing the harsh realities of competitive corporate economies. In addition, although they may feel prepared, they may not realize that they still may be unprepared in relation to poor grammar, weak communication, and deficient networking skills (Baas, 2019; Sawir, 2005). Students assume a role similar to a football in the educational industrial complex where complex systems present in the technologically advanced societies have taken undue advantage. Finally, Bernstein (1964) informs us that students with restricted codes cannot survive the sociological pressures in the event of developing restricted codes arising from low communication patterns (Singh, 2015).

METHODOLOGY

The author used Fairclough and Wodak's (1997) three-dimensional approach of critical discourse analysis (CDA) to explore the micro, meso, and macroscale of the professional, social, and societal exclusion of international students based on language patterns (Bernstein,1964)—more specifically, the structurally weak patterns of their technical English communication. The author used CDA as a methodological approach where grammar, intertextuality, vocabulary, content, and rhetorical structures and literary devices (Kobayashi, 2019) were closely evaluated in the context of technical communication.

The author employed CDA (Fairclough & Wodak, 1997; Van Dijk, 2015) as a research methodology to study the role of linguistics (Given, 2008) in technical communication classes and educational sociology (May & Hornberger, 2017). Some researchers explore social issues via CDA, others unearth power relations between groups, and a great many extrapolate narratives through employment of metadata and secondary data from nuances present in society and culture under the researcher's critical microscope (Given, 2008). In this connection, the author has analyzed 50 international students' assignments submitted on Flipgrid, Blackboard, Zoom presentations, and Microsoft Word and PowerPoint artefacts.

The researcher kept the ethical considerations for this research via confidentiality and anonymity by not linking any assignment or Flipgrid video footage to the study (Panel on Research Ethics, 2018) and removing students' names from assignments and randomly selected names via multiple technologies and applications where it may prompt readers to relate whatsoever to the study (Panel on Research Ethics, 2018). For example, Blackboard randomizes the names of the students via a group-making tab. Similarly, Blackboard also anonymized discussion posts so no one can identify the names of students. Moreover, the researcher also asked students to anonymize documents by only recording their voice versions as opposed to video recording. The principal investigator was even unable to see the names of students on their assignments, which provided an extra layer of anonymity for metadata and its interpretation through the lens of CDA in this study.

Gee (2011) maintains that CDA "treat[s] social practices, not just in terms of social relationships, but also in terms of their implications for things like status, solidarity, the distribution of social goods and power" (p. 28). Moreover, the researcher did investigate 50 international students' assignments through the lens of CDA. The researcher randomly chose the assignments in technical communication classes taught in a college.

CDA is mostly used in journalism but underused in the field of education. Most recently, educational researchers started using CDA in the sociolinguistic and linguistic evaluation of student communication patterns (Rogers, 2011). Key figures in the "ethnography of communication" paradigm have written extensively about how language differences cause social inequalities (e.g., Cazden et al., 1970; Cook-Gumperz, 1986; Gumperz & Hymes, 1986; Hymes, 1980). Interestingly, Labov (1972) illuminated the notion that "nonstandard speakers were somehow linguistically deficient" (p. x), resulting in issues of social inequalities.

The researcher used Flipgrid, Zoom, and Blackboard assignments of 50 international students, mainly from India, China, Nigeria, and Iran. The study evaluated their writing, speaking, reading, and listening skills to scrutinize their assignments solely written in English. Here, the researcher used randomized secondary data as the first evaluation point, barring issues of Research Ethics Board approval for the current study. The study employed CDA on technical communication of these international students on writing, reading, and speaking assignments. The study used metadata of students' assignments as a secondary data source by employing CDA as a research methodology to construct themes from 50 international students' assignments, Flipgrid videos, and Zoom presentation videos submitted for grading for their technical communication and English communication courses

RESULTS

The researcher used CDA for data analysis (Fairclough & Wodak, 1997; Flick, 2014) and adopted a Bernsteinian lens of elaborated code and restricted code (Bernstein, 1964). The findings reveal that international students' poor technical communication skills coupled with deficiencies in writing, speaking, and reading are a matter of great concern. It was also noted that international students are not fully aware that: (a) technical English is different from cultural English; (b) both cultural and technical communication skills are needed to survive either postsecondary tenure or in the professional market; and (c) competencies such as understanding of technical communication, assignments, official emails, workplace ethical issues, and networking are the most critical skills other than academic skills to survive in the competitive higher education environment.

Writing

Upon critical analysis of metadata available through writing assignments of international students, it appeared that they are unable to write well enough the technical pieces that may expand their subject knowledge. In this connection, their grammatical structures and syntax comprehension encompass weak sentences, so much so that they are sometimes incapable of producing assignments correctly. The following themes emerged from the analysis of writing assignments.

Inability to Connect Operations

For most international students, technical writing assignments was not a palatable activity because they were not creative enough (giving them some room for writing whatever they wanted) nor were they able to produce a sufficiently descriptive document of a technical nature. Most technical writing assignments were verbal illustrations of devices. For example, the international students' writing texts show that they were unable to connect thoughts coherently. The lack of transition words (e.g., firstly, secondly, thirdly; however; moreover; in conclusion) shows their mental processes are not aware of systematic breakdown and coherent writing approaches. Moreover, well-coordinated sentences heavily capitalize upon transition words to bring more logical connection to the text, prompting the readers to flow smoothly from one topic to another (Slack et al., 1993). In addition, extensive evaluation of the writing text provides solid evidence that although testing credentials such as IELTS, TOEFL, and CELPIP may be good options to segue them into more technical writing tasks, such language testing exams should not be viewed as sufficient yardsticks for technical courses such as engineering design, computer science, and artificial intelligence.

The most interesting aspect of these international students' writing appeared paradoxical when they spoke fluent English but at the expense of technical jargon. Although explanation of technical knowledge should be transparent and visually clear, international students were contrary to what has been assumed in academia. Furthermore, it is writing that helped them gain greater command over technical aspect of their professional lives (Wall, 1943)

Weak Cognitive Structures

The evaluation of technical workplace writing tasks further revealed that most international students were unable to engage technically with the technical texts, developing weak cognitive structures in their minds (Gibbs, 1995). What this means is that their cognitive abilities such as reasoning, evaluation, problem-solving, and decision-making were of no relevance to the tasks at hand. Communicating technically with the given texts stems from well-established metamemory and metacomprehension (Martinez, 2006). When the researcher evaluated their technical description portfolios, it was obvious that poor meaning making in terms of technical knowledge was lacking in coherent thought processes. These incoherent thoughts that international students used further revealed that their mind is unable to read the given technical data statistically and analytically as highly technical professionals may use and exploit the same given data at their workplace to their utmost advantage. Similarly, the students were not able to interpret highly technical data for these technical reports, so much so that they were not finding knowledge gaps in the critical analysis of the two products they were given to analyze as a recommendation report for an imaginary employer.

Poor Command Over Organization

The textual production by international students lacked some basic organizational rules for technical writing. Their grammatical error analysis was poorly constructed. For example, the researcher asked them to edit some content of a major technical report. Students mostly were at a loss to edit the simple document. Grammatical errors were overlooked, resulting in a poor-quality document. Grammatical and punctuation errors, spelling mistakes, and the design of the formal report showed that most students would face severe problems if they were tasked with the development of technical documents at a workplace owing to their inadequate formatting skills.

Speaking

When writing is poor, the resultant impact will be on speaking which consequently builds upon language chunks accumulated slowly and gradually (Chafe & Tannen, 1987). The researcher evaluated Flipgrid oral communication assignments through the lens of CDA and found that these students' background knowledge is insufficient to a point where they exhaust all their articulatory channels (Riemer, 2007) whereby their thoughts are either inconsistent, cursive, or baseless, leaving a huge gap to fill in their cognitive structures. In this connection, the themes discussed in this section stemmed from the analysis of Flipgrid assignments submitted for oral communication grades. The researcher applied a technique of self-evaluation and debriefing on international students' Flipgrid tasks whereby students had submitted assignments by self-criticizing their homework. The researcher listened to these recordings to observe the linguistic strengths in their oral communication. Following themes came from the evaluation.

Inapt Technical Communication

The researcher gave the students some prompts based on technical description of products such as pulse oximeter, digital caliper, and digital micrometer. The engineering students were asked to describe these tools for technical-description assignment purposes. Almost all international students mechanically regurgitated facts at the cost of finding some gaps in these products. Their spoken language was dependent on the object's straightforward description rather than problem-solving mechanics of these products. In addition, they were not able to handle the technical aspect of these products (Donnell et al., 2011). For example, when the researcher asked engineering students to explain vividly the exploded diagram, almost all engineering students were at a loss either due to deficient product knowledge or it was because almost all students had not used those mechanical products in their home countries (such as India, Nigeria, China, and Iran).

Lack of Content Knowledge

When the researcher asked international students to explain content knowledge via a Flipgrid oral assignment, most of the students were not aware of the discipline-related concepts, theories, and principles, raising a question about their prior knowledge base or schema. Although most of these students had prior engineering degrees from their home countries, their irrelevance was apparent from their communication patterns. For example, when the international students were asked to explain certain sophisticated soldering robots that do repeatable routine work, none of them were able to touch upon the delicacy and subtlety of the custom program. When the researcher evaluated the reason behind this lack of information via another Flipgrid assignment (Yong & Ashman, 2019), the international students' assignment revealed that they lacked information around the given topic. Even these students were unaware of the basic engineering design which may be attributed to the fact that they were not taught the same advance concepts in their home countries.

Highly Layman Language

Engineering students' prior knowledge flows from the fundamentals such as mathematics, design principles, and physics, to name only a few (Derr et al., 2018). It was opposite to what most international students presented in their oral communication assignment through the Flipgrid application. They did not touch upon the critical areas that needed clarification and a clear thought process. Moreover, their language structures were vacuous in terms of content, context, trigger, and structures. Most of the international students used either culturally induced English such as slang or colloquialisms in their oral assignments. Technical English is not about phonology but rather about vocabulary, pragmatics, and discourse (Ibbotson, 2009), which any successful engineering students must acquire during their engineering tenure.

Insufficient Technical Vocabulary

The Flipgrid assignment also revealed that most international students had an insufficient technical vocabulary base. Here it is important to note that the researcher assessed international students via Flipgrid assignment as to how they use some prefixes, infixes, and suffixes to coin new engineering words for exploring the product's functionality, usability, accessibility, durability, and design. Ninety-five percent of these students' oral communication assignments either plagiarized the concepts or communicated that the assignment is incomprehensibly difficult. Instead of using logical replies on vocabulary assignments, students communicated the concepts that had not matched the assignment rubrics.

Thought Inconsistencies

Most international students showed poor intellectual coordination of their technical knowledge, so much so that their whole Zoom presentations were out of context. For example, the researcher gave students a topic of "Communication Barriers in Canadian Workplace" (Adler et al., 2016). Most of the students touched upon the superficial meaning of the given topic where their sentence structures displayed little to almost no proficiency in the content knowledge of the topic. Here the researcher also evaluated the Flipgrid speaking assignments of international students. These assignments also indicated their cognitive dissonance to a great extent while maintaining their communication patterns in technical communication speaking presentations.

According to Dawson (1999), people show cognitive dissonance when they experience an existential crisis that they are unable to deal with. Here it should be a question of extreme concern for higher education administrators and policy makers to identify what these international students may face in what Hune-Brown (2021) deems higher education's "shadowy business of international students."

Notwithstanding the thought inconsistencies observed in their Zoom and Flipgrid assignments, these students' command over technical communication and knowledge was deeply questionable as they were evaluated by international language testing bodies nominated internationally as standardized gatekeepers for competitive criteria for Canadian universities.

Reading

The researcher designed a reading test on Blackboard and analyzed the responses. Although the reading questions were multiple choice, the measurement of reading comprehension was qualitative (Oded & Walters, 2001) where verbal competencies of these international students were measured on five highly technical passages. The researcher excerpted the five technical passages from engineering books (Abdulla & Kumar, 2016). The following themes emerged from the evaluation of reading assignments.

Unfamiliarity With Deep Context

The processing of reading comprehension was contextualized with the international students' speaking Flipgrid assignment and Zoom presentations. Almost all international students showed poor comprehension skills of these technical reading passages. The problem may be attributed to thought inconsistencies or unfamiliarity with context (Clements, 2007). In other words, if students had no prior knowledge, their cognition may not evolve resulting in metacognition in language skills such as speaking, writing, listening, or reading. According to Nan (2018), there is a very deep connection between all these English language skills in the constructive making of English language learners. If one skill is poor, it would have indirect or indirect poor reflection on the rest of the language skills. For example, students cannot show good command over the content knowledge of the scientific discipline if they are poor in speaking and excellent in reading and writing, because writing stems from integrating all other language skills.

Lack of Metacognition

As mentioned earlier, reading comprehension was a critical issue around highly technical comprehension topics. International students appeared to lack deep cognitive structures around the relevant topic and their prior knowledge base was insufficient to answer highly technical analysis on chosen topics.

It was assumed that the way international students answered their questions could flow from superficial perspectives on engineering knowledge. The researcher gave two reading comprehension tasks to evaluate students' prior knowledge on topics such as pulse oximeter and laser distance measurement. Similarly, these two reading tasks were connected to writing and speaking whereby students had to write short answers. These reading, speaking, and writing tasks correlated where mastery over one task means that one could have mastery over another. It was noted via reading comprehension error analysis that there was asymmetry in their grades. Some students did good in writing whereas some did good in reading but neither outperformed in either of the tasks. It could mean that they had cognitive deficiency leading to the weak metacognition or cognition was not well-established around highly technical topics. They were unable to extrapolate on given topics so much so that they did not forecast upcoming speaking tasks.

The researcher also evaluated secondary reading assignment data through Blackboard where international students' learning experience in the past could be blamed because not having enough knowledge around technical topics could result from lack of prior interaction with relevant pieces. In addition, international students were also given open textbook timed reading quizzes in the computer labs. Some did good whereas some were completely unable to do these highly technical comprehension tasks.

DISCUSSION

Bernstein (1964) maintained that students with elaborated codes make longer sentences, use complex language, elaborate more, and plan circumstantially, whereas students with restricted codes have unplanned discursive knowledge dissemination, produce weak educational materials, lack background information, and are poor interlocutors (Apple, 1995).

Most university or college faculty members assume that international students come with authentic international testing credentials such as IELTS, CELPIP, and TOFEL. Here, it is important to note that the international students have serious technical English communication barriers as this study reveals, which was also indicated by their lack of technical communication patterns used in speaking, writing, and reading assignments (Arkoudis et al., 2009). One the one hand, they were able to culturally communicate sound English; on the other hand, they had troublesome experiences in explaining simple technical pieces (Morais, 2002). For example, the individual presentation tasks assigned to present technical devices on Flipgrid turned out to be crucial because almost all international students completed the 5-minute activity in as few as 2 or 3 minutes (the average presentation time was 2 minutes 30 seconds). Most international students were completely aware of the criticality of the tasks because they were advised to follow guided instructions.

Deficiency in reading comprehension of international students (Bernstein, 2001, 2019) shows that either their English language experiences were limited in their home countries or they were unable to establish deep connections with reading texts, resulting in uncritical knowledge consumption and consequently low skills and deficient entrepreneurial flair, as Wright (2008) argues.

Most international students were unaware of the technical jargon around the topics. The researcher gave another Flipgrid assignment to self-evaluate their language performance. Almost all international students explained these tasks in simple plain English without bothering about the technical aspect and surmised that the Flipgrid activities were the hardest, exposing their technical communication weaknesses to a great extent. Furthermore, the Flipgrid assignment shed more light on their "technical communication barriers" (Song, 2019) in highly technical workplaces. According to Sakamoto et al. (2010), Canadian workplaces are fast-paced, intense, and highly technical. If a worker is slow in communication, he or she may stall not only production lines but also the overall work environment due to their incompatible workplace behaviour needed to creatively energize production (Hackett & Kline, 1998).

When the researcher assessed international students' Zoom group presentations, it appeared that they lacked coordination skills or logistical awareness, leaving them vulnerable in the Canadian fast-paced work environment. The reason behind Zoom presentations was multifold, such as teaching them virtual coordination skills, developing their technical conversation skills, evolving their metacognition (Martinez, 2006), and finally helping them navigate a technical workplace environment. Factually, their cognitive structures lack metacognition (Martinez, 2006) that could assist them in highly loaded topics at work. However, they were able to fully explain cultural topics of some relevance in their Zoom presentation assignments. Similarly, it can be noted that these students' ways of knowledge transfer are not technical enough to meet demanding employment opportunities in a Canadian economy that is globally transformative and locally competitive (Arthur & Flynn, 2011).

Most data on the Flipgrid speaking assignment indicate that international students' cognitive structures are not wired technically to create fresh knowledge perspectives on any given products via class assignments. For example, when the researcher asked students to explain highly technical and course-relevant exploded diagrams of some specific products used in the industry, their explanations had little technical relevance resulting in more knowledge gaps in their minds and low-level knowledge structures for highly competitive economies such as Canada (Figel, 2006).

That assignment was designed to be presented on the Flipgrid app. Evaluation of the Flipgrid assignment revealed that most of these students were unable to extrapolate products clearly in relation to product deficiencies, so much so that they either submitted 5-minute assignments halfway or in just under 2 minutes. Here it was notable that their English language skills were good but not technical enough to land a job in a highly technical workplace environment. In addition, international students' focus on course material is not conducive to innovating something new for the knowledge economy such as Canada. Most international students appeared to have not been involved in proper assessment since their plain and simple speaking language skills may be good to meet temporary economy job demands (e.g., Walmart, call center jobs) but not enough to innovate something new for the knowledge hungry, capitalist Canadian economy.

Similarly, the researcher also asked via Flipgrid assignment from international students to expand on the topics related to market economy. Almost all were unable to understand the complex phraseology employed by the researcher for their basic technical assignment; their communication patterns stemmed either from colloquial English or non-technical jargon needed to survive in the workplace environment. Here Bernstein's (1964) critical views on poor communication skills of students can be replicated for international students who are devoid of Bernsteinian elaborated codes needed to survive in capitalist economies such as Canada.

The critical evaluation of students' Flipgrid assignment further reveals that if international students had not been directed in terms of technical English, they may have failed during the course of action (Hune-Brown, 2021). Moreover Bernstein (2001) also indicated that students from low-income households produce less complicated and poorly articulated sentences. The same holds true for international students whose financial status in relation to Canadian living standards (Hune-Brown, 2021) is not equal to that of domestic Canadian students of the same age.

The Flipgrid speaking test data also showed that international students were not comfortable with the tasks, so much so that they recorded more than nine times on average their given slots. Mostly fillers such as ah, oh eh, mm huh, and uh were the most frequently used expressions in their technical speaking assignments. It can be argued here that instead of using only fillers, an expert uses some highly technical diction (Amiridze et al., 2010), which would indicate that they are proficient enough to explain the prompt/ product or concept and shows that their working memory (Martinez, 2006) is capable enough of taking cues from their metacognition. Consequently, it further illustrates that experts' theoretical knowledge base is fundamentally sound and able enough to communicate both the technicality and commerciality of any product or concept, an ability that was missing in international students.

Finally, the Flipgrid speaking assignment was also used to evaluate international students' technical vocabulary on a scale of 1 to 10, with 1 indicating that a student had not used any technical diction and 10 indicating that a student had used completely all the tested technical vocabulary in a given Flipgrid assignment. Here the researcher also intentionally emphasized to the students that they would be evaluated on a list of 50 technical vocabulary items test. Almost none of the international students used the list despite pre-information and clear instructions, which is completely opposite to the Hawthorne effect in which participants show their awareness in case they are consciously instructed to carry out any workplace task increasing production cycles manifold (Adair, 1984).

The researcher evaluated the writing tasks via Blackboard-generated assignments on highly technical topics. For example, students were asked to write a description of a product, instructions on the operationality of a product, and writing a report on a topic in the end. Finally, these students were asked to write a proposal on the same topic. Most international students were not able to write coherent and consistent pieces, so much so that their assignments were completely asymmetrical and incompatible with the prior thoughts and inconsistent in terms of technical communication. Despite telling them repeatedly the implication of the assignments, they casually submitted them for the course grading.

The international students' ways of technical writing also were not analytically predictive in terms of audiences. The reason may be that the commercial course pack does not recommend anything close to real-world scenarios and is generalized too much in a direction that is not course-specific but rather adopts an all-sizes-fits-all approach (Mathews, 2007). When the researcher evaluated the sentence structure of these documents submitted by the international students, none of the international students were using highly technical vocabulary needed to explain particular technical documents or ideas for specific audiences. Their sentence structures were weak and did not flow from discipline-specific metacognition generated during a given course where they may have learned some appropriate diction. For example, students were not handling writing assignments according to the technical requirements and needs of the audience.

Similarly, an appropriate technical document depends on course-specific diction but this was missing in their technical projects (Hoft, 1995).

Here a parallel is drawn between IELTS exams and their technical assignments; the technical assignment needs more deep learning and comprehension of the highly scientific content whereas IELTS writing exams evaluate students merely on two simple tasks (Xu, 2021). For example, the first writing task requires students to write a pictorial description whereas the second task requires an argument on some proposition. However, technical writing is demandingly complex where students must evaluate a product to offer an assumed audience some guidance and direction. Interestingly, most students were employing rhetorical rather than technical vocabulary, which indicates that their task-specific cognitive structures are not loaded with technical diction. For instance, the researcher asked students to write a description of a pizza slicer as an assignment. Almost all used plain English by employing a rhetorical mode of communication; this may be good but not appropriate for engineering students. Students were unable to understand the greater context of the assignments despite several videos and class explanations; and therein lies another possible issue. The students may have internalized weak knowledge hierarchies based on previous informational listening aspects.

When the researcher evaluated the Flipgrid speaking assignments based on pre-recorded questions provided by the researcher, it was noted that international students' capacity of unpacking the technical questions was not supported appropriately by their communication responses. Information listening comes from well-established cognitive knowledge structures that support one's explanations on a given topic. If the knowledge base is weak, the responses are completely decontextualized and irrelevant.

RECOMMENDATIONS AND CONCLUSION

Most studies corresponding to international students focus on success, immigration prospects, residential difficulties, and poor communication skills. However, the current study reveals international students' technical communication deficiencies in reading, listening, writing, and speaking. These communication deficiencies become complex when international students are unable to transition into successful career paths in the aftermath of their respective higher educational journeys.

Keeping in mind the challenges faced by international students in their highly technical and complex classrooms in Canadian institutions, the research also reveals that international students' writing, speaking, listening, and reading communication may be good but not technically sound enough to survive in a highly industrialized workplace. Their cultural English may be appropriate but their deficient technical communication skills in writing, speaking, and reading put them at a serious disadvantage according to Bernstein (2001), who notes that students with restricted codes informally exploit the English language whereas those who use elaborated codes explicitly communicate with enhanced syntactic and semantic range. This whole process further indicates that ill-informed knowledge consumers may produce low-level knowledge hierarchies resulting in more employment pressures locally, regionally, and nationally. For instance, their metacognition may not be loaded to think critically and solve problems (Martinez, 2006). Moreover, if the knowledge consumers are not aware of their rightful knowledge consumption behaviours, this process of inappropriate knowledge consumption by chief consumers of society's knowledge may cause industrial economies such Canada as to grow as fast its institutional production.

It is recommended that all international students should record pre-arrival videos (Willems & Gonzalez-DeHass, 2012) that could be matched with their international testing credentials. For example, IELTS or TOFEL speaking scores could be matched with these pre-arrival videos on Flipgrid 5-minute assignments. The research reveals deep structural issues around testing bodies as these students are evaluated on cultural English as opposed to highly technical English used in Canadian higher education. This whole process of virtual admission criteria will save not only higher education recruiters but also future faculty members a lot of precious time. The researcher also discovered that international students' willingness to excel and deep reluctance to recoil from failures would make them a great fit for the 21st century entrepreneurial-based knowledge economy. This assumes that they have good English language skills yet the present study surmises that it may be good to test international students on highly technical bases rather than just through a flashy recruitment drive (Hune-Brown, 2021) to be based on scanty assumptions that IELTS or TOELF (Willems & Gonzalez-DeHass, 2012) are gatekeepers. This may be true, but not in the context of technical communication skills needed to survive highly troublesome navigation.

For example, teaching international students is indeed a daunting task because of their implicit and explicit English language skills assumed in academia. On the one hand, professors think these international students bring required English language skills; on the other hand, the market requirements of technical communication skills are completely a different story. The researcher has discussed, for instance, that the sentence structures of international students in writing assignments are different from their oral communication assignments. These students use short sentences in oral communication assignments recorded in the Flipgrid app with a lot of non-technical vocabulary. Their discipline-specific diction is poorly selected, whereas their writing assignments are heavily technical. This dichotomy in speaking and writing is a problem, and it also helps detect their plagiarism issues (Fatemi & Saito, 2020; Gunnarsson et al., 2014).

Previous studies (e.g., Fatemi and Saito, 2020; McGowan 2008) focus more on social aspects of student success whereas this study sheds light on students' intellectual issues in relation to being non-technical in their respective fields, more specifically in computer science, nursing, data science, biomedical engineering, and robotics. If we relate the critical aspect of technical English communication to the broader Canadian knowledge society, their sustainable integration may help explain how international students could bring the economy around by comprehending scientific topics of relevance.

CONFLICTS OF INTEREST

The author declares no conflicts of interest regarding the publication of this paper.

REFERENCES

Abdulla, M. D., & Kumar, S. A. (2016). Blooming English language skills for budding engineers to flourish in global environment. *Journal of English Language and Literature, 3*(1), 58–63. http://joell.in/wp-content/uploads/2016/03/BLOOMING-ENGLISH.pdf

Adair, J. G. (1984). The Hawthorne effect: A reconsideration of the methodological artifact. *The Journal of Applied Psychology, 69*(2), 334–345. doi:10.1037/0021-9010.69.2.334

Adler, R. B., Rodman, G. R., & Du Pré, A. (2016). *Understanding human communication* (13th ed.). Oxford University Press.

Aina, J. K., Ogundele, A. G., & Olanipekun, S. S. (2013). Students' proficiency in English language relationship with academic performance in science and technical education. *American Journal of Educational Research, 1*(9), 355–358.

Amiridze, N., Davis, B. H., & Maclagan, M. (Eds.). (2010). *Fillers, pauses and placeholders*. John Benjamins., doi:10.1075/tsl.93

Andrade, M. S. (2006). International students in English-speaking universities: Adjustment factors. *Journal of Research in International Education, 5*(2), 131–154. doi:10.1177/1475240906065589

Apple, M. W. (1995). Education, culture and class power: Basil Bernstein and the neo-Marxist sociology of education. In A. R. Sadovnik (Ed.), *Knowledge and pedagogy: The sociology of Basil Bernstein* (pp. 45–66). Ablex.

Arkoudis, S., Hawthorne, L., Baik, C., Hawthorne, G., O'Loughlin, K., Leach, D., & Bexley, E. (2009). *The impact of English language proficiency and workplace readiness on the employment outcomes of tertiary international students: Executive summary.* Centre for the Study of Higher Education, University of Melbourne. https://tinyurl.com/2m7ejse6

Arthur, N., & Flynn, S. (2011). Career development influences of international students who pursue permanent immigration to Canada. *International Journal for Educational and Vocational Guidance, 11*(3), 221–237. doi:10.100710775-011-9212-5

Baas, M. (2019). The education-migration industry: International students, migration policy and the question of skills. *International Migration (Geneva, Switzerland), 57*(3), 222–234. doi:10.1111/imig.12540

Bernstein, B. (1964). Elaborated and restricted codes: Their social origins and some consequences. *American Anthropologist, 66*(6, Part 2), 55–69. doi:10.1525/aa.1964.66.suppl_3.02a00030

Bernstein, B. (2001). Symbolic control: Issues of empirical description of agencies and agents. *International Journal of Social Research Methodology, 4*(1), 21–33. doi:10.1080/13645570118017

Bernstein, B. B. (2019). Social class, language and socialisation. In *Linguistics and adjacent arts and sciences* (pp. 1545–1562). De Gruyter Mouton. doi:10.1515/9783110811278-003

Caissie, K. B. (1978). *A handbook for teaching technical English* (Master's thesis, SIT Graduate Institute). SIT Digital Collections. https://digitalcollections.sit.edu/ipp_collection/248/

Canadian Bureau for International Education. (2020, February 21). *International students in Canada continue to grow in 2019* [Press release]. https://cbie.ca/international-students-in-canada-continue-to-grow-in-2019/

Cazden, C., Hymes, D., & John, V. (Eds.). (1970). *Functions of language in the classroom.* Teachers College Press.

Chafe, W., & Tannen, D. (1987). The relation between written and spoken language. *Annual Review of Anthropology*, *16*(1), 383–407. doi:10.1146/annurev.an.16.100187.002123

Choi, Y., Crossman, E., & Hou, F. (2021, June 23). *International students as a source of labour supply: Transition to permanent residency.* Statistics Canada. doi:10.25318/36280001202100600002-eng

Clements, D. (2007). Prior knowledge of mechanics amongst first year engineering students. *Teaching Mathematics and Its Applications*, *26*(3), 119–123. doi:10.1093/teamat/hrm005

Cook-Gumperz, J. (1986). Interactional sociolinguistics in the study of schooling. In J. Cook-Gumperz (Ed.), *The social construction of literacy* (pp. 45–68). Cambridge University Press.

Dawson, L. L. (1999). When prophecy fails and faith persists: A theoretical overview. *Nova Religio*, *3*(1), 60–82. doi:10.1525/nr.1999.3.1.60

Derr, K., Hübl, R., & Ahmed, M. Z. (2018). Prior knowledge in mathematics and study success in engineering: Informational value of learner data collected from a web-based pre-course. *European Journal of Engineering Education*, *43*(6), 911–926. doi:10.1080/03043797.2018.1462765

Donnell, J. A., Aller, B. M., Alley, M., & Kedrowicz, A. A. (2011, June 26–29). *Why industry says that engineering graduates have poor communication skills: What the literature says* [Conference session]. ASEE Annual Conference & Exposition, Vancouver, BC, Canada. https://tinyurl.com/3kbhe7av

Fairclough, N., & Wodak, R. (1997). Critical discourse analysis. In T. van Dijk (Ed.), *Discourse studies: A multidisciplinary introduction* (Vol. 2, pp. 258–284). SAGE.

Fatemi, G., & Saito, E. (2020). Unintentional plagiarism and academic integrity: The challenges and needs of postgraduate international students in Australia. *Journal of Further and Higher Education*, *44*(10), 1305–1319. doi:10.1080/0309877X.2019.1683521

Figel, J. (2006, April 3). *International competitiveness in higher education—A European perspective* [Conference session]. AHUA Conference, Oxford, UK.

Flick, U. (2014). Mapping the field. In U. Flick (Ed.), *The SAGE handbook of qualitative data analysis* (pp. 3–18). SAGE. doi:10.4135/9781446282243.n1

Freimuth, H. (2013). *Cultural bias on the IELTS examination: A critical realist investigation* (Doctoral dissertation, Rhodes University). SEALS Digital Commons. http://hdl.handle.net/10962/d1012088

Gee, J. P. (2011). Discourse analysis: What makes it critical? In R. Rogers (Ed.), *An introduction to critical discourse analysis in education* (2nd ed., pp. 23–45). Lawrence Erlbaum Associates.

Gibbs, R. W. Jr. (1995). Idiomaticity and human cognition. In M. Everaert, E.-J. van der Linden, A. Schenk, & R. Schreuder (Eds.), *Idioms: Structural and psychological perspectives* (pp. 97–116). Lawrence Erlbaum Associates.

Given, L. M. (Ed.). (2008). *The SAGE encyclopedia of qualitative research methods.* SAGE. doi:10.4135/9781412963909

Goldring, L., Berinstein, C., & Bernhard, J. K. (2009). Institutionalizing precarious migratory status in Canada. *Citizenship Studies, 13*(3), 239–265. doi:10.1080/13621020902850643

Gopal, A. (2016). Visa and immigration trends: A comparative examination of international student mobility in Canada, Australia, the United Kingdom, and the United States. *Strategic Enrollment Management Quarterly, 4*(3), 130–141. doi:10.1002em3.20091

Gumperz, J., & Hymes, D. (Eds.). (1986). *Directions in sociolinguistics* (2nd ed.). Blackwell.

Gunnarsson, J., Kulesza, W. J., & Pettersson, A. (2014). Teaching international students how to avoid plagiarism: Librarians and faculty in collaboration. *Journal of Academic Librarianship, 40*(3–4), 413–417. doi:10.1016/j.acalib.2014.04.006

Hackett, R. D., & Kline, T. (1998). Editorial: Industrial-organizational psychology and emerging needs of the Canadian workplace: Traversing the next millennium. *Canadian Psychology, 39*(1–2), 1–2. doi:10.1037/h0092483

Harrison, M. (2011). Supporting the T and the E in STEM: 2004–2010. *Design and Technology Education: An International Journal, 16*(1), 17–25. https://eric.ed.gov/?id=EJ916493

Hoft, N. L. (1995). *International technical communication: How to export information about high technology.* Wiley.

Hune-Brown, N. (2021, September/October). The shadowy business of international education. *The Walrus.* https://thewalrus.ca/the-shadowy-business-of-international-education/

Hymes, D. (1980). *Language in education: Ethnolinguistic essays.* Center for Applied Linguistics.

Ibbotson, M. (2009). *Professional English in use—Engineering with answers: Technical English for professionals.* Cambridge University Press.

Immigration, Refugees and Citizenship Canada. (2020). *Canada—Study permit holders with a valid permit on December 31st by province/territory of intended destination and study level, 2000–2020* [Data set]. https://www.cic.gc.ca/opendata-donneesouvertes/data/IRCC_M_TRStudy_0008_E.xls

Jackman, J. A., Gentile, D. A., Cho, N.-J., & Park, Y. (2021). Addressing the digital skills gap for future education. *Nature Human Behaviour, 5*(5), 542–545. doi:10.103841562-021-01074-z PMID:33707657

Kobayashi, A. (Ed.). (2019). *International encyclopedia of human geography* (2nd ed.). Elsevier.

Labov, W. (1972). *Language in the inner city.* University of Pennsylvania Press.

Lewington, J. (2019, November 4). Why universities are trying to recruit overseas students from as many places as possible. *Maclean's*. https://www.macleans.ca/education/why-universities-are-trying-to-diversify-where-overseas-students-come-from/

Martinez, M. E. (2006). What is metacognition? *Phi Delta Kappan, 87*(9), 696–699. doi:10.1177/003172170608700916

Mathews, J. (2007). Predicting international students' academic success... may not always be enough: Assessing Turkey's foreign study scholarship program. *Higher Education, 53*(5), 645–673. doi:10.100710734-005-2290-x

May, S., & Hornberger, N. H. (Eds.). (2017). *Encyclopedia of language and education*. Springer.

McGowan, U. (2008). International students: A conceptual framework for dealing with unintentional plagiarism. In T. Roberts (Ed.), *Student plagiarism in an online world: Problems and solutions* (pp. 92–107). IGI Global. doi:10.4018/978-1-59904-801-7.ch007

Mirel, B., & Spilka, R. (Eds.). (2002). *Reshaping technical communication: New directions and challenges for the 21st century*. Routledge. doi:10.4324/9781410603739

Morais, A. M. (2002). Basil Bernstein at the micro level of the classroom. *British Journal of Sociology of Education, 23*(4), 559–569. doi:10.1080/0142569022000038413

Nan, C. (2018). Implications of interrelationship among four language skills for high school English teaching. *Journal of Language Teaching and Research, 9*(2), 418–423. doi:10.17507/jltr.0902.26

National Academies of Sciences, Engineering, and Medicine. (2018). *English learners in STEM subjects: Transforming classrooms, schools, and lives*. National Academies Press.

Oded, B., & Walters, J. (2001). Deeper processing for better EFL reading comprehension. *System, 29*(3), 357–370. doi:10.1016/S0346-251X(01)00023-9

Panel on Research Ethics. (2018). *TCPS 2 (2018)—Chapter 5: Privacy and confidentiality*. https://ethics.gc.ca/eng/tcps2-eptc2_2018_chapter5-chapitre5.html#d

Qiang, Z. (2003). Internationalization of higher education: Towards a conceptual framework. *Policy Futures in Education, 1*(2), 248–270. doi:10.2304/pfie.2003.1.2.5

Rashed, H. (2017). *The relationship between federal citizenship and immigration policies and the internationalization of higher education in Canada* (Doctoral dissertation, University of Western Ontario). Scholarship@Western. https://ir.lib.uwo.ca/etd/4676

Reave, L. (2004). Technical communication instruction in engineering schools: A survey of top-ranked U.S. and Canadian programs. *Journal of Business and Technical Communication, 18*(4), 452–490. doi:10.1177/1050651904267068

Riemer, M. J. (2007). Communication skills for the 21st century engineer. *Global Journal of Engineering Education, 11*(1), 89–100. http://www.wiete.com.au/journals/GJEE/Publish/vol11no1/Riemer.pdf

Rogers, R. (2011). Becoming discourse analysts: Constructing meanings and identities. *Critical Inquiry in Language Studies, 8*(1), 72–104. doi:10.1080/15427587.2011.545768

Sá, C. M., & Sabzalieva, E. (2018). The politics of the great brain race: Public policy and international student recruitment in Australia, Canada, England and the USA. *Higher Education*, *75*(2), 231–253. doi:10.100710734-017-0133-1

Sageev, P., & Romanowski, C. J. (2001). A message from recent engineering graduates in the workplace: Results of a survey on technical communication skills. *Journal of Engineering Education*, *90*(4), 685–693. doi:10.1002/j.2168-9830.2001.tb00660.x

Sakamoto, I., Chin, M., & Young, M. (2010). "Canadian experience," employment challenges, and skilled immigrants: A close look through "tacit knowledge." *Canadian Social Work*, *12*, 145–151. https://tspace.library.utoronto.ca/handle/1807/94782

Sawir, E. (2005). Language difficulties of international students in Australia: The effects of prior learning experience. *International Education Journal*, *6*(5), 567–580. https://files.eric.ed.gov/fulltext/EJ855010.pdf

Scott, C., Safdar, S., Trilokekar, R. D., & El Masri, A. (2015). International students as "ideal immigrants" in Canada: A disconnect between policy makers' assumptions and the lived experiences of international students. *Comparative and International Education*, *43*(3), 5. Advance online publication. doi:10.5206/cie-eci.v43i3.9261

Slack, J. D., Miller, D. J., & Doak, J. (1993). The technical communicator as author: Meaning, power, authority. *Journal of Business and Technical Communication*, *7*(1), 12–36. doi:10.1177/1050651993007001002

Song, X. (2019). "Chinese students syndrome" in Australia: Colonial modernity and the possibilities of alternative framing. *Higher Education*, *79*(4), 605–618. doi:10.100710734-019-00426-z

Van Dijk, T. A. (2015). Critical discourse analysis. In D. Tannen, H. E. Hamilton, & D. Schiffrin (Eds.), *The handbook of discourse analysis*. Wiley. doi:10.1002/9781118584194.ch22

Wachsmuth, D., & Kilfoil, P. (2021). Two logics of regionalism: The development of a regional imaginary in the Toronto–Waterloo Innovation Corridor. *Regional Studies*, *55*(1), 63–76. doi:10.1080/00343404.2020.1817362

Wall, F. E. (1943). The importance of technical writing in chemical education. *Journal of Chemical Education*, *20*(12), 580–586. doi:10.1021/ed020p580

Willems, P. P., & Gonzalez-DeHass, A. R. (2012). School–community partnerships: Using authentic contexts to academically motivate students. *School Community Journal*, *22*(2), 9–30. https://www.adi.org/journal/2012fw/WillemsDeHassFall2012.pdf

Wright, S. (2008). Demanding knowledge–marketing and consumption. In D. Epstein, R. Boden, R. Deem, F. Rizvi, & S. Wright (Eds.), *Geographies of knowledge, geometries of power: Framing the future of higher education* (pp. 181–189). Routledge.

Xu, S. (2021). Processes and effects of test preparation for writing tasks in a high-stakes admission test in China: Implications for test takers. *Studies in Educational Evaluation*, *70*, 101015. Advance online publication. doi:10.1016/j.stueduc.2021.101015

Yong, E., & Ashman, P. J. (2019). Integration of the structured development of communication skills within a chemical engineering curriculum at the University of Adelaide. *Education for Chemical Engineers*, *27*, 20–27. doi:10.1016/j.ece.2018.12.002

Zhang, Z., & Zhou, G. (2010). Understanding Chinese international students at a Canadian university: Perspectives, expectations, and experiences. *Comparative and International Education*, *39*(3), 5. Advance online publication. doi:10.5206/cie-eci.v39i3.9162

Zhou, G., Yu, Z., Rideout, G., & Smith, C. (2021). Why don't they participate in class?: A study of Chinese students' classroom participation in an international master of education program. In V. Tavares (Ed.), *Multidisciplinary perspectives on international student experience in Canadian higher education* (pp. 81–101). IGI Global. doi:10.4018/978-1-7998-5030-4.ch005

ADDITIONAL READING

Aarrevaara, T., Finklestein, M. J., Jones, G. A., & Jung, J. (Eds.). (2021). *Universities in the knowledge society: The nexus of national systems of innovation and higher education*. Springer. doi:10.1007/978-3-030-76579-8

Dooey, P., & Oliver, R. (2002). An investigation into the predictive validity of the IELTS Test as an indicator of future academic success. *Prospect, 17*(1), 36–54. http://www.ameprc.mq.edu.au/docs/prospect_journal/volume_17_no_1/17_1_3_Dooey.pdf

Intaraprawat, P., & Steffensen, M. S. (1995). The use of metadiscourse in good and poor ESL essays. *Journal of Second Language Writing*, *4*(3), 253–272. doi:10.1016/1060-3743(95)90012-8

Macedo, D., Dendrinos, B., & Gounari, P. (2015). *Hegemony of English*. Routledge. doi:10.4324/9781315634159

Maxwell, A., Curtis, G. J., & Vardanega, L. (2006). Plagiarism among local and Asian students in Australia. *Guidance & Counselling, 21*(4), 210–215. https://researchrepository.murdoch.edu.au/id/eprint/9914/

McLean, M., Murdoch-Eaton, D., & Shaban, S. (2013). Poor English language proficiency hinders generic skills development: A qualitative study of the perspectives of first-year medical students. *Journal of Further and Higher Education*, *37*(4), 462–481. doi:10.1080/0309877X.2011.645461

Olsen, L. A., & Huckin, T. H. (1990). Point-driven understanding in engineering lecture comprehension. *English for Specific Purposes*, *9*(1), 33–47. doi:10.1016/0889-4906(90)90027-A

Robertson, M., Line, M., Jones, S., & Thomas, S. (2000). International students, learning environments and perceptions: A case study using the Delphi technique. *Higher Education Research & Development*, *19*(1), 89–102. doi:10.1080/07294360050020499

Singh, P. (2015). Performativity and pedagogising knowledge: Globalising educational policy formation, dissemination and enactment. *Journal of Education Policy*, *30*(3), 363–384. doi:10.1080/02680939.2014.961968

Valencia, C. (2009). "Oh, no, I failed math, I have to be an English major now": Features of how engineering students construct a relational identity. *The McNair Scholars Journal, 8*, 319–334. http://depts. washington.edu/uwmcnair/wp-content/uploads/2015/12/2009-Journal.pdf

KEY TERMS AND DEFINITIONS

Critical Discourse Analysis: Critical discourse analysis is much informed by Fairclough's three-dimensional model that encourages researchers to evaluate discursive events, discursive practices, and social structures. Here the critical analysis of texts such as grammar, structure, vocabulary, intertextuality, and rhetorical or literary devices is carefully executed to find critical nuances in the text.

Cultural English: A language with greater cultural than academic relevance. Much in cultural English flows from norms, values, and surroundings, and is thus easier to enact than technical English, which is more scientific.

Elaborated Code: This concept was promoted by Basil Bernstein, an English sociologist who denotes elaborated code to middle-class speakers who are linguistically proficient and can produce rich linguistic content. The speakers are able to produce abstract reasoning, critical thinking, and technical knowledge.

Knowledge Economy: 21st-century societies live on knowledge as a staple diet as opposed to traditional economies of the bygone century. Traditional economies were sustainably inviable and depleted the natural resources to the point of national diversification drive; for example, Saudi Arabia Vision 2030 is one but a simple example of Saudi society's hunger for knowledge.

Pedagogizing: Making the teaching and learning content pedagogically suitable for learners so they can consume knowledge easily and comfortably in knowledge economies.

Restricted Code: Bernstein talks about restricted code as poor syntactic and semantic production of language from lower-working-class speakers. This could produce social class differences.

Technical Communication: Communication of scientific and highly technical knowledge. The processing of information in terms of technical communication should be clear and loaded with technical pieces or discipline-specific vocabulary, but most international students are not aware of this aspect of technical communication.

Technical English: Technical English is driven by technical jargon and is based on highly scientific content. In addition, technical English also relies on research-based vocabulary for technological innovation.

Section 3
Teaching About Academic Integrity

Chapter 9

Putting Plagiarism Under Scrutiny:
Punjabi International Students and Barriers Within Canadian Higher Education

Lilach Marom

ⓘ https://orcid.org/0000-0003-3534-5212

Kwantlen Polytechnic University, Canada

ABSTRACT

This chapter focuses on the concept of plagiarism through a case study of Punjabi international students (PS) in Canadian higher education. While plagiarism by international students is often seen as a sign of deficiency and a lack of academic abilities, this chapter aims to conceptualize and contextualize the phenomenon of plagiarism. The quick association of international students with cases of plagiarism overlooks structural and academic barriers that push some students to commit plagiarism. This chapter also distinguishes between unintentional and intentional plagiarism; while the first is often rooted in academic and language barriers, the second reflects wider structural barriers. Understanding the factors underlying plagiarism can help institutions provide relevant support for international students rather than invest in increased surveillance mechanisms.

INTRODUCTION

This chapter is part of a wider research project focused on the experiences of Punjabi international students (hereafter PS) in higher education through a case study of Kwantlen Polytechnic University (KPU), a teaching university in British Columbia (BC) (Marom, 2021, forthcoming). As such, it does not aim to provide a full analysis of the complex and multi-layered phenomenon of internationalization in higher education, but rather, to highlight a sub-set of the data that intersected with the issue of plagiarism.

DOI: 10.4018/978-1-7998-8921-2.ch009

Plagiarism committed by international students is often seen as a sign of their deficiency and lack of academic abilities (Baas, 2010; Birrell, 2005; Caluya et al., 2011; Sidhu, 2006). A recent *The Globe and Mail* article titled "Why Many International Students get a Failing Grade in Academic Integrity" stated that "At some Canadian schools, an alarming number of the accused [plagiarists] share one characteristic: they came from abroad to study here" (Bradshaw & Baluja, 2021, para. 1).

This perception overlooks underlying causes for plagiarism that I explore in this chapter: mainly, differences between diverse educational systems as well as the multiple barriers that international students face in admission and retention in higher education. I argue that there is a need to conceptualize and contextualize the phenomenon of plagiarism in order to understand what might be driving some international students to plagiarize. Such analysis could help institutions of higher education in providing relevant support for international students rather than investing in increased surveillance mechanisms.

Caluya et al. (2011) suggest that literature on international students "tends to isolate pedagogic issues from the larger structural contexts within which the international student market and hence international students are formed" (p. 86). In the current chapter, PS experiences are analysed as underlined by structural and institutional mechanisms operating in a global, neoliberal higher education market. While this chapter is focused on PS, as members of a racialized group of international students coming from a non-Western education system, their experiences could reflect challenges experienced by other groups of international students of similar backgrounds.

This chapter starts with the wider framework of internationalization in higher education since these underlying structures are reflected in many of the experiences of PS, followed by context for the phenomenon of plagiarism. It then provides the background for PS at KPU and presents the methodological design of this study. The Findings section distinguishes between intentional and unintentional cases of plagiarism and analyses the main issues underlying them. The Solutions section recommends ideas for addressing these issues on a policy, institutional, and pedagogical level.

BACKGROUND

Internationalization in Higher Education

The term internationalization in higher education is used in multiple ways by scholars, reflecting different perspectives and analyses (de Wit, 2002; Harman, 2005; Knight, 2003). While internationalization can be driven by academic, social, political, or economic motives, the internationalization of higher education must be analysed as part of a wider realignment of social institutions toward a global, neoliberal knowledge economy (Grubb & Lazerson, 2009; Weis & Dolby, 2011). This shift was accompanied by the strengthening of global players such as the OECD that promote policies constructing higher education as a form of human capital, intending "to support national competitiveness in global knowledge economies" (Sellar & Gale, 2011, p. 1).

The neoliberal shift in education shrunk government funding and constructed global universities as competitors, aiming to increase revenues through expansion into the international market (Harvey, 2005; Olssen & Peters, 2005). This was accompanied by a shift "from aid to trade" (Harman, 2004): From providing education to students in developing countries as a public good to recruiting international students as a revenue stream (Connell, 2013; Mazzarol & Soutar, 2002). As Connell (2013) explains,

Increasingly, education has been defined as an industry, and educational institutions have been forced to conduct themselves more and more like profit-seeking firms... higher education [was redefined] as an export industry, extracting income from overseas students, rather than educating them for free as development aid by a rich country. (p. 102)

When higher education is at the service of a competitive job market, it sees a negative impact to access, admissions, and retention of international students.

Punjabi International Students in Canada

The Canadian government is heavily invested in international education in the hope that it will both contribute to a declining population and meet the needs of a changing job market. This is reflected in Canada's "Building on Success: International Educational Strategy 2019-2024," which states that "international education fuels the people-to-people ties crucial to international trade in an increasingly interconnected global economy" (Government of Canada, 2019b, p. 3).

In recent years (pre-COVID-19), there has been a steep increase in the enrolment of international students at all levels of Canadian education (Canadian Bureau for International Education [CBIE], 2018; Universities Canada, 2017). Between 2010-2019, Canada saw a 185% increase in international students (CBIE, 2020). Since 2015, the proportion of international students from India has grown considerably, from 16% to 27% in total, with 67% growth at the college level (CBIE, 2018; Vanderklippe, 2019). Prior to COVID-19, "In colleges, India was the top source of international enrolment in most broad program areas" (Frenette et al., 2020, para. 8).

Key factors underlying the growth in international students from India include the expedited visa procedures for students from India under the Student Direct Stream (SDS), which provides student visas within 20 calendar days (Government of Canada, 2019a); expansion of the global higher education market; Canada's relatively easy route to immigration post-graduation; and the political climate and education policies in other countries (Baas, 2010; Beech, 2018; Migration Advisory Committee, 2018).

PS come from a segment of the Indian population that traditionally did not send their kids to higher education abroad. In recent years, the younger generation of Punjabis are being sent to study abroad in large numbers in order to provide better life trajectories for themselves and their families. Many PS come from a farming background, and their families have been impacted by the decline and instability of the agriculture sector in Punjab (Government of Punjab, 2020).

Another factor that contributes to the large efflux of students from Punjab to Canada is the drug crisis in Punjab. The Chief Minister of Punjab argued, "If Punjab is made a drug-free state, then there will be no need for parents to send their children abroad (cited in the *Hindustan Times*, 2018, para. 3); "Parents, worried about losing their young sons to drugs, are left with no choice but to send them away" (Mehra, 2019, para. 4).

Since in Canada being an international student is an easy route to immigration (Vanderklippe, 2019), international students are often perceived as seeking immigration opportunities rather than as "real students." Indeed, for some PS, particularly those from marginalized groups, international education is a means to gain entry to Canada for the purpose of obtaining permanent residency (PR), and their main concern is not necessarily the quality of their education (Wadhwa, 2016). While it is tempting to criticize such students, one must keep in mind that Canadian policies and economic interests have created this loophole where the route to immigration and international education are conflated (Government of

Canada, 2019a). Furthermore, hoping to obtain an education while having immigration aspirations is not inherently contradictory. Many PS come to study abroad with aspirations to immigrate, yet they also want to pursue education that will lead to a better personal and professional trajectory (Tran & Thao, 2016).

Plagiarism and International Students

The increase in international students reflects global neoliberal trends in Canadian higher education that have reconstructed universities in Canada as entrepreneurial enterprises. Canadian universities were pushed to increase their marketing efforts to attract international students, who are seen as "cash cows" that pay higher tuition fees. The Canadian Bureau for International Education warns that while "Internationalization is important to the financial sustainability of many institutions, [it] should not be undertaken without adequate allocation of resources, [and that] the financial imperatives must not dictate the internationalization agenda" (CBIE, 2014, p. 2). Yet many universities, particularly those not in the elite category, have become highly dependent on international tuition as a main source of revenue (CBIE, 2018; Marginson, 2004).

The increasing dependency of universities on international tuition pushes universities to accept students with low or mismatched credentials to meet their cost recovery targets without providing adequate academic and mental support, which leaves students struggling. This cycle also leads to international students' being subjected to deficit terminology at host universities where they are constructed as of "lesser quality" (Caluya et al., 2011; Houshmand et al., 2014). As Caluya et al. argue, "Academic teaching staff regularly complain about poor language skills, improper learning styles and poor motivation. Committees, sub-committees and inquiries are increasingly established to explore "the international student problem" (Caluya et al., 2011, p. 85).

As part of this "deficit perception," international students are often seen as the cause for an increase in cases of plagiarism. The overlapping discourses about international students and plagiarism is evident in multiple recent news reports in Canadian media outlets, where plagiarism is discussed in the context of international students, often specifically Indian students (Todd, 2019a/b). Bradshaw and Baluja's (2021) article in *The Globe and Mail* claims that "The disproportionate number of international students accused of plagiarism or cheating on exams is raising red flags in university administrations and legal aid offices" (para. 2). Similarly, an article about Cape Brenton University describes issues with "academic integrity," citing faculty members' discussing "students who seem unfamiliar with Canadian standards for academic citation" (Friesen, 2019, para. 36). Another article featuring Niagara College describes "a crisis on campus," where thousands of international students from India could not cope academically, which led to suspicions of forgery of their English proficiency test IELTS (LaFleche et al., 2019). Indeed, an investigation by a Punjabi radio journalist further exposed education agents selling IELTS scores (Kainth, 2016).

While such reports raise red flags, it is important to look beyond the catchy headlines and public perceptions in order to unpack underlying patterns that contribute to plagiarism, rather than "stigmatis[ing] some students as 'blatant plagiarists'" (The Higher Education Academy, 2014, p. 2).

Studies demonstrate how differences between academic systems and in academic expectations can lead to unintentional plagiarism. Such differences can be invisible to insiders of a specific academic culture, but experienced by those new to it (Carroll, 2008). Studies further identify epistemic differences between notions of intellectual ownership and authorship between Western and non-Western cultures (Sutherland-Smith, 2008). While in a Western context higher education is conceptualized as the pursuit of individual excellence, in other contexts, it can be seen as a collective endeavour serving a public good (Sillitoe et al., 2005).

On a more pragmatic level, studies challenge the assumption that international students cheat more than domestic students do, arguing that some modes of plagiarism employed by international students are easier to detect (Bull et al., 2001). For example, international students tend to use "patchwriting" (Pecorari, 2005), incorporating large segments of text into their writing that are easier to detect by software than more sophisticated methods of plagiarism (Zobel & Hamilton, 2002). However, such writing techniques can also be seen as tools for developing writing competencies for second language speakers, rather than automatically be deemed cheating (Schmitt, 2005).

In the case of international students, a more nuanced and contextualized understanding of plagiarism is needed. Also of importance in discussions about plagiarism is identifying whether the plagiarism is done intentionality or unintentionally (Carroll, 2007). In this chapter I examine both scenarios.

METHODOLOGY

Data Sources

While many institutions in BC admit large numbers of international students from India, KPU is recognized as a particularly attractive and affordable destination in the Canadian teaching universities category (see for example, ApplyBoard, 2021). KPU is appealing for Indian students from the Punjab region because its main campus is in Surrey, BC, which is home to a large Punjabi Canadian diasporic community (Statistics Canada, 2016). Many PS have extended families that have immigrated to Surrey, and they recommend KPU to families and friends back home, which creates an expanding circle of new PS applicants (Beech, 2015).

This case study was designed to focus on the experiences of PS at KPU (see Marom, 2021; forthcoming). The main source of data was interviews with 16 PS (see Table 1 for summary of information about the participants) that were focused on their experiences as KPU students inside and outside the university. Each participant was asked a set of questions regarding their experiences at various stages of their academic trajectory and with various stakeholders (e.g., peers, administrative staff, and faculty).

The PS interviewees in this study had several features in common. They had arrived in Canada within the last three years and were between the ages 19-21. Most interviewees were Sikh, with varying degrees of religiosity (two students were Hindu). These PS were first generation to attend a post-secondary institution in Canada. A large number of them came from farming households and grew up in villages and rural towns in Punjab. All the participants were working part time in addition to being full-time students. All the students indicated that they received some financial support from their parents in India in order to attend KPU.

KPU faculty and staff were also interviewed. These included two faculty members with extensive experience teaching PS and four senior administrators in the KPU International office working in areas such as recruitment, admissions, academic support, and student services. These interviews help unpack the wider institutional mechanisms framing PS' experiences.

In addition, five professionals who work or volunteer in organizations that provide resources and support for international students, many of whom are PS, were interviewed. These organizations include One Voice Canada and South Asian Mental Health Alliance. One Voice Canada (OVC) was founded in

2019 as a non-profit organization to bridge gaps between the local populations and international students. OVC advocates for international students and connects them to appropriate resources and support services related to exploitation, mental health, immigration, etc. (One Voice Canada, 2021). The South Asian Mental Health Alliance is a non-profit organization that serves the South Asian community specifically, fostering mental health awareness and connecting individuals to mental health resources (South Asian Mental Health Alliance, 2021). The interviews with volunteers from these two organizations provided a wider perspective on and context for the individual stories shared by PS.

To maintain the participants' anonymity, pseudonyms have been used for PS and titles (e.g., Faculty, Administrator) for professional interviewees. In addition to the interviews, KPU policies, meeting minutes, and public documents, as well as policies regarding international education and international students in Canada and BC, contributed to the findings of this case study. Finally, media and social media resources regarding international students, and PS in particular, were considered. These were used as a means of triangulation.

Data Analysis

In the first stage of the data analysis process, interviews were transcribed verbatim, and all sources of data organized (e.g., senate documents, KPU's student newsletter, policies, and media resources). In the second stage, the data was analyzed using NVivo software, with a focus on repeating threads and patterns. In the coding process, a list of topics that were repeated in the interviews emerged (e.g., agents, plagiarism, tuition, work, personal challenges, Indo-Canadian community); topics also emerged from the theoretical framework (e.g., marketization, neoliberalism, immigration). In the final stage, the topics were assembled under several key themes, which were searched for connections and relationships.

A main theme that emerged from the data was pedagogical, academic, economic, and structural challenges as they pertain to the issue of plagiarism. While this theme intersects with other key categories such as the marketization of international higher education and intra-cultural tensions between PS and the local Punjabi community (Marom, 2021; forthcoming), it deserved a more detailed analysis, which is the focus of this chapter.

PUTTING PLAGIARISM UNDER SCRUTNY

This chapter presents two key issues underlying plagiarism: 1) Language and academic barriers and 2) structural and economic barriers. Both categories are discussed with the aim to unpack the complexity of plagiarism and move beyond deficit (as the cause) and surveillance (as the solution) discourses while highlighting different aspects of plagiarism: The first explores the differences between higher education systems and demonstrates how PS can unintentionally commit plagiarism if they are not provided with enough academic preparation and learning support; the second focuses on structural and economic barriers that many PS face and that can drive them, in some cases, to take the route of intentional plagiarism.

Language and Academic Barriers

Gaps between the Education Systems in Punjab and BC

International students and students from marginalized groups often experience challenges in Western academic institutions; these challenges are not necessarily a reflection of lesser abilities, but rather, of issues such as gaps in prior education. In the case of PS, there are significant differences between the school systems in India and in Canada in areas such as structure, academic tracks, and pedagogy.

The majority of PS came from two large public schoolboards in Punjab: Punjab School Education Board (PSEB) and Central Board of Secondary Education (CBSE). These schoolboards are more traditional in their pedagogy and mostly reliant on final exams. Thus, many PS lacked some of the competencies gained in Canadian high schools, such as inquiry and research skills. Arshdeep compared the two school systems: "[In India] the thing that is tested is your memory. You are just given lots of notes. You have to just memorize them and then copy. But here... teachers are looking for your knowledge, rather than your memory." Paramjeet shared, "My first semester was not that easy...I didn't feel confident speaking in class. ...It took a few semesters to understand everything—the plagiarism, all the [APA] style, how to write research papers. These are completely different, new things for me." A member of OVC who has supported many PS shared the following observations:

There's such a big gap between secondary education in Punjab and post-secondary education in Canada; it's a huge leap. I'm not sure if secondary education [in India] is necessarily preparing people for post-secondary education in Canada...I have been talking to PS, and they mentioned that they've never done a research paper in their life and the first time they're doing it is in a college in Canada.

In the above examples, PS stated that they were used to a more traditional way of learning rooted in memorization and listening to lectures rather than the active learning and inquiry-based engagement that is prevalent in Canadian schools (Carroll, 2008; Marom, 2017). Notably, a report by Deloitte (2017) points out that there is a "significant shortfall of quantity and quality research being conducted at the universities in India" (p. 13).

In addition, underfunding of government schools in India affects the level of educational technology available in Punjab secondary schools: Among government schools, less than 12% had internet in 2019-20 while less than 30% had functional computer facilities" (Mehra, 2021, para. 1). Shivehare (2017) argues that "lack of internet penetration may obstruct adoption of education technology in Indian schools significantly" (para. 6). Hence, many PS were not used to the excessive usage of technology in class and online learning in Canadian higher education. Manpreet shared some of the differences in pedagogy and in the usage of technology:

For the first couple of classes I was totally confused...Because in India ...teachers used to explain everything and then write it on the board. But here, whether it's an online class or not, we are just working on technology every time, like on laptops, PowerPoint, and all. So, it was quite challenging for me.

As emerged from the above statements, the differences between the education systems demands adjustment and academic support, yet there is no mandatory academic preparation course offered to international students. While there are support services offered by KPU's Learning Centre and International Office, many new students do not access these services because of language and cultural barriers (Bradshaw & Baluja, 2021).

Gaps in English Proficiency

Another barrier emerged from gaps in English proficiency. KPU is an "open access" university, which means that admission is granted based on English proficiency and a high school diploma. The recent influx of international students has challenged KPU's open access policy because of the incompatibility of report cards from non-Western school systems with Canadian ones. As a result, with international student admissions, the greatest weight rests on English exams such as IELTS.

Punjabi native speakers' scores were at the bottom of the IELTS ranking in 2019 (IELTS, 2019), triggering a booming industry of English coaching centres. Punjab is estimated to have more than 5,000 IELTS coaching centres, the vast majority unregulated (Roy, 2019). The desire to come to Canada has become so intense that IELTS has become ingrained in mainstream pop culture, with songs and films produced about IELTS (Kahlon, 2021, p. 8). The IELTS industry has been connected to cases of forgery, which raises concerns for Canadian institutions (Bradshaw & Baluja, 2021; Keung, 2018; LaFleche et al., 2019). A volunteer at OVC echoed these concerns:

We hear stories about these English training centers and how they're being used. You drive down the street and there are boards all over the place. "Come here to study," with pictures of the Niagara Falls... It's a kind of advertisement that says that you can come to be a student basically as a way to get PR.

Another volunteer in OVC discussed cases of marriage based on the IELTS score of the bride. Following the marriage, the bride comes to Canada as an international student and later brings her spouse to Canada. Chabba (2020) explains that "The agreement is that the girl scores well in English language proficiency tests and gets admitted into a foreign educational institution. The groom's family then pays for the girl's education and for the couple to move abroad" (para. 4).

These stories demonstrate the entanglement of international higher education with the migration industry (Baas, 2010; Beech, 2018; Wadhwa, 2016). There is an inherent flaw in a Canadian higher education admission system that conflates migration-seeking applicants with applicants who might be interested in migration but have an interest in quality education as well. This conflation has a negative impact on the experiences of PS in Canadian higher education. For example, PS said that when they seek academic guidance, they do not get individualized support and were seen as members of a deficient group of students who are more focused on work and immigration. Sukhamdeep shared, "Some students just want to go and take a diploma, go to work. But some actually want to build up careers. So, for them, it's like a drawback because they're also given the same advice, like, general advice, not customized advice."

In a study on international students in lower-tier universities in Australia, Tran and Thao (2016) argue that since the students are perceived by administrators and faculty as "PR hunters," international students are put in a vulnerable position, leaving many feeling disconnected and marginalized. The authors argue that because many international students are seeking PR, their individuality and personal goals are ignored. However, the students' desire for PR does not negate the need to attend to their academic trajectory.

On the receiving end, KPU is struggling to determine admission requirements that will maintain the flow of international students while supporting students' academic success. IELTS as the only admission requirement has proven to be an insufficient indication of academic readiness (LaFleche et al., 2019).

Admitting PS without knowing their level of academic preparedness and without support systems in place has turned into an academic trap for many students.

Gaps in Expectations and Unintentional Plagiarism

It seems that many cases of plagiarism were committed unintentionally as a result of gaps in expectations between the academic systems in Canada and Indian generally, and in academic writing specifically. A volunteer at OVC explained the typical perception that PS hold that does not apply in the context of Canadian higher education:

It's a switch from the Indian education system because, in India, we don't have that much strictness. We are much more lenient with [copying from books] which, here, is considered plagiarism. So, students, they've never heard of it...and they get into trouble.... In India, you have the final exam, which weighs [the most] and the rest, it's pretty lenient... it's handwritten, and no one checks for plagiarism. So, when PS come here, and a course has 20% for final exam and 80% for assignments, they don't know how to deal with that.

The PS interviewees echoed this observation. Pravinder shared, "I had some challenges regarding citations because back in my country, we didn't do citations. We just took the stuff from everywhere and just put the link." Hermandeep explained, "The plagiarism thing is a totally new concept that was introduced to me... I was terrified...I started crying. I remember, like, 'I don't know what's happening in this class. I don't know what's going on.'" Navjot expressed the problem succinctly: "There is no word for 'plagiarism' in Indian schools. No word."

The lack of understanding of academic expectations could lead PS to unintentional acts of plagiarism, as Harvir shared:

More than half of this course was Punjabis, and they didn't even know how to cite. So, the majority of the class was plagiarizing.... So, I submitted three assignments on the same day, and I got a plagiarism on all three...I heard from some older students that if you get plagiarized for the first time, it's a zero on an assignment. Second time, it's a zero in the course. And the third time you get expelled from university. I was not sure if [what I had done] was considered one plagiarism or three... I was so worried that I would have to move back to my country and get expelled from college.

The segments above demonstrate that many PS were not familiar with the concept of plagiarism nor with the academic requirements in Canadian universities (Handa & Power, 2005; Maxwell et al., 2008;). Since there is no mandatory academic preparation course for international students at KPU, PS had to adjust on their own, which led to high levels of stress and feelings of overwhelm. Jashanpreet shared,

I did statistics in India. That was so fun for me...But here...I didn't pass that course. That was a horrible time for me. I was like, "It's my first semester, and I didn't pass that course. How am I going to study my further courses?"

It is important to understand that many PS did not have a security net so when they experienced academic challenges, it was harder for them to get back on track. PS were worried about needing to repeat a course and pay more tuition, about being put on academic probation (which could lead to a loss of their work permit and PR prospect), and about disappointing their families. An Administrator shared,

There may be students who can't afford to repeat any more courses...Their families have very limited financial resources. Oftentimes we have students whose family members get loans to support these studies. And how can an international student say to their family members, "Oh, I failed this course, and I have to repeat. Give me a thousand dollars more just to do that."

Such pressures can lead students to intentionally commit plagiarism, especially when they felt trapped in an academic system they could not successfully navigate, as I discuss next.

Structural and Economic Barriers

Barriers in Admission

In India, the admission process to universities abroad is dominated by "agents," who are the middle persons between universities and potential students. The term "education agent" refers to an "individual or organization offering education advising services to students and their parents in exchange for a fee (paid by students and their families) and/or a commission (paid by an [educational] institution they represent...)" (Council of Ministers of Education, Canada, 2013, p. 6). Beech (2018) explains that "Over time and as a result of the benefits that they can bring, agents have become integral to international student recruitment, with both universities and students viewing agents as gatekeepers to international students and higher education opportunities, respectively" (p. 611). India has the highest number of agents (30%), followed by China (25%), used in Canadian education (Council of Ministers of Education, Canada, 2013).

While education agents can act as "cultural mediators," bridging the gap between the home and host countries (Robinson-Pant & Magyar, 2018), educational considerations do not necessarily play a central role in the admission process (Baas, 2010; Caluya et al., 2011). A KPU administrator shared how market considerations can be embedded in the agents' choice of universities offered: "Some agents, they only have contracts with certain universities. So, when they're doing promotions, they only promote these schools. They would not even mention other schools because they are not going to get a commission." PS were often admitted to institutions or programs that were not a good fit for them or enrolled by agents in the wrong courses. Manpreet shared,

My agent didn't tell me that I had to select my courses by myself. So only when I came here for my orientation, I became aware that I was already enrolled in some courses... The orientation leader told me, "You have to check by going to this site." So, I came to know that I was enrolled in Psych 1100 and 1200. That was quite amazing for me.

An OVC volunteer who is also an immigration consultant and has worked with many PS summarized the problems with an agent dependent admission system: "The agent wants to make the commission; the student wants to come to Canada. But when they come here, they have no idea what the course or what the program is. They're setting themselves up for failure."

Economic Barriers

Misalignment in the admission process can have long term repercussions since there are economic implications to switching a program or repeating a course (Marom, forthcoming). An OVC volunteer explained that agents often told PS and their families that there is a fixed sum of money needed to study abroad (i.e., the Guaranteed Investment Certificate (GIC) - the initial deposit and tuition fees required by the Canadian Government; Government of Canada, 2021); as a result, many PS did not fully comprehend the ongoing expenses involved in studying abroad.

Gagandeep shared,

It's a lot of money for my family to pay. Because...the only person who earns in my family is my father... I have a younger brother, and my mother, she's an asthma patient. So, most of the time she's sick. So eventually it will be an additional burden if I keep asking them for money for every little thing.

Jashanpreet explained, "Parents' sacrifice, yeah, their [own] wishes for their kids--so they can get a good life."

As mentioned earlier, most PS came from small villages and farming families, and their parents had paid significant amounts of money, some selling their lands or taking loans in order to send their kids to higher education, all in the hope that it would lead to a better career and life trajectory. That is, studying in Canada was a high-stake investment made by families, which put pressure on PS to make it work at all costs. Simran shared,

The very first semester I was on academic warning. I failed four courses...I haven't told my family yet about that. So, I was scared. How will I arrange my fees...? The next month I tried my best. I cleared one course, then I took three and, again, I failed! It's my first year.... I wasn't able to manage the job and the study together.

Intentional Plagiarism as a Sign of Distress

The challenges described above had a negative impact on PS' engagement in their academic studies. A faculty member shared her perspective on how financial struggles impact PS' engagement in their coursework:

It all becomes about "How am I going to pay for my tuition as quickly as I can." And it seems that education sacrifice is a result because they're spending so much of their time and energy towards work... I've had a couple students who've maybe come to two classes this whole semester because they're busy working to pay for their education... I keep saying to students, "What is your priority? ...You came here. It should be school." But it's not, because they have to pay for school.

Another faculty member shared:

Many PS have said that when they first decided to come to KPU and they were accepted, they were following their dream of what they wanted to do in their preferred future, but that when they came here, their dream changed. Right now, it's all about how to survive.

For many international students such as PS and their families, higher education has become part of a bigger plan for immigration (Beech, 2015, 2018). This puts significant pressure on students to do well since much is at stake. This may also lead some students to attempt to plagiarize in situations where they feel trapped and are worried about failing a course that they do not have the funds to re-take. They also fear being put on academic probation and many other scenarios that endanger their future in Canada.

An instructor articulated the difference between intentional and unintentional plagiarism:

I do want to distinguish between accidental plagiarism—thinking that they could copy and paste (in their home country they were rewarded for doing something like that) and then coming here and not really understanding the [academic] differences—and intentional plagiarism. I hear sob stories from students saying, "I'm taking 5, 6, or even 7 courses. I'm just trying to make ends meet. Please don't do this to me."

Another instructor shared,

I have quite a few students that are in their last semester that have plagiarized. And they should know, in their last semester at KPU, about plagiarism. But the reason that I hear over and over again as to why they're committing plagiarism is they don't have the time and energy to put into the work. It's because either they're working too much or they're not managing their time effectively. I feel that education is not their priority, and so plagiarism becomes a big issue.

It is important to take into account the challenges that PS face in order to understand why some plagiarize. While plagiarism is never justified, it is understandable that when some students feel that they are left with few options, they do whatever it takes to remain students and not risk their life trajectory in Canada.

SOLUTIONS AND RECOMMENDATIONS

In order to profoundly address plagiarism in higher education there is a need to identify its root causes and to provide relevant solutions for instances of both unintentional and intentional plagiarism. While solutions to the first are mainly in the pedagogical and instructional domain, solutions to the second demand more substantial changes on a policy and an institutional level.

Unintentional plagiarism is often an outcome of gaps in preparation and in limited understanding of Western academic expectations rather than a desire to cheat; as a result, it is important for faculty members to be aware of these gaps and provide appropriate support in their courses.

Without education for faculty, it is easy to develop a deficit perception toward international students. Faculty education should focus on both academic differences and barriers that international students experience. Designing courses in more accessible ways could also help international students in transitioning to higher education; for example, courses could include scaffolding for assignments. Faculty should also discuss the concept of plagiarism with students, not only in the form of a warning, but in a deeper sense of understanding authorship. Such discussions combined with diverse modes of assessment could support international students in identifying and developing their academic voice.

While some faculty members can be resistant toward change, it is important to keep in mind that as the student body is changing, teaching must also. As Tran and Thao (2016) argue, while universities claim to want international students to enrich their institutions, their "pedagogic practices" suggest that international students are *not* ideal students and, as a consequence, they are Othered. Intercultural teaching pedagogies offer multiple ways to draw on the diversity of the students as a source of strength and enrichment to the curriculum (Lee et al., 2012; Sleeter, 2011).

Since adjusting to multiple changes can be overwhelming, international students would also appreciate designated transition courses to help them adjust to a new academic system and its requirements before they enrol in regular courses. Such courses could be provided by universities prior to arrival in Canada in order to help students adjust to future expectations.

In order to decrease intentional plagiarism, there is a need to address some of the structural barriers in admission and retention in higher education. Universities can no longer justify the assumption that the market will regulate the global economy and, therefore, they carry no responsibility for the academic trajectory of international students. There is an inherent distortion in the promise of education when it is subjected to the market (Brown et al., 2011), and the price is paid by students, particularly those in vulnerable positions such as PS.

On the policy level, it is important to regulate the international student market to both protect students and keep universities accountable to their stated academic mission. Higher education should not be a route for low skilled immigration, and universities should provide support for the students they admit. A necessary part of this process is to regulate international tuition fees and protect students from extreme tuition hikes. Universities also need to make sure that prospective students get sufficient information about admission, enrollment, and tuition so they can make informed decisions.

When admitting international students, it is not enough to consider their academic trajectory; Canadian institutions must also consider other aspects of living abroad, such as work and housing. One repeated suggestion from interviewees was to provide more work opportunities on campus as well as student housing to create a more holistic support system for international students and protect them from exploitation off campus.

FUTURE RESEARCH DIRECTIONS

Further research is needed to explore the effects of the disruption of Covid-19 and the shift online on the learning experiences of international students from marginalized groups.

For those of us who are committed to the idea of higher education as a human right, the pandemic uncertainty and the shift to online education are no reason to forget what we stand for. In fact, they provide a reason to look even more closely at the barriers and challenges that many international students face and to consider how we can make education more accessible and inclusive in these uncertain times.

CONCLUSION

This chapter argues for the need to examine plagiarism as part of the bigger phenomenon of the international market of higher education. It is possible to develop more sophisticated mechanisms to detect plagiarism and to turn faculty members into police officers; yet such direction overlooks the root cause of the issue, separating it from underlying institutional injustice. The quick association of international students with an increase in cases of plagiarism likewise overlooks the overlapping reasons that push some students to commit plagiarism.

Table 1. PS participants

	Pseudonym	M/F	From	Family Background	Semester in KPU	Changed Program	Want to Immigrate
1	Ravneet	F	Small city	Father owns store	6th	No. Business Management Diploma	Yes
2	Navjot	F	Small city	Father owns store	8th	Associate Degree in Horticulture to General Studies (GS) Diploma	Yes
3	Pravinder	F	Small city	Farming background, own a store	6th	No. HR Management Diploma	Yes
4	Prabhjeet	F	City	Father lawyer Mother teacher	4th	No. Computer Information Systems	Yes
5	Sukhamdeep	F	City	Father government job	6th	Associate Degree in Science to Post-Bac HR Management	Yes
6	Jashanpreet	F	Small village	Farmers	6th	Computer Information Systems to Business to GS Diploma	Undecided
7	Arshdeep	F	City	Farming background, moved to city to start businesses	1st	Associate Degree in Science	Yes
8	Gagandeep	F	Small city	Father government job	1st	Associate Degree in Science	Yes
9	Amritveer	M	Village	Farmers	6th	Business to GS Diploma	Yes
10	Rajiv	M	Village	Farming background, father police officer	6th	IT to GS Diploma	Yes
11	Paramjeet	F	Village	Farmers	7th	IT to General Business Diploma	Yes
12	Harvir	M	Small city	Mother teacher, Father doctor	7th	Business Associate Degree to GS Diploma.	Yes
13	Hermandeep	F	City	Writers	Graduated 2-year diploma	No. Computer Information Systems	Yes
14	Rajdeep	M	City	Farmers	Graduated 2-year diploma	No. Diploma in Business Management	Undecided
15	Simran	F	Small city	Clothing business	7th	Business to GS Diploma	Yes
16	Manpreet	F	Small city	Farming background/ own store	1st	Associate Degree in Psychology	Yes

In the case of PS, plagiarism was an indication of the disconnect between the Canadian academic system and their previous educational experiences. Understanding this disconnect becomes even more important when the shift to online education pushes universities to consider implementing further surveillance technologies (Harwell, 2020). While online learning bypasses geographic borders, it is by no means the "great equalizer" when it comes to the socioeconomic conditions and support systems available to students.

It is important to make it clear that this chapter is not a justification for plagiarism of any sort. Plagiarism is a breach of the academic code of conduct. However, the academic code of conduct is a two-way relationship between universities and students, and universities should take seriously their part of that relationship. When universities accept international students for their tuition fees and are not committed to their academic success, they not only betray their mission, but can also put students in vulnerable situations with few choices. However, while individual students can be easily punished, universities can get away with maintaining a mechanism that continues to fail many international students. As a member of OVC reminds us,

Schools need to understand that if PS are suspended for a year, or for three months, they lose out on their visa, and that's a big thing.... We jeopardize their lives, and we don't understand the implications of jeopardizing the student's life because you don't have time to listen or to understand. What if it was your child in that position? They've come across the world to a foreign country. They have no support. They're already being exploited by employers and then by the school. They're vulnerable.

ACKNOWLEDGMENT

I want to thank KPU for its continuous support of my research project. This study was funded by KPU's professional development fund. I want to thank the PS participants in this study who shared their knowledge and experiences with me, and the faculty members and administrator participants who work to improve education and services for international students. My appreciation to the participants who volunteer in organizations supporting PS on their journey in Canada.

REFERENCES

ApplyBoard. (2021, September 24). *KPU*. https://www.applyboard.com/schools/kwantlen-polytechnic-university-surrey

Baas, M. (2010). *Imagined mobility: Migration and transnationalism among Indian students in Australia.* Anthem Press.

Beech, S. E. (2015). International student mobility: The role of social networks. *Social & Cultural Geography, 16*(3), 332–350. doi:10.1080/14649365.2014.983961

Beech, S. E. (2018). Adapting to change in the higher education system: International student mobility as a migration industry. *Journal of Ethnic and Migration Studies, 44*(4), 610–625. doi:10.1080/1369183X.2017.1315515

Birrell, B. (2005). *Immigration rules and the overseas student market in Australia*. IDP Education Australia Limited.

Bradshaw, J., & Baluja, T. (2021). Why many international students get a failing grade in academic integrity. *The Globe and Mail*. https://www.theglobeandmail.com/news/national/education/why-many-international-students-get-a-failing-grade-in-academic-integrity/article4199683/

Brown, P., Lauder, H., & Ashton, D. (2011). *The global auction: The broken promises of education, jobs, and incomes*. Oxford University Press.

Bull, J., Collins, C., Coughlin, E., & Sharpe, D. (2001). *Technical review of plagiarism detection software report*. Academic Press.

Caluya, G., Probyn, E., & Vyas, S. (2011). "Affective eduscapes": The case of Indian students within Australian international higher education. *Cambridge Journal of Education*, *41*(1), 85–99. doi:10.1080/0305764X.2010.549455

Canadian Bureau for International Education. (2018). *International students in Canada*. https://cbie.ca/wp-content/uploads/2018/09/International-Students-in-Canada-ENG.pdf

Canadian Bureau for International Education. (2020). *Infographic*. https://cbie.ca/infographic

Carroll, J. (2008). Assessment issues for international students and for teachers of international students. *The enhancing series case studies: International learning experience*, 1-13.

Chabba, S. (2020, May 5). "IELTS marriages" — India's "ideal bride" is proficient in English. *Deutsche Welle*. https://www.dw.com/en/ielts-marriages-indias-ideal-bride-is-proficient-in-english/a-53341947

Connell, R. (2013). The neoliberal cascade and education: An essay on the market agenda and its consequences. *Critical Studies in Education*, *54*(2), 99–112. doi:10.1080/17508487.2013.776990

Council of Ministers of Education. Canada. (2013). *The role of education agents in Canada's education system*. https://www.cmec.ca/Publications/Lists/Publications/Attachments/326/The-Role-of-Education-Agents-EN.pdf

de Wit, H. (2002). *Internationalization of higher education in the United States of America and Europe: A historical, comparative, and conceptual analysis*. Greenwood Press.

Deloitte. (2017, November). *Annual Status of Higher Education of States and UTs in India*. https://www2.deloitte.com/content/dam/Deloitte/in/Documents/public-sector/in-ps-ashe-2017-noexp.pdf

Frenette, M., Choi, Y., & Doreleyers, A. (2020). *International student enrolment in postsecondary education programs prior to COVID-19*. Statistics Canada. https://www150.statcan.gc.ca/n1/pub/11-626-x/11-626-x2020003-eng.htm

Friesen, J. (2019, October 9). In Cape Breton, a dramatic rise in international students has transformed a school and a community. *The Globe and Mail*. https://www.theglobeandmail.com/canada/article-how-the-world-came-to-cape-breton-university/

Government of Canada. (2019a). *Student direct stream: About the process*. https://www.canada.ca/en/immigration-refugees-citizenship/services/study-canada/study-permit/student-direct-stream.html

Government of Canada. (2019b). *Building on success: International educational strategy 2019-2024.* https://www.international.gc.ca/education/assets/pdfs/ies-sei/Building-on-Success-International-Education-Strategy-2019-2024.pdf

Government of Canada. (2021). *Study permit: Get the right documents.* https://www.canada.ca/en/immigration-refugees-citizenship/services/study-canada/study-permit/get-documents.html

Government of Punjab. (2020). *Punjab economic survey 2019-20.* https://www.esopb.gov.in/static/PDF/EconomicSurvey-2019-20.pdf

Grubb, W. N., & Lazerson, M. (2009). *The education gospel.* Harvard University Press.

Handa, N., & Power, C. (2005). Land and discover! A case study investigating the cultural context of plagiarism. *Journal of University Teaching & Learning Practice, 2*(3), 64–84. doi:10.53761/1.2.3.8

Harman, G. (2004). New directions in internationalizing higher education: Australia's development as an exporter of higher education services. *Higher Education Policy, 17*(1), 101–120. doi:10.1057/palgrave.hep.8300044

Harman, G. (2005). Internationalization of Australian higher education: A critical review of literature and research. In P. Ninnes & M. Hellstén (Eds.), *Internationalizing higher education: Critical explorations of pedagogy and policy* (Vol. 16, pp. 119–140). Springer Netherlands. doi:10.1007/1-4020-3784-8_7

Harvey, D. (2005). *A brief history of neoliberalism.* Oxford University Press. doi:10.1093/oso/9780199283262.001.0001

Harwell, D. (2020). Mass school closures in the wake of the coronavirus are driving a new wave of student surveillance. *The Washington Post.* https://www.washingtonpost.com/technology/2020/04/01/online-proctoring-college-exams-coronavirus/

Hindustan Times. (2018, July 31). *Parents sending kids abroad for studies due to drug menace: Punjab CM.* https://www.hindustantimes.com/punjab/parents-sending-kids-abroad-for-studies-due-to-drug-menace-punjab-cm/story-UoRAI4JuMegM81ni7mo02K.html

Houshmand, S., Spanierman, L. B., & Tafarodi, R. W. (2014). Excluded and avoided: Racial microaggressions targeting Asian international students in Canada. *Cultural Diversity & Ethnic Minority Psychology, 20*(3), 377–388. doi:10.1037/a0035404 PMID:25045949

IELTS. (2019). *Test taker performance 2019.* https://www.ielts.org/for-researchers/test-statistics/test-taker-performance

Kahlon, B. (2021). *Report on the realities for international students.* One Voice Canada. https://onevoicecanada.org/wp-content/uploads/2021/05/The-Realities-of-International-Students-Evidenced-Challenges_Full-Report-2.pdf

Kainth, S. (2016, December 30). *IELTS score for sale in India: SBS Punjabi investigates.* SBS Punjabi Radio. https://www.sbs.com.au/language/english/audio/ielts-score-for-sale-in-india-sbs-punjabi-investigates

Keung, N. (2018, December 8). More than 400 students in India told to retake language tests after Niagara College flags concerns. *The Star*. https://www.thestar.com/news/canada/2018/12/08/400-students-in-india-told-to-retake-language-tests-after-niagara-college-flags-concerns.html

Knight, J. (2003). Updating the definition of internationalization. *Industry and Higher Education, 33*(3), 2–3. doi:10.6017/ihe.2003.33.7391

LaFleche, G., Keung, N., & Teotonio, I. (2019, September 28). The test said they were good enough to get in, but they were failing in class. How Niagara College tackled an international student crisis. *The Toronto Star*. https://www.niagarafallsreview.ca/news/niagara-region/2019/09/28/they-passed-the-admissions-test-but-they-were-failing-in-class-how-niagara-college-tackled-an-international-student-crisis.html

Lee, A., Poch, R., Shaw, M., & Williams, R. (2012). *Engaging Diversity in Undergraduate Classrooms: A Pedagogy for Developing Intercultural Competence*. John Wiley & Sons.

Marginson, S. (2004). National and global competition in higher education. *Australian Educational Researcher, 31*(2), 1–28. doi:10.1007/BF03249517

Marom, L. (2017). Eastern/Western conceptions of the "Good Teacher" and the construction of difference in teacher education. *Asia-Pacific Journal of Teacher Education, 45*(6), 1–17. doi:10.1080/1359866X.2017.1399982

Marom, L. (2021). Outsiders-insiders-in between: Punjabi international students in Canada navigating identity amid intraethnic tensions. *Globalisation, Societies and Education*. Advance online publication. doi:10.1080/14767724.2021.1882291

Maxwell, A., Curtis, G. J., & Vardanega, L. (2008). Does culture influence understanding and perceived seriousness of plagiarism? *International Journal for Educational Integrity, 4*(2), 25–40. doi:10.21913/IJEI.v4i2.412

Mazzarol, T., & Soutar, G. (2002). *The global market for higher education: Sustainable competitive strategies for the new millennium*. Edward Elgar Publishing.

Mehra, A. (2019, December 1). Why mini-Punjabs sprout in distant lands. *The Hindu*. https://www.thehindu.com/opinion/open-page/why-mini-punjabs-sprout-in-distant-lands/article30124230.ece

Migration Advisory Committee. (2018). *Impact of international students in the UK*. https://assets.publishing.service.gov.uk/government/uploads/system/uploads/attachment_data/file/739089/Impact_intl_students_report_published_v1.1.pdf

Olssen, M., & Peters, M. A. (2005). Neoliberalism, higher education and the knowledge economy: From the free market to knowledge capitalism. *Journal of Education Policy, 20*(3), 313–345. doi:10.1080/02680930500108718

One Voice Canada. (2021). *About Us*. https://onevoicecanada.org/about-us-2/

Pecorari, D. (2003). Good and original: Plagiarism and patchwriting in academic second-language writing. *Journal of Second Language Writing, 12*(4), 317–345. doi:10.1016/j.jslw.2003.08.004

Robinson-Pant, A., & Magyar, A. (2018). The recruitment agent in internationalized higher education: Commercial broker and cultural mediator. *Journal of Studies in International Education*, 22(3), 225–241. doi:10.1177/1028315318762485

Roy, V. (2019, February 23). Foreign dreams make IELTS coaching Rs 1,100-cr industry. *The Tribune*. https://www.tribuneindia.com/news/archive/foreign-dreams-make-ielts-coaching-rs-1-100-cr-industry-733521

Sellar, S., & Gale, T. (2011). Globalisation and student equity in higher education. *Cambridge Journal of Education*, 41(1), 1–4. doi:10.1080/0305764X.2011.549652

Sidhu, R. (2006). *Universities and globalization: To market, to market*. Lawrence Erlbaum Associates Publishers. doi:10.4324/9781410617217

Sillitoe, J., Webb, J., & Zhang, M. C. (2005). Postgraduate research: The benefits for institutions, supervisors and students of working across and between cultures. In J. Carroll & J. Ryan (Eds.), Teaching international students: Improving learning for all (pp. 130-136). Routledge.

Sleeter, C. E. (2011). *The academic and social value of ethnic studies. A research review*. NEA. https://files.eric.ed.gov/fulltext/ED521869.pdf

South Asian Mental Health Alliance. (2021). *About Us*. http://samhaa.org/about

Statistics Canada. (2016). *Census profile Surrey and BC*. https://www.statcan.gc.ca/eng/start

Sutherland-Smith, W. (2008). *Plagiarism, the internet and student learning: Improving academic integrity*. Routledge. doi:10.4324/9780203928370

The Higher Education Academy. (2014). *Addressing plagiarism*. https://www.aqa.ac.nz/sites/all/files/addressing_plagiarism.pdf

Todd, D. (2019a, December). An inside look at Indian students in Canada. *The Vancouver Sun*. https://vancouversun.com/news/staff-blogs/an-inside-look-at-indian-students-in-canada

Todd, D. (2019b, September 3). Over-reliance on students from India and China sparks Ottawa reaction. *The Vancouver Sun*. https://vancouversun.com/opinion/columnists/douglas-todd-feds-to-address-over-reliance-on-students-from-india-and-chinaSun

Tran, T., & Thao, T. (2016). 'I'm not like that, why treat me the same way?' The impact of stereotyping international students on their learning, employability, and connectedness with the workplace. *Australian Educational Researcher*, 43(2), 203–220. doi:10.100713384-015-0198-8

Universities Canada. (2017). *Canada's global moment: Students from around the world choose Canada*. https://www.univcan.ca/media-room/media-releases/canadas-global-moment-students-around-world-choose-canada/

Vanderklippe, N. (2019, March 1). In a shift on Canadian campuses driven by Trump policies, Indian students now outnumber Chinese. *The Globe and Mail*. https://www.theglobeandmail.com/world/article-in-a-shift-on-canadian-campuses-driven-by-trump-policies-indian/

Wadhwa, R. (2016). Students on move: Understanding decision-making process and destination choice of Indian students. *Higher Education for the Future, 3*(1), 54-75. https://journals.sagepub.co/doi/10.1177/2347631115610221

Weis, L., & Dolby, N. (Eds.). (2011). *Social class and education: Global perspectives*. Routledge.

Zobel, J. & Hamilton, M. (2002). Managing student plagiarism in large academic departments. *Australian Universities Review, 45*.

Chapter 10
Academic Integrity and the Inclusion of East Asian International Students in Canadian Higher Education

Phoebe Eunkyung Kang

Ontario Institute for Studies in Education, Canada & University of Toronto, Canada

ABSTRACT

This chapter discusses academic integrity issues affecting East Asian international students in Canadian higher education contexts and further highlights the importance of addressing academic integrity issues to improve the inclusion of East Asian international students. The student body has shifted with the increasing number of international students in Canadian higher education contexts and the number of East Asian international students plays a significant role with the shift. East Asian international students bring in their unique cultural backgrounds to the teaching and learning environments in the Canadian higher education landscape. This chapter draws on the autoethnographic approach to discuss the persistence of the academic integrity issues East Asian international students have been facing. The chapter further makes practical and future research recommendations from a transnational educator's perspective.

Every educational institution in Canada, and across the world, experiences issues with academic integrity (McKenzie, 2018, p.40)

INTRODUCTION

How is the Canadian higher education landscape being shaped by the growing numbers of international students from East Asia? As these students seek integration into local higher education institutions, what academic integrity issues do they face, and with what linguistic, cultural, pedagogical and policy implications? These are the questions that puzzled me during a decade of teaching international students,

DOI: 10.4018/978-1-7998-8921-2.ch010

primarily from East Asia, in English for Academic Purposes programs and English preparation programs in the university and college sector in Canada. I came to these questions not only as a result of my professional experiences as a trained educator but based on my own lived experiences as a non-native English speaker who immigrated to Canada initially as an international student from East Asia. As I sought my own path to inclusion in Canadian higher education, I came to understand the importance of academic integrity as crucial for student success. For me, then, these issues are both personal and professional. Furthermore, academic integrity – which I use interchangeably in this chapter with related terms such as plagiarism, cheating, academic honesty, and academic dishonesty – is an issue of growing concern that has multifaceted implications for international learners, for teaching methods and content, and for institutional policymaking.

In this chapter, I bring together the challenges of academic integrity with equity and inclusion issues facing international students by intertwining my own trajectory together with that of the East Asian international student body in the Canadian higher landscape. To do this, I use autoethnography as both theoretical framework and method, which I discuss in the next section. I then set out the intersections of academic integrity and East Asian international students in Canadian higher education in three ways. First, by examining higher education institutions' (HEIs) policies on academic integrity; second, charting the rise of East Asian international students in Canada, and third, connecting academic integrity as an issue of inclusion when it comes to East Asian students. Here, East Asia refers to students from China, South Korea, Japan, Hongkong and Taiwan. I, then, compare the findings from the literature to the findings of my own autoethnography by analyzing the implications of the study in order to provide recommendations for teaching practice and for further research.

AUTOETHNOGRAPHY AS THEORETICAL FRAMEWORK AND METHOD

This chapter utilizes autoethnography as both theoretical framework and method. Autoethnography is "a highly personal process" yet "it carefully examines how the researcher interacted with other people within their socio-cultural contexts and how social forces have influenced their lived experiences" (Chang, 2013, p.107). Spry (2001) states that autoethnography is "a self-narrative that critiques the situatedness of self with others in social, political, economic and cultural context" (p.710). Jones (2005) states that "autoethnography involves setting a scene, telling a story, weaving intricate connections among life and art, experience and theory, evocation and explanation ... hoping for readers who will bring the same careful attention to our words in the context of their own lives" (p.765). While there are various understandings of autoethnography as a theoretical and/or a methodological framework, Chang (2013) summarizes some of the common characteristics of autoethnography as follows:

- "Autoethnography uses the researcher's personal experiences as primary data;
- Autoethnography intends to expand the understanding of social phenomena;
- Autoethnography processes can vary and result in different writing products." (p.108)

Autoethnography deals with researchers' personal, professional, relational and socio-cultural stories in relation to the social phenomena that the researcher is investigating in (Chang, 2008; Chang, 2013; Ellis 2004). In this chapter, my autoethnographic approach aligns with Chang in that I combine my personal experiences as primary data with academic literature on the topic of academic integrity in order to offer an expanded understanding of this phenomenon as it relates to the East Asian international students. As such, academic integrity is a highly personal, professional, relational and socio-cultural issue to me.

ACADEMIC INTEGRITY POLICIES IN CANADIAN HIGHER EDUCATION INSTITUTIONS

Academic integrity represents the culture of academic and curricular norms in university teaching and learning environment. While research on institutional academic integrity policies of higher education appears to be lacking in Canada, one exception may be found in Stoesz and Eaton (2020) conducted a policy analysis of academic integrity policies from the 24 publicly funded universities in the four Western provinces in Canada, British Columbia, Alberta, Saskatchewan and Manitoba. The study found that while values of integrity and/or educative approach were emphasized as the foundation of the policy, the procedures laid out were instead rather punitive and emphasized policing, reporting, investigating and sanctioning student engagement in academic misconduct. In Stoesz and Eaton's study (2020), they also found the rhetoric around "academic integrity and academic misconduct is largely based on morality" (p.14). This moral discourse leads to the "use of law-or-crime-related language (e.g. theft, breach, copyright)" (Adam et al., 2017, p.19 as cited in Stoesz & Eaton, 2020). This tendency in institutional academic integrity policies is congruent with a study on publicly funded colleges across Ontario, Canada (Stoesz, et al., 2019). This tendency shows that the issues around academic integrity is prevalent in Canadian higher education. This further highlights the importance for institutions to pay more attention to foster a culturally sensitive way in interpreting the policies when international students arrive in Canadian higher education institutions.

The interpretation and application of academic integrity in Canada operates on a level that is both different and potentially conflictual with the cultural expectations that East Asian students may bring with them. In Thompson et al's study (2017), international students from three Asian cultures reported that they view knowledge as something to be shared rather than focusing on rights of ownership of the knowledge. These students' cultural association with a sense of morality heavily influences their understanding of academic integrity. Considering this in the North American educational environment, Song and Cadman (2013) assert the need for university leadership to show their willingness to provide training on the academic literacy necessary to succeed in their environment. Beyond the specificity of East Asian international students' cultural background, another important characteristic was that the relevant policy documents are not easily found (Song & Cadman, 2013). It is problematic if academic integrity policies are perceived to be unimportant as the policy documents are difficult to locate while the reality of increasing academic integrity incidents persists.

EAST ASIAN INTERNATIONAL STUDENTS IN THE CANADIAN HIGHER EDUCATION LANDSCAPE

A notable development of Canadian higher education internationalization has been the ever-increasing enrolment of international students. As of 2019, Canadian Bureau of International Education (CBIE) reports that there are over 600,000 international students in Canada in all levels of studies. The overall number of international students in tertiary level almost tripled from 142,000 in 2010/2011 to 389,000 in 2019/2020 (Statistics Canada, 2021). According to CBIE (2018), the number of international students from East Asian countries (e.g. China, South Korea, Japan and Taiwan) make up over 30% of the total number of the inbound students, making them one of the largest groups across all education sectors in Canada. International students encounter a variety of integration challenges as a result of language and cultural barriers, academic and financial difficulties, interpersonal problems, racial discrimination, loss of social support, and alienation and homesickness (Yeh & Inose, 2003; Stein, 2018; Smith, 2016; Guo & Guo, 2017). Border closures related to the global COVID-19 pandemic in 2020 and 2021 have left many international students isolated from their home countries and elevated many of the struggles faced by international students in Canadian higher education settings (Vandeville, 2020). In addition, they may be experiencing academic challenges as the learning has fully converted into virtual spaces.

With the limitations on student mobility, international students will likely experience more pronounced inequities, such as educational access issues and prolonged study processes, which ultimately have impact on multiple aspects including their finances and study plans. Fully online learning due to COVID-19 constraints may have exposed a new set of challenges and needs for East Asian international students, such as the inconvenience of learning from the opposite time zones, the difficulty to access university social and academic supports, which may have limited the exposure and access to learn about academic integrity conventions in Canadian universities (Kang, 2020). Chinese international students in Zhang and Zhou's study (2010), language proficiency was mentioned by many participants as one factor that influenced their full engagement in the academic and social life on and off campus, it was often cultural differences that affected their lives to feel inclusive in the academic and social communities that they were living in. In addition to the academic barriers, even prior to the COVID-19 outbreak, East Asian international students experience international students in Canada already experienced social exclusions, overt racist aggression, and cultural barriers (Firang & Mensah, 2022; Zhang & Zhou, 2010), although Canadian schools and universities promote multiculturalism on their campuses. Therefore, an approach to create an inclusive learning environment affecting East Asian international students requires a more attention. While more and more academic institutions are putting an emphasis on academic and social support for international students, their learning issues specifically about academic integrity and/or academic misconduct are still under-investigated practically and scholarly.

ACADEMIC INTEGRITY AND INCLUSION OF EAST ASIAN INTERNATIONAL STUDENTS

The Canadian higher education teaching and learning environment has shifted with the increased number of international students but these changes are not widely reflected in the curriculum and in policies and procedures to support the integration of East Asian international students (Smith et al, 2019; Eaton & Christensen Hughes, 2022). This is a longstanding issue: over 20 years ago, it was argued that, in Western institutions, "many current approaches to internationalization of the curriculum in higher education are ad hoc, tokenistic, and inadequate" (Kelly, 2000, p.163). While pointing out the importance of internationalization for international and domestic students to help prepare them to be global citizens, many scholars highlight the dearth of research on internationalization of curriculum (Svensson & Wihlbord, 2010, Clifford, 2009, Sawir, 2013; Foster & Anderson, 2015; Leask, 2015). In Guo and Guo's (2017) study, Asian undergraduate international students in a Canadian university reported that they did not see teaching materials reflecting their experiences. They cite one international student who said "It is more like I need to adapt myself to fit into the program. I feel like there is less understanding" (Guo and Guo, 2017, p.859).

For many newly arrived international students, academic integrity in the hosting university is a foreign topic. Some literature discusses the complications arising when international students face different conventions in the Western educational system. For example, when international students are expected to quote and reference their teacher's opinion and when Canadian domestic students are expected to reference other author's opinion, they may take the approach entirely differently. In East Asian cultures, knowledge is something that is received by students from their teacher, but not necessarily something that they themselves may be positioned to disseminate through citation of other scholars' work or by putting forward their own perspectives. This has a profound impact on students' approach to education in Western systems, for instance as witnessed by teachers in the lower level of class participation by East Asian students. Another area is where knowledge content has received more emphasis than knowledge delivery itself (Gu, 2010; Song-Turner, 2008). International students experience linguistic challenges requiring special help to avoid plagiarism and its consequences if they have limited experience in writing in English, especially in the academic contexts (Amsberry, 2010; Chen &Van Ullen, 2011). Academic integrity violation cases caused by international students have various contributing factors. While students' inadequate English proficiency is one of the main contributing factors, there are also many other factors beyond the language deficiency issue. Zhang and Zhou (2010) asserted that Chinese international students have difficulties not only in academic English but also in collaboration and cooperation in team projects due to the exam-based learning environment in China.

Thompson et al (2017) pointed out the importance of helping international students understand their host university's expectations regarding academic honesty. Yet faculty perceptions may also preclude East Asian and other international students from being able to integrate into Canadian higher education norms. MacLeod and Eaton (2020) found that faculty members perceived international students as unprepared, as struggling with language issues in the Canadian academic context and embedding or perpetuating a culture of cheating. Faculty respondents reported that students who are unprepared for university-level work often cheat because they do not know how, or do not care, and are unable to function effectively in English (MacLeod & Eaton, 2020). Faculty members in this study further cited international students as major contributors to academic dishonesty (MacLeod & Eaton, 2020). Other studies have reinforced this portrayal of East Asian students as lacking academic skills including English proficiency, academic writing skills, and critical thinking ability (Lin & Scherz, 2014).

Instead of a deficit focused approach towards international students, recent research highlights the need to rethink how knowledge is generated and to see international students as knowledge producers, not as passive consumers of Eurocentric knowledge. (Guo & Guo, 2017; Stein, 2017). The lack of a nuanced cultural approach towards curriculum may have an impact on the international students' understanding of academic integrity policies. In Fass-Holmes' (2017) study, it was reported that among reported academic integrity violations, undergraduates outnumbered graduate students, males outnumbered females, and Chinese nationals outnumbered other nationalities. Does this result mean that this phenomenon is a problem of Chinese male undergraduate students? Or could it suggest that the hosting HEIs need to study what might be the root cause of the heightened number of academic misconduct incidents with this particular student group?

THE PERSISTENT ISSUE OF ACADEMIC INTEGRITY: A PERSONAL TRAJECTORY

To support the examination of the root causes of academic misconduct suggested above, in this section I turn to my own journey through Canadian higher education. As outlined by Chang (2013), I argue that by relating my own experiences, I can expand understanding of broader phenomena – in this case, why academic integrity is perceived as an issue among East Asian international students in Canadian higher education and why this issue has persisted over time. I have played three different roles in Canadian higher education: a) as an international graduate student coming from South Korea, b) as a transnational non-native English language educator, and c) as a doctoral researcher on the topic of East Asian international students in Canada.

Arriving in Canada as an East Asian International Graduate Student

In 2003, I came to Canada as an international graduate student to pursue my Master of Education degree after finishing my undergraduate studies back home in South Korea. I was admitted directly with my TOEFL score and did not have any prior English as a Second Language or academic English preparation program experience. My English proficiency level met the university admissions requirement and I did not experience particular difficulties following class materials or understanding academic English in class. However, one thing that I noticed instantly were the Canadian rules about writing styles and in particular the APA referencing that all written assignments and academic presentations had to follow. This was an academic convention that neither the TOEFL exam nor my prior English language education in South Korea had prepared me for.

To adapt to these different academic conventions, my first strategy was to read prolifically. I read numerous journal articles, dissertations, and other types of written forms that employed the APA style in order to be exposed to this academic convention as much as possible. Second, I was very fortunate to have a professor in my program who prioritized students' understanding of APA style guide rules. He incorporated APA style guide presentations as part of his curriculum, so each student had to pick a topic, such as citation, capitalization, reference lists from the most updated APA style guide. This assignment was designed for both domestic and international students. Many years after completing this assignment, I still remember the topic and my presentation as I had to study and research word by word precisely how to do the referencing and the rules of in-text citation. The fact that I still recall this assignment speaks to the importance of the APA style in academic writing in Canada (at least in my discipline). This exercise also provided me with an opportunity to examine the rules from an academic perspective, and this has impacted my learning and later teaching experiences.

From International Student to Teaching East Asian International Students in Canada

While I was completing my Master's degree, I began to work at the university, first as an ESL Instructor and later as an Academic Coordinator, a role that included teaching in the English for Academic Purposes (EAP) program. Overall, I worked in these positions at the same university for 15 years, more than sufficient time to witness the different kinds of struggles faced by other East Asian international students.

EAP programs are academic bridging or transition program has a unique positionality in universities in Canada. Often, international students who do not meet the language requirements (IELTS 6.5 for the majority of Canadian university programs) are admitted to an EAP program and the exit requirements of the highest level of the program are usually designed to meet the university's required level of English proficiency. These programs are primarily intended to be revenue generating units in universities and are often used as the pipeline generating international students for the degree programs. In my teaching context, the tension between adequately preparing students linguistically and culturally in the university academic context for the degree programs versus advancing students to the degree programs quickly to meet the international student enrolment target was persistent. Pressure from the university administration to advance more students to degree programs tipped the scale of the tension to sometimes pass the students who may not have achieved the stated English proficiency level. The advancement of underprepared students to the degree program was frequent, such that I would call it a systemic problem. The consequences of student under-preparedness fell to faculty in the degree programs to deal with. For example, students would struggle with participating in the seminars expressing their opinions effectively in English or face challenges in academic writing when writing essays or writing exams not being to properly paragraph, summarize or reference the articles they use to support their arguments.

Building on Previous Study and Professional Experience as a Doctoral Researcher in Canada

While I approached academic integrity issues from the academic cultural convention and from the linguistic perspective in my two previous roles, in my current role as a doctoral researcher, I am engaging in academic integrity issues by East Asian international students as part of the focus of my doctoral research. While the focus on academic integrity was not my initial intention, the topic emerged from the interviews I conducted. In my research, I interviewed East Asian first year international students, faculty and staff and found that academic integrity issues were raised by all three groups. Students generally expressed their lack of familiarity around academic integrity and copyright conventions in the Canadian university environment. Faculty and staff maintained a supportive attitude yet expressed frustration around the persistent number of academic integrity violation cases they deal with on a regular basis. Both faculty and staff believe that there are intercultural aspects that need to be addressed when implementing the academic integrity related policies. The findings of my research demonstrate the need for culturally sensitive measures to be implemented as an educative approach for the students rather than approaching the issue with a punitive measure after the violation has already been detected. For East Asian international students, a successful acculturation process to Canadian life academically and socially may be a long journey. However, a concerted effort from the institutions to educate and raise awareness to East Asian international students about academic integrity especially through the first year transition time would be crucial for their academic success in Canadian universities.

IMPROVING THE INCLUSION OF EAST ASIAN INTERNATIONAL STUDENTS IN THE CANADIAN CLASSROOM

Based on the literature and my own lived experiences, this discussion section considers the linguistic, cultural, pedagogical and policy implications of academic integrity for East Asian international students.

Smith (2016) provides four key suggestions for academic support for international students outside of the classroom: a) peer academic advising b) frequent and early academic intervention to better prepare for classroom expectations, internship placements, communication skills c) inform and educate academic integrity standards, and d) provide language assistance for better verbal and written communication. As Smith (2016) assert, the language support can be provided for both domestic and international students. International graduate students could use specific language support for their thesis writing. I argue that language and academic support measures, such as providing academic writing workshops, and academic writing editing help have to go hand-in-hand with measures to address academic integrity issues for international students.

Pedagogically, faculty members can use three approaches to internationalize their course curriculum, thereby integrating an international and intercultural dimension into the course content as well as teaching and learning activities (Bond et al 2003). First, an add-on approach usually means adding a reading or an assignment to the existing course content while the main body is untouched. This is a simple low-stakes approach from the faculty perspective. Second, an infusion approach involves infusing international content in the selection of course materials and integrating student experiences into learning activities. This requires more preparatory work from the faculty but is a great way to increase student engagement in the learning. Third, the transformation approach aims to enable students to move between two or more worldviews and requires a shift in how we understand the world. This approach maybe the most rare and difficult, yet it is the one that may have the most impact on changing people and genuinely leading to inclusion of international students.

I believe all these three approaches are optimal options for faculty members to incorporate in their course curricula to address academic integrity issues as learning through their course work could help international students help understand the importance of the issues. I have personally experienced the add-on approach when the professor in my master's program added an assignment on the APA style guide as part of the course requirements. I found that this successfully raised awareness of academic integrity for both domestic and international students and it also provided an opportunity for the students to examine a variety of examples using the APA rules. Faculty members have an integral role to promote academic integrity in students' learning and in order to to create a truly inclusive learning environment for all students. Beyond detecting and reporting academic violations from students of colour or students' whose first language is not English, it is probably worth noting the fact that "promoting academic integrity is about more than upholding rules and policies, especially when they perpetuate systems of privilege for some and oppression for others" (Eaton, 2022, pp. 6-7).

With the increasing number of international students in HEIs in Canada, there is a growing need for a better understanding of intercultural communication between students, university faculty or staff, especially when it comes to topics of academic integrity and plagiarism. As the literature review showed, the practices of academic integrity and plagiarism are often believed to be influenced by cultural values from both hosting universities and the origin of the international students. As such, it is important and beneficial to international students when providing training and discussions on academic honesty issues to approach these from a nuanced and cultural perspective (Thompson et al, 2017). However, while the demographic composition of students in the classroom has rapidly changed over the last decade in Canada, the assumptions and expectations of higher education leadership or university faculty and staff members may have remained the same in terms of academic integrity issues, which may have resulted in the disconnect between the written institutional policies and the application of the policies (MacLeod & Eaton, 2020). Rather than the policy making and implementation having a top-down approach, students voices from different cultural groups should be reflected in the policy making and implementation process. Perhaps, with the added diversity in the classroom, one size fits all policy approach no longer is effective.

There are also policy implications for the way that institutions support faculty members when academic integrity issues occur. It is important to note that when an academic integrity issue has been detected, it is not a problem that one faculty member can solve. It is a much more complicated issue that involves individual, institutional and policy levels. According to the surveys from MacLeod and Eaton's study (2020), faculty members expressed their concerns about ineffective application of academic integrity policies, added workload due to increased numbers of academic dishonesty incidents, and frustration caused by the inconsistent institutional responses. As Stoesz and Eaton (2020) assert, "policies only have a chance of being effective if all stakeholders including students are well aware of them" (p.4). They also emphasize the need for educating students through a robust orientation process before they begin their first year as a postsecondary student (Stoesz and Eaton, 2020).

This should apply to both domestic and international students. In terms of international students' case, a more concerted effort to make sure the international students are aware and understand the academic integrity policies is essential. This could be possible by providing mandatory online modules, workshops and via rigorous academic advising or academic support activities (Smith, 2016; Smith et al, 2019). Based on my three roles and experiences associated as an international student, a transnational language educator and a researcher, academic integrity issues for East Asian international students remain as a persistent academic challenge the students face in Canadian universities. I believe that through these intentional measures of training and academic support activities, international students will not only be made aware of the existence of the academic integrity policies but also help understand the intentions of the policies which then are not 'lost in translation'. Reflecting international students' voices in curriculum design and course delivery as well as policy documents themselves and the translation of the policies from a culturally sensitive approach is essential to help ensure academic success for the East Asian international students that Canadian universities are eager to recruit and host and provide an adequate support for transition and integration (Guo & Chase, 2011).

MOVING BEYOND A DEFICIT APPROACH

It is neither sustainable nor equitable to continue to label East Asian international students under the culturally and linguistically deficit focused lens from an institutional perspective. A more culturally relevant pedagogy (Ladson-Billings, 2014) and culturally and linguistically relevant policy interpretation and implementation are required amongst the university stakeholders including faculty, instructional staff, and policy makers. East Asian international students bring "unique educational background and learning preferences", therefore "university authorities and teaching staff need to consider the learning differences of international students in the curriculum design and course delivery" (Zhou & Zhang, 2014, p.14).

Canadian HEIs should develop comprehensive programs to address the academic integrity challenges that East Asian international students are faced with in order to help ensuring academic success of the students. As Heng (2017) notes, institutions should shift their paradigm on perspectives towards international students to address issues around academic integrity. And, as Smith (2020) rightfully points out, going beyond enrolling international students to meet the goals of achieving, diversity, inclusivity, and internationalization means paying attention to enhancing the international student academic experience. For example, they should lessen their authoritative and deficit-minded approaches towards international students and empower international students by making them part of decision-making process specifically on policy making and policy implementation. HEIs can also view academic integrity as equity related concerns factoring in unique socio-cultural contexts international students bring rather than treating the issues from a punitive viewpoint.

CONCLUSION

In this chapter, I used an autoethnography approach to bring the literature on East Asian international students and academic integrity into conversation with three perspectives on this topic from my own lived experiences. By doing so, I highlighted some of the challenges, possibilities and the emergent need to address the issues of academic integrity for East Asian international students. I shed light on the need for a more concerted effort in internationalizing the curriculum in higher education in Canada, specifically by addressing academic integrity related policies and pedagogies.

While this chapter contributes to knowledge by weaving together findings from the literature as well as my personal journey, it would have additionally benefited from empirical data from East Asian international student perspectives. Canada currently lacks scholarship investigating student voices on the challenges they experience in applying academic integrity in their written and oral communication in their academic contexts. As such, future research could incorporate the views of students from various levels of programs including English Preparation Programs and graduate courses. Another possibility for future research would be to concentrate on academic integrity issues relative to students from specific countries in the East Asian regions. While the East Asian countries share some level of common cultural backgrounds rooting from Confucian influences, they have unique cultures and linguistic backgrounds that may influence on the students' learning and outlook differently.

In addition, further studies on the institutional policy and support system to address the disconnect between the written policies and the application of the policies are needed. This could result in positive learning opportunities for newly arrived international students rather than labeling them as the problem. In addition, more specific research on what a culturally sensitive approach in addressing academic integrity concerns for faculty, staff and students could entail is also worthy of further investigation. At the same time, it is important to maintain a delicate balance between respecting Canadian university academic standards and values and implementing culturally sensitive approach.

Academic integrity is a growing concern in higher education in Canada and beyond. Issues around academic integrity are associated with one of the inequities affecting East Asian international students in higher education. Addressing these concerns is crucial in teaching and learning if all students are to be given equal opportunities for academic success and true inclusion in higher education.

REFERENCES

Altbach, P. G. (2002). Perspectives on International Higher Education. *Change, 34*(3), 29–31. doi:10.1080/00091380209601852

Amsberry, D. (2010). Deconstructing Plagiarism: International Students and Textual Borrowing Practices. *The Reference Librarian, 51*(1), 31–44. doi:10.1080/02763870903362183

Bond, S. (2003). *Untapped Resources, Internationalization of the Curriculum and Classroom Experience: A Selected Literature Review*. Canadian Bureau for International Education.

Bond, S., Qian, J., & Huang, J. (2003). *The Role of Faculty in Internationalizing the Undergraduate Curriculum and Classroom Experience*. Canadian Bureau for International Education.

Canadian Bureau for International Education. (2018). *Canada's Performance and Potential in International Education 2018*. Retrieved from: https://cbie.ca/media/facts-and-figures/

Canadian Bureau for International Education. (2020). *International Students in Canada 2020*. Retrieved from: https://cbie.ca/infographic/

Chang, H. (2008). *Authoethnography as Method*. Left Coast Press.

Chang, H. (2013). Individual and Collaborative Autoethnography as Method: A Social Scientist's Perspective. In *Handbook of autoethnography* (pp. 107-123). Springer. doi:10.4324/9781315427812

Chen, & Zhou, G. (2019). Chinese International Students' Sense of Belonging in North American Postsecondary Institutions: A Critical Literature Review. *Brock Education, 28*(2), 48–63. doi:10.26522/brocked.v28i2.642

Chen, Y.-H., & Van Ullen, M. K. (2011). Helping International Students Succeed Academically through Research Process and Plagiarism Workshops. *College & Research Libraries, 72*(3), 209–235. doi:10.5860/crl-117rl

Clifford, V. A. (2009). Engaging the Disciplines in Internationalising the Curriculum. *The International Journal for Academic Development, 14*(2), 133–143. doi:10.1080/13601440902970122

Eaton, S., & Christensen Hughes, J. (2022). *Academic Integrity in Canada : An Enduring and Essential Challenge*. Springer International Publishing AG. doi:10.1007/978-3-030-83255-1

Ellis, C. (2004). *The ethnographic I: A methodological novel about autoethnography*. AltaMira Press.

Fass-Holmes, B. (2018). International Students Reported for Academic Integrity Violations: Demographics, Retention, and Graduation. *Journal of International Students, 7*(3), 644–669. doi:10.32674/jis.v7i3.292

Firang, D., & Mensah, J. (2022). Exploring the Effects of the COVID-19 Pandemic on International Students and Universities in Canada. *Journal of International Students, 12*(1), 1–18. doi:10.32674/jis.v12i1.2881ojed.org/jis

Foster, M., & Anderson, L. (2015). Editorial: Exploring Internationalisation of the Curriculum to Enhance the Student Experience. *Journal of Perspectives in Applied Academic Practice., 3*(3), 1–2. doi:10.14297/jpaap.v3i3.206

Foltýnek, T., & Glendinning, I. (2015). Impact of Policies for Plagiarism in Higher Education across Europe: Results of the Project. *Acta Universitatis Agriculturae et Silviculturae Mendelianae Brunensis, 63*(1), 207–216. doi:10.11118/actaun201563010207

Gu, Q. (2010). Variations in Beliefs and Practices: Teaching English in Crosscultural Contexts. *Language and Intercultural Communication, 10*(1), 32–53. doi:10.1080/14708470903377357

Guo, S., & Chase, M. (2011). Internationalisation of Higher Education: Integrating International Students into Canadian Academic Environment. *Teaching in Higher Education, 16*(3), 305–318. doi:10.1080/13562517.2010.546524

Guo, Y., & Guo, S. (2017). Internationalization of Canadian Higher Education: Discrepancies between Policies and International Student Experiences. *Studies in Higher Education, 42*(5), 851–868. doi:10.1080/03075079.2017.1293874

Heng, T. (2017). Voices of Chinese International Students in USA Colleges: "I want to tell them that…. *Studies in Higher Education, 42*(5), 833–850. doi:10.1080/03075079.2017.1293873

Jones, S. H. (2005). Autoethnography: Making the Personal Political. In Denzin & Lincoln (Eds.), Handbook of Qualitative Research (3rd ed.). Thousand Oaks, CA: Sage.

Kang, P. (2020). Towards Sustainable Internationalization in Post-COVID Higher Education: Voices from Non-Native English-Speaking International Students in Canada. *Migration and Language Education, 1*(2), 60–73. doi:10.29140/mle.v1n2.383

Kelly, P. (2000). Internationalizing the Curriculum: For Profit or Planet. In S. Inayatullah & J. Gidley (Eds.), *The University in Transformation: Global Perspectives on the Futures of the University*. Bergin and Harvey.

Ladson-Billings, G. (2014). Culturally Relevant Pedagogy 2.0: A.k.a. the Remix. *Harvard Educational Review, 84*(1), 74–84. doi:10.17763/haer.84.1.p2rj131485484751

Leask, B. (2015). *Internationalizing the Curriculum*. Routledge. doi:10.4324/9781315716954

MacLeod, P. D., & Eaton, S. E. (2020). The Paradox of Faculty Attitudes toward Student Violations of Academic Integrity. *Journal of Academic Ethics, 18*(4), 347–362. doi:10.100710805-020-09363-4

McKenzie, A. (2018). Academic Integrity across the Canadian Landscape. *Canadian Perspectives on Academic Integrity, 1*(2), 40–45.

Sawir, E. (2005). Language Difficulties of International Students in Australia: The Effects of Prior Learning Experience. *International Education Journal, 6*(5), 56780.

Smith, C. (2016). International Student Success. *Strategic Enrolment Quarterly, 4*(2), 61–73. doi:10.1002em3.20084

Smith, C. (2020). International Students and Their Academic Experiences: Student Satisfaction, Student Success Challenges, and Promising Teaching Practices. In Rethinking Education Across Borders (pp. 271–287). Springer. doi:10.1007/978-981-15-2399-1_16

Smith, C., Zhou, G., Potter, M., & Wang, D. (2019). Connecting Best Practices for Teaching Linguistically and Culturally Diverse International Students with International Student Satisfaction and Student Perceptions of Student Learning. *Advances in Global Education and Research, 3*, 252-265. https://scholar.uwindsor.ca/educationpub/24

Song, X., & Cadman, K. (2013). Education With(out) Distinction: Beyond Graduate Attributes for Chinese International Students. *Higher Education Research & Development*, *32*(2), 258–271. doi:10.1 080/07294360.2012.673573

Song-Turner, H. (2008). Plagiarism: Academic Dishonesty or 'Blind Spot' of Multicultural Education? *Australian Universities Review*, *50*(2), 38–50.

Spry, T. (2001). Performing Autoethnography: An Embodied Methodological Praxis. *Qualitative Inquiry*, *7*(6), 706–732. doi:10.1177/107780040100700605

Statistics Canada. (2021). *Distribution of International Student Enrolments, by Level of Tertiary Education.* Statistics Canada. https://www150.statcan.gc.ca/

Stein, S. (2018). National Exceptionalism in the "EduCanada" Brand: Unpacking the Ethics of Internationalization Marketing in Canada. *Discourse (Abingdon, England)*, *39*(3), 461–477. doi:10.1080/0 1596306.2016.1276884

Stoesz, B., & Eaton, S. E. (2020). Academic Integrity Policies of Publicly Funded Universities in Western Canada. *Educational Policy*, *00*(0), 1–20. doi:10.1177/0895904820983032

Stoesz, B., Eaton, S. E., Miron, J. B., & Thacker, E. (2019). Academic Integrity and Contract Cheating Policy Analysis of Colleges in Ontario, Canada. *International Journal for Educational Integrity*, *15*(1), 1–18. doi:10.100740979-019-0042-4

Svensson, L., & Wihlborg, M. (2010). Internationalising the Content of Higher Education: The Need for a Curriculum Perspective. *Higher Education*, *60*(6), 595–613. doi:10.100710734-010-9318-6

Thompson, B., Bagby, J. H., Sulak, T. N., Sheets, J., & Trepinski, T. M. (2017). The Cultural Elements of Academic Honesty. *Journal of International Students*, *7*(1), 136–153. doi:10.32674/jis.v7i1.249

Yeh, C., & Inose, M. (2003). International Students' Reported English Fluency, Social Support Satisfaction, and Social Connectedness as Predictors of Acculturative Stress. *Counselling Psychology Quarterly*, *16*(1), 15–28. doi:10.1080/0951507031000114058

Vandeville, G. (2020). *The biggest resource we have is each other.* https://www.utoronto.ca/news/biggest-resource-we-have-each-other-how-u-t-s international-students-are-coping-covid-19

Zhang, A., & Zhou, G. (2010). Understanding Chinese International Students at a Canadian University: Perspectives, Expectations, and Experiences. *Comparative and International Education*, *39*(3), 1–16. doi:10.5206/cie-eci.v39i3.9162

Zhou, G., & Zhang, Z. (2014). A Study of the First Year International Students at a Canadian University: Challenges and Experiences with Social Integration. *Comparative and International Education/Éducation Comparée et Internationale*, *43*(2), 7.

Section 4
Student Development and Support

Chapter 11

Developing Fruitful Communication:
How to Lead Culturally and Linguistically–Diverse International Students With Emotional Intelligence

Rakha Zabin

Brock University, Canada

ABSTRACT

To smoothly transition to the educational platforms and integrate into the new country, especially after the heinous impact of the COVID-19 pandemic, international students need adequate support from the leaders of educational institutions. Leaders not only refer to the administrative leaders but also include the teachers who lead these students in their regular classes. Leaders may also refer to their peers and even the students themselves, who make decisions about their own lives and lead themselves. The toolkit of emotional intelligence (EQ) is valuable for all leaders because it is a multifaceted ability that helps individuals apply the power of emotions as a source of trust, communication, and influence. This chapter focuses on an account of the learning experience of one international doctoral student's transition within a new cultural context. Self-reflection on the hurdles experienced and the importance of respectful communication during the evolution to becoming an international doctoral student in Ontario informs the analysis.

INTRODUCTION

COVID-19 has drastically changed the educational landscape for millions of university students around the world, and international students have their own set of unique challenges. International students worry about things, such as visa and graduation status, optional practical training opportunities being harder to obtain or canceled, whether to go home (if that is even an option, due to border closings), living far from loved ones, not having a strong support network, having to find a place to live (if dormitories

DOI: 10.4018/978-1-7998-8921-2.ch011

closed), and finances (Firang, 2020; Keung & Teotonio, 2020; Wong et al., 2020). Even in the post-pandemic stages, some of these challenges might persist, requiring some adjustments to better cater to these international students.

Leaders in academia are also going through a challenging time, working through new processes for ensuring student progress and holding graduations. There is no doubt that "leadership will be one of the most heavily tested skills throughout the coronavirus pandemic" (Murray, 2020, para. 3). Communication is critical in such adverse situations, for both leaders and international students, to develop a bond of support and understanding during this unprecedented time. These communications can be made more fruitful, with the aid of emotional intelligence (EQ). The ability to perceive and express emotions, assimilate emotions in thought, understand and reason with emotions, and regulate emotions in oneself and others is what experts defined as emotional intelligence (EQ) (Clayton, 2012; Goleman, 2006; Mayer et al., 2000). The five components (self-awareness, self-regulation, empathy, motivation, and social skill) embedded within EQ may work solely, or collectively, to develop fruitful communications among students and leaders. This chapter aims to highlight the importance of developing fruitful communications with culturally and linguistically diverse international students employing emotional intelligence (EQ).

BACKGROUND

The evolution of the internationalization of higher education in Canada is happening at a rapid pace, which is worthy of attention (Guo & Guo, 2017; Heringer, 2020; Knight, 1997; Knight, 2003). Every year, many international students are flying to Canada from all over the world to pursue their future academic and career goals in a multicultural, global setting (Knight, 2015). It is true that international student enrollment in Canada has been hit hard by the COVID-19 pandemic (International Consultants for Education and Fairs, 2020; Keung & Teotonio, 2020), as most of the universities are moving into an online format (Ross, 2020). International students who are already here are also going through severe challenges, being a vulnerable minority, and bearing the impact on their well-being during the current global health crisis. Wong et al. (2020) interviewed three international students from India, the Netherlands, and Mauritius, and they shared how they have been continuing to study and stay connected to their classmates and families during this critical time of the pandemic. Staying connected and having effective communications stands as a vital source of support for these international students.

Keung and Teotonio (2020) share disorienting stories of international students, as colleges and universities were abruptly halted, due to travel restrictions imposed in the wake of the global COVID-19 health crisis. Border closures, flight cancellations, shuttered language testing sites, and closed visa offices are posing major challenges. A growing number of international students who intended to come to Canada in the next few months are now deferring their study plans. "I am afraid to be in a country where I do not know anyone and have nowhere to go during this pandemic. I don't think it would be mentally healthy for me to go to a place for the first time, alone, with all these problems," says Olaifa, a potential international student, as cited by Keung and Teotonio (2020, para. 4). As the health crisis drags on, colleges and universities are asking the federal government to allow all international students to do online courses while in their own country.

These are some highlights of international-student challenges during the pandemic. The challenges for international students precede the pandemic and are likely to continue post-pandemic. International students have been struggling for a long time. Past research shows that disorienting experiences are common among most international students, for as students reported, instances of facing racial dynamics, outsider status, risk-taking behaviours, and power relations (Liu, 2016; Trilokekar, Safdar, El Masri, & Scott, 2014), both in the realms of the academic and the job market (Trilokekar & Kukar, 2011), were portrayed. Despite the promoted potential benefits of having a multicultural campus, students reported, internationalizing higher education requires more than the physical presence of international students (Heringer, 2020). Adjustment difficulties about language abilities, poor connectedness to host communities, and perceived employer discrimination against international students hinder international students' integration into Canadian society, as well as into the academic and labour markets (Trilokekar et al., 2019; Yi, 2018).

Effective communications with leaders from educational organizations may be helpful for these culturally and linguistically diverse groups of international students, with the aid of emotional intelligence, as it consists of elements beneficial to deal with stress and adverse situations. According to Goleman's article, in *HBR's 10 Must Reads on Leadership* (2011), emotional intelligence is one crucial way that makes all effective leaders alike. Goleman (2011) further says that all individuals are leaders of themselves, as they lead themselves in making decisions of critical real-life situations to move on in life. Emotional intelligence is at the core of being able to make significant behavioural shifts and ultimately helping individuals attain all those adjectives describing stellar leadership (Goleman et al., 2001). The components are supportive of both the students and the leaders, and can work solely and collectively, depending upon the context.

EMOTIONAL INTELLIGENCE

Emotional intelligence (EQ) deals with managing stress, communicating effectively, empathizing with others, overcoming challenges, and defusing conflict (Goleman & Boyatzis, 2008). These are personal, and professional, significant parts of a person's life. International students have such usual and unusual situations to deal with, and EQ helps these diverse groups of students to increase their emotional self-awareness, emotional expression, creativity, tolerance, trust, and integrity. It also helps them to improve relations, and, eventually, aid them in making social and psychological adjustments. "The emotional dimensions are key elements in regulating oneself, and the surrounding stimulating environment," writes (Goleman, 2011, p. 9). These are essential factors that are often ignored, which gave rise to the importance of this research. In this challenging year, stress levels in many people have increased further (Harmey, 2021), and international students are, in fact, one of the most vulnerable populations suffering from mental health and wellness challenges (Lai et al., 2020), as they deal with a unique set of circumstances which may be catered well, with effective communications, using emotional intelligence.

The current uncertainties of COVID-19 have made the situation more challenging for international students, with occurrences of stressful disruptions (Murray, 2020), and the toolkit of emotional intelligence would be more vital for them in such situations. Such a dynamic instrument may help multicultural international students handle several adverse situations, which are more apparent, due to the pandemic.

According to Canada's International Education Strategy (2019-2024), Canada is focusing on growing and sustaining the international education sector. The strategy builds on the attributes that have made Canada a destination of choice for international students: strong schools and programs of study, welcoming and diverse communities with an enviable quality of life, and opportunities to start careers and pursue permanent residency. However, most students shared perplexing experiences that often lead to traumatic effects and psychological reactions, such as depression, anxiety, and acute stress disorder, which was further amplified during this pandemic (Browning et al., 2021; Song et al., 2021). Immigration, Refugees and Citizenship Canada (2020) states that the government of Canada also took several measures to support international students during the COVID-19 pandemic. However, international students are still struggling, and these stressful situations may be better coped with by using effective conversations, based on emotional intelligence.

"There is a significant association of emotional intelligence and stress coping styles," stated two leading scholars (Fteiha & Awwad, 2020, p. 4) in their study conducted using Goleman's (1996) theory of emotional intelligence. Another research article, titled, '*Emotional Intelligence as Predictor of Mental, Social, and Physical Health in University Students*, conducted by Fernández-Berrocal and Extremera (2016), illustrates that a higher level of emotional intelligence is positively and significantly related to dealing with increased anxiety and depression situations. Goleman (2006) developed five key emotional intelligence skills that are linked to everything from decision-making to academic achievement: self-awareness, self-regulation, social skills, empathy, and motivation.

Emotional intelligence involves understanding and managing emotions, and its five components play an essential role in handling even the most challenging life situations with grace. Emotional intelligence is beneficial for students, because it helps them empathize with others and themselves, and deal with difficult situations without getting frazzled (Fernández-Berrocal & Extremera, 2016). It affects relationships, academic performance, and even the way students handle pressure. For international students, especially during the pandemic, emotional intelligence would be more crucial in managing their adaptive processes and regulating their emotions better. Emotional intelligence is essential to have better overall health and wellbeing. Employing EQ is vital for international students, and can aid in effective communication, both in class, and outside of the classroom. Leadership and teaching strategies used by administrators and professors dealing with a diverse group of international students can be curated with EQ elements to develop fruitful communications. Emotional intelligence is key to leadership, and it plays a critical role in helping others get through these tough times.

International Student Challenges

According to the American College Health Association (ACHA, 2014), 61% of graduate students report more than average or tremendous stress, which is higher than the average rate (55%) among all college students. The problem is more dominant among these international students, as there is a vast difference in their culture, language, food, weather, and other factors from here to their own countries.

El Masri et al. (2015), in their report, state that there is a need for more programs that enhance interactions between international and domestic students, as well as for programs that support ongoing language competency. It is also noted that there is a lack of integration of programs and services, which is necessary to build a sense of community and belonging for these international students. There is also a lack of communication and coordination between departments, so that not all services are known to staff, nor clearly advertised on institutional websites, thus, hindering accessibility and awareness. These gaps are, indeed, making the lives of international students more difficult and leading to greater transitional challenges.

Lu et al. (2018) carried out research focusing on the aspects of positive adjustments of Chinese international graduate students. Results of the study show that "academic and sociocultural challenges tended to be temporary, whereas social and employment challenges tended to be more long-standing"

(Lu et al., 2018, p. 998). Other than these, the research results also showed that emotional and psychological well-being and sociocultural difficulties are great challenges that international students must fight. For international students, the challenges are greater compared to those of others. This is because of their experiences of social isolation and employment barriers. Lu et al. (2018) shed further light on the issue, and say that "in their narratives, they tend to attribute individual challenges to psychological (e.g., personality, motivation, effort) and cultural factors (e.g., language barriers)" (p. 998), which are challenges unique to international students.

Chen and Zhou (2019) illustrate that an increasing number of Chinese international students have been entering North American universities, and many have experienced issues with a sense of belonging, which can, in turn, impact their academic, social performance, and psychological well-being. Another, similar research study, conducted by Zhou et al. (2017), highlights the challenges of Chinese international graduate students in Canadian universities, and both these research studies portray issues of the language barrier that were key challenges for almost all the Chinese international students. Lack of exposure to English, during their own educational journey, created this challenging setting for Chinese students. After conducting the in-depth examinations, Zhou et al. (2017) explicitly state:

The culture and educational differences between Canada and China were reported to be significant challenges. In our study, participants had difficulties in communicating with domestic peers and instructors in English. Such inadequate language proficiency and cultural differences limited their experience in building social networks, fitting into the community, participating in classes, and connecting with instructors. (pp. 225-226)

These research results offer valuable insights for future international students to have greater exposure to the language, in order to make a smoother linguistic transition, and also, for universities to provide additional assistance to support the language development of international students, who find it challenging to grapple with these language barriers (Burel et al., 2019; Chen & Zhou, 2019; Zhou et al., 2017), as Ontario provides more assistance for English language learners in its elementary and secondary educational systems (Li, 2016).

Cooper and Yarbrough (2016) carried out research using the bio-cultural model of human adaptation and photo-voice methodology to study the reflecting behaviour of the physical or mental health of Asian-Indian female international students. The photographs and the narratives of the students showed that one of the greatest challenges was "addressing fear and anxiety related to loneliness and separation from home and family" (Cooper & Yarbrough, 2016, p. 1045), which was depicted in the photos of several participants.

For these students, mental/emotional wellness and competencies are more important, because of the diverse change between the current context and culture, compared to the one of their home. Cooper and Yarbrough (2016) say that several participants presented pictures "representing loneliness mixed with some degree of anxiety" (p. 1045). Emotional makeup is an important aspect for these students' adjustments, because otherwise, they suffer from psychological disorders, as many of them come from very crowded cities and are plunged into loneliness as they land here. Support services for these emotional aspects are very important, because stress is associated with academia and work, which needs proper balance and nurturing (Cooper & Yarbrough, 2016).

Duncan (2020) reflects on the survey conducted by IDP Connect, the B2B division of international education specialists. Noting how IDP Education and its research examined nearly 6,900 international student applicants' attitudes and motivations for studying in Australia, Canada, New Zealand, the United Kingdom, and the United States, in light of COVID-19. The research focused on students' views on commencement dates, perceptions of safety, and online versus face-to-face delivery. The survey results reveal that:

Thirty-one percent of respondents stated that they would be willing to start their course online and move to face-to-face learning at a later date, but by far the greatest preference was to defer to January 2021, if this meant face-to-face learning would be possible. (Duncan, 2020, para. 8)

Of the students who stated that they would prefer to defer than study online, 69 percent said that they believed it lacked international exposure, and 47 percent stated that the standard of online teaching was a concern. Duncan (2020) further shares that the IDP Chief assures the international students by saying that they are working together to find the right solutions, through effective partnerships and technologies, that create a new bridge for international students to achieve their global goals.

According to the International Consultants for Education and Fairs (2020), international students ' exploring-destination preferences are also interesting, in terms of how the competitive dynamic among destinations could shift, as the pandemic runs its course. Given the strong underlying demand for in-person instruction, for example, destinations that are seen to have a stronger public-health response and can move more quickly to open borders and campuses, will likely earn a greater market share, by attracting students who had originally intended to study elsewhere. This would be an added challenge for international students to keep this new aspect in mind, along with a truckload of other factors, while choosing their ultimate higher-educational institution.

International students who are already here are also going through severe challenges, being a vulnerable minority group of people, and bearing the impact on their well-being during the current global health crisis. Wong et al. (2020) interviewed three international students from India, the Netherlands, and Mauritius, and they shared how they have been continuing to study and stay connected to their classmates and families during this critical time of the pandemic. In answer to this question: How has the pandemic changed you? one of the students answered,

It has reinforced my belief that I am studying the right things. We are seeing how opinion is so divided and there are such global disparities. We studied these things in the classroom, and now we are watching them unfold in real-time. (Wong et al, 2020, para. 7)

Wong et al. (2020) illustrate that these students shared that the situation escalated quickly. Some of them preferred taking a flight at a higher cost, and moved back to their home country, because they desired to be with family, rather than being stuck in the dorm. For some others, flying home was not an option; with closed borders and financial stress, they had to stick around, experiencing the pandemic in a different way.

Okwuosa (2021) shares that Ottawa has updated its policy for international graduates, but advocates say that it has not gone far enough to address longstanding issues and new pandemic realities. While job loss and underemployment have been a province-wide challenge during the pandemic, international graduates looking for skilled work face a specific set of stresses, as their ability to remain in the country hangs in the balance. As a result of the pandemic, a number of international graduates have taken up work in warehouses and grocery stores to earn money but working in jobs considered low-skilled and high-risk does not bring them closer to their dream of settling permanently in Canada. "None of this work counts toward permanent residency, because it's not valued, but this is the work that, as we have seen through COVID-19, sustains our communities and keeps the economy moving" (Okwuosa, 2021, para. 8).

Emotional Competencies and Mental Health of Young Adults

The role of EQ is vital in making social and emotional adjustments, as its dimensions play a crucial role in developing one's own self with components of self-awareness, motivation, and social skills (Goleman, 2006). The components of EQ are indispensable for these students, as they are the upcoming leaders of tomorrow in leading themselves and others (Tracy, 2017). EQ is a set of qualities or competencies that captures a broad collection of individual skills and dispositions that are outside the traditional thought of knowledge, like professional skills, technical knowledge, or academic intelligence. Brackett, Rivers, and Salovey (2011) illustrate that emotions are an intrinsic part of our biological makeup. They help to regulate ourselves during various stressful situations and influence our behaviour to cope with them.

Blakemore (2018) states that all our characteristics are reflections of important stages of our brain development. Referring to this age group, she says, "adolescence isn't an aberration; it is a crucial stage of our becoming individuals and human beings (Blakemore, 2018, p.13). She also says that the start of adolescence is measured biologically, but the end is done socially, or may even be arbitrary. She explains that the age of adolescence is seen differently in western culture, compared to other cultures. Some perceive it to approach along with puberty, but many others see it as the age of change and adjustment to the culture around, which even includes parents and family. Young people who are in their 20s, and even later, are in that stage of development where they are constantly fighting with the thought of being accepted, or not, by the society, and at times, even by their parents. The development of the brain is merely a physical aspect, but, during this period, it is more of cultural and emotional development (Blakemore, 2018).

Kong et al. (2019) investigated the role of social support and affective experience in the relationship between EI and life satisfaction. The study included a large group of Chinese adult participants, who completed the Wong Law Emotional Intelligence Scale, the multi-dimensional scale of perceived social support, the Positive Affect and Negative Affect Scale, and the Satisfaction with Life Scale. As a result, it is seen that "structural equation modeling demonstrated that social support, positive affect and negative affect independently mediated the effect of trait emotional intelligence on life satisfaction, consistent with the social network and affective meditation models" (Kong et al., 2019, Discussion section). The study states that for young adults, as well as general adults, EI plays a vital role in shaping their satisfaction of day-to-day life and activities.

Psychological and social impulses play a vital role, as "the complexity of self and surrounding emotions tends to focus on the young individual's ability to recognize themselves, and other people, as psychological and emotional beings" (Bosacki, 2016, p. 83). The emotional self, referring to one's self-development and emotional regulation, especially in the stage of adolescence and young adulthood, is met with regulatory and coping behaviours carved from individual thoughts, experiences, and attachment relations. Young people may self-evaluate themselves, depending on how others judge their actions.

Bosacki (2016) further illustrates the importance of virtues and principles, and says "the moral imperatives derived from spiritual beliefs may impact their attitudes and behaviours, leading to positive or negative self-adjustment" (p. 87). Complex emotional understanding might hinder the cognitive abilities, but linkage between the emotional and social abilities might be helpful for this age group of early adolescence and young adulthood. Due to this reason, "to a large extent, emotional processes help to guide young people's social interactions and relationships and are needed to help create constructive solutions in personally and socially challenging situations" (Bosacki, 2016, p. 96). This means that the multidimensional process of self-image negotiation and co-construction, with others, help to shape our social, cognitive, and emotional worlds (Bosacki, 2016).

International students are drowned into an ocean of emotional and social challenges. The challenges for international students precede the pandemic and are likely to continue post-pandemic. International students have been struggling for a long time, and this pandemic just amplified their challenges even further. A closer insight of a personal log will assist in reflecting better on some of these challenges.

Account of Personal Narrative

Clandinin (2007) describes narrative inquiry as "the researchers usually embracing that assumptions that the story is one, if not the fundamental unit, that accounts for human experiences" (p. 5). With the emphasis on the narrative, the stories become both the method and phenomena of the study. This narrative account includes stories of transition of an international doctoral student beginning the doctoral program in the time of the pandemic, reflecting on the hurdles of the new academic and cultural contexts. "Through the attention to methods for analyzing and understanding stories lived and told, it can be connected and placed under the label of qualitative research method" (Clandinin, 2007, p. 6). Smith (2017) adds to the importance of qualitative research methods, particularly narrative inquiry, by stating, "stories teach us who we are by constituting our identities and sense of self" and that "people need stories because of the work they do for us, which primarily, is to help make the world meaningful" (p. 505).

A narrative in temporality, "refers to events under study in transition" (Connelly & Clandinin, 2000, p. 479). Giving attention temporally directs inquirers to the past, present, and future of the people, places, things, and content being studied. This narrative is such, as it displays multiple layers of consciousness. An autobiographical narrative inquiry is a special form of narrative inquiry and is closely linked to auto-ethnography. Understanding 'life as narrative' led Bruner (2004) to posit, "the stories we tell about our lives are our autobiographies" (p. 691). However, Phillips (1999) made the distinction between the autoethnography and autobiography that confirmed the research component. An autobiography shows a linear correlation between the person and his or her past experiences. An autoethnography allows for a self-story that voices a "narrative oriented inquiry" honouring the told, the re-telling, and the teller (Hiles et al., 2017, p. 8). Nevertheless, narrative inquirers understand that telling stories is not an unbridled process. How people tell their stories is shaped by cultural conventions and language usage, and reflects the stories of possible lives that are a part of one's culture (Bruner, 2004).

My Story

I am an international student from Bangladesh. I started my doctoral journey at an Ontario university in the summer of last year (2020), just amid the COVID-19 pandemic. Being an international student, and starting a doctoral program in a foreign land among most of the native students, is in itself certainly stressful. However, I was more anxious, because the program began online, and I was restricted from the in-person exposure. I am a strong believer in collaborative learning and engagement, and the beginning of my doctoral journey online made me more conscious of that missing piece. I started wondering how I would collaborate with my peers and the instructors, to that extent, if it is all through the screen. I was also nervous about whether or not I had enough technical skills to conduct my doctoral coursework online. I come from a developing country, Bangladesh–a country with a huge population, which is still struggling to strengthen its technological infrastructure. Although there have been significant improvements to education that resulted in nearly universal access to primary education, a literacy rate estimated at over 78% of the young adult population, and greater gender equality in primary and secondary education, which have taken place in Bangladesh in the last decade, learning outcomes and completion rates have not kept pace with the advances in participation and gender parity, despite investments in infrastructure and improvements in teacher training, curriculum revision, and textbook provision (Bangladesh Ministry of Primary and Mass Education, 2015, Islam, 2020).

Even after getting enrolled in the program, I was continuously questioning my abilities about whether I would be able to begin such a rigorous program online or not. I was also conscious of my lacking technological skills, and whether it would be possible for me to adapt to the new learning environment. These worries drowned me in a world of emotional stress and challenges. Although I was already residing in Canada for the last few years, and was getting adapted to this foreign land, this pandemic just changed the whole scenario. I was so lonely and isolated, being home all day long and worrying about all these hurdles. Previously, I used to share my apartment with two other flatmates, who left to live with their families, after the closure of the campus. I could not travel back home due to border closures, and traveling within Canada was also restricted to a great extent. The hope of vaccination was mere, and although I did not worry about traveling to Canada for my classes, I was stressed, as I was already in Canada and things were online, which meant that I could have been in my home country, doing my classes from there. This would have saved me all my living costs, and would have allowed me to be with my family during this crucial period. Neither could I go back home, nor could someone come to visit me. All I could do was get stuck on the screen for fifteen hours a day for my online commitments, and feel isolated and lonely at the end of the day. Going out to restaurants, gyms, and swimming, in order to socialize and get an emotional boost were also not options. I was indeed drowned in the world of academic, emotional, and social challenges that were to be bridged in order to transition to the new normal smoothly.

Leading with Emotional Intelligence

The current COVID-19 pandemic is testing leaders worldwide, exposing deficits in crisis communication, leadership, preparedness, and flexibility. It has impacted the effectiveness of communication and has imposed ethical dilemmas and emotional stress on leaders (Christian et at., 2021). Leaders refer to leadership in business organizations, educational institutions, and classrooms (educators, peers, and students who are leading themselves). It is easy to read articles about how leaders "should" or "should not" behave or "be." In real practice, however, behavioural changes are hard and take practice, little by little (Murray, 2020). EQ is at the core of being able to make these behavioural shifts, and ultimately help leaders attain all those aspects that describe stellar leadership.

Every individual is primarily a leader of leading themselves. Only if someone is effective in leading oneself, can he or she look into coaching, managing, and mentoring others using the "L.I.V.E.S. model" (Novak et al., 2014, p.14). Leading oneself might seem an effortless job, but it is challenging, especially during times of uncertainty. These elements promote the leaders' core authenticity in being more inviting to support the L.I.V.E.S. model, and help maintain the fundamental consistency between one's values, goals, and actions. International students coming to Canada are leaders of themselves; they make decisions regarding academics, finances, social community, etc. They are leading themselves in understanding the new world that they are exposed to.

They are motivating themselves intrinsically and continually, trying to boost their inner self. When this author reflected on the beginning phase of her doctoral journey within the COVID-19 pandemic, she can vividly remember how she kept motivating herself with all the challenges. Motivation from her teachers and peers acted as her emotional booster. Communication with her teachers, who were compassionate towards her, made her feel that she was not alone. As a result, she was treating herself with more kindness, compassion, and care. As Neff (2020b) illustrates, being kind and compassionate to oneself adds to one's resilience during challenging times and helps one understand his or herself-worth. Compassion helped this author develop fruitful communication with her teachers and peers, and helped her to calm herself during her emotional disruptions.

This idea of being one's leader, and inviting oneself to live an educational life, presented through the L.I.V.E.S. model, and aligned with the emotional intelligence elements, can be vividly intertwined with this study. Knowing oneself better, foreseeing the possibilities ahead, and building the social connections are very helpful in the difficult phases, which are seamlessly applicable for international students. Treating oneself with kindness during a difficult time, believing in a better tomorrow, and extending empathy towards oneself and the surrounding community are helpful food for the international students who are leading themselves through this challenging situation. While leading a diverse group of international students, whose lives are full of uncertainties, leaders may treat them with kindness and help them adapt and be hopeful for tomorrow. During the times of crisis, communications from leaders should be empathetic, honest, transparent, and understandable, able to build trust, and foster resilience and compassion (Christian et al., 2021).

Neff (2020a) states that people should treat themselves with the same kind of kindness, care, and compassion as they would treat those they care about: their good friends and their loved ones. This is self-compassion. He also says that that self-compassion also provides a sense of self-worth. It is intertwined with mindfulness, which assists in coping and the growth of resilience. These connect clearly to this author's own experience, because resilience was the core of her coping strategies during the pandemic. Neff et al. (2020) presented a series of research on developing and validating the Self-Compassion Scale—Youth version (SCS-Y). Results show significant association with mindfulness, happiness, life satisfaction, depression, and resilience, and achievement of goal orientation in expected directions. Overall, findings suggest that the SCS-Y is a reliable and valid measure of self-compassion for use with youths.

Neff (2020) explores self-compassion, and states that self-compassion means being kind and understanding to oneself when confronted with personal failure, instead of mercilessly judging and criticizing oneself for various inadequacies or shortcomings. Giving up at the painful times of adjustment challenges was something easier for this author. Feeling that she was not fit for this new environment was the most common thought inside her mind, because she constantly thought that she was not the right person for this. This author was trying to treat herself with kindness, patience, and motivation–all in alignment with the E.Q. areas, to cope with her challenges, and all these, in return, from the people around her, was immensely valuable.

SOLUTIONS AND RECOMMENDATION

The key findings from the analysis show that EQ can play a vital role in dealing with disruptive impulses and stressful situations. Components of EQ (i.e., self-awareness, motivation, empathy, and self-regulation) are of great assistance in fostering one's emotional and social skills, which is a prerequisite in situations, like adaptation and assimilation in a foreign land and culture. When leading a group of diverse individuals from different backgrounds, it is critical that leaders employ components of EQ, in their communication, to develop fruitful relationships. Fabio and Kenny (2019) state that healthy relationships at school and the workplace help newcomers deal better with their stress and loneliness. Healthy relationships cannot be built by the students themselves to help them stay motivated, self-regulated, social, et cetera. Institutions play a dominant role in creating a healthy environment for students. The role of leaders is vital in leading fruitful communications that employ the components of EQ, such as self-awareness, motivation, empathy, and so on. Leaders leading themselves and those leading others, communications with one's own self or communication with others, the role of emotional intelligence and its components are all critical in leading culturally and linguistically diverse international students.

This means that if institutions reshape their strategies and create support services to develop mindfulness, self-awareness, emotional regulation, and management, which align with the core theory of EQ, international students will benefit the most in making their adjustments when dealing with psychological stress and anxiety. From the narrative account, it is clear that when the author was undergoing stressful and uncertain circumstances, the aspects of EQ were of tremendous help in making adjustments and dealing with emotional breakdowns.

Along with the academic resources, and the suggestions that the teachers and administrators offer, leaders should provide international students with a platform for respectful communication, that fosters emotional entities, so that these students can share their challenges, without any hesitation, to make their adaptation phase easier.

The implications of the study are to guide future educators to understand the theory of EQ, and to understand its practice and applications among international students, as they deal with the adjustment challenges they face during their settlement. It will also act as a guide for the policy actors to reshape the internationalization policies, and develop better support services to assist students in developing their social and emotional domains, which are equally important as the academic factors, regarding their assimilation.

The scope of the study is to increase international graduating students' awareness of their use of EQ, and strengthen it, by involving them in programs, such as mental health workshops, communication clubs, and so on. This will also help these students to deal with stressful, emotional situations at the workplace and in family life in the future.

CONCLUSION

Leaders should focus on the emotional paradigms and the components of emotional intelligence, while leading a group of diverse students, and the institutions must aid them with services based on mindfulness and compassion. Appel, Park, Wortmann, and Schie (2019) talk about the struggles of spiritual and religious violation in the stressful phases of life. In these situations, discrepancies rise the most within the individual's mind, which is the common case for international students. Programs based on mindfulness, mental wellness, and cultural awareness should be targeted at international students, in order to promote their cultural competence and social-emotional/mental health.

Educators and administrators should practice empathy and compassion while dealing with this vulnerable group of society. Universities should also include programs and provide resources for faith-based support, as faith beliefs and spiritual health are often connected to mental health and cultural competence. "Religion is often a driving force in negative attitudes" (Anderson & Deslandes 2019, p. 128), which further explains that in a situation of trauma and stress, religion can help in building tolerance, or intolerance towards oneself, as well as the surrounding circumstances. Leaders should be respectful of the religious and linguistic differences of international students, and assist in creating an integrative culture for them to openly communicate regarding any of these issues. Cetin (2019) states, "Participation in social life and feeling included in the host country can play an important role on well-being" (p. 64), by which he meant that religious participation and social inclusion greatly affect the immigrants and refugees, and ease many of their difficulties. University programs could also provide more opportunities for students to connect with nature in their host culture (e.g., programs could offer nature walks, meditative and contemplative programs within the outdoors, outdoor activities, gardening/sports, etc.). Adams (2019) illustrates the importance of spiritual space and experiences that can be provoked by nature. A moderated meditation model can add a lot to the psychological well-being, personal aspiration, learning environment, and one's meaning in life (Mairean et al., 2019; Zhang et al., 2019). Connections with nature, spirit, and religion shape relationships with oneself, his or her tradition, and relationships with the surrounding people. In traumatic situations, regulating one's own emotions is a key aspect for every individual, and leaders should be understanding of all these elements, and employ emotional intelligence, while leading such diverse communities.

EQ can be a good aid for individuals to regulate their emotions under stressful and challenging circumstances. It can be a valuable tool kit for the leaders who are leading a diverse group of individuals, and the individual themselves who are leading themselves. According to Fabio and Kenny (2019), "the 21st century is characterized by a rapidly changing world, where challenges and transitions are ever more frequent, with regard to the workplace and society overall" (p. 6). and in this situation, the role of emotional intelligence acts as a key element. Larsen (2015) states that "internationalization is a key feature of higher education in the early 21st century, and Canadian universities are no exception to this global trend" (p. 101). With this higher rate of internationalization, there is a higher rate of international student flow whose needs are essential, and need to be addressed by these universities, as they suffer from many and various challenges during this time. The universities are prone to internationalization, and are shaping their policies to adapt to these students' educational needs, but there is a significant lacking in addressing their emotional concerns. When these students move to this land, in order to pursue their higher education, they come across stressful situations regarding their settlement, which can be supported by cultivating their emotional strengths and management.

This chapter explored the elements of EQ, and how it can be connected to leadership in developing healthy and fruitful communications, in order to help international students make a smoother transition when studying in a foreign country. The chapter concludes that the nurturing components of EQ can surely assist these students in a better way, by regulating their disruptive impulses. Educators teaching these diverse groups of international students can nurture the EQ elements themselves for better self-awareness and self-regulation, and may also practice components like motivation and empathy, while interacting with the students. It is recommended that universities that are disposed to internationalization should take the initiative and create opportunities for mental health workshops and training sessions in self-awareness and mindfulness, for the benefit of both the institutional leaders, as well as the students. In this way, students can handle their traumatic situations and make better adjustments to the new setting, and universities can also have greater student enrollment and global engagement, by providing them not only with education, but all other required resources as well.

REFERENCES

Adams, K. (2019). Navigating the spaces of children's spiritual experiences: Influences of tradition(s), multidisciplinary and perceptions. *International Journal of Children's Spirituality, 24*(1), 29–43. doi:1 0.1080/1364436X.2019.1619531

American College Health Association. (2014). *National College Health Assessment II: Spring 2014 Reference Group Executive Summary*. https://www.acha.org/documents/ncha/ACHA-NCHA-II_Refer-enceGroup_ExecutiveSummary_Spring2014.pdf

Anderson, J. R., & Deslandes, C. (2019). Religion and prejudice toward immigrants and refugees: A meta-analytic review. *The International Journal for the Psychology of Religion, 29*(2), 128–145. doi:1 0.1080/10508619.2019.1570814

Appel, J. E., Park, C. L., Wortmann, J. H., & Schie, H. T. (2019). Meaning violations, religious/spiritual struggles, and meaning in life in the face of stressful life events. *The International Journal for the Psychology of Religion, 29*(2). Advance online publication. doi:10.1080/10508619.2019.1611127

Bangladesh Ministry of Primary and Mass Education. (2015). EFA 2015 national review: Bangladesh. *UNESDOC Digital Library*. https://unesdoc.unesco.org/ark:/48223/pf0000230507

Blakemore, S. J. (2018). *Inventing ourselves: The secret life of the teenager brain*. Public Affairs Books.

Bosacki, S. L. (2016). *Social Cognition in Middle Childhood and Adolescence: Integrating the Personal, Social and Educational Lives of Young People*. Wiley.

Brackett, M. A., Rivers, S. E., & Salovey, P. (2011). Emotional intelligence: Implications for Personal, Social, Academic, and Workplace Success. *Social and Personality Psychology Compass, 5*(1), 88–103. doi:10.1111/j.1751-9004.2010.00334.x

Browning, M. H. E. M., Larson, L. R., Sharaievska, I., Rigolon, A., McAnirlin, O., Mullenbach, L., Cloutier, S., Vu, T. M., Thomsen, J., Reigner, N., Metcalf, E. C., D'Antonio, A., Helbich, M., Bratman, G. N., & Alvarez, H. O. (2021). Psychological impacts from COVID-19 among university students: Risk factors across seven states in the United States. *PLoS One, 16*(1), e0245327. doi:10.1371/journal.pone.0245327 PMID:33411812

Bruner, J. (2004). Life as Narrative. *Social Research: An Educational Quarterly, 71*(3), 691–710. https://ewasteschools.pbworks.com/f/Bruner_J_LifeAsNarrative.pdf

Burel, M., Graser, M., & Park, S. (2019). Exploring the international student experience: Providing insight through a mixed-methods approach. *Journal of Library Administration, 59*(2), 149–174. doi:10 .1080/01930826.2018.1562804

Canada's International Education Strategy. (2020). *Building on Success: International Education Strategy (2019-2024).* https://www.international.gc.ca/education/strategy-2019-2024-strategie.aspx?lang=eng

Cetin, M. (2019). Effects of religious participation on social inclusion and existential well-being levels of Muslim refugees and immigrants in Turkey. *The International Journal for the Psychology of Religion, 29*(2), 64–76. doi:10.1080/10508619.2019.1580092

Chen, J., & Zhou, G. (2019). Chinese international students' sense of belonging in North American postsecondary institutions: A critical literature review. *Brock Journal of Education, 28*(2), 48–63. doi:10.26522/brocked.v28i2.642

Christian, M. B., Lutz, E. L., Matthias, B., Richard, D. U., Markus, M. L., & Frank, S. (2021). Leadership in a time of crisis: Lessons learned from a pandemic. *Best Practice & Research. Clinical Anaesthesiology, 35*(3), 405–414. doi:10.1016/j.bpa.2020.11.011 PMID:34511228

Clandinin, D. J. (Ed.). (2007). *Handbook of narrative inquiry: Mapping a methodology.* Sage Publications, Inc., doi:10.4135/9781452226552

Clayton, M. (2012, January 24). *There is more to emotional intelligence than Daniel Goleman* [Web log post]. Management Pocketbooks. https://www.pocketbook.co.uk/blog/2012/01/24/theres-more-to-emotional-intelligence-than-daniel-goleman/

Connelly, F. M., & Clandinin, D. J. (1990). Stories of experience and narrative inquiry. *Educational Researcher, 19*(5), 2–14. doi:10.3102/0013189X019005002

Cooper, C., & Yarbrough, S. (2016). Asian-Indian female international students: A photovoice study of health and adaptation to the immigration experience. *The Qualitative Report, 21*(6), 1035–1051. https://nsuworks.nova.edu/tqr/vol21/iss6/3/

Duncan, C. (2020, May 4). New research shows international students keeping study dreams alive, for now. *IDP Connect.* https://www.idp-connect.com/newspage/international-student-crossroads-demand-for-on-campus-education-amidst-covid-19-apac/

El Masri, A., Choubak, M., & Litchmore, R. (2015, Nov. 5). *The Global Competition for International Students as Future Immigrants: The role of Ontario universities in translating government policy into institutional practice.* Higher Education Quality Council of Ontario. https://heqco.ca/wp-content/uploads/2020/03/Global-Competition-for-IS-ENG.pdf

Fabio, A. D., & Kenny, M. E. (2019). Resources for enhancing employee and organizational well-being beyond personality traits: The promise of emotional intelligence and positive relational management. *Personality and Individual Differences, 151,* 1–11. doi:10.1016/j.paid.2019.02.022

Fernández-Berrocal, P., & Extremera, N. (2016). Ability Emotional Intelligence, Depression, and Well-Being. *Emotion Review, 8*(4), 311–315. doi:10.1177/1754073916650494

Fteiha, M., & Awwad, N. (2020). Emotional intelligence and its relationship with stress coping style. *Health Psychology Open, 7*(2). Advance online publication. doi:10.1177/2055102920970416 PMID:33224513

Goleman, D. (2006). *Emotional intelligence: Why it can matter more than IQ* (10th ed.). Bantam.

Goleman, D. (2011). *HBR's 10 must reads on leadership*. Harvard Business Review Press.

Goleman, D., & Boyatzis, R. (2008). Social intelligence and the biology of leadership. *Harvard Business Review*, *86*(9), 74–81. http://files-au.clickdimensions.com/aisnsweduau-akudz/files/inteligencia-social-y-biologia-de-un-lider.pdf PMID:18777666

Goleman, D., Boyatzis, R., & McKee, A. (2001). Primal leadership: The hidden driver of great performance. *Harvard Business Review*, *79*(11), 42–53. https://hbr.org/2001/12/primal-leadership-the-hidden-driver-of-great-performance

Guo, Y., & Guo, S. (2017). Internationalization of Canadian higher education: Discrepancies between policies and international student experiences. *Journal of Studies in Higher Education*, *42*(7), 851–868. doi:10.1080/03075079.2017.1293874

Harmey, S. (2021). Responses to Educating Students at Risk During the COVID-19 Pandemic Special Issue Editorial for Journal of Education for Students Placed at Risk. *Journal of Education for Students Placed at Risk*, *26*(2), 87–90. doi:10.1080/10824669.2021.1906252

Heringer, R. (2020). From Enrolment Rates to Collaborative Knowledge Production: A Critique to the Internationalization of Higher Education in Canada. *Higher Education for the Future*, *7*(2), 169–186. doi:10.1177/2347631120930838

Hiles, D., Ermk, I., & Chrz, V. (2017). Narrative inquiry. In C. Willig & W. S. Rogers (Eds.), *The SAGE Handbook of Qualitative Research in Psychology* (pp. 157–175). Sage. doi:10.4135/9781526405555.n10

Immigration, Refugees and Citizenship Canada. (2020). *Facilitative measures to support international students affected by the COVID-19 pandemic*. https://www.canada.ca/en/immigration-refugees-citizenship/news/2020/08/facilitative-measures-to-support-international-students-affected-by-the-covid-19-pandemic.html

International Consultants for Education and Fairs. (2020, May 6). New insights on how international students are planning for the coming academic year. *ICEF Monitor*. https://tinyurl.com/yc5sgry7

Islam, S. M. R. (2020). Achievements and challenges in Bangladesh education. *The Financial Express*. https://www.thefinancialexpress.com.bd/views/achievements-and-challenges-in-bangladesh-education-1577975979

Keung, N., & Teotonio, I. (2020, April 8). "Billions of dollars are at risk." Colleges and universities scramble to protect international student sector amid COVID-19 pandemic. *The Star*. https://tinyurl.com/yay5ewp9

Knight, J. (1997). A Shared Vision? Stakeholders' Perspectives on the Internationalization of Higher Education in Canada. *Journal of Studies in International Education*, *1*(1), 27–44. doi:10.1177/102831539700100105

Knight, J. (2003). Updated Definition of Internationalization. *Industry and Higher Education*, (33). Advance online publication. doi:10.6017/ihe.2003.33.7391

Knight, J. (2015). Internationalization: A decade of changes and challenges. *International Higher Education: A Quarterly Publication*, 50. doi:10.6017/ihe.2008.50.8001

Kong, F., Gong, X., Sajjad, S., Yang, K., & Zhao, J. (2019). How is emotional intelligence linked to life satisfaction? The mediating role of social support, positive affect and negative affect. *Journal of Happiness Studies*, *20*(8), 2733–2745. Advance online publication. doi:10.100710902-018-00069-4

Lai, A. Y., Lee, L., Wang, M. P., Feng, Y., Lai, T. T., Ho, L. M., Lam, V. S., Ip, M. S., & Lam, T. H. (2020). Mental Health Impacts of the COVID-19 Pandemic on International University Students, Related Stressors, and Coping Strategies. *Frontiers in Psychiatry*, *11*, 584240. doi:10.3389/fpsyt.2020.584240 PMID:33329126

Larsen, M. A. (2015). Internationalization in Canadian higher education: A case study of the gap between official discourses and on-the-ground realities. *Canadian Journal of Higher Education*, *45*(4), 101–122. doi:10.47678/cjhe.v45i4.184907

Li, X. (2016). Ontario, Canada and Hawaii, USA: Who makes stronger vertical equity efforts? *International Studies in Educational Administration*, *44*(1), 71–84.

Liu, J. (2016). Internationalization of higher education: Experiences of intercultural adaptation of international students in Canada. *Antistasis, 6*(2), 1-11. https://journals.lib.unb.ca/index.php/antistasis/article/view/25433

Lu, Y., Chui, H., Zhu, R., Zhao, H., Zhang, Y., Liao, J., & Miller, M. J. (2018). What does "good adjustment" mean for Chinese international students? A qualitative investigation. *The Counseling Psychologist*, *46*(8), 979–1009. doi:10.1177/0011000018824283

Mairean, C., Turliuc, M. N., & Arghire, D. (2019). The relationship between trait gratitude and psychological wellbeing in university students: The mediating role of affective state and the moderating role of state gratitude. *Journal of Happiness Studies*, *20*(5), 1357–1377. doi:10.100710902-018-9998-7

Mayer, J. D., Salovey, P., Caruso, D. R., & Cherkasskiy, L. (2011). Emotional intelligence. In R. J. Sternberg & S. B. Kaufman (Eds.), *The Cambridge handbook of intelligence* (pp. 528–549). Cambridge University Press. doi:10.1017/CBO9780511977244.027

Murray, L. K. (2020). *How to Lead With Emotional Intelligence in the Time of COVID-19*. https://publichealth.jhu.edu/2020/how-to-lead-with-emotional-intelligence-in-the-time-of-covid-19

Neff, K. D. (2020a). Guided Self-Compassion Meditations. *Self-Compassion*. https://self-compassion.org/the-three-elements-of-self-compassion-2/

Neff, K. D. (2020b). Commentary on Muris and Otgaar (2020): Let the empirical evidence speak on the Self-Compassion Scale. *Mindfulness*, *11*(8), 1900–1909. Advance online publication. doi:10.100712671-020-01411-9

Neff, K. D., Bluth, K., Tóth-Király, I., Davidson, O., Knox, M. C., Williamson, Z., & Costigan, A. (2020). Development and validation of the Self-Compassion Scale for Youth. *Journal of Personality Assessment*. Advance online publication. doi:10.1080/00223891.2020.1729774 PMID:32125190

Novak, J., Armstrong, D., & Browne, B. (2014). *Leading for educational lives: Inviting and sustaining imaginative acts of hope in a connected world*. Sense Publishers. doi:10.1007/978-94-6209-554-0

Okwuosa, A. (2021, February 24). What it's like for international students graduating during COVID-19. *TVO Current Stories.* https://www.tvo.org/article/what-its-like-for-international-students-graduating-during-covid-19?utm_source=cpc&utm_medium=google&utm_campaign=cov&utm_content=&gcl id=CjwKCAjw9MuCBhBUEiwAbDZ-7uBum58fEZ4lHCd91sCrEHXcIUkvDGI3Dn7NRo75l0wC-GHX6ZeHCuxoCCdQQAvD_BwE

Phillips, A. (1999). *Darwin's Worms.* Faber & Faber.

Ross, S. (2020, May 11). McGill and Concordia universities plan to move most classes online for fall term. *CTV News.* https://tinyurl.com/yb8sprsy

Smith, B. (2017). Narrative inquiry and autoethnography. In M. L. Silk, D. L. Andrews, & H. Thorpe (Eds.), *Routledge Handbook of Physical Cultural Studies* (pp. 505–515). Routledge. doi:10.4324/9781315745664-51

Song, B., Zhao, Y., & Zhu, J. (2021). COVID-19-related Traumatic Effects and Psychological Reactions among International Students. *Journal of Epidemiology and Global Health, 11*(1), 117–123. doi:10.2991/jegh.k.201016.001 PMID:33605116

Tracy, B. (2017, October 30). Why emotional intelligence is indispensable for leaders [Web log post]. *Forbes.* https://www.forbes.com/sites/forbescoachescouncil/2017/10/30/why-emotional-intelligence-is-indispensable-for-leaders/amp/

Trilokekar, R., & Kukar, P. (2011). Disorienting Experiences During Study Abroad: Reflections of Pre-service Teacher Candidates. *Teaching and Teacher Education, 27*(7), 1141–1150. doi:10.1016/j.tate.2011.06.002

Trilokekar, R., Safdar, S., El Masri, A., & Scott, C. (2014). *International education, labour market and future citizens: prospects and challenges for Ontario.* Unpublished Report, Ontario Human Capital Research.

Trilokekar, R. D., Thomson, K., & El Masri, A. (2019). *Open borders, closed minds: The experiences of international students in the Ontario labour market. In Internationalization and Employability in Higher Education.* Routledge. doi:10.4324/9781351254885-8

Wong, J., Hian, B. T. C., Haldmann, A., & Agrawal, A. (2020, May 11). *Interviews with international students in Canada about the Covid-19 situation.* The World University Rankings. https://www.timeshighereducation.com/student/blogs/interviews-international-students-canada-about-covid-19-situation#

Yi, S. (2018). Why am I here? A self-study of an international art education student lost in transition. *International Journal of Education through Art, 14*(2), 197-210. doi:10.1386/eta.14.2.197_1

Zhang, H., Chen, K., Chen, C., & Schlegel, R. (2019). Personal aspirations, person-environment fit, meaning in work, and meaning in life: A moderated mediation model. *Journal of Happiness Studies, 20*(5), 1481–1497. doi:10.100710902-018-0005-0

Zhou, G., Liu, T., & Rideout, G. (2017). A study of Chinese international students enrolled in the Master of Education program at a Canadian university: Experiences, challenges, and expectations. *International Journal of Chinese Education, 6*(2), 210–235. doi:10.1163/22125868-12340081

ADDITIONAL READING

Ashkanasy, N. M., & Dasborough, M. T. (2003). Emotional awareness and emotional intelligence in leadership teaching. *Journal of Education for Business*, *79*(1), 18–22. doi:10.1080/08832320309599082

Butler, C. J., & Chinowsky, P. S. (2006). Emotional intelligence and leadership behavior in construction executives. *Journal of Management Engineering*, *22*(3), 119–125. doi:10.1061/(ASCE)0742-597X(2006)22:3(119)

Greenockle, K. M. (2010). The New Face in Leadership: Emotional Intelligence. *Quest*, *62*(3), 260–267. doi:10.1080/00336297.2010.10483647

Heifetz, R., Grashow, A., & Linsky, M. (2009). *The practice of adaptive leadership: Tools and tactics for changing your organization and the world*. Harvard Business School Press.

Kaden, U. (2020). COVID-19 school closure-related changes to the professional life of a K-12 teacher. *Education Sciences*, *10*(6), 165. doi:10.3390/educsci10060165

Netolicky, D. M. (2020). School leadership during a pandemic: Navigating tensions. *Journal of Professional Capital and Community*, *5*(3/4), 391–395. Advance online publication. doi:10.1108/JPCC-05-2020-0017

Northouse, P. G. (2019). *Leadership: Theory and practice* (8th ed.). Sage Publishing.

Parrish, D. R. (2015). The relevance of emotional intelligence for leadership in a higher education context. *Studies in Higher Education*, *40*(5), 821–837. doi:10.1080/03075079.2013.842225

Rada-Florina, H., Simona, S., Rita-Monica, T., & Michaela, R. C. (2012). About emotional intelligence and leadership. *Annals of Faculty of Economics*, *1*(2), 744–749. http://anale.steconomiceuoradea.ro/volume/2012/n2/113.pdf

KEY TERMS AND DEFINITIONS

COVID-19: Coronavirus disease (COVID-19) is an infectious disease caused by the SARS-CoV-2 virus.

Emotional Intelligence: The capacity to be aware of, control, and express one's emotions, and to handle interpersonal relationships judiciously and empathetically.

Empathy: The ability to understand and share the feelings of another.

Hurdle: An obstacle or difficulty.

International Students: Temporary residents who come to a foreign country from anywhere in the world to pursue education.

Internationalization of Higher Education: The process of integrating an international, intercultural, or global dimension into the purpose, functions, or delivery of postsecondary education.

Mindfulness: The quality or state of being conscious or aware of something.

Transition: The process or a period of changing from one state, or condition, to another.

Chapter 12
Sense of Belonging:
Rethinking Chinese International Student Engagement in Canadian Higher Education

Meng Xiao

ⓘD https://orcid.org/0000-0001-9561-8919

Univerisity of Toronto, Canada & Ontario Institute for Studies in Education, Canada

ABSTRACT

This research offers a critical understanding of Western-dominant student engagement in terms of rethinking the sense of belonging of Chinese international graduate student populations. The Western perspective on student engagement in Canadian higher education fails to recognize the broader social and cultural inclusivity and diversities of student sense of belonging. Specifically, this research explores the challenges faced by Chinese international students engaging in Canadian graduate schools towards their sense of belonging. This study offers inclusive ways of rethinking Chinese international students' sense of belonging and engagement by deconstructing Western ideology on student experiences in Canadian higher education. Faculties, institutions, and university communities need to redefine the desired content of student engagement based on social justice values in terms of empowering democratic, inclusive, and diverse student experiences and strengthening their sense of belonging with the landscape of internationalization.

INTRODUCTION

With the landscape of internationalization, the number of Chinese international students pursuing their graduate study has rapidly increased each year globally (Calder, Richter, Mao, Kovacs Burns, Mogale & Danko, 2016; Xiang, 2017). Up until 2017, Chinese students represented the largest group of international students in Canada, constituting 28.4% of the total (Canadian Bureau for International Education, 2021).

This rapid growth of Chinese international students in Canada warrants the examination of their experiences in Canadian schooling and their engagement matters to Canadian higher education. The increasing number of Chinese international students have been entering North American universities,

DOI: 10.4018/978-1-7998-8921-2.ch012

and many of them have experienced issues with a sense of belonging that has negatively impacted their academic and social engagement and mental health (Chen & Zhou, 2020; Xiang, 2017). Raising the awareness of Chinese international graduate students' challenges towards their sense of belonging includes understanding how they perceive their sense of belonging and what challenges they have been facing. This acknowledgement will empower those students' experiences in Canada and initiate support from Canadian institutions at the teaching pedagogy and the policy level.

The dominant approach to understand student engagement characterizes it as a way of engagement impacted by Western cultural norms. However, this Western perspective fails to recognize the broader social and cultural inclusivity and diversities of student engagement. This negatively impact their sense of belonging in Canadian higher education. Specifically, Chinese international graduate students in Canada face different social and cultural challenges including their sense of belonging while being situated within the Chinese and Canadian educational systems after studying in Canada. The sense of belonging is a socio-cultural construct that influences students' engagement and success (Xiang, 2017; Yao, 2015). Impacted by Chinese values and culture, those Chinese international graduate students have been stereotyped as less engaged and lack of belonging in and beyond classrooms in Canada schooling (Liu, 2001; Xiang, 2017). Their ways of engagement and their sense of belonging for better student experience and success need to be examined.

LITERATURE REVIEW

This research draws on theories examining students'sense of belonging and their engagment (Flowerdew & Miller, 1995; Grabke, 2013, Tsai, 2016; Xiang, 2017) from a critical comparative analysis. Many research show students' sense of belonging is known to be strongly associated with student successful engagement at universities (Ahn & Davis, 2020; Carales & Nora 2020; Gillen-O'Neel, 2021).

Some existing literature on sense of belonging assumes Western dominant ways of interpreting these concepts, which lacks a broader understanding the sense of belonging based on diverse socio-cultural considerations. For example, this taken-for-granted approach using Western educational values reflects better sense of belonging as positive interactions (Flowerdew & Miller, 1995; Grabke, 2013), while Chinese culture embodies sense of belonging as passive interactions (Chen & Zhou, 2019; Tsai, 2016; Xiang, 2017).

Cultural identities are imperative to students' sense of belonging. Duran, Dahl, Stipeck, and Mayhew (2020) found students' belonging are significantly impacted by different racial identities and their college generation statuses based on the research data from 7,888 students in the U.S. Ahn and Davis (2020) argue that there are two neglected domains to support the full range of students' sense of belonging: the surroundings including students' living space, and geographical and cultural location, and personal spaces referring to students' satisfaction, identity, and interests. Carales and Nora (2020) indicated that the racial attitudes and psychosocial experiences and beliefs crucially influence some Latina/o student's sense of belonging at a Hispanic Serving Institution.

Chinese identity has been "an embodied racialized identity in Canadian history, and it continues to be in contemporary Canadian society through the discursive reproduction of racist discourse" (Cui, 2015, p. 1157). All of these impact Chinese international students, who try hard to fit into the community of native English speakers in terms of being accepted and regarded as engaged in and beyond classrooms. Thus, some Chinese students adjust their Chinese accents and writing styles that imperatively reflect

Chinese history, culture, and identity (Wang, 2009). This way of adjusting their accents and writing style can make them better understood so that they can be better fit into the western education. Similarly, some underrepresented students in US institutions need to abandon their cultural identities to "assimilate to the mainstream campus culture" (Tinto, 1993). Some Chinese students feel less engaged and belonging to the community in and beyond classrooms and do not interact with native English speakers and the local community because they cannot be as fluent as native English speakers (Wang, 2009).

Some research highlighted the importance of strengthening students' sense of belonging in Canadian education system for better student experiences, Erb and Drysdale (2017) pointed out that the relationship between sense of belonging, persistence in higher education and well-being are imperative to mature and traditional age students' motivation and success. Marshall, Zhou, Yang and Jing (2021) pointed out some Chinese international students' limited English language proficiency including is a challenging factor to impact their sense of belonging. This limited language proficiency include "understanding teaching content, hesitation in participating in classroom discussion, incompetence to answer questions during presentation, spending more time on reading materials, and frustration in writing term papers" (p.133). Gervan, and Wiebe (2012) found that the students' perceptions of sense of belonging in Canadian higher education are multi-layered and context-dependent, impacted by classroom pedagogy, and social, cultural, and linguistic factors.

Although the international student experience has been studied, there is little research about Chinese students' engagement and how they belong to the communities in Canadian graduate schools. This study aimed to generate a better understanding about Chinese student engagement experiences in their graduate life that relates to the particular context of Western schools. In this paper, I focus on the sense-of-belonging challenges faced by Chinese international graduates, including how students' sense of belonging and engagement can be interpreted within the Canadian contexts, how these challenges have been reproduced by the Western cultural norms, and how a new understanding of student engagement can enhance better student experience in Canadian graduate schools. I argue that student engagement now presents a Western ideological understanding on students' sense of belonging that values social and active engagement based on the dominant culture.

This research examines how Chinese graduate student sense of belonging is interpreted with the notion of student engagement in Western social-cultural and local contexts. I also examined how these ways of illustrating students' sense of belonging can be implemented to empower student experiences by investigating three empirical questions:

1. How is Chinese international graduate sense of belonging perceived in and beyond classrooms in Canadian higher education?
2. What are the determining factors that influence Chinese international graduate students' sense of belonging in Canadian higher education?
3. What are the needs of Chinese international graduate students for enhancing their sense of belonging in Canadian higher education?

There is a need to interpret the sense of belonging based on the concept of integration for international students' diverse cultural experience. As Tinto (1993) argued, making the assumption that students in the non-dominant culture can effectively and easily increase their sense of belonging by accessing and infiltrating the dominant cultural group can be problematic. According to the sense of belonging, international students' voice and experiences needs to be heard and empowered. For instance, there is a need to clarity international Chinese graduate students' sense of belonging and to explore how their sense of belonging depends on their socio-cultural identities and their circumstances before coming to Canada. Institutions need to redefine the desired content of students' sense of belonging based on diverse student groups with the landscape of internationalization.

METHODOLOGY

This study is based on the qualitative data examining the lived experiences of Chinese international students regarding their sense of belonging in and beyond classrooms in Canadian higher education. I conducted twelve interviews with six students and six university staff at three graduate faculties in one Canadian university. In addition, I gathered historical data, policies, and artifacts in China and Canada. The data were collected through one-on-one interviews and questionnaires from participating students drawn from various faculties. The inquiries include how factors in Canadian higher education have been influencing the sense of belonging of Chinese international graduate students who have been impacted by Chinese educational system and culture.

I adopted a case study approach to explore the Chinese international graduate students' sense of belonging in and out of the classroom in a Canadian university. The case study approach provides insight into the perspectives of current Canadian graduate schools in terms of equity and inclusive pedagogy and education policy enactment and the perspectives of students, teachers, and universities administrative professionals in university communities.

I asked Chinese international graduate students and the staff in their departments, and central university staff to share their stories and experiences of understanding and approaching students' sense of belonigng in Canadian universities. Six Chinese international graduate students, three student service staff from three different departments, and three student service staff from university service sectors at this university were interviewed using some guiding questions to elicit their experiences with regards to their engagement in Canadian graduate schools.

To ensure that the participants could effectively help me explore Chinese graduate students' engagement in Canada and the socio-cultural factors that affect their participation, I recruited the participants through the following strategies.

1. The participants of this study were ethnic Chinese who were born and grew up in Mainland China before they began their studies in Canada. This meant Chinese students who were born and received their education in Canada were excluded from the study.
2. The participants of this study have earned a post-secondary degree in the Mainland China before they began their studies in Canada. Additionally, those who had any form of relationship with the investigator were also excluded.
3. When they begin their graduate study in Canada, the participants had not studied in Western graduate schools before and must have had no previous learning and practicing experience in Canada, North America, or other English-speaking countries.

For the sake of confidentiality and to protect the identities of the participants, only pseudonyms were used in the discussion. Thus, the names of the female-identified, male-identified, and queer-identified international student participants were substituted with IF1, IF2, IF3, IF4, IM1, IQ1, while the female-identified and male-identified student service staff participants were described as SF1, SF2, SM1, SM2, SM3, SM4. For student participants, IF1 is a profession-based Master parent student with social science background from Education, and IQ1 is a research-based Ph.D. student with social science background from Education; IF2 and IM1 are profession-based Master students with science background from Engineering; IF3 is a profession-based Master student with business background and IF4 is a research-based Ph.D. student with business background. For student service staff participants, SF1 is from business; SF2 is from the graduate school; SM1 is from Education; SM2 is from Engineering; SM3 is from the international student Center; and SM4 is from the student life services. The information chart regarding participants is as follows (Figure 1).

Figure 1. Participant information in this study

Participants	Student/Staff	Program/Background	Research-based/Profession-based	Identity
IF1	Student	Education	Profession-based, master degree	Chinese; Female-identified; Parent Student
IQ1	Student	Education	Research-based, Ph.D.	Chinese; Queer-identified
IF2	Student	Engineering	Profession-based, MEng	Chinese; Female-identified
IM1	Student	Engineering	Profession-based, MEng	Chinese; Male-identified
IF3	Student	Business	Profession-based, MBA	Chinese; Female-identified
IF4	Student	Business	Research-based, Ph.D.	Chinese; Female-identified
SF1	Staff	Business		Non-Chinese; Female-identified
SF2	Staff	Graduate Studies		Non-Chinese; Female-identified
SM1	Staff	Education		Chinese Canadian; Male-identified
SM2	Staff	Engineering		Non-Chinese; Male-identified
SM3	Staff	International Student Center		Non-Chinese; Male-identified
SM4	Staff	Student Life Center		Non-Chinese; Male-identified

FINDINGS OF THE STUDY

Perceptions of Chinese International Graduate Students' Sense of Belonging in Classrooms

When inquiring their general experience of the level of Chinese international graduate students' sense of belonging in classrooms, six student participants shared varied stories about engagement in classrooms and their communities in Canadian higher education. However, all of them shared some of their concerns and challenges during the process of engaging in classrooms.

In terms of their own experience in classrooms, IF1 from the social science background stated that she did not think she was engaged and felt the strong sense of belonging at the first several months but felt less pressure for doing something wrong and gained confidence with the support from professors and peers. The other student with a social science background IQ1 opined that he is very cautious about a lot of things when actively engaging in classroom, stating:

First of all, I do not want to be the only Chinese who talks. I am also aware that I am a cis-male. So I do not take a lot of verbal spaces for talking too much. I am also cautious about different personalities. I am the kind of person who just talks in classrooms. I am saying that because I do talk when I would like to share my ideas with other people, even though they might seem not agree with what I am talking about.

As one of the two student participants with a science background, IF2 shared the opinion that she is not engaged in classrooms as she would prefer to actively communicate with the professor outside of class. The male with a science background, IM1, stated that he engages in classrooms with his Chinese friends and feels some sense of belonging only by doing some course project and form a group with Chinese students to finish the team project.

With her business background, IF3 pointed out she would ask questions to her professors and her group peers and voice her opinions to engage in classrooms whenever they are necessary. Another business student, IF4, explained how her sense of belonging has been gradually changing in the graduate classroom:

[Y]ou have to talk about your feelings, your thoughts, or your opinions. I think that really challenges me by the same time also changes me a lot in a lot of ways.... Maybe because of the Chinese culture, you are not allowed to even express your opinions sometimes. At the beginning, it was very tough.... But I think as you go on, you speak more, and then you become reinforce to the value and feel more sense of belonging.

Based on their observation on Chinese international graduate student classroom engagement, half of student interviewees shared the common idea that Chinese international graduate students participated less than some domestic students in the courses in their programs. IF3 opined that, in her classroom, it was usually students from India and North America who constructively participate more in classroom work and feel a stronger sense of belonging, followed by the South Americans, and the Asian students. IF4 stated that some Chinese students in her class ask relatively fewer questions compared to other people. Maybe this is because Chinese students are a little bit shy, but they talk a lot after the class, but not during the class. IM1 also noted that some Chinese students like him do not engage in class discussions and still feel a strong sense of belonging in his program.

However, the other half of student participants held different views with regards of their Chinese classmates' engagement in the class. Given the fact that there is such a high percentage of Chinese international students in the classes, IQ1 noted some of them are quite active like him, some of them are not but he is not sure why. IQ1 noted that there are so many factors about why some students vigorously participate in class activities while others sit and listen to the professors passively. For instance, some Chinese students are more used to listening quietly but taking detailed notes and effectively learn from the professor and the class. They found their sense of belonging through non-oral engagement. These factors resulting in students' different behaviors towards engagement will impact those students' sense of belonging in some degree. IF1 highlighted the culture differences that he perceives affect Chinese students' sense of belonging in the class, noting:

[T]his classroom is really diverse, and everybody gets accustomed to such a diverse culture. Even we are exceptional in this mainstream culture, but some uniqueness does not mean we are inferior to them. So I do appreciate the differences between different cultural ideologies, which broaden our mind to a different society. They are [engaged] but we can be open-minded and vibrant.

Similarly, IF2 gave her perspective that students in different majors engage very differently. Some students in social science may be engaged in the group discussions in classrooms while some students in the science programme may be more engaged with group assignments out of the classroom. Based on her observation, if students who wanted to do research or they may have a lot of interest in specific subjects, they will tend to communicate with professors more and join the professors' labs so that they will feel more sense of belonging.

Perceptions of Chinese International Graduate Students' Sense of Belonging beyond Classrooms

When inquiring their general experience of the level of Chinese international graduate students' engagement out of the classroom, one student interviewee, IF1, who has family responsibility, shared her varied ways of engaging out of the classroom, stating:

Recently, I took a Yoga class every Wednesday trying to socialize as well as to do mindfulness because mindfulness is a very fantastic way to release the pressure and to regulate your mind zone and feel your belonging to the surrounding. Also, I attended most of my children's friends' birthday party and their activities. I took a part-time job even I am busy with my study and family.

IF1 found her strong sense of belonging to the community where she was actively engaged out of the classroom. Identified as a queer person, IQ1 shared his opinion of find communities to engaging out of the classroom through doing work-study, being engaged in Asian queer communities, and connecting with his supervisor to get involved in racialized communities.

The other four student interviewees from science and business background shared their varied ways and views towards student out-of-classroom engagement. Two students from science backgrounds held different opinion engaging out of classroom. IF1 opined that she spent a lot of time on trying to make

Canadian friends and to improve her English. In this way, she can communicate better with them and get out of her comfort zone of staying at home for better belonging to the community.

IM1 said that he was not engaged much out of the classroom and feels little sense of belonging because some university community events did not fit into his interests. IF4, a Ph.D. student from business background, claimed she engaged to a very great extent with her peers and advisor out of classroom and found her sense of social belonging to her school community because she believed that social interactions are important to one's mental health. She noted:

I feel like Ph.D. is such a long and lonely experience. Sometimes you sit there for a couple of days, not talking to anyone. I think maybe because my background is psychology, I know that social connections and social interactions are very crucial for our well-being, so we have to talk to other people. I am the type of person if I feel lonely, I would knock on my adviser's door, "Hey, can we chat?"

The other business student IF3 noted that her personality, interest, purpose of engagement plays a crucial part to affect her sense of belonging and involvement out of the classroom. She mentioned:

As I mentioned, I focus on marketing. So, for those marketing associations that I found strong sense of belonging, whenever they have those case competitions, I will selectively sign up, because I know that would be good for my own experience accumulation. Whenever I wish to be alone, I would not sign up for those activities if I do not really like and feel my belonging to this event.

Based on their observation on Chinese international graduate student classroom engagement, half of student interviewees shared the common idea that Chinese international graduate students from their own departments engage in many out-of-classroom activities and found their sense of belonging to their school communities. IF2 stated that those students engaged often in these activities because they like spending time with non-Chinese students where they feel that they belong to a community. These activities include going to the supermarket or hanging out to do different things in the weekends or learning about the North American holidays. The connection time engaging in cultural activities helps the Chinese students to learn the context of the conversations with non-Chinese students.

Both IF3 and IM1 shared the common opinion that they do not engage in out of classroom activities but that other Chinese students from their programs actively engage in their communities. IF3 believed that Chinese students are never afraid of taking part in any of those out-of-classroom activities and those students were doing quite well and also have a strong sense of belonging. She shared, "For example, in one of the global business competitions that I was involved in, for the first, second, and third prizes, most of the participants are Chinese students, even if it is a competition for all students". IM2 mentioned that the school provides diverse activities that fit into some Chinese students' interests so that his Chinese friends can actively engage out-of-classroom activities and find their sense of belonging through the friendship with others within these activities.

Two Ph.D. student interviewees shared their common opinions that most Chinese students prefer to have their own circle of friends to engage with Chinese people and communities where they do not feel strong sense of belonging in the same way, which has excluded some Chinese students from engaging in experiences that they would normally have had and limiting their sense of belonging in Canadian institutions. IQ1 claimed:

I think there are some Chinese students' clubs where there are just Chinese students. I have never been to these events because it is quite triggering for me, and most of them are quite heteronormative so I do not really feel I am belonging to there even though we are all Chinese. I think a lot of Chinese international graduate students have their own circles. I think that is fine and that is their community. Although they talk in Chinese, I do not feel that I belong there.

Similarly, IF4 gave her perspectives on engaging out of the classroom only speaking with Chinese, which may be perpetuating one's views. She claimed:

I feel like Chinese people engage with Chinese people often. They have their own circles, and they talk about their own, like our own shows. We have our own opinions of the society, but we do not really talk to non-Chinese. I would not say that it is a bad thing, but it has its limits. Because if you do not really talk to other people, you do not really know how they are feeling about that, and you are just stuck in your own circle. It is like a chamber.

Both IQ1 and IF4 stated some Chinese students remained their comport zone by speaking their mother tongue or interacted with students from similar cultural backgrounds in order to feel their sense of community belonging so that their identities are much represented.

On the other hand, based on staff interviewees' observation of Chinese international graduate student classroom engagement in the lectures, three of these interviewees from different programs held similar opinion of Chinese students. SF1 from business programs stated that, in her faculty, Chinese international graduate students are very active engaged in the clubs, noting that those students are active in the regional clubs as well, especially the ones for the Asian Business club. They get involved very much outside the classroom because they understand how important it is to develop some skills such as communication and leadership skills to develop the community relationships such as teamship and friendship and then strengthen their sense of belonging.

SM2 from the science programs claimed that he met some Chinese students who are very engaged. He also highlighted the importance of university student support services offering different ways to engage those students in terms of the outside classroom such as project and volunteering opportunities, noting:

To introduce students to different projects, we hosted a showcase where professors or Post docs will come in and present their work and MASc students have a chance to kind of meet, learn, and ask questions.... [T]hey can also engage when they want to participate and take part in volunteering for something. That is a way for them to gain experience and also meet new people as well.

Similarly, staff SM4 from the student life center, based on the limited data that he saw, claimed that it looks like Chinese international graduate students are better participating in some of the out-of-class activities than domestic students at most of the time, stating:

Why might that be? Maybe because [domestic students] are looking to develop some experiences, networks, and relationships; maybe people are just generally interesting curiously, in a way that people like me who have lived here are less interested or curious about these; maybe people see it more as a way to have a good social experience and sense of belonging to the community.

The frequency of involving in those activities may enhance the sense of belonging of those students.

Staff interviewee SM1 from social science programs believed Chinese students' engagement out of the classroom in his faculty really varies and these different levels impact their sense of belonging. In general, some students are very active getting involved by taking leadership positions at student organizations; but more people prefer not engaging and not very socializing with others out of their social circle so that they feel less belonging to the community.

Factor Influencing Sense of Belonging in Classrooms

Teamwork experience in Canadian classrooms has been a factor influencing Chinese graduate classroom sense of belonging. One student participant IM1 opined that he did feel a strong sense of belonging because, whenever he needs to do group work, he does not know the non-Chinese students so that he does not feel comfortable to say hi to non-Chinese students and form in the same group with them. Moreover, he is also afraid of starting a friendship with non-Chinese students to do group work because he does not have experience interacting with people from different cultural backgrounds. These challenges impact his sense of belonging to the group. Another student participant, IF2, also shared her main challenges of doing group works when being engaged in classrooms and finding her sense of belonging based on different cultural habitats:

The challenges will especially rise when I need to make up groups and do group work, because people are from different study backgrounds and they have different ways to communicate. So, when I have to make a group who are not Chinese, it is difficult to really communicate well. But I work well with Chinese because we can talk and understand each other. I feel much belonging to my Chinese group.

Similarly, one staff participant SF1 pointed out some Chinese international graduate students prefer to stay in their comfort zone by connecting with their own group of people from the same country to do the group work and those students may only have their sense of belonging to their Chinese community circle. It can be difficult for them to branch out and make new friends from the different parts of the world. SM4 claimed that, when international students have group work, wondering how often domestic students are willing to work sometimes with international students. Some international students and also domestic students may remain in their different comfort zone to feel a better sense of belonging.

Other staff participants shared the common idea that lack of belonging may challenge an international student classroom experience in Canada. SM1 mentioned:

Being an international student, you may not know the local cultural, whatever is that trendy with your peers, and what they are talking about because they are talking about something local. If you are not customized to the culture here, if you do not watch news, if you do not read what is happening in the community, you probably do not know what is going on. When we have that kind of conversation, you feel left out.

Similarly, SM4 highlighted how the community, faculty members, and domestic students see international students also impact their sense of belonging:

[I]n the class who identified as being an international student, I think if someone who has already done one degree in Canada, or the U.S., and the western context, it is a little bit less challenging. They have a little bit understanding of classroom dynamics of faculty expectations.... I also think about professors. I do not know how many professors taught international students in classrooms before. I do not know how often they make the students feel welcome or included in classrooms.

SM4 highlighted that a graduate school faculty's awareness about international students' sense of belonging and the relationship between those international students and their teachers are imperative.

The positive student-faculty interactions can significantly contribute to students' academic goal pursuits and their sense of belonging (Glass, Kociolek, Wongtrirat, Lynch & Cong, 2015). The inclusive classroom and the community environment that empower the different ways of graduate students can be engaged can be a great support to strengthen those students' sense of belonging. SF2 also gave her perspectives that it is not the case that every faculty member is doing a good job of supporting international students and supporting their community belonging. Institutions ought to be able to support students' sense of belonging through a strong awareness of international students' cultural experiences, their transition into the new educational system, and the evaluation for their student success, and in other inclusive ways by developing a sense of belonging once a student is here. Caligiuri, DuBois, Lundby and Sinclair (2020) suggested that semester-long classroom experiential activities supporting international students' social interaction be created with domestic students. This can foster international students' sense of belonging, since some international students had lower levels of openness at the beginning of their study.

Factor Influencing Sense of Belonging beyond Classrooms

Inclusivity and sense of belonging matters when Chinese international graduate students are engaging out of the classroom. Speaking to inclusivity and accessibility, student IM1 mentioned that, how the school activities were sent and what content of the platform was provided for Chinese international graduate students matter. How to access the school activities and whether the platform is provided based on inclusivity influences IM1's decision of engaging in and belonging to the community. Student IQ1 also shared his opinion of accessibility and inclusivity, highlighting the digital gap that may marginalize Chinese international graduate students' experience and lower their sense of belonging. He claimed:

I think the access to how to engage and then find the sense of belonging is a factor. I think a lot is happening on Facebook but a lot of Chinese students have been using Wechat. This is the digital gap between the Canadian context and the Chinese context. It is not that you have to but unfortunately, a lot of things happen on Facebook and other events that you might be interesting and find you feel connected to a community.

Speaking to accessibility and inclusivity, staff interview SM4 stated that the first thing to consider is whether international students are accessing good information about opportunities to improve their sense of belonging. For example, institutions need to be aware of what matters is those international graduate students from China towards their sense of belonging, including "are they getting good concise, easy-to-read and timely information about the things that are available?", "what emails do students read, where do they find information, where do they find good information, and how many places? Are Chinese students getting good information about opportunities or getting resources to enhance their sense of belonging?" Similarly, SM3 highlighted the context or the setting when someone decides to participate in an activity that contributes to their sense of belonging.

The sense of belonging is highlighted by two staff interviewees. SF1 believed an inclusive, safe, welcome, and supportive environment created by the faculty and the community is crucial to creating the sense of belonging for enhancing Chinese international graduate students' sense of belonging out of classroom. She noted:

I think the factors include that we try to really engage these students, all students to participate. Secondly, an inclusive environment helps as well. [We] value diversity very much so that we talk about diversity a lot, we talk about inclusion, and we talk about respecting another opinion. Then I think having an environment that is supportive, which I think maybe goes hand in hand. [Those] three are very important in ensuring that Chinese students feel wanted and engaged, and that we value their opinion as well.

Similarly, SM3 believed that feeling welcomed is a key factor affecting student out-of-classroom engagement and being aware of how to create the environment to make those students want to engage, and to feel a strong sense of belonging. She stated:

Do the presenters make the environment welcoming and open? Do they let people participate or not participate? Do they force people to participate, which is maybe not always the way that people want to engage? Is the content relevant not just for domestic students but also for international students? Are they doing things in the workshop or the event? That makes it easier for people to participate.

Speaking about Chinese international graduate students, SM3 held the opinion that:

It might be about how welcoming that spaces are and do they see other Chinese students there? Sometimes this is another stereotype - that Chinese international students only hang out together, which I think is untrue, but I do think your confidence level changes when you see someone there who can help you navigate ambiguity.

A welcome and inclusive environment in and out of the classroom will increase students' sense of belonging by strengthening their confidence and creating more opportunities and possibilities to empower their socio-cultural stories.

Needs towards Students' Sense of Belonging

In this study, student participants showed varied needs to enhance their sense of belonging in Canadian higher education. These needs include enhancing the language skills and cultural experiences that will greatly increase their sense of belonging. For instance, based on her engagement, IF1 has been improving the language skills and experiencing more culture so that she can feel her sense of belonging gradually strengthened.

IQ1 shared how valuable of finding the sense of community and having a supportive supervisor is. As a Chinese international Ph.D. queer-identified student, he stated that:

To summarize, I would say you stumble and then you finally find your own community where you belong. Then I stumbled like what I said to my supervisor. [With the help of my supervisor], I connected with so many radical people and not all of them are good; some of them are problematic. But I do find people that I love and that we stick together and we have a collective queer diaspora. So we stumbled and finally realized instead of finding communities, it is probably more productive to just create your own.

Those experiences have made him see how injustice is done to him structurally and interpersonally and how an agency for change impacts on him. All of those motivate him to being a research and activist in those injustice issues. He stated:

I am definitely queer but that is where I am different from some of the other Chinese students. But for that side, I do feel things that people talk about towards structural issues such as racism, patriarchy, inequality, and economic inequality.... I used to just focus and create activism but now I am more interested in broader issues, not just queer people but everybody who is marginalized.

IF2 also shared her experience that she had made much progress since she came to her graduate study, highlighting the great support from her TA and the friendship with people from different countries has helped her with the academic and community engagement and sense of community belonging:

I feel [my TA] gave me some feeling like they are there to help me instead of judging my homework or me. So it totally changes in my attitude to the professors and teaching assistants out of the classroom.... Out of the classroom, it is nice to talk with different people to know why they come here and what they are doing here, and to talk about my country, and myself and to go to a Chinese restaurant, and to introduce Chinese dishes to them.

These experiences have made her to have a more positive attitude to communicate with different people to have more confident in herself and strengthen her social skills and sense of community belonging.

IM1, another student participant, shared his own experience stating that the out-of-classroom social activities and clubs from his program and the good sense of belonging helped him to get involved and engaged:

I think some activities in the courses I have talked about are the [university] Transition. They organized activities like Toast in a club. All of the students and teachers go to the club and toast, and this is just a very exciting party; this is the first and only party I engaged in, so this is just my best experience of social activities.

These experiences helped him find the fact that the non-Chinese students are willing to help and to make friends with him, and he has more confidence to talk with other and the motivation of strengthening language skills in order to engage in the community.

IF4, a student from the business background, shared how her program and community have been opportunities of supporting her to understanding student engagement in a broader way. She shared her experience of "engagement as interaction than exams or tests" based on her presentation transition, as a person who are not good at making presentation and hates presentation before:

I think if it is engagement in classrooms, I used to hate presentations. I feel like the presentation is such a formality where you just have to present whatever you know. But now even my adviser was asking me to do a presentation, I will say, "Yes, for sure". This is because I see engagement is more like interaction than exams or tests [now]. The new way I think about engagement that really changed my life including strengthening my sense of belonging in classrooms.

Those experiences have supported her to change her attitude of presentation from negatively to passively and rethink the meaning of being "perfect". In this way, she enhanced her sense of belonging by not being so hard on herself. She noted:

Because, for Chinese people, our culture is that we were always taught to be perfect. You have to be perfect in the district area. But I feel like sometimes just being open, nobody's perfect, right? I think now I was just like, "I love discussion. I will try to my best to address your question, but I am happy to discuss after presentation if not satisfied". I think that really makes me feel much better of a presentation in general and easier to connect to the community.

IF3, another student from the business background, shared that the power of being confident on communication and her own strength and the support including positive feedback and encouragement of her coworkers make her more belonging to the community and engaged in and beyond classrooms in the studying and working environment:

My experience is always my coworkers are very friendly and they appreciate what you contribute to the projects. [My] coworkers gave me positive feedback that my opinions and contributions really impress them and they all remember what I did for all of the projects. So these positive feedbacks really encouraged me to contribute more to small communities and let me know that I have my own strength even I am new to this country.

As a first-year graduate student, she believes those experience help her identify what her strength is in a community in the Canadian context.

FINDINGS AND DISCUSSION

Chinese international graduate students' classroom and out-of-classroom engagement and their sense of belonging in this study is influenced by many factors and these student and staff interviewees described the situation by sharing some of their experiences and stories. Some of their perceptions and stories align with the views of scholars while other do not.

All of the twelve participants were interviewed to give their own perceptions of student engagement and how they belong to the communities in Canadian higher education. Based on their experiences, the perceptions of student engagement and their sense of belonging vary in different settings and from different participants. This study shows that Chinese international graduate students' engagement and their sense of belonging in and out of the classroom in this university can significantly be impacted by their interests and motivation, their programs, their Chinese-cultural-rooted background, and the relationship between students and their teachers, peers, and communities in this study. These findings are similar to other researchers' findings that a strong teacher-student relationship and the inclusive community environment imperatively impact the levels of students' sense of belonging (Chan, 1999; Glass et.al, 2015; Liu, 2001; Tsai, 2016). It is also consistent with the findings of Curtin, Stewart, and Ostrove (2013) and Le, LaCost, and Wismer (2016) about the positive relationship between advisor support and sense of belonging among international and domestic graduate students.

In Canadian university education, student engagement and their sense of belonging emphasize socially engaging in activities in and beyond classrooms such as extra-curricular engagement, community activities, and students' communications and interactions, and relationship with the community and societies. In previous studies, student engagement in and beyond classrooms in the Western contexts similarly indicates a strong motivation for social practice reflected by student experiences (Ams & Archer, 1988; Bernard, 2010; Blumenfeld & Paris, 2004; Grabke, 2013). This also supports Grabke (2013)'s findings that students' sense of belonging can be improved by better social engagement experiences. Similarly, Chen and Zhou (2019) and Heng (2017) found that a sense of belonging as an imperative predictor of social performance motivates universities to create a supportive environment for students' strong sense of belonging and better social engagement.

All of the student participants agree with the notion that students' sense of belonging are impacted by the involvement in and out of the classroom and the relationship between students, teachers, schools, communities, and societies. Student participants and student service staff in this study stated that students' sense of belonging can be significantly influenced by how students engage in and out of the classroom, how students feel their sense of belonging when they engage in the communities, and how students perceived their sense of belonging based on their cultural backgrounds and socio-cultural experiences. This finding is consistent with the findings of Willms, Friesen and Milton (2009), and Yang and Jing (2021) that how students are belonging to community is impacted by how students feel regarding their relations to their communities including their teachers and peers.

Portelli (2015)'s critical perspectives on student engagement and their sense of belonging that "not all learners that seem to be engaged from the perspective of the teacher are necessarily engaged, and not all learners that seem to be disengaged are necessarily disengaged" (p. 76) seems true of many participants in this study. For instance, one student participant stated that some students do not want to talk, but it does not mean they are not engaged or belonging to the community. The different ways that students' engagement, willingness to participate and the climate in classrooms are imperative to perceive the genuine notion of sense of belonging in classrooms.

According to the level of Chinese international graduate students' engagement and how they belong in classrooms, six student participants shared varied stories about sense of belonging in classrooms with regarding to their own experience and their perceptions of Chinese international graduate student engagement in Canada. However, all of them shared that some of their experience has been interpreted as passive and negative during the process of engaging in the Canadian classroom and of belonging to the community. This is because they were not actively talking about their ideas or engaging in the group discussion or showing their sense of belonging. Their infrequent oral engagement based on feelings, deep thinking and minds, and different expressions was not recognized as engaging and belonging in Western Canadian graduate schools.

It is consistent with the understanding of some research (Tsai, 2016; Yao, 2015; Zhao, 2017) regarding the challenges and stereotypes of Chinese international graduate students in North American universities including their marginalizing cultural experiences indicated in my prior analysis. This also reflects Liu's (2001) finding of the 'silent' performance of some Chinese international students in class have been evaluated as less engaged and belonged to the communities in Canadian higher education.

The practice of criticizing students for their silence resulting in a low sense of belonging in classrooms is unfair. It does not take into account the cultural differences that the student may have to assess their sense of belonging. Students may have good reasons why they do not talk and how they belong. Students may feel valued and empowered through different ways of interactions, which supports their sense of belonging and their desire to succeed when they build relationships (García, Garza, & Yeaton-Hromada, 2019). Thus, the fact that they do not talk does not mean that they are not engaged intellectually in the issues at hand or they feel they do not belong to the communities. These definitions of sense of belonging, and their student experience indicate a dominant ideology of understanding student engagement only as orally actively engaging or showing sense of belonging in classrooms. Similarly, Tweed and Lehman (2002) pointed out that Asian students' tendency not to speak out in class, assuming that speaking is conducive to learning and engaging while not speaking, is a lack of engagement or belonging.

No matter in or beyond classrooms, the need of belonging is a fundamental motivation for students. Liu and Littlewood (1997) stated that East Asian students' passive attitude that they are regarded to have towards classroom engagement in English-speaking countries even they are willing to participate in class discussions. Many Chinese internationals are eager to understand the local culture, make local friends, and get involved in their communities if they can gain support (Heng, 2017).

With regards to Chinese international graduate students' engagement in classrooms, two students from social science background shared some of their positive experience or concerns and challenges during the process of engaging in classrooms. Based on their observations of Chinese international graduate student classroom engagement, two of the six student interviewees from Engineering and Business programs and two of the six staff interviewees from the Engineering department and the Student Life Center shared the common idea that Chinese international graduate student from their own departments engage in out-of-classroom activities a lot. This finding is different from the findings from other scholars who noticed that Chinese international students have lower engagement and less sense of belonging in North American's schooling (Grabke, 2013; Tsai, 2017; Xiang, 2017) and Chinese students as "passive" learners seems to be lower engaged in and out of the classroom (Chang, 1997; Zhao & McDougall, 2005). Some Chinese students engage in the non-oral or non-verbal interactions or with deep thoughts regarding as "passive" engagement does not mean that they are less engaged or feel a lower sense of belonging as shown in this study.

The findings in this study show that Chinese international students are engaged as passive learners and lower engagement were disadvantaged and their sense of belonging can be better enhanced and supported by institutions in Canadian higher education. This study shows some international students from a social science background stated that some students feel less engaged and a sense of belonging when they began their study. However, those students gradually increase their sense of belonging by feeling that they might do something wrong and gain confidence with the support from the professors and peers as they spend more time in Canada.

The sense of belonging can be viewed as "the sense of transformation" based on students' cultural identities (Le, LaCost, &Wismer, 2016, p.146). Le, LaCost and Wismer (2016), in their explanation of the sense of transformation, described the experiences of international female graduate students at a Midwestern university in the U.S. as they tried to make the best of their situations based on their strong sense of belonging that transfers their difficulties into motivation to try harder.

Most participants in this study described their transitioning from lower to higher engagement and indicated that a sense of belonging and community inclusivity can effectively enhance the engagement of Chinese international graduate student in and out of the Canadian classrooms. This finding supports the argument of McDowell and Montgomery (2006) that some international students have experienced difficulties on social exchanges and interactions such as feeling challenging to share their culture, being reluctance to low sense of belonging in and beyond classrooms.

In this study, half of the student participants stated that they choose to come to Canada and this urban university to study because they believe Canadian multiculturalism can empower their cultural experiences and identities. However, after they came to Canada, they did experience lots of exclusion, a lack of sense of belonging, and feel less engaged in and beyond classrooms. This is consistent with the statement of Brown and Holloway (2008) that some international postgraduate students engaging at an English university experience depression, loneliness, anxiety, and stressed originated from cultural differences, especially at the beginning of their transition period. There are lots of factors that negatively impacted their sense of belonging including the preference of western ways of student engagement, the lack of knowledge of Chinese student engagement, and the stereotypes of Chinese international students.

The democratic and inclusive community can encourage students in the minority to examine the inequitable structures and oppressive relationships in solidarity towards their engagement reflected in the previous study (McInerney, 2009; Portelli, 2015). In this study, one student participant suggested that the supporting resources for Chinese international graduate students can include the learning and practice knowledge about the Indigenous cultural and worldview to rethink the collaborative relationship between international students and indigenous students so that they can enhance their sense of belonging by share cultural similarities.

All of the student interviewees reported that the sense of belonging and inclusivity makes them feel confident, welcomed, and encouraged in classroom group work and out-of-classroom activities. Half of the student and staff interviewees highlighted a welcome and inclusive environment that supports different engaging ways, different accents, different writing style contributes to better classroom engagement of Chinese international graduate students in Canadian schools. This supports the statement of Hare and Portelli (2015) on student voice, that we should not only prefer to allow students to speak, but that voice should be associated with educational reform in the interests of disadvantaged and minority students. To increase student engagement in classrooms, it is important encourage teachers and students to develop democratic educational practices against the dominant reform rhetoric.

Students' sense of belonging that occurs in classroom and communities is described as a way to enhance student engagement. It is consistent with the findings of Neild et al. (2008) that the sense of belonging to the community has a significant effect on student engagement. This also supports the argument of Rosenfeld, Richman and Bowen (2000) highlighting that the more positive relationships to the community that students have, the better student experience would have in their school community.

One student interviewee indicated that information inclusivity matters when Chinese international graduate students are engaged out of the classroom. The influence will be how the school activities were sent and what content of the platform is provided for Chinese international graduate students to engage and enhance their sense of belonging towards engaging in out-of-classroom activities on campus to ensure their needs be met and their voice be heard. Their voice includes their engagement in and out of the classroom, their relationship with the communities, their cultural perceptions of sense of belonging are imperative, and their socio-cultural sense of belonging based on their international student identities. This supports Fielding's (2012) finding that schools and institutions deliberately develop "more participatory and less hierarchical forms of engagement and decision making" (p. 15) to make different voices of students be listened to through community participation. Maramba (2008) pointed out that institutions could engage their sociocultural consciousness within community involvement in order to engage diverse students.

The awareness and practice of creating an inclusive and diverse engaging environment are highlighted in the staff participants' experiences as shown in this study. One staff claimed that feeling welcomed is a key factor in affecting student out-of-classroom engagement as well as being aware of how to create an environment to encourage those students to want to engage. This is consistent with student engagement based on student voice within democratic communities stated by Fielding (2012). Thus, student voice with a learning and practical community in more inclusive settings supports Chinese international graduate students to engage in schooling and to make their different voices be heard in the communities. In this way, students will have the stronger sense of belonging that supports their engagement in and out of the classroom.

CONCLUSION

Given the magnitude of current global challenges facing Chinese international student engagement, this research provides valuable insights and effective ways of supporting Chinese international graduate student experiences with regards to increasing their sense of belonging and engagement in Canadian higher education. This study provides some implications for the teaching pedagogy to improve the engagement of Chinese students in the Canadian education system. This study provides some evidence for faculty and staff having a holistic look at international students especially those Chinese graduate students and their challenges they encounter while attending university in Canada. The results of this study can also help Western institutions become aware of the efforts currently undertaken by the Canadian education system and the cost in terms of resources, capacity, pedagogical changes entailing for the Canadian educators and institutions for better Chinese international student sense of belonging. This awareness helps educators and institutions build a broader understanding of Chinese international students' sense of belonging in Canada higher education and their engagement. Future research is suggested to include Chinese graduate students' peers and professors to investigate their perceptions of Chinese graduate students' sense of belonging in Canadian universities. Studies should be conducted to examine concrete proposals for the teaching pedagogy to improve the sense of belonging of Chinese international students in the Canadian education system. In this way, those Canadian institutions can have a more inclusive academic environment and support Chinese international students' sense of belonging in and beyond classrooms.

REFERENCES

Adamuti-Trache, M., & Sweet, R. (2010). Adult immigrants' participation in Canadian education and Training. *Canadian Journal for the Study of Adult Education, 22*(2), 1.

Ahn, M. Y., & Davis, H. H. (2020). Four domains of students' sense of belonging to university. *Studies in Higher Education, 45*(3), 622–634. doi:10.1080/03075079.2018.1564902

Ballard, B., & Clanchy, J. (1997). *Teaching international students: A brief guide for lecturers and supervisors*. IDP Education Australia.

Batido, H. M. (2001). The Endangered Languages of Africa, A Case Study from Botswana. In On Bicultural Diversity, linking language, knowledge and the environment. Smithsonian Institute Press.

Calder, M. J., Richter, S., Mao, Y., Kovacs Burns, K., Mogale, R. S., & Danko, M. (2016). International Students Attending Canadian Universities: Their Experiences with Housing, Finances, and Other Issues. *Canadian Journal of Higher Education*, *46*(2), 92–110. doi:10.47678/cjhe.v46i2.184585

Caligiuri, P., DuBois, C. L., Lundby, K., & Sinclair, E. A. (2020). Fostering international students' sense of belonging and perceived social support through a semester-long experiential activity. *Research in Comparative and International Education*, *15*(4), 357–370. doi:10.1177/1745499920954311

Canadian Bureau for International Education. (2021). *Canada's performance and potential in international education*. Retrieved from http://www.cbie.ca/about- ie/facts-and-figures/

Carales, V. D., & Nora, A. (2020). Finding place: Cognitive and psychosocial factors impacting Latina/o students' sense of belonging. *Journal of Student Affairs Research and Practice*, *57*(4), 355–370. doi:10.1080/19496591.2019.1662795

Chen, J., & Zhou, G. (2019). Chinese international students' sense of belonging in North American postsecondary institutions: A critical literature review. *Brock Education Journal*, *28*(2), 48–63. doi:10.26522/brocked.v28i2.642

Cui, D. (2015). Capital, distinction, and racialized habitus: Immigrant youth in the educational field. *Journal of Youth Studies*, *18*(9), 1154–1169. doi:10.1080/13676261.2015.1020932

Curtin, N., Stewart, A. J., & Ostrove, J. M. (2013). Fostering academic self-concept: Advisor support and sense of belonging among international and domestic graduate students. *American Educational Research Journal*, *50*(1), 108–137. doi:10.3102/0002831212446662

Duran, A., Dahl, L. S., Stipeck, C., & Mayhew, M. J. (2020). A Critical Quantitative Analysis of Students' Sense of Belonging: Perspectives on Race, Generation Status, and Collegiate Environments. *Journal of College Student Development*, *61*(2), 133–153. doi:10.1353/csd.2020.0014

Erb, S., & Drysdale, M. T. (2017). Learning attributes, academic self-efficacy and sense of belonging amongst mature students at a Canadian university. *Studies in the Education of Adults*, *49*(1), 62–74. doi:10.1080/02660830.2017.1283754

Flowerdew, J., & Miller, L. (1995). On the notion of culture in L2 lectures. *TESOL Quarterly*, *29*(2), 345–373. doi:10.2307/3587628

García, H. A., Garza, T., & Yeaton-Hromada, K. (2019). Do we belong? A conceptual model for international students' sense of belonging in community colleges. *Journal of International Students*, *9*(2), 460–487. doi:10.32674/jis.v9i2.669

Gillen-O'Neel, C. (2021). Sense of belonging and student engagement: A daily study of first-and continuing-generation college students. *Research in Higher Education*, *62*(1), 45–71. doi:10.100711162-019-09570-y

Glass, C. R. (2018). International students' sense of belonging-locality, relationships, and power. *Peer Review: Emerging Trends and Key Debates in Undergraduate Education, 20*(1), 27–30.

Glass, C. R., Kociolek, E., Wongtrirat, R., Lynch, R. J., & Cong, S. (2015). Uneven Experiences: The Impact of Student-Faculty Interactions on International Students' Sense of Belonging. *Journal of International Students, 5*(4), 353–367. doi:10.32674/jis.v5i4.400

Grabke, S. V. R. (2013). *Institutional strategies and factors that contribute to the engagement of recent immigrant adult students in Ontario post-secondary education* [Unpublished dissertation]. York University.

Heng, T. T. (2017). Voices of Chinese international students in USA colleges: 'I want to tell them that…' *Studies in Higher Education, 42*(5), 833–850. doi:10.1080/03075079.2017.1293873

Kamens, D. H. (2015). A maturing global testing regime meets the world economy: Test scores and economic growth, 1960–2012. *Comparative Education Review, 59*(3), 420–446. doi:10.1086/681989

Klees, S. J. (2016). Human capital and rates of return: Brilliant ideas or ideological dead ends? *Comparative Education Review, 60*(4), 644–672. doi:10.1086/688063

Le, A. T., LaCost, B. Y., & Wismer, M. (2016). International Female Graduate Students' Experience at a Midwestern University: Sense of Belonging and Identity Development. *Journal of International Students, 6*(1), 128–152. doi:10.32674/jis.v6i1.485

Liu, J. (2001). *Asian Students' Classroom Communication Patterns in American Classrooms*. Greenwood Publishing Group.

Marshall, S., Zhou, M., Gervan, T., & Wiebe, S. (2012). Sense of belonging and first-year academic literacy. *Canadian Journal of Higher Education, 43*(3), 116–142. doi:10.47678/cjhe.v42i3.2044

McInerney, P. (2009). Toward a critical pedagogy of engagement for alienated youth: Insights from Freire and school-based research. *Critical Studies in Education, 50*(1), 23–35. doi:10.1080/17508480802526637

Pintrich, P. R., & Schrauben, B. (1992). Students' motivational beliefs and their cognitive engagement in classroom academic tasks. *Student Perceptions in the Classroom, 7*, 149–183.

Portelli, J. P., & Konecny, C. P. (2013). Neoliberalism, Subversion and Democracy in Education. *Encounters on Education, 14*, 87–97. doi:10.24908/eoe-ese-rse.v14i0.5044

Portelli, J. P., & Sharma, M. (2014). Uprooting and settling in: The invisible strength of deficit thinking. *LEARNing Landscapes, 8*(1), 251–267. doi:10.36510/learnland.v8i1.684

Ryan, J. (2010). 'The Chinese learner': Misconceptions and realities. *International education and the Chinese learner*, 37-56.

Tinto, V. (1993). Building community. *Liberal Education, 79*(4), 16–21. PMID:10124451

Tsai, S. C. (2016). Perceptions of East Asian Students in Canadian Graduate Schools: What They May Indicate about a Chinese Model of Education. In C. P. Chou & J. Spangler (Eds.), *Chinese education models in a global age* (pp. 217–230). Springer. doi:10.1007/978-981-10-0330-1_16

Wang, F. (2009). Student experiences of English language training: A comparison of teaching in UK and Chinese contexts. *English Language Teaching*, 2(3), 237–242. doi:10.5539/elt.v2n3p237

Xiang, B. (2017). *Classroom engagement and participation among Chinese international graduate students: A case study*. Academic Press.

Yang, W., & Jing, X. (2021). Chinese Graduate Students at a Canadian University: Their Academic Challenges and Coping Strategies. In Multidisciplinary Perspectives on International Student Experience in Canadian Higher Education (pp. 120-136). IGI Global.

Yao, C. W. (2015). *Sense of belonging in international students: Making the case against integration to US institutions of higher education*. Academic Press.

Yao, C. W. (2015). *Sense of belonging in international students: Making the case against integration to US institutions of higher education*. Academic Press.

Zhao, N., & McDougall, D. (2008). Cultural Influences on Chinese Students' Asynchronous Online Learning in a Canadian University. *Journal of Distance Education*, 22(2), 59–79.

Chapter 13

Effective Teaching Strategies for Chinese International Students at a Canadian University:
An Online Reading–Writing Support Program

Xiangying Huo
https://orcid.org/0000-0001-8165-1486
University of Toronto, Scarborough, Canada

Elaine Khoo
https://orcid.org/0000-0001-5672-0419
University of Toronto, Scarborough, Canada

ABSTRACT

Challenges that Chinese international students with low academic English proficiency encounter in academic reading and writing were exacerbated by remote learning during the COVID-19 pandemic. Qualitative and quantitative data were collected and analyzed from an online reading-writing support program at a Canadian university to examine Chinese students' challenges, perceptions of learning, as well as the impact of culturally responsive pedagogy (CRP) used in the program. The study indicates the benefits of CRP in improving language proficiency and critical thinking, facilitating student experience and satisfaction, constructing identities, promoting learner agency, and enhancing transformative inclusivity. The study also provides insights into effective online teaching pedagogies to help instructors better support low-proficiency international students in coping with academic challenges. In addition, the study suggests teaching practices for empowering international students studying remotely from various global locations, with potential applicability to different teaching contexts.

DOI: 10.4018/978-1-7998-8921-2.ch013

INTRODUCTION

With increasing internationalization, which results in high mobility, more international students study in English-speaking countries such as Canada and the United States. Chinese international students, as one of the largest overseas student groups, comprise 33.86% and 12.68% of the total Chinese international student population in the U.S. and Canada respectively (Tao & Hu, 2013). Chinese overseas student population is on the rise, constituting 18.5% of all overseas students 2009-2010, 21.8% 2010-2011, and 25.4% during 2011 and 2012 (Institute of International Education, 2014). Due to different "linguistic and cultural norms" in the mainstream classrooms, Chinese international students do not have a sense of belonging in the host country (Huo, 2020, p. 2). Chinese international students' cultural challenges, language barriers, socialization issues, and adjustment difficulties (Smith et al., 2019; Zhang & Zhou, 2010) were exacerbated by the pandemic as international students have to learn remotely from their home countries while immersed in their home languages. Despite the correlation shown between pedagogy and student satisfaction and perceptions (Smith et al., 2019), there is an inadequate supply of teachers with intercultural competence who are capable of acting as "border crossers" (Giroux, 1992) to teach culturally and linguistically diverse international students, including Chinese students. This paper aims to investigate potential teaching strategies that work effectively for international students (e.g., Chinese students) in the online teaching and learning environment to help them develop their competence with academic English (e.g., reading and writing) skills needed for academic work. With the paucity of research on sustained learner-centered or learner-driven programs to achieve this goal, the paper will contribute pedagogical insights gained from taking an innovative approach (i.e., Culturally Responsive Pedagogy) to supporting students in developing these skills.

LITERATURE REVIEW

Challenges Chinese International Students Face

Sociocultural Challenges

Culture affects learning (Tweed & Lehman, 2002) and students' perceptions (Koul & Fisher, 2005), such as different cultural beliefs, educational norms, instruction approaches, and learning styles (Henze & Zhu, 2012; Zhang & Zhou, 2010). Culture shock is the biggest cultural challenge that Chinese students encounter (Zhang & Zhou, 2010) caused by differences and conflicts between individualism held by Westerners and collectivism valued by Asian people (Marginson, 2014; ; Sawir et al., 2008; Tsai et al., 2000) which upholds conformity (Chan, 1999). Students' cultural backgrounds (Zhang & Zhou, 2010) and former learning strategies (Levinsohn, 2007) influence their academic transition and success. As teachers are regarded as authoritative figures, Chinese students are not encouraged to ask questions (Biggs, 1996; Biggs & Watkins, 2001) or think critically (O'Sullivan & Guo, 2010). By contrast, in the West, students' participation and engagement are essential to learning (Liu, 2016). Varying lecture delivery methods, classroom organization, learner-centeredness, and interaction-based mode by encouraging inquiries and discussions are challenging for Chinese students who are from the teacher-centered education system (Zhang & Zhou, 2010). Rote learning was prevalent among Chinese students in their previous years of studies, making deep learning and thinking difficult for most Chinese students in the mainstream classroom

(Ballard & Clanchy, 1991; Henze & Zhu, 2012). Being accustomed to their past "Confucian-influenced learning" (Foster & Stapleton, 2012, p. 302) or "traditionally behaviourist oriented" pedagogy (Zhang & Zhou, 2010, p. 45), Chinese students are at a loss facing the Western "Socratic-influenced learning" (Foster & Stapleton, 2012, p. 302) or "social-constructivist" teaching approach (Zhang & Zhou, 2010, p. 45) which involves students' own knowledge construction (Levinsohn, 2007). As a result, Chinese international students are regarded as passive learners in class (Huang, 2005; Liu, 2016) leading to their struggles in the mainstream classroom.

International students encounter more sociocultural challenges than domestic students, including adjustment, socialization, and communication challenges (Ammigan & Jones, 2018; Wu et al., 2015). According to Chen (2011), nearly 25% of Mandarin-speaking students face adjustment challenges. In fact, 40% of international students in the United States, 56% in Canada, and 67% in the UK do not have local friends (Canadian Bureau for International Education, 2014). International students are marginalized by stereotypes (Henze & Zhu, 2012; Zhang & Zhou, 2010) and othered by their instructors and fellow students (Beck, 2013). Chinese international students feel lonely and isolated in the host country (Henze & Zhu, 2012). Following Sawir et al. (2008), loneliness is largely caused by language proficiency. To summarize: Students' previous learning experiences and cultural influences (e.g., cultural values, norms, teaching methods, and learning styles) have affected their academic transition and led to the many sociocultural challenges that they faced.

Language Challenges

Language challenges rank top among the difficulties for international students (Yeh & Inose, 2003); Chinese students are no exception. Chinese international students are overwhelmed by academic reading and writing assignments which are different from their prior teacher-centered education systems and norms (Ching et. al, 2017; Turner, 2006). Coupled with their limited English language skills, they are often stressed and unconfident about succeeding in the host society (Bertram et al., 2014; Khawaja & Stallman, 2011). Chinese international students are particularly fearful of committing errors (Ching et. al, 2017). Wang (2003) attributes Chinese students' language barriers to insufficient cultural knowledge and inadequate English proficiency, practice, and language learning experiences. These barriers can be exacerbated by deficit models of language proficiency which devalue international students as linguistic losers, using standardized English as reference (Mackenzie, 2014). Because of unfamiliar and dominant "Eurocentric" curricula and teaching methods, international students wrestle with their academic studies in the host country (Huo, 2020, p. 7). Consequently, these international students' confidence is weakened (Beck, 2009) which has a negative impact on their studies (Clifford, 2010).

Student Satisfaction

Recent studies have demonstrated the close connection between teaching practices and international students' learning experience and satisfaction (Smith et al., 2021). A key dimension of student satisfaction is linked to teachers' motivation, support, engagement, care, enthusiasm, and feedback, students' communication with teachers, and effective teaching approaches (Shea et al.,2004). Such an approach to teaching can also be applied to satisfaction in online teaching and learning contexts (Bangert, 2006; Kéri; 2021). As student satisfaction plays a vital role in generating successful learning practices and outcomes (Elshami et al., 2021) to help international students achieve academic success, attention needs to be paid to students' "success factors" and teachers' pedagogical strategies to enhance students' perceptions and satisfaction (Smith et al., 2019, p. 253; Smith, 2020, p. 271) which reflect students' learning experience (Astin, 1993).

Culturally Responsive Pedagogy

The efficacy of the Culturally Responsive Pedagogy (CRP) is not only displayed in traditional classrooms (Smith et al., 2019; Smith, 2020), but also in virtual environments (Artze-Vega & Delgado, 2019; Rider, 2019). CRP "is defined as using the cultural characteristics, experiences, and perspectives of ethnically diverse students as conduits for teaching them more effectively" (Gay, 2002, p. 106). CRP is "inclusive," "empowering," "transformative," "emancipatory," and "humanistic" (Gay, 2018, pp. 38-44) with five key strategies: cultural bridging, personalized feedback, learner autonomy, teachers as collaborators, and humanistic teaching (Krasnof, 2016).

Culturally responsive teachers "build bridges" between students' existing knowledge and new knowledge, and between students' previous life experience with their new academic experience (Kilburn et al., p. 12 2019; Krasnof, 2016). CRP is "inclusive" (Gay, 2018, p. 38) as it takes students' diverse needs into consideration by providing customized feedback. CRP is also "empowering" and liberating (Gay, 2018, pp. 40-42) and supports learner autonomy which enhances student satisfaction and perception. Additionally, when teachers regard themselves as co-educators with students, the learning becomes reciprocal since students are power-sharing partners. Furthermore, CRP is ethical (Gay, 2018, pp. 44-45) because culturally responsive teachers respect students' differences and humanize learning with care and compassion.

METHODOLOGY

This study is an investigation of the application of the Culturally Responsive Pedagogy that was incorporated into a compressed four-week online version of a long-running, eight-week non-credit program to support students who were globally distributed during the COVID-19 pandemic. This co-curricular program aims to develop students' academic English reading, writing, and critical thinking skills.

Research Questions

1. What are Chinese international students' major challenges at Canadian universities?
2. What is the efficacy of the Culturally Responsive Pedagogy in coping with Chinese students' academic challenges?
3. What are Chinese international students' perceptions of the Culturally Responsive Pedagogy?

Research Context

The research was conducted in a fully online program run by a Center for Teaching and Learning during the COVID-19 pandemic at a large comprehensive university, located in a cosmopolitan city in southern Ontario, Canada. The support center serves students from linguistically, culturally, and ethnically diverse backgrounds, including Chinese international students who constitute a high percentage of the university's international students.

This fully online program was a re-envisioned iteration of a learner-driven, instructor-facilitated Reading and Writing Excellence (RWE) program that addressed students' language and identity (Bucholtz & Hall, 2005) and self-regulation (Zimmerman, 2002), and offered a relational pedagogy that made each student understand that they mattered (Gravett & Winstone, 2020). Since participation in this program is voluntary, students are free to withdraw at any time. RWE students are expected to read for 40 minutes and write about their readings for 20 minutes daily to the assigned writing instructor. The writing instructor then provides personalized responses intended to motivate students to keep writing and gain accelerated language and identity development from one-to-one support. The student meets with the instructor in a 30-minute online meeting every two weeks. CRP was applied in one of nine regular RWE groups as an enhancement to the standard relational pedagogy of the program by emphasizing individualized and dialogical support, students' voice and strength, learner-centeredness, and care.

In winter 2021, one group of students took part in a one-month CRP-enhanced intervention. As Chinese students constitute the largest proportion of international students whose first language has a written script and grammar very different from English, it is pertinent to identify ways of better supporting these students by developing their abilities to cope with academic writing. In this group of 21 students, 14 were Chinese students aged 20 to 27 years. All students in this group had low Academic English proficiency as identified by their performance in the Diagnostic English Language Needs Assessment (DELNA) Screening test (n.d.), a post-entry learning assessment that is provided risk-free and at no charge so that students have an early alert about their language needs and can enrol in support programs like this (i.e., RWE).

Table 1. Demographic features of Chinese international students

Anonymized Student ID	Year of Study	Program
HW018	1	Management
HW016	1	Management
HW015	1	Management
HW022	1	Arts Culture and Media
HW020	1	Management
HW021	1	Management
HW011	1	Arts Culture and Media
HW024	3	Political Science
HW017	1	Management
HW023	3	Psychology
HW008	1	Management
HW013	1	Physical and Environmental Science
HW009	1	Management
HW019	2	Critical Development Studies

Data Collection and Analysis

All student-instructor asynchronous interactions took place through the learning management system (LMS) by way of dedicated discussion threads created for students to write their daily journal entries, and for the instructor to respond to the students. As a result, the LMS provided data of student engagement. For this study, students' data from the CRP-enhanced group were extracted from the winter term 2021 dataset for analysis.

Quantitative Method

The volume of Chinese students' written output in a one-month cycle indicates written language practice and progress. In addition, word count has also been established as a measure of fluency of output (Crossley et al., 2013; De Angelis & Jessner, 2012; González, 2017). Therefore, the word count of each student's journal entries was tallied.

Qualitative Method

Students' daily reflective journals, end-of-program reflections, emails, as well as teaching notes and instructor feedback were analyzed. Students' reflective journals were extracted from the dataset downloaded from LMS. The instructor's teaching notes recorded students' cultural challenges, namely adjustment and socialization challenges. As the instructor met each student biweekly during the program, she had a chance to chat with students in synchronous online sessions which enabled her to learn about her students' concerns and struggles.

FINDINGS

Research Question 1: What are Chinese international students' major challenges at Canadian universities?

Qualitative Data

Both teaching notes and journal data were employed to report students' challenges. Teaching notes reflect students' major issues (e.g., cultural challenges) based on the instructor's conversations with students while journal data reveal students' self-identified challenges in their journal entries.

Instructor Teaching Notes

Teaching notes were the notes taken by the CRP instructor during the interaction with students in synchronous online sessions, at the end of the sessions, or the notes about the students' struggles, learning styles, or academic goals in the program.

Cultural Challenges

The CRP instructor's teaching notes recorded students' cultural challenges, namely adjustment and socialization challenges. As the CRP instructor met each student biweekly during the program, she had a chance to chat with students in asynchronous online sessions which enabled her to learn about students' concerns and struggles.

Adjustment: *She looked aside and sighed. Then she said slowly, "I am a new student here. I did not attend high school in Canada and feel the adjustment is really challenging for me. Everything is new, overwhelming. Really challenging. It is so hard to fit in…I am struggling all the time."*

Socialization: *He was a first-year student. Although he told me that he had never studied abroad before, he spoke fluent English, "I was outgoing and sociable in my home country. I have been in Canada for several months, but I do not have any friends. I often feel I am isolated. No friends and I do not know how to make friends with my classmates born here."*

Student Journal Data

Language Challenges

Language poses a major challenge to Chinese international students (Zhang & Zhou, 2010). Five themes emerged from the analysis of students' journal entries for the language challenges they faced: class participation, reading, writing, vocabulary, and communication. These challenges illustrate the severity of linguistic obstacles that impact students' classroom performances and academic skills related to achieving success.

Class Participation. The data indicate that Chinese students encountered challenges in class discussion, due to their fear of giving wrong answers in class or lack of confidence.

There are twenty to thirty students in one class, the teacher will ask each student to answer the question, because I was afraid of answer in wrong, therefore I often skipped class.

I dare not participate in class and do not ask questions. I think I will be more confident to share my ideas and attend professors' office hours more frequently.

Reading. The biggest barriers in reading were found to be low reading speed, comprehension, and translation.

But compared with Chinese reading, my reading speed in English is much slower. However, there are a number of readings required to complete every week, and it takes a long time.

I need to spend a lot of time on reading textbooks because I have to translate the academic vocabulary into my first language (Mandarin).

I am also a slow reader. I have tried different reading strategies such as skimming and scanning, but I found that I have trouble remembering the ideas. I often have to re-read the passage again to understand the text.

Writing. Students reported that grammar was one of the major concerns in their academic writing.

Due to English is my second language, I am not comfortable with my writing skills where every time before summiting an essay or a writing project I need to meet up with a tutor for proofreading. My English grammar is not very strong where I will always make some grammar mistakes while writing, and I don't really know how I can improve it. Despite the grammar, sometimes, my wording and sentence structure might be confusing, and can't fully deliver my opinions.

Students also mentioned that they lacked critical thinking skills in their academic writing.

I think my essays are informal and the whole essay is incoherent which lacks connections between each paragraph. Another problem of my writing skills is critical thinking. The discussions in my essays are not supportive enough.

Vocabulary. According to students, vocabulary was one big obstacle to academic English, not only hampering their reading efficiency, but also their writing abilities.

I am aware that my vocabularies and sentence structures are limited while I am writing no matter essays or reports.

I always struggle with writing essays which I think I am so slow and inefficient in finding the right words to express and develop an idea fluently. I have to put more effort and spend more time searching for the right words to construct my sentences.

It's a little bit hard for me to write in an academic style and express my idea using sufficient vocabulary.

Communication. As discussed in the literature review, the sociocultural challenges of adjusting to expectations and ways of communication in the Western culture are significantly different from those in Chinese culture, students' lack of language proficiency makes it even challenging to mitigate the academic demands on them. Chinese students indicated they had difficulty in communicating both in verbal and written forms.

Communicating with people and express ideas are challenge for me, especially in one of my courses. In this course, we had to turn on the camera and communicate with the teaching assistant in front of the entire class. I am very worried about people not understanding my spoken language and making it difficult for others to understand.

I doubt my ability to express my ideas in a clear way no matter in oral or in writing.

Research Question 2: What is the efficacy of the Culturally Responsive Pedagogy in coping with Chinese students' academic challenges?

To address the second research question, both qualitative and qualitative data were collected. Qualitative data include teacher responses and students' journal entries written at different stages of the program (e.g., at the beginning and at the end of the program) to examine student improvement in their writing and critical reading skills. The excerpts of teacher feedback and quantitative data will be presented later (Tables 2 and 3)—the volume of writing produced by these Chinese international students and their frequency of writing.

Teacher Written Feedback on Student Journal Entries

The following excerpts include the instructor's customized support, motivation, and development of critical thinking that attend to the features of CRP.

Personalized Feedback

I also agree that free shipping could attract more customers…However, when you mentioned the "several psychological tricks" in your summary, you could introduce them or list them briefly so that it would be clearer to your readers…Do you agree?

It is also good to compare the article with the previous chapters in the textbook. My question is: In your summary, what are "a range of patterns"? List them to be more concrete. In Journal 20, you need more explanation and clarity. There are two sentences: "…and one is due to the <u>group society</u>, and another is because of <u>authority</u>"… Because your readers have not read this chapter, you need to explain the underlined parts clearly.

Motivation and Encouragement

You did a very good job in writing your journals. I can see your potential. Both your structure and language are clear. You well planned your journals with claims and relevant evidence to support the major arguments. I also like your responses, interesting and reflective. You not only discussed the strengths of these articles, but also their weaknesses. Well-done!

You should feel proud of yourself now as you have conquered your biggest challenge—critical thinking! You are making thoughtful reflections and you are good at making judgment and assessment! Very impressive!

Critical Thinking

When responding to students' journals about their readings and reflections on different topics, the instructor offers specific comments about students' ideas, poses questions or comments, elicits their authentic voices, and encourages them to continue the exploration of thoughts.

The following feedback shows the instructor's responses to students where there was a greater focus on developing the type of clarity and precision needed in academic writing.

Moreover, dig more in your reflection parts, such as your responses in Journal 7 and Journal 9. In Journal 7, think about the question: If it is a lie and plus parents also know it is a lie, why did they lie to their kid? … Excavate the deeper meanings to make your comments more profound.

You mentioned that loneliness increased the possibility of depression which was another cause of Alzheimer. Do you agree or disagree? Why (not)? Can you analyze the reasons from the perspective of psychology or with the theories learned in your course or in this textbook/article? Any other relevant examples? If you can include your answers to these questions in your journal, your responses will be reflective.

In fact, the topic you chose for Journal 8 is very interesting. There are a lot of things to talk about. For example, do you agree with the claim "being parents reduces the marital satisfaction?" What are your reasons? Any examples from other articles or the couples around you? Also, what is your opinion on the statement that "...a child might be the reason for the deterioration of the couple's relationship"? Is that true or fair? Additionally, are couples with higher salaries are really happier? There are the possible questions you may start to think about and comment on. If you could answer all of them, your response paragraph will not be one sentence long any more.

Student Journal Entries: Student Improvement

Students' journals written at the beginning and the end of the program were compared to investigate the differences in students' academic English skills, improvement in their academic writing and critical thinking skills, as well as the efficacy of Culturally Responsive Pedagogy.

Beginning of the Program (Journal #3)

There is a student sample which shows the absence of reflection. It is more like a mere summary of the text rather than a reflective journal as required by the program.

The main topic of the section that I have read in the textbook PSYA02 is about the "prenatal develop-ment". It separates the pregnant process into three periods, such as, zygote (0-2 weeks), embryo (2-8 weeks) and fetus (week of 9-childbirth). The first 2 weeks is waiting for the zygote to implant on the uterine wall. Meanwhile, completing the genetic inheritance by cell division. After that, the next around 6 weeks is the main process for fetus to develop organs and body structures from inside to outside and top to tail. Furthermore, these 6 weeks is a crucial time for pregnant woman to avoid teratogens, which might make disastrous results on fetus. Teratogens are ingredients that from the outside world and lead the fetus to abnormalities, such as, drugs, alcohol, toxins. Finally, for the rest of weeks is the time for fetus to grow and finish development in the brain (Altman, et al.).

However, after daily critical reading-into-writing practice with the instructor's feedback, in Journal #25, this student demonstrates rapid progress in making reflections and critiques.

End of the Program (Journal #25)

I like the example of egg and chicken because it an accurate explanation of the attitude and behavior and I agree with this relationship. I did not know the attitude is acquired since I used to think it is nurtured and natured. However, it is easy to have the same point of view as reading through life experi-ence. For example, everyone has their own views and attitudes to objects, and this is actually related to our families because they are related to our parental upbringing. For the second discussion, I like the example of contextualization. The author used the cult group to demonstrate the theory as the result of cult leader said did not happen but the group members still loyal to the cult (Altman et al., 2017). This theory makes people feel worse since their actions and thoughts are opposite, so the cult members still follow the cult. There are many examples in daily life. For example, I stay up late a lot, and I know this is bad for my health and other life aspects and this is a "cognitive dissonance" (Altman et al., 2017). The reading did not show the result whether attitude or behavior comes first and it probably because there is no consequence yet but it gives me a feeling of not having finished reading. There is another problem of this discussion is the reading focused on attitude but did not relate it to the behavior. I suggest adding a discussion of behavior, which would allow the reader to better relate behavior and attitudes.

In Journal #25, the student not only states the author's stance, provides rationale and examples, but also compares the course reading to those with other topics which "contain many academic discussions." As well, the student links the reading material to the psychology course. In Journal #25, as compared with the earlier writing (e.g., Journal #3), the student focuses on reflection. The student not only comments on the "egg and chicken" and "contextualization" examples, but also critiques the weakness of the chosen text, indicative of dramatic improvement in reading, writing, and critical thinking positively benefiting from Culturally Responsive Pedagogy.

Quantitative Data

Quantitative data were used to triangulate the qualitative data (i.e., teaching notes, teacher response, students' journal entries, emails, and end-of-program reflections).

Word Count as an Objective Measure of Volume of Language Practice

In order to quantify how much practice students have engaged in their one-month program, the word count of their journal entries is the most direct and objective measure of students' efforts at expressing their thoughts on disciplinary topics in written English instead of in their mother tongues. For students with low English proficiency, this practice writing is essential to prepare them for their assignment writing. Students' total written output over the four-week program ranged from 1,309 words to 14, 845 words (Table 2).

Frequency of Writing

Using the target language daily helps students acquire disciplinary vocabulary and develop competence for academic communication. An expectation of this program was for students to write a daily journal entry as consistent daily practice would help develop their abilities for academic writing (i.e., intermittent writing or writing a large amount within a day is not acceptable).

Table 3 shows that 57.1% of the low-proficiency students wrote at least 25 journal entries and 21.4% students wrote 13-24 journals within 28 days of the support program. In total, 78.5% of these low-proficiency Chinese student were willing to put in the effort to write almost every day or at least half the time in the program. Only three students did not participate fully, and as such their average sum total was 1,854 words as compared with the students who wrote almost every day (11,454 words).

Table 2. Sum of words written by each student over four weeks

Anonymized Student ID	Sum of Words Written in Journal Entries
HW020	14,845
HW009	12,767
HW015	12,450
HW008	11,918
HW023	11,638
HW016	11,029
HW024	9,491
HW019	7,497
HW022	8,137
HW013	6,570
HW021	4,605
HW018	2,854
HW017	1,398
HW011	1,309

Table 3. Frequency of student writing within one month

Frequency of Student Writing	Number of Students	Average Total Number of Words Written per Student
A.Students who wrote at least 25 journal entries within 28 days of the support program	8 (57.1%)	11,454 words
B.Students who wrote 13-24 journal entries within 28 days of the support program	3 (21.4%)	6,437 words
C.Students who wrote 12 or fewer journal entries during the support program	3 (21.4%)	1,854 words

Research Question 3: What are Chinese international students' perceptions of Culturally Responsive Pedagogy?

End-of-program reflections were analyzed to study students' perceptions of learning in this program and their satisfaction with Culturally Responsive Pedagogy. Student perception is displayed in the following excerpts. Students have addressed their improvement in academic writing, critical thinking, reading skills, and vocabulary development, as well as their satisfaction with the CRP approach used in the program.

Academic Writing

In academic writing, after receiving reading-to-writing training with the CRP approach, students' major improvement was shown in their expression of ideas, flow, and structure.

The quality of my writing has also improved significantly.

I think I am starting to write better ideas of writing in a more logical and comprehensive way.

With the help of tutor, the structure and sentence pattern of my article have been corrected and improved.

My sentence becomes more condensed and precise in expressing my idea.

There were many problems in the structure and wording of my articles, but now I feel that I can express my ideas more fluently.

Critical Thinking

All respondents mentioned rapid progress in their critical thinking abilities.

My critical thinking skill has improved and I can write more compared to the beginning. My critical thinking has been developed and began to think in a deeper perspective.

In terms of critical thinking, I am thinking deeply now after I read a new article. This helps me think independently without researching a lot, also helps me to generate my creative thinking.

I have longer critique paragraphs because I used to have only 2 sentences. However, my criticism is longer than my summary now.

Students perceive their rapid improvement in critical thinking skills as higher volume of critical written output, heighted awareness of the importance of critical thinking, "deeper perspective," independent, and "creative thinking" which is a significant breakthrough in their one-month journeys in the program with the support of the CRP teaching strategy.

Reading

Concerning academic reading skills, respondents made rapid progress in reading speed, comprehension, reading strategy, and "willingness to read."

I have more confidence to read a complete English academic or news article and I can finish reading an article faster and more accurately.

I also have more patience and willingness to read and keep practice.

I have different reading method than before, since I started to think when I am reading and not just read the information in the line.

Vocabulary

Students noticed their progress in vocabulary in terms of vocabulary span and the use of a variety of words in expression. They also addressed the intersection between their writing and vocabulary development. Students demonstrated a relationship between the volume of writing and the need to use more extensive vocabulary. As a result, with a wider range of vocabulary, the writing became "more coherent" and "smoother."

The vocabularies increase a lot. The structure of the articles became much clearer than before.

...I also tried to use more vocabulary to avoid repeating the same wording.

Furthermore, when I am writing now, my essay is more coherent and my writing is smoother. I have more flexible vocabulary than before, since daily journals forced me to use diverse words and phrases in order to make my essays look fresh everyday.

Communication

Through regular instructor-student interactions, students are more capable of conveying their ideas with more ease. The CRP approach has made students feel comfortable and eager to engage in academic communication and integrate their instructor's customized feedback with each of subsequent journals to improve their skills. This comfort and (internalized) willingness empowered students.

During writing the journals, I have followed the instructions that my instructors gave to me, which helps me a lot when I write quality journals. Since everyday, she can see my changes and improvements.

One of the impressive things that I have learned from Dr. XX is she also gives me a lot of useful suggestions for my essay assignment. Not directly, but the skill is required.

I carefully read the feedback from Dr. XX and take notes. I then apply them in my next journal. Dr. XX also notices it. For instance, she suggests that if I add examples to my ideas, it would be more convictive, and I should simply explain new concept to make my readers easily understand my ideas, etc.

Confidence

Students expressed a sense of enhanced confidence in academic reading and writing which was conductive to their "willingness to read," readiness to write, and "sharper mindset about writing."

I am more confident at constructing and writing long essay, rather than being stressful. I also have more patience and willingness to read and keep practice. I consider that I have developed a positive mind on academic writing.

I used to be a student who was very afraid of writing. After participating in this project, I became more confident in writing after following the advice.

I have better writing skills and not be afraid of writing as before. I have sharper mindset about writing.

As compared with students' initial challenges when they first joined the program, after the implementation of the CRP approach, students' challenges became their strengths. The evolution of students' perceptions is indicative of students' productivity, empowerment, and self-transformation.

Email Data

Email data collected from students to their instructor reinforce students' perceptions of and satisfaction with the teaching practices and the approach.

Dear Dr XX,

How are you? I am very happy that I have already completed 25 journals under your help and encouragement! Thank you very much for all these useful suggestions and I will keep applying more in my future writings! Thank you again for your helping and it has been a great time spending with you within this month and I hope we could meet in the campus! I will keep writing journals in the future and will keep in mind all your advice!

DISCUSSION AND CONCLUSION

Having a sufficiently high level of language proficiency is fundamental to student's academic success. Chinese international students living in their home countries were particularly challenged to function across different time zones in a culture quite different from their own. Supporting them online through a combination of personalized asynchronous and asynchronous interactions resulted in a high volume of language usage practice, and a strong sense of learner autonomy, achievement, and transformation.

Challenges Faced by Low-English Proficiency Students

Summarizing RQ1 data, the impact of low Academic English ability has far-reaching consequences particularly for reading academic texts. As students mentioned "reading slowly," "translat[ing]e the academic vocabulary into my first language (Mandarin)," and "re-reading" multiple times, it is a concern that these students face difficulty in reading course materials. Depending on their disciplines, students can be expected to read at least forty pages per course each week and write at least twenty pages over the semester to develop critical thinking skills (Arum & Roksa, 2011; Evans & Andrade, 2015). This volume of expected reading is challenging for students with limited vocabulary as every few words could be unfamiliar. Research has established that knowing at least 98% of the words on the page is necessary to comprehend content (Nation, 2006). However, many students with limited vocabulary try to translate most of the words in a text. This is an unsustainable strategy as the process takes too long and students fall behind with the reading each week which will result in the failure to process or engage in deep learning of the course content. This gives rise to a great deal of stress. Hence, establishing conducive conditions that facilitate exponential academic and technical vocabulary expansion (Coxhead, 2020; Liu & Lei, 2020) as well as gaining familiarity with reading academic texts are keys to empowering students to address their challenges. In this program, the relational pedagogy enhanced by CRP motivated students to sustain almost daily acquisition of academic and technical vocabulary from reading and writing about their course texts since the instructor encouraged and modeled the vocabulary use that would be helpful to students.

In addition to vocabulary and reading, Chinese international students also struggle with academic writing, communication, and participation in class. Having students articulate their concerns and challenges at the outset is significant as it enables the instructor to engage in cultural bridging when supporting students. Given the risk-free teaching-learning environment in this program to express ideas, the instructor could work collaboratively with students to address these needs, supporting students in constructing knowledge and expressing their opinions in the ways that are valued within the Western academic discourse community (Tang, 2012). The instructor supports and encourages students' "self formation" (i.e., constructing their identities on their own instead of by the instructor) (Marginson & Sawir, 2011, p. 149) using the CRP tenets of personalized, culturally oriented, and humanized interactions. The instructor took on the roles of being a cultural informant, cheerleader, and coach to raise learners' awareness of the fact that that "different is not deficient" (Heng, 2018b, p. 22). The instructor also helped connect students lived experiences to their expected participatory roles at university to contribute their diverse perspectives, including dealing with disciplinary topics related to their courses.

Efficacy of Culturally Responsive Pedagogy

As overcoming the challenges that Chinese international students face is contingent on their ability to quickly develop competence and confidence to communicate in English for academic purposes, the efficacy of using Culturally Responsive Pedagogy to elicit voluntary engagement with daily reading and writing related to their course materials is examined. In other words, the focus here is to examine how well the incorporation of CRP into the program has engaged students in target language practice where they systematically and deliberately work on developing knowledge and language skills (DeKeyser, 2007).

Practice is the key to language development since vocabulary acquisition is incremental and dependent on frequent usage to achieve mastery of lexical items (Schmitt, 2010). Thus, engaging students in the daily practice of reading, summarizing academic texts, drawing inferences, and expressing their perspectives help them develop their writing skills. To study the impact of the practice, students who wrote at least 25 out of 28 days were placed into category A, and students who wrote at least half the time (i.e., at least 13 journal entries and up to 24 journal entries) were placed into Category B. The remaining students who engaged in relatively little practice were placed into Category C.

The frequency and volume of writing suggest that most students were enthusiastic about the learning and writing process. 78.5% of these low English proficiency Chinese students wrote almost every day or at least half the time in the program, implying that they valued the opportunity. The written output measured by the total word count (Table 3) shows that students in Category A and Category B found the engagement so meaningful that they wrote far more than the minimum number of the words required.

The high percentage of students in Category A (51.7%) and Category B (21.4%) indicates that students managed to take up the challenge of reading their academic texts for 40 minutes almost every day. Since English and Chinese belong to different language systems, Chinese students need practice to gain fluency in cognitively processing alphabetic texts. Altogether, 73.1% (Categories A and B) students' engagement with the daily task of reading and writing is indicative that these Chinese students have recognized the value of this reading and writing practice.

According to the data, Chinese students need to learn to think critically about the texts they read. Chinese students expressed that they lacked the essential critical thinking skills required for their courses stemmed from their previous exam-oriented educational system which restricted "divergent thinking as students were 'very afraid of making mistakes' and taking risks" (Heng, 2018b, p. 29). Learning to read critically is not a problem for Chinese students alone when transitioning from high school to university. Evans and Andrade (2015) have identified faculty frustration about students' tendency to "read texts like a novel and not evaluating their understanding of the information that they are exposed to" (p. 104).

Reading their own course texts and writing daily about what they have learned in those texts benefit Chinese students in at least three ways which may explain the pattern of their willingness to produce high written output: exposure to disciplinary terminologies and discourses, acquisition of academic vocabulary and expansion of active vocabulary repertoire, and opportunities to "talk" to an instructor in a risk-free context. Unlike their previous exam-oriented culture where students feared taking risks or engaging in divergent thinking, students in this program read for a purpose – to summarize and discuss what they had learned. During the pandemic, remote learning from their home countries may mean that the instructor in Canada might be the only person that students were communicating with in English without the fear of being evaluated negatively.

To make the daily writing task manageable, students were asked to write at least 250 words for each journal. The word count produced is much higher than the minimum written output expected if students wrote for 25 days (i.e., 250 x 25 = 6,250 words). Table 3 illustrates that students in Category A and Category B found the benefit of the practice. Consequently, they wrote far more than expected in their respective categories. Students in Category A wrote on average of 11,454 words, while those in Category B wrote 6,437 words and those three students in category C wrote 1,854 words. In the case of Category B students who wrote 13-24 journal entries, if they wrote the minimum of 250 words for their journal entries, then, the word range the researchers expect to see for this category would be 2,750-3,000 words. In fact, Category B students actually wrote on average 6,437 words—beyond the minimum range. Although Category C students wrote only an average of 1,854 words for one month, this is still considered as a forward step as these students would likely not have read their course texts to write if they were not in this conducive condition to read and write and be accountable to a supportive instructor. Since students analyzed in this study were identified through the DELNA Screening test to have extremely low English proficiency, this high volume and frequency of output speak to the positive match between the pedagogy and students' willingness to invest in their academic development.

Engaging students in daily reading of course texts not only helps facilitate vocabulary acquisition through the reading of materials which are meaningful to students, but also develops students' writing skills as more input propels higher output. In addition, gaining the confidence to write extended texts is important as it provides students with the training that they need to complete their various assignments. Being able to write fluently and express their thoughts coherently is the key to meeting students' course expectations. A main focus of the program is to help students mobilize their language resources (e.g., active vocabulary) when they participate in class discussions or in high-stakes situations like answering their exam questions. As a result, the instructor offered students constructive feedback to improve clarity and logic of their ideas rather than corrective feedback that focuses on accuracy of form for remedial purposes. In terms of critical thinking skills, which they have never practiced, or have been exposed to or trained in, the transition is not easy without scaffolding. Besides getting practice with acquiring the vocabulary and language use in academic English, Chinese students also need to shift their mindsets from being expected to reproduce knowledge to being able to critique and transform knowledge (Heng, 2018b; Tang, 2012). The instructor provided Chinese students with supportive feedback by nudging students' critical thinking about their chosen texts through a series of questions in a dialogic written exchange. Students appreciated that as it made them think more deeply and "have a sharper mindset" (as seen in some of the excerpts related to Research Question 3).

Students' Perceptions

As seen in students' written reflections, as a result of the program, there was a transformation in how they perceived themselves as participants in their new academic community. Students were able to identify a shift towards being more capable of thinking critically, reading fast, and writing more fluently. Given that language is the site of struggle for language learners, these students who voluntarily wrote on average 6,000-11,000 words within one month submitted to their instructor crossed that threshold of fear, anxiety, and the language obstacles that they expressed to be their issues at the start of the program. The data from this study suggest that the approach to supporting Chinese students is empowering them so that they are capable of mitigating their possible "tremendous stress, self-doubt, dip in confidence, anxiety and depression" (Heng, 2018a, p. 4).

Although one month is certainly not long enough for language development, the positive experience of being able to sustain effective communication with their instructor and receive regular and continuous support through Culturally Responsive Pedagogy has amplified the foundational inclusive learner-driven, instructor-facilitated approach of the program. The CRP approach appears to have transformed these low-proficiency Chinese international students and helps them discover and explore their numerous ideas that they could express about their course materials.

Implications

The findings in this study show Chinese students' readiness to put in the effort for practicing their language skills with such disciplined engagement and achieving the transformation they have perceived are in alignment with other findings on Chinese students' abilities to be agentic and resilient when coping with new academic expectations (Heng, 2021)

The analysis of students' improvement in their academic English during this one-month in the program and their reflections on their learning experience illustrate how the prevalent tendency to think of Chinese international students in deficit terms could be addressed and reversed. The findings provided in this chapter about the pedagogy and teaching-learning dynamics seem conducive to students in bringing their cultural differences into the academic arena, and also providing them with the experience of having positive identities instead of the deficit ones so often imposed on them.

This program also develops students' confidence in bringing their diverse lived experience to learning and has thus achieved transformative inclusivity with learner centeredness, learner autonomy, and a sense of belonging. It sheds light on the application of Culturally Responsive Pedagogy to the teaching practice in the online context.

Limitations

As researchers chose to analyze the winter cohort of students in order to gain pedagogical insights into developing effective ways of supporting low-proficiency Chinese international students, the small sample size of 14 undergraduate students may not be representative of Chinese international students studying in other English-speaking countries. Furthermore, there were no interviews or focus groups conducted to learn more about students' motivation for engagement.

Recommendations

Based on the pedagogical insights gained from this research, the following are several key aspects of effective teaching strategies to facilitate learning for Chinese international students especially with those with low English language proficiency. This approach could be expanded to support other international students from diverse backgrounds with low proficiency in academic English.

- Create a conducive teaching and learning environment that is risk-free to enable students to learn about expectations at university and engage them in practice which will enable them to develop their competence and confidence in communication in academic English.
- Provide customized support to enable the scope for cultural bridging that meets individual student needs.
- Prioritize accelerated language development that is learner-driven so that the practice is inherently motivating students.
- Capitalize on students' work ethics arising from their previous training in their educational and cultural backgrounds.
- Use Culturally Responsive Pedagogy to amplify program pedagogy that emphasizes positive feedback and learner agency.

Future Research Directions

Since having stronger lexical resources comprising not only of single-word vocabulary items but also competence in lexical bundles (e.g., "as a result of," "on the other hand") would enable students to write more fluently and confidently, future research could explore an additional lexical dimension incorporated into this proactive learner-driven, instructor facilitated approach to developing students' writing skills. A study of (a) the volume of new single word vocabulary and lexical bundles that students integrate with their daily writing and which they track over the period of intervention, and (b) students' self-perception of their lexical dexterity at the start and the end of the one-month program could provide insights for instructors into the optimal development of students' lexical competence for writing.

REFERENCES

Ammigan, R., & Jones, E. (2018). Improving the student experience: Learning from a comparative study of international student satisfaction. *Journal of Studies in International Education*, *22*(4), 283–301. doi:10.1177/1028315318773137

Artze-Vega, I., & Delgado, E. P. (2019). Supporting faculty in culturally responsive online teaching: Transcending challenges and seizing opportunities. In L. Kyei-Blankson, J. Blankson, & E. Ntuli (Eds.), *Care and culturally responsive pedagogy in online settings* (pp. 22–41). IGI Global. doi:10.4018/978-1-5225-7802-4.ch002

Arum, R., & Roksa, J. (2011). *Academically adrift: Limited learning on college campuses*. University of Chicago Press.

Astin, A. W. (1993). *What matters in college: Four critical years revisited*. Jossey-Bass.

Ballard, B., & Clanchy, J. (1991). *Teaching students from overseas*. Longman.

Bangert, A. W. (2006). Identifying factors underlying the quality of online teaching effectiveness: An exploratory study. *Journal of Computing in Higher Education, 17*(2), 79–99. doi:10.1007/BF03032699

Beck, K. (2009). Questioning the emperor's new clothes: Towards ethical practices in internationalization. In R. D. Trilokekar, G. A. Jones, & A. Shubert (Eds.), *Canada universities go global* (pp. 306–336). James Lorimer & Company Ltd.

Beck, K. (2013). Making sense of internationalization: A critical analysis. In Y. Hebert & A. A. Abdi (Eds.), *Critical perspectives on international education* (pp. 43–59). doi:10.1007/978-94-6091-906-0_2

Bertram, D. M., Poulaski, M., Elsasser, B. S., & Kumar, E. (2014). Social support and acculturation in Chinese international students. *Journal of Multicultural Counseling and Development, 40*(2), 107–124. doi:10.1002/j.2161-1912.2014.00048.x

Biggs, J. (1996). *Academic development in Confucian heritage culture* [Paper presentation]. The International Symposium on Child Development, Hong Kong.

Biggs, J., & Watkins, D. A. (2001). *The paradox of the Chinese learner and beyond*. Comparative Education Research Center.

Bucholtz, M., & Hall, K. (2005). Identity and interaction: A sociocultural linguistic approach. *Discourse Studies, 7*(4-5), 585–614. doi:10.1177/1461445605054407

Canadian Bureau for International Education (CBIE). (2014). *A world of learning Canada's performance and potential in international education*. The Canadian Bureau for International Education.

Chan, S. (1999). The Chinese learner – A question of style. *Education + Training, 41*(6/7), 294–304. doi:10.1108/00400919910285345

Chen, B. (2011). *An emerging trend of Mandarin-speaking international students* [Paper Presentation]. The American Psychological Association Annual Meeting, Washington, DC, United States.

Ching, Y., Renes, L. S., McMurrow, S., Simpson, J., & Strange, T. A. (2017). Challenges facing Chinese international students studying in the United State. *Educational Research Review, 12*(8), 473–482. doi:10.5897/ERR2016.3106

Clifford, V. (2010). The international curriculum: (Dis)locating students. In E. Jones (Ed.), *Internationalization and the student voice: Higher education perspectives* (pp. 169–180). Routledge.

Coxhead, A. (2020). Academic vocabulary. In S. A. Webb (Ed.), *The Routledge handbook of vocabulary studies* (pp. 97–110). Routledge.

Crossley, S. A., Cobb, T., & McNamara, D. S. (2013). Comparing count-based and band-based indices of word frequency: Implications for active vocabulary research and pedagogical applications. *System, 41*(4), 965–981. doi:10.1016/j.system.2013.08.002

De Angelis, G., & Jessner, U. (2012). Writing across languages in a bilingual context: A dynamic systems theory approach. In R. Manchón (Ed.), *L2 writing development: Multiple perspectives* (pp. 47–68). De Gruyter., doi:10.1515/9781934078303.47

DeKeyser, R. (Ed.). (2007). *Practice in a second language: Perspectives from applied linguistics and cognitive psychology.* Cambridge University Press. doi:10.1017/CBO9780511667275

DELNA. (n.d.). *Diagnositc English langauge needs assessment.* https://www.auckland.ac.nz/en/students/student-support/delna.html

Elshami, W., Taha, H. M., Abuzaid, M., Saravanan, C., Kawas, A. S., & Abdalla, E. M. (2021). Satisfaction with online learning in the new normal: Perspective of students and faculty at medical and health sciences colleges. *Medical Education Online, 26*(1), 1920090. doi:10.1080/10872981.2021.1920090 PMID:33974523

Evans, N. W., & Andrade, M. S. (2015). Understanding challenges, providing support: ESL readers and writers in higher education. In N. W. Evans, N. J. Anderson & W. Eggington (Eds.), ESL readers and writers in higher education: Understanding challenges, providing support (pp. 3-17). Routledge.

Foster, D. K., & Stapleton, M. D. (2012). Understanding Chinese students' learning needs in Western business classrooms. *International Journal on Teaching and Learning in Higher Education, 24*(3), 301–313.

Gay, G. (2002). Preparing for culturally responsive teaching. *Journal of Teacher Education, 53,* 106–116.

Gay, G. (2018). *Culturally responsive teaching: Theory, research, and practice* (3rd ed.). Teachers College Press.

Giroux, H. (1992). *Border crossings: Cultural workers and the politics of education.* Rutledge.

González, M. C. (2017). The contribution of lexical diversity to college-level writing. *TESOL Journal, 8*(4), 899–919. doi:10.1002/tesj.342

Gravett, K., & Winstone, N. E. (2020). Making connections: Authenticity and alienation within students' relationships in higher education. *Higher Education Research & Development,* 1–15.

Heng, T. T. (2018a). Coping strategies of international Chinese undergraduates in response to academic challenges in U.S. colleges. *Teachers College Record, 120*(Feb), 1–42. doi:10.1177/016146811812000202

Heng, T. T. (2018b). Different is not deficient: Contradicting stereotypes of Chinese international students in US higher education. *Studies in Higher Education, 43*(1), 22–36. doi:10.1080/03075079.2016.1152466

Heng, T. T. (2021). Socioculturally attuned understanding of and engagement with Chinese international undergraduates. *Journal of Diversity in Higher Education.* Advance online publication. doi:10.1037/dhe0000240

Henze, J., & Zhu, J. (2012). Current research on Chinese students studying abroad. *Research in Comparative and International Education, 7*(1), 90–104. doi:10.2304/rcie.2012.7.1.90

Huang, J. Y. (2005). Challenges of academic listening in English: Reports by Chinese students. *College Student Journal, 39*(3), 553–569.

Huo, X. Y. (2020). *Higher education internationalization and English language instruction: Intersectionality of race and language in Canadian universities.* Springer. doi:10.1007/978-3-030-60599-5

Institute of International Education. (2014). *Project Atlas/international students in the United States.* https://www.iie.org/Services/Project-Atlas/United-States/International-Students-In-US

Kéri, A. (2021). Online teaching methods and student satisfaction during a pandemic. *Journal of Educational and Pedagogical Sciences, 15*(4), 373–379.

Khawaja, N. G., & Stallman, H. M. (2011). Understanding the coping strategies of international students: A qualitative approach. *Australian Journal of Guidance & Counselling, 21*(2), 203–224. doi:10.1375/ajgc.21.2.203

Kilburn, M., Radu, B. M., & Henckell, M. (2019). Conceptual and Theoretical Frameworks for CRT Pedagogy. In L. Kyei-Blankson, J. Blankson, & E. Ntuli (Eds.), *Care and culturally responsive pedagogy in online settings* (pp. 1–21). IGI Global.

Koul, R., & Fisher, D. (2005). Cultural background and students' perceptions of science classroom learning environment and teacher interpersonal behaviour in Jammu, India. *Learning Environments Research, 8*, 195–211.

Krasnof, B. (2016). *Culturally responsive teaching: A guide to evidence-based practices for teaching all students equitably.* Region X Equity Assistance Center at Education Northwest.

Levinsohn, R. K. (2007). Cultural differences and learning styles of Chinese and European trades student. Institute for Learning Styles Journal, 1.

Liu, D., & Lei, L. (2020). Technical Vocabulary. In S. A. Webb (Ed.), *The Routledge handbook of vocabulary studies* (pp. 111–124). Routledge.

Liu, D. F. (2016). Strategies to promote Chinese international students' school performance: Resolving the challenges in American higher education. *Asian-Pacific Journal of Second and Foreign Language Education, 1*(8).

Mackenzie, I. (2014). *English as a lingua franca: Theorizing and teaching English.* Routledge.

Marginson, S. (2014). Student self-formation in international education. *Journal of Studies in International Education, 18*(1), 6–22.

Marginson, S., & Sawir, E. (2011). *Ideas for intercultural education.* Palgrave Macmillan.

Nation, I. S. P. (2006). How big a vocabulary is needed for reading and listening? *Canadian Modern Language Review, 63*(1), 59–82.

O'Sullivan, M., & Guo, L. (2010). Critical thinking and Chinese international students: An east-west dialogue. *Journal of Contemporary Issues in Education, 5*(2), 53–73.

Rider, J. (2019). E-relationships: Using computer-mediated discourse analysis to build ethics of care in digital spaces. In L. Kyei-Blankson, J. Blankson, & E. Ntuli (Eds.), *Care and culturally responsive pedagogy in online settings* (pp. 192–212). IGI Global.

Sawir, E., Marginson, S., Deumert, A., Nyland, C., & Ramia, G. (2008). Loneliness and international students: An Australian study. *Journal of Studies in International Education, 12*(2), 148–180.

Schmitt, N. (2010). *Researching vocabulary: A vocabulary research manual.* Palgrave Macmillan.

Shea, P., Fredericksen, E., Pickett, A., & Pelz, W. (2004). Faculty development, student satisfaction and reported learning in the SUNY Learning Network. In T. Duffy & J. Kirkley (Eds.), *Learner centered theory and practice in distance education* (pp. 343–377). Lawrence Erlbaum.

Smith, A. C., Zhou, G., Potter, M., & Wang, D. (2019). Connecting best practices for teaching linguistically and culturally diverse international students with international student satisfaction and student perceptions of student learning. *Advances in Global Education and Research, 3*, 252–265.

Smith, C. (2020). International students and their academic experiences: Student satisfaction, student success challenges, and promising teaching practices. In U. Galuee, S. Sharma, & K. Bista (Eds.), *Rethinking education across borders: Emerging issues and critical insight on globally mobile students* (pp. 271–287). Springer Nature.

Smith, C., Zhou, G., Potter, M., Wang, D., Menezes, F., & Kaur, G. (2021). Connecting best practices for teaching international students with student satisfaction: A review of STEM and non-STEM student perspectives. In V. Tavares (Ed.), Multidisciplinary perspectives on international student experience in Canadian higher education (pp. 63-80). IGI Global.

Tang, R. (Ed.). (2012). *Academic writing in a second or foreign language: Issues and challenges facing ESL/EFL academic writers in higher education contexts.* Continuum.

Tao, Y., & Hu, R. J. (2013). Challenges and problems of overseas Chinese students socializing into international academic settings. In *Proceedings of the 2013 Conference on Education Technology and Management Science.* Atlantis Press.

Tsai, J. L., Ying, Y., & Lee, P. A. (2000). The meaning of "being Chinese" and "being American": Variation among Chinese American young adults. *Journal of Cross-Cultural Psychology, 31*(3), 302–332.

Turner, Y. (2006). Chinese students in a UK business school: Hearing the student voice in reflective teaching and learning practice. *Higher Education Quarterly, 60*(1), 27–51.

Tweed, R. G., & Lehman, D. R. (2002). Learning considered within a cultural context: Confucian and Socratic approaches. *The American Psychologist, 57*(2), 89–99.

Wang, Y. (2003). *The contextual knowledge of language and culture in education: Exploring the American university experiences of Chinese graduate students.* https://aquila.usm.edu/theses_dissertations/2631/

Wu, H. P., Garza, E., & Guzman, N. (2015). International student's challenge and adjustment to college. *Education Research International.* doi:10.1155/2015/202753

Yeh, C. J., & Inose, M. (2003). International students' reported English fluency, social support satisfaction, and social connectedness as predictors of acculturative stress. *Counselling Psychology Quarterly, 16*(1), 15–28.

Zhang, Z., & Zhou, G. (2010). Understanding Chinese international students at a Canadian university: Perspectives, expectations, and experiences. *Comparative and International Education, 39*(3), 1–16.

Zimmerman, B. (2002). Becoming a self-regulated learner: An overview. *Theory into Practice, 41*(2), 64–70.

ADDITIONAL READING

Carroll, J., & Ryan, J. (Eds.). (2007). *Teaching international students*. Routledge. doi:10.4324/9780203696132

Gay, G. (2010). *Culturally responsive teaching: Theory, research, and practice*. Teachers College Press.

Jones, E. (2017). Problematizing and reimagining the notion of "international student experience." *Studies in Higher Education, 42*(5), 933–943. doi:10.1080/03075079.2017.1293880

Kyei-Blankson, L., Blankson, J., & Ntuli, E. (2019). *Care and culturally responsive pedagogy in Online Settings*. IGI Global. doi:10.4018/978-1-5225-7802-4

KEY TERMS AND DEFINITIONS

Academic Writing: Formal writing used in academic contexts, such as university writing, journal articles, research papers, and academic books in a scholarly way.

Challenges: Obstacles or problems that one encounters or faces.

Chinese International Students: Chinese students who study in foreign countries other than China.

Critical Thinking: Active, rational, and skeptical synthesis and analysis of facts, information, arguments, and situations to make judgments and reach effective conclusions.

Culturally Responsive Pedagogy: A learner-centered approach by placing students' cultural strength at the core of teaching and learning.

Perceptions: Ideas or understanding of something.

Reading: It is a cognitive process of reading written or printed materials and acquiring meaning.

Student Satisfaction: Students' attitudes as a result of their learning experience and learning outcomes.

Chapter 14
Navigating the Australian Education System Refugees and New Arrivals:
An Insider's View

Alfred Mupenzi

https://orcid.org/0000-0002-5299-4719

Western Sydney University, Australia

ABSTRACT

The chapter highlights students' initial contacts with the Australian formal education system, the deficit logic that underpins underachievement, and provides a discourse around what can be done to make the Australian education landscape more inclusive and accommodating to refugees and new arrivals. The author employs a storytelling/narrative approach that focuses on three research participants to explore factors that enable students to successfully navigate the Australian education system. The discussion explores themes drawn from the narratives of participants and are supported by scholarly research. In addition to the participants' narratives, the author provides an insider's narrative with a strong emphasis on the view that 'no one can tell the lived experience of refugees and new arrivals in Australia more accurately than themselves'. Narratives about lived experiences of refugees have frequently been told in the third person because many of the studies that were carried out used methodologies that kept participants passive rather than active.

BACKGROUND

It is widely held that the role of education and training institutions is to nurture and support students so that they reach their full potential. More importantly, through thoughtful and more equitable discourses, they should work to engage and empower vulnerable students. One of the most challenging experiences for practitioners or service providers is regarding how to best engage refugees and asylum seekers (new arrivals)[1] in an appropriate and empathetic manner while maintaining fair and inclusive strategies and

DOI: 10.4018/978-1-7998-8921-2.ch014

practices. Refugee background students often face difficulties in forming their new identities. This is concerning as how they view the world is vital to their settlement and integrations processes, particularly when it comes to enrolling in formal education. Their perceptions of the world is often that it is unfair, many too, carry the pain of having suffered through injustices for the vast majority of their lives. According to Kiramba and Oloo, (2019, p2) there is 'misrecognition of refugees' translingual and transcultural competencies especially competencies that do not align with normative school literacy.' Students are often not regarded for the most part as actors in their own rights, with their own agency or resourcefulness, but as people whose perspectives do not matter and from whom we could not learn to see in new ways (Orellana, 2016; Shapiro & MacDonald, 2017).

Australia has a long-standing commitment to recognising the rights of refugees. Before Covid-19, Australia had the third largest humanitarian program in the world, after the USA and Canada (Parliament of Australia, 2016). Indeed, Australia's humanitarian program increased from 12,000 to 18,750 places from 2018–19 (Refugee Council of Australia (RCOA), 2018). Over the last decade, the nationalities of refugees resettled in Australia has remained relatively consistent, with Burma, Iraq, and Afghanistan featuring in the top five countries of origin accepted via the humanitarian program. This reflects the continuing unrest and violence in those countries. African nations (including the Democratic Republic of Congo, Sudan, Liberia, Somalia) have also featured consistently. There has been concern that responses to mass displacement resulting from violence in the Middle East has seen Australia (and other resettlement countries) overlooking the needs of African refugees (RCOA, 2017).

In Australia, the influx of a large number ethnic minority groups has created an educational system that is 'a complex social site for intercultural relations requiring a unique educational approach' and has led to tensions that shows itself in the form of verbal and physical racial abuse (Mansouri & Jenkins, 2010). Even with low occurrences, studies have shown that personal or general experiences with discrimination can lower an individual's self-esteem and ability to bond at school (Dotterer, McHale and Crouter, 2009).

The educational experience of refugees and new arrivals in Australia is often viewed by educators and policy makers from a deficit approach, that is from the perspective of what is lacking in their educational experiences rather than on what they can bring to the western education system (Mupenzi, 2018). For Sovic and Blythman (2013, p.3); "It would not be an overstatement to note that language inadequacy, associated with the much-contested concept of 'cultural differences', is far too often offered as a simplistic explanation for the learning deficiency of international students". Indeed, at the school or tertiary level, there is frequently a lack of culturally diverse student voices informing policies, and practices. Thus, this study is a reflection on the meanings attached to diverse educational experiences of refugees and new arrivals in the Australian education system. However, first I will unpack the perceptions, stereotypes and misconception which form the deficit logic when it comes to refugees and asylum seekers in Australia. These deficit ideologies, low expectations, and negative stereotyping are discussed in the next section.

DEFICIT DISCOURSE

The deficit framing/labelling of refugees and new arrivals in the Australian education system is concerning. According to Harris, Marlowe, and Nyuon (2015), the deficit framing model covers: 'low educational expectations, low tolerance of educators for different needs, inability to see education success or career-track options where they exist, attenuated migrant families who can't quite understand, support or assist their aspirational children who would like to achieve in the western educational context' (p.

1228). In the deficit model, students with a refugee background are viewed as 'tabula rasa with no history, past experience, culture, anticipation skills…refugees in general are treated as if they are starting from scratch and this denies them agency' (Hatoss & Huijser, cited in Harris et al. 2015, p. 1234). In other words, refugees are seen only one-dimensionally, they are not looked at as people who have both a history and past experiences that inevitably shape their present. For instance, in their study, Earnest, Joyce, De Mori, & Silvagni, (2010, p.167) found that, "some participants felt that they had experienced some form of prejudice from academic staff who assumed that students from refugee backgrounds possess basic or little knowledge, skills and education, despite some refugees having had degrees in their former countries". Overwhelmingly refugees and new arrivals have not been given the space to speak about their educational support needs. This results from using a deficit model lens to interpret educational underachievement for these students based on social status attributes like being victims, suffering trauma and having language challenges (Naidoo, Wilkinson, Langat, Adoniou, Cunneen, & Bolger, (2015); Uptin, Wright, & Harwood, 2016). Uptin, et al., 2016. states that the Australian education system 'quickly relabel[s] young former refugees with deficit terms rather than opening up a discourse to include the intricate complexities of each refugee experience' (p. 598). Some other scholars believe that refugees and new arrivals 'can contribute to, as well as benefit from, the further development of a high quality socially inclusive university system' (Terry, Naylor, Nguyen, & Rizzo, 2016, p. 7). Current educational researchers reject 'the focus on "deficit" models for refugee background students which do not acknowledge the social and cultural capital that these students carry with them' (Terry et al., 2016, p. 14). Taylor, Gillborn, and Ladson-Billings (2009) highlight that, 'the assumptions of white superiority are so ingrained in political, legal, and educational structures that they are almost unrecognizable' (p. 4). This relates to education in that 'we learn to value the Western literary canon and Eurocentric curriculum as superior to the traditions developed by oppressed groups' (Zamudio, Russell, Rios, & Bridgeman, 2011, p. 4). Those very beliefs are also embedded in our education system meaning that students of colour often find themselves tangled in the middle of all these racialized (i.e., race based) social relationships, structures, institutions, ideologies, and beliefs.

Other non-academic perceptions and challenges for refugees and new arrivals emerging from practitioners can include prejudice, stereotypes and assumptions. Most of these negative perceptions result from political debates and hyperbolic media messaging. Harris et al. (2015) states that, 'media discourses of deficit, dangerous and traumatised people are limiting potential…' (p.1227). These scholars therefore call upon successful tertiary refugee background students to speak back to such reductive notions of failure. Such social injustices and prejudices coming from political debates and the media are a source of distress and discomfort for students with a refugee background, moreover they are frequently experienced in addition to their existing learning challenges (Onsando & Billett, 2009).

Scholars agree that there is need to demystify assumptions and stereotypes around what it means to be a refugee and more importantly, to acknowledge the struggles students with a refugee background may encounter in their endeavours to access and participate in Australian tertiary education. Critical Race Theory (CRT) can be used as a basis of understanding the above deficit discourse. CRT is 'an epistemological and methodological tool, intended to help analyse the experiences of historically underrepresented populations across their particular educational experiences' (Delgado & Stefancic, 2012, p. 12). In this case, the experiences are those of refugees and asylum seekers (new arrivals) in Australia while they try to navigate the education system. Scholars indicate that education provides an opportunity for socialization of the young into the norms of the society (Oloo, 2012), thus, schools form key spaces where refugees and asylum seekers students build, mold, and reinvent their identities and self-image, often in opposition to marginalization, othering, and exclusionary discourses (Obsiye & Cook, 2016). Therefore, educators, policy makers and the host communities of these students should resist the temptation of believing preconceived notions about refugees and asylum seekers. The media messaging has influenced what people say to and about them and shape how teachers and peers see them, often through a deficit lens. This book chapter highlights Critical race theory (CRT) as a relevant tool in interpreting inequalities associated with the different forms of injustices and conflicts that emerged as a result of imagined and real threats about shared space and limited resources.

There is need to acknowledge resilience and tenacity demonstrated by refugees and asylum seekers while navigating the education system. This can be done using a strength-based approach as opposed to a deficit lens; 'a strengths-based philosophical approach stands in opposition to a deficit approach because it does not focus on a person's so-called shortcomings, deficits or dysfunction, nor does it label or disempower a person' (McCaskey cited in Hutchinson & Dorsett, 2012, p. 66). A strengths perspective draws on a 'power with' approach rather than 'power over' approach, viewing refugees as the experts on their own lives and situations (Hutchinson & Dorsett, 2012, p. 66). Scholars with this perspective believe that labelling these students as 'refugees' has a negative connotation that holds them back in life, restricting them to a life as a refugee rather than including them as equal members in society. As a result of this labelling, refugee people can experience 'internalised oppression' (Australian Psychological Society, 1997, p. 22).

ACCEPTING THE BITTER TRUTH: REFUGEES AND NEW ARRIVALS NEED ADDITIONAL SUPPORT

International agencies like the United Nations High Commission for Refugees (UNHCR) have shown that 'the chances of a refugee completing secondary school are slim and the chances of reaching university indicate a low probability because of the challenges associated with forced displacement' (Pflanz, 2016, p. 1). In fact, only one in every 100 of the world's refugees goes on to tertiary education (UNHCR, 2016). The difficulties involved in completing tertiary education by refugee background students include the lack of a student identity along with a lack of ability to match the required skills, knowledge and demands of being a student: 'The knowledge of how to "be a student", and indeed look like one, entails many skills, behaviours, formative experiences and a great deal of knowledge' (Miller, Mitchell, & Brown, 2005, p. 25). As such, it is likely that students with a refugee background: will leave school early, will never participate fully in society or in the decision-making processes of government, and that they will neither enjoy the benefits of good health, nor experience the upward mobility needed as adults to make them full contributors and partners in shaping and participating in the larger society (Biscoe & Ross, 1989, p.586). In resettlement countries like Australia, refugee and asylum seekers (New arrivals) are exposed to several other challenges such as placement into classrooms that are age appropriate rather than appropriate to their academic level. This often leads to these students facing social isolation, bullying, stress, and academic failure (Ferfolja, Vickers, McCarthy, Naidoo, & Brace, 2011). Despite the many challenges, some refugee background students have displayed remarkable resilience and capacity to learn and eventually some of these students become strong survivors. They go to school every day, they persist, and they never give up. They work very hard, they value education highly and some refugee and asylum seekers background students are able to progress to university and higher education and build a strong career pathway (Ferfolja, Vickers, McCarthy, Naidoo, & Brace, 2011). This research has allowed individuals to tell their unique stories in order to challenge the homogenous stereotypes that are applied on them in the Australian education system. Evidently, there is value in drawing upon the rich backgrounds of diverse refugees and asylum seekers experiences and through their stories, we learn about their perceptions of experiences and knowledge, dispositions and skills that could be useful to educators, policy makers, parents, and communities in welcoming and giving chance to such groups of vulnerable youth in Australia.

Initial Contact with Formal Education in Australia

Upon arriving in Australia and enrolling in school for the first time, the initial prospect of attending school or of achieving education success in Australia is exciting for refugees and new arrivals in Australia. Students' education dreams, aspirations and expectations are often high and unrealistic. For example, 'it is common for these students to declare strong ambitions to become engineers, doctors, nurses, teachers and the like; however, as they go along their path in education several challenges start to emerge and only few are able to sustain the journey' (Brace, 2001, p.93). In their study, Khawaja, N. G., White, K. M., Schweitzer, R., & Greenslade, J., (2008, p. 503) found that barriers to education in post-resettlement included 'a lack of environmental mastery, financial difficulties, social isolation and the impact of perceived racism'. For Shakespeare-Finch and Wickham (2010, p. 33), barriers included 'a lack of survival needs, disease, and the lack of security and safety, racism and racial discrimination, employment difficulties, financial difficulties, and inadequate/inappropriate assistance, [and] difficulties with the English language for refugees. English language learning in Australia for refugees and new arrivals is vital for attending school and entering tertiary education, yet these levels require a much higher level of proficiency than many students of refugee backgrounds have acquired. Poor levels of English skills create a substantial barrier to education and also limit employment options (Brown, J., Miller, J., & Mitchell, J. (2006); Hatoss, A., O'Neill, S., & Eacersall, D. (2012)). Scholars have found that language courses provided on arrival through the Integrated Humanitarian Settlement Strategy (IHSS) do not adequately prepare potential refugee students for university study (Joyce, A., Earnest, J., de Mori, G., & Silvagni, G., 2010, p. 95). In addition to lacking English language proficiency, students also lacked 'Australian cultural knowledge' (Brown, J., Miller, J., & Mitchell, J., 2006). Such knowledge includes Australian current affairs and cultural norms, moreover, they also experience unfamiliarity with teaching techniques involving use of videos and group work, and they lack complex skills required for learning such as listening, summarizing and note-taking (Windle & Miller, 2013). At the school level, refugee background students often show a lack of 'topic-specific vocabulary of academic subjects, social understandings of how to be in the classroom, and learning strategies to process content' (Windle & Miller, 2013, p. 178). According to Naidoo (2010) 'upon their arrival in Australia, many of these refugee students are placed in classrooms that are age appropriate rather than appropriate to their academic level and this increases the pressure on both students and school officials as both have to produce passing scores on standardized tests to achieve high school success' (p. 140). For Ferfolja et al. (2011) 'upon enrolling in high school, refugee students are required to negotiate the Australian education system; developing social networks, familiarizing oneself with schooling cultures and practices, and negotiating one's progression through these' (p. 4). Weekes, Phelan, Macfarlane, Pinson & Francis (2011) state that 'most secondary schools, in particular, are busy places with each student having multiple teachers for different subjects and moving from room to room in a day, this becomes challenging for these refugee background students who have not grown up in this type of education system' (p. 312).

Refugees and new arrivals in Australia will form a number of subcategories of students both in secondary and tertiary education. For example, many refugee children arrive in Australia from countries where their education has been hampered and interrupted by civil war and conflicts (Miller et al., 2005; Olliff & Couch, 2005). Therefore, many of these students will have faced challenges ranging from sociocultural dissonances, distress due to personal histories, academic and financial challenges and experiences of social exclusion (Earnest, J., Joyce, A., de Mori, G., & Silvagni, G. (2010); (Joyce, A., Earnest, J., de Mori, G., & Silvagni, G. (2010); Onsando, 2013). In their pursuit of education, these students are exposed to unfamiliar pedagogical practices that ignore their personal histories and sociocultural backgrounds. Additionally, they experienced racial discrimination (Onsando, 2009; Onsando, 2013; Onsando & Billett, 2009). Nevertheless, despite the challenges, some scholars have applauded the motivation and aspirations towards education exhibited by this cohort of students. For instance, Earnest et al. (2010) states that 'despite multiple difficulties involved in commencing and completing tertiary education, the dedication and resilience of these students in education is indisputable' (p. 172). Lived experiences of refugee background students in higher education attests to their capacities and skills of adaptation, resilience, aptitude and a willingness to look forward (McMahon, 2007; Schoorman & Bogotch, 2010; Shah, 2008). Understanding refugees and new arrivals in Australia requires creating a space for them to tell their life stories and having their voices heard. This greater insight can in turn become the basis for establishing the appropriate support required for educational attainment. In the next section, this book chapter explains the story telling approach to understanding refugees and asylum seekers.

STORY TELLING/NARRATIVES

Fundamentally, 'research is about furthering understanding, increasing the universal sum of knowledge, and making better sense of whatever it is that is being studied' (Sikes & Goodson, 2017, p. 66). Storytelling methodology does this through foregrounding accounts of lived experiences as the source of knowledge building. The methodology draws out what Atkinson (2001) suggests is of the most importance to participants and their experiences. He says that:

I have felt that it is important, in trying to understand other persons' experiences in life or their relations to others, to let their voices be heard, to let them speak for and about themselves first. If we want to know the unique perspective of an individual, there is no better way to get this than in that person's own voice. I am also interested in having the person tell his or her story from the vantage point that allows the individual to see his or her life as a whole, to see it subjectively across time as it all fits together, or as it seems discontinuous, or both. It is, after all, this subjective perspective that tells us what we are looking for in all our research efforts. (p. 125)

Providing an opportunity for people to tell their own stories reduces the colonising aspect of having others tell your own story and, according to Goodson, Biesta, Tedder, and Adair (2010, p. 33) 'it reduces the research power imbalance because, in narrative research, the researcher has less control over the participants while they are narrating their stories'. In addition to giving power to the narrator, the individual story of lived experiences counteracts the assumptions and stereotypes that are advanced in meta-narratives about other cultures. For example, that all people of a particular cultural group have had similar experiences with similar results. This can be challenged by listening to narratives of that particular culture in this case refugees and new arrivals in Australia.

Internationalism and multiculturalism defines the Australian classroom today. The diversity that exists among the student body is a rich investment into the sense of belonging and identity. Building a life in the Australian education system and later in the employment and career sector, is a story that has been left out of many narratives, especially in the world of academia. Therefore, the voices and narratives of refugees and new arrivals will create a firm and solid foundation for policy and pedagogical changes in the Australian education system. Stories of these students will bring together collective insights, strengthen relationships and collaboration among all stakeholders in education and ultimately in the employment sector. As the workforce in Australia continues to grapple with cultural diversity in workspaces, emphasis has been put on hiring based on culturally diverse employees to acknowledging the global experience. However, few investigations have been carried out to understand the fabric of the workforce in Australia mostly in classrooms where majority teaching staff are dominantly English, White and Middle class (Adams, 2014).

Whereas Australia registers graduates from culturally and linguistically diverse background each year, there is limited record of which sectors receives them most. The emphasis in recent years has been placed on measuring and reporting some quantifiable data, but the lived experiences of those in marginalised communities cannot rely only on statistics. A qualitative study will bring to the surface the entirety of experiences and thus could provide the basis for policy change. Therefore, the teaching of culturally diversity requires a more human-centred approach. We all know that numbers matter but how many of those marginalised students tell their stories? We can keep quantifying but without having the tough conversations, nothing will happen.

Following ethics approval and consent from the participants I used semi-structured interview as conversations guided by open-ended research questions to explore experiences of the three participants in this study. I recorded the participants' life experiences in great detail and covered three main life phases: 1) prior to displacement; 2) in transit countries; and 3) after resettlement in Australia. As a result of the data collected, the researcher employed several strategies to create meaning out of the narratives. The first strategy was reporting the contextual life story of the participant in their own words. The second strategy was 'collaboration' with the participants whereby each participant agreed with the researcher on the content in his/her narrative. Critical events were further developed by the researcher using information from the transcribed data. The third strategy was tracing the educational life journeys of participants from the transcribed data with a particular emphasis on motivational factors that enabled them to continue with their education through primary, secondary and tertiary stages. In this study the intention has been to treat the participants as intimate knowers of their experiences who, by participating, could become more aware of their own agency and personal strengths or resilience. Furthermore, through this study participants have begun to produce counter narratives to the dominant meta-narratives about students of refugee backgrounds. According Clandinin and Rosiek (2007) "Stories people live and tell . . . are a result of the confluence of social influences on a person's inner life, social influences on their environment, and their unique personal history" (p. 41). As such, participant stories are shaped by societal influence including sociocultural and historical situations where their experiences occurred and continue to unfold. However, "Words themselves may not be sufficient, but the process, the story, is everything" (Fox, 2018, p. 2). This study utilizes stories as vehicle for telling and retelling and making sense of lived experiences.

NAVIGATING PARTICIPANTS' EDUCATIONAL TRAJECTORIES

Participant 1: Fatima's Vignette

Fatima was born in Ethiopia to Sudanese parents in 1988. Her parents migrated to Ethiopia following the civil war in the Sudan. In 1991, political instability in Ethiopia resulting from border conflicts between Eretria and Ethiopia saw Fatima's family return to Southern Sudan where they stayed for six years. Her father joined the military and served in the Southern Sudan military. Her father's service in the army changed the trend of events because they never got to see him on a regular basis again. The civil war in Sudan intensified and so her mother, sister and herself had to flee to Kenya where they were settled in Kakuma refugee camp. After securing refugee status, her mother moved them to Nairobi so that her daughters could get good education. They stayed in Kenya for eight years and were resettled in Australia-Adelaide in 2006.

Navigating Education Systems

Before coming to Australia, Fatima was enrolled in high school. Her motivation to be in school was purely through the support of her mother and uncle but Fatima also was motivated to be in school because of her friends. She loved making friends and she also loved reading story books. In Australia, Fatima and her sister started an Intensive English course at a High School in Adelaide, South Australia. She says that the students there were friendly, and the school prepared her well for high school. After a year she finished with a Certificate III in English as a Second Language and was able to join year 10. At that time, Fatima was focused, and she had great commitment to school, so much so that she passed her year 10 subjects successfully to the surprise of her teachers. When she was promoted to year 11, she became distracted and had a friend who misled her to parting and drinking as opposed to giving priority to her education. She responded to the demands of peer pressure and was always in conflict with her mother. As a result, she lost interest in school, started oversleeping and frequently reported late to school. She was very disoriented and lost focus. Because she had excelled in year 10 and had done more subjects at that level, in year 11 she was only doing three subjects. Even with a reduced load, she did not pass them easily. Her performance deteriorated completely in year 12. She did not finish and did not want to continue with the option of year 13 to finish those subjects. Instead, she dropped out of school. In Sydney, Fatima went to TAFE and did Certificate III in Aged Care and Certificate III in Disability Care. Fatima reinvigorated her courage to push on in education because she did not want to take it for granted anymore. Fatima experienced a turnaround in her education at tertiary level. By the time of our interview, she had enrolled for a degree in Business Studies. She is now determined to finish her degree and she is motivated because she wants to be a role model for those girls who might face challenges like hers. She is looking into being an inspiration to the young girls who need to finish their education. Her inspiration has also resulted from other people she has met, and she believes in surrounding herself with people who will positively influence her decisions. She says:

Experience has taught me that, when you surround yourself with good people, you have a choice to make; either you learn good things or bad things from them. Knowing God and learning from the past mistakes makes me a better person. Even if I don't have a lot of things in terms of status I don't mind as long as I am focused on what I want to be.

By the time of the interview, Fatima had started pursuing her dreams in education and was enrolled in a business course. Her future aspiration of helping other girls who might be experiencing what she went through is one reason she had gone back to school. Her motivation therefore according to her is the 'next generation'. She thinks that if she has to encourage other girls experiencing what she went through then she has to also exhibit some level of resilience and show how she never succumbed to failure.

Participant 2: Biruk's Vignette

Biruk was born in 1996 in Ethiopia. His mother was Eritrean and Father Ethiopian. Because of his mother's background, when the border conflicts between Ethiopia and Eritrea began in 1998, his family became divided. His mother, together with his sister, went to Eritrea and his father and himself remained in Ethiopia. The two years of border conflict that lasted from 1998 to 2000, claimed the lives of thousands both in Eritrea and in Ethiopia. His mother and sister fled from Eritrea to Kenya while his father, and himself were airlifted by the United Nations High Commission for Refugees to Kenya. Biruk' mother and sister were temporarily settled in Kakuma refugee camp in Kenya and when him and his father reached Kenya, they stayed in the same camp for some time and later moved to Nairobi. In 2003, after a period of two years, Biruk's whole family of four was resettled in Australia. Resettlement in Australia became a turning point for Biruk's family because they were able to stay together as a family again. 'We were given accommodation together as opposed to the way we were living in Kenya because my father and I were in Nairobi while my mother and sister were in Kakuma refugee camp'. Ever since they arrived here, they have been bonded together as a family and this has laid the foundation for their vision. Biruk and his sister were enrolled in school. His father too went back to university and in 2012 he graduated with a degree in nursing. He is currently working as a Registered Nurse (RN), supporting his family and Biruk able to go to school because of his support but above all because of his father's motivation.

Navigating Education System

Biruk's father was a schoolteacher back in Ethiopia. After resettlement in Australia in 2012, he graduated in Australia as a Registered Nurse (RN). Biruk takes his father's achievement as a turning point in his life because it has influenced his desire to achieve a good education. Because my father was able to make it, then I have to as well. He is my example, and he was almost the only person who managed to graduate in his cohort and age mates. 'My father has motivated many to go back to school including me.' In Australia, Biruk attended English classes as Second Language in addition to school support programs including home-based support and afterschool care which helped him to catch up with the rest of the kids. Biruk went to Maryland East Public School and later to St. Mary Mother Primary School where he finished year six. After year six of primary school, Biruk went to Mt. Druitt Coptic College and then to St. Mary's Senior High School where he finished year twelve. Biruk's motivation to be in school and finish high school was based on a favourable school learning environment where he had good peer relationships and encouraging teachers. Biruk had one year off after high school and visited his surviving family members in Ethiopia. He came back and enrolled at Western Sydney University and at the time of his interview he was in his second year doing a Bachelor of Health Science. Biruk says this: 'My heart's desire is to help people and this degree equips me to help them overcome and prevent injuries and I am passionately looking forward to working and helping patients who sustain injuries and come to the hospitals for treatment'. I like helping people and I am doing a health science degree which will help me to fulfil my passion.

Participant 3: Alhassan's Vignette

Alhassan was born in Guinea Conakry in 1996 to a Guinea Conakry family. In the year 2007, Guinea Conakry started facing a lot of uncertainties resulting from the repatriation of Sierra Leonean refugees who had stayed in Guinea for many years. In 2002, Sierra Leone was declared a peaceful country by the international community and refugees were repatriated. In addition to the challenges associated with repatriating Sierra Leonean refugees, the political turmoil in Guinea also resulted from violent power struggles and there were nationwide strikes in the months of January and February 2007. Hundreds of people lost their lives and many more were displaced as a result of the strikes. Alhassan's uncle who was working with refugees, supported his family to take refuge among the Sierra Leonean refugees in the refugee camp and in 2009, together with Sierra Leoneans they were resettled in Australia.

Navigating Education Systems

Alhassan came to Australia when he was in year 9 of secondary school. Alhassan went to Evans High School. He had to start in Year 9 and each class had different streams named Year 9A, Year 9B, Year 9C and Year 9D. Year 9A was considered to be for the brilliant students and Alhassan was put in the lowest class, that is Year 9D. He had to catch up with a lot of reading and subject content. At the end of the academic year, he sat for exams and his results came back with good grades and as result he was put into the second highest level stream. He kept working hard and progressing, although it was difficult. He says: "I was scared and shy, not that I am a shy person but in class I could not read audibly. I used to get teased about my pronunciation and accent and I became timid whenever I compared my reading skills to other students". It took me a lot more effort to understand what the teachers were trying to say and this affected my performance in the tests and the exams. However, I had teachers who believed in me, who kept pushing me and motivated me and at the end of year ten, I emerged the best in some subjects like PDHPE and Sports Science. He further says that 'my good performance came as a surprise to many people and as a result I was able to join year 11 and 12 at St. Mary's Senior High School where I graduated from high school in 2014'. Although language was always a barrier, finding good friends made it fun for Alhassan and he looked forward to going back to school every day. Evidently his personality, influence of teachers and peers motivated him to remain in school. As a result of hard work at high school, at the time of the interview Alhassan was completing his second year of a Bachelor of Health Sciences at the University of Sydney. Alhassan says 'you cannot just be an average performer in a country like Australia, if you want to get somewhere, you have to aim higher'. He further adds that, 'the only way I can get something out of this country is to get education and get a degree. I had to learn the language because to get something from anybody you have to communicate to them in the language they best understand. This has been my motivation to be in school. My dream is basically to get a degree from here first and hopefully do a Masters degree in physiotherapy'.

AN INSIDER'S VIEW – ALFRED' VIGNETTE

In 2013, I arrived in Australia as an international student from Rwanda. Entering the Australian education system was completely strange in terms of demands and outlook, but I was also struck by the independence and the abundance of the available resources and student support services at the university. Although I started from scratch in a completely new system, I'll never forget the welcoming and caring supervisor who made me feel at home from day one.

In my early years, growing up in a Refugee Camp in Uganda, higher education was not an option. We were able to acquire primary education which was offered within the refugee camp under the support of United Nations High Commission for Refugees (UNHCR). As a result, growing up, education was the only thing I ever wanted which I can now say I have acquired from both in Uganda and Australia. I understand the significance of high-quality education and what it can provide. Most importantly, the stability and economic independence it can provide for people from disadvantaged backgrounds. In 2018, I graduated with a Doctorate of Philosophy (PhD) from Western Sydney University and for the past three years I have been teaching pre-service teachers. In my professional work, I have worked with so many intelligent, resilient, and ambitious refugee and new arrival students in Australian high schools and tertiary education (TAFE and University).

Providing refugees and new arrivals in Australia with the option of higher education is so empowering. Shifting the perceptions of young, refugee and asylum seekers towards higher education, has always been the biggest highlight of my work at Western Sydney University. I have witnessed so many students we worked with in high schools, go on to university and even work in the University Student Ambassador pool and this leaves an amazing feeling! I am a big believer in honouring the sacrifices people have made to get you to where you are. For me, like many other families – it is the migration story to Australia in search for better opportunities not just for me but for my family. A friend of mine (Ana Setiu Tuala) once said "Someone planted a seed years ago so that you could sit in the shade today." Through the work that we do, I hope we are planting the seeds of education in the minds of every young people we engage with.

What stands out the most in my teaching and engagement work is witnessing the struggles students go through while trying to internalise the demands of the Australian education system including meeting the demands of the curriculum, teacher pedagogies, education policies and schooling practices. My daily work has been to challenge these students to discover their strength and passion and to try to manage the deficit discourse that can often define their circumstance and ambitions. It takes an effort to recognise that the Australian education system provides support systems and builds on the strengths that refugees and new arrivals may have. It is also true that most people will never fully understand the experience of those who have experienced war and are not allowed to fully exercise their basic human rights especially the right to education. My lived experience has shaped the person I am today, and it has taught me many lessons. Education is an empowering tool and when adopted to the needs of people it become so rewarding. My own experience as a former refugee exemplifies the diverse and complex narratives that impact on educational trajectories. Many of my research participants (Biruk, Alhasan and Fatima) can identify with aspects of my story and together we have co-constructed narratives that speak to the world about the particulars of our own experiences, the injustices we have suffered and the impacts of ongoing mass displacements.

My education journey was enriched by the guidance I received from two important scholars I met in Australia: Associate Professor Loshini Naidoo and Associate Professor Susanne Gannon. They were my supervisors and they saw me through thick and thin. Their gift to inspire me, to value my strengths and our connections to each other was the inspiration for completing my degree and a constant source of energy. Despite the challenges I faced in my educational background, my supervisors did not pity me but rather motivated me to keep on and this reminded me of Deveson's statement that, 'when compassion turns to pity, people are generally rendered ineffective and powerless, that dominant cultures colonise weaker ones, sapping their natural resilience' (2003, p. 127). My supervisors rekindled my natural resilience and welcomed me on a round table discussion to address the challenges I was facing and thus each year was a year of progress until the end. As a refugee child you tend to lose self-esteem and confidence and your aspirations are influenced by the desire to regain the lost esteem and confidence. Despite the many challenges, some refugee, and new arrivals in Australia, have displayed remarkable resilience and capacity to learn and eventually some of these students become strong survivors. They go to school every day, they persist, and they never give up. They work very hard, they value education highly and some are able to progress to university and higher education and build a strong career pathway (Ferfolja et al., 2011).

DISCUSSION OF FINDINGS

Displacement Experiences

Refugees and new arrivals come to Australia from a difficult past, most of them will have struggled from their country of origin to circumnavigate not only the education system but also with other challenges including; family separation and many years of living in refugee camps where they had limited access to social services. This is clearly evident in this chapter from narratives of the research participants; For instance, Biruk's family was separated for some time during the war and conflicts in his home country, "when the border conflicts between Ethiopia and Eritrea began in 1998, my family became divided…" As for Alhassan, "…the political turmoil in Guinea resulted from violent power struggles and there were nationwide strikes in the months of January and February 2007…' and Fatima could not be protected by her Father who was in the military of South Sudan and instead her and her mother fled to Kenya. "The civil war in Sudan intensified and so my mother, my sister and I had to flee to Kenya, and we were settled in Kakuma refugee camp" Fatima. When it comes to the education of refugee and new arrivals, their experiences present complex and vexing issues on which there in no agreement between policy and practice. For example, teachers claim that these students are difficult to educate because their life history challenges spill into the classroom environment. These students are challenged by 'a set of dispositions that they carry with them which influence their attitudes, behaviour and how they see themselves' (Webb, Schirato & Danaher 2003, p.27). This was however different for Alhassan; "…Year 9A was for the brilliant students and Alhassan was put in the lowest class, that is Year 9D. He had to catch up with a lot of reading and subject content. At the end of the academic year, he sat for exams and his results came back with good grades and as result he was put into the second highest level stream…" Evidently refugees and new arrivals defy the odds of life and excel in their education pursuits.

In the refugee camps, education is not a priority. For instance, the author of this chapter highlights 'in his early years, growing up in a Refugee Camp in Uganda, higher education was not an option. refugees were able to only acquire primary education which was offered within the refugee camp under the support of United Nations High Commission for Refugees (UNHCR)." For Biruk "[h]is mother and sister were temporarily settled in Kakuma refugee camp in Kenya and when my father and I reached Kenya we stayed in the same camp for some time and later my father and I moved to Nairobi in order for him to get some education". Nonetheless, education as the main resource grants refugees and new arrivals rights and attributes that increase their confidence and self-esteem. Education also helps them operate successfully within the cultural norms and expectations of the dominant groups. For example, ways of speaking, and relating to the social world and shaping interpersonal relationships where language is the code. Fatima, for example, has regained her confidence and enrolled into university where she is pursuing her degree in Business studies. Alhassan and Biruk are looking forward to pursuing their masters in Physiotherapy and are building strong career pathways. Education increases the network which enhances life possibilities for individuals. This is echoed by Mckinney that 'improving attainment and achievement in schools for children from poor families is expected to enhance life chances and wellbeing and provide opportunity for social mobility' (2014, p.209).

Education in Australia

Evidently, the main theme of this book chapter is on the Australian education system and how the school and tertiary institutions welcome and impacts on refugees and new arrivals aspiration to access and finish their educational aspirations. Student's experiences at school can significantly enhance or undermine their sense of self. Refugees and new arrivals in Australia, need to feel emotionally safe in order to learn effectively. This was true for Alhassan, "I had teachers who believed in me, who kept pushing me and motivated me and at the end of year ten, I emerged the best in some subjects like PDHPE and Sports Science" Although language was always a barrier, finding good friends made it fun for Alhassan and he looked forward to going back to school every day. Evidently his personality, influence of teachers and peers motivated him to remain in school. According to (Luecke, 2011, p.117). "Welcoming and supportive schools where bullying and teasing is not permitted and children are actively taught to respect and celebrate difference is the ideal environment for all children."

One of the purposes of implementing the Australian Professional Teaching Standards (2018) was to "improve educational outcomes for all students" (p. 2). This outcome is still employing a deficit-thinking which includes treating students differently based on their culture, excluding them from class discussions, focusing on their weaknesses instead of their strengths and maintaining low expectations (Buxton, 2017). Mills and Keddie, (2012) reveal that these deficit constructions create a culturally disconnected classroom, and as a result, it affects children's perceptions of different cultures (p.10). For example, if a teacher begins to discriminate against an ethnic child, students will see that type of behaviour as permissible because they look up to the teacher as a guide and as someone they admire. Accordingly, this will affect student's perceptions of students from different cultures, and as such, they will maintain these prejudicial attitudes around members of society.

Culturally responsive pedagogies are essential as their implementation allows students from varying cultural backgrounds to reach their academic potential regardless of the differences held by them. It is crucial that teachers are aware of different cultural backgrounds as it can help prevent conflict from arising by input of culturally diverse students and how they draw upon their learning. In mainstream schooling, it is expected of students to abandon their style of speech and learning and conform to the correct language and culture (Rahman, 2013, p. 661)

Navigating Australian education for refugees and new arrivals will require implementing policy documents like Multicultural Education policy which according to Watkins (2018, p. 163) refers to the pedagogies that are designed and implemented within schools, that have the intention to "meet the needs of migrant and refugee students and their families and to promote intercultural understanding".

These pedagogies lead to better educational prospects for culturally diverse students. NSW Government Multicultural Education Policy (NSW Government, 2021) "Responsibilities and Delegations 4.4 'all staff members are responsible for ensuring their practices are consistent with the policy" therefore, reinforcing that whilst the above requirements are mandated, it is dependent on the classroom teacher to ensure that their individual practices are aligned with the policy. Although, teachers are provided with several resources and programs as seen within the Multicultural Plan 2019-2022 (NSW Department of Education, n.d), it can be argued that this does not entirely assist in the achievement of statement 4.4.

Expectations and Support Services

Refugees and new arrivals, like asylum seekers, have experienced difficulties and challenges related to their identity and belonging. Service providers lower their expectation of students from a refugee background instead of revising their perception and establishing strategies to meet or accommodate their needs. This leaves refugees and new arrivals on their own to challenge these perceptions and stereotypes. For Alhassan is a good example of a self-motivated as he narrates his experience of the perceptions teachers had on him: 'Year 9A was considered to be for the brilliant students and Alhassan was put in the lowest class, that is Year 9D. He had to catch up with a lot of reading and subject content. At the end of the academic year, he sat for exams and his results came back with good grades and as result he was put into the second highest level stream. Alhassan was convinced that 'you cannot just be an average performer in a country like Australia, if you want to get somewhere, you have to aim higher' no wonder he was able to excel. On the contrary, at school, Fatima had an encounter with friends who influenced her in a negative way. She says that: 'A friend of mine who had a lot of family challenges distracted me from school and together we started dealing with emotional problems and making wrong choices. We started having boyfriends, going for parties, clubbing, and drinking and I did not prioritise my education as I had originally intended'. Such behaviour affected her education and that is why she did not finish year twelve. When Fatima lost interest in school, she started having conflicts with her mother. As a result, she moved from Adelaide to Sydney to start a new life. Fatima does not indicate any support system that come to her aid when she couldn't make good choices. The education system at the time of interview did not provide aid teachers or support teacher as it is today where every school now employees aid teachers to support struggling students. At the university level there are a number of support services including disability and students wellbeing.

Expectations put on a student, whether high or low, can have a huge bearing on how a student will perform academically. Students who have been nurtured and supported by parents, teachers and peers will have a vastly different experience when navigating the Australian education system. For example, Fatima found herself in conflict with her mother due to the expectations her mother had for her. For Biruk a nurturing environment at home gave him a reason to work hard toward his degree. In general participants stories call for a paradigm shift of looking at refugee students as people least deserving to being viewed as a community that needs support. At University, students have been able to access support services. The author of this chapter works with widening participation programs and is the lead for Refugee, New and Emerging communities. 'Western Sydney University's Widening Participation programs engage with schools and community groups to provide students with a taste of higher education, raise their academic confidence and prepare them for tertiary study. Programs aim to provide access to higher education and promote the successful participation of students who are underrepresented in the current education system and practices. Activities target communities and schools identified as disadvantaged by multiple socio-economic indicators, all modes of intervention are assessed against refined measures of success and regularly reviewed. The Widening Participation evaluation method considers (i) developing program objectives; (ii) formalising evaluation questions; (iii) adopting methodology; (iv) utilising evaluation materials; (v) selecting sampling techniques; (vi) evaluating data analysis; and (vii) reporting.' Jim Micsko, Manager, Widening Participation Programs (The Higher Education Participation and Partnerships Program (HEPPP) Report 2021)

Perceptions and Stereotypes

At a global level, stereotypes and assumptions have impacted identity, belonging and agency among refugees and new arrivals (both asylum seekers and migrants). One example is after the September 11, 2001 attack in the US, 'perceptions about refugees and increased deep suspicion, and even fear, of refugees' (Frelick 2007, p.37). Australian attitudes have also been shaped by political factors such as boat arrivals and offshore detention policies by successive governments that have influenced public opinion. From these observations, several conclusions can be drawn about current assumptions and stereotypes about refugees and how these have impacted on education for students with a refugee background. For instance, 'the newcomer in Western countries has often been categorised as undeserving, and depending on the factors at play, asylum seekers may be constructed as the migrants least deserving of state support' (Kissoon, 2015, p. 12). As such, education for refugees and new arrivals remains at stake because the perceptions, assumptions and stereotypes that host communities hold affects their integration and acculturation. This applies not only in host communities but in schools and tertiary institutions. More damagingly refugees are often viewed as people in need of protection and assistance but as potential threats to national security and even as a potential source of armed terror' (Loescher, 2003, p. 31). In such cases, these students become victims of circumstances and their education is hampered because of the way they are perceived in the general refugee community. According to Dowtry and Loesher 'these irregular migrants [are viewed] as something akin to human missiles, penetrating national defences (borders) and attacking state sovereignty and security, the domestic economy and social cohesion' (1996, p.43).

In developing countries—which host greater numbers of refugees, it is common to hear refugees frequently associated with problems such as crime, banditry, prostitution, alcoholism, and drugs. 'In many instances, host countries do not have the capacity or willingness to maintain law and order in the remote areas where the largest numbers of refugees are often to be found' (Newman & Van Selm, 2003, p. 35). Loescher highlights that, 'refugees become the scapegoat for many of the host country's ills, and governments and opposition groups are prone to use the refugees' presence to encourage nationalistic and xenophobic sentiments' (Loescher, 2003, p. 35). In some cases, host states have themselves armed or helped to arm refugee fighting groups as a weapon against the country of origin, but then found that they were unable to control the consequences of having done so. This occurred in the Great Lakes region of Africa particularly with Uganda supporting Rwandan refugees, resulting in the destabilization of the entire region in the late 1990s.

RECOMMENDATIONS

There is a need for research studies to identify durable and effective programs to support the needs of individual refugee background students entering tertiary education in Australia. There is also a need to convince policy makers and advocates to ask respective governments to improve the support available for students with a refugee background in Australia. Addressing racism and discrimination within schools and the broader community is challenging. Every school, every student, every staff member and every community are at a different stage of the journey, and have a unique context (CMY, 2021). For refugees and new arrivals to succeed in the Australian education system, it is important to encourage positive discourses around culture and ethnicity. The highly researched and well documented consequences of discrimination and bullying against refugees and new arrivals may be consolidated as anxiety-related disorders, conduct disorders, suicidal thoughts, academic difficulties, aggressive and anti-social behaviors among others and sometimes leading to school dropouts (Protogerou & Flisher, 2012).

School context and teacher's attitudes are significant for minority ethnic groups like the migrants and refugees in a White community like that of Australia (Brown & Chu, 2012). Teachers tend to treat students differentially in their day-to-day interactions and in the assessment, processes based on the preconceived ideas about the students' ability or inability attributing it to their ethnic background (Mohamed's story Center for Multicultural Youth, 2021). As a result, students develop a sense of educational futility, that is students feeling incapable of having control over their educational outcomes (D'hondt, Eccles, Van Houtte, & Stevens, 2016). Chan (2007) concludes that without a culturally sensitive curriculum, academic and social performances of students are at stake. Saha (2014) also highlights that the absence of a unified national curriculum in Australia fuelled by the authority of each state and territory being able to pass their own educational policies has potential implications for students from refugees and new arrivals.

The main attribute of ethnic identity is feeling a strong sense of attachment to one's ethnic group which can promote higher self-esteem and mental health in the face of discrimination (Wong, C.A., Eccles, J.S., & Sameroff, A. (2004). Development of this strong identity depends on how implicitly schools promote multiculturalism (Brown, 2017), teachers assist students in their identity exploration journey, make connections with the families about their ethnic identity and explores ethnic histories, traditions and customs as part of the learning (Branch, 2020). D'hondt et al. (2016) reminds that given the seriousness and complexity in addressing this issue, it becomes vital that the targets of ethnic discrimination are empowered by parents, teachers, principals and policy makers alike. This can be done by maintaining high expectations for all students resulting in positive school climate and supportive student-teacher relationships which in turn will also reduce peer victimization (Konold, T., Cornell, D., Shukla, K., & Huang, F., 2017).

Policy level changes are needed to specifically address the discrimination faced by ethnic groups and refugees as these students' access to proper education is limited to policies regarding ESL, multiculturalism or 'students at risk' (Taylor, 2008). Schools need to find balance in positioning ethnic minority teachers as 'cultural experts (Basit & Santoro, 2010) and build a socially cohesive and inclusive environment by deliberately seeking to recruit teachers of diverse background to better support students from minority backgrounds (Keddie, 2010).

An essential aspect of culturally responsive pedagogy is understanding students' cultural identities and agency within their learning. To implement culturally responsive pedagogy, teachers must be adequately supported by their initial teacher education, curriculum, educational policies and schooling practices to ensure that equitable education can be delivered to their students. A key aspect of culturally responsive teaching is the commitment of teachers to consistently evaluate and recognise their privilege and "cultural positions" before and during their time in the classroom to ensure that their privilege and implicit biases are not negatively impacting their students (Burnett & Lampert, 2018, p.86).

Teacher pedagogies can enhance or hinder learning. As most Australian pre-service teachers identify as Anglo-Australian and come from a middle-class background, there is an overwhelming lack of teachers who come from a refugee and new arrivals background. Research suggests that a teacher's pedagogical practices within the classroom, are significantly linked to how well a student performs academically (Skourdoumbis, 2014). Some teachers are in their position because they have passion and want to encourage students to succeed. Conversely, some teachers can be swayed by more money and better facilities and seek employment where student success is but only a responsibility. Keddie (2011, p. 9) reinforces the idea of the Education System being "incongruent with the experiences of children from refugee backgrounds who have had little prior experience of western schooling". This, therefore, demonstrates that migrant students are already experiencing inequities on the level of everyday communication, which serves to reinforce the capacity for educational disadvantage they face.

Cultural inclusivity, cultural competency, equality and advance educational outcomes for ethnically diverse students. On an individual level teaching staff should engage on a deep level with their culturally and ethnically diverse students, parents and caregivers. This can take the form of parent-teacher meetings. This is where teachers will gain insight and understanding into their student's cultural background and communicate the best practices within the classroom to support their student's ethnicity and culture.

On an institutional level, the education system needs to move away from teacher training programs based on a "simplistic categorisation of students backgrounds" (Watkins, 2011, p. 844). Thus, preparing teachers to the best degree to provide learning experiences and curriculums that support, empower, and respect differing ethnicities and cultures within the classroom. Moreover, the education system should mandate more university courses focused on multicultural education, ethnicity and teaching. Through this analysis, it is evident that teachers' perspectives, knowledges and privileges have the potential to create inequities within the classroom for students of ethnically diverse backgrounds.

By setting aside the notions of deficit and colorblindness, teachers and policy makers can provide an accessible and inclusive environment to students where their ethnic identity is strengthened. When students realize that schools are places where they can walk in with confidence and that they will not be judged based on any attributes relating to their ethnicity and their ethnic heritage will be celebrated, they will connect and flourish as individuals who can contribute positively to the society. Educators working with diverse ethnic groups can draw from the words of the former Secretary-General of the United Nations, Kofi Annan (2016), "We may have different religions, different languages, different colored skin, but we all belong to one human race".

CONCLUSION

This chapter has presented the stories of and lived experiences of my research participants. The narratives in this chapter are compressed and distilled from long interviews. The distilled narratives of my participants are organized to show the complexities of their journeys, the obstacles they have overcome, the resources they have drawn upon and the educational trajectories they experienced through multiple languages, school systems, vocational and tertiary institutions. These stories show the varied and challenging journeys that each participant experienced. In theory, a developed country like Australia should offer similar schooling and educational outcomes throughout all classrooms, regardless of the background of students. This is because there is a curriculum, syllabus, and teaching standards that must be followed. According to Hage, (2003), Social research is neither capable nor ought to attempt to define ready-made political paths, "It can, however, through its capacity to listen with and through people to the echoes of social suffering, furnish tools for rethinking political efficacy in a world as traumatising as ever for those who lack the social means to cope with its rapid changes" (2003, p.25). Therefore, there is need to overcome the prevailing or the dominant narrative about refugees and increase on productive diversity in Australian education system. Stories in this chapter bring us back to the centrality of alternative ways to articulate admission and acceptance of refugees in the education sector and challenges us to appreciate the life trajectories of refugees by recognising what refugees have overcome in terms of their tragedies and traumas. Character building through education will empower refugees and new arrivals and challenge the systems and structures to move away from wishful thinking to actual impactful actions. This way, we will move away from deficit labelling of refugees as vulnerable to viewing them as people that have demonstrated resilience, ingenuity and with a sense of agency. Refugees are resilient and have learned to fight with both their heart and mind. They know that what they overcome in their life trajectory is a good example of what they can overcome today and in future. They are always prepared and willing to do more than the what the media and public discourse display. They are creative and innovating in so many ways. They can navigate any education system and beat all odds of life.

REFERENCES

Atkinson, R. (2001). The life story interview. In G. F. Jaber & H. A. James (Eds.), *Handbook of interview research* (pp. 120–140). SAGE Publications.

Australian Psychological Society. (1997). *Racism and prejudice: Psychological perspectives.* Available at https://www.psychology.org.au/Assets/Files/racism_position_paper.pdf

Basit, T. N., & Santoro, N. (2010). Playing the role of 'cultural expert': Teachers of ethnic difference in Britain and Australia. *Oxford Review of Education, 37*(1), 37–52. doi:10.1080/03054985.2010.521621

Brace, E. (2001). *Crossing borders to create supportive educational spaces for refugee youth. In Crossing borders: African refugees, teachers and schools.* Common Ground Publishing Inc.

Branch, A. J. (2020). Promoting ethnic identity development while teaching subject matter content: A model of ethnic identity exploration in education. *Teaching and Teacher Education, 87,* 102918. Advance online publication. doi:10.1016/j.tate.2019.102918

Brown, C. S., & Chu, H. (2012). Discrimination, ethnic identity and academic outcomes of Mexican immigrant children: The importance of school context. *Child Development, 83*(5), 1477–1485. doi:10.1111/j.1467-8624.2012.01786.x PMID:22966916

Brown, J., Miller, J., & Mitchell, J. (2006). Interrupted schooling and the acquisition of literacy: Experiences of Sudanese refugees in Victorian secondary schools. *Australian Journal of Language and Literacy, 29*(2), 150–162.

Burnett, B., & Lampert, J. (2018). Destabilising privilege: Disrupting deficit thinking in white pre-service teachers on professional experience in culturally diverse, high-poverty schools. In T. Ferfolja, C. J. Diaz, & J. Ullman (Eds.), *Understanding sociological theory for educational practices* (2nd ed., pp. 85–101). Cambridge University Press. doi:10.1017/9781108378482.007

Buxton, L. (2017). Ditching deficit thinking: Changing to a culture of high expectations. *Issues in Educational Research, 27*(2), 198–214.

Chan, E. (2007). Student experience of a culturally sensitive curriculum: Ethnic identity development amid conflicting stories to live by. *Journal of Curriculum Studies, 39*(2), 177–194. doi:10.1080/00220270600968658

Clandinin, D. J., & Rosiek, J. (2007). Mapping a landscape of narrative inquiry: Borderland spaces and tensions. In D. J. Clandinin (Ed.), *Handbook of narrative inquiry: Mapping a methodology* (pp. 35–75). doi:10.4135/9781452226552.n2

CMY. (2021). *The Schools Standing Up to Racism site Schools Standing Up To Racism*. Centre For Multicultural Youth. cmy.net.au

D'hondt, F., Eccles, J. S., Van Houtte, M., & Stevens, P. A. J. (2016). Perceived Ethnic Discrimination by Teachers and Ethnic Minority Students' Academic Futility: Can Parents Prepare Their Youth for Better or for Worse? *Journal of Youth and Adolescence, 45*(6), 1075–1089. doi:10.100710964-016-0428-z PMID:26861710

Delgado, R., & Stefancic, J. (Eds.). (2012). *Critical race theory: An introduction*. New York University Press.

Deveson, A. (2003). *Resilience*. Allen & Unwin.

Dotterer, A. M., McHale, S. M., & Crouter, A. C. (2009). Sociocultural factors and school engagement among African American youth: The roles of racial discrimination, racial socialization, and ethnic identity. *Applied Developmental Science, 13*(2), 61–72. https://bit.ly/3vjpSuh. doi:10.1080/10888690902801442 PMID:27134516

Fox, G. (2018, February 21). *Words to live by*. Retrieved from http://www.nybooks.com/daily/2018/02/21/words-to-live-by/

Goodson, I., Biesta, J. G., Tedder, M., & Adair, N. (2010). *Narrative Learning*. Routledge. doi:10.4324/9780203856888

Harris, A., Marlowe, J., & Nyuon, N. (2015). Rejecting Ahmed's 'melancholy migrant': South Sudanese Australians in higher education. *Studies in Higher Education, 40*(7), 1226–1238. doi:10.1080/03075079.2014.881346

Hatoss, A., O'Neill, S., & Eacersall, D. (2012). Career choices: Linguistic and educational socialization of Sudanese-background high-school students in Australia. *Linguistics and Education, 23*(1), 16-30. doi:10.1016/j.linged.2011.10.003

Hutchinson, M., & Dorsett, P. (2012). What does the literature say about resilience in refugee people? Implications for practice. *Journal of Social Inclusion, 2*(3), 55–78. doi:10.36251/josi.55

Joyce, A., Earnest, J., de Mori, G., & Silvagni, G. (2010). The experiences of students from refugee backgrounds at universities in Australia: Reflections on the social, emotional and practical challenges. *Journal of Refugee Studies, 23*(1), 82–97. doi:10.1093/jrs/feq001

Keddie, A. (2010). Pursuing justice for refugee students: Addressing issues of cultural (mis)recognition. *International Journal of Inclusive Education, 16*(12), 1295–1310. doi:10.1080/13603116.2011.560687

Khawaja, N. G., White, K. M., Schweitzer, R., & Greenslade, J. (2008). Difficulties and coping strategies of Sudanese refugees: A qualitative approach. *Transcultural Psychiatry, 45*(3), 489–512. doi:10.1177/1363461508094678 PMID:18799645

Luecke, J. (2011). Working with Transgender Children and Their Classmates in Pre-Adolescence. *Just Be Supportive. Journal of LGBT Youth, 8*(2), 116–156. doi:10.1080/19361653.2011.544941

Mansouri, F., & Jenkins, L. (2010). Schools as Sites of Race Relations and Intercultural Tension. *The Australian Journal of Teacher Education, 35*(7). Advance online publication. doi:10.14221/ajte.2010v35n7.8

Mckinney, S. (2014). The relationship of child poverty to school education. *Improving Schools, 17*(3), 203–216. doi:10.1177/1365480214553742

McMahon, B. (2007). Educational administrators' conceptions of whiteness, anti-racism and social justice. *Journal of Educational Administration, 45*(6), 684–696. doi:10.1108/09578230710829874

Miller, J., Mitchell, J., & Brown, J. (2005). African refugees with interrupted schooling in the high education, inequality and society. *British Journal of Sociology of Education, 25*(4), 457–471. doi:10.1080/0142569042000236952

Mills, C., & Keddie, A. (2012). 'Fixing' student deficit in contexts of diversity: Another cautionary tale for pre-service teacher education. *International Journal of Pedagogies & Learning, 7*(1), 9–19. doi:10.5172/ijpl.2012.7.1.9

Mupenzi, A. (2018). *Narratives of displacement, resilience and education: Experiences of African students with a refugee background in Australian tertiary education* (Thesis). Western Sydney University.

Naidoo, L. (2004). Fields and institutional strategy: Bourdieu on the relationship between higher education, inequality and society. *British Journal of Sociology of Education, 25*(4), 457–471. doi:10.1080/0142569042000236952

Naidoo, L. (2010). Engaging the refugee community of Greater Western Sydney. *Issues in Educational Research, 20*(1), 47–56.

Naidoo, L. (2011). School-university-community partnerships. In *Crossing borders: African refugees, teachers and schools* (pp. 73–90). Common Ground Publishing.

Naidoo, L., Wilkinson, J., Langat, K., Adoniou, M., Cunneen, R., & Bolger, D. (2014). *Supporting school-university pathways for refugee students' access and participation in tertiary education: an implementation guide for universities*. University of Western Sydney.

Naidoo, L., Wilkinson, J., Langat, K., Adoniou, M., Cunneen, R., & Bolger, D. (2015). *Case study report: Supporting school-university pathways for refugee students' access and participation in tertiary education*. University of Western Sydney.

NSW Department of Education. (n.d.). *Multicultural Plan 2019-22*. Retrieved May 8th, 2021, from https://library.westernsydney.edu.au/main/guides/referencing-citation/i%3aCite

NSW Education Standards Authority (NESA). (2018). *Australian Professional Teaching Standards for Teachers*. Author.

NSW Government. (2021). *Multicultural Education Policy*. Policy Library. Retrieved May 8th, 2021, from https://policies.education.nsw.gov.au/policy-library/policies/multicultural-education-policy

Olliff, L., & Couch, J. (2005). Pathways and pitfalls: The journey of refugee young people in and around the education system in Greater Dandenong, Victoria. *Youth Studies Australia, 24*(3), 42–46.

Oloo, J. A., & Kiramba, L. K. (2019). *A narrative inquiry into experiences of Indigenous teachers during and after teacher preparation*. Race Ethnicity and Education. https://digitalcommons.unl.edu/teachlearnfacpub/342/ doi:10.1080/13613324.2019.1604507

Onsando, G. (2014). Refugee immigrants: Addressing social exclusion by promoting agency in the Australian VET sector. *2013 Postgraduate Research Papers: A Compendium*, 76-96.

Onsando, G., & Billett, S. (2009). African students from refugee backgrounds in Australian TAFE institutes: A case for transformative learning goals and processes. *International Journal of Training Research, 7*(2), 80–94. doi:10.5172/ijtr.7.2.80

Orellana, M. (2016). *Immigrant children in transcultural spaces: Language, learning, and love*. Routledge.

Parliament of Australia (APH). (2016). *Refugee resettlement to Australia: What are the facts?* https://www.aph.gov.au/About_Parliament/Parliamentary_Departments/Parliamentary_Library/pubs/rp/rp1617/RefugeeResettlement

Protogerou, C., & Flisher, A. (2012). *Bullying in schools*. https://bit.ly/3oNUKk7

Rahman, K. (2013). Belonging and learning to belong in school: The implications of the hidden curriculum for indigenous students. *Discourse (Abingdon, England), 34*(5), 660–672. doi:10.1080/01596306.2013.728362

Refugee Council of Australia (RCoA). (2017). *New refugee statistics highlight need for greater Australian support for Africa*. https://www.refugeecouncil.org.au/media/new-refugee-statistics-highlight-need-greater-australian-support-africa/

Refugee Council of Australia (RCoA). (2018). *Recent changes in Australian refugee policy*. https://www.refugeecouncil.org.au/publications/recent-changes-australian-refugee-policy/

Saha, L. J. (2014). Australia. In P. A. J. Stevens & A. G. Dworkin (Eds.), *The palgrave handbook of race and ethnic inequalities in education* (pp. 39–69). Palgrave Macmillan. doi:10.1057/9781137317803_3

Schoorman, D., & Bogotch, I. (2010). Moving beyond 'diversity' to 'social justice': The challenge to reconceptualise multicultural education. *Intercultural Education, 21*(1), 79–85. doi:10.1080/14675980903491916

Shah, S. (2008). Leading multi-ethnic schools: Adjustments in concepts and practices for engaging with diversity. *British Journal of Sociology of Education, 29*(5), 532–536. doi:10.1080/01425690802263684

Shakespeare-Finch, J., & Wickham, K. (2010). Adaptation of Sudanese refugees in an Australian context: Investigating helps and hindrances. *International Migration (Geneva, Switzerland), 48*(1), 23–46. doi:10.1111/j.1468-2435.2009.00561.x

Shapiro, S., & MacDonald, M. T. (2017). From deficit to asset: Locating discursive resistance in a refugee-background student's written and oral narrative. *Journal of Language, Identity, and Education, 16*(2), 80–93. doi:10.1080/15348458.2016.1277725

Sikes, P., & Goodson, I. F. (2017). What have you got when you've got a life story? In I. F. Goodson, A. Antikainen, P. J. Sikes, & M. Andrews (Eds.), *International handbook on narrative and life history* (pp. 60–71). Routledge.

Sovic, S., & Blythman, M. (2013). *International Students Negotiating Higher Education: Critical perspectives*. Routledge.

Taylor, E., Gillborn, D., & Ladson-Billings, G. (2009). *Foundations of critical race theory in education*. Routledge.

Taylor, S. (2008). Schooling and settlement of refugee young people in Queensland: '…The challenges are massive'. *Social Alternatives, 27*(3), 58–65. https://bit.ly/3hWSTIt

Terry, L., Naylor, R., Nguyen, N., & Rizzo, A. (2016). *Not yet there: an investigation into the access and participation of students from humanitarian refugee background in the Australian Higher ducation System*. Centre for the Study of Higher Education, The University of Melbourne.

Traoré, R. L. (2004). Colonialism continued: African students in an urban high school in America. *Journal of Black Studies, 34*(3), 348–369. doi:10.1177/0021934703258986

Uptin, J., Wright, J., & Harwood, V. (2016). Finding education: Stories of how young former refugees constituted strategic identities in order to access school. *Race, Ethnicity and Education, 19*(3), 598–617. doi:10.1080/13613324.2014.885428

Watkins, M. (2011). Complexity reduction, regularities and rules: Grappling with cultural diversity in schooling. *Continuum, 25*(6), 841–856. doi:10.1080/10304312.2011.617876

Watkins, M. (2018). Culture, hybridity and globalisation: Rethinking multicultural education in schools. In Understanding Sociological Theory for Educational Practices (pp. 159-175). Cambridge University Press.

Webb, J., Schirato, T., & Danaher, G. (2002). Understanding bourdieu. *Sage (Atlanta, Ga.)*.

Weekes, T., Phelan, L., Macfarlane, S., Pinson, J., & Francis, V. (2011). Supporting successful learning for refugee students: The Classroom Connect project. *Issues in Educational Research, 21*(3), 310–329.

Windle, J., & Miller, J. (2013). Migration integration: The reception of refugee-background students in Australian schools. In L. Bartlett & A. Ghaffar-Kucher (Eds.), *Refugees, immigrants, and education in the global south: Lives in motion* (pp. 196–209). Routledge.

Wong, C. A., Eccles, J. S., & Sameroff, A. (2004). The influence of ethnic discrimination and ethnic identification on African American adolescents' school and socioemotional adjustment. *Journal of Personality, 71*(6), 1197–1232. doi:10.1111/1467-6494.7106012 PMID:14633063

Zamudio, M., Russell, C., Rios, F., & Bridgeman, J. L. (2011). *Critical race theory matters: Education and ideology*. Routledge. doi:10.4324/9780203842713

ENDNOTE

[1]   I will use refugees and new arrivals in this chapter to refer to students from a refugee and asylum seekers background. Asylum seekers are new arrivals and are also sometimes grouped as boat people or illegal migrants both in education and social service system in Australia.

Section 5
Online Teaching and Learning

Chapter 15
Massive Open Online Courses:
Promoting Intercultural Communication

Shikha Gupta

https://orcid.org/0000-0002-0121-572X

Shaheed Sukhdev College of Business Studies, University of Delhi, India

Samarth Gupta

Shiv Nadar University, India

ABSTRACT

Multimedia technology and the internet have revolutionized the delivery and the reach of education through massive open online courses (MOOCs). Starting in 2011 when professors from Stanford University took a lead in starting such courses, teaching/learning through MOOCs has become a revolution of sorts with the professors and the higher education institutions (HEIs) realizing the benefits of several thousand students registering for an online course. Today, more than 11000 MOOCs are available from various countries spanning diverse cultures and languages, disrupting the teaching/learning models in the HEIs. This chapter outlines the history of MOOCs. It also suggests research questions towards the use of MOOCs in promoting international/intercultural communication. A critical assessment of the impact of online learning and MOOCs in the COVID-19 era is also presented.

INTRODUCTION

The COVID-19 pandemic propelled educators everywhere to shift from the traditional methods of imparting education through classroom teaching to a solely online approach using the current day's technologies. Online learning has its roots in the concept of distance learning that started with the goal of delivering education. *Distance learning* is a method where the teacher and the learner are separate in space and possibly time (Keegan, 1995), (Blieszner & Teaster, 1999). Initially relying on postal services and later supplemented by radio broadcasting, distance learning engages students, often on an individual basis, who cannot be physically present in a traditional educational setting such as classrooms. It dates

DOI: 10.4018/978-1-7998-8921-2.ch015

back at least as early as 1728 when an advertisement was placed in the Boston Gazette by Caleb Phillips seeking students for lessons on the new method of Short Hand (Gupta, Taneja, & Kumar, 2015).

Online education is the modern form of distance learning where the Internet often unites the distance learning instructor with the learner. Audio, video, computer, and networking technologies are often combined to create a multifaceted instructional delivery system. In comparison to the mature methods of distance learning such as the correspondence course method of education delivery, or the television method, or the video-conferencing method, the online learning method has a requirement of the content being delivered partially or fully based on the Internet. The strength of an online system is its flexibility in allowing students to take lessons at their pace and schedule. All the lectures are recorded, thereby allowing students to repeat the lessons. Also, this form of teaching greatly reduces the load on resources like classrooms, parking areas, and traveling time. While the technology provides the necessary support for online learning, the delivery mechanism does not define the pedagogical practice. An online class is not simply a digitized version of a traditional classroom. Rather, an online instructor must utilize the technology to implement the best pedagogy. As opposed to only listening to and learning, a highly interactive and engaging environment is more suitable for student learning. Experiential and interactive exercises as online assignments help in reinforcing concepts and testing a student's knowledge. That is, a student-centered learning approach with active learning activities is an effective online pedagogy (O'Neil, 2013).

In the last decade, the lure of online learning in providing more flexible access to content and instruction at any time and from any place, motivated universities across all continents to create Massive Open Online Courses (MOOCs). Massive Open Online Courses (MOOCs) are open to students across the world without any limitations on the number of seats, geography, or qualifications. A wide array of choices is available to the students, each student having the freedom to decide the university and the professor. Many online courses also offer opportunities for the students to interact with the professors teaching the course. In turn, the huge volume of students has been motivating many universities to compete to offer better education options. The advent of the MOOC era has made accessible the intellect and knowledge of the likes of Stanford, MIT, and Harvard professors to every enthusiastic learner who wants to achieve higher goals in education. The analysis is supported using the data of growth of the MOOC movement in the last decade (Table 1) from Class Central, a search engine and reviews site for free online courses (Shah, 2012), (Shah, 2013), (Shah, 2014), (Shah, 2015), (Shah, 2016), (Shah, 2017), (Shah, 2018), (Shah, 2019), (Shah, 2020).

The advantages of online education have persuaded students from diverse backgrounds and circumstances to enrol in online programs to pursue their education. An upward growth trend is observed in the number of students enrolled in MOOC courses (Figure 1). It can be argued that classroom teaching cannot be replaced entirely by automated programs, and the interactions of the students with the teachers and their peer group serve as a key component of learning. However, one cannot deny that online education has opened new frontiers that allow the melting of geographical boundaries and do not restrict learners due to their circumstances (Gupta, Taneja, & Kumar, 2015). Indeed, the anticipation that the information revolution will change the structure of higher education became a reality during the COVID-19 lockdown situation. While the number of new learners joining MOOC courses started declining after 2015, the lockdown in many countries due to the pandemic in 2020 became a motivating factor for these numbers to rise again (Figure 2).

Table 1. Growth of MOOCs: data across all MOOC providers

Year	# Students (millions)	# Universities	# Courses (thousands)	# New Students (millions)	# New Courses (thousands)
2020	180	950	16.3	60	2.8
2019	120	900	13.5	19	2.5
2018	101	900	11.4	20	2
2017	81	800	9.4	23	2.55
2016	58	700	6.85	23	2.6
2015	35	500	3.914	35	1.8
2014	17	400	2.042	18	1.19
2013	8	150	.852	6	.7
2012	2	40	.108	1.7	.105
2011	.3	1	.003	.3	.003

With the greater integration of MOOCs in the pedagogy of learning, it is worth noting that MOOCs allow the instructor and the students to span international and intercultural boundaries. One can even say that MOOCs are becoming an asset in reinforcing an institution's communication strategy while also improving its international scope. However, the diversity visible in the MOOC setup may involve both challenges and learning opportunities arising from the language and cultural differences. In this chapter, we explore MOOCs as a tool in promoting international/intercultural communication.

The rest of the paper is organized as follows: Section 2 outlines the evolution of MOOCs; Section 3 gives a brief discussion on international/intercultural communication; In section 4, we present the research questions on the use of MOOCs for international/intercultural communication; Section 5 is a critique on the impact of online learning in the era of COVID-19 pandemic. Section 6 concludes the paper.

EVOLUTION OF MASSIVE OPEN ONLINE COURSES (MOOCS)

George Siemens and Stephen Downes (Boven, 2013) are credited with the creation of the first MOOC in 2008, called "Connectivism and Connective Knowledge (CCK08)" (Downes, 2012), which eventually had 2200 enrolled students. The first MOOCs (now termed cMOOCs) used collaborative tools, blogs, and discussion boards with participants managing their own time, resources, and learning paths (Qian & Bax, 2017). The connectivist approach emphasizes the power of networking with other individuals to learn from their diverse opinions. cMOOCs provide an environment for the learners to define their objectives and collaboratively create and share knowledge via their social networks outside the learning platform (Mohamed, Yousef, Schroeder, Wosnitza, & Jakobs, 2014). This setup requires the learners to be fluent in digital literacies and abilities such as collaboration, creativity, communication, critical thinking, and information media skills path (Qian & Bax, 2017). Grading of assignments is through peer assessment based on pre-defined parameters that contribute to the learning of all the participants (Mohamed, Yousef, Schroeder, Wosnitza, & Jakobs, 2014). That is, the learners are the focus of the learning process. The nature of cMOOCs makes it difficult for official certification of the knowledge acquired by the participant (Qian & Bax, 2017).

Figure 1. Number of students enrolled in MOOC courses (Shah, 2012), (Shah, 2013), (Shah, 2014), (Shah, 2015), (Shah, 2016), (Shah, 2017), (Shah, 2018), (Shah, 2019), (Shah, 2020)

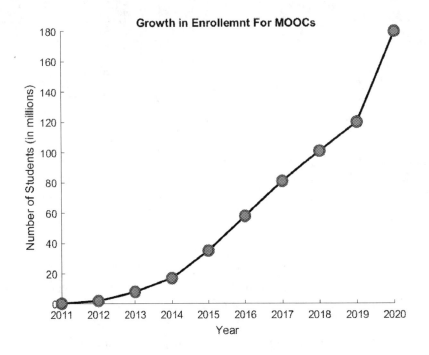

Figure 2. Number of new students enrolled in MOOC courses (Shah, 2012), (Shah, 2013), (Shah, 2014), (Shah, 2015), (Shah, 2016), (Shah, 2017), (Shah, 2018), (Shah, 2019), (Shah, 2020)

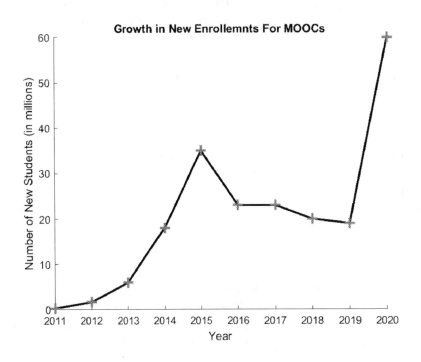

More recently, a new scheme of MOOC, termed xMOOC, has become popular. xMOOCs are more 'behaviourist' in nature and emphasize the content rather than on connections between the learners. The xMOOCs derived their name from the open course model of MITx. Joined by other universities, it later evolved into edX. Initially offering courses with a fixed duration and clear deadlines, many xMOOCs evolved to a more flexible approach where the students may pursue the course at their pace. The learning objectives are pre-defined by the teacher, and video lecture mode is used to impart knowledge. The participants can participate without a high competence in digital literacy. The assessment is usually done via online grading of quizzes, projects. Peer assessment may also be used. While the participants may interact via the online discussion boards, xMOOCs provide limited communication space between the participants (Mohamed, Yousef, Schroeder, Wosnitza, & Jakobs, 2014). xMOOCs emphasize the content with a fixed learning path for all the learners and tend to mirror the traditional learning environment more closely. However, as MOOCs have developed and become more widespread, the distinction between the two types, namely cMOOCs, xMOOCs, has become blurred (Qian & Bax, 2017). Table 2 (Mohamed, Yousef, Schroeder, Wosnitza, & Jakobs, 2014), (Qian & Bax, 2017) outlines some of the characteristics of cMOOCs and xMOOCs.

Table 2. Characteristics of cMOOCs and xMOOCs (Mohamed, Yousef, Schroeder, Wosnitza, & Jakobs, 2014), (Qian & Bax, 2017)

Characteristic	cMOOC	xMOOC
General	Self-organized, Networked, Connectivist approach	Teacher-organized, Centralized, Behaviorist approach
Assessment	Self-assessment, Peer-assessment, Online test	Teacher defined, Peer-assessment, Online quiz/test/projects
Content	Learner generated, distributed, notes, videos	Teacher generated, central repository, notes, videos
Learning goals	Learner decided	Teacher decided
Communication	Open networking, Outside MOOC platform, Extensive peer interaction and learning	Within the MOOC platform, Limited peer interaction through discussion boards
Certification	Not possible	Possible
Example	Connectivism and Connective Knowledge Course (CCK11) (Downes, Welcome to CCK11, 2011)	Machine Learning Course on Coursera (Machine Learning, 2012)

Some of the earliest popular platforms to provide e-content include MIT OpenCourseWare (Massachusetts Institute of Technology, 2002) and Stanford Engineering Everywhere (SEE) (Stanford University, 2011). They offered several free online courses through instructional videos, reading lists, and assignments. In Fall 2011, the Stanford Engineering Everywhere (SEE) program was expanded to offer online courses in Machine Learning, Artificial Intelligence, and Databases, leading to the birth of xMOOCs. Each of these courses had an enrolment of more than 100,000 students. The students were required to register to view the courses, raise queries and submit online assignments (Gupta, Taneja, & Kumar, 2015). A statement of accomplishment signed by the professor was awarded to the successful students. Some examples of MOOC hosting platforms that have seen success in the past decade (Table 3) are Coursera (Coursera, 2012), Udacity (Udacity, 2011), edX (edX, 2012), and FutureLearn (Future Learn, 2012).

Table 3. Number of students (in millions) for the earliest MOOC providers (Shah, 2012), (Shah, 2013), (Shah, 2014), (Shah, 2015), (Shah, 2016), (Shah, 2017), (Shah, 2018), (Shah, 2019), (Shah, 2020)

Year	Coursera	EdX	Udacity	FutureLearn
2020	76	35	14 (Dalporto, 2021)	16
2019	45	24	11.5	10
2018	37	18	10	8.7
2017	30	14	8	7.1
2016	23	10	5	5.3
2015	17	6	4	3
2014	10.5	3	1.5	.8
2013	5.7	1	1.6	.115
2012	2	.605	.753	-

Figure 3. Subject-wise distribution of MOOCs (Shah, 2012), (Shah, 2013), (Shah, 2014), (Shah, 2015), (Shah, 2016), (Shah, 2017), (Shah, 2018), (Shah, 2019), (Shah, 2020)

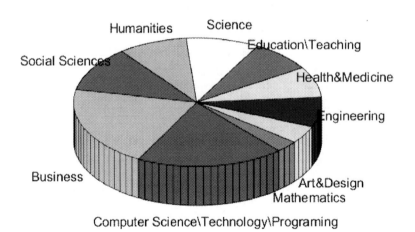

MOOC Distribution by Subject in 2020

Today, several premier universities like Stanford, Cambridge, Princeton, University of Michigan, University of Edinburgh, University of Pennsylvania, California Institute of Technology, Duke University offer many paid degree/certificate online courses along with a free audited version. These courses span diverse subject areas including Language, Humanities, Medicine, Biology, Social Sciences, Mathematics, Business, and Computer Science (Figure 3, Table 4).

More and more students are engaging in MOOCs to enhance their knowledge. Also, higher education institutes like MIT and Harvard have been using MOOCs in addition to their mainline curriculum (Bates, 2013). A flipped classroom model was experimented with at San Jose University with classroom time spent on problem-solving and MOOC lectures pursued by the students outside the class. Furthermore,

MOOCs are being taken seriously by employers as a "parallel learning universe" (Carey, 2012). In summary, with over 100 million worldwide learners (Figure 1) enrolled in more than 11000 MOOCs (Figure 5) launched by over 900 universities (Figure 4) with new courses (Figure 6) added annually, it cannot be denied that the MOOC movement is a disruptor in the traditional approach to learning.

Table 4. Yearly distribution (%) of MOOC courses by subject (Shah, 2012), (Shah, 2013), (Shah, 2014), (Shah, 2015), (Shah, 2016), (Shah, 2017), (Shah, 2018), (Shah, 2019), (Shah, 2020)

Year	Social Sciences	Business	Computer Science & Technology & Programing	Mathematics	Art & Design	Engineering	Health & Medicine	Education & Teaching	Science	Humanities
2020	11.4	20.4	19.3	2.9	4.4	7.6	7.7	7.9	9.5	9.1
2019	11	19.7	19.8	2.9	5.2	7.8	7.4	8	9.2	8.9
2018	11.5	18.2	20.4	3.1	5	7	7.2	8.6	9.4	9.4
2017	10.6	18.5	19.9	3.3	5.5	7.1	7.2	8.5	10	9.5
2016	9.82	19.3	17.4	3.64	6.47	6.32	7.68	9.26	10.4	9.82
2015	10.8	16.8	17.18	4.09	6.73	6.11	8.27	9.36	11.3	9.41

Figure 4. Number of Universities Offering MOOCs (Shah, 2012), (Shah, 2013), (Shah, 2014), (Shah, 2015), (Shah, 2016), (Shah, 2017), (Shah, 2018), (Shah, 2019), (Shah, 2020)

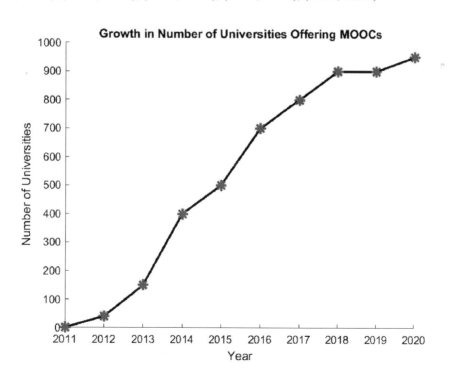

Figure 5. Number of MOOC Course MOOCs (Shah, 2012), (Shah, 2013), (Shah, 2014), (Shah, 2015), (Shah, 2016), (Shah, 2017), (Shah, 2018), (Shah, 2019), (Shah, 2020)

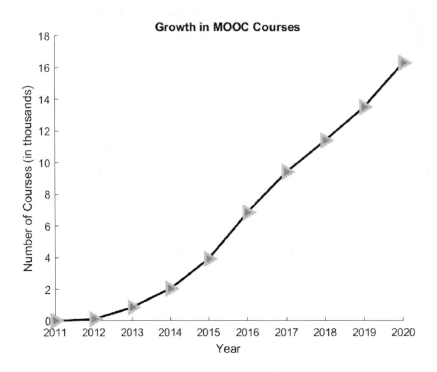

Figure 6. Number of new MOOC courses MOOCs (Shah, 2012), (Shah, 2013), (Shah, 2014), (Shah, 2015), (Shah, 2016), (Shah, 2017), (Shah, 2018), (Shah, 2019), (Shah, 2020)

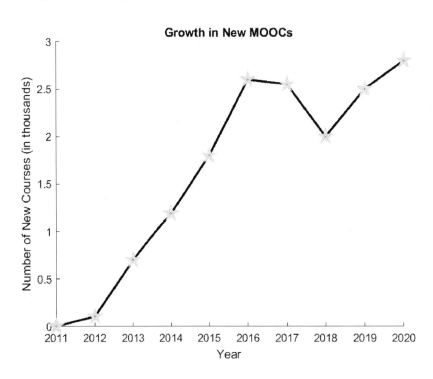

INTERNATIONAL/INTERCULTURAL COMMUNICATION

Globalization has resulted in the melting of the barriers of countries/continents, creating interaction and even interdependence between people belonging to different cultures. Intercultural and international communication is a necessity for a global society (Carey, 2012).

Arguably culture is an important factor in deciding how individuals encode messages, what medium they choose for transmitting them, and the way messages are interpreted (Lauring, 2011). These differences become important in situations where people from different cultural backgrounds interact. Intercultural communication (or cross-cultural communication) is a discipline that studies the effect of culture on communication across different cultures and social groups. It describes the wide range of communication processes and problems that naturally appear within an organization or social context made up of individuals from different religious, social, ethnic, and educational backgrounds. In this sense, it seeks to understand how people from different countries and cultures act, communicate and perceive the world around them. In the present context, owing to the high volume of international and intercultural trade and personnel interchange, international communication may be perceived as a particularly useful skill in international business (Rogers, Hart, & Miike, 2002).

The study of communication across cultures and nations first appeared as a part of communication study in the late 1960s. Before the mid-1960s, it was believed that international communication meant mastering English conversation and that this was enough for a person to be an effective international communicator. Edward T. Hall emphasized that international interaction, rather than being a mere exchange of words, involved understanding cultural systems of beliefs, values, and worldviews. Intercultural communication competence is defined as the ability to communicate effectively and appropriately in various cultural contexts (Rice, 2021). That is, intercultural communication requires an understanding of language skills and also requires an understanding that different cultures have different customs, standards, social norms, and even thought patterns. Good intercultural communication skills require a willingness to accept differences and adapt to them.

The last few decades witnessed an ever-increasing number of internationally mobile students and many higher education institutions attempting to become more international (Kelly & Moogan, 2012). The globalization of higher education institutions brings together, learners and teachers from heterogeneous cultures, languages, ages, experiences, and countries into the same classroom, for a duration. Internationalized universities in their culturally diverse settings provide opportunities for the students, through interactions with students and staff from international backgrounds, to develop the skills required to be productive members of the world community (Leask, 2009). Although this may prove to be an inspiring experience, it does create language and cultural problems that must be solved if a benefit is to be derived from diversity. However, many HEIs expect foreign students to themselves adapt to the new educational environment. This may potentially lead to lower performance, at least initially, for the international students as compared to the home country students (Kelly & Moogan, 2012).

Cultural consciousness is learned and transmitted through generations and reflects in the patterns of knowledge, beliefs, and behaviours of individuals. Issues arising from differing cultural backgrounds include inequities arising from cultural values, the potential miscommunications among students and/ or instructors during online interaction, participant group formation based on cultural homophily, the anxiety of students in a multicultural learning setup. When the instructors work with an awareness of the cultural backgrounds, values, and performance styles of ethnically diverse students, their learning environment can be made more effective. Collaborative activities can be used to encourage students from diverse backgrounds to participate in class discussions. Providing an environment where the students can learn and appreciate the diverse culture of their peers can build a more inclusive environment (Kumi Yeboah, Dogbey, & Yuan, 2020).

MOOCS FOR INTERNATIONAL/INTERCULTURAL COMMUNICATION

In today's age of global knowledge and technology, an interconnected network and global awareness are increasingly viewed as sought-after assets. With the current labour market requiring graduates to have international, foreign language, and intercultural skills to be able to interact in a global setting, institutions are placing more importance on internationalisation (Qian & Bax, 2017). The trend towards globalization resulting in the melting of national boundaries and the concepts of global citizenship and responsibility has brought new dimensions for the pursuit of knowledge in higher education (Kim, et al., 2015). The English language is dominating new programmes and campuses are being built to welcome an increasing number of students from emerging economies. New forms of institutions, programmes and teaching methods are being set up (Hénard, Diamond, & Roseveare, 2012).

Students/professionals preparing to study/work internationally need to work on developing an understanding of the different cultures, languages, and customs of people. In this regard, it can be argued that exposure to professionals from different countries can help in practical learning. With courses in at least 19 languages (Shah, 2018), MOOCs have the potential to provide educational opportunities for a very wide multilingual and multicultural audience and can extend the reach of the institution, thereby, improving its international scope. Also, with more than 100 courses teaching the English language (Shah, 2018), a category of MOOCs called a foreign language massive open online courses (LMOOCs) has emerged. LMOOCs are defined as "dedicated web-based online courses for second languages with unrestricted access and potentially unlimited participation" (Qian & Bax, 2017).

The heterogeneous social structure of the students in a given course provides opportunities for explicit social inclusion, where the members of the learning community are collectively learning about the subject of the course, and implicit social inclusion, where people from different backgrounds are mixing and working together online (Read & Barcena, 2019). The global reach and open aspects of MOOCs imply that HEIs will have to address extremely varied types of audiences. For example, by September 2019, Coursera had 196 partners across 46 countries offering 3,770 courses. Depending on the type of courses offered, HEIs can expect to reach a diverse audience that is not limited to those who are connected to the related domains and may include students/professionals trained in a completely unrelated domain, institutions, and anyone from the general public. The institutions offering the MOOCs also have to address the complexities added due to the geographical and language diversity of both the instructors and the audiences. On the flip side, since the MOOCs cannot be tailor-made to one community of students, they do retain the cultural and national impact of the instructors/university offering the course. Therefore, it can be postulated that MOOCs can provide a training ground for students to get acclimatized to an international learning environment.

For international students, language and communication barriers often prevent them from effectively interacting in online classrooms. Many MOOC platforms provide speech-to-text translation to produce subtitles in multiple languages. It can be daunting for instructors to address and promote cultural diversity and equity in online learning. Instructors have reported encountering several challenges including the fear of stereotyping students, inability to identify students' cultural backgrounds, language and communication barriers, time constraints, and the lack of skills to design multicultural online courses to enrich students' academic experiences in online learning (Kumi Yeboah, Dogbey, & Yuan, 2020).

In the light of the above discussion, the following questions can be asked for future research: 1) What are the most important issues in intercultural communication that the MOOCs should address? 2) How should the instructors identify the students' cultural backgrounds in an online learning environment? 3) What will be the best activities or practices that will help the students from diverse backgrounds to succeed in the online classes? 4) What will be the best pedagogical practices for MOOCs that encounter international students? 5) What issues need to be addressed for online assessment when encountering multicultural students? For example, will peer-review be an effective strategy for the assessment?

COVID-19 AND ONLINE EDUCATION: A CRITIQUE

The lockdown imposed after the worldwide outbreak of COVID-19 became an important factor in the increase in enrolments in online courses and MOOCs. Some of the MOOC platforms, such as Coursera, provided zero-cost access to certificate courses during this period. The number of new learners enrolling in MOOCs (Figure 2), which was steadily dropping since 2015, suddenly skyrocketed during the pandemic motivated lockdown. In the pre-pandemic era, the online mode of learning was steadily gaining importance and was mostly used to supplement face-to-face classroom learning. The COVID-19 pandemic fast-forwarded the process of many years and the education system moved to mostly online mode in a span of a few weeks (Adedoyin, 2020).

The sudden transformation to a completely online mode resulted in logistical challenges for the institutions such as the availability of digital infrastructure and content, digital competence of the teachers and the learners. Many students and teachers relied on the use of the digital infrastructure provided by the institution. Closure of institutions due to pandemic withdrew this support. The complete dependence of online learning mode on digital equipment resulted in denial of access to teaching/learning for the instructors/students with outdated devices, poor internet connectivity. The problems were more pronounced in developing countries, especially in the rural areas (Adedoyin, 2020), (Lockee, 2021). During the lockdown arising from the global pandemic, many families experienced higher stress levels due to constant engagement with each other and competing needs for the use of home technology (Pokhrel & Chhetri, 2021).

Many pre-COVID studies conducted to compare the face-to-face and online learning environments found no significant difference in the learning success of students between online and traditional classroom setups (Paul & Jefferson, 2019). However, the studies did not have the experience of a 100% online mode. Although the advantages of time flexibility of teaching the online course cannot be denied, it is also true that traditional offline learning setup raises social skills and awareness besides being fun for the students. Increased and unstructured time spent on virtual platforms can expose children to potentially harmful and violent content and leave the students vulnerable to online exploitation (Pokhrel & Chhetri, 2021). In addition, the apprehensions of the faculty members related to unfamiliarity with the e-learning medium have to be addressed with formal training and workshops on using various technological methods and platforms for strengthening the e-learning activities (Zalat, 2021).

Various studies have also noted that the workload for online courses is more than for face-to-face courses. Though automated exams in an online course save the effort and time of the online instructors, many observational and participatory evaluations, and informal assessments of online/distance learning are challenging (Zalat, 2021). Additionally, online teaching provides a limited scope of supervision and regulation in the evaluation process. Limited peer group interaction and support brings about the tendency for procrastination, lower concentration and performance, and a high rate of dropouts. This may ultimately result in bringing down the quality of learning and a higher rate of issues of mental health and wellbeing (Adedoyin, 2020).

With the entire world caught in the grip of COVID-19 lockdown, the technical teams were burdened with the task of quickly providing online learning systems. Many institutions turned to popular online unified communication and collaboration virtual learning platforms and social media forums such as Google Classroom, Microsoft Teams, Zoom, Cisco Webex, Canvas, Blackboard, Elias, Moodle, Big-BlueButton and Skype, Piazza, Telegram, Messenger, WhatsApp, and WeChat. The platforms include options of workplace chat, video meeting, content repository management, sharing, and tracking of student learning and assessment by using quizzes, and rubric-based assessment of submitted assignments. The flipped classroom model became the popular pedagogical practice where the instructors provided learning resources such as articles, pre-recorded videos, and YouTube links before the class, and the online classroom time was used to deepen understanding through discussion with faculty and peers (Pokhrel & Chhetri, 2021).

However bleak the circumstances, the education system brought out innovative solutions such as institutions sending the infrastructure to the homes of the learners, school bus serving as a WI-FI hotspot, sharing of study material via mail, use of broadcast systems for delivering content, virtual experiential learning, and virtual labs. The force of the times served as a rare opportunity to move away from our attachment to the old ways and to think anew about the educational pedagogy. With the academic year 2020-21 in our rear-view mirror, educators have become more open to considering online education in a hybrid and flexible mode for learners of all age groups, new evaluation and assessment strategies, and a collaborative learning environment (Lockee, 2021). However, one needs to assess the suitability of the online mode of learning with specific disciplines. Many educators have contended the applicability of online teaching strategies in the fields requiring hands-on lab experiences like medical science, engineering, and pure sciences (Adedoyin, 2020).

DISCUSSION

The last decade has seen a proliferation of blended and online modes of learning. Online courses, especially MOOCs, are uniquely posited to bring together participants and educators from diverse cultures and expose the students to new ideas and values from peers with different backgrounds. However, many students experience social and cultural tensions when working with diverse peers. As such, teachers in online programmes face challenges in encouraging participation and interaction among peers from vastly different backgrounds. The internationalization of the online academic content can encourage individual-level participation and decrease the disparity of participation within small groups when the content is situated in countries that are personally relevant to students' backgrounds (Mittelmeier, Rienties, Tempelaar, Hillaire, & Whitelock, 2018).

The COVID-19 pandemic has created the largest disruption of education systems in human history. Lockdown and social distancing measures due to the COVID-19 pandemic led to the closure of education facilities in most countries. During these trying times, the online learning environment became the elixir despite the challenges posed to both educators and learners. Transitioning from traditional face-to-face learning to solely online learning as an emergency response proved to be very different from blended learning. Nevertheless, the education community proved its resilience and tried its hardest to evolve. In this process, many challenges and research areas were identified including issues of affordability and accessibility for learners of varied economic backgrounds, development of integrated online learning environments, tools for authentic assessments and timely feedback, and effective pedagogy for online teaching. A lesson learned from the COVID-19 pandemic is that teachers and learners should be oriented on the use of different online educational tools and should continue using them to enhance teaching and learning even when the normal classes resume (Pokhrel & Chhetri, 2021).

CONCLUSION

Global interconnectedness that allows people to travel to different countries/continents necessitates intercultural and international communication. Recognizing, understanding, and adapting to cultural differences is now considered a requirement to be effective in intercultural communication. The last decade has seen a proliferation in the popularity of Massive open online courses (MOOCs). MOOCs contribute to institutional diversity, improve motivation for learning, and also contribute towards the internationalisation of the institutions. Further, since the MOOCs retain the cultural and national flavour of the university offering them, they can also be considered as a tool to provide the necessary international exposure, both through the online language courses and through the interactions with international peers/teachers. The chapter traces the evolution of MOOCs and suggests some future research questions towards the use of MOOC platforms for promoting international communication.

The year 2020 brought a paradigm shift in teaching/learning as an emergency response to the prolonged lockdown resulting from the COVID-19 pandemic. As we move forward, it is becoming evident that online learning can be sustainable in a hybrid format provided the challenges experienced by the educational institutions during the pandemic are addressed.

ACKNOWLEDGMENT

This research received no specific grant from any funding agency in the public, commercial, or not-for-profit sectors.

REFERENCES

Adedoyin, O. B. (2020). Covid-19 pandemic and online learning: The challenges and opportunities. *Interactive Learning Environments*, 1–13.

Arasaratnam, L. A. (2005). Intercultural communication competence: Identifying key components from multicultural perspectives. *International Journal of Intercultural Relations*, 29(2), 137–163.

Bates, T. (2013). *Harvard's current thinking on MOOCs. Harvard Magazine.*

Blieszner, P. B., & Teaster, R. (1999). Promises and pitfalls of the interactive television approach to teaching adult development and aging. *Educational Gerontology, 25*(8), 741–753.

Boven, D. (2013). The next game changer: The historical antecedents of the MOOC movement in education. *E-learning Papers, 33*, 1–7.

Carey, K. (2012). The siege of academe. *The Washington Monthly*.

Coursera. (2012). Retrieved from Coursera: https://www.coursera.org/in

Dalporto, G. (2021). *Udacity 2020: The Year in Review*. Retrieved from Udacity: https://www.udacity.com/blog/2021/01/udacity-2020-the-year-in-review.html

Downes, S. (2011). *Welcome to CCK11*. Retrieved 10 1, 2021, from Connectivism and Connective Knowledge 2011: http://cck11.mooc.ca/

Downes, S. (2012). *Creating the Connectivist Course*. Retrieved 08 15, 2019, from Knowledge, Learning, Community: https://www.downes.ca/cgi-bin/page.cgi?post=57750

edX. (2012). Retrieved from edX: https://www.edx.org/

Future Learn. (2012). Retrieved from Future Learn: https://www.futurelearn.com/

Gupta, S., Taneja, S., & Kumar, N. (2015). Redefining the Classroom: Integration of open and classroom learning in higher education. In Macro-level learning through massive open online courses (MOOCs): Strategies and predictions for the future (pp. 168-182). IGI Global.

Hénard, F., Diamond, L., & Roseveare, D. (2012). Approaches to internationalisation and their implications for strategic management and institutional practice. *IMHE Institutional Management in Higher Education, 11*(12), 2013.

Keegan, D. (1995). *Distance Education Technology for the New Millennium Compressed Video Teaching. ZIFF Papiere 101*. ERIC.

Kelly, P., & Moogan, Y. (2012). Culture shock and higher education performance: Implications for teaching. *Higher Education Quarterly*, 24–46.

Kim, B., Ying, W., Pushpanadham, K., Yamada, T., Lee, T., & Fadzil, M. (2015). *MOOCs and Educational Challenges around Asia and Europe* (B. Kim, Ed.). KNOU Press. Retrieved from http://asemlllhub.org/fileadmin/www.asem.au.dk/publications/MOOCs_and_Educational_Challenges_around_Asia_and_Europe_FINAL.pdf

Kumi Yeboah, A., Dogbey, J., & Yuan, G. (2020). Cultural Diversity in Online Education: An Exploration of Instructors' Perceptions and Challenges. *Teachers College Record, 122*(7).

Lauring, J. (2011). Intercultural organizational communication: The social organizing of interaction in international encounters. *The Journal of Business Communication*, 231-255.

Leask, B. (2009). Using formal and informal curricula to improve interactions between home and international students. *Journal of Studies in International Education, 13*(2), 205–221.

Lockee, B. B. (2021). Online education in the post-COVID era. *Nature Electronics*, 5-6.

Machine Learning. (2012). Retrieved 2019, from Coursera: https://www.coursera.org/learn/machine-learning

Massachusetts Institute of Technology. (2002). Retrieved from MIT Open Courseware: https://ocw.mit.edu/index.htm

Mittelmeier, J., Rienties, B., Tempelaar, D., Hillaire, G., & Whitelock, D. (2018). The influence of internationalised versus local content on online intercultural collaboration in groups: A randomised control trial study in a statistics course. *Computers & Education*, 82–95.

Mohamed, A., Yousef, F., Schroeder, U., Wosnitza, M., & Jakobs, H. (2014). MOOCs. A Review of the State-of-the-Art. *CSEDU 2014-6th International Conference on Computer Supported Education.*

O'Neil, C. A. (2013). *Developing online learning environments in nursing education.* Springer Publishing Company.

Paul, J., & Jefferson, F. (2019). A comparative analysis of student performance in an online vs. face-to-face environmental science course from 2009 to 2016. *Frontiers of Computer Science*, *1*, 7.

Pokhrel, S., & Chhetri, R. (2021). A literature review on impact of COVID-19 pandemic on teaching and learning. *Higher Education for the Future*, *8*(1), 133–141.

Qian, K., & Bax, S. (2017). *Beyond the language classroom: researching MOOCs and other innovations.* Research-publishing.net.

Read, T., & Barcena, E. (2019). A Role for Inclusive MOOCs in Societal Change. EADTU.

Rice, T. S. (2021). Retrieved 10 01, 2021, from Intercultural Communication Competence: https://socialsci.libretexts.org/@go/page/55556

Rogers, E. M., Hart, W. B., & Miike, Y. (2002). *Edward T. Hall and The History of Intercultural Communication: The United States and Japan.* Keio Communication Review.

Shah, D. (2012). *The MOOC Juggernaut: One Year Later.* Retrieved from Class Central: https://www.classcentral.com/report/growth-of-moocs/

Shah, D. (2013). *The MOOC Juggernaut: Year 2.* Retrieved from Class Central: https://www.classcentral.com/report/the-mooc-juggernaut-year-2/

Shah, D. (2014). *Online Courses Raise Their Game: A Review of MOOC Stats and Trends in 2014.* Retrieved from Class Central.

Shah, D. (2015). *By The Numbers: MOOCS in 2015.* Retrieved from Class Central: https://www.classcentral.com/report/moocs-2015-stats/

Shah, D. (2016). *By The Numbers: MOOCS in 2016.* Retrieved from Class Central: https://www.classcentral.com/report/mooc-stats-2016/

Shah, D. (2017). *By The Numbers: MOOCS in 2017.* Retrieved from Class Central: https://www.classcentral.com/report/mooc-stats-2017/

Shah, D. (2018). *By The Numbers: MOOCs in 2018*. Retrieved 08 15, 2019, from Class Central: https://www.classcentral.com/report/mooc-stats-2018/

Shah, D. (2019). *By The Numbers: MOOCs in 2019*. Retrieved from Class Central: https://www.class-central.com/report/mooc-stats-2019/

Shah, D. (2020). *By The Numbers: MOOCs in 2020*. Retrieved from Class Central: https://www.class-central.com/report/mooc-stats-2020/

Siemens, G. (2003). *Connectivism by Siemens*. Retrieved from http://www.ceebl.manchester.ac.uk/events/archive/aligningcollaborativelearning/Siemens.pdf

Stanford University. (2011). Retrieved from Stanford Engineering Everywhere: https://see.stanford.edu

Udacity. (2011). Retrieved from Udacity: https://www.udacity.com/

UNESCO. (2011). *WSIS Knowledge Commons*. Retrieved from http://www.wsiscommunity.org/pg/groups/14358/open-educational-resources-oer/

Zalat, M. M. (2021). The experiences, challenges, and acceptance of e-learning as a tool for teaching during the COVID-19 pandemic among university medical staff. *PLoS One, 16*(3), e0248758.

ADDITIONAL READING

Annabi, C. A., & Muller, M. (2016). Learning from the adoption of MOOCs in two international branch campuses in the UAE. *Journal of Studies in International Education, 20*(3), 260–281. doi:10.1177/1028315315622023

Bergmann, J., & Sams, A. (2012). *Flip your classroom: Reach every student in every class every day.* International Society for Technology in Education.

Conole, G., & Brown, M. (2018). Reflecting on the Impact of the Open Education Movement. *Journal of Learning for Development, 5*(3), 187–203.

Daniel, J. (2012). Making sense of MOOCs: Musings in a maze of myth, paradox and possibility. *Journal of Interactive Media in Education, 2012*(3), 18. doi:10.5334/2012-18

Hall, E. T. (1960). The silent language in overseas business. *Harvard Business Review, 38*(3), 87–96.

Leask, B. (2007). *International teachers and international learning.* Routledge.

Ong, B. S., & Grigoryan, A. (2015). MOOCs and universities: Competitors or partners? *International Journal of Information and Education Technology (IJIET), 5*(5), 373–376. doi:10.7763/IJIET.2015.V5.533

Otten, M. (2003). Intercultural learning and diversity in higher education. *Journal of Studies in International Education, 7*(1), 12–26. doi:10.1177/1028315302250177

Ryan, J. (2005). Improving teaching and learning practices for international students. *Teaching international students: Improving learning for all*, 92-100.

Wilkins, S. (2013). The future of transnational higher education: What role for international branch campuses. *Possible futures: The next, 25*, 182-186.

KEY TERMS AND DEFINITIONS

Connectivism: According to George Siemens, "Connectivism is a learning theory for the Digital Age." In Connectivism, learning is a process that occurs based upon a variety of continuously shifting elements. The "starting point of learning is the individual who feeds information into the network, which feeds information back to individuals who in turn feed information back into the network as part of a cycle" (Siemens, 2003).

Distance Learning: Distance learning is a method where the teacher and the learner are separate in space and possibly time (Hénard et al., 2012; Bates, 2013).

Intercultural Communication: "Intercultural" encompasses ethnic, religious, cultural, national, and geographic variances, and "communication" is perceived to be a verbal exchange of ideas and messages through the use of language, and involves an element of understanding on the part of the participants (Arasaratnam, 2005).

Internationalisation of the Curriculum: Internationalisation of the curriculum is the incorporation of an international and intercultural dimension into the content of the curriculum as well as the teaching and learning processes and support services of a program of study (Leask, 2009).

MOOC: Massive open online courses (MOOCs) are online courses that are accessible to anyone with internet access, irrespective of their location. MOOC courses do not limit the number of participants and may allow thousands or even millions of learners.

Online Education: Online education is the modern form of distance learning with the Internet often uniting the distance learning instructor with distance learner.

Open Educational Resources: Open educational resources are defined as teaching, learning, or research materials that are in the public domain or released with an intellectual property license that allows for free use, adaptation, and distribution (UNESCO, 2011).

Chapter 16

A "Glocal" Community of Practice to Support International ELT (English Language Teaching) Students in the UK:
Project BMELTET

Marina Orsini-Jones
https://orcid.org/0000-0001-5250-5682
Coventry University, UK

Abraham Cerveró-Carrascosa
https://orcid.org/0000-0002-3545-1085
Florida Universitària, Spain

Kyria Rebeca Finardi
Federal University of Espirito Santo, Brazil

ABSTRACT

This chapter reports on the project 'Blending MOOCs (Massive Open Online Courses) into English Language Teaching (ELT) Education with Telecollaboration (BMELTET)'. BMELTET aims to foster reflection on ELT with a COIL (Collaborative Online International Learning) MOOC blend. It promotes the engagement of international students based in the UK and studying on a Master's degree in ELT, with students and staff based in universities in Brazil, China, and Spain and with the participants on the MOOC from all over the world. BMELTET aims to debunk the myth of the 'native speaker' as the ideal teacher of English language, thus decolonising ELT through dialogic online intercultural exchanges in a safe 'third space'. Data were collected via two online surveys, the analysis of the 'live' Zoom exchanges, and focus groups with self-selected groups of students. This chapter reports on the impact that BMELTET had on the international students involved in it.

DOI: 10.4018/978-1-7998-8921-2.ch016

INTRODUCTION

This chapter reports on project BMELTET 2020-2021 (Blending MOOCs–Massive Open Online Courses–for English Language Teacher Education with Telecollaboration) in its September-December 2020 cycle (see Orsini-Jones et al., 2018; Orsini-Jones & Cerveró-Carrascosa, 2019; Orsini-Jones et al., 2020 with reference to previous action-research cycles). Staff and students at four Higher Education Institutions (HEIs) in Brazil, China, Spain, and the UK took part in the project. The students were from the following undergraduate and postgraduate teacher education courses: BA in Primary English Education and MA in TEFL at Florida Universitària (FU), Spain; MA TESOL at Sichuan International Studies University, China; and MA in English Language Teaching and Applied Linguistics (ELTAL) at Coventry University (CU), UK. Only one member of staff took part in the project from Brazil, from the Federal University of Espirito Santo, in Victoria.

The project repurposed the FutureLearn MOOC *Understanding Language: Learning and Teaching* (designed by the University of Southampton in collaboration with the British Council) by incorporating it into existing teacher education curricula. As in previous cycles, this took the form of a blended learning model of MOOC-COIL (Collaborative Online International Learning) whereby students participated in the COIL while simultaneously joining a global English Language Teaching community of practice on a MOOC that had over 200,000 participants from all over the world (FutureLearn, 2020). COIL is also known as Virtual Exchange (VE), telecollaboration, or Online Intercultural Exchange (OIE) (O'Dowd, 2020; Lewis & O'Dowd, 2016). These terms are used interchangeably in this work (even if there is a debate about whether or not they can be, e.g. Colpaert, 2020; O'Dowd, 2021). This specific type of curricular integration is relatively new but has been done before. For example, Sandeen (2013) was one of the first supporters of the merge between existing curricula and 'off the shelf' MOOCs, defining such an approach as a MOOC 3.0 distributed flip model. More recently, De Lima-Guedes (2020) discusses how an 'off the shelf' MOOC is merged into a curriculum that covers the same or similar topics.

The integration of COIL/telecollaboration into the curriculum addressed the need to develop new approaches to teaching and learning that include the internationalization of the curriculum, to enable students to develop competencies that can equip them for the demands and challenges of the 21st Century.

Project BMELTET aimed to provide its participants with the opportunity to discuss English language teacher education topics within global communities of practice in a decolonised 'Third Space'.

GENERAL BACKGROUND

Coventry University's strong internationalization ethos and commitment to 'intercultural and international engagement' is one of the pillars of the university group strategy (Gearing, 2015, p.6). This commitment is validated by the fact that, for 6 years running, Coventry University has been rated the best university in the UK for providing students with international experiences, according to the Higher Education Statistical Agency (HESA) (from 2015-2016 to 2020-2021), even in the year of the lockdown caused by the pandemic (2020-2021).

Internal data from admissions at Coventry University (CU) show that over 3000 overseas students enrolled on CU courses in September 2021. This means that educators in this institution need to explore and implement what Smith et al. define as 'promising teaching practices for teaching linguistically and culturally-diverse international students' (2019, p. 252). It also means that all staff need to become more sensitive to diversity and not assume that their international students have knowledge that comes from a traditional British syllabus background. The Research Centre for Global Learning (GLEA) at Coventry University, where one of the authors of this paper is a research associate, explores the theme of 'Education without boundaries' which includes widening participation, inclusion and ethical ways of internationalising the curriculum (GLEA, n.d.). The influx of overseas students who bring different perspectives and backgrounds has indeed made it more urgent to create an inclusive curriculum.

The Master's degree in English Language Teaching (renamed English Language Teaching and Applied Linguistics in 2018) was launched at Coventry University in academic year 2009-2010. In its first years, it mainly recruited British and European (EU) students. Since 2014, the majority of students attracted to the course are international ('overseas' in the Coventry University terminology which since 2021, post-Brexit, also includes EU students). Many of these students are classified as 'BAME' (Black, Asian and Minority Ethnic) in the UK system. The term BAME is arguably quite reductionist and does not represent the variety of backgrounds that these students are from. Various central initiatives try to address their specific needs at Coventry University, such as the training of staff in inclusive curriculum design. An example of this is the way a new academic skills component was added to the existing MA ELT curriculum in 2015. Staff worked with BAME students to explore how they could be supported with their academic writing skills. Coventry University has a dedicated Centre for Academic Writing, but the students asked for more tailored interventions than the Centre could offer. This resulted in the collaborative creation of an integrated academic skills component, designed with them and addressing their needs and 'wants' (Orsini-Jones et al., 2015).

More recently, staff on the MA have explored inclusive ways of internationalising the curriculum to foster intercultural awareness through COIL (Wimpenny & Orsini-Jones, 2020). It may sound like a paradox, but engaging overseas students with other students located outside the UK to discuss topics relating to their degree course has proven to be a positive and inclusive experience for most.

While most participants from the UK were from overseas in BMELTET 2020-2021, the 'make up' of students involved in the BMELTET project from Spain and China was very different on the other hand. All students from the Chinese partner university were of Chinese nationality and Mandarin L1 and all students but one (who was dual nationality Spanish/British) based in Spain were Spanish—bilingual in Valencian and 'standard' Castilian Spanish. There were no student participants from Brazil in this BMELTET project cycle. There was one Brazilian scholar of English, who joined BMELTET both for the purpose of knowledge-sharing to start their own telecollaborative/COIL exchanges in their own HE institution (Federal University of Espirito Santo – UFES - in the state of Victoria) and to support the project with a session on one of their areas of expertise: Global Englishes. The Spanish, Chinese and Brazilian partners involved in BMELTET valued this unique experience of ELT knowledge-sharing and internationalization of the curriculum. Although there are telecollaborative studies in Brazil (e.g. Salomao, 2011; Telles, 2015), there are no other studies where MOOCs and COIL/Telecollaboration have been integrated in the way they were in the BMELTET project discussed here.

COIL AT COVENTRY UNIVERSITY

The Coventry University definition of COIL is that:

- It involves a cross-border collaboration or interaction with people from different backgrounds and cultures.
- It requires students to engage in some sort of online interaction, whether it is asynchronous or synchronous.
- It is driven by a set of internationalised learning outcomes aimed at developing global perspectives and/or fostering students' intercultural competences.
- It requires a reflective component that helps students think critically about such interaction (O'Brien, 2018).

COIL is utilised here as a synonym of 'telecollaboration' and/or Virtual Exchange (VE). COIL has grown exponentially since it was set up as an institutional tool to provide internationalization experiences in 2013 (Wimpenny & Orsini-Jones, 2020). The COIL figures for 2020-2021 are as follows: 7233 Coventry students participated in 171 COIL projects with 134 institutions, in 52 countries, in comparison with only three projects with five countries in 2013 (personal communication with a member of staff in the Centre for Global Engagement, CU, 2021). This growth is supported by the strong central drive towards COIL: it is an institutional target that every course in the University should include a COIL project. Coventry University also provides a support infrastructure which includes the recording of COIL projects, the regular provision of COIL training and the appointment of dedicated internationalization leaders (Associate Heads for Global Engagement and Associate Deans for Global Engagement) tasked with promoting and disseminating COIL to staff in their schools and faculties.

The reasons behind this strong support for COIL are numerous. COIL situates students in a learning space that activates inter-connected competencies such as 'critical cultural adaptation and relationship building' and provides graduates with a foundation of resilience and responsiveness 'within situations of uncertainty' (Wimpenny & Orsini-Jones, 2020, p. 14). COIL can also be used to harness students' critical digital literacies so that they may become active, deep thinkers and creators. For example, Orsini-Jones et al. (2018) discuss how the integration of their MOOC-COIL blend into the teacher education curriculum became a conduit for trainee teachers to become reflective practitioners. Students were simultaneously immersed in the synchronous online environment in BMELTET (the Coventry University 'safe' institutional version of Zoom was the main platform) (https://coventry-ac-uk.zoom.us/), in conjunction with the asynchronous MOOC environment, as further discussed below.

LITERATURE REVIEW

According to Ladson-Billings, we now live in an era affected by four pandemics: 1. COVID-19, 2. systemic racism, 3. economic crisis, 4. climate crisis. Residual effects of these four pandemics increase and expose the long-standing disparities in our education systems calling for reflection and action in a hard re-set fashion (2021: 68-78).

This re-set or re-imagination of systems requires access to transformative teaching and learning: creating a Third Space for the encounter and clash of different languages, cultures and knowledges thus contributing to the visibility and appreciation of difference, diversities and minorities. Third Space, as coined by Bhabha (2004), is conceptualized here as a place of exchange, clash, contrast, rearticulation, and negotiation rather than as a space of resolution (Helm, 2013; Orsini-Jones & Lee, 2018). As such,

Third Space emphasizes the ambivalence that questions authoritarian and colonial discourses as well as the systems that reproduced them (Bhabha & Rutherford, 2006).

There are many examples of telecollaboration/COIL/VE used for English Teacher education (e.g. Gutiérrez et al., 2021; Dooly & Vinagre, 2021; O'Dowd & Dooly, 2021; Sadler & Dooly, 2016;), but they do not extend the telecollaborative online community of practice via the integration of a MOOC, like BMELTET did. Similarly, there are examples of MOOC integration into existing curricula (see De Lima Guedes, 2020 on this), but without the added value of the telecollaboration element.

The BMELTET project's focus was to provide students with alternative perspectives on ELT through interconnected local and global online communities of practice. Topics such as the role of English in the world, the role of ELT and 'Global Englishes' were discussed while questioning notions of authority and normativity to decolonise ELT (Finardi, 2014, 2019; Kumaravadivelu, 2006; Rubdy, 2015). The dynamic and dialogic online exchanges in BMELTET reflect the interplay of 'glocal'—that is, global and local—forces that act on each other within a 'Third Space. Drawing from Bhabha's conceptualisation of the Third Space (2004), Guimarães and Finardi (2021) describe how telecollaboration facilitates the creation of a safe area and a fertile ground for intercultural and decolonised encounters in Higher Education. The coining of the term 'glocal' is attributed to Robertson (1995) as a sociological concept; it is used here to highlight the awareness that teachers of English need about the interactions between their local teaching contexts and the global realities that will impact on them and their teaching practice. The effect of the COVID pandemic on education is an example that well illustrates the importance of 'glocal' considerations.

One of the main aims of BMELTET was to debunk the myth of the 'native speaker' as the ideal teacher of a language, as exemplified in Macedo's (2019) seminal work urging the dissolution of colonial linguistic oppression in language teaching. Finardi's work (2014, 2019) on decolonization from the perspective of the Global South also illustrates well how new voices need to be heard in the field of ELT. Indeed, all the English teacher educators involved in the project were non L1 English speakers (their first language–L1–was not English). The project enabled students to work towards developing a critical awareness of their own 'right to teach English'. This was achieved through the fusion of multifaceted reflections: meta-reflection 'in' action on technical aspects of teaching and learning English online; reflection 'on' action on lessons learnt from the experience; and reflection 'for' action on the application of these lessons to their future practice (Mann & Walsh, 2018; Schön, 1983). This process gradually built the confidence of the international students involved–both those on the MA in ELT and those joining them via telecollaboration from Spain and China–to believe in themselves as 'competent teachers of English', even if they were not L1 English speakers.

The reflections 'in' action are illustrated by the notes taken by participants while carrying out collaborative tasks in Zoom breakout rooms (BoRs) and shared via the 'wall' on the Padlet tool (https://padlet.com/premium/backpack, see Figure 3 below). They enabled everyone to discuss the intercultural dimensions of ELT and explore different country-specific contextual perspectives on it. The reflections 'on' action delved into how online classes could benefit teacher education and how a MOOC/COIL-blend integrated into the curriculum could support this. The students were appreciative of feeling part of a 'global ELT village' where it became evident that the majority of English language teachers are L2 speakers. Finally, 'for' action discussions allowed pre-service and in-service teachers to envisage future actions based on the promotion of creativity, the role of digital tools in classes or the blending of MOOCs into professional development. There were visible ontological (becoming English language teachers in the digital age) and epistemological (learning new literacies, acquiring new technological knowledge relating to the ELT online dimension) shifts resulting from participation in BMELTET 2020.

However, as pointed out before (Wimpenny & Orsini-Jones, 2020) BMELTET can take students out of the comfort zone of the traditional teaching and learning settings they are used to, more so at a time when said zone is also being put to the test by the pandemic. While the encounter with the online Third Space of the telecollaborative project proved to be empowering for some students, others found it troublesome, and this was possibly also in relation to the effects of the epistemological and ontological shifts mentioned above. Before the pandemic, virtual spaces could be used as an alternative to physical reality, but the physical distancing measures imposed by the pandemic rendered virtual space the only real space for connections, thus blurring the borders between virtual, physical, and 'real'. Despite this, all students agreed it was a powerful intercultural knowledge-sharing space. The conclusion illustrates the lessons learnt from this cycle of the project carried out during the challenging time of the pandemic and proposes how we can support international students with a blended learning experience like BMELTET.

Also, previous cycles of BMELTET have ascertained that many international students still perceive technology as a troublesome area of their educational experience, both as learners and as future teachers of English (Orsini-Jones et al., 2020, p. 262). Thus a further aim of the project aimed at lowering anxiety towards technology while fostering the development of teachers' online digital competencies. These competencies for teachers of English language—what Moorhouse et al. (2021) call 'e-Classroom Interactional Competencies' (e-CIC)—are essential to teach English effectively in a pandemic and post-pandemic scenario and include: technological competencies, online environment management competencies and online teacher interactional competencies.

The next section will dwell further into how BMELTET 2020-2021 was implemented and why.

BMELTET: DETAILS

The BMELTET project is rather unique in its integration of COIL with an existing 'off-the-shelf' MOOC because it creates 'ripples' of communities of practice (CoPs) (Wenger, 1998) that is to say:

- The MA classroom for module Theories and Methods of Language Learning and Teaching at Coventry University (originally face-to-face in the first cycles, online synchronous via Zoom during the Covid 19 pandemic) and the cycle discussed here.
- The partner students and courses in Spain (BA TEFL – Teaching English as a Foreign Language) and China (MA TESOL – Teaching English to Speakers of Other Languages).
- The large MOOC community of practice (see Figure 1).
- The 'expert visiting scholars' from Spain, Brazil and China.

A lesson outline (inclusive of some pre-tasks) was provided before each session, based on the relevant MOOC topic, e.g.:

- BMELTET week 1

- ○ 9-9.10. Introductions (each staff and student to say their name and country on camera in Zoom), then staff will explain the task on Padlet: https://coventryunionline.padlet.org/marinaorsini1/ac8zi6bih8ac403h
- ○ 9.10-9.30. Breakout rooms (BoRs) for 20 minutes: what is there to learn (self/MOOC), write on the Padlet and get to know each other.
- ○ 9.30-9.40. Groups to report back (around 2 minutes for each of the 5 groups, each group to choose a spokesperson).
- ○ 9.40-9.55. Brief Socrative quiz on week 1: MOOC revision.
- ○ 9.55-10. Task for next week: prepare task-based language learning section from the MOOC, be prepared to talk about that in the MOOC next week at 9.

Figure 1. Zee map of the participants' location on the MOOC understanding language learning and teaching (FutureLearn/University of Southampton and British Council (2020), courtesy of Kate Borthwick, University of Southampton)

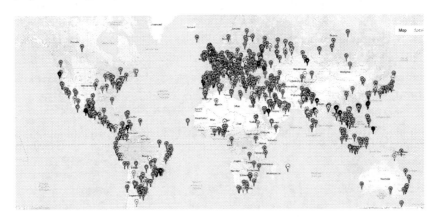

The topics covered mirrored those in the MOOC and in the respective syllabi in each country and were delivered in the courses below by the following lecturers:

- Abraham Cerveró (Spain): Content and Language Integrated Learning (CLIL).
- Wulin Ma (China): Creating and integrating MOOCs for ELT in China.
- Kyria Finardi (Brazil): Global Englishes.
- 'local' UK-based Marina Orsini-Jones – British/Italian: Intercultural Communicative Competence for Global Citizenship.

The assessment in all the courses involved was partially linked to the COIL exchange and required a demonstration of reflection on practice on the lessons learnt from the COIL experience.

METHODOLOGY

The research design was mainly qualitative and 'grounded'. 'Thick data' were collected and safely stored in secure and password-protected areas. Explicit informed consent was sought from all participants. As in the previous cycles of BMELTET, participants' consent forms were coded and all data were treated anonymously.

The 15 students based at Coventry University were mainly international: 3 Chinese, 2 British, 1 Polish, 1 French, 4 Pakistani, 1 South African/Belgian, 1 Cypriot, 2 Romanian. The 25 students from Florida Universitària, Spain were all Spanish except one who was dual nationality Spanish/British. The 9 participants from Sichuan International Studies University were all Chinese.

Participation in BMELTET involved:

- Registration on the FutureLearn MOOC *Understanding Language: Learning and Teaching* (The MOOC opened on 12/10).
- Around 2 hours of engagement per week with the MOOC's set activities for the four weeks of their duration.
- Reflection on individual beliefs on online and blended learning through:
  ○ A pre-BMELTET and a post-BMELTET survey designed with Online Surveys (formerly Bristol Online Survey) consisting of Likert-scale type statements and open-ended questions.
  ○ COIL engagement through Zoom meetings (synchronous task-based discussions) and Padlet tasks.
  ○ COIL engagement through synchronous discussions with the partners through Microsoft Teams/Zoom/Wechat (small group).
  ○ Completion of specific collaborative tasks in small groups by students from the four universities involved.
- Participation in focus group interviews at the end of the project (self-selected participants).

A mixed-method approach was adopted for the data analysis and data were collected via the two surveys and the analysis of the Zoom exchanges and focus groups after ethics clearance was obtained through ethics governance at Coventry University.

'Action Research' (AR) was used to implement the BMELTET cycle and reflect on the data collected. AR is an expression first coined by the social psychologist Kurt Lewin (1946). It is problem-focused, context-specific and future-oriented. It involves a change intervention and a cyclic process in which research, action and evaluation are interlinked. It aims at improvement and involvement and is underpinned by the adoption of a will to embrace transformation and change on a continuous basis.

The AR model utilised here is Kemmis and McTaggart's 'participatory action research' (2005) which was inspired in turn by educational research principles proposed by Argyris and Schön (1974) and Schön (1983). This AR model is seen as a 'classic' in AR literature and is, according to Burns (2010, p. 8), also the best known and most widely adopted because it succinctly summarises all the phases of the action research cycles:

- A problematic issue is identified.
- Change is planned collaboratively to address the issue.
- The change process is implemented: 'acted out'.

- All agents involved in the change process reflect upon its outcomes, both while it is happening and at the end of the first phase of implementation.
- A new cycle starts.

In view of the results from the AR cycle that preceded this one (Orsini-Jones et al., 2020, p. 263), it was agreed that the following changes would be implemented for BMELTET 2020-2021:

- An element of gamification would be added.
- The use of Open Moodle as an asynchronous repository would be discontinued (it proved difficult to access outside the UK).
- Padlet (https://en-gb.padlet.com/) would be used for both synchronous and asynchronous reflections on the project.
- Zoom and its BoRs would be used for synchronous exchanges instead of Skype (N.B. Zoom was not yet available at institutional level at the time of the October 2019-Feb 2020 exchange).
- The project would be linked to summative assessment in each country.

The research questions for the BMELTET project were:

RQ1: Can BMELTET support English language teachers to adopt a holistic approach to the integration of technology into their practice?

RQ2: Can BMELTET promote intercultural awareness in the field of English language teacher education?

RQ3: Can BMELTET support the identification of troublesome areas in English language teacher education with particular reference to critical digital literacy development?

RQ4: Can BMELTET support reflection on practice?

RQ5: Can BMELTET support the integration of international students in an overseas learning setting?

This chapter will focus on RQ5.

Issues, Controversies, Problems: The Pre-Project Survey Results

The very fact that BMELTET was managed and ran successfully despite the various personal circumstances of the MA ELTAL students (some of whom had not managed to reach the UK and were connecting remotely while others were joining while in lock down in the UK) indicates that it managed to support the inclusion of students. This unusual experience was scaffolded by the controlled interactions via Zoom in BoRs with questions that addressed topics covered in the MOOC and in the course lectures. These synchronous exchanges seemed to have provided participants with a sense of a safe environment, a safe intercultural knowledge-sharing Third Space.

Furthermore, gamification elements were included in each class to lower students' anxiety. Kahoot (https://kahoot.com/) and Socrative (https://b.socrative.com/login/student/) were used as quiz tools to check participants' knowledge and learning. Despite the fact that not all participants were familiar with these tools, they found them useful and engaging (even if students at CU preferred Socrative while students from FU and China preferred Kahoot). Staff noticed that the Kahoot and Socrative quizzes increased students' motivation towards the contents explored in the MOOC and during the lectures.

The themes that emerged from the findings are illustrated below with quotes from the participants. These are all recorded *verbatim*, with word stress in bold by the authors, and numbers randomly allocated by the survey tool).

Doubts about the Value of Online Learning

Despite the fact that BMELTET 2020 took place during a pandemic, when many aspects of life had become 'remote', 86% of participants stated that they had not completed an online training course before. This meant that most participants in this cycle of the project were having their first experience with online and blended approaches and admitted in the Pre-Project survey that they were not sure it would be a motivating way of engaging in teacher education. Below, a participant highlights issues that seem to be related to the digital divide:

*Pre_CU_194: I think it is a double-edged way of learning. On one side it is a precious tool that helps to keep learning in those special circumstances. It also **allows to virtually meet and exchange with people from all around the world**. On the other side there are some obstacles. For example depending on the area you can have **some connexion problem that can prevent the proper functioning** of the online learning. Linked to that the fact that some people don't have the same access to internet, a computer makes the system a little bit precarious. Moreover obviously even if the online learning works well it lacks this kind of immediacy that can be necessary, in particular for the teacher.*

There were also positive remarks though:

*Pre_FU_ 665: I think online learning it's **a good way to know other people because of the pandemic**.*

*Pre_FU_659: I think that online **learning is very useful and it is a good opportunity for meeting new people**.*

Oher participants were aware of this kind of learning experience but expressed their lack of enthusiasm for it:

*Pre_ FU_653: It could be more difficult to learn I that way and **it is not as efficient as being in a class**.*

*Pre_CU_886: Online learning is good as it's highly accessible. However, **I prefer face to face learning**.*

Apprehension about Future Online Practice

Another issue that emerged was the anxiety related to the integration of online teaching and learning practices in the participants' future teaching. Interestingly however, this was paired with the willingness to learn more:

*Pre_CU_275: A bit **terrified, but looking forward to it**.*

Pre_CU_328: It is extremely relevant and becoming more so with **the development of technology** *and its increased use in general, especially* **amongst younger generations**.

The majority of students' contributions were in line with the two reported above; nevertheless, some participants held the belief that classroom human interaction is always better than interaction facilitated by technology, as demonstrated below:

Pre_ FU_064: We cannot deny the usefulness of technology but when it comes to learning I do believe **the human factor is essential**.

Pre_FU _664: I think **everything is better with a pencil and a paper** *but to be honest technology has helped us a lot lately.*

In sum, it seemed that the Covid-19 pandemic boosted the reliability of online teaching and the participants' responses suggest that they were aware of this.

Lack of Participation

Another issue that arose is students' lack of contributions to the BMELTET tasks. This had previous been identified in the BMELTET 2019-2020 cycle: some students found it face threatening or even intimidating to take part (Orsini-Jones et al., 2020). In previous cycles, online synchronous discussions had scarcely taken place, as Zoom was not available at that time and class-to-class Skype webinars were utilised. Skype did not offer the opportunity of separating students into BoRs, like Zoom, so the sessions were 'whole group' to 'whole group', and an extra challenge to effective communication consisted in the fact that the Chinese partners struggled to join through Skype. Also, when students presented their collaborative tasks, it was not possible to comment on them via a Padlet, so the Skype experience became very tutor-centred. The tutors involved had hoped that the asynchronous engagement on the dedicated BMELTET Open Moodle discussion threads created for the project (https://openmoodle.coventry.ac.uk/) would support collaborative work, but it did not work effectively. The participants from Spain and China declared in the focus groups that took place at the end of the 2019-2020 cycle of the project that they did not feel confident enough to post in English in Open Moodle.

In the 2020 cycle discussed here, BMELTET was designed so that students would have mostly synchronous interaction in BoRs in each of the four weekly sessions. While the dynamic nature of the interaction on Zoom was positive, it was challenging for lecturers to manage BoRs with members from all three universities because they all needed scaffolding and moderation. For this reason, structured MOOC-based questions were introduced as 'warmers' that entailed group interactions with online and offline support from lecturers when needed. However, lecturers could not be present at all times and some participants did not manage to contribute in their groups due to a variety of factors, such as the language barrier, not having completed the MOOC activities or feeling too shy or overly exposed to inter-act. Having said this, once all participants from Spain and China realised that they were communicating with a majority of L2 speakers of English studying in Britain, their interactional confidence improved.

SOLUTIONS AND RECOMMENDATIONS: THE POST-PROJECT SURVEY RESULTS

The Post-Project surveys illustrate that by the end of the project, 80% of participants found their engagement in BMELTET motivating despite initial negative attitudes towards online learning and teaching, as Figure 2 demonstrates (Post-Project survey that closed on 12/12/2020).

Figure 2. Post-Project participants' feelings on the statement 'Learning about language learning and teaching online can motivate EFL future teachers'

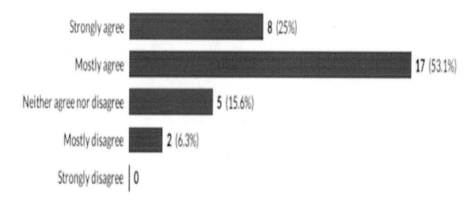

1. *A positive shift in attitude*

It would appear that using a MOOC and collaborating with participants located in three different countries increased students' sense of progress towards understanding the ELT topics covered on their syllabi. The award of a Coventry University COIL certificate and the optional extra certification via FutureLearn supported their motivation towards the project, despite initial doubts:

Post _FU_858: It has been different to what I was used to while studying my degree at university, been **engage in a MOOC with students from other universities around the world has been really interesting and helpful.**

Post _CU_648: I enjoyed the opportunity to acquire the extra certificate which worked as an extrinsic motivational factor. Although self-paced learning can be a double-edged sword, I found that **taking time to discuss the MOOC together during lectures was extremely beneficial to consolidate what we have learnt and to keep us accountable in progression**. *The combination was essential to help me feel that I was getting the most possible experience with the content.*

To sum up, BMELTET participants' initial reservations about online learning had mostly dissipated. The synchronous interaction was highly regarded and considered as a type of face to face communication. Moreover, the self-paced learning on the MOOC was deemed to be a positive experience.

2. *Online teaching: a necessary evil?*

Even though some participants were well aware of the fact that they needed to acquire online teaching skills, they still preferred face to face environments:

Post _CU_ 273: As far as I'm concerned I thought it could be hard for me to get used to online learning and teaching particularly because I was not used to it. **But eventually I get to appreciate it as it allows to connect to more people.** *Nevertheless I think I am still more attracted to face-to-face teaching and learning but I understand and acknowledge the interest of getting to know online learning and teaching.*

3. *Unique affordances of online learning*

Reflection and metareflection (Flavell, 1979) are at the heart of BMELTET which has provided solid ground for 'on' practice considerations and changes in initial beliefs, as seen below:

Post _CU_648: I discovered **many benefits that online classes offer which face-to-face cannot** *(e.g. the opportunity to re-watch lectures, particularly if I forgot what was said later on).*

Moreover, considerations 'for' future practice were also identified:

Post _FU_824: As a teacher, I soon realized **it was very effective and left room for creativity.**

Post _FU_450: We discovered a lot of new resources and ways of communication and I think that it was very positive. Now, **we are able to create and develop and online class and we have more tools than before.**

These statements are reinforced by one of the participants whose views on online education had changed:

Post _CU_648: I thought that online learning was exclusively asynchronous which is something I would struggle with, however, I have **really enjoyed some of the things we have been able to do with online resources during live-online classes which I found myself bringing into face-to-face** *classes when possible.*

Participants also reflected on the impacts of online learning on their personal circumstances:

Post _CU_052: I enjoy online learning as I can organise my learning according to my preferred times and study at my own pace. It **provides opportunities to engage with learners across the world and share experiences.**

Other reflections captured the concept of the safe virtual Third Space:

Post _CU_648: I found that I have become more open to online learning, and have enjoyed many of the benefits and freedom which it has allowed. **I found participating in group activities easier online than in person.**

Post _CU_ 201: I have to say that at the beginning it was a bit uncomfortable because of talking with strange people from different countries and in addition, in a language that it's not your first one. Finally **the experience became great and in my opinion successful as well**, *so I am happy with the experience.*

These findings suggest that BoRs seem to be a reliable solution for 'online face to face interaction'. The possibility of international students interacting with their peers in these rooms with scaffolding mediation by lecturers is viewed as an asset of BMELTET.

One of the discussion strategies in BMELTET 2020-2021 was the use of Padlets as a live 'virtual wall' (see Figure 3 below). After discussing a topic in groups, students were asked to post a summary of what had been said, or simply their own individual reflections. The Padlets became a way to support participants' meta-reflections on context-specific issues that triggered different ways of putting ELT approaches into action. The discussion and synthesis on the potential applications of Content and Language Integrated Learning (CLIL) approaches can be seen in Figure 3.

Figure 3. Screenshot of participants' reflections on CLIL on Padlet

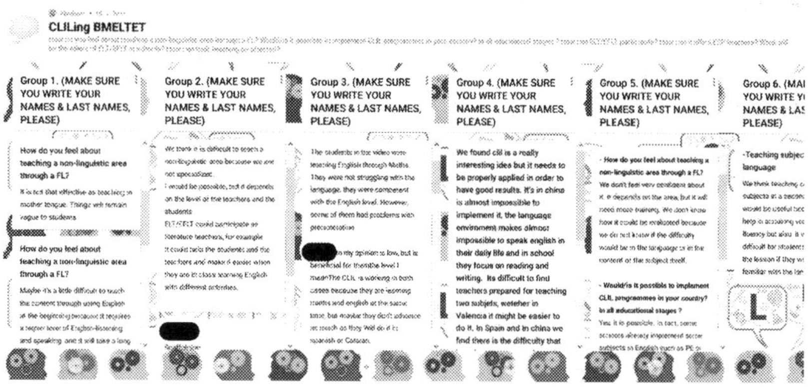

4. A truly 'glocal' experience

As reported by some of the participants, BMELTET contributed to the expansion of their ideas about teaching. It seemed to accentuate the use of English in real communication and to provide wider insights on their conceptualization of other worldviews.

Post _CU_ 824: As a student, I could have never expected expanding my knowledge on online learning this much. **Thanks to the BMELTET we engaged with other students around the world and we got to know more English and more about other cultures.**

The response below may well summarise the 'glocality' that BMELTET aimed to achieve:

Post _CU_162: I came to enjoy online learning as much as I liked the face-to-face. The opportunity of **synchronous learning with students and teachers from China and Spain was inspiring.**

Finally, the value of intercultural interaction was recognised:

Post _CU_ 052: I think it **provided a great opportunity particularly to develop intercultural communication competence***. It was a great experience.*

FUTURE RESEARCH DIRECTIONS

It would appear from the results gathered that the online dimension is still causing some initial discomfort despite the fact that we have been forced into online teaching and/or hybrid teaching by a pandemic for a considerable number of months. It is undeniable that the online space can feel alienating.

The future direction of research is to investigate further how to support international students in English language teacher education with interacting in the online Third Space of COIL in general and in BoRs in particular, both in terms of current learning and future teaching practice. A deeper exploration of the three e-Classroom Interactional Competencies identified by Moorhouse et al. (2021) is needed, namely: technological competencies; online environment management competencies and online teacher interactional competencies. A worthwhile addition to these competencies is the further development of the intercultural competencies that can be gained from a project like BMELTET. It is also important to note that strategies need to be employed to manage the expectations of sceptical participants who feel suspicious of this 'unknown' Third space.

In addition to this, at a time in which many overseas students could not reach the UK due to the pandemic, the theme of digital poverty emerged. Some students did not appear to have a laptop and/or a robust Internet connection in their country of residence. This affected their resilience and their ability to engage fully with the project. Therefore an additional future direction for research could be to explore how to foster resilience and build on international students' psychological capital. This is 'an individual's positive psychological state of development' that is characterised by:

- Self-efficacy: having confidence to take on and put in the necessary effort to succeed at challenging tasks.
- Optimism: making a positive attribution about succeeding now and in the future.
- Hope: persevering toward goals and, when necessary, redirecting paths to goals in order to succeed.
- Resilience: when beset by problems and adversity, sustaining and bouncing back and even beyond to attain success (Luthans et al., 2007, p. 3).

CONCLUSION

It would appear that BMELTET contributed to lowering the majority of its participants' anxiety about online learning and facilitated a 'glocal' intercultural dialogue in a safe Third Space where both local and global ELT issues were discussed and reflected upon. The Third Space is a source of inspiration for students' future EFL teaching practice and an asset for their future continuous professional development actions. Reflection 'in' action, 'on' action and 'for' action took place here, as well as discussions on the decolonisation of ELT. By the end of the project, there appeared to be less diffidence towards online learning and teaching than that encountered in previous cycles of BMELTET, possibly because the pandemic has 'normalised' (Bax, 2018) technology use and Zoom has made interaction more dynamic.

The live Zoom interactions were conducive to healthy discussions on who can or should be a teacher of English language and the Global North/South dialogue made participants aware of the limitation of certain approaches in relation to their learning and teaching contexts. However, some participants still felt uneasy about their online presence and their level of digital literacy; their lack of engagement was made more visible in BoRs by their poignant 'black mute box' on screen. In view of the discomfort that some international students still appeared to feel in the online COIL Third Space, despite the overall positive results, more research needs to be carried out on how to support international students in teacher education to become resilient online during and after a pandemic.

ACKNOWLEDGMENT

We would like to thank all the colleagues and students who participated in this project, and our colleagues Prof Bin Zou and Prof Wulin Ma in China in particular.

Abraham Cerveró-Carrascosa acknowledges Florida Universitària for including him in its Research Support Scheme (2021-2022).

Kyria Rebeca Finardi wishes to also acknowledge financial help in the form of the Productivity Scholarship by Cnpq-Bolsa de Produtividade em Pesquisa (PQ).

Some of the material included here was published as part of the conference proceedings for the International Teaching Online Symposium in Windsor, Ontario (Canada) 17-18 June 2021 and some descriptions reflect those reported in Wimpenny and Orsini-Jones (2020).

REFERENCES

Argyris, M., & Schön, D. (1974). *Theory in practice. Increasing professional effectiveness*. Jossey-Bass.

Bhabha, H. K. (2004). *The location of culture*. Routledge.

Bhabha, H. K., & Rutherford, J. (2006). Third space. *Multitudes*, *26*(3), 95–107. doi:10.3917/mult.026.0095

Bax, S. (2018). MOOCs as a new technology: approaches to normalising the MOOC experience for our learners. In M. Orsini-Jones & S. Smith (Eds.), Flipping the blend through MOOCs, MALL and OIL – new directions in CALL (pp. 9-16). Research-publishing.net. doi:10.14705/rpnet.2018.23.785

Burns, A. (2010). *Doing action research in English Language Teaching: A guide for practitioners*. Routledge.

Colpaert, J. (2020). Editorial position paper: How virtual is your research? *Computer Assisted Language Learning*, *33*(7), 653–664. doi:10.1080/09588221.2020.1824059

De Lima-Guedes, K. K. (2020). Integrating MOOCs into traditional UK higher education: Lessons learnt from MOOC-blend practitioners. In K. Borthwick & A. Plutino (Eds.), Education 4.0 revolution: Transformative approaches to language teaching and learning, assessment and campus design (pp. 29-36). Research-publishing.net. doi:10.14705/rpnet.2020.42.1084

Dooly, M., & Vinagre, M. (2021). Research into practice: Virtual exchange in language teaching and learning. *Language Teaching*, 1–15. doi:10.1017/S0261444821000069

Finardi, K. R. (2014). The slaughter of Kachru's five sacred cows in Brazil: Affordances of the use of English as an international language. *Studies in English Language Teaching*, 2(4), 401–411. doi:10.22158elt.v2n4p401

Finardi, K. R. (2019). *English in the South*. Editora da Universidade Estadual de Londrina.

Flavell, J. H. (1979). Metacognition and cognitive monitoring: A new area of cognitive–developmental inquiry. *The American Psychologist*, 34(10), 906–911. doi:10.1037/0003-066X.34.10.906

FutureLearn. (2020). *Understanding language: Learning and teaching*. University of Southampton & British Council. https://www.futurelearn.com/courses/understanding-language

Gearing, L. (2015). *Coventry University Group education strategy 2015-2021*. Coventry University Higher Education Corporation.

Guimarães, F. F., & Finardi, K. R. (2021). Global citizenship education (GCE) in internationalization: COIL as alternative Thirdspace. *Globalisation, Societies and Education*, 19(5), 641–657. doi:10.1080/14767724.2021.1875808

Gutiérrez, B. F., Glimäng, M. R., O'Dowd, R., & Sauro, S. (2021). *Mentoring handbook for virtual exchange teachers. Strategies to help students achieve successful synchronous and asynchronous online intercultural communication*. Stevens Initiative. https://www.stevensinitiative.org/resource/mentoring-handbook-for-virtual-exchange-teachers/

Helm, F. (2013). A dialogic model for telecollaboration. *Bellaterra Journal of Teaching & Learning Language & Literature*, 6(2), 28–48. doi:10.5565/rev/jtl3.522

Kemmis, S., & McTaggart, R. (2005). Participatory action research: Communicative action and the public sphere. In N. Denzin & Y. Lincoln (Eds.), Handbook of qualitative research. Sage.

Kumaravadivelu, B. (2006). Dangerous liaison, globalization, empire and TESOL. In J. Edge (Ed.), *Relocating TESOL in an age of empire* (pp. 1–26). Palgrave Macmillan.

Ladson-Billings, G. (2021). I'm here for the hard re-set: Post pandemic pedagogy to preserve our culture. *Equity & Excellence in Education*, 54(1), 68–78. doi:10.1080/10665684.2020.1863883

Lewin, K. (1946). Action research and minority problems. *The Journal of Social Issues*, 2(4), 34–46. doi:10.1111/j.1540-4560.1946.tb02295.x

Lewis, T., & O'Dowd, R. (2016). *Online intercultural exchange*. Routledge.

Luthans, F., Youssef, C. M., & Avolio, B. J. (2007). *Psychological capital: Developing the human competitive edge*. Oxford University Press.

Macedo, D. (2019). Rupturing the yoke of colonialism in foreign language education: An introduction. In D. Macedo (Ed.), *Decolonizing foreign language education: The misteaching of English and other colonial languages* (pp. 1–49). Routledge. doi:10.4324/9780429453113-1

Mann, S., & Walsh, S. (2017). *Reflective practice in English language teaching: Research-based principles and practices.* Routledge. doi:10.4324/9781315733395

Moorhouse, B. L., Li, Y., & Walsh, S. (2021). E-classroom interactional competencies: Mediating and assisting language learning during synchronous online lessons. *RELC Journal.* Advance online publication. doi:10.1177/0033688220985274

O'Brien, R. (2018). *COIL at Coventry University.* Coventry University Higher Education Corporation.

O'Dowd, R. (2020). A transnational model of virtual exchange for global citizenship education. *Language Teaching, 53*(4), 477–490. doi:10.1017/S0261444819000077

O'Dowd, R. (2021). Virtual exchange: Moving forward into the next decade. *Computer Assisted Language Learning, 34*(3), 209–224. doi:10.1080/09588221.2021.1902201

O'Dowd, R., & Dooly, M. (2021). Exploring teachers' professional development through participation in virtual exchange. *ReCALL, 34*(1), 21–36. doi:10.1017/S0958344021000215

Orsini-Jones, M., & Cerveró-Carrascosa, A. (2019). BMELTET – Blending MOOCs into English language teacher education with telecollaboration. In A. Plutino, K. Borthwick & E. Corradini (Eds.), New educational landscapes: Innovative perspectives in language learning and technology (pp. 47-53). Research-publishing.net. doi:10.14705/rpnet.2019.36.955

Orsini-Jones, M., Cerveró-Carrascosa, A., & Zou, B. (2020). The trouble with telecollaboration in BMELTET. In K. Frederiksen, S. Larsen, L. Bradley & S. Thouësny (Eds.), CALL for widening participation: Short papers from EUROCALL 2020 (pp. 259-265). Research-publishing.net. doi:10.14705/rpnet.2020.48.1198

Orsini-Jones, M., Conde, B., Borthwick, K., Zou, B., & Ma, W. (2018). *BMELTT: Blending MOOCs for English language teacher training.* ELT Research Papers 18.02, British Council.

Orsini-Jones, M., & Lee, F. (2018). *Intercultural communicative competence for global citizenship: Identifying rules of engagement in telecollaboration.* Palgrave MacMillan. doi:10.1057/978-1-137-58103-7

Orsini-Jones, M., Wang, X., & Zhao, J. (2015). Study skills for Masters' level 'through the looking glass' of Chinese students on the MA in English language teaching at Coventry University. Case study. In P. Kneale (Ed.), *Masters level teaching, learning and assessment: Issues in design and delivery* (pp. 97–100). Palgrave MacMillan.

Research Centre for Global Learning (GLEA). (n.d.). *Focus of our research.* Coventry University. https://www.coventry.ac.uk/research/areas-of-research/global-learning/global-learning-education-without-boundaries/

Robertson, R. (1995). Glocalization: Time-space and homogeneity-heterogenity. In M. Featherstone, S. Lash, & R. Robertson (Eds.), *Global Modernities* (pp. 25–44). Sage. doi:10.4135/9781446250563.n2

Rubdy, R. (2015). Unequal Englishes, the native speaker, and decolonization in TESOL. In R. Tupas (Ed.), *Unequal Englishes* (pp. 42–58). Palgrave Macmillan. doi:10.1057/9781137461223_3

Sadler, R., & Dooly, M. (2016). Twelve years of telecollaboration: What we have learnt. *ELT Journal*, *70*(4), 401–413. doi:10.1093/elt/ccw041

Salomão, A. C. B. (2011). The education of teacher educators: Perspectives of collaboration between undergraduate and graduate students in the Project Teletandem Brazil. *Revista Brasileira de Lingüística Aplicada*, *11*, 653–678.

Sandeen, C. (2013). Integrating MOOCs into traditional higher education: The emerging "MOOC 3.0" era. *Change: The Magazine of Higher Learning*, *45*(6), 34–39. doi:10.1080/00091383.2013.842103

Schön, D. (1983). *The reflective practitioner: How practitioners think in practice*. Basic books.

Smith, C., Zhou, G., Potter, M., & Wang, D. (2019). Connecting best practices for teaching linguistically and culturally diverse international students with international student satisfaction and student perceptions of student learning. *Advances in Global Education and Research*, *3*, 252–265.

Telles, J. A. (2015). Learning foreign languages in teletandem: Resources and strategies. *Documentação de Estudos em Lingüística Teórica e Aplicada*, *31*(3), 603–632. doi:10.1590/0102-4450226475643730772

Wenger, E. (1998). *Communities of practice: learning, meaning, and identity*. Cambridge University Press. doi:10.1017/CBO9780511803932

Wimpenny, K., & Orsini-Jones, M. (2020). Innovation in collaborative online international learning: A holistic blend. In D. Burgos (Ed.), Radical Solutions in eLearning (pp. 1-25). Springer. doi:10.1007/978-981-15-4952-6_1

ADDITIONAL READING

De Wit, H. (2019). Internationalization in higher education, a critical review. *Simon Fraser University Educational Review*, *12*(3), 9–17. doi:10.21810fuer.v12i3.1036

De Wit, H. (2020). Internationalization of higher education: The need for a more ethical and qualitative approach. *Journal of International Students*, *10*(1), i–iv. doi:10.32674/jis.v10i1.1893

De Wit, H., Hunter, F., Howard, L., & Egron-Polak, E. (2015). *Internationalisation of higher education*. European Parliament.

Finardi, K. R., & Ortiz, R. A. (2015). Globalization, internationalization and education: What is the connection? *International E-Journal of Advances in Education*, *1*(1), 18–25. doi:10.18768/ijaedu.16488

Guimarães, F. F., Mendes, A. R. M., Rodrigues, L. M., Paiva, R. S. dos S., & Finardi, K. R. (2019). Internationalization at home, COIL and intercomprehension: For more inclusive activities in the global South. *Simon Fraser University Educational Review*, *12*(3), 90–109. doi:10.21810fuer.v12i3.1019

Li, Y., Zhang, M., Bonk, C. J., & Guo, N. (2015). Integrating MOOC and flipped classroom practice in a traditional undergraduate course: Students' experience and perceptions. *International Journal of Emerging Technologies in Learning., 10*(6), 4–10. doi:10.3991/ijet.v10i6.4708

Lloyd, E., Cerveró-Carrascosa, A., & Green, C. (2018). A role-reversal model of telecollaborative practice: the student-driven and student-managed FloCo. In M. Orsini-Jones & S. Smith. (Eds.), Flipping the blend through MOOCs, MALL and OIL – new directions in CALL (pp. 51-58). Research-publishing. net. doi:10.14705/rpnet.2018.23.790

Mann, S., & Walsh, S. (2017). *Reflective practice in English language teaching: Research-based principles and practices*. Routledge. doi:10.4324/9781315733395

Orsini-Jones, M., Cerveró-Carrascosa, A., & Finardi, K. (2021). *Digital critical literacy development and intercultural awareness raising 'in' action, 'on' action and 'for' action in ELT*. International teaching online symposium. https://pure.coventry.ac.uk/admin/files/44675476/Digital_critical_literacy_development_and_intercultural_awareness.pdf

KEY TERMS AND DEFINITIONS

Blended Learning: This definition is becoming more flexible. It is used to indicate a mix of face-to-face and online learning experiences, but post COVID-19 pandemic it is not easy to define a synchronous live session, so the blend can now include various types of online experiences now and might not include a face-to-face element.

BoRs: Breakout rooms are virtual seminar rooms where students/participants can carry out tasks in smaller groups while on Zoom.

Collaborative Online International Learning (COIL): Online collaboration between students and staff in different geographical locations/countries in the world to discuss common topics of interest through an intercultural lens.

CoPs: Communities of practice as groups of people willing to knowledge-share for a collective reflection on how to improve learning through practice and situated learning. CoPs are underpinned by a social-collaborative learning model.

E-CIC: Electronic Classroom Interactional Competencies are the competencies teachers in general, and English Language Teachers in particular, need to develop to become competent in the synchronous online learning and teaching environment.

EFL: English as a Foreign Language.

ELT: English Language Teaching.

MOOC: Massive Open Online Course. These are freely available for a certain period of time worldwide (some require payment from the moment one joins).

Telecollaboration: This term is associated with language learning and teaching carried out online and at a distance and, in the context of this chapter, it is used interchangeably with COIL and VE.

TESOL: Teaching English to Speakers of Other Languages.

Third Space: A fertile ground for intercultural and decolonised encounters in Higher Education.

VE: Virtual Exchange.

Chapter 17

Perceived Learning Effectiveness and Student Satisfaction:
Lessons Learned From an Online Multinational Intensive Program

Alexandre Duarte

 https://orcid.org/0000-0002-2665-864X

Centro de Estudos Comunicação e Sociedade, Universidade do Minho, Portugal

Kirstie Riedl

FH Wien, Austria

ABSTRACT

In 2020, the COVID-19 pandemic turned the world upside down and forced a redesign of the work models of most organizations, including educational institutions that urgently needed to adapt their teaching practices. This chapter reports the CBBC project, an event organized by six European universities with the objective to solve a real business challenge, in international teams, via a 360° communication campaign, analyzing the student's satisfaction and discusses it in light of a unique multi-cultural, online project. The findings contribute to support the validity of the online assessment model and some insights can help education managers and marketing academics to better understand the students learning percep-tions in a multi-cultural/multi-national online environment. Also, as proposed by Stallings, it is of utmost importance to identify the aspects that students feel are important in their online learning environment, so the conclusions will enhance the knowledge about how educational tools can be improved to increase overall student satisfaction.

DOI: 10.4018/978-1-7998-8921-2.ch017

INTRODUCTION

In March 2020, the Covid-19 pandemic turned the world upside down and forced a redesign of the forms of activity and work models of most organizations. Educational institutions were not immune to this wave of change and, all over the globe, urgently needed to adapt their teaching practices, for which most were not prepared (Chakraborty et al., 2020; Bahasoan et al., 2020). According to UNESCO (2020), due to the pandemic more than 1.5 billion students in all levels of education had their classes suspended or reconfigured, which represents more than 90% of all students world-wide. Although HEI (Higher Education Institutions) have recently "embraced the internet as an important vehicle for delivering courses and programs to a wide array of audiences" (Peltier et al., 2007, p. 140), in reality this recent global event has taken this trend to another level. Bachelor and Master degrees, Doctoral programs, Postgraduate courses, intensive programs, in fact all the academic programs had to urgently reorganize themselves in order to adapt to this new situation, fulfil their purpose and adapt to the students' needs during the lockdown.

This was also the case for the Intensive Program CBBC (Cross Border Brand Communications), an annual event organized by six European Universities that brings together students from each country named by the institutions, tutored by lecturers. Its objective is to solve a real communication challenge, via a creative 360° communication campaign, in multidisciplinary and international teams that compete against each other. This program, detailed in Duarte and Riedl (2021), was just one, amongst many others that needed to change from a face-to-face to online format, in a short period of 2 months. This chapter reports on a small-scale survey carried out after the project, which evaluated student satisfaction and discusses this in light of the unique multicultural, online project and proposes elements, which require more due consideration on the part of instructors and course designers to ensure student satisfaction and the fulfillment of learning objectives.

MULTIFACETED DIFFERENCES

This new "knowledge economy", as Domingues and Araújo (2010) coin it, requires us to reflect on the importance of developing competencies in order to be at the level of acquiring skills on a global scale. As a consequence of globalization students are required to have mastered global competences and international multicultural skills over and above traditional academic expectations. Briguglio (2007) suggests current students must acquire, in addition to the curricular contents, other transversal skills, of which the internationalization of the curriculum is highlighted as a critical success factor for new future professionals. To many scholars, education is not understood as an isolated area, but as a permanent process of building bridges between schools and the globalized universe that characterizes the current reality, where the internationalization of education is now an irreversible phenomenon and the demand for education across borders is a perfectly common fact (Duarte, 2013).

Universities play a key role in nurturing these multicultural skills[1] and this is often manifested in the universities' internationalization efforts and strategies, which as Deardorff (2006) points out, should lead to more inter-culturally competent students. Research has shown that multicultural competent persons display superior job performance and have a positive impact on their co-workers (Leung, Ang & Tan, 2014). University internationalization is defined as "the intentional process of integrating an international, intercultural or global dimension into the purpose, functions and delivery of post-secondary education, in order to enhance the quality of education and research for all students and staff and to make a meaningful contribution to society" (Wit 2020). It is mostly implemented across two pillars, through staff and student mobility on the one hand and internationalization at home which involves weaving international aspects into the curriculum for local students who may not be able to go abroad, which is where such projects like the online CBBC are promoted and supported.

The nature of the CBBC project is of difference – difference in subject, language, culture, and format and therein lies the unique opportunity for a truly enriching learning experience. However, this does not come without considerable challenges, and it is the responsibility of the tutors to navigate these, particularly when the stakes are high and the students are tasked with solving a real client problem.

PEDAGOGIC PRACTICES

As the classic industrialist models of teaching and learning, presented in linear ways, that emphasize an assembly of facts to be remembered on tests are no longer enough to provide the skills that young graduates will need in the context of globalization and creative economies (Saebø et al., 2007), a new standard of learning environment is absolutely necessary. Although discipline-specific facts are important, even more fundamental is to know how to think critically and creatively to solve problems, collaborate in teams, use rhetoric to aptly construct an argument, and enact social-emotional skills (Vanada, 2016).

Specifically in one area of social sciences, business education, there has been a shift in pedagogic practices due to the changes in the global and digital economy and the burgeoning student population. An increasingly popular pedagogic practice in this discipline is the so-called "studio" format, which helps students to learn from their own experiences rather than from formal frontal teaching. This learning environment is designed so that students can actively engage in creative work under the guidance of an instructor that use a learner-centered approach rather than a teacher-centered approach (Sawyer, 2017). In these studio classes, the instructor acts not as an authority figure who presents information as the expert, but rather as a guide and facilitator, and where both instructors and students mutually determine the flow of the session. A core element of this approach is the environment that instructors create where they and students are peers and attempt to avoid the traditional classroom dynamic where the teacher is a power figure (Salazar, 2013). In these classes, students play an important role in the learning system, since the teacher role shifts to becoming a co-learner and guide, and responsibility for learning is placed in the hands of the students who are active, not passive, participants in the construction of their own knowledge along the process (Weimer, 2002, as cited in Vanada, 2016). Particularly in business education, working on real-life problems with real clients has become crucial for students to be exposed to real business issues. Not only do they learn practical skills but having worked on such projects is key for their curriculum vitae and future employment.

Although all the students in the CBBC project come from the social sciences field, each of the participating universities practice different techniques in teaching, coaching and in the extent and use of studio classes. This is also due to the diverse participation of different types of universities in the CBBC project. Universities of Applied Sciences (UAS) are predominantly European tertiary education institutions that have their roots in the 1980s and flourished due to restructuring of vocational institutions. They are positioned differently to Research Universities (RUs) and are termed differently locally: for example, in German speaking countries they are referred to as *Fachhochschulen* (FHs), in Finland *Ammattikorkeakoulus*, in Portugal, *Politécnicos* and in Dutch speaking countries *Hogescholen*. UASs are generally smaller, more numerous and more regional than RUs (Lepori & Kyvik, 2010, p. 298).

The crucial differentiating factors to RUs are the vocational character and the focus on teaching rather research, although this divide is becoming increasingly blurred with UASs in recent times engaging more frequently with "use-inspired" research (Lepori & Kyvik, 2010, p. 296).

MULTICULTURAL TEACHING

A review of relevant and current literature confirms that many researchers have attempted to explain and define multicultural education. Most scholars agree that it encompasses an intellectual concept whereby all students should enjoy the same opportunities with no racial, ethnic, social class, or gender discrimination (e.g. Banks, 2001a, 2001b; Mwonga, 2005). It is also considered a reformist movement and process, aiming to improve and sustain democracy and liberal, fair, and egalitarian social structure (Kim, 2011; Polat, 2009).

Professionals in all fields of business are increasingly required to work in multicultural environments and teaching these multicultural skills are now part of the "core business of universities" (McAllister et al., 2006, p. 367). Working in multicultural teams can be challenging as Turner (2009, p. 248) reports issues include unequal language skills, leadership ambiguity, communication issues, conflict, unequal commitment to time-keeping, differing expectations and over-talking. Notwithstanding this, it has also been shown that heterogeneous teams can be more creative in solving problems and come up with innovative solutions (Distefano & Maznevski, 2000). For universities to be competitive they need to equip students with multicultural skills and this is particularly the case in the field of business education. As designers of meaningful experiences and student engagement (Vanada, 2016), instructors naturally have a pivotal role in facilitating this multicultural education. Gehrke and Abermann (2016, p. 2) propose that "teachers must have a defined level of intercultural competence to integrate a variety of learning, communication and conflict styles" and they must navigate challenges in the multicultural classroom to achieve the learning outcomes with suitable course design and implementation. This echoes Gay´s (2013) notion of culturally responsive teaching which is defined as "using the cultural knowledge, prior experiences, frames of reference, and performance styles of ethnically diverse students to make learning encounters more relevant to and effective for them" (Gay, 2013, pp. 49-50). Sharma (2011, p. 54) suggests that effective teaching in a multicultural classroom not only requires cultural sensitivity strategies but also the creation of equal opportunities for academic success and personal development. The onus on the success therefore also lies with the instructor´s perceptions and beliefs.

The challenges in the multicultural classroom are compounded as literacy and learning through the medium of another language is indisputably different from doing that in the mother tongue. Mostly in these settings, as in the CBBC, English is used as a Lingua Franca (ELF[2]), and there is extant research in the applied linguistic community on learning in English as a Medium Instruction (EMI).

As learning through the medium of English is often a new phenomenon for university students, it follows that this takes some time for these skills to develop. Insights from a study in Hong-Kong indicate that first year students have more issues in the EMI classroom, which improve with time due to diligence, motivation and effective learning strategies (Evans & Morrison, 2011). Other researchers investigating students' experience of learning in English have found that they display some comprehension problems, participate less in class and find the associated workload harder to manage (e.g. Knapp, 2011; Tatzl, 2011). Researchers have also endeavoured to see if student learning outcomes in EMI classes are equivalent to the mother tongue, but mostly the results have been inconclusive with some researchers pointing to inferior learning outcomes (e.g. Sert, 2008; Pulcini & Campagna, 2015; Arkin & Osam, 2015) whereas some have shown that students performed even better (e.g. del Campo et al., 2015; Dafouz & Camacho-Miñano, 2016). As such, success does not only depend on student maturity, but the learning experience in EMI and linguistic competence has to be taken into consideration when reviewing such research, as well as the delivery of content by the instructors. Klassen (2001) looked into the relationship between effective lecturing behaviour and students´ learning results and found that "student´s learning experiences do not only depend on their listening comprehension capacities, but also depends on their experiences of the lecture situation and, in particular, on the lecturing behaviour of the lecturer" (Klassen, 2001, p. 144).

In conclusion, students in multicultural teams not only deal with the differences in educational culture but using ELF with different degrees of proficiency considerably affects the interactivity and communication in such international projects. Additionally, students in this CBBC project are from different courses (some more strategic, some more focused in marketing, others in media and finally, some with a more creative focus), and are in different semesters in their degree program, so the extent of their own maturity skills are at different stages of development.

ONLINE LEARNING

From an organizational point of view, online learning has various advantages, such as the low cost, the convenience and flexibility, the unlimited number of students at the same time, the opportunity to adapt fast to the latest developments, the use of interactive tools, and the possibility to be accessed from anywhere and anytime, among others. But what about the student's perspective? Are they really satisfied with this format? Do they feel it as an advantage comparing to face-to-face classes?

There have been many investigations into student satisfaction with online learning with inconclusive results about whether students prefer online or face-to-face (e.g. Allen & Seaman, 2015; Aguilera-Hermida, 2020) and the effectiveness of online learning compared to face-to-face (e.g. Markova et al., 2017; Tseng & Walsh, 2016). Scholars have also looked into teaching qualities required in the online format. The review by Marks et al. (2005) found that instructor-student interaction is the most important factor, twice that of student-student interaction, and that some student-content interaction is significantly related to perceived learning. This echoes the findings from Woo and Reeves (2007), who also summarize that "meaningful interaction" is key. Similarly, Shea et al. (2006) name "teaching presence" as crucial. Other authors who have studied the perceived learning effectiveness and students' satisfaction in an online environment (e.g. Peltier et al., 2003; Marks et al., 2005; Chyung & Vachon, 2005; Bahasoan et al., 2020; Chakraborty et al., 2020) point to some consensual conclusions: the interaction among students and between students and instructors, the course content and pedagogical tools used to deliver it, and the communication conditions are among the most cited factors.

Recent studies investigating learning outcomes in the enforced online learning due to the Covid-19 pandemic have indicated that outcomes are varied with some pointing to similar student satisfaction (e.g. Jia et al., 2020). However, an investigation by Chakraborty et al. (2020) looking into undergraduate student perceptions of online learning at an Indian university showed that 65.9% of the students felt that they learn better in physical classrooms than through online education, and 75.1% felt that they can interact better with professors in a physical classroom, echoing Aguilera-Hermida (2020) who reported also that students prefer face-to-face interaction with professors. Others showed declines in learning (e.g.

Orlov et al., 2021; Pezenka et al., 2020) whereas the findings of Bahasoan et al. (2020) concluded that the online learning system carried out during the COVID-19 pandemic was effective but inefficient. The review of the 2020 edition of the CBBC by Duarte and Riedl (2021) indicated that although the learning outcomes in the online format were almost the same, the student experience was inferior to face-to-face interaction.

Furthermore, the capacity to apply ideas creatively in new contexts, requires that learners have opportunities to actively develop their own representations of information to convert it to a usable form (DeHaan, 2009) and this is one of the reasons why social interactions, networking, partying, or simply enjoying each other's company is fundamental in the creative process among young people. This is naturally very difficult in the online format. The specific nature of CBBC, i.e. the studio-like classes and its practical nature with the anticipated creative output, the support of the instructors as coaches instead of content lecturers meant that this was a considerable challenge online. This, coupled with the fact that the students work intensively for one week with new peers from other countries, other cultures, who speak different languages, meant the transition to an online format was even more formidable.

McWilliam and Dawson (2008) remind us that all university students should be engaged in work that is less focused on solving routine problems and more focused on interactivity, navigation skills, creating relationships, coping with new challenges and synthesis of 'overview' scenarios for the purpose of adding a competitive business advantage. It is for this reason that the CBBC project is organized so that the students are placed into multidisciplinary and multicultural teams. This way, every student has the possibility to work with different skills, personalities, culture, language and ways of thinking, enhancing their own capacities, while each one contributes to the development of the creative outcome from their own domain as well as helping one another mutually. This learning approach is aligned with the most recent research, which has found that such pedagogies are more effective at fostering better learning outcomes (Nathan & Sawyer, 2014).

DATA SET AND METHODOLOGY

The 2021 CBBC was meant to take place in The Netherlands, hosted by Breda University of Applied Sciences, however a decision was made in January 2021 to host it online due to the continuing Covid-19 pandemic and the travel restrictions this brought.

Students from European universities in Lisbon (Portugal), Paris (France), Breda (Netherlands), Antwerp (Belgium), Vienna (Austria) and Espoo (Finland) were nominated and participated. Of those, four are universities of applied sciences and two are research universities. The students were from the 4th and 6th semester of their studies. It was held mid-May and students were informed to make sure they had permission from their study program to attend the full week.

Based on the literature review, an investigation was undertaken to assess the perceived effectiveness of learning outcomes from the multicultural students in this new online version of this project. After having participated in the CBBC in person for several years and online once, the coaches were particular mindful of the importance of capturing feedback and curious about student perceptions in this challenging environment.

The authors adapted the "online education model" (see figure 01), proposed by Peltier et al. (2003, p. 264) to create an online survey. This identifies six dimensions to assess overall perceived learning ef-

Figure 1. Online education model, Peltier et al. (2003, p. 264)

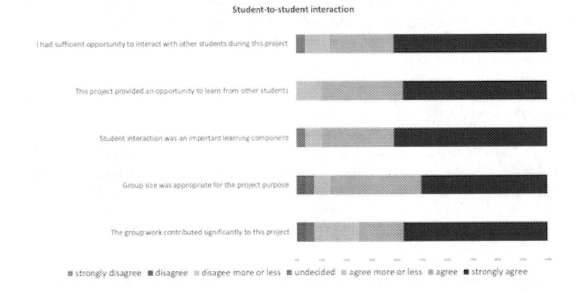

fectiveness: 1) student-to-student interactions; 2) student-to-instructor interactions; 3) instructor support and mentoring; 4) information delivery technology; 5) course content; and 6) course structure.

As the dimension "information delivery technology" did not apply, as Microsoft Teams software was used throughout the project, this item was eliminated. A 7-point Likert scale was used to grade each question from strongly disagree to strongly agree and some minor adaptations were made to fit and adjust to this multidisciplinary and international project (e.g. the sentence "I've interacted with *my* professor" was changed to "I've interacted with *the* professors"; "this *course* included applied learning" was changed to "this *project* included applied learning" and "existing *classroom technology* was used effectively" to "*Microsoft Teams software* was used effectively"). Students were invited to add some general reflection on their experience in the open questions, which also enriched the findings. One week after the second online CBBC edition in 2021, a link with this online survey was emailed to all the participant students. Of the 36 students that participated in the 2021 edition of the CBBC, 28 students responded, with at least 4 from each institution. At the same time, a zoom meeting with all the instructors took place to discuss the pros and cons of the whole project.

RESULTS

Divided in 5 major areas, each dimension was evaluated with several statements inspired by the Peltier et al. (2003) *online education model*, and two additional areas were included to evaluate both the perceived effectiveness of the educational experience and the of the learning outcomes. The results are presented here and discussed in the next section.

In the dimension *Support and Mentoring,* 12 statements were offered, with the large majority of the participants answering with "agree" or "strongly agree" to most of the items (figure 02). 64.3% of the participants agreed and strongly agreed that the tutors played an important role in facilitating learning during the project, and 67.8% agreed and strongly agreed that the tutors helped them to apply the theory to solve problems.

When asked if the tutors had explained difficult content clearly, 78.6% agreed or strongly agreed while 71.5% agreed or strongly agreed that tutors had maintained rapport with the group. Almost half of the students (42.9%) agreed that the tutors contributed to the discussions, with 28.9% strongly agreeing and 25% more or less agreeing. 3 out of 4 participants reported an agreement or strong agreement when asked if tutors were actively helpful when students needed it. There were a few slightly critical voices with 64.3% agreeing or strongly agreeing that tutors provided sufficient feedback in every step of the project.

When asked if the tutors had motivated the students to do their best, 60.7% agreed or strongly agreed while 28.6% agreed more or less. Regarding the question as to whether the tutors identified major points in the project 42.9% agreed and 14.3% strongly agreed. Almost all respondents (92.9%) agreed or strongly agreed that they had interacted with the tutors, 82.1% agreed or strongly agreed that tutors empathized relationships between and among topics and finally, 67.9% agreed or strongly agreed that many methods were used to involve students in the learning process.

Figure 2. Instructors support and mentoring

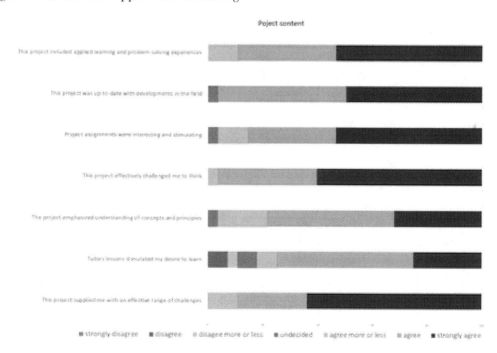

Regarding the dimension *Project Content*, all the 7 sentences were very highly evaluated by the respondents, with percentages reaching 90% and more (figure 03). The first item enquired how the project had supplied the students with an effective range of challenges, where 87.3% agreed or strongly agreed and 75% agreed or strongly agreed that the lessons stimulated the student's desire to learn. 78.5% answered with agreed or strongly agreed that the project emphasized understanding of concepts and principles, and almost all students (96.4%) reported that they agreed or strongly agreed (60.7%) that the project effectively challenged them to think. When asked about the interest level of the project assignments, 85.7% agreed or strongly agreed, 96.4% agreed or strongly agreed that the project was up-to-date with developments in this field and 89.3% agreed or strongly agreed that this project included applied learning and problem-solving experiences.

Figure 3. Project content

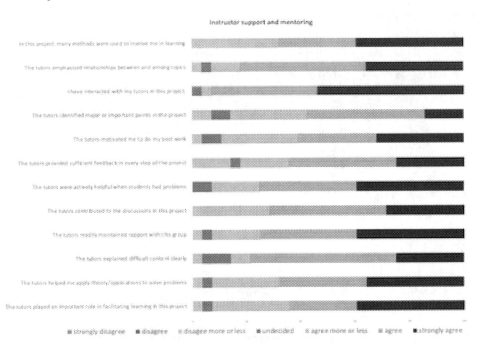

When looking at the *Project Structure*, 4 statements were evaluated (figure 04). In this dimension, the results were more distributed, but the majority were still positive with more than half of the participants evaluating all the items with agreed or strongly agreed. In the first question about how students felt that each step was well prepared and organized, 60.8% agreed or strongly agreed. Concerning the question about if they felt that the assignments were clearly explained, 78.6% agreed or strongly agreed and the question about if the technology were used effectively 57.1% agreed or strongly agreed while 21.4% agreed more or less. The final statement refers to the feeling that students perceived from what's expected on their part and 85.8% agreed (42.9%) or strongly agreed (42.9%).

In the dimension *Student-to-student interaction*, 5 statements were evaluated. In the first one "the group work contributed significantly to this project", 57.1% answered that they strongly agree, while 17.9% answered agreed, the same percentage of those who answered that they agreed more or less to the statement "The group size was appropriate for the project purpose", half of the students said strongly agree and 35.7% answered agree. The last 3 sentences of this dimension evaluated how students perceived the interaction as an important learning component of the project with 79.3% saying that agreed (28.6%) or strongly agreed (60.7%). The statement as to whether the project provided an opportunity to learn from other students, 89.2% answered agreed or strongly agreed and the last one asked if students felt that had sufficient opportunity to interact with other students during the project. 60.7% answered strongly agree and 25% agreed (table 28).

Figure 4. Project structure

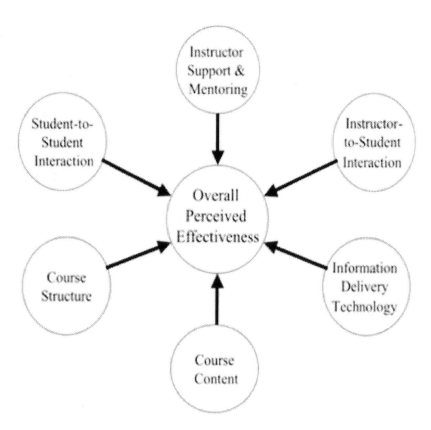

The *Tutor-Student Interaction* dimension evaluated 5 statements (figure 06). In this item, 78.5% answered that they agreed or strongly agreed about the freedom of asking questions throughout the project, 89.3% agreed or strongly agreed that the tutors responded in a timely manner and 96.4% agreed or strongly agreed with the easily access to tutors. 78.5% agreed or strongly agreed that they felt free to express and explain their own views about the project and finally, and 3 out of 4 students expressed agreement or strongly agreement about the clarity of the daily feedback on the final objectives.

When directly evaluating the *effectiveness of the online educational experience*, 3 statements were created (figure 07). 100% agreed or strongly agreed that they would recommend this project to friends/colleagues, 82.1% agreed or strongly agreed that they had learnt a lot with this project and 96.4% agreed or strongly agreed that they had enjoyed taking part in the project.

The last dimension evaluated the *perceived learning outcomes* (figure 08). To access that, 8 statements were created. When asked about the possibility to apply the acquired knowledge to a real job in a professional context, 78.5% agreed or strongly agreed and 82,2% agreed or strongly agreed that this project analyzed a real-world oriented communication approach. While 78.6% agreed or strongly agreed that the online version of the CBBC defines objectives, strategies and communication measures in a coherent concept and develop feasible solutions, 82.2% agreed or strongly agreed that this project allowed then to implement a real-world relevant information into a concept.

Figure 5. Student-to-student interaction

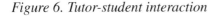

Figure 6. Tutor-student interaction

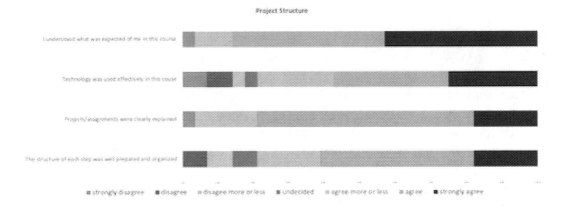

Other items refer to the perception of how this project allowed students to present and argue in favor of concepts in a convincing manner, with 85.7% answered agree or strongly. Regarding the question about how participants understood if the project reflected on conclusions from the coaching process and draw conclusions, 86.1% agreed or strongly agreed and 92.8% agreed or strongly agreed that this project had allowed them to collaborate and co-operate with students from other countries and help them to understand different cultural backgrounds. The last statement asked if students felt that they had work effectively with appropriate and strategies online, where 82.2% agreed or strongly agreed, and 10.7% more or less agreed.

Figure 7. Effectiveness of the online educational experience

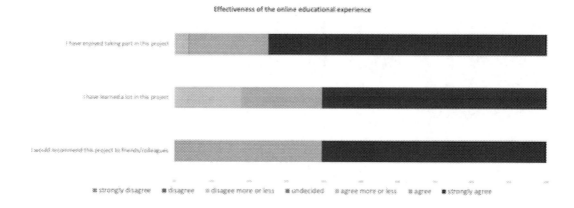

Figure 8. Perceived learning outcomes

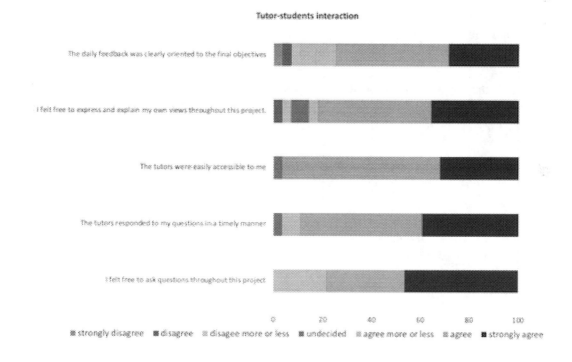

In the two last open questions, students were asked about their satisfaction with the project and if they thought that the CBBC would have been better in person instead of the online version. In a general evaluation, students were overwhelmingly positive in their answers about the satisfaction with the CBBC week. This positive feedback includes very encouraging statements such as:

"Yes, happy with the outcome and what I achieved"

"I am satisfied and I had a ton of fun"

"Yes, it was a very pleasant experience and the lectures were very informative and interesting. Also interacting with students from different universities made consider more [sic]point of view which will definitely stand me in good stead in my future projects! Thank you for the opportunity!"

"Yes! I really, really enjoyed it and I definitely did not expect to be able to learn SO much in just 5 days!"

"Yes, it was good to be able to work and share ideas with people from other countries and develop a project."

Notably the only negative statements referred to the online aspect:

"Yes and no, I loved it because I got to work with students from different countries and no because I missed the social interaction."

And with regards to language issues:

"Yes, it was intensive, but I have learned to do work in a short time limit and I met new people! despite the language barrier which limits the investment in the debate, it was a very enriching week"

Furthermore, there was one mention about the project intensity:

"Yes, but it was a lot of work in a short-time period"

In the other open question, participants were asked about if they thought the CBBC would be better in person, and why. Some of the answers referred to the lack of social interaction due to the online environment:

"Although our team was great and we still communicate. I do still think that in person the team synergy could have been better and getting to know new people would have been easier"

"Totally, it would allow more interaction, be more efficient and it facilitates dialogue"

"Yes! Working online is so much more tiring and boring and we really missed social interaction. We could have had much more fun in person"

"Yes, because we would have the opportunity to learn from different cultures and the work would be more efficient"

One student made an interesting observation and considered the online environment might have led to better project outcomes:

"I think it worked really well online, but I would have loved to have met the other students in person. However, I also think that we were really productive online - I wonder if we would have been as productive, had we worked in person"

Looking at these answers it is clear that all of the participants believe that a face-to-face experience would be better, especially on the social, communication and relationship aspects of the project.

As for the opinion of the teachers involved, the second online edition in a row had improved a lot from the first one in several aspects. The lessons learned from the previous online edition have revealed to be very useful especially in the project organization, tasks attribution, working methodology, communication, controlling student's expectations and in the final work outputs. Since every university started to work on the research analysis of the briefing about two months before, the students become involved in an early stage and the instructors soon clarified the main purpose of the project. When the get together finally happened, teachers organized the teams through complementary skills of the students, lectured inspiring sessions every morning, provided clear goals for each daily task and coached by listening and giving feedback to every team twice a day. This way, students felt more willing and confident to evolve.

DISCUSSION AND CONCLUSION

Our literature review pointed to multifaceted challenges in the multicultural and online learning environment. When students come together in a new international environment working in multicultural teams, instructors need to navigate students through the potential difficulties experienced due to different degree programs and different university types that bring different methods of instruction in different countries. Students in CBBC are from different semesters in their programs and so display different levels of cognitive maturity. They have all different levels of English language proficiency with some having been taught in EMI classes before, and for some this would have been completely new.

Learning in an online environment exacerbates the challenges in such projects as social interaction is missing and this is compounded by potential stunted interaction in comparison to a face-to-face project. However, it is precisely all of these challenges which the authors believe can really provide the students a profound learning opportunity. As pointed out, the difficulty of spending one entire week working with colleagues that they never met before, with different backgrounds, culture and expectations, and doing all of that online, throughout screens, had strengthen their capacities of resilience and maturity.

The online experience also facilitated multicultural connections during the students' learning process, as physical distance exacerbated differences and, as communication was much more difficult without a face-to-face contact, students had to find strategies and common contact points to be able to work and develop the project.

Instructors participating in the CBBC had been doing so for many years and as such experience from previous projects helped them to create a week with a clear structure and guidelines. Students received a timetable with exact instructions of tasks at the beginning of the week and the team work sessions were dotted with lectures and Q&A sessions for students to participate in as the project progressed.

A high-stake project such as this with a real client briefing is naturally daunting for a student, even more so working with a team of people who they do not know in terms of working style and cultural background. Instructors of the CBBC are likewise mindful of these critical challenges and had dedicated a whole week for the students to ensure they are optimally coached and guided. This has proven crucial in previous projects both online and face-to-face and so the instructors were well-versed in preparing a clear structure.

Bearing in mind that some students were not used to studio-like classes, having teachers working with them as coaches instead of traditional content lecturers, the online format was a considerable challenge for the instructors too. They had to create the entire interaction dynamic, content, and methodology to fulfil the expectations of the students and accomplish the learning goals. Therefore, a pedagogical strategy based on a more empathic approach, a simpler and clear communication and a bigger sense of proximity with students were fundamental to create a positive and confident learning environment. This was highly valued as shown in the positive survey results for this section.

Both the statements and the open questions in the survey clearly indicated that the social interaction would have enriched this experience, corroborating the literature review that clearly indicates that networking, partying and being in each other's company is a fundamental component of the creative process among young adults. This is even more pressing since the Covid-19 pandemic struck, as in the aftermath of the pandemic there continues to be a real thirst for live interaction both from student-to-student and coach-to-student.

Notwithstanding this, the students reported that their experience was overwhelmingly positive which was achieved due to the highly structured nature and the dedication of the lecturers for the entire time. The students reported that the tutor support and mentoring as well as interaction was crucial for the project success, with 96% agreeing that they learnt a lot in the week and that the learning outcomes were met.

Our results corroborate some previous research, which states that the perceived learning effectiveness is a multi-dimensional phenomenon but also points to the possibility that online learning can be as successful as face-to-face. This contrasts to the findings of Duarte & Riedl (2020), where students suggested that the experience was inferior to how they believe the project would have been in person. The success of the 2021 CBBC edition can be attributed to the fact that students had become used to the online environment a year into the pandemic. At the same time, the clear effort, guidelines and structure provided by the instructors were certainly a contributing factor. This echoes the recommendations reported by Jia et al. (2020, p. 15) who suggest that social, cognitive and teaching presence as well as capturing and sustaining attention and meaningful interaction are key components for success.

The findings of this study contribute to support the validity of the online assessment model (Peltier et al., 2003) and some of the insights and lessons learned can help education managers and marketing academics to a better understanding of the student's learning perceptions in a multicultural and multinational online environment.

LIMITATIONS AND POSSIBILITIES FOR FURTHER INVESTIGATION

As proposed by Stallings (2002), it is of utmost importance to identify the aspects that students feel are relevant in their online learning environment.

The authors believe that the findings of this study based on a multicultural and multinational project could help to enhance the knowledge about how educational tools can be improved to increase overall student satisfaction, at the same time point to some of the best practices in pedagogical strategies.

Although the survey was small-scale in nature, the depth and breadth of the questions has shed light on student perceptions of this specific multicultural, online learning experience.

Notwithstanding this, a deeper analysis focused on the advantages or disadvantages of this multicultural projects could be addressed by investigating the ways the students' multicultural interactions enhance or hinder the learning effectiveness and its pedagogical implications. This could be achieved through the analysis of the differences in the outputs of the creative proposals and through the quality and deep level of interactions among students or by examining the specific differences between the multicultural connections online versus a face-to-face.

REFERENCES

Aguilera-Hermida, A. P. (2020). College students' use and acceptance of emergency online learning due to COVID-19. *International Journal of Educational Research Open, 1,* 100011. doi:10.1016/j.ijedro.2020.100011 PMID:35059662

Allen, I. E., & Seaman, J. (2015). *Grade Level: Tracking Online Education in the United States.* Babson College.

Arkın, E., & Osam, N. (2015). 8. English-medium higher education: A case study in a Turkish university context. In *English-medium instruction in European higher education* (pp. 177–200). De Gruyter Mouton. doi:10.1515/9781614515272-010

Bahasoan, A. N., Ayuandiani, W., Mukhram, M., & Rahmat, A. (2020). Effectiveness of online learning in pandemic COVID-19. *International Journal of Science, Technology & Management, 1*(2), 100–106.

Banks, J. A. (2001a). Multicultural education: Goals, possibilities and challenges. In C. F. Diaz (Ed.), *Multicultural education in the 21st century* (pp. 11–22). Addison-Wesley.

Banks, J. A. (2001b). History, characteristics and goals. In J. A. Banks & C. A. M. Banks (Eds.), *Handbook of research on multicultural education* (pp. 3–29). Wiley.

Briguglio, C. (2007). Educating the Business Graduate of the 21st Century: Communication for a Globalized World. *International Journal on Teaching and Learning in Higher Education, 19*(1), 8–20.

Chakraborty, P., Mittal, P., Gupta, M. S., Yadav, S., & Arora, A. (2021). Opinion of students on online education during the COVID-19 pandemic. *Human Behavior and Emerging Technologies, 3*(3), 357–365. doi:10.1002/hbe2.240

Chyung, S. Y., & Vachon, M. (2013). An Investigation of the profiles of satisfying and dissatisfying factors in e-learning. *Performance Improvement Quarterly, 26*(2), 117–140. doi:10.1002/piq.21147

Dafouz, E., & Camacho-Miñano, M. M. (2016). Exploring the impact of English-medium instruction on university student academic achievement: The case of accounting. *English for Specific Purposes, 44,* 57–67. doi:10.1016/j.esp.2016.06.001

Deardorff, D. K. (2006). Identification and assessment of intercultural competence as a student outcome of internationalization. *Journal of Studies in International Education, 10*(3), 241–266. doi:10.1177/1028315306287002

Del Campo, C., Cancer, A., Pascual-Ezama, D., & Urquía-Grande, E. (2015). EMI vs. Non-EMI: Preliminary Analysis of the Academic Output within the INTE-R-LICA Project. *Procedia: Social and Behavioral Sciences, 212,* 74–79.

DeHaan, R. L. (2009). Teaching Creativity and Inventive Problem Solving in Science [Fall]. *CBE Life Sciences Education*, *8*(3), 172–181. doi:10.1187/cbe.08-12-0081 PMID:19723812

DiStefano, J. J., & Maznevski, M. L. (2000). Creating value with diverse teams in global management. *Organizational Dynamics*, *29*(1), 45–63. doi:10.1016/S0090-2616(00)00012-7

Domingues, J., & Araújo, E. R. (2010). *Hibridismo y Transnacionalidad en contexto Erasmus. El caso de los estudiantes Erasmus en la Universidad de La Coruña*. Paper presented at the X Congreso Español de Sociología, Pamplona.

Duarte, A. (2013). *A Atração Da Educação: O Impacto do Estereótipo Nacional na Intenção de Escolha do Destino de Estudo no Contexto do Ensino Superior Europeu: O Caso de Portugal* (Doctoral dissertation). http://hdl.handle.net/1822/29965

Duarte, A. & Riedl, K. (2021). 'Virtually' the same learning outcomes. A case study of a virtual client briefed communication project across borders, *Icono 14, 19*(2), 155-177. doi:10.7195/ri14.v19i2.1724

Evans, S., & Morrison, B. (2011). Meeting the challenges of English-medium higher education: The first-year experience in Hong Kong. *English for Specific Purposes*, *30*(3), 198–208. doi:10.1016/j.esp.2011.01.001

Gay, G. (2013). Teaching to and through cultural diversity. *Curriculum Inquiry*, *43*(1), 48–70. doi:10.1111/curi.12002

Gehrke, I., & Abermann, G. (2016). *The Multiculural Classroom-A Guaranteed Intercultural Learning Space*. Academic Press.

Holm, G., & Zilliacus, H. (2009). Multicultural education and intercultural education: Is there a difference. *Dialogs on diversity and global education*, 11-28.

Jia, C., Hew, K. F., Bai, S., & Huang, W. (2020). Adaptation of a conventional flipped course to an online flipped format during the Covid-19 pandemic: Student learning performance and engagement. *Journal of Research on Technology in Education*, 1–21. doi:10.1080/15391523.2020.1847220

Kim, E. (2011). Conceptions, critiques and challenges in multicultural education reform the U.S. *KEDI Journal of Educational Policy*, *8*, 201–218.

Klassen, R. (2001). *The international university curriculum: Challenges in English-medium Engineering education* [Doctoral dissertation]. Delft University of Technology.

Knapp, A. (2011). When comprehension is crucial: Using English as a medium of instruction at a German university. *English in Europe today: Sociocultural and educational perspectives*, 51-70.

Lepori, B., & Kyvik, S. (2010). The research mission of universities of applied sciences and the future configuration of higher education systems in Europe. *Higher Education Policy*, *23*(3), 295–316.

Leung, K., Ang, S., & Tan, M. L. (2014). Intercultural competence. *Annual Review of Organizational Psychology and Organizational Behavior*, *1*(1), 489–519. doi:10.1146/annurev-orgpsych-031413-091229

Markova, T., Glazkova, I., & Zaborova, E. (2017). Quality Issues of Online Distance Learning. *Procedia: Social and Behavioral Sciences*, *237*, 685–691. doi:10.1016/j.sbspro.2017.02.043

Marks, R. B., Sibley, S. D., & Arbaugh, J. B. (2005). A structural equation model of predictors for effective online learning. *Journal of Management Education, 29*(4), 531–563. doi:10.1177/1052562904271199

McAllister, L., Whiteford, G., Hill, B., Thomas, N., & Fitzgerald, M. (2006). Reflection in intercultural learning: Examining the international experience through a critical incident approach. *Reflective Practice, 7*(3), 367–381. doi:10.1080/14623940600837624

McWilliam, E., & Dawson, S. (2008). Teaching for creativity: Towards sustainable and replicable pedagogical practice. *Higher Education, 56*(6), 633–643. doi:10.100710734-008-9115-7

Mauranen, A. (2018). Second language acquisition, world Englishes, and English as a lingua franca (ELF). *World Englishes, 37*(1), 106–119. doi:10.1111/weng.12306

Mwonga, C. (2005). *Multicultural education: new path toward democracy*. Merrill.

Nathan, M. J., & Sawyer, R. K. (2014). Foundations of the learning sciences. In R. K. Sawyer (Ed.), *The Cambridge handbook of the learning sciences* (2nd ed., pp. 21–43). Cambridge University Press. doi:10.1017/CBO9781139519526.004

Orlov, G., McKee, D., Berry, J., Boyle, A., DiCiccio, T., Ransom, T., Rees-Jones, A., & Stoye, J. (2021). Learning during the COVID-19 pandemic: It is not who you teach, but how you teach. *Economics Letters, 202*, 109812. doi:10.1016/j.econlet.2021.109812

Peltier, J. W., Drago, W., & Schibrowsky, J. A. (2003). Virtual communities and the assessment of online marketing education. *Journal of Marketing Education, 25*(3), 260–276. doi:10.1177/0273475303257762

Peltier, J. W., Schibrowsky, J. A., & Drago, W. (2007). The interdependence of the factors influencing the perceived quality of the online learning experience: A causal model. *Journal of Marketing Education, 29*(2), 140–153. doi:10.1177/0273475307302016

Pezenka, I., Rußmann, U., Schwarzbauer, T., & Bernhard, J. (2020). 100% Distance Learning von heute auf morgen – eine Umfrage unter Studierenden an der FHWien der WKW im April 2020. *FNMA Magazin*, 38–41.

Polat, S. (2009). Öğretmen adaylarının çokkültürlü eğitime yönelik kişilik özellikleri [Probationary teachers' level of inclination to multicultural education]. *International Online Journal of Educational Sciences, 1*, 154–164.

Pulcini, V., & Campagna, S. (2015). Controversy in Italian higher education. *English-medium instruction in European higher education, 4*, 65.

Saebø, A. B., McCammon, L. A., & O'Farrell, L. (2007). Creative Teaching—Teaching Creativity. *Caribbean Quarterly, 53*(1-2), 205–215. doi:10.1080/00086495.2007.11672318

Salazar, S. M. (2013). Laying a foundation for artmaking in the 21st century: A description and some dilemmas. *Studies in Art Education, 54*(3), 246–259. doi:10.1080/00393541.2013.11518897

Sawyer, R. K. (2017). Teaching creativity in art and design studio classes: A systematic literature review. *Educational Research Review, 22*, 99–113. doi:10.1016/j.edurev.2017.07.002

Sert, N. (2008). The language of instruction dilemma in the Turkish context. *System, 36*(2), 156–171. doi:10.1016/j.system.2007.11.006

Sharma, S. (2005). Multicultural education: Teachers perceptions and preparation. *Journal of College Teaching and Learning, 2*(5). Advance online publication. doi:10.19030/tlc.v2i5.1825

Shea, P., Sau Li, C., & Pickett, A. (2006). A study of teaching presence and student sense of learning community in fully online and web-enhanced college courses. *The Internet and Higher Education, 9*(3), 175–190. doi:10.1016/j.iheduc.2006.06.005

Stallings, D. (2002). Measuring success in the virtual university. *Journal of Academic Librarianship, 28*(1-2), 47–53. doi:10.1016/S0099-1333(01)00300-7

Tatzl, D. (2011). English-medium masters' programmes at an Austrian university of applied sciences: Attitudes, experiences and challenges. *Journal of English for Academic Purposes, 10*(4), 252–270. doi:10.1016/j.jeap.2011.08.003

Tseng, H. W., & Walsh, E. J. Jr. (2016). Blended vs. traditional course delivery: Comparing students' motivation, learning outcomes, and preferences. *Quarterly Review of Distance Education, 17*(1).

Turner, Y. (2009). "Knowing me, knowing you," is there nothing we can do? Pedagogic challenges in using group work to create an intercultural learning space. *Journal of Studies in International Education, 13*(2), 240–255. doi:10.1177/1028315308329789

UNESCO. (2020). *Education: From disruption to recovery.* Retrieved from https://en.unesco.org/covid19/educationresponse

Vanada, D. I. (2016). An equitable balance: Designing quality thinking systems in art education. *International Journal of Education & the Arts, 17*(11).

Wit, H. D. (2020). Internationalization of higher education: The need for a more ethical and qualitative approach. *Journal of International Students, 10*(1), 1–4.

Woo, Y., & Reeves, T. C. (2007). Meaningful interaction in web-based learning: A social constructivist interpretation. *The Internet and Higher Education, 10*(1), 15–25. doi:10.1016/j.iheduc.2006.10.005

ENDNOTES

[1]   This chapter predominantly uses the term multicultural education although some authors refer to the term as inter-cultural and sometimes both terms are used as synonyms. In Europe, the term inter-cultural is used more often whereas in North America and Asia the idea of multicultural education is predominant. For an in-depth review and discussion about this, see Holm and Ziliacus (2009).

[2]   for a detailed description of this see Mauranen (2018).

Chapter 18

Collaborative Online International Learning (COIL) Case Study:
Canadian and Spanish Classes Develop Intercultural Competencies

Jody-Lynn Rebek
Algoma University, Canada

Victor del-Corte-Lora
ⓘD https://orcid.org/0000-0002-7571-170X
Universitat Jaume I, Spain

Eunjung Riauka
Algoma University, Canada

ABSTRACT

The COVID-19 pandemic posed challenges, including travel restrictions that limited opportunities for student exchange. One solution to promote intercultural learning amongst students in different countries was COIL. This chapter presents a collaborative online international learning (COIL) case study that engaged students from Canada and Spain in an intercultural learning experience. Professors worked collaboratively to design a five-week program of co-instruction within their higher education course schedules. Using technology and a combination of asynchronous and synchronous opportunities, students engaged in the course content and learned about their unique cultural applications and perspectives in relation to the content as they engaged in activities via cross-cultural teams. Administrators, students, and faculty found the benefits far outweigh the improvements needed. This chapter shares the details of this experience from administrative, faculty, and student perspectives.

DOI: 10.4018/978-1-7998-8921-2.ch018

INTRODUCTION

Before the pandemic, travelling inspired students' appreciation and value for cultural experiences and opened up a whole new world of learning. During the COVID-19 pandemic, student opportunities to travel abroad or participate in intercultural exchanges were non-existent. This hindered the ability of students to develop intercultural competencies. These intercultural educational experiences nurture cultural relations that extend beyond the classroom and have the potential to "indirectly affect participants' families, neighbours, and communities" (Fantini, 2000). To engage students and to remain competitive, higher education institutions will need to ensure opportunities integrate intercultural competency development into educational program teaching, activities, pedagogy and assessment (Islam & Stamp, 2020). This paper presents a case study that engaged students from universities in Canada and Spain in Collaborative Online International Learning (COIL). This case study fills a gap in the research, as it presents valuable information from institutions that have successfully engaged diverse students across modes of internationalization (Islam & Stamp 2020). Using technology students connected their classrooms, and engaged in intercultural learning. This case study investigated the COIL experience and evaluated how students and faculty experienced COIL and cultural competency development. We present the positive feedback students and faculty shared via a case study that focused on program evaluation (gathering quantitative and qualitative data). First, we present a literature review, then we outline the methods used to implement the courses. We then describe student and faculty perspectives about their COIL experience and then present the data analysis. Finally, we reflect on the results and the applicability of COIL as an innovative pedagogy: to complement physical mobility programs, enhance learning, develop intercultural competencies among students and faculty and contribute to the internationalization of higher education curriculum.

LITERATURE REVIEW

This literature review focuses on intercultural learning within higher education. We will present the value of cultural competence in higher education learning, define intercultural competence, outline the benefits of this complex but powerful mode of learning, and connect these methods to Internalization at home (IaH) and Virtual Exchange (VE).

The world is becoming more interconnected, and those individuals that exhibit intercultural competence are becoming more valuable (Ceo-DiFrancesco & Bender-Slack, 2016). Currently, higher education is focused on teaching content outlined in the syllabus as a guide, and also, preparing students to face globalization by giving them different perspectives of diversity and inclusion (Zhang & Pearlman, 2018). Students are required to gain knowledge about the content, and methodologies, along with how to apply them in different situations. With various points of view in an interconnected world, students are expected to develop and maintain relationships with different cultures (Fantini, 2000). Apart from preparing the students for the global world, some universities find that cultural diversity also improves the quality of education or research, promotes a better reputation, and offers financial benefits (Barbosa & Neves, 2020). For these reasons, the internationalization of higher education is a priority for universities.

One of the benefits of internationalization occurs through the offering of exchange opportunities at post-secondary institutions. Exchange programs put emphasis on academics and on how students can benefit from studying in foreign countries, including discussions that reveal different viewpoints. Sharing different perspectives with students from socially, culturally and economically different backgrounds in the host institution will enhance and foster Canadian students' cross-cultural understanding and world views (Sowa, 2002). COIL-VE is a specific pedagogy within the umbrella of virtual exchange, and its curriculum integrates internationalization and responds to globalization by (a) fostering global citizenship among students, faculty and staff, (b) providing accessibility, (c) encouraging mobility between and among educational institutions through academic collaborations and (d) promoting international research, teaching and learning. It is important to differentiate between the international program and provider mobility (IPPM) from student and faculty mobility programs. IPPM involves programs and higher education institutions moving to where the interested students are located, whereas mobility programs mobilize students and faculty to foreign countries for their academic programs, research or teaching (Knight & Liu, 2019).

Having classmates from around the world helps students become more self-aware of their own culture by contrasting it with the knowledge they gather from their peers' culture (Deardorff, 2006; Kahn & Agnew, 2017). Bloom's (1969) taxonomy highlights "affect" (or attitude) to knowledge (or cognition), while Freire (1998) called awareness "critical consciousness" and asserted that it is the most important task of education. Focusing on Bloom's (1969) three levels of knowing, students could engage in evaluation and deepen their self-understanding. Self-awareness has been shown to raise students' consciousness about how they think, feel and behave–past, present and future (Fantini, 2000; Rebek, 2019). Students who had opportunities to reflect assessed and applied their self-understanding and deepened how meaning was assigned, including concepts of privilege, racism, classism, sexism (bias and societal perspectives), discrimination, and oppression (Abrums & Leppa, 2001; Fantini, 2000). Offering opportunities to become self-aware, and evaluate and confront an individual's underlying issues, perspectives and biases in higher education, has been shown to be an important first step in developing cultural competence (Abrums & Leppa, 2001). Cultural competence provided individuals with awareness, a sensitivity to cultural differences that promote the formation of healthy ethnic relations, and an ability to be more effective in their chosen profession (Fantini, 2000). The intercultural competencies and skills students acquired were shown to be necessary for academic success and, even more importantly, success in life. Higher education institutions should then shift focus from what is learned (the outcomes) to the learning process itself so that students benefit from these valuable competencies that prepare them for the real world (Kahn & Agnew, 2017).

Even though there exists "a lack of clarity about the nature of intercultural communicative competence (ICC)," Fantini (2019) presents multiple facets to help define ICC: "(1) a variety of characteristics; (2) three areas or domains; (3) four dimensions; (4) host language proficiency; and (5) degrees of attainment that evolve through a longitudinal and developmental process" (p. 271). We present a summary here:

1. ICC **characteristics**: openness, suspension of judgment, flexibility, patience, humour, curiosity, interest, and tolerance for ambiguity, among others.
2. **Three domains** as shared (Fantini, 2000) from past research by Martin (1989) and Wiseman and Koester (1993): to develop and maintain relations, to "communicate effectively and appropriately with minimal loss or distortion" (Fantini, 2000, p. 27), and to engage in team collaboration effectively by better understanding people from different cultural backgrounds (Fantini, 2019).
3. **Four dimensions** were found: "awareness, attitudes, skills, knowledge (A+ASK)" (Fantini, 2000). As participants develop in self-knowledge and cultural knowledge, they also develop positive at-

titudes and skills, which furthers their personal development (Fantini, 2019). Awareness is the keystone to all dimensions and also enhances their development (Fantini, 2000).

4. Increased **host language proficiency** and the ability to communicate and connect students open up possibilities to learn. Lack of proficiency in the host language alternatively limits the student's ability to understand the host culture. The process of grappling with different languages reinforces other modes of communication and can be a humbling experience (Fantini, 2019).

5. **Degrees of attainment** are complex and require multiple assessment strategies. "Global (using performance criteria), discrete (assessing specific items typical of quizzes, examinations, etc.), direct (when attention is focused on the evaluation process itself), and indirect (when attention is focused on an activity that can be used concurrently for assessment purposes)" (Fantini, 2019, p. 274).

Bennet (2008) defines intercultural competence as consisting of three core competencies: (a) *Mindset* or cognitive competencies, especially those related to identity and cultural knowledge; (b) *Skillset* or behavioural competencies, which leads to managing social interactions, such as listening, conflict resolution, etc.; and (c) *Heartset* or affective competencies, which are prone to discovering new cultures: curiosity, initiative, risk-taking, etc.

All these concepts could easily be learned by students by visiting another university in another culture, integrating themselves in multicultural teams and exposing themselves to a new reality with a different lens. However, there are some circumstances that might hinder the possibility for students to study abroad, such as financial issues, family, work or, lately, the COVID-19 pandemic. In situations where students are unable to study abroad, COIL (Collaborative Online International Learning) promotes an opportunity for students to be immersed in an intercultural project without having to travel. In a way, COIL also has strong ties to Internationalization at home (IaH) and Virtual Exchange. Virtual exchange (VE) is an educational practice that involves the engagement of groups of learners in extended periods of online intercultural interaction and collaboration with international peers as an integrated part of their educational programmes and under the guidance of educators and/or facilitators (O'Dowd, 2021). IaH is the purposeful integration of international and intercultural dimensions into the formal and informal curriculum for all students within domestic learning environments (Beleen & Jones, 2015, P. 59). IaH can also serve as a means to promote common values and closer understandings between different peoples and cultures, enhance cooperation between post-secondary institutions in their internationalization efforts, and also improve the educational quality of the sector and human resources through mutual learning, comparison, and exchange of good practice (Almeida & Morosini, 2019). Some other approaches that have been used as VE tools include the following (O'Dowd, 2017):

- **Subject-specific Virtual Exchange-Language learning**: Teachers connect students with other students in different countries so they can interact with native speakers.
- **Subject-specific Virtual Exchange-Business initiatives**: Mainly, the International Business and International Marketing subjects use *Global Virtual Teams (GVTs)*. GVT connects members who represent diverse cultural backgrounds, using the Internet, to collaborate on business concepts (Taras et al., 2013).

COIL is a more comprehensive form of virtual exchange (VE). According to the State University of New York (SUNY) COIL Center, COIL is a new teaching and learning paradigm that promotes the development of intercultural competence across shared multicultural learning environments (Rubin & Guth, 2016). Using technology, COIL fosters meaningful exchanges between university faculty and students with peers in geographically distant locations and from different lingua-cultural backgrounds. COIL courses are team-taught by educators who remotely collaborate to develop a shared syllabus emphasizing experiential and collaborative student-centred learning (Starke-Meyerring & Wilson, 2008). COIL focuses on student collaboration in teams, interactive learning assignments, and cultural knowledge. The COVID-19 pandemic accelerated personal and professional use of online learning technologies and video communications. As a result, students did not have to travel to participate in intercultural learning, so COIL provided a unique opportunity (Stevens Institute, 2021).

Barriers to international travel were lifted for students as they engaged in collaborative video communication tools to share and exchange their cultural experiences, a unique opportunity during the COVID-19 pandemic (Ceo-DiFrancesco & Bender-Slack, 2016; Katre, 2020). COIL provided an exciting virtual experience for faculty and students in higher education to engage interculturally, increase their global awareness and gain intercultural competencies. Teams are formed by members of two or more universities from different regions or countries (Zhang & Pearlman, 2018). Collaboration engaged students from different countries, often speaking different languages and using support material such as pictures and videos from their respective countries, which helped to improve their intercultural competencies (Scales et al., 2006). COIL uses a collaborative methodology to help foster positive interdependence, helping students to understand better, increase their engagement and improve their problem-solving skills (Johnson et al., 2014). Learning is not restricted to the boundaries of the classroom, giving the possibility to the students to have access to international education (Khan et al., 2020).

How does COIL work? COIL can be co-developed by faculty in any discipline. Often, the best collaboration occurs from interdisciplinary courses offered in higher education institutions. In this case study, COIL was facilitated through Algoma University's Experiential Learning and International Affairs Department. Applications from professors at Algoma and partner universities from all over the world were required and vetted by this department. Professors were matched based on their applications and worked together to co-create COIL modules. The modules were developed for at least five weeks within the professor's existing course designs. Faculty co-taught during this time, and students formed teams comprised of a balance of members from each university. Students and professors worked together over the five weeks to complete assignments and learn from each other. Students were assessed collaboratively by professors who worked together to assign final grades. Following the course, administrators and professors met to debrief key learnings, what worked, and what could be improved to enhance future instances of COIL. We will now turn to explore the methods we used to better understand our COIL case study.

METHODS

The COIL project was presented by Algoma University (Canada) from December 2020 to April 2021, during the COVID-19 lockdown for many countries in the world. In December 2020, Algoma University arranged some virtual meetings looking for three partners to develop a COIL project with them. Applicants uploaded basic information about their subject/course, their intentions, a CV, and their university coordinates, and attended a meeting to determine suitability. After the meeting, three partners were chosen, two from Universitat Jaume I (Spain) and one from Soonchunhyang University (South Korea). Before starting the project, three professors from Canada were matched with one of the professors from Spain or South Korea. Professors in Canada also had to apply to illustrate their ability, willingness and interest in co-teaching and intercultural competency development (both for themselves and their students). In the case of this COIL course, both professors instructed within the business program and had complementary fields: Management and Marketing. All COIL faculty (six in total) were coached on developing COIL courses, and faculty/students were invited to complete pre-and post-surveys online (see Appendix 1).

The process was initiated by four coaching sessions (between January and February 2021). These sessions were held by a subject matter expert (Jon Rubin) who guided faculty to set up their COIL course. During this time, professors had to co-create the following for their five-week intercultural course component, which was provided within their existing course schedules:

- Learning objectives
- Course content
- Timetable
- Methodology and tools to be used
- Assessment methods

The learning objectives and content had to integrate the core knowledge of the course or subject, and also the intercultural competencies that students would need to demonstrate. The COIL learning objectives established for students in both courses were:

- Develop intercultural understanding as evidenced by knowledge sharing about our cultures and sports marketing strategies,
- Apply interpersonal skills to form teams and communicate effectively from different perspectives as demonstrated by the team agreement and presentations,
- Demonstrate critical thinking in the development of a marketing strategy and plan for a sports case study, including cultural components and questions posed on team presentations.

The content was a blend of two subjects: *Strategy and Policy*, a 4th year subject from Canada, and *Fundamentals of Marketing*, a 2nd year subject from Spain. Both subjects were from the same field–business. The timetable for students was restricted to two compulsory sessions and three optional sessions. Two of the compulsory sessions were synchronous and all the students had to attend. The remaining three sessions were asynchronous, and students could complete these course activities at a mutually convenient time while arranging to work in their teams independently.

Collaboratively administrators and faculty provided an online platform and organized teams that balanced student members from each country (Canada and Spain), and teams were taken through technology-enhanced team development processes to establish safe online learning spaces. It is important to note that team building for faculty and students was an essential component of the COIL program. There were 24 students from Canada and 22 students from Spain. For both the course in Canada and the course in Spain, students were split into eight teams (of two or three students). This made it easy for professors to form intercultural teams (of five or six students) by matching and amalgamating the eight teams from each class (e.g., team #1 from Canada joined team #1 from Spain). The relationships developed allowed both the COIL course, cultural competency development, and student assignments to be implemented smoothly.

The course started with sharing the COIL schedule, learning activities, and project instructions, along with video introductions, which were all shared online using *Padlet*. These videos were done in teams for students and professors to introduce themselves and present the Canadian city and Spanish cities where they lived. The students were invited to pose questions to other students to learn about their culture and answer questions that students asked. The professors also explained the framework of the course and distributed the pre-survey to students (this was a brief survey that asked faculty and students about their expectations regarding the COIL experience). Then, students had to complete modules with asynchronous lessons. Professors uploaded videos to explain the content and methods they used for analysis. Students watched videos and were instructed to complete assignments collaboratively in groups. Students could meet in teams whenever they wanted and many shared they used various online Smartphone apps to connect with each other (i.e., *Whatsapp, Google Hangouts*). The last lesson was the presentation of team project results. Students were instructed to reflect on how applications would differ in each country and share key learnings about the other country. Both professors graded assignment submissions independently and then reviewed each other's feedback, coming to a mutual agreement on the final grade (typically an average taken from professors' independent assessment). Lastly, students and faculty were invited to complete the post-survey to reflect on the experience (quantitative and qualitative questions).

During the course, the professors used several tools. For the synchronous classes, they used Zoom, as it allowed them to see all the students on the same screen, share documents, or split them into teams via breakout rooms. In addition, recordings to the Cloud also created fairly accurate transcripts that were shared alongside the video recording. The professors also used Padlet to share documents and videos publicly with all students easily, engage in online dialogue, and allow students to pin videos or documents. Finally, Google Drive was used to receive assignments privately from each team for summative feedback and assessment. It appeared that many were excited about this unique learning experience since there were almost no issues with student engagement throughout (apart from one student missing a class) and at the conclusion of the course.

RESULTS

To evaluate student and faculty experiences, we developed pre and post- COIL reflection surveys that were adapted from Stevens Initiative Cohort (Appendix I). Although a textual analysis could be undertaken to code the writing for a more comprehensive analysis, students were asked to quantify the results, which would still require a second layer of analysis. For the short time frame, we decided to conduct an online survey to encourage student reflection, which was the most important aspect of intercultural learning through COIL.

Canadian students' response rate from the Pre-COIL survey was 71% and Spanish students' response rate was 51%. We asked four (4) questions in our Pre-COIL Survey as follows:

1. Did you have any concerns when you learned that your course will be COILing with a class from a partner school?
2. What do you COIL from this COIL experience?
3. How do you think your interaction with students from another country might impact what you learn in this course?

4.   How do you think the way you see and understand the world might change by connecting with students in another country?

Students' responses to Pre-COIL survey questions were mostly positive. For example, for the first question on whether or not students had any concerns about their course being COILed, seventy percent (70%) of students who responded said "No," and said that they were very excited about this opportunity. Thirty (30%) of the students who responded were somewhat concerned about time zone differences, language barriers, and were simply feeling nervous about working with students from different countries (Figure 1). In terms of expectations (second question), students wanted international experiences, cross-cultural learning, language, people and exposure to a different culture. Some expressed that they wanted to learn how to work better as a diverse team to communicate with others. Some were excited about meeting new people, seeing how they thought differently about the subject matter, learning about the culture their international peers are engaged with, and gaining a better viewpoint of the world from this experience. For the third question around learning, students stated that they hoped to have an enhanced experience through the interaction with people from different countries, would gain insight into how social constructs, education systems or business practice work in different parts of the world, and would change existing thoughts with new perspectives about the world. The last question regarding student perspectives about the world might change by connecting with students in another country. The students shared that once they learned about their peers' country, people and culture, their basic knowledge and view toward their peers' country might change, which would broaden their own perspectives and respect for other cultures.

Figure 1. Pre-survey COIL - Algoma University 2021

Pre-Survey COIL - Algoma University 2021

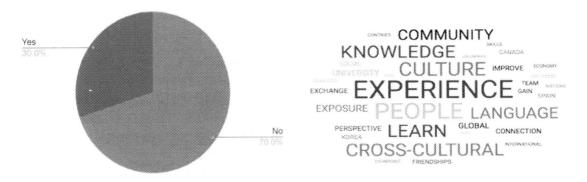

Note: This provides an overview of the key theme's students reported in the pre-survey.

Note: The pie chart shows students' responses to the question of whether they had any concerns about their courses being COILed. The word art provides an overview of the key themes students reported to the question in the pre-survey on what students wanted to learn from their COIL experience.

In terms of student engagement, the response rate dropped from 71% to 35% for Canadian students whereas it increased slightly from 51% to 56% for Spanish students after COIL courses concluded. This may be due to the fact that Canadian students were under enormous pressure to finish their winter courses and were preparing for final exams during the survey period. We asked six (6) questions for the post-COIL survey. Questions included:

1. What were the most important skills and knowledge you feel you gained from this COIL course?
2. Given your online interactions with students from another country, describe any key changes that occurred in how you view the world, your own culture or the culture of your partner country? In other words, what surprised you the most about the COIL experience?
3. How did the assumption of your partner school's culture or course subject influence your perspective after your interaction and collaborating with your partner(s)?
4. Was there any aspect of this COIL-enhanced course that was challenging in any way? If so, please describe this challenge and what you learned from it?
5. What do you want to explore further as a result of this connection to students from another country? For example, does this experience encourage you to study abroad or engage in another virtual exchange opportunity?
6. If these courses are offered again in the future, do you have any suggestions on how they could be enhanced?

The first question on the most important skills and knowledge students felt they gained from COIL, included the following responses:

- greater understanding into different perspectives shared,
- extended knowledge by applying concepts explored in class in a global setting,
- increased connection with different people that promoted extroversion and the ability to talk to other people,
- increased engagement in learning since the communication and connections made the class more exciting, and
- ability to break down language barriers and work with different time zones more effectively.

Did COIL courses encourage students to study abroad and in other virtual intercultural learning opportunities in the future? Sixty (60%) percent of students wanted to study abroad, 32% wanted to engage in another virtual intercultural learning opportunity, and 8% of students wanted to learn more about their partner country's social structure, education system and politics, to visit the country, and to work abroad in the future (Figure 2). In essence, students would still prefer physical mobility versus virtual exchange if they had to choose, even though virtual exchanges are a great alternative and solution during the pandemic.

It was also interesting to learn from the students' pre-COIL survey that language barriers and time differences were some of their concerns but the students' post-COIL survey didn't identify them as a hindrance to working together.

Figure 2. Post-survey COIL - Algoma University 2021

Post-Survey COIL - Algoma University 2021

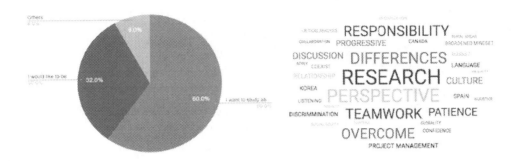

Note. This provides an overview of the key theme's students reported in the post-survey.

Note. The pie chart shows students' responses to whether or not the COIL courses encouraged students to study abroad or engage in other virtual intercultural learning opportunities. The word art provides an overview of the key themes students reported were the most important skills and knowledge they felt they gained from COIL courses in the post-survey.

Considering both *Algoma University* and *Universitat Jaume I* had never offered a COIL course in the past, both institutions felt that their COIL pilot was extremely successful. To the question about the "language or cultural differences that might lead you to choose a partner from a different culture next time" the faculty responded one-hundred percent (100%), "no". One-hundred percent (100%) of faculty shared that COIL was a success, they would conduct a COIL course again, and they would work with their COIL partner again. In terms of student engagement, the post-survey reported a 600% increase in students' virtual intercultural engagement and a 350% increase in underrepresented student group participation (especially Indigenous students). Note: the pre-COIL survey had 70 participants and the post-COIL survey had 53 participants. One-hundred percent (100%) of faculty participated in both the pre-and post-surveys.

The students and faculty felt that through this COIL experience, they:

- Improved intercultural awareness by working closely with students and faculty from different cultures. For most students, this was their first experience working with students from different countries, so it was an exciting and motivating experience. Students learned about other cultural locations, discussed different views of society and had many opportunities to see themselves more clearly through the lens of other students.
- Increased interest in study abroad and future intercultural learning opportunities for students.
- Enhanced accessibility of underrepresented student groups.
- Developed digital literacy skills, especially for working in virtual teams.

Students have stated that they've been able to put into practice what they learned in class. However, both institutions did experience some challenges along the way.

- Difficulty planning COIL due to the short time frame. Normally, COIL course development takes at least eight months before launching. This COIL project development and implementation was done in three months and did not provide enough time to prep registered students on COIL.
- Difficulty finding a collaborative online platform. A suitable e-learning platform that worked for both institutions was difficult, and with the GDPR (The General Data Protection Regulation) compliance in Europe, and FIPPA (Freedom of Information and Protection of Privacy Act) compliance in Canada, posed challenges. Some faculty felt that e-learning platforms like Moodle would have been better than Google Drive.
- The time difference between the two partnering countries, with Spain but particularly with South Korea, was a challenge. However, despite this challenge, students had the best engagement when they were working synchronous versus asynchronous.
- Also, in some cases, different communication styles coupled with using English as a Second Language were a challenge for some participants.

Overall, students and faculty felt that COIL was a worthwhile experience that enhanced their learning, as it enriched the content taught and improved students' interpersonal and intercultural skills. COIL improvements will continue to be integrated and evaluated.

CONCLUSION

If designed effectively, COIL provided an engaging, mutually beneficial and equitable learning opportunity for participants and enhanced Internationalization-At-Home and Diversity Abroad initiatives for Canadian Post Secondary Education Institutions, and their counterparts abroad. Our results suggested that COIL improves intercultural competence, as students shared an increase of Bennet's (2008) competencies: intercultural awareness and their desire to study abroad (*heartset* or affective); adoption of different perspectives (*mindset*); and behavioural changes (*skillset*) illustrated by the communication skills developed during the course.

COIL provided accessibility to those students, especially underrepresented student groups, who would have not been able to travel for quality international learning opportunities. Many factors impact a low student participation rate such as not having financial resources to travel, work/home obligations, and other socio-economic factors. Although VE programs can never replace the in-person experiences of traditional exchange and study abroad programs, COIL-VE, if offered in tandem with physical mobility programs, has proven to be valuable and, going forward, an integral part of Internationalisation-At-Home strategies.

COIL requires commitment and collaboration from all key stakeholders in higher education and depends on three key pillars – active partnerships, flexible institutional policies and innovative pedagogies, to be successful (O'Dowd, 2021). Higher Education leaders should understand that running a successful VE requires careful planning, resource dedication, capacity building, common intentions, and thoughtful relationships, none of which is achieved quickly. Incorporating all perspectives and building trust amongst partners from the earliest stages of planning may not seem possible when time constraints exist but are warranted and beneficial. In addition, engaging students in cultural awareness prior to COIL courses primes student engagement, which was one improvement of this case study. This may involve completing a cultural assessment, engaging students in self-reflection, dialogues with peers about self-identified areas of growth, and participating in cultural sensitivity training. In this way, students identify, learn and prepare to grow by addressing cultural biases prior to engaging with COIL partners. COIL is a worthy approach to student learning, as it promotes inclusion and diversity, and will continuously improve through continued evaluation, reflection and learning. COIL offers opportunities for enriched student learning experiences in higher education and enhances self-awareness in a way that can not be offered by other traditional learning strategies.

Future research could explore a comparative study between online and in-person intercultural experiences, the integration of intercultural competencies into the core curriculum, and/or interdisciplinary applications. Future research could also consider: (a) applying social and justice theoretical perspectives, (b) investigating effective teaching strategies and curriculum design of global and intercultural competency development to create a framework for excellence, and (c) discovering better ways of measuring intercultural competence to further advance pedagogical practices and learning outcomes of intercultural competency development (Islam & Stamp, 2020). Intercultural competency development is an "institution's responsibility rather than a goal if we consider higher education as a tool for preparing students to live purposeful lives as engaged citizens" (p. 71). This requires intentionally articulated, integral and measurable components of all curricula with intercultural experiences. Though intercultural communication competence has not been clearly defined, competencies must be explicitly linked to the course and unique approaches to assessing competencies could improve intercultural competency development (Fantini, 2019). Courses that integrate intercultural learning within the context of content and curricula strengthen students' confidence in subject matter knowledge and cultural competence.

REFERENCES

Abrums, M. E., & Leppa, C. (2001). Beyond cultural competence: Teaching about race, gender, class, and sexual orientation. *The Journal of Nursing Education, 40*(6), 270–275. doi:10.3928/0148-4834-20010901-07 PMID:11554461

Almeida, J., Robson, S., Morosini, M., & Baranzeli, C. (2019). Understanding Internationalization at Home: Perspectives from the Global North and South. *European Educational Research Journal, 18*(2), 200–217. doi:10.1177/1474904118807537

Barbosa, M. L. O., & Neves, C. E. B. (2020). Internationalization of Higher Education: Institutions and knowledge diplomacy. *Sociologias, 22*(54), 22–44. doi:10.1590/15174522-104425

Beelen, J., & Jones, E. (2015). Redefining internationalization at home. In A. Curai, L. Matei, R. Pricopie, J. Salmi, & P. Scott (Eds.), *The European Higher Education Area: Between Critical Reflections and Future Policies* (pp. 59–72). Springer. doi:10.1007/978-3-319-20877-0_5

Bennet, J. (2008). On becoming a global soul: A path to engagement during study abroad. In V. Savicki (Ed.), *Developing intercultural competence and transformation: Theory, Research and Application in International Education* (pp. 12–31). Stylus.

Bloom, B. S. (1976). *Human characteristics and school learning*. McGraw-Hill.

Ceo-DiFrancesco, D., & Bender-Slack, D. (2016). Collaborative Online International Learning: Students and professors making global connections. In A. K. Moeller (Ed.), *Fostering Connections, Empowering Communities, Celebrating the World Fostering Connections, Empowering Communities, Celebrating the World* (pp. 147–174). Robert M. Terry.

Deardorff, D., Guth, S., Rubin, J., & Church, A. (2017). *Prompts for student reflections in COIL-enhanced modules* [Unpublished manuscript]. Developed for COIL Stevens Initiative Cohort 2. https://docs.google.com/document/d/1Ghe8QtJczuLd0qdWOCl1ZXB1JFKZREIT/edit

Deardorff, D. K. (2006). Identification and assessment of intercultural competence as a student outcome of internationalization. *Journal of Studies in International Education*, *10*(3), 241–266. doi:10.1177/1028315306287002

Fantini, A. E. (2000). A central concern: Developing intercultural competence. In A. E. Fantini (Ed.), *Addressing International Education Training & Service* (pp. 25–42). School for International Training.

Fantini, A. E. (2012). Language: An essential component of Intercultural Communicative Competence. In J. Jackson (Ed.), *The handbook of language and intercultural communication* (pp. 273-288). Routledge. https://docuri.com/download/the-handbook-of-language-and-intercultural-communication_59c1e904f5 81710b286cfba3_pdf#page=274

Fantini, A. E. (2019). *Intercultural communicative competence in educational exchange: a multinational perspective*. Routledge. doi:10.4324/9781351251747-2

Freire, P. (1970). *Pedagogy of the Oppressed*. Continuum.

Freire, P. (1973). *Education for Critical Consciousness*. Continuum.

Freire, P. (1998). *Teachers as cultural workers: Letters to those who dare teach*. Westview Press.

Islam, M. S., & Stamp, K. (2020). A reflection on future directions: Global international and intercultural competencies in higher education. *Research in Comparative and International Education*, *15*(1), 69–75. doi:10.1177/1745499920901951

Johnson, D. W., Johnson, R. T., & Smith, K. A. (2014). The power of cooperative learning for university classes: The interrelationships among theory, research, and practice. *Journal on Excellence in College Teaching*, *25*(4).

Kahn, H. E., & Agnew, M. (2017). Global learning through difference: Considerations for teaching, learning, and the internationalization of Higher Education. *Journal of Studies in International Education*, *21*(1), 52–64. doi:10.1177/1028315315622022

Katre, A. (2020). Creative Economy Teaching and Learning–A Collaborative Online International Learning Case. *International Education Studies*, *13*(7), 145. doi:10.5539/ies.v13n7p145

Kealey, D. J. (1990). *Cross-Cultural Effectiveness: A Study of Canadian Technical Advisors Overseas*. Canadian International Development Agency.

Khan, S., Haleem, A., & Khan, M. I. (2020). Enablers to implement circular initiatives in the supply chain: A Grey DEMATEL Method. *Global Business Review*. Advance online publication. doi:10.1177/0972150920929484

Knight, J., & Liu, Q. (2019). International program and provider mobility in higher education: Research trends, challenges and issues. *Comparative and International Education*, *48*(1). Advance online publication. doi:10.5206/cie-eci.v48i1.9335

Kohls, L. R. (1979). *Survival Kit for Overseas Living*. Intercultural Network/SYSTRAN Publications.

O'dowd, R. (2017). Virtual exchange and internationalising the classroom. *Training. Language and Culture*, *1*(4), 8–24. doi:10.29366/2017tlc.1.4.1

O'Dowd, R. (2021). Virtual exchange: Moving forward into the next decade. *Computer Assisted Language Learning*, *34*(3), 209–224. doi:10.1080/09588221.2021.1902201

Rebek, J. L. (2019). *Mindful leader development of undergraduate students* [Unpublished doctoral dissertation]. Lakehead University: Knowledge Commons.

Rubin, J., & Guth, S. (2015). Collaborative online international learning: An emerging format for internationalizing curricula. In *Globally Networked Teaching in the Humanities*. Theories and Practices.

Scales, P. C., Roehlkepartain, E. C., Neal, M., Kielsmeier, J. C., & Benson, P. L. (2006). Reducing academic achievement gaps: The role of community service and service-learning. *Journal of Experiential Education*, *29*(1), 38–60. doi:10.1177/105382590602900105

Sowa, P. A. (2002). How valuable are student exchange programs? *New Directions for Higher Education*, *2002*(117), 63–70. doi:10.1002/he.49

Starke-Meyerring, D., & Wilson, M. (2008). Learning environments for a globally networked world: emerging visions. Designing globally networked environments: Visionary partnerships, policies, and pedagogies.

Stevens Initiative. (2021). *2021 Survey of the Virtual Exchange Field Report*. The Aspen Institute.

Taras, V., Caprar, D., Rottig, D., Sarala, R. M., Zakaria, N., Zhao, F., Jiménez, A., Wankel, C., Lei, W. S., Minor, M. S., Bryla, P., Ordeñana, X., Bode, A., Schuster, A., Vaiginiene, E., Froese, F. J., Bathula, H., Yajnik, N., Baldegger, R., & Huang, V. Z. (2013). A global classroom evaluating the effectiveness of global virtual collaboration as a teaching tool in management education. *Academy of Management Learning & Education*, *12*(3), 414–435. Advance online publication. doi:10.5465/amle.2012.0195

Zhang, J., & Pearlman, A. M. G. (2018). Expanding access to international education through technology-enhanced collaborative online international learning (COIL) courses. *International Journal of Technology in Teaching and Learning*, *1*(14), 1–11. doi:10.37120/ijttl.2018.14.1.01

Zhang, X., & Zhou, M. (2019). Interventions to promote learners' intercultural competence: A meta-analysis. *International Journal of Intercultural Relations*, *71*, 31–47. doi:10.1016/j.ijintrel.2019.04.006

KEY TERMS AND DEFINITIONS

Internationalization-at-Home: Internationalization at home (IaH) is the purposeful integration of international and intercultural dimensions into the formal and informal curriculum for all students within domestic learning environments (Beleen & Jones, 2015). Internationalization at Home can also serve as a means to promote common values and closer understandings between different peoples and cultures, enhance cooperation between post-secondary institutions in their internationalization efforts, while also improving the educational quality of the sector and human capacity through mutual learning, comparison and exchange of good practice (Almeida & Morosini, 2019).

Virtual Exchange (VE): Virtual exchange (VE) is an educational practice that involves engaging groups of learners in extended periods of online studies. This intercultural interaction and collaboration with international peers is an integrated part of educational programs and is guided by educators and/ or facilitators (O'Dowd, 2021).

APPENDIX - SURVEY QUESTIONS

Pre-COIL Survey

1. Did you have any concerns when you learned that your course will be COILing with a class from a partner school? (20 words)
2. What do you want from this COIL experience? (20 words)
3. How do you think your interaction with students from another country might impact what you learn in this course? (20 words)
4. How do you think the way you see and understand the world might change by connecting with students in another country? (20 words)

Post-COIL Survey

1. What were the most important skills and knowledge you feel you gained from this COIL course? (min. 20 words)
2. Given your online interactions with students from another country, describe any key changes that occurred in how you view the world, your own culture or the culture of your partner country? In other words, what surprised you the most about the COIL experience? (min. 30-50 words)
3. How did the assumption of your partner school's culture or course subject influence your perspective after your interaction and collaborating with your partner(s)? (30-50 words)
4. Was there any aspect of this COIL-enhanced course that was challenging in any way? If so, please describe this challenge and what you learned from it? (30-50 words)
5. What do you want to explore further as a result of this connection to students from another country? For example, does this experience encourage you to study abroad or engage in another virtual exchange opportunity? (Please select all that apply)
   - I want to study abroad in the future
   - I would like to be engaged in another virtual exchange opportunity
   - I would like to register for another COIL course, if available, in the future semester
6. If these courses are offered again in the future, do you have any suggestions on how they could be enhanced? (min. 20 words)

Chapter 19
Best Practices of Teaching and Engaging International Students in Online Learning:
An Australian Perspective

Jasvir Kaur Singh Nachatar Singh
La Trobe University, Australia

ABSTRACT

Teaching international students can be challenging, either online or face-to-face. However, it can also be fruitful if one knows how to engage with international students in the learning and teaching environments, especially online. In Australia, traditional delivery of teaching was still going on for schools and higher education institutions until the end of March 2020, but this changed within weeks to remote or online methods due to the COVID-19 pandemic. At La Trobe University, Australia, teaching was paused for a week to cope with the learning and teaching 'shock' – that is to re-orientate teaching from face-to-face to completely offering courses remotely to international and domestic students. The symbiotic relationship between learning and teaching, as well as between students and teachers, must go on although through online medium. This chapter illustrates the journey of reflections of an early-career international academic unpacking the online practices of teaching and engaging international students in online learning environment at La Trobe University, Australia.

INTRODUCTION

Australia had been steadily attracting international students from around the world up until the pandemic in 2020. There were 177,155 international students in 2019 but only 136,138 in 2020 studying at Australian higher education institutions (Department of Education, Skills and Employment, 2021). These international students came largely from Asian countries: 38.4% were of Chinese background, followed by Indians (19%) and Nepalis (7.8%) (Department of Education, Skills and Employment, 2021). International education was worth $40.3 billion to the economy in 2019 (Department of Education, Skills

DOI: 10.4018/978-1-7998-8921-2.ch019

and Employment, 2020) and was the largest services export. Higher learning institutions in Australia have been attracting international students mainly to generate revenue to support their operational costs due to progressively reduced government funding (Hoang & Rojas-Lizana, 2015).

On the other side, international students seek studies aboard for a number of reasons. One of the earliest studies in understanding the reasons for their seeking international education was by Mazzarol and Soutar (2002), who developed the push and pull model that encapsulated Asian students' reasons to study in Western countries such as Australia, New Zealand, the United Kingdom, and the United States of America. Generally, push factors refer to the features of the home environment that are considered by students as unsatisfactory; these may include unstable social or political conditions, inability of local educational institutions to provide suitable programs, places, funding, resources to accommodate all students, and poor career possibilities in the home countries. Pull factors include what prospective students may consider attractive features of a host country, such as good academic reputation, quality academic and non-academic services and facilities, availability of funding in the form of scholarships, lower costs and fees and cost of living, the opportunity to live in a diverse culture and acquisition of a global view of the world, and better employment prospects.

More recently, scholars (Singh & Jack, 2018; Singh & Jamil, 2021) have found that international students seek international education because they want to experience international life. Such students in Singh and Jack (2018) envision gaining inter-cultural experiences via attending international cultural programs, language-support programs and local homestay programs. International students also want to enhance their career outcomes globally through gaining an international qualification (Pham et al., 2019), develop their personal and professional skills, such as research skills and their soft skills, and contribute to their home, host or third countries based on their international qualifications and skills (Singh & Jamil, 2021). Therefore, it is vital for teaching staff to provide a meaningful, supportive and safe learning and teaching environment for international students to engage with and to achieve academic success.

Pre-pandemic, most of the learning and teaching for students, including international students, was conducted either in traditional mode (face-to-face lectures, tutorials) or 'flipped' classroom mode (a combination of online and face-to-face). However, in the early days of COVID-19 in 2020, on a global scale higher education learning and teaching was moved online with immediate effect (Bozkurt & Sharma, 2020). This situation has impacted the learning and teaching process of students, including international students, at higher education level. The purpose of this chapter is to unpack reflections of an early-career international academic on the synchronous online strategies adopted to engage international students during COVID-19.

LITERATURE REVIEW: INTERNATIONAL STUDENTS' ACADEMIC CHALLENGES

In the main, a wide range of research focusses on international students' academic and social adjustment challenges (Singh, 2021). Underpinning these academic and social challenges is students' deficits in English proficiency (Haugh, 2016; Rao, 2017; Sherry et al., 2010). Brown's (2008) ethnographic study of such students found that they face problems when they communicate in English in both academic and social settings, whether written or oral. International students fear their accents may be ridiculed by others and prefer to stay silent in both settings (Rao, 2017). Although international students have enrolled in their courses with a minimum level of IELTS 6, the majority felt disadvantaged by having poor

English skills (Brown, 2008), since they could not express their arguments or perspectives eloquently in class or group discussions (Liu et al., 2010). Hence Xu (1991) concluded that TOEFL/IELTS scores were in themselves not accurate indicators of language abilities of international students in an academic environment.

Brown (2008) further reported problems experienced by international students in an academic setting, such as "insufficient comprehension of lectures, seminar discussion and day-to-day conversation; limited fluency, grasp of grammar and vocabulary" (p. 77), and that these impeded participation in the classroom and resulted in poor reading and writing skills. Rao (2017) added that international students found their professors' accents difficult to understand or the teaching material hard to comprehend fully, which were underpinned by lack of English competency. There wee lecturers who did not engage adequately with international students' learning because these academics were underprepared, they lacked teaching experience or they had no passion for teaching (Arkoudis et al., 2019). Consequently, international students have encountered non-timely completion of assignments, thesis chapters, examinations and tests, which then impede their academic success (Campbell & Li, 2008; Kim, 2007). Andrade (2006) also confirmed that high competency in English is an important factor for international students in achieving their academic success in terms of obtaining good grades in their courses (Li et al., 2002). Haugh (2016) argued that international students lack confidence or are shy in corresponding in English and that this situation has been mistakenly perceived as international students lacking ability to communicate in English.

Apart from language challenges, international academics also face pedagogical challenges in their learning. For example, international students from certain cultures, such as Asia and the Middle-East, may not be familiar with the pedagogical environment that Western universities typically showcase, which promote discussion-based activities such as case studies, debates and open class discussions (Rao, 2017). Through these activities, skills such as independent and critical thinking, problem solving, interpreting information, and communicating knowledge are developed and enhanced (Smith et al., 2019). However, international students are more comfortable with passive learning styles, such as engaging in non-participatory activity: sitting in on lectures or tutorials, taking notes, listening to discussion and memorizing learning materials (Huang, 2012; Robertson et al., 2000). As a result, international students prefer to not challenge their teachers or other students in discussion-based activities or provide critical and analytical comments or even ask diagnostic questions of others (Fell & Lukianova, 2015; Liu et al., 2010; Zhou et al., 2008). International students also prefer individual assignments over group assignments, as they feel their opinions are undervalued by other students, especially domestic students (Elliott & Reynolds, 2014). Due to these differing learning cultures, international students are often labelled as non-active learners, slow or disengaged in the learning process (Huang, 2012).

Online learning has also presented its own challenges for international students during pre-pandemic times. For instance, Chinese international students studying business had difficulty understanding which points were important and which ones wee not, because the faculty member did not recap the key points for them, unlike in China, where the academic staff member would summarise vital arguments (Liu et al., 2010). It proved difficult, too, to schedule a synchronous workshop, because international students were spread around the globe across different time zones (Liu et al., 2010), and at times they would miss the workshop due to its being held at odd hours. In addition, as learning materials were not provided in advance to international students, they felt that they could not prepare for the lessons to the best of their ability (Liu et al., 2010).

In terms of social challenges relating to language, international students in Kim's (2007) study made mistakes in wording their sentences and their improper grammar usage frustrated them in expressing their ideas in English with their friends. Language limitations also interfered with their daily conversations in their social space. International students in Malaysia have also experienced friendship barriers with local students (Malaklolunthu & Selan, 2011) and these barriers were related more to communication gaps: thus, Malaysian students were reluctant to converse in English with international students (Asgari & Borzooei, 2014); and, although Malaysian students were polite and friendly, they spoke the national language (Malay) among themselves and international students felt completely ignored and isolated.

TEACHING INTERNATIONAL STUDENTS: STRATEGIES

Smith (2020) has argued that curriculum and teaching staff development are considered lower priorities for host higher education institutions because they are *busy* recruiting international students without giving appropriate consideration to providing meaningful learning and teaching experiences for international students. However, Smith predicted that "this is expected to change as more institutions are developing academic-related internationalization initiatives" (p. 272) in order to satisfy international students' learning outcomes and to promote diversity and inclusion in teaching practices. Indeed, to develop inclusive universities, it is important for teaching staff members to be "engaged in internationalization efforts by paying more attention to international student success factors along with satisfaction of international students within the classroom and across the student experience" (p. 272).

According to Smith et al. (2019), faculty members have been able to improve their teaching of international students, resulting in high levels of student learning via promising teaching practices: for example, providing opportunities for classroom interaction and participation between international and domestic students, offering specific learning and study methods, providing international context and experiences in the classroom discussions and a supportive learning environment for international students (Huang, 2012). Students in Smith et al. (2019) appreciated teaching approaches that were student-centered, the use of interactive teaching methods such as games, "specific and prompt feedback, use of practical experiences, pleasant learning environment, and methods that support the learning of additional language learners" (p. 261). The latest findings by scholars (Li et al., 2021) are that academic staff members during COVID-19 online teaching did pay attention to international students via increased interaction with them and finding time to assist them, and by extensive resource preparation as well as their passion for teaching, which positively affected international students' online learning.

International students in Arkoudis et al.'s (2019) research were concerned about the inadequate teaching skills of academic staff members at Australian higher education institutions. For the former, they "seek to be engaged in their learning and are critical of teachers who they perceive to are not engaged with their teaching" (p. 805). There is a mismatch of intercultural teaching and learning expectations from international students (Zhou et al., 2008). Hence international students in Rao's (2017) research proposed that professors should offer detailed and developmental feedback, "encourage nurturing environments, and provide informal feedback for all assignments" (p. 1012), so that international students were able to understand and improve their work for future assignments. In reality, international students often just received an overall score for their work and with limited direction on how to improve it academically (Rao, 2017). Based on this, "international students are seeking a supportive learning environment where they can work collaboratively with their professors" (p.1012) and engage in their learning environment;

it is important for teaching staff members to accommodate international students preferred pedagogical needs. Rao further argued that "perhaps a modification in the pedagogies might be extremely helpful as the educational classrooms of today in most western nations reflect such student diversity" (p. 1012). For example, since international students still prefer classes in lecture format, "it might be helpful to lecture or present key concepts of chapters/subjects as it might alleviate some of the learning anxiety experienced by international students" (p. 1013) in absorbing knowledge.

In teaching international students, international academics have had a significant impact on the students' learning because they offer "a rich source of cultural, pedagogic and academic experience" (Minocha et al., 2019, p. 943) due to their international backgrounds. International academics provide international or global dimensions in their teaching through "problem-based teaching and project-based learning, using rich media in the classroom and embedding international case studies" (p. 952). VeLure Roholt and Fisher (2013) strongly suggest that academic staff members could facilitate meaningful classroom and online discussions by especially using international experiences that allow the experiential content to emerge with international students to support their learning. Minocha et al. (2019) observed that, as a result, such pedagogic approaches promote collaborative learning between international and domestic students in the classroom.

However, limited research had been conducted in exploring specific strategies adopted by higher education institutions and academic staff members to teach international students (Lomer & Mittelmeier, 2021) during the pandemic, and there are limited scholarly studies focusing on classroom pedagogies involving international students. Scholars (e.g., Chalmers & Volet, 1997; Leask & Carroll, 2011) have labelled international students passive and highly reluctant learners when it comes to participation in academic and social activities, either in or outside the classroom environment. As a result, international students are normally seen as being a deficient rather than resilient student cohort (Singh, 2021a). Accordingly, teaching strategies for international students are not always assessed appropriately in scholarly research (Lomer & Mittelmeier, 2021) in order to understand the underlying problem of academic failure or disengagement of international students in the higher education learning and teaching environment (Singh, 2020).

To address the gap in the literature in exploring online teaching approaches dedicated to international students during a time of crisis, the research question of this study is: *What are the successful synchronous online strategies adopted to engage international students during COVID-19?* The purpose of this chapter is to highlight several successful online teaching strategies adopted in a synchronous online learning environment by an early-career teaching academic to engage international students in the online learning and teaching environment as a result of COVID-19 impacts – and in an environment very different from that in the academic's home country.

METHODS

This study uses autoethnography as the method to encapsulate an early-career international academic's online teaching experiences and reflections during COVID-19 in 2020. Autoethnography falls under the interpretivist research paradigm and illustrates an individual's personal experience in a systematic manner to develop sociological understanding (Farrell et al., 2015). It is "an autobiographical genre of writing and research that displays multiple layers of consciousness, connecting the personal to the cultural" (Ellis & Bochner, 2000, p. 39). According to Stahlke Wall (2016, p.1), "personal experience methods can offer a new and unique vantage point from which to make a contribution to social science". Therefore, this method has provided the space for the author as an early-career international academic (with nearly nine years' teaching experience in Australia) to reflect upon her online teaching practices adopted in a synchronous online learning environment in COVID-19 and how the author has engaged international students in their learning experience. Reflection is an important aspect of autoethnography study. Rao et al. (2018) have defined early-career teaching academics as usually within their first ten years of their teaching journey. For the purposes of this chapter, international academics are individuals born overseas, "educated and enculturated in one system of education and currently teaching and re-searching in another" (Walker, 2015, p. 61), and therefore the author also falls into this category, because she was born and educated in Malaysia but currently works as a senior lecturer at La Trobe University, Melbourne and resides in Australia.

The sudden change to teaching fully online, and that too during the pandemic, was a new orientation and transition for the author and these challenging experiences are captured extensively in Singh (2021b) and in Singh and Chowdhury (2021).

In this study, the author wrote her individual recollections independently in a diary immediately after teaching, over a period of two semesters in 2020, so that she did not lose any insights and strategies that seemed to be beneficial in engaging international students in online workshops. The author specifically reflected on synchronous teaching strategies that engaged international students in the online learning environment, following this writing prompt – the central question: *What are the successful synchronous online strategies adopted to engage international students during COVID-19?* In analysis and interpretation of the data based on the diary entries, the author followed a thematic analysis approach to identify emerging themes from the collected data. This involved individual coding addressing the research question and then reaching several common themes in answering it. The effort to ensure the credibility and trustworthiness of data collection and analysis was embedded in the research process in two meaningful ways: (1) triangulating a variety of data from different sources and types (individual data of personal memory, the credibility of the author in reflecting the experience, and self-reflection based on journal entries) (Ellis & Bochner, 2000); and (2) placing the author's experiences within the larger body of scholarly studies.

The author then adopted a narrative style of writing (Ellis, 2004), where a first-person voice is utilised to describe personal experiences in the narrative.

Research Site and Positionality

The author started her academic career as a teaching tutor (sessional staff member) at several Australian universities from 2012. Upon PhD completion, the author was offered a contract position as an Associate Lecturer at La Trobe Business School in the Department of Management and after two years was appointed to a continuing (tenured) position as a lecturer. Just recently, the author was promoted to senior lecturer. The author mainly taught subjects relating to Management, Human Resources, Leadership, Negotiation and Organisational Behaviour.

The author has extensive experience in providing face-to-face lectures, tutorials and workshops. Since 2016, La Trobe has been offering subjects via the 'flipped' classroom approach and the author has experience in designing and delivering subjects under this *new* approach. The author and other teaching staff members at the university have uploaded and revised from time-to-time related learning and teaching materials, such as lectures, slides, reading materials and podcasts, complemented by delivering face-to-face workshops (mainly activity-based) to students. The flipped classroom model is underpinned by the active learning framework, where, Andrews et al. (2011) argue, active learning "occurs when an instructor stops lecturing and students work on a question or task designed to help them understand a concept" (p. 394) in the workshops. Students need to review concepts via reading online materials prior to the workshop and then engage in the workshop discussions to fully understand these concepts. McLean and Attardi (2018) further state that the instructor acts a moderator, rather than an information-deliverer in this flipped classroom approach.

Prior to 2020, the author had limited experience in online teaching' having never taught and co-ordinated online subjects. The author has been teaching students via the flipped classroom approach adopted at La Trobe University in 2016, due to the technological revolution. The flipped classroom model was introduced at La Trobe, with reading materials such as reading lists, podcasts, recorded lectures, slides, and other learning online materials provided via online platform such as the Learning Management System (LMS), to be viewed individually by students, and classroom time devoted to workshop activities and discussions (Abeysekera & Dawson, 2015).

However, due to the pandemic, the author started teaching remotely in March 2020 at La Trobe University. The author was given the responsibility to co-ordinate and teach two new subjects in 2020. She taught and co-ordinated a Human Resource Development subject in Semester 1 (March to May 2020) and a Negotiation subject in Semester 2 (July to October 2020). These subjects were undergraduate level in the La Trobe Business School. Pre-Covid, there were around 9,000 international students enrolled at the University, mainly drawn from India and China. Reflecting on the students' demographics, the author had a substantial number of international students from China and India enrolled in her subjects over both semesters. In Semester 1, the author taught two workshops and three in Semester 2. The workshops were activity-based and conducted for two hours for 12 weeks in Semester 1 and another 12 weeks in Semester 2. Students need to actively participate in the workshop activities, as they had prior knowledge of the topic through engaging with the online materials. In Semester 1, the author taught 78 students, of whom six international students were from China, and in Semester 2, the author taught 120 students, of whom five international students were from China and two from India.

RESULTS

Due to the COVID-19 outbreak, face-to-face teaching moved to remote or online teaching within a week at the author's university in March 2020. All teaching staff members only had a week to convert their face-to-face workshop-related teaching materials to suit the online delivery mechanism. Underpinned by the active learning framework, the face-to-face workshops are now offered online. The in-class workshops activities have been modified to be delivered online. Therefore, international students are still expected to be active learners in this modified flipped classroom approach during the pandemic. According to Singh et al. (2019), the flipped classroom learning environment "has shifted its focus from the traditional, one-way teaching to engage students in meaningful learning activities which supports the active learning principle" (p. 1311). A recent study by Singh et al. (2019) argues that international students are active learners during face-to-face workshops, where they interact with other students and the lecturer, as a result of engaging with the online materials before coming to workshops. McPhee and Pickren (2017) found that international students do review online materials in their own time at their own pace, and they do take ownership of their learning process seriously. From these research findings, we infer that international student are not disengaged in the classroom due to their low English proficiency levels (Rao, 2017).

Hence, in order to engage international students in the author's online workshops, the author adopted two major teaching strategies, mainly using Zoom functions and online games to engage international students in the synchronous online workshops. The teaching-related reflections are underpinned by the author's experiences as former international student and international academic in Australia. In this circumstance, the author does understand the anxiety, fear and discomfort experienced by international students in their learning in a completely new context. Therefore, the reflections are focused on the author's personal practices of online teaching in engaging international students in a synchronous online learning environment over two semesters in 2020.

Zoom Chat

During the pandemic, at La Trobe Zoom was used as the teaching tool to replace face-to-face contact hours with students. As the author only had a week to convert the face-to-face teaching materials to online and learn how to deliver workshops online, she had to quickly learn how to use the Zoom functions effectively to include international students in the online teaching. The author certainly did not want international students to feel disadvantaged via this new way of learning. The author, herself an international academic, observed that, in the first few workshops, international students were comfortable in communicating via the chat function as opposed to talking to the author directly during the workshop. This behaviour emulates what usually happened in face-face-face teaching prior to the pandemic, when international students would ask questions or clarifications not in the classroom itself but either before or after the class, in private.

Upon reflection, the author therefore used the chat function frequently to communicate with international students and also used it to provide workshop materials for students. This action especially benefited international students, as they were able to read and comprehend the material prior to the workshop activity:

During the synchronous online delivery via Zoom, I have used the chat function regularly, as I observed that international students prefer to communicate with me one-on-one via this function. Furthermore, I have provided information, messages and uploads/downloads of relevant files on the online learning activity via the chat function, as I understand international students will need time to read due to their English proficiency levels. (Semester 1 - Week 4, 2020)

The chat function is not only used to provide information on the learning activity; it is also used as a chatting function, not only with the workshop facilitator but also with other students. As an international academic, the author is mindful to provide discussion-based questions that take into account worldwide issues so that international students are able to provide their perspective easily:

I have noticed that international students also use it to send instant messages on concepts that they do not understand or to seek clarification on assignment questions. The function assisted international students who did not wish to share their questions with other classmates, especially for those feeling peer pressure, but who were motivated to engage in the online workshop. Also, I have noted that international students provide answers via the chat function to my broad questions in the online workshop – at times they sent them directly to me. (Semester 1 - Week 5, 2020)

The chat feature has been utilised as a non-verbal communication tool for international students to ask questions, seek clarifications, address questions posed in the workshop and also communicate with other students and the workshop facilitator.

Zoom Screen Sharing Function

Zoom has a screen sharing function which allows the author to display PowerPoint slides, and view related videos and other reading materials, so that international students are able to follow the topic under discussion during the workshop. As an international teaching academic, the author is aware that international students do prefer to read short notes and slides, an observation also supported by Singh et al. (2021), who argue that international students face problems with lengthy reading material because English is their second language.

In addition, to create active engagement in the online workshop and promote interactivity, Zoom screen sharing was also used to generate discussion via the annotate function. For example:

I have used screen annotation intensively so that international students are able to engage innovatively with the content shared on screen. For instance, I provide a question for students to answer and international students commonly use the annotate tool, such as text or draw (lines, arrows, and shapes) in composing answers to address the question asked by me. I perceive that they are much more confident in participating in the written discussion. (Semester 1 - Week 7, 2020)

The author noted that international students were interested in participating in online workshop activities as long as they were able to write on the screen as opposed to verbal communication. In addition, the author was also mindful of the importance of providing workshop activities such as case studies that were universal in context and were not skewed towards Australia alone, so that international students would be able to feel included and participate in the discussion unreservedly.

Demuyakor (2020) argued that successful and effective online learning is mainly dependent on how the workshop facilitator appreciates students' work and the availability of learning materials. Hence, in this context, the author usually saves the student answers as a screenshot in the workshop slides and the slides are shared on the LMS. This is to ensure that students are able to review the answers to the questions posed in the workshop activities:

I then normally saved the screen with all the annotations (i.e., answers to the questions asked) as a screenshot and included the screenshot in the slides which I will later share on the LMS upon completion of the Zoom workshop, so that international students could review materials for further understanding and assignment purposes. (Semester 1 - Week 6, 2020)

Singh et al. (2019) found that international students engage with online material in their own time and at their own pace for assignment purposes. Flexibility in learning is important to international students, because they are able to comprehend and deliberate further on the reading materials better without time pressure.

Zoom Breakout Room Tool

The breakout room is also vital to emulate small face-to-face group discussions in an online learning environment. Although the author does understand that international students prefer passive learning method or teacher-centred modes of learning, it is important for international students to have a supportive learning environment with their peers. Hence, the author has used the Zoom breakout room function purposely to promote integration between domestic and international students in the online workshop discussion. The author randomly allocated students for a short breakout room activity that took a maximum of 10 minutes to address case study questions. This was to encourage both cohorts of students to take full advantage in learning and engaging with one and another:

I have frequently used the breakout room tool in my weekly online workshops. I will randomly allocate students to different breakout rooms every week, as it provides domestic and international students with the opportunity to learn how to discuss and engage with each other and those they may have ignored in a face-to-face classroom otherwise. Based on my observation, in the face-to-face workshops domestic and international students will sit with their friends and not allow themselves to move around the entire semester. (Semester 1 - Week 8, 2020)

The breakout room function is also used to aid group assignment interactions and online peer-to-peer support, especially for assignment purposes. As many of the international students were studying from their respective home countries, the time difference was a hindrance for group members to have discussion on their assignment outside of the workshop time. Hence the author took note of that and provided a weekly consultation time for group assignment discussion during the workshops, usually the last 30 minutes before the workshop ended. This approach was received very well among students:

I also use the breakout room function to facilitate group assignments. I will usually provide a substantial amount of time for students to discuss their group assignment in the workshop itself, as I know that, due to the time difference, international students might be left out in the group discussion outside of the dedicated workshop time. Many international students were in their home countries due to the pandemic. (Semester 2 - Week 5, 2020)

The author also utilised breakout rooms to facilitate one-on-one drop-in sessions for any queries from students in regard to their individual or group assignments. The author discovered that numbers of emails from international students plummeted because of the drop-in session provided to them before the assignment's due date. The author deduced that international students understood the assignment requirement better during the breakout room discussions:

I have provided a drop-in session via the breakout room function for all group members to participate in separate rooms to discuss their group assignment extensively with me. This session was conducted a week before their group assignment was due, and this has reduced the number of emails from international students seeking extra guidance on their group assignment. (Semester 2 - Week 9, 2020)

Online Games

As an international academic, the author is sensitive to international students' learning experiences. For students not to be bored with similar weekly online workshop activities and to understand important concepts of the week, the author has been mindful of rotating activities with online games. For students to understand and grasp certain concepts, the author has created online games for students to engage with in the online workshops. The author has utilised many game-based learning platform such as Mentimeter and Quizzzzzzz but Kahoot! was mostly used to promote student engagement and fun in their learning. Kahoot! was the most requested game by students:

I have personally developed questions for my online games for students to engage with the weekly learning materials. I have used several online games platforms such as Mentimeter and Quizzzzzzz but it did not attract students to get involved as they would do in Kahoot! Therefore, upon reflection, I mostly use a game-based online activity - Kahoot! International students are fond of this game, as it promotes learning, but in a fun way. I usually have a multiple-choice questions quiz, which takes about 15 minutes of online class time and was conducted a few times during the semester. (Semester 2 - Week 4, 2020)

The author usually created questions that allowed students to think on their feet at times for a few seconds and at times longer – just to spice up their learning. International students chose to participate in this game as the questions were short and they were able to read and understand the questions quickly and also just choose one answer without any verbal communication. The author also provided feedback after each question was attempted and that made the learning more interesting since the students were able to understand the rationale and reasoning of the right answer.

Because the quiz is ungraded, I have observed that international students welcomed the use of this fun game, because they were able to answer most of the questions correctly and contribute to their learning. Immediate or real-time feedback after every question was provided to further clarify and explain the answers, which at times stirred excellent discussions between the students and myself. (Semester 2 - Week 10, 2020)

The fun and feel-good factor was extremely important in teaching during the COVID-19 lockdown as it gave a break to international students to be happy during online learning.

DISCUSSION

In the main, scholarly articles (Rao, 2017; Smith et al., 2019; Smith, 2020) have focused on international students' learning experiences pre-pandemic. This study contributes new empirical insights relating to online teaching strategies adopted by an early-career international academic to engage international students in the online learning and teaching environment during COVID-19. Using the author's experiences as former international student and current international academic in Australia, it observes that, when the faculty member is excited and enthusiastic about a new teaching approach, students' learning is enhanced (Smith et al., 2019) and this is the more so when international students are able to relate to international academic staff member rather than only with domestic staff members. Students who find faculty members valuing diverse culture, and being supportive and jovial, appreciate this and the learning experience is enhanced (Smith et al., 2019). According to Smith et al. (2019) one of the vital elements for teaching international students is to create an inclusive learning environment for international students to thrive and engage in their learning process in their host countries.

According to Cooney and Darcy (2020), it is important for staff members to effectively use Zoom functions such as annotate, chat, poll and breakout room tools to engage students online. The navigation of these functions is important; it must be learned and used creatively to engage students in the synchronous online workshop and learn the week's content in a fun way. Based on the reflections of an early-career international academic at an Australian university, there are several Zoom functions such as the chat, screen sharing and breakout room tools that were predominately utilised innovatively to engage international students in the weekly synchronous online workshop over two semesters in 2020. In addition to the Zoom functions, the academic also incorporated online games into the weekly workshops to provide a sense of fun in learning and inclusiveness for international students to be engaged in their online learning environment. Where possible in the workshop activities, the international academic provided examples and activities such as case studies that wee not skewed towards understanding Australian contexts alone but were worldwide. The intention was for international students to be able to feel included in the learning process and participate in the discussion as well as learning the subject content with wide knowledge and application.

Previous research (Asgari & Borzooei, 2014; Brown, 2008; Kim, 2007) has indicated that international students have low confidence in communicating in the English language and are regarded as passive learners in the traditional learning mode (face-to-face) due to their differing learning styles (Rao, 2017). During COVID, as face-to-face learning shifted online, international students were reflecting their behaviour of not strongly communicating verbally either in individual or group discussions due to fears about their accents and low English proficiency (Rao, 2017). Therefore, after reflecting on this, the academic used the chat function effectively in communicating, providing vital information relating to students' learning materials and assignment clarifications, and this was the able to engage international students in online workshop discussions. The latest research by Li et al. (2021) during COVID-19 has argued that international students demonstrated their engagement levels by participating in online discussions and message postings, as well as by reviewing lessons before online workshop, which is similar to the observations made by the early-career international academic in this study. Correspondingly, a recent study by Stanchevici and Siczek (2019) found that, by regularly posting through the chat function, "students practice writing and participate in class discussions more deeply and consistently than they do in oral conversations in the classroom" (p. 148). In addition, social engagement with other students is also enhanced via the chat function. Such interactions are an important indicator to further develop social relationships in an online class, but for it to be successful Stanchevici and Siczek suggest that "online interactions must be guided with clear instructions and requirements" (p. 148) from the workshop facilitator.

In addition to the chat function, the international academic also used the screen sharing function to share learning materials such as the PowerPoint slides, watch related videos and access other reading materials. International students in Smith et al. (2019) appreciated the provision of the slides before they started their class, as this reduced their anxiety in the classroom. The international academic also utilised the annotate feature to include international academics in the class discussion by writing their answers against the question(s) posed. International students in Rinehart and Cong (2011) were much more confident in participating in online discussion because they have had more time to reflect, consider, and read other posts, as well as editing and proof reading their own posts, thus providing a greater active voice in the online setting. Moreover, students need to address the questions with short answers using annotate function, therefore, creating less dependency on their English ability, unlike writing or speaking in long sentences (Brown, 2008).

The breakout room function is a useful tool for facilitating collaborative learning and effective interaction between students and facilitators, according to Chandler's (2016) advice. Although the international academic observed that international students are comfortable to learn passively due to their cultural pedagogic values, which is similar to Rao's (2017) findings, it is vital for international students to be active learners in the online learning environment in order to gain much knowledge and skills to be applied in the global employment market. Chandler (2016) further argued that "interaction in an online tutorial also provides students learning at a distance with a rare opportunity for peer-to-peer contact, which can be invaluable in building relationships and confidence" (p. 16), especially for international students who are shy and do not communicate with domestic students in the face-to-face traditional learning mode (Rao, 2017). Online intervention via breakout rooms provides more personal opportunity for students to have a dialogue together and facilitate independent work (Chandler, 2016). In particular, international students can be at ease, "knowing that their input to a discussion can only be heard by the small group of their peers present in the room and the discussion cannot be recorded" (Chandler, 2016, p.16). Breakout rooms were used also for students to discuss and finalise their group assignments (Quezada et al., 2020). Chandler (2016) found that students had the time to plan with one and another to tackle their assignment topic together.

Many international students still prefer the combination of traditional methods of teaching, where the lecturer provides the content knowledge coupled with active interaction between both parties – students and lecturer via interactive teaching methods (Singh et al., 2021; Smith et al., 2019). But in these unprecedented times, Chandler (2016) has argued that learning how to use breakout room enhances student engagement and makes sessions more interactive, as opposed to the facilitator having a whole online class discussion. It can be quite boring for students to hear facilitator's voice only and international students usually then become silent participants in the whole group discussion because of their lower level of English competency (Rao, 2017).

In addition to the utilisation of Zoom functions to engage international students, the international academic incorporated online games for students to understand important concepts of the weekly learning content. Rather than giving a short lecture on the weekly content, the academic was creative in using game-based learning platforms to engage students to study the concepts. She did use several other game-based learning platforms, such as Mentimeter and Quizzzzzzz, but upon deep reflection measuring student engagement, Kahoot! was the preferred mode of learning requested by international students. Correspondingly, as noticed by Martín-Sómer et al. (2021), that the transfer from face-to-face to remote teaching could result in a general decrease in interest of students to engage and learn online could be mitigated by using digital technology applications such as the Kahoot! games. For example, Donkin and Rasmussen (2021) reported that "in the first quarter of 2020 the game-based software Kahoot! reported a threefold increase in players and a fivefold increase in asynchronous learning globally" (p. 572). Kahoot! is a fun-based activity designed to further review and support students' knowledge and learning in an online setting (Plump & LaRosa, 2017; Wang & Tahir, 2020). Therefore, Kahoot! was chosen as an online gaming platform by the international academic in this study to enhance students' engagement and learning in the COVID-19 environment.

International students engaged with the Kahoot! quiz because it was easy for them to understand the questions in a very short time and that motivated them to be more attentive and become more engaged online, similar to Muhridza et al.'s (2018) findings. It also created a more 'relaxed' learning environment (Smith et al., 2019). Interestingly, Mada and Anharudin (2019) found that Kahoot! was able to increase students' learning motivation because it provided benefits to students in being able to recall the material given, "making them more excited, feeling happy, not feeling bored and being able to actively participate in doing the exercises" (p. 426). Further, the discussion following completion of the Kahoot! quiz adopted by the international academic "gave students feedback to immediately correct their own mistakes, knowing if they got an answer right or wrong, and more importantly, why" (Licorish et al., 2018, p. 16); "exploring the answers and understanding why they were right or wrong generated a deeper understanding that strongly aided participants' engagement and retention of knowledge" (p. 16). However, the international academic also noticed that, when students were not involved in the game, this was due to only one barrier, which was unstable internet connections or internet networks (Mada & Anharudin, 2019).

CONCLUSION

This chapter has recorded how an early-career international academic teaching in one of Australia's higher education institutions adopted online teaching practices in a synchronous online learning environment that engaged international students during COVID-19. It was not an easy task to teach online subjects, and that too during the pandemic, because the teaching staff member had never taught any online subjects or even experienced learning via online mechanism either at home or in a host country. Further, changing the mode of teaching from face-to-face to online in just a week due to the pandemic was challenging as the international academic was mindful of providing inclusive online learning environment to international students. Underpinned by deep reflection on as well as trial and error in using several Zoom functions effectively in weekly online workshop activities and incorporating online games platform such as Kahoot! and providing workshop activities that captured worldwide contexts, international students were engaged in the synchronous online learning environment during COVID-19.

Given that the research findings are based on a relatively small-scale autoethnography study, it is important to note that the emergent themes of teaching strategies adopted to engage international students during COVID-19 are neither definitive or comprehensive: they reflect the lived experiences of an early=career international academic teaching in a university in Victoria, Australia. Hence, they are not generalisable, since they do not represent the lived experiences of all early-career international teaching academics in Australia. Future studies should consider the inclusion of a larger sample size of international academics through a more strategic sampling approach and with a focus on triangulation. A quantitative approach that enables the examination of a larger international academic population in relation to their teaching-related strategies to include international students in their virtual classrooms in Australia should be considered. A comparative study with Canada, the United States and United Kingdom is also recommended, because the findings and discussions will have relevance globally, given that the international academic population is also growing in these countries. In addition, future research work might also want to include international students in gauging their engagement experiences through the synchronous learning experience during COVID.

There are a number of important practical implications that arise from these findings for early career international academic themselves and for Australian higher education institutions. For early-career international teaching staff members, meaningfully including and engaging international students in their learning and teaching process are vital. Students feel they belong not only to the subject or course that they are studying in but also to the university if they are able to engage meaningfully in the classroom as well as outside the classroom environment. The exploration of the author's personal teaching experience as an international academic contributes a voice to the underrepresented early-career international teaching staff members in the higher education system. As Singh and Chowdhury (2021) say, it is important "for international academics to feel comfortable and to adjust to the new learning and teaching environment, especially during times of crisis, so that they are able to provide the best learning experience to students" (p. 13). For Australian higher education institutions, these findings imply that ongoing and sustainable teaching-related support mechanisms should be in place to assist international academics to thrive in their teaching during the pandemic. As such, teaching-related training and development programs, as well as mentorship guidance, are vital factors for international academics in order to foster their teaching capabilities and provide an inclusive learning and teaching environment for students.

REFERENCES

Abeysekera, L., & Dawson, P. (2015). Motivation and cognitive load in the flipped classroom: Definition, rationale and a call for research. *Higher Education Research & Development, 34*(1), 1–14. doi:10.1080/07294360.2014.934336

Andrade, M. S. (2006). International students in English-speaking universities: Adjustment factors. *Journal of Research in International Education, 5*(2), 131–154. doi:10.1177/1475240906065589

Andrews, T. M., Leonard, M. J., Colgrove, C. A., & Kalinowski, S. T. (2011). Active learning not associated with student learning in a random sample of college biology courses. *CBE Life Sciences Education, 10*(4), 394–405. doi:10.1187/cbe.11-07-0061 PMID:22135373

Arkoudis, S., Dollinger, M., Baik, C., & Patience, A. (2019). International students' experience in Australian higher education: Can we do better? *Higher Education, 77*(5), 799–813. doi:10.100710734-018-0302-x

Asgari, M., & Borzooei, M. (2014). Evaluating the perception of Iranian students as educational tourists toward Malaysia: In-depth interviews. *Interdisciplinary Journal of Contemporary Research in Business, 5*(9), 81–109.

Bozkurt, A., & Sharma, R. C. (2020). Emergency remote teaching in a time of global crisis due to CoronaVirus pandemic. *Asian Journal of Distance Education, 15*(1), i–vi.

Brown, L. (2008). Language and anxiety: An ethnographic study of international postgraduate students. *Evaluation and Research in Education, 21*(2), 75–95. doi:10.1080/09500790802152167

Campbell, J., & Li, M. (2008). Asian students' voices: An empirical study of Asian students' learning experiences at a New Zealand university. *Journal of Studies in International Education, 12*(4), 375–396. doi:10.1177/1028315307299422

Chalmers, D., & Volet, S. (1997). Common misconceptions about students from South-East Asia studying in Australia. *Higher Education Research & Development, 16*(1), 87–99. doi:10.1080/0729436970160107

Chandler, K. (2016). Using breakout rooms in synchronous online tutorials. *Journal of Perspectives in Applied Academic Practice, 4*(3), 16–23. doi:10.14297/jpaap.v4i3.216

Cooney, A., & Darcy, E. (2020). 'It was fun': Exploring the pedagogical value of collaborative educational games. *Journal of University Teaching & Learning Practice, 17*(3), 1–15. https://ro.uow.edu.au/jutlp/vol17/iss3/4. doi:10.53761/1.17.3.4

Demuyakor, J. (2020). Coronavirus (COVID-19) and online learning in higher institutions of education: A survey of the perceptions of Ghanaian international students in China. *Online Journal of Communication and Media Technologies, 10*(3), 1–9. doi:10.29333/ojcmt/8286

Department of Education, Skills and Employment. (2020b). *Education export income by country 2019.* Retrieved from https://internationaleducation.gov.au/research/research-snapshots/Documents/RS%20Education%20export%202019.pdf

Department of Education, Skills and Employment. (2021). *End of Year Summary of International Student Data 2020.* Retrieved from https://internationaleducation.gov.au/research/international-student-data/Documents/Monthly%20Summaries/2020/Full%20year%20summary.pdf

Donkin, R., & Rasmussen, R. (2021). Student perception and the effectiveness of Kahoot!: A Scoping review in Histology, Anatomy, and Medical Education. *Anatomical Sciences Education, 14*(5), 572–585. doi:10.1002/ase.2094 PMID:33900041

Elliott, C. J., & Reynolds, M. (2014). Participative pedagogies, group work and the international classroom: An account of students' and tutors' experiences. *Studies in Higher Education, 39*(2), 307–320. doi:10.1080/03075079.2012.709492

Ellis, C. (2004). *The ethnographic I: A methodological novel about autoethnography.* Altamira Press.

Ellis, C., & Bochner, A. (2000). Autoethnography, personal narrative, reflexivity: Researcher as subject. In N. K. Denzin & Y. S. Lincoln (Eds.), *Handbook of qualitative research* (2nd ed., pp. 733–768). Sage Publications, Inc.

Farrell, L., Bourgeois-Law, G., Regehr, G., & Ajjawi, R. (2015). Autoethnography: Introducing 'I' into medical education research. *Medical Education, 49*(10), 974–982. doi:10.1111/medu.12761 PMID:26383069

Fell, E. V., & Lukianova, N. A. (2015). British universities: International students' alleged lack of critical thinking. *Procedia: Social and Behavioral Sciences, 215*, 2–8. doi:10.1016/j.sbspro.2015.11.565

Haugh, M. (2016). Complaints and troubles talk about the English language skills of international students in Australian universities. *Higher Education Research & Development, 35*(4), 727–740. doi:10.1080/07294360.2015.1137878

Healey, M., Flint, A., & Harrington, K. (2014). *Engagement through partnership: Students as partners in learning and teaching in higher education.* HEA.

Hoang, T. V. Y., & Rojas-Lizana, I. (2015). Promotional discourse in the websites of two Australian universities: A discourse analytic approach. *Cogent Education*, 2(1), 1011488. Advance online publication. doi:10.1080/2331186X.2015.1011488

Huang, Y. (2012). Transitioning challenges faced by Chinese graduate students. *Adult Learning*, 23(3), 138–147. doi:10.1177/1045159512452861

Kim, Y. (2007). Difficulties in quality doctoral academic advising: Experiences of Korean students. *Journal of Research in International Education*, 6(2), 171–193. doi:10.1177/1475240907078613

Leask, B., & Carroll, J. (2011). Moving beyond 'wishing and hoping': Internationalisation and student experiences of inclusion and engagement. *Higher Education Research & Development*, 30(5), 647–659. doi:10.1080/07294360.2011.598454

Li, M., Baker, T., & Marshall, K. (2002). Mismatched expectations: A case study of Asian students in New Zealand. *New Zealand Journal of Applied Business Research*, 1(1), 137–156.

Li, W., Gillies, R., He, M., Wu, C., Liu, S., Gong, Z., & Sun, H. (2021). Barriers and facilitators to online medical and nursing education during the COVID-19 pandemic: Perspectives from international students from low-and middle-income countries and their teaching staff. *Human Resources for Health*, 19(1), 1–14. doi:10.118612960-021-00609-9 PMID:33980228

Licorish, S. A., Owen, H. E., Daniel, B., & George, J. L. (2018). Students' perception of Kahoot!'s influence on teaching and learning. *Research and Practice in Technology Enhanced Learning*, 13(1), 1–23. doi:10.118641039-018-0078-8 PMID:30595732

Liu, X., Liu, S., Lee, S. H., & Magjuka, R. J. (2010). Cultural differences in online learning: International student perceptions. *Journal of Educational Technology & Society*, 13(3), 177–188.

Lomer, S., & Mittelmeier, J. (2021). Mapping the research on pedagogies with international students in the UK: A systematic literature review. *Teaching in Higher Education*, 1–21. doi:10.1080/1356251 7.2021.1872532

Mada, R. D., & Anharudin, A. (2019). How online learning evaluation (Kahoot) affecting students' achievement and motivation (Case Study on it Students). *International Journal for Educational and Vocational Studies*, 1(5), 422–427. doi:10.29103/ijevs.v1i5.1494

Malaklolunthu, S., & Selan, P. S. (2011). Adjustment problems among international students in Malaysian private higher education institutions. *Procedia: Social and Behavioral Sciences*, 15, 833–837. doi:10.1016/j.sbspro.2011.03.194

Martín-Sómer, M., Moreira, J., & Casado, C. (2021). Use of Kahoot! to keep students' motivation during online classes in the lockdown period caused by Covid 19. *Education for Chemical Engineers*, 36, 154–159. doi:10.1016/j.ece.2021.05.005

Mazzarol, T., & Soutar, G. N. (2002). "Push-pull" factors influencing international student destination choice. *International Journal of Educational Management*, 16(2), 82–90. doi:10.1108/09513540210418403

McLean, S., & Attardi, S. M. (2018). Sage or guide? Student perceptions of the role of the instructor in a flipped classroom. In Active learning in higher education (pp. 1–13). doi:10.1177/1469787418793725

McPhee, S., & Pickren, G. (2017). Blended learning with international students: A multiliteracies approach. *Journal of Geography in Higher Education*, *41*(3), 418–433. doi:10.1080/03098265.2017.1331208

Minocha, S., Shiel, C., & Hristov, D. (2019). International academic staff in UK higher education: Campus internationalisation and innovation in academic practice. *Journal of Further and Higher Education*, *43*(7), 942–958. doi:10.1080/0309877X.2018.1429582

Muhridza, N. H. M., Rosli, N. A. M., Sirri, A., & Samad, A. A. (2018). Using game-based technology, KAHOOT! for classroom engagement. *LSP International Journal*, *5*(2), 37–48. doi:10.11113/lspi.v5n2.77

Pham, T., Tomlinson, M., & Thompson, C. (2019). Forms of capital and agency as mediations in negotiating employability of international graduate migrants. *Globalisation, Societies and Education*, *17*(3), 394–405. doi:10.1080/14767724.2019.1583091

Phan, A. N. Q. (2021). Sojourning as a wife, a mother and a daughter: A critical autoethnography of a Vietnamese doctoral student in New Zealand. *Journal of Gender Studies*. Advance online publication. doi:10.1080/09589236.2021.198853

Plump, C. M., & LaRosa, J. (2017). Using Kahoot! in the classroom to create engagement and active learning: A game-based technology solution for e-learning novices. *Management Teaching Review*, *2*(2), 151–158. doi:10.1177/2379298116689783

Quezada, R. L., Talbot, C., & Quezada-Parker, K. B. (2020). From bricks and mortar to remote teaching: A teacher education programme's response to COVID-19. *Journal of Education for Teaching*, *46*(4), 1–12. doi:10.1080/02607476.2020.1801330

Rao, N., Yeh, C. S. H., Hosein, A., & Kinchin, I. (2018). Academics' international teaching journeys: An introduction. In A. Hosein, N. Rao, C. S. H. Yeh, & I. M. Kinchin (Eds.), *Academics' International Teaching Journeys: Personal Narratives of Transitions in Higher Education* (pp. 1–12). Bloomsbury Publishing.

Rao, P. (2017). Learning challenges and preferred pedagogies of international students. *International Journal of Educational Management*, *31*(7), 1000–1016. doi:10.1108/IJEM-01-2016-0001

Rinehart, E., & Cong, Y. (2011). Chinese international students' experience of studying online in New Zealand. *Waikato Journal of Education*, *16*(1), 93–105.

Robertson, M., Line, M., Jones, S., & Thomas, S. (2000). International students, learning environments and perceptions: A case study using the Delphi technique. *Higher Education Research & Development*, *19*(1), 89–102. doi:10.1080/07294360050020499

Roy, R., & Uekusa, S. (2020). Collaborative autoethnography: "Self-reflection" as a timely alternative research approach during the global pandemic. *Qualitative Research Journal*, *20*(4), 383–392. doi:10.1108/QRJ-06-2020-0054

Sherry, M., Thomas, P., & Wing, C. H. (2010). International students: A vulnerable student population. *Higher Education*, *60*(1), 33–46. doi:10.100710734-009-9284-z

Singh, J. K. N. (2017). Human capital or talent development? A paradigm shift by Malaysian higher education. In H. de Wit, J. Gacel-Ávila, E. Jones, & N. Jooste (Eds.), *The globalization of internationalization: Emerging voices and perspectives*. Routledge.

Singh, J. K. N. (2020). Academic Failure: Unspoken Experiences by International Postgraduate Students in a Malaysian University. *IAFOR Journal of Education: Studies in Education, 8*(4), 79-94. https://eric.ed.gov/?id=EJ1279427

Singh, J. K. N. (2021a). Academic resilience among international students: Lived experiences of postgraduate international students in Malaysia. *Asia Pacific Education Review, 22*(1), 129–138. doi:10.100712564-020-09657-7

Singh, J. K. N. (2021b). Online learning and best teaching practices in COVID-19 environment: A case study in Australia. *SEAMEO Journal, 2,* 47-53. https://www.seameo.org/img/Publications/SEAMES/SEAMEO%20Journal%202020%20%20V2%20Special%20Issue.pdf

Singh, J. K. N., & Chowdhury, H. (2021). Early-career international academics' learning and teaching experiences during COVID-19 in Australia: A collaborative autoethnography. *Journal of University Teaching & Learning Practice, 18*(5), 1–17. doi:10.53761/1.18.5.12

Singh, J. K. N., & Jack, G. (2018). The benefits of overseas study for international postgraduate students in Malaysia. *Higher Education, 75*(4), 607–624. doi:10.100710734-017-0159-4

Singh, J. K. N., Jacob, J., Nagpal, S., & Inglis, S. (2021). Undergraduate international students' challenges in a flipped classroom environment: An Australian perspective. *Innovations in Education and Teaching International*, 1–12. Advance online publication. doi:10.1080/14703297.2021.1948888

Singh, J. K. N., & Jamil, H. (2021). International education and meaningful contributions to society: Exploration of postgraduate international students' perspectives studying in a Malaysian research university. *International Journal of Educational Development, 81*, 102331. Advance online publication. doi:10.1016/j.ijedudev.2020.102331

Singh, J. K. N., Nagpal, S., Inglis, S., & Jacob-John, J. (2019). International students' experiences in a flipped classroom environment: An Australian perspective. *International Journal of Educational Management, 33*(6), 1303–1315. doi:10.1108/IJEM-11-2018-0362

Smith, C. (2020). International students and their academic experiences: Student satisfaction, student success challenges, and promising teaching practices. In *Rethinking education across borders* (pp. 271–287). Springer. doi:10.1007/978-981-15-2399-1_16

Smith, C. A., Zhou, G., Potter, M., & Wang, D. (2019). Connecting best practices for teaching linguistically and culturally diverse international students with international student satisfaction and student perceptions of student learning. *Advances in Global Education and Research, 3,* 252-265. https://scholar.uwindsor.ca/educationpub/24

Stahlke Wall, S. (2016). Toward a moderate autoethnography. *International Journal of Qualitative Methods, 15*(1), 1–9. doi:10.1177/1609406916674966

Stanchevici, D., & Siczek, M. (2019). Performance, interaction, and satisfaction of graduate EAP students in a face-to-face and an online class: A comparative analysis. *TESL Canada Journal, 36*(3), 132–153. doi:10.18806/tesl.v36i3.1324

VeLure Roholt, R., & Fisher, C. (2013). Expect the unexpected: International short-term study course pedagogies and practices. *Journal of Social Work Education, 49*(1), 48–65. doi:10.1080/10437797.20 13.755416

Waller, V., Farquharson, K., & Dempsey, D. (2015). *Qualitative social research: Contemporary methods for the digital age.* Sage Publications.

Wang, A. I., & Tahir, R. (2020). The effect of using Kahoot! for learning–A literature review. *Computers & Education, 149*, 1–22. doi:10.1016/j.compedu.2020.103818

Xu, M. (1991). The impact of English-language proficiency on international graduate students' perceived academic difficulty. *Research in Higher Education, 32*(5), 557–570. doi:10.1007/BF00992628

Zhou, Y., Jindal-Snape, D., Topping, K., & Todman, J. (2008). Theoretical models of culture shock and adaptation in international students in higher education. *Studies in Higher Education, 33*(1), 63–75. doi:10.1080/03075070701794833

Chapter 20
A Systematic Review of Online Learning of International Students

Thi Kim Thu Le

HCMC University of Technology and Education, Vietnam & University of Windsor, Canada

Khanh Van Pham

HCMC University of Technology and Education, Vietnam

ABSTRACT

In response to COVID-19, universities have increasingly adopted online teaching to expand students' access to education. Integrating technology into online teaching is considered one of the best teaching practices since it provides international students with multiple benefits. Through a systematic review, this chapter goes through a critical analysis and synthesis process to explore the benefits technology brings to international students, leading to a more comprehensive understanding of how technology works best and what students' preferences truly are in an online context. Drawing on 20 selected articles, the review finds that there are five main benefits of online learning. It also provides conceptual work by identifying a taxonomy of three crucial values of technology integration to teaching international learners in an online environment. Implications are made with regards to the best teaching practices to reshape policies and curriculum designs. The study calls for further studies pertaining to featured factors of teachers and student and stakeholder focuses.

INTRODUCTION

In this review, international students are used to describe those who "have left his or her country, or territory of origin, and moved to another country or territory with the singular objective of studying" (UNESCO Institute for Statistics, 2009, p. 36). However, in response to the Covid-19 pandemic, international students can be referred to foreign students as "non-citizens enrolled at an institution of education

DOI: 10.4018/978-1-7998-8921-2.ch020

outside their home country, but who have not necessarily crossed a border to study" (OECD & UIS, 2006, p. 351). Therefore, these two terms are used interchangeably throughout the review.

Online learning (also called web-based learning, computer-mediated learning, e-learning) has become more accessible thanks to rapid technological advancements (McBrien et al., 2009). It is defined as a learning experience in synchronous or asynchronous contexts using various devices with internet access, where students can be anywhere (independent) in these spaces to learn and connect with their teachers and peers (Singh & Thurman, 2019). According to Dhawan (2020), in online learning environments, a great deal of student-centeredness, innovation and flexibility are found to be escalated within the teaching and learning process.

However, online teaching and learning has also posed numerous major challenges that stakeholders have to take into consideration. Without the actual presence of the teachers and students in the online study environment, interactions between teachers and learners and among learners themselves have been becoming more and more sluggish, which is unexpectedly contradictory to students' desire for two-way interaction (Dhawan, 2020). According to Baber (2021), a shortage of interaction in virtual classes is one of the barriers minimizing the effectiveness of teaching and learning processes. Moreover, students believe that the primary challenges to online learning are a lack of a sense of community, technological issues, and difficulty comprehending educational goals (Song et al., 2004). On account of that, Smith et al. (2019a) states that teaching practices highly accommodating students' learning needs are supposedly to obtain students' high perception of studying levels. Those teaching practices, including "academic integrity, assessment, assignments, clarifying expectations, communicating outside of the classroom, lecture design and delivery, verbal communications, and visual communications," could lead to highly expected rates of either student satisfaction or student perceptions of studying (Smith et al., 2019a, p. 256). In the trend of today's educational context, appropriate teaching activities incorporating educational technology are widely supposed to make education more meaningful, exciting, and relevant to students, dramatically enhancing the students' learning experience (Dhawan, 2020; Gray et al., 2010; Karasavvidis & Kollias, 2014; King et al., 2014; Li & Zhang, 2015; Smith et al., 2021). The intensive integration of technological tools into virtual classes appears to be a fundamental way to connect teachers and students together, making the teaching and learning process meaningful and fruitful.

This systematic review aims to investigate to what extent various employed research methods are applicable in a number of chosen articles and whether the integration of technologies into teaching international students online can be effective or not. The review seeks for answers to the following research questions.

1. What are the research methods that are featured in the collected articles within the systematic review?
2. What are the benefits of online learning with the use of different technological tools to teaching international learners online in published literature over the last two decades?

This paper makes several remarkable contributions to the existing body of literature. It is among the first to provide a big picture of how effective the use of technological tools is to teaching international students in an online learning environment. Online learning has gained its increasing popularity, hence, this review also offers educational implications and crucial considerations that researchers, technical designers, and teachers teaching international students online would likely take into account. Finally, by critically analyzing different research methods used in the selected articles, this review explores insights into the appropriate use of a particular research design in helping to answer the research questions and solve research problems. In doing so, this study contributes to the theoretical work pertaining to the core values of online learning in preparing international students' essential skills, knowledge, and attitudes for future personal and professional development.

The rest of the review is organized as follows: The next section describes the methodology, followed by a section that presents and discusses the major findings from selected papers. The last section concludes the paper with a summary of five key benefits of an online learning environment and a taxonomy of the core values that integrating technology into online teaching brings to international students, followed by some educational implications and further research avenues.

METHODOLOGY

With the aim of examining the available literature in such a way that it allows a clear conclusion on what is known and what is not about the reviewed topic (Denyer & Tranfield, 2009), this review adapted the framework of Xiao and Watson (2017) by following three main stages with eight steps.

Figure 1. Process of a systematic literature review (Xiao & Watson, 2017)

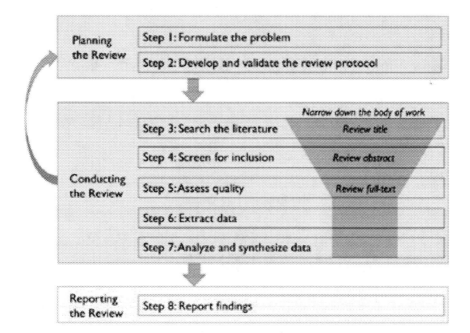

Step 1: Formulate the Research Problems

The main researcher of the paper, currently an international student in the joint PhD program at a university in Canada, is experiencing online studying in a culturally and linguistically diverse learning environment. After reading the article related to the best teaching practices for the teaching of international students conducted by Smith et al. (2019a), she has gained more interest in investigating international student learning experiences in an online environment, which has inspired her to conduct a thorough and systematic review on the topic.

Step 2: Develop and Validate the Review Protocol

This was a very crucial step since it determined the rigorousness and helped enhance the quality of the review. In this step, the researchers identified research aims, research questions, inclusion criteria, search strategies, quality assessment criteria and screening procedures, and strategies for data extraction, synthesis, and reporting.

Step 3: Searching for Literature

A range of 20-year investigations between 2000 and 2021 have been considered. The articles were collected from different peer-reviewed journals such as Scopus, Elsevier, Web of Science, JSTOR, SAGE, Springer, Taylor and Francis, and Wiley with the following codes:

International students/learners and online learning
Foreign students/learners and online learning
Technology and international students/learners
Technological tools + International students/learners

Step 4: Screening for Inclusion and Step 5: Assessing Quality

In these steps, based on the research aims, questions, and methodology, the researchers screened the titles, abstracts, and keywords according to the inclusion and exclusion criteria that had been established in Step 2. If the abstract did not provide enough information, the researcher could also read the entire study, especially the conclusion section. The articles are selected with the following requirements: (1) methodology designs could be a literature review, qualitative, quantitative, or mixed methods; (2) research participants must be post-secondary international students, and (3) the study context was online learning.

Step 6: Extract Data and Step 7: Analyze and Synthesize Data

Identified and selected articles were thoroughly read, classified, and analyzed through/by the researchers. The extracted data included: author, years of publication, research design/methods used, technological tools used, key concepts/themes. The data were presented and described in tables for the regression analysis based on contingent design in which different descriptive themes were used to answer two research questions in this review (Sandelowski, Voils, & Barroso 2006).

Step 8: Report Findings

As the final step, there were five key themes pertaining to the international student learning experience in an online environment, including satisfaction, engagement, communication and interaction, academic performance, and educational equity.

FINDINGS

The Research Methods That Are Featured in The Collected Articles Within the Systematic Review

The research methods used in the twenty studies were classified into qualitative, quantitative, mixed method, and literature review, see Figure 2.

Figure 2. Research designs applied in the selected articles

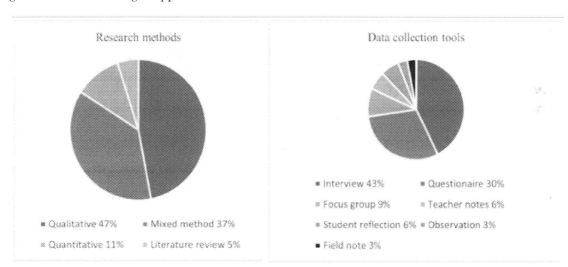

This figure demonstrates that the vast majority of the studies adopted the qualitative method (n=9, 47%), followed by the mixed method (n=8, 37%). The quantitative method and literature review accounted for the smallest portion, at n=2, 11%, and n=1, 5%, respectively. The findings mean that the selection of research methods was inconsistent but had a tendency to apply qualitative and mixed methods. However, the selection of research methods depends on research goals, helping solve the research problems and answer the research questions.

Table 1 below describes twenty selected articles with different research methods and data collection tools. The only literature review by Alexander (2002) was selected since it was related to all sections of the paper (Chen et al., 2016), and it described a "fully professional grasp of the background theory" (Phillips & Pugh, 1987, p. 53). Drawing on the scholarship of Alexander (2002) on the range of issues and challenges associated with provision of online learning, the researchers had an overview of the increasing use of the Internet to facilitate teaching and learning opportunities and a number of benefits to international students in particular and to higher education institutions in general.

Eight studies adopting mixed methods included Garrett and Cutting (2012), Gray, Chang, and Kennedy (2010), Karkar-Esperat (2018), King and So (2014), Li and Zhang (2015), Smith et al. (2019), Sadykova (2014), and finally Zhu et al. (2021) with various data collection tools such as surveys, interviews, focus group discussions, document analysis, field notes, Google analytics, student reflections, and researcher's journal entries. The similarity among these studies was the research scope, particularly a research project between two universities in two countries (Garrett & Cutting, 2012; Li & Zhang, 2015), a study project for an international symposium (Smith et al., 2019b), or two consecutive studies with many rounds of data collection (Gray, Chang & Kennedy, 2010; King & So, 2014; Sadykova, 2014; Zhu et al., 2021). The general research purpose was another similarity among the studies. Creswell and Creswell (2018) noted that the reasons for choosing mixed methods were to compare different perspectives drawn from quantitative and qualitative data, and to understand the research results by incorporating the perspectives of individuals. Particularly, by collecting data from questionnaires, interviews, focus group discussions, and student and teacher reflections, Garrett and Cutting (2012), Li and Zhang (2015), Sadykova (2014), and Karkar-Esperat (2018) wanted to explore a collaboration project and an education program in depth, and to examine the details of the research setting and subject in order not only to conclude their studies but to develop ideas for further study. In their mixed method study, Smith et al. (2019b) explored and identified promising teaching practices for teaching linguistically and culturally diverse learners so as to develop an understanding of needed changes for this international student group. In a paper reporting on two studies, Gray, Chang, and Kennedy (2010), and King and So (2014) investigated the benefits of an intervention involving Web 2.0 technology and a virtual learning community, analyzing data from online surveys and student interviews/reflections.

The qualitative method was the most popular research method selected by nine researchers, including Chen and Bennett (2012), Khali (2019), Kumi-Yeboah et al. (2020), Pimpa (2011), Rodrigues-Manzanares (2012), Sleeman, Lang, and Dakich (2019), Smith et al. (2021), Wang and Reeves (2007), and finally Zhang (2013). As Bryman and Bell (2019) state, the interview was the most widely used method (p. 240), being applied in all these qualitative studies with different types such as open-ended, structured, semi-structured, and conducted in different modes including online, phone, face-to-face, or as a self-report. The use of interviews as a data collection method required researchers to play a very significant role in "using special protocols for recording data, analyzing the information through multiple steps of analysis, and mentioning approaches for documenting the methodological integrity or accuracy - or validity - of the data collected" (Creswell & Creswell, 2018, p. 254). Among these studies, the ones conducted by Chen and Bennett (2012), Khali (2019), Rodrigues-Manzanares (2012), Sleeman, Lang and Dakich (2019), Wang and Reeves (2007), and Zhang (2013) illustrated a very clear and detailed explanation and rationale for the development of the interview protocol and procedures, steps for data analysis, coding protocol, and data review process to obtain a sense of the information. Although studies by Kumi- Yeboah et al. (2020), Pimpa (2011) and Smith et al. (2021) lacked these components, they provided a clear recruitment strategy for research sites and individuals. Pimpa gave specific reasons and rationale for why interviews were used to collect data in his qualitative phenomenography approach.

Among twenty selected articles, two studies conducted by Hannon and D'Netto (2007), and Smith et al. (2019b) adopted quantitative research methods with the main research tool of an online survey. Quantitative research was not so popular in social, especially educational studies; however, the use of surveys was of significance since it allowed "for standardization in the asking and the categorization of the answers given" (Bryman & Bell, 2019). These two criteria were applied in the research aims of the two studies by Hannon and D'Netto (2007), and Smith et al. (2019b). The factor of standardization and categorization in Smith et al.'s research was the variability of student satisfaction by individual student characteristics (e.g., level of study, year of study, age, gender, field of study, country of origin, length of time studying outside country of origin, parents' educational level, and study location), while that of Hannon and D'Netto was cultural factors that impact learners' engagement with online learning.

Table 1. Research methods adopted in the collected studies

No.	Articles (n=20)	Qualitative	Quantitative	Literature review	Data collection tools
1	Garrett & Cutting (2012)	*	*		Online questionnaire Online focus group discussion Interviews Google analytics
2	Li & Zhang (2015)	*	*		Online survey Focus group discussion
3	Rodrigues-Manzanares (2012)	*			Open-ended interviews
4	Smith et al. (2021)	*			Phone interview
5	Smith et al. (2019a)	*	*		Online questionnaire Online focus group discussion Individual interviews
6	Smith et al. (2019b)		*		Online questionnaire
7	Alexander (2002)			*	
8	Chen & Bennett (2012)	*			Focus group discussion Interviews with students and teachers
9	Gray, Chang & Kennedy (2010)	*	*		Online survey Interviews
10	Hannon & D'netto (2007)		*		Survey
11	King & So (2014)	*	*		Survey Student reflection
12	Pimpa (2011)	*			Phenomenography approach applying interviews
13	Sleeman, Lang & Dakich (2019)	*			Interviews as self-report method
14	Khali (2019)	*			Semi-structured interviews
15	Kumi-Yeboah et al. (2020)	*			Semi-structured interviews
16	Zhu et al. (2021)	*	*		Online questionnaire Email interviews
17	Sadykova (2014)	*	*		Survey Online interviews Reflective journal Document analysis
18	Karkar-Esperat (2018)	*	*		Online questionnaire Focus group discussion Semi-structured interviews Field notes Researcher's journal entries
19	Wang & Reeves (2007)	*			Semi-structured interviews Observation
20	Zhang (2013)	*			Face-to-face interviews

Table 2. The advantages of online learning with the use of technological tools for teaching international students

No.	Articles	Satisfaction	Engagement	Communication/ Interaction	Academic performance	Equity
1	Garrett & Cutting (2012)	- a fun, exploratory learning environment - a sense of globalization	- engagement in thought-provoking topics - interest in non-academic fields including cultures - making international contacts	- view sharing & developing perspectives - building connections & reaching agreement/ consensus	- positive effects of social media for educational use - further unrelated discussion beyond the course	- left behind students
2	Li & Zhang (2015)	- a constructive and nurturing forum, empowering students emotionally, socially, and cognitively - immigrants' cultural & linguistic exploration	- attractive discussions	- sharing of personal experiences associated with students' own experience in sociocultural sensitive topics		- use of other ideas to construct own comprehension & self-evaluation - most effective elimination of discrimination or separation in education
3	Rodrigues-Manzanares (2012)	- a chance for cultural interaction but incomplete - a lack of consideration because of unfamiliar cultural references	- flexibility & convenience	- online social network but not effective - mostly course-related interaction, focusing on studying, assignments…	- independent learning enhancement	
4	Smith et al. (2021)	- isolated & stressful online learning environment - a lack of community online - a lack of instructors' control over students' discussion boards - questions & interactions encouraged in class. - preference for group projects		- poor communication, unclear assignment instructions - a shift from communication outside of the classroom to online - satisfaction with classroom communication		- fairness in group project assessment - low grades for students who are uncomfortable to join - unfair & disorganized evaluation by teaching assistants - no discrimination
5	Smith et al. (2019a)	- effective teaching practices result in high student perception of learning levels				- preferred teaching practice by students: supportive learning environment
6	Smith et al. (2019b)	- various learning preferences - international students' less satisfaction with online education in Canada				

continues on following page

Table 2. Continued

No.	Articles	Satisfaction	Engagement	Communication/ Interaction	Academic performance	Equity
7	Alexander (2002)	- importance of cultural awareness - advantages of new technologies: economic benefits, time reduction to market, international collaboration & educational benefits		support/convenience for content via email/computer conferencing		
8	Chen & Benett (2012)			- the Net Generation's blurred boundaries between school & socializing - blogging as an online communication tool	- social software is suitable for educational purposes	
9	Gray, Chang & Kennedy (2010)	- online identity management - a sense of security - blog eradicates misunderstandings between various parties & promotes harmony	- a chance for creativity - a chance for sharing - deeper insight into understanding internationalization	- social software tools support effective online learning communities	- content creation	- students' critical reflection on their own learning
10	Hannon & D'netto (2007)	- high satisfaction with technologies - students' different abilities to use online educational technologies contingent on various cultural backgrounds				
11	King & So (2014)	- online discussion forum (ODF) participation is highly appreciated - a chance to exercise critical thinking - strong motivation to be well prepared for discussions. - raised confidence in online communication - increased level of comfort to save face virtually - convenient & time-saving logistic	- strong engagement in dialogues - differences deemphasized & more active participation than in traditional setting	- peer connections enable international student success		- an equal chance for international students to take part in the ODF - adoption of practices for students' quality educational experience regardless of cultural or language differences

continues on following page

Table 2. Continued

No.	Articles	Satisfaction	Engagement	Communication/ Interaction	Academic performance	Equity
12	Pimpa (2011)	- a chance to share and exchange academic matters & life experience - vivid, modern & worldly experience in online discussion	- online environment encourages "sophistication" of group discussion - added practical experiences in lectures encourages students' discussion - students' engagement in learning is influenced by personal experience within a particular cultural context.	- interaction, conversation, group debates or online case studies as key activities & experience - a variety of forms & tools make students highly interactive in online learning		- Lecturers as encouragers are able to respond effectively to a wide range of learners' needs - free & open discussions about issue of race, ethnicity & other "sensitive" issues thanks to anonymous identities
13	Sleeman, Lang & Dakich (2019)			- friendship establishment - the need of online establishing social interactions varies	- academic adjustment can be easily carried out - an improvement on writing skill with linguistic help	- Educators' provision of more strategic guidance on to enhance social connections
14	Khalil (2019)	- a lack of sense of online community - cultural & linguistic backgrounds/ previous educational experiences affect online participations & interactions - linguistic problems: more easily overcome online - online discussion: research/ ask others to proofread before giving ideas	Recommendations for online course design: - consideration of cross-cultural instructional design of an online course - online courses associated with social presence - collaborative group projects included	- isolation & loneliness due to a lack of social presence & interaction - hesitation to communicate - desired socialization		- specific standards & requirements to online courses' structure on cultural awareness
15	Kumi-Yeboah et al. (2020)	- Technologies as a means of engaging students in online learning	- tools and applications motivate students to participate in learning collaboratively		- digital technologies advanced knowledge acquisition online	
16	Zhu et al. (2021)	- additional professional development needed for MOOC instructors to make more personally engaging MOOC courses				- an adaptation of both course design and delivery to better address cultural diversity.

continues on following page

Table 2. Continued

No.	Articles	Satisfaction	Engagement	Communication/ Interaction	Academic performance	Equity
17	Sadykova (2014)	- a class built on student-centered practices that encourage peer-to-peer interactions - valuable group activities for the ability to connect with peers, learn from their experiences, and take advantage of their knowledge of field of study				- peer assistance in collaborative activities set up by their instructors - assign tasks that incorporate everyday culture into the course content
18	Karkar-Esperat (2018)	- teacher's lack of preparation makes students overwhelmed, discouraged & unable to meet the course requirements - flexibility & convenience - helpful online support group	- a decrease in students' engagement due to teacher's ill preparedness	- preference for face-to-face class to avoid miscommunication & receive immediate feedback - lack of communication & interaction		- online classes built on students' needs - clear instructions to students on different activities
19	Wang & Reeves (2007)	- comfort & convenience: no physical campus attendance - useful online classes but still need traditional ones		- limited ways of communication - a lack of facial expression		- clear rules of using use message board - online classes erase differences of race, class, gender, and ethnicity
20	Zhang (2013)	-Confucian-heritage culture, especially power distance, might affect students' online participation & interaction - online discussion makes a more democratic learning environment	- more engagement in online discussions	- Communication with instructors as a formal activity - interaction with peers as more comfortable activity		- equal opportunities for each student to participate in online discussions - additional efforts to approach international students to bring students together - additional learning opportunities among students in online discussion.

The quality of research findings is ensured by the research design and distinctive research strategy that involve particular steps and rationales, helping answer research questions and solve research problems. There is no best research method, but the most appropriate one for particular research aims. Since studies on the benefits of technology application to teaching international students in an online environment are in association with various factors, including organization, use of technological tools, course design, online instructors, learner access to the technology, and learner characteristics, they should be conducted by adopting a mixed-method design. As Creswell and Creswell (2018) state, a mixed method study should be considered to "develop a stronger understanding of the research problem and questions and overcome the limitations of each" (p. 337). Also, the use of different data collection tools with a triangulation data analysis process such as survey/questionnaire, interview, and teachers' notes provide different types of information, giving the fact that more insight into a problem is to be gained. However, conducting mixed methods research takes lots of time, so researchers should rigorously consider all the nature and its essential characteristics to begin a good mixed methods procedure. Based on different data collection and analysis, and aims, researchers should also choose different types of mixed methods designs as being classified by Creswell and Plano Clark (2018).

Benefits of Online Learning with the Use of Technological Tools to Teaching International Students in Published Literature Over the Last Two Decades

As demonstrated in Table 2, the benefits of technology integration for teaching international students online were divided into five categories, including satisfaction, engagement, communication and interaction, academic performance, and equity.

A great level of satisfaction was similarly found in a majority of investigated studies by Alexander (2002), Garrett and Cutting (2012), Gray, Chang and Kennedy (2010), Hannon and D'netto (2007), King and So (2014), Kumi-Yeboah et al. (2020), Li and Zhang (2015), Pimpa (2011), and Sadykova (2014). Technology could help meaningfully build up a fun and exploratory online learning environment in which international students were able to get to know a diversity of cultures and also sharpened their language competence (Garrett & Cutting, 2012; Li & Zhang, 2015). A sense of globalization and a chance for international collaboration were truly treasured by international students when educators capitalized on the use of technologies in an online learning environment, providing students with a chance to share and exchange academic matters and non-academic experiences (Alexander, 2002; Garrett & Cutting, 2012; Pimpa, 2011). To be specific, students could significantly gain insight into and interact with a large diversity of cultures from all over the world (Li & Zhang, 2015; Rodrigues-Manzanares, 2012), which was consequently believed to eradicate misunderstandings between teachers and students, and among students themselves (Gray, Chang & Kennedy, 2010). According to Li and Zhang (2015), most of the online course participants were reported to highly appreciate the chance to take part in the online discussion forums that were described as constructive and nurturing platforms for students. In effective online discussion forums, students likely had a golden opportunity to have their critical thinking exercised and ideas well prepared for discussions (Khalil, 2019; King & So, 2014). Online group activities, offering a valuable learning and sharing experience, were another outstanding feature of the online learning environment, bringing about high satisfaction for students (Sadykova, 2014; Smith et al., 2021). In Zhang (2013), online discussion particularly created a more democratic learning environment; that was the platform in which students highly appreciated the convenience and flexibility (Alexander 2002; Karkar-Esperat, 2018; King & So, 2014). Apart from the convenient nature of online learning platforms, a strong emphasis on comfort and a sense of security were manifested since students felt at ease managing their virtual identities, saving their faces, and gradually adapting to new learning cultures (Gray, Chang & Kennedy, 2010; King & So, 2014; Zhang, 2013). Smith et al. (2019a) focused on effective teaching practices that may likely result in high student perceptions of learning levels. On the downside, very little to no satisfaction could be seen in the other reviewed research on online learning contexts (Karkar-Esperat, 2018; Khalil, 2019; Rodrigues-Manzanares, 2012; Smith et al., 2019b; Smith et al.; 2021; Wang & Reeves, 2007; Zhang, 2013). The findings from Smith et al. (2021) revealed that international students found online learning environments extremely isolated and stressful due to a lack of sense of community and instructors' control over students' discussion boards. This lack of sense of community in online learning platforms was quite in line with the findings from Khalil (2019). In addition, Karkar-Esperat (2018) mentioned teachers' lack of preparation as a destructive factor for online learning, making students overwhelmed, discouraged, and unable to fulfill the course requirements successfully. It is true that students' cultural and linguistic backgrounds or previous educational experiences strongly affected online participation and interactions (Khalil, 2019; Zhang, 2013). Although students felt comfortable when studying online at home, attending traditional classes remained quite essential (Wang & Reeves, 2007). In the viewpoint of Rodrigues-Manzanares (2012), while taking online classes could be a valuable opportunity for cultural interaction, it seemed incomplete.

In terms of engagement, throughout the theme-based analysis of the collected research, students are much more attracted to discussions about nonacademic and thought-provoking topics, especially cultures (Garrett & Cutting, 2012; Gray, Chang & Kennedy 2010; Li & Zhang, 2015; Pimpa, 2011; Zhang, 2013). Students were reported to be more involved in online discussions and dialogues where differences were more deemphasized than in traditional classes (King & So, 2014). According to Gray, Chang, and Kennedy (2010), students' engagement in the online learning environment was developed thanks to the benefits they could gain from it. These were described as a great chance for creativity and sharing, and an exploratory process of digging into internationalization. On top of that, Garrett and Cutting (2012) also added that when taking online courses, making international contact was regarded as a significant contribution to students' engagement in their classes. Kumi-Yeboah et al. (2020) stated that students were motivated by tools and applications integrated into online classes, making them willingly participate in collaborative learning activities, while Rodrigues-Manzanares (2012) emphasized the flexibility and convenience of the online learning environment. However, what made students less determined in their learning was teachers' poor preparation (Karkar-Esperat, 2018). Therefore, teachers played a critical role in their students' involvement. To promote students' engagement, teachers should add practical experiences in lectures to encourage students' discussion (Pimpa, 2011). According to Khalil (2019), a concern about cross-cultural instructional design of an online course could help improve the situation. Furthermore, the researcher suggested that social presence and collaborative group projects were key factors for students' engagement into online learning.

When it comes to the third benefit of technology integration for teaching international students online, there appears to be an effective communication/interaction aspect which could be considered the most significant to students. It was an actual shift from communication in traditional classes to an online learning environment (Smith et al., 2021). Of all the selected studies in this review, the communication/interaction aspect could be categorized into two opposite sides since just around half of them demonstrated positivity (Alexander, 2002; Chen & Benett, 2012; Garrett & Cutting, 2012; Gray, Chang & Kennedy, 2010; King & So, 2014; Li & Zhang, 2015; Pimpa, 2011). Technology, including a series of forms and tools such as blogs, social software, emails, and computer conferencing, could definitely be beneficial to students as it made online communication quite convenient and fluent (Alexander, 2002; Chen & Bennett, 2012; Gray, Chang & Kennedy, 2010; Pimpa, 2011). It is stated by King and So (2014) that peer connections could boost international students' success; as a result, a thirst for a sense of online learning community was always among students. Throughout this community, Li and Zhang (2015), and Pimpa (2011) agreed that students were empowered with a chance to raise their voices, develop different perspectives, debate in groups, and share their personal experiences on sociocultural sensitive topics. In light of this, they could build connections and reach consensus with their peers (Garrett & Cutting, 2012). All the afore-mentioned activities among students proved that there existed a desire for social-ization in the virtual world where friendship establishment happened (Khalil, 2019; Sleeman, Lang & Dakich, 2019). That could be clearly seen as a common fact because interaction with their peers was a more comfortable activity with their peers than their instructors (Zhang, 2013). On the contrary, online social networks were found to be ineffective in the rest of the reviewed studies (Karkar-Esperat, 2018; Khalil, 2019; Rodrigues-Manzanares, 2012; Smith et al., 2021; Wang & Reeves, 2007). Online learning platforms made it hard for students to interact with their teachers due to the fact that course and assign-ment instructions were normally unclear to them (Smith et al., 2021) and formal communication with their teachers was usually less favored among them (Zhang, 2013). In relation to online interaction with their classmates, isolation and loneliness were what students might experience due to a lack of social preference, facial expression, and interaction (Karkar-Esperat, 2018; Khalil, 2019; Wang & Reeves, 2007). Furthermore, this might be because most interaction in an online learning environment was all about the course-related content or assignments, causing students' boredom (Rodrigues-Manzanares, 2012).

Academic performance enhancement was another merit that some of the reviewed studies have shown. The most significant was that learner autonomy was proven to escalate when students studied online (Rodrigues-Manzanares, 2012). Moreover, digital technologies could meaningfully enhance students' knowledge acquisition (Kumi-Yeboah et al., 2020). In Gray, Chang and Kennedy (2010), content creation was another outstanding point that students could achieve in online learning platforms. Additionally, their academic writing skills were supposed to improve with the support from others in the discussion forum (Sleeman, Lang & Dakich, 2019).

Speaking of educational equity, Cook-Harvey et al. described it as "the policies and practices that pro-vide every student access to an education focused on meaningful learning that teaches the deeper learning skills contemporary society requires in ways that empower students to learn independently throughout their lives'' (p. 1, 2016). Enhancement of learning occurred only when learning activities were linguisti-cally and culturally meaningful and related to students from diverse backgrounds (Lee, 2003). Based on those above-mentioned ideas about equity in education, findings from the investigated studies pointed out a range of equity in online learning environments for international students. Generally speaking, online classes could erase differences of race, class, gender, and ethnicity, bringing about educational equity for international students (Wang & Reeves, 2007). On account of this, they were thought to be the most effective elimination of discrimination or separation in education (Li & Zhang, 2015; Smith et al., 2021). These online classes were supposedly to meet students' actual needs (Karkar-Esperat, 2018). According to King and So (2014), and Zhang (2013), international students were provided with an equal chance to participate in online discussions which Pimpa (2011) considered as open and free discussions for students about race, ethnicity, and other sensitive issues thanks to anonymous identities. These were also "virtual places" for all students to fairly use others' ideas to construct their own comprehension, self-evaluation, and self-reflection (Gray, Chang & Kennedy, 2010; Li & Zhang, 2015). Garrett and Cutting (2012), on the other hand, noted that students who fall behind in an online learning environment were common. Moreover, unfair and disorganized assessment by teaching assistants could be problematic for international students (Smith et al., 2021). To promote equity for international students in an online learning environment, teachers as encouragers needed to adopt a wide range of appropriate teaching practices for students' quality educational experience and students' needs regardless of the differences in their cultural and linguistic backgrounds (King & So, 2014; Pimpa, 2011). A set of teaching practices should include clear instructions to students on different activities, clear rules of using message boards, fairness in group project assessment, peer assistance in collaborative activities (Karkar-Esperat, 2018; Sadykova, 2014; Smith et al., 2021; Wang & Reeves, 2007). Besides, instructors needed to assign tasks linking with daily culture into the course content, adapted both course design and delivery to effectively address cultural diversity, set up specific standards and requirements for online course structures on cultural awareness, and provided more strategic guidance on how to enhance social connections (Khalil, 2019; Sadykova, 2014; Sleeman, Lang & Dakich, 2019; Zhu et al., 2021).

DISCUSSION

Key findings from twenty selected studies have been presented and described in the previous section. It is clear that the technology in an online class brings about various meaningful benefits in terms of international students' satisfaction, engagement, communication and interaction, academic performance, and equity. Especially, there is an emphasis on cultural factors which are considered as the core concept determining these values in these analyzed articles.

First, the values that an online class bring to international students can be explained by two terms: (1) "public engagement", which is defined by Arendt in *The Human Condition* as "a person emerges in the public realm in a general sense whenever he or she takes a position on an effort or issue common to a group of people that both "relates and separates" them at the same time." (Cited by Schutz & Sandy, p. 25, 2015), and (2) "sociological imagination", which is how we bridge the gap between ourselves and the imagined other within the arc of history, enabling us to "grasp history and biography and the relationship between the two in society" (Mills, 1959, p. 6). In particular, although international students are from different corners of the world and have different distinctive cultural features, they are members of society, representing their world and lived experiences within the classroom. Whether they are related to or separated from each other, it is the awareness of their positionalities that helps them to engage in different learning activities and inspires them to communicate with each other, bridging their cultural differences. It is in the online environment where students have equal rights to have their voice heard that brings them the chance to be more involved and engaged in learning activities. In addition, an understanding of how such differences affect learning would solve the gap, resulting in meeting learners' needs. It is well noted that the features of a technology-enhanced classroom, such as a discussion forum, a blog, or social media page where everyone has equal opportunities to express their agreement or disagreement, vote for the ideas with shared positionalities, and address their difficulties, can address the problems caused by the gap among international students in an online environment, including access, preparedness (including language skills), appropriate tutorial mechanisms to resolve high attrition, discrimination, academic equity, and communication/interaction. The more students get involved in the learning activities, the better the academic performance they make, as the U.S. statesman Benjamin Franklin and the Chinese philosopher Confucius once expressed, "Tell Me and I Forget; Teach Me and I May Remember; Involve Me and I Learn" (n.d). Thus, students' involvement in their own learning process has been considered as an influential approach to education, promoting their academic performance and reaching the best learning outcomes.

Second, culturally responsive teaching theory, defined by Gay as "using the cultural knowledge, prior experiences, frames of reference, and performance styles of ethnically diverse students to make learning encounters more relevant to and effective for them" (2018, p. 29) also significantly elaborates the crucial role of technology in teaching international students. Students seize an opportunity to achieve equity and equality when studying in an online environment where technology is applied with culturally responsive teaching theory. This helps students to hold high expectations and build the strengths they bring to school from their homes and communities. The application of this theory with the use of technology is an asset for many international students. Also, with the help of technology, they can create complex and linguistically hybrid multimodal texts to negotiate transnational relationships, develop their advanced 21st century literacy skills, and affiliate with communities, enabling their success.

Third, it is worth pointing out that the aspect of technology in an online environment not only bridges cultures together in a multicultural classroom, develops essential skills for learner readiness in the modern world, hone students' academic knowledge, it also supports learning by improving learner attitudes toward learning, increasing their participation and self-confidence. By establishing cooperative learning environments, students may contribute to the learning community to gain acceptance and enhance their self-esteem so that they may not feel like "outsiders". Cooperative learning with technology helps international students to get more involved in the classroom discussions, providing them with opportunities to express their strengths and gain class status. According to Vygotsky (1978), learning is socially constructed and mediated through interaction and communication. In other words, human learning is largely a social process which focuses not only on how adults and peers influence individual learning via interaction, but also on how cultural beliefs and attitudes affect how learning takes place. Hence, in a technology-enhanced classroom, the role of the teacher in planning, organizing, and designing their instructions and lessons, using hints, prompts, and direct instructions, and scaffolding should be prioritized.

All in all, drawing on the for-going discussions, the researchers formulate a new framework to conceptualize three outstandingly remarkable values of technology integration in teaching international students in an online learning environment: a preparation for 21st century skills, a positive attitude toward online learning, and an improved academic performance (See Fig.3).

CONCLUSION

In spite of several problems that online learning encounters such as a lack of two-way communication and a sense of community, technical issues, difficulties in comprehending instructional goals, drawing on the analysis of twenty selected articles, this paper critically reviews international student learning experience in an online learning environment. Two research questions are addressed, pertaining to the benefits of online learning with the integration of different pedagogical technological tools and the application of different research methods. The key findings offer exploratory insights into different core values that international students benefit from online learning, including satisfaction, engagement, communication and interaction, academic performance, and equity. The paper has shed light on the crucial and significant roles of technology in getting students more involved and engaged in learning activities, promoting communication and interaction, enhancing academic performance, and guaranteeing equity and equality among international students from the lens of social imagination, culturally responsive teaching theory, and constructivist learning theory.

Figure 3. The map of the benefits of technology integration in teaching international students within this systematic review

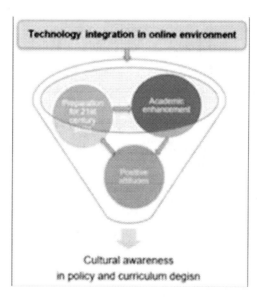

Besides, a range of research methods, from the most frequently adopted qualitative approach to the least favored literature review, have been identified. Although every single used method possesses its own perks, mixed methods of research appear to be highly recommended throughout the paper as a means of developing a complete understanding of the research problem and questions, leading to a deep exploration of different aspects of student learning experiences in an online learning environment.

Based on the perceived findings, a valuable taxonomy is put forwarded by grouping five benefits into three vital dimensions including increased cultural, linguistic, and academic knowledge, must-have 21st century skills, and professional attitudes that help noteworthily systemize the positive aspects of online teaching and learning contexts. By taking a meticulous look at the used research methods and what might become advantages of teaching international students from a wide variety of cultural and linguistic backgrounds, the conceptual work will significantly elaborate on a new perspective and scholarship on the integration of technology into online teaching for international students, which other researchers, technical designers, and teachers might take reference from for their future explorations.

RECOMMENDATION FOR FUTURE RESEARCH AND TEACHING PRACTICE

This review appreciably recommends some future research directions and teaching practices involved in virtual education embracing technology for international students. A worthwhile proposed scenario for online course design consisting of thoughtful consideration of cross-cultural instructional design and a sense of online learning community can be seen as the most appropriate to accommodate international students' learning and sharing needs. To achieve that, teachers are those who should be present socially and academically in the course, giving prompt feedback and showing their interest and engagement with students. Moreover, a vigorous emphasis should be placed on collaborative learning activities that lend a helping hand to students' socialization and globalization. This can be carried out effectively only when teachers instruct, initialize, follow up and provide timely assistance to their students in an online learning environment. Therefore, international students might feel that they are not isolated and lonely in the virtual world and have an incredible chance to establish their commonalities and international connections. Another paramount issue teachers should take into account is providing culturally inclusive instructions and abolishing cultural and linguistic boundaries among international students in order to develop culturally sensitive online environments and assure educational equity. This is firmly accredited to an enhancement of students' learning motivation and engagement. All of the previously indicated points could be even much more propitiously achieved in accordance with stakeholders' assistance. In a broader vision, online instructors should be well-trained to be better prepared for what it really takes in an online teaching and learning environment. According to Khalil (2019), specific set standards and requirements to online courses' structure on cultural awareness and working with international students by educational institutions are truly of significance to teachers. Aside from the provision of necessary training for teachers, culturally inclusive and inter-cultural curriculum design and development are key roles in the accomplishment of educating internationally in a virtual learning environment.

This paper has suggested some questions in need of investigation in the following areas. Further research should elaborate on teachers' perspectives of their preferences for types of applications employed for their online classes and of a set of necessary criteria when opting for them. The next step should be placed on students' readiness for the use of technology in their study, emphasizing their tech skills. More research is also required to examine how the relationship between linguistic and cultural inclusion and course-content design could influence the quality of online study. Stakeholders, including institutions, administrators, and technical course designers, should be the focus of further research on the making of a successful online learning and teaching environment.

REFERENCES

Alexander, S. (2002). Designing learning activities for an international online student body: What have we learned? *Journal of Studies in International Education*, 6(2), 188–200. doi:10.1177/1028315302006002007

Baber, H. (2021). Social interaction and effectiveness of online learning: A moderating role of maintaining social distance during the pandemic COVID-19. *Asian Education and Development Studies*. doi:10.1108/AEDS-09-2020-0209

Bryman, A., & Bell, E. (2019). *Social Research Methods* (5th ed.). Oxford University Press.

Chen, R. T.-H., & Bennett, S. (2012). When Chinese learners meet constructivist pedagogy online. *Higher Education*, 64(5), 677–691. doi:10.100710734-012-9520-9

Chen, D.-T. V., Wang, Y.-M., & Lee, W. C. (2016). Challenges confronting beginning researchers in conducting literature reviews. *Studies in Continuing Education*, 38(1), 47–60. doi:10.1080/015803 7X.2015.1030335

Cojocariu, V.-M., Lazar, I., Nedeff, V., & Lazar, G. (2014). SWOT ANALYSIS of e-learning educational services from the perspective of their beneficiaries. *Procedia: Social and Behavioral Sciences, 116*, 1999–2003. doi:10.1016/j.sbspro.2014.01.510

Cook-Harvey, C. M., Darling-Hammond, L., Lam, L., Mercer, C., & Roc, M. (2016). *Equity and ESSA: Leveraging educational opportunity through the every student succeeds act.* Learning Policy Institute. Retrieved from https://learningpolicyinstitute.org/product/equity-essa-report

Creswell, J. W., & Creswell, J. D. (2018). *Research design: Qualitative, quantitative, and mixed methods approach* (5th ed.). SAGE Publications.

Creswell, J. W., & Plano Clark, V. L. (2018). *Designing and conducting mixed methods research* (3rd ed.). Sage.

Denyer, D., & Tranfield, D. (2009). Producing a systematic review. In D. Buchanan & A. Bryman (Eds.), *The Sage Handbook of Organizational Research Methods* (pp. 671–689). Sage Publications.

Dhawan, S. (2020). Online learning: A panacea in the time of covid-19 crisis. *Journal of Educational Technology Systems, 49*(1), 5–22. doi:10.1177/0047239520934018

Gay, G. (2018). *Culturally responsive teaching: Theory, practice, and research.* Teachers College Press.

Garrett, B. M., & Cutting, R. (2012). Using social media to promote international student partnerships. *Nurse Education in Practice, 12*(6), 340–345. doi:10.1016/j.nepr.2012.04.003 PMID:22595660

Gray, K., Chang, S., & Kennedy, G. (2010). Use of social web technologies by international and domestic undergraduate students: Implications for internationalizing learning and teaching in Australian universities. *Technology, Pedagogy and Education, 19*(1), 31–46. doi:10.1080/14759390903579208

Hannon, J., & D'Netto, B. (2007). Cultural diversity online: Student engagement with learning technologies. *International Journal of Educational Management, 21*(5), 418–432. doi:10.1108/09513540710760192

Karasavvidis, I., & Kollias, V. (2014). Technology integration in the most favorable conditions: findings from a professional development training program. In C. Karagiannidis (Ed.), *Research on e-learning and ICT in education* (pp. 197–224). Springer.

Karkar-Esperat, T. M. (2018). International Graduate Students' Challenges and Learning Experiences in Online Classes. *Journal of International Students, 8*(4), 1722–1735. doi:10.32674/jis.v8i4.227

Khalil, S. (2019). *International students' perspectives of building communities in online learning environments* (Publication No. 27663440) [Doctoral dissertation, New Mexico University]. ProQuest Dissertations and Theses Global.

King, C., & So, K. K. (2014). Creating a virtual learning community to engage international students. *Journal of Hospitality & Tourism Education, 26*(3), 136–146. doi:10.1080/10963758.2014.936255

Kumi-Yeboah, A., Sallar, A. W., Kiramba, L. K., & Kim, Y. (2020). Exploring the use of digital technologies from the perspective of diverse learners in online learning environments. *Online Learning, 24*(4), 42–63. doi:10.24059/olj.v24i4.2323

Lee, O. (2003). Equity for linguistically and culturally diverse students in science education: A research agenda. *Teachers College Record, 105*(3), 465–489. doi:10.1111/1467-9620.00247

Li, J., & Zhang, Z. (2015). An Intercontinental inquiry on multicultural education: Canadian and Hong Kong university students connected through a Web 2.0 learning environment. *Intercultural Education, 26*(6), 562–583. doi:10.1080/14675986.2015.1109773

McBrien, J. L., Cheng, R., & Jones, P. (2009). Virtual spaces: Employing a synchronous online classroom to facilitate student engagement in online learning. *The International Review of Research in Open and Distributed Learning, 10*(3). Advance online publication. doi:10.19173/irrodl.v10i3.605

Mills, C. W. (1959). The promise. In *The Sociological Imagination* (pp. 3–24). Oxford University Press.

Pimpa, N. (2011). Engaging international business students in the online environment. *International Journal of Management Education, 9*(3), 77–89. doi:10.3794/ijme.93.323

Rodrigues-Manzanares, M. A. (2012). *Portraits of the activity systems of postsecondary international students in online learning: from tensions to transformations in activity* (Master thesis). Memorial University of Newfoundland. https://research.library.mun.ca/

Sadykova, G. (2014). Mediating knowledge through peer-to-peer interaction in a multicultural online learning environment: A case of international students in the US. *The International Review of Research in Open and Distributed Learning, 15*(3). Advance online publication. doi:10.19173/irrodl.v15i3.1629

Sandelowski, M., Voils, C. I., & Barroso, J. (2006). Defining and designing mixed research synthesis studies. *Research in the Schools, 13*(1), 29–40. PMID:20098638

Schutz, A., & Sandy, M. G. (2015). Friendship and the public stage: Revisiting Hannah Arendt's resistance to "political education". *Educational Theory, 65*(1), 21–38. doi:10.1111/edth.12093

Sleeman, J., Lang, C., & Dakich, E. (2019). International students' transition to university: Connection and disconnection in online group work interactions. *Student Success, 10*(2), 35–45. doi:10.5204sj.v10i2.1300

Smith, C. A., Zhou, G., Potter, M., & Wang, D. (2019a). Connecting Best Practices for Teaching Linguistically and Culturally Diverse International Students with International Student Satisfaction and Student Perceptions of Student Learning. *Advances in Global Education and Research, 3*, 252-265. https://scholar.uwindsor.ca/educationpub/24/

Smith, C., Zhou, G., Potter, M., Wang, D., Pecoraro, M., & Paulino, R. (2019b). Variability by individual student characteristics of student satisfaction with promising international student teaching practices. *Literacy Information and Computer Education Journal, 10*(2), 3160–3169. doi:10.20533/licej.2040.2589.2019.0415

Smith, C., Zhou, G., Potter, M., & Ammar, F. (2021). Engaging diverse international students: Promising online teaching practices. In J. Christensen Hughes, J. Mighty, & D. Stockley (Eds.), *Taking stock 2.0: Transforming and learning in higher education.* Society for Teaching and Learning in Higher Education.

Song, L., Singleton, E. S., Hill, J. R., & Koh, M. H. (2004). Improving online learning: Student perceptions of useful and challenging characteristics. *The Internet and Higher Education, 7*(1), 59–70. doi:10.1016/j.iheduc.2003.11.003

OECD. (2008). *Education at a Glance 2007: OECD Indicators*. OECD.

Vygotsky, L. (1978). *Mind in society* (M. Cole, Trans.). Harvard University Press.

Wang, C. M., & Reeves, T. C. (2007). Synchronous online learning experiences: The perspectives of international students from Taiwan. *Educational Media International, 44*(4), 339–356. https://doi.org/10.1080/09523980701680821

Xiao, Y., & Watso, M. (2019). Guidance on conducting a Systematic Literature Review. *Journal of Planning Education and Research, 39*(1), 93–112. https://doi.org/10.1177%2F0739456X17723971

Zhang, Y. L. (2013). Power distance in online learning: Experience of Chinese learners in U.S. higher education. *The International Review of Research in Open and Distributed Learning, 14*(4). https://doi.org/10.19173/irrodl.v14i4.1557

Zhu, M., Sabir, N., Bonk, C. J., Sari, A., Xu, S., & Kim, M. (2021). Addressing learner cultural diversity in MOOC design and delivery: Strategies and practices of experts. *Turkish Online Journal of Distance Education*, 1-25. doi:10.17718/tojde.906468

402

Compilation of References

Abdulla, M. D., & Kumar, S. A. (2016). Blooming English language skills for budding engineers to flourish in global environment. *Journal of English Language and Literature*, *3*(1), 58–63. http://joell.in/wp-content/uploads/2016/03/BLOOMING-ENGLISH.pdf

Abeysekera, L., & Dawson, P. (2015). Motivation and cognitive load in the flipped classroom: Definition, rationale and a call for research. *Higher Education Research & Development*, *34*(1), 1–14. doi:10.1080/07294360.2014.934336

Abrums, M. E., & Leppa, C. (2001). Beyond cultural competence: Teaching about race, gender, class, and sexual orientation. *The Journal of Nursing Education*, *40*(6), 270–275. doi:10.3928/0148-4834-20010901-07 PMID:11554461

Adair, J. G. (1984). The Hawthorne effect: A reconsideration of the methodological artifact. *The Journal of Applied Psychology*, *69*(2), 334–345. doi:10.1037/0021-9010.69.2.334

Adams, T., Leventhal, M., & Connelly, S. (2012). International student recruitment in Australia and the United States: approaches and attitudes. In D. K. Deardorff, H. d. Wit, & J. D. Heyl (Eds.), *The SAGE handbook of international higher education* (pp. 399-416). SAGE Publications, Inc. https://www.doi.org/10.4135/9781452218397.n22

Adams, K. (2019). Navigating the spaces of children's spiritual experiences: Influences of tradition(s), multidisciplinary and perceptions. *International Journal of Children's Spirituality*, *24*(1), 29–43. doi:10.1080/1364436X.2019.1619531

Adamuti-Trache, M., & Sweet, R. (2010). Adult immigrants' participation in Canadian education and Training. *Canadian Journal for the Study of Adult Education*, *22*(2), 1.

Adedoyin, O. B. (2020). Covid-19 pandemic and online learning: The challenges and opportunities. *Interactive Learning Environments*, 1–13.

Adjei, R (2018). Accreditation and Development of Employable Skills in Graduates. *Accreditation News*, (1).

Adler, N. (1991). *International Dimensions of Organizational Behaviour* (2nd ed.). PWS-Kent Publishing Company.

Adler, R. B., Rodman, G. R., & Du Pré, A. (2016). *Understanding human communication* (13th ed.). Oxford University Press.

Adu-Gyamfi, A. B. (n.d.). Graduate Unemployability in Ghana: Views of Unemployed Graduates. *Patrick Darkwa Department of Management Studies University of Cape Coast Ghana.*

Aguilera-Hermida, A. P. (2020). College students' use and acceptance of emergency online learning due to COVID-19. *International Journal of Educational Research Open*, *1*, 100011. doi:10.1016/j.ijedro.2020.100011 PMID:35059662

Ahn, M. Y., & Davis, H. H. (2020). Four domains of students' sense of belonging to university. *Studies in Higher Education*, *45*(3), 622–634. doi:10.1080/03075079.2018.1564902

Aina, J. K., Ogundele, A. G., & Olanipekun, S. S. (2013). Students' proficiency in English language relationship with academic performance in science and technical education. *American Journal of Educational Research, 1*(9), 355–358.

Akanwa, E. E. (2015). International students in western developed countries: History, challenges, and prospects. *Journal of International Students, 5*(3), 271–284. doi:10.32674/jis.v5i3.421

Al Fahim, M. A. J. (2013). *From Rags to Riches. A Story of Abu Dhabi.* Makarem LLC.

Alexander, S. (2002). Designing learning activities for an international online student body: What have we learned? *Journal of Studies in International Education, 6*(2), 188–200. doi:10.1177/1028315302006002007

Alfred, M. V. (2009). Nonwestern immigrants in continuing higher education: A sociocultural approach to culturally responsive pedagogy. *The Journal of Continuing Higher Education, 57*(3), 137–148. doi:10.1080/07377360903262168

Alkandari, N. Y. (2021). Students anxiety experiences in higher education institutions. In V. V. Kalinin, C. Hocaoglu, & S. Mohamed (Eds.), *Anxiety disorders: The new achievements* (pp. 1–11). IntechOpen. doi:10.5772/intechopen.92079

Allen, I. E., & Seaman, J. (2015). *Grade Level: Tracking Online Education in the United States.* Babson College.

Allote, N. (2016). Misunderstanding in verbal communication. In A. Rocci & L. de Saussure (Eds.), *Verbal communication* (Vol. 3, pp. 487–507). Walter de Gruyter GmbH & Co KG. doi:10.1515/9783110255478-025

Almeida, J., Robson, S., Morosini, M., & Baranzeli, C. (2019). Understanding Internationalization at Home: Perspectives from the Global North and South. *European Educational Research Journal, 18*(2), 200–217. doi:10.1177/1474904118807537

Altbach, P. G. (2002). Perspectives on International Higher Education. *Change, 34*(3), 29–31. doi:10.1080/00091380209601852

Altbach, P., & Knight, J. (2007). The internationalization of higher education: Motivations and realities. *Journal of Studies in International Education, 11*(3–4), 290–305. doi:10.1177/1028315307303542

Alter, R. (2010). *The Wisdom Books: Job, Proverbs, and Ecclesiastes. A translation with commentary.* W.W. Norton & Company.

Alumran, J. (2008). Learning styles in relation to gender, field of study, and academic achievement for Bahraini University students. *Individual Differences Research, 6*(4), 303–316.

American College Health Association. (2014). *National College Health Assessment II: Spring 2014 Reference Group Executive Summary.* https://www.acha.org/documents/ncha/ACHA-NCHA-II_ReferenceGroup_ExecutiveSummary_Spring2014.pdf

Amiridze, N., Davis, B. H., & Maclagan, M. (Eds.). (2010). *Fillers, pauses and placeholders.* John Benjamins., doi:10.1075/tsl.93

Ammigan, R. (2019). Institutional satisfaction and recommendation: What really matters to International students? *Journal of International Students, 9*(1), 262–281. doi:10.32674/jis.v9i1.260

Ammigan, R., & Jones, E. (2018). Improving the student experience: Learning from a comparative study of international student satisfaction. *Journal of Studies in International Education, 22*(4), 283–301. doi:10.1177/1028315318773137

Ammigan, R., & Langton, D. (2018). *The International student experience in Australia: Implications for administrators and student support staff.* International Education Association of Australia.

Amoako, G. K., & Okpattah, B. K. (2018). Unleashing salesforce performance: The impacts of personal branding and technology in an emerging market. *Technology in Society, 54*, 20–26. doi:10.1016/j.techsoc.2018.01.013

Amsberry, D. (2010). Deconstructing Plagiarism: International Students and Textual Borrowing Practices. *The Reference Librarian*, *51*(1), 31–44. doi:10.1080/02763870903362183

Anderson, J. R., & Deslandes, C. (2019). Religion and prejudice toward immigrants and refugees: A meta-analytic review. *The International Journal for the Psychology of Religion*, *29*(2), 128–145. doi:10.1080/10508619.2019.1570814

Andrade, M. S. (2006). International students in English-speaking universities: Adjustment factors. *Journal of Research in International Education*, *5*(2), 131–154. doi:10.1177/1475240906065589

Andrews, T. M., Leonard, M. J., Colgrove, C. A., & Kalinowski, S. T. (2011). Active learning not associated with student learning in a random sample of college biology courses. *CBE Life Sciences Education*, *10*(4), 394–405. doi:10.1187/cbe.11-07-0061 PMID:22135373

Appel, J. E., Park, C. L., Wortmann, J. H., & Schie, H. T. (2019). Meaning violations, religious/spiritual struggles, and meaning in life in the face of stressful life events. *The International Journal for the Psychology of Religion*, *29*(2). Advance online publication. doi:10.1080/10508619.2019.1611127

Appiah-Kubi, P., Annan, E. (2020). A Review of Collaborative Online International Learning. *International Journal of Engineering Pedagogy*, *10*(1), 109-124. doi:10.3991/ijep.v10i1.11678

Apple, M. W. (1995). Education, culture and class power: Basil Bernstein and the neo-Marxist sociology of education. In A. R. Sadovnik (Ed.), *Knowledge and pedagogy: The sociology of Basil Bernstein* (pp. 45–66). Ablex.

ApplyBoard. (2021, September24). *KPU*. https://www.applyboard.com/schools/kwantlen-polytechnic-university-surrey

Arasaratnam, L. A. (2005). Intercultural communication competence: Identifying key components from multicultural perspectives. *International Journal of Intercultural Relations*, *29*(2), 137–163.

Archer, W., & Davison, J. (2008). *Graduate employability*. The Council for Industry and Higher Education.

Argyris, M., & Schön, D. (1974). *Theory in practice. Increasing professional effectiveness*. Jossey-Bass.

Arkın, E., & Osam, N. (2015). 8. English-medium higher education: A case study in a Turkish university context. In *English-medium instruction in European higher education* (pp. 177–200). De Gruyter Mouton. doi:10.1515/9781614515272-010

Arkoudis, S., Hawthorne, L., Baik, C., Hawthorne, G., O'Loughlin, K., Leach, D., & Bexley, E. (2009). *The impact of English language proficiency and workplace readiness on the employment outcomes of tertiary international students: Executive summary*. Centre for the Study of Higher Education, University of Melbourne. https://tinyurl.com/2m7ejse6

Arkoudis, S., Dollinger, M., Baik, C., & Patience, A. (2019). International students' experience in Australian higher education: Can we do better? *Higher Education*, *77*(5), 799–813. doi:10.100710734-018-0302-x

Arkoudis, S., Watty, K., Baik, C., Yu, X., Borland, H., Chang, S., Lang, I., Lang, J., & Pearce, A. (2013). Finding common ground: Enhancing interaction between domestic and international students in higher education. *Teaching in Higher Education*, *18*(3), 222–235. doi:10.1080/13562517.2012.719156

Arthur, N., & Flynn, S. (2011). Career development influences of international students who pursue permanent immigration to Canada. *International Journal for Educational and Vocational Guidance*, *11*(3), 221–237. doi:10.100710775-011-9212-5

Artze-Vega, I., & Delgado, E. P. (2019). Supporting faculty in culturally responsive online teaching: Transcending challenges and seizing opportunities. In L. Kyei-Blankson, J. Blankson, & E. Ntuli (Eds.), *Care and culturally responsive pedagogy in online settings* (pp. 22–41). IGI Global. doi:10.4018/978-1-5225-7802-4.ch002

Arum, R., & Roksa, J. (2011). *Academically adrift: Limited learning on college campuses*. University of Chicago Press.

Asgari, M., & Borzooei, M. (2014). Evaluating the perception of Iranian students as educational tourists toward Malaysia: In-depth interviews. *Interdisciplinary Journal of Contemporary Research in Business, 5*(9), 81–109.

Astin, A. W. (1993). *What matters in college: Four critical years revisited.* Jossey-Bass.

Atkinson, R. (2001). The life story interview. In G. F. Jaber & H. A. James (Eds.), *Handbook of interview research* (pp. 120–140). SAGE Publications.

Australian Psychological Society. (1997). *Racism and prejudice: Psychological perspectives.* Available at https://www.psychology.org.au/Assets/Files/racism_position_paper.pdf

Australian Trade and Investment Commission. (2021). *YTD March 2021 international student data released.* https://www.austrade.gov.au/australian/education/news/data/ytd-march-2021-international-student-data-released

Awang-Hashim, R., Kaur, A., & Valdez, N. P. (2019). Strategising inclusivity in teaching diverse learners in higher education. *Malaysian Journal of Learning and Instruction, 16*(1), 105–128. doi:10.32890/mjli2019.16.1.5

Aydin, C. H., & Kayabas, B. K. (2018). Designing culturally sensitive massive open online courses: Learning culture and MOOCs in Turkey. In E. Toprak & E. Kumtepe (Eds.), *Supporting multiculturalism in open and distance learning spaces* (pp. 208–221). IGI Global. doi:10.4018/978-1-5225-3076-3.ch011

Baas, M. (2010). *Imagined mobility: Migration and transnationalism among Indian students in Australia.* Anthem Press.

Baas, M. (2019). The education-migration industry: International students, migration policy and the question of skills. *International Migration (Geneva, Switzerland), 57*(3), 222–234. doi:10.1111/imig.12540

Baber, H. (2021). Social interaction and effectiveness of online learning: A moderating role of maintaining social distance during the pandemic COVID-19. *Asian Education and Development Studies.* doi:10.1108/AEDS-09-2020-0209

Bahasoan, A. N., Ayuandiani, W., Mukhram, M., & Rahmat, A. (2020). Effectiveness of online learning in pandemic COVID-19. *International Journal of Science, Technology & Management, 1*(2), 100–106.

Ballard, B., & Clanchy, J. (1991). *Teaching students from overseas.* Longman.

Ballard, B., & Clanchy, J. (1997). *Teaching international students: A brief guide for lecturers and supervisors.* IDP Education Australia.

Bandura, A. (1977). *Social learning theory.* Prentice-Hall.

Bandura, A. (1978). The self system in reciprocal determinism. *The American Psychologist, 33*(4), 344–358. doi:10.1037/0003-066X.33.4.344

Bandura, A. (1989). Human agency in social cognitive theory. *The American Psychologist, 44*(9), 1175–1184. doi:10.1037/0003-066X.44.9.1175 PMID:2782727

Bangert, A. W. (2006). Identifying factors underlying the quality of online teaching effectiveness: An exploratory study. *Journal of Computing in Higher Education, 17*(2), 79–99. doi:10.1007/BF03032699

Bangladesh Ministry of Primary and Mass Education. (2015). EFA 2015 national review: Bangladesh. *UNESDOC Digital Library.* https://unesdoc.unesco.org/ark:/48223/pf0000230507

Banks, J. A. (2001a). Multicultural education: Goals, possibilities and challenges. In C. F. Diaz (Ed.), *Multicultural education in the 21st century* (pp. 11–22). Addison-Wesley.

Banks, J. A. (2001b). History, characteristics and goals. In J. A. Banks & C. A. M. Banks (Eds.), *Handbook of research on multicultural education* (pp. 3–29). Wiley.

Barbosa, M. L. O., & Neves, C. E. B. (2020). Internationalization of Higher Education: Institutions and knowledge diplomacy. *Sociologias*, *22*(54), 22–44. doi:10.1590/15174522-104425

Basit, T. N., & Santoro, N. (2010). Playing the role of 'cultural expert': Teachers of ethnic difference in Britain and Australia. *Oxford Review of Education*, *37*(1), 37–52. doi:10.1080/03054985.2010.521621

Bates, T. (2013). *Harvard's current thinking on MOOCs. Harvard Magazine.*

Batido, H. M. (2001). The Endangered Languages of Africa, A Case Study from Botswana. In On Bicultural Diversity, linking language, knowledge and the environment. Smithsonian Institute Press.

Bauler, C. (2019). Speech Acts and Cross-Cultural Pragmatics. In N. Erdogan & M. Wei (Eds.), *Applied Linguistics for Teachers of Culturally and Linguistically Diverse Learners* (pp. 223–238). IGI Global. doi:10.4018/978-1-5225-8467-4. ch009

Bax, S. (2018). MOOCs as a new technology: approaches to normalising the MOOC experience for our learners. In M. Orsini-Jones & S. Smith (Eds.), Flipping the blend through MOOCs, MALL and OIL – new directions in CALL (pp. 9-16). Research-publishing.net. doi:10.14705/rpnet.2018.23.785

Beck, K. (2009). Questioning the emperor's new clothes: Towards ethical practices in internationalization. In R. D. Trilokekar, G. A. Jones, & A. Shubert (Eds.), *Canada universities go global* (pp. 306–336). James Lorimer & Company Ltd.

Beck, K. (2013). Making sense of internationalization: A critical analysis. In Y. Hebert & A. A. Abdi (Eds.), *Critical perspectives on international education* (pp. 43–59). doi:10.1007/978-94-6091-906-0_2

Beech, S. E. (2015). International student mobility: The role of social networks. *Social & Cultural Geography*, *16*(3), 332–350. doi:10.1080/14649365.2014.983961

Beech, S. E. (2018). Adapting to change in the higher education system: International student mobility as a migration industry. *Journal of Ethnic and Migration Studies*, *44*(4), 610–625. doi:10.1080/1369183X.2017.1315515

Beelen, J., & Jones, E. (2015). Redefining internationalization at home. In A. Curai, L. Matei, R. Pricopie, J. Salmi, & P. Scott (Eds.), *The European Higher Education Area: Between Critical Reflections and Future Policies* (pp. 59–72). Springer. doi:10.1007/978-3-319-20877-0_5

Belford, N. (2017). International Students from Melbourne Describing Their Cross- Cultural Transitions Experiences: Culture Shock, Social Interaction, and Friendship Development. *Journal of International Students*, *7*(3), 499–521. doi:10.32674/jis.v7i3.206

Belkhodja, C., & Esses, V. (2013). *Knowledge synthesis: Improving the assessment of international students' contribution to Canadian society.* Pathways to Prosperity. http://p2pcanada.ca/library/knowledge-synthesis-improving-the-assessment-of-international-students-contribution-to-canadian-society/

Benedict, R., & Mead, M. (1972). Rumanian culture and behavior. Colorado State University.

Benedict, R. (1943). *Rumanian culture and behavior.* Institute for International Studies.

Bennet, J. (2008). On becoming a global soul: A path to engagement during study abroad. In V. Savicki (Ed.), *Developing intercultural competence and transformation: Theory, Research and Application in International Education* (pp. 12–31). Stylus.

Bernstein, B. (1964). Elaborated and restricted codes: Their social origins and some consequences. *American Anthropologist*, *66*(6, Part 2), 55–69. doi:10.1525/aa.1964.66.suppl_3.02a00030

Bernstein, B. (2001). Symbolic control: Issues of empirical description of agencies and agents. *International Journal of Social Research Methodology, 4*(1), 21–33. doi:10.1080/13645570118017

Bernstein, B. B. (2019). Social class, language and socialisation. In *Linguistics and adjacent arts and sciences* (pp. 1545–1562). De Gruyter Mouton. doi:10.1515/9783110811278-003

Bertram, D. M., Poulaski, M., Elsasser, B. S., & Kumar, E. (2014). Social support and acculturation in Chinese international students. *Journal of Multicultural Counseling and Development, 40*(2), 107–124. doi:10.1002/j.2161-1912.2014.00048.x

Best Colleges. (2019). *2019 Online Education Trends Report.* https://res.cloudinary.com/highereducation/image/upload/v1556050834/BestColleges.com/edutrends/2019-Online-Trends-in-Education-Report-BestColleges.pdf

Bhabha, H. K. (2004). *The location of culture.* Routledge.

Bhabha, H. K., & Rutherford, J. (2006). Third space. *Multitudes, 26*(3), 95–107. doi:10.3917/mult.026.0095

Biggs, J. (1996). *Academic development in Confucian heritage culture* [Paper presentation]. The International Symposium on Child Development, Hong Kong.

Biggs, J., & Watkins, D. A. (2001). *The paradox of the Chinese learner and beyond.* Comparative Education Research Center.

Birenbaum, M., DeLuca, C., Earl, L., Heritage, M., Klenowski, V., Looney, A., Smith, K., Timperley, H., Volante, L., & Wyatt-Smith, C. (2015). International trends in the implementation of assessment for learning: Implications for policy and practice. *Policy Futures in Education, 13*(1), 117–140. doi:10.1177/1478210314566733

Birrell, B. (2005). *Immigration rules and the overseas student market in Australia.* IDP Education Australia Limited.

Blakemore, S. J. (2018). *Inventing ourselves: The secret life of the teenager brain.* Public Affairs Books.

Blieszner, P. B., & Teaster, R. (1999). Promises and pitfalls of the interactive television approach to teaching adult development and aging. *Educational Gerontology, 25*(8), 741–753.

Bloom, B. S. (1976). *Human characteristics and school learning.* McGraw-Hill.

Blunkett, D. (2001). *Education into employability: The role of the DfEE in the economy.* Speech at the Institute of Economic Affairs, London, UK.

Boadu, G. (2021). Historical significance and the challenges of African historiography. *Pedagogy, Culture & Society.* Advance online publication. doi:10.1080/14681366.2020.1843070

Bond, S. (2003). *Untapped Resources, Internationalization of the Curriculum and Classroom Experience: A Selected Literature Review.* Canadian Bureau for International Education.

Bond, S., Qian, J., & Huang, J. (2003). *The Role of Faculty in Internationalizing the Undergraduate Curriculum and Classroom Experience.* Canadian Bureau for International Education.

Bonnet, D. (1982). Le proverbe chez les Mossi du Yatenga (Haute Volta). Société d'études linguistiques et anthropologiques de France – SELAF.

Boronat, T., Quiles-Carrillo, O. F., Ivorra-Martinez, J., & Montanes, N. (2021). Do You Study or Work? Project based learning as an enriching experience in education. In M. Carmo (Ed.), Education Applications & Developments, Advances in Education and Educational Trends Series (pp. 159-166). InScience Press. doi:10.36315/2021ead13

Bosacki, S. L. (2016). *Social Cognition in Middle Childhood and Adolescence: Integrating the Personal, Social and Educational Lives of Young People.* Wiley.

Bossio, E., & Bylyna, C. (2006). *Semester 2: Benchmarks report: Community worker outreach and development.* Unpublished manuscript, Colleges Integrating Immigrants to Employment, Ontario Ministry of Citizenship and Immigration, Toronto, Ontario, Canada.

Boven, D. (2013). The next game changer: The historical antecedents of the MOOC movement in education. *E-learning Papers, 33*, 1–7.

Bozkurt, A., & Sharma, R. C. (2020). Emergency remote teaching in a time of global crisis due to CoronaVirus pandemic. *Asian Journal of Distance Education, 15*(1), i–vi.

Brace, E. (2001). *Crossing borders to create supportive educational spaces for refugee youth. In Crossing borders: African refugees, teachers and schools.* Common Ground Publishing Inc.

Brackett, M. A., Rivers, S. E., & Salovey, P. (2011). Emotional intelligence: Implications for Personal, Social, Academic, and Workplace Success. *Social and Personality Psychology Compass, 5*(1), 88–103. doi:10.1111/j.1751-9004.2010.00334.x

Bradshaw, J., & Baluja, T. (2021). Why many international students get a failing grade in academic integrity. *The Globe and Mail.* https://www.theglobeandmail.com/news/national/education/why-many-international-students-get-a-failing-grade-in-academic-integrity/article4199683/

Branch, A. J. (2020). Promoting ethnic identity development while teaching subject matter content: A model of ethnic identity exploration in education. *Teaching and Teacher Education, 87*, 102918. Advance online publication. doi:10.1016/j.tate.2019.102918

Braun, V., & Clarke, V. (2006). 2006/01/01). Using thematic analysis in psychology. *Qualitative Research in Psychology, 3*(2), 77–101. doi:10.1191/1478088706qp063oa

Brazill, S. (2021). Narrative inquiry into Chinese international doctoral students' journey: A strength-based perspective. *International Journal of Doctoral Studies, 16*, 395–428. doi:10.28945/4785

Briguglio, C. (2007). Educating the Business Graduate of the 21st Century: Communication for a Globalized World. *International Journal on Teaching and Learning in Higher Education, 19*(1), 8–20.

Briguglio, C., & Smith, R. (2012). Perceptions of Chinese students in an Australian university: Are we meeting their needs? *Asia Pacific Journal of Education, 32*(1), 17–33. doi:10.1080/02188791.2012.655237

Brown, C. S., & Chu, H. (2012). Discrimination, ethnic identity and academic outcomes of Mexican immigrant children: The importance of school context. *Child Development, 83*(5), 1477–1485. doi:10.1111/j.1467-8624.2012.01786.x PMID:22966916

Brown, G., Brown, G. D., Brown, G. R., Gillian, B., & Yule, G. (1983). *Discourse analysis.* Cambridge University Press. doi:10.1017/CBO9780511805226

Browning, M. H. E. M., Larson, L. R., Sharaievska, I., Rigolon, A., McAnirlin, O., Mullenbach, L., Cloutier, S., Vu, T. M., Thomsen, J., Reigner, N., Metcalf, E. C., D'Antonio, A., Helbich, M., Bratman, G. N., & Alvarez, H. O. (2021). Psychological impacts from COVID-19 among university students: Risk factors across seven states in the United States. *PLoS One, 16*(1), e0245327. doi:10.1371/journal.pone.0245327 PMID:33411812

Brown, J., Miller, J., & Mitchell, J. (2006). Interrupted schooling and the acquisition of literacy: Experiences of Sudanese refugees in Victorian secondary schools. *Australian Journal of Language and Literacy, 29*(2), 150–162.

Brown, L. (2008). Language and anxiety: An ethnographic study of international postgraduate students. *Evaluation and Research in Education, 21*(2), 75–95. doi:10.1080/09500790802152167

Brown, P., Lauder, H., & Ashton, D. (2011). *The global auction: The broken promises of education, jobs, and incomes.* Oxford University Press.

Bruner, J. (2004). Life as Narrative. *Social Research: An Educational Quarterly, 71*(3), 691–710. https://ewasteschools.pbworks.com/f/Bruner_J_LifeAsNarrative.pdf

Bryman, A. (2016). *Social research methods* (5th ed.). Oxford University Press.

Bryman, A., & Bell, E. (2019). *Social Research Methods* (5th ed.). Oxford University Press.

Bucholtz, M., & Hall, K. (2005). Identity and interaction: A sociocultural linguistic approach. *Discourse Studies, 7*(4-5), 585–614. doi:10.1177/1461445605054407

Bull, J., Collins, C., Coughlin, E., & Sharpe, D. (2001). *Technical review of plagiarism detection software report.* Academic Press.

Burel, M., Graser, M., & Park, S. (2019). Exploring the international student experience: Providing insight through a mixed-methods approach. *Journal of Library Administration, 59*(2), 149–174. doi:10.1080/01930826.2018.1562804

Burnett, B., & Lampert, J. (2018). Destabilising privilege: Disrupting deficit thinking in white pre-service teachers on professional experience in culturally diverse, high-poverty schools. In T. Ferfolja, C. J. Diaz, & J. Ullman (Eds.), *Understanding sociological theory for educational practices* (2nd ed., pp. 85–101). Cambridge University Press. doi:10.1017/9781108378482.007

Burns, A. (2010). *Doing action research in English Language Teaching: A guide for practitioners.* Routledge.

Buxton, L. (2017). Ditching deficit thinking: Changing to a culture of high expectations. *Issues in Educational Research, 27*(2), 198–214.

Cacciaguidi-Fahy, S., & Cunningham, J. (2007). The Use of Strategic Metaphors in Intercultural Business Communication. *Managing Global Transitions International Research Journal, 5*(2), 133–155.

Caissie, K. B. (1978). *A handbook for teaching technical English* (Master's thesis, SIT Graduate Institute). SIT Digital Collections. https://digitalcollections.sit.edu/ipp_collection/248/

Calder, M., Richter, S., Mao, Y., Kovacs-Burns, K., Mogale, R., & Danko, M. (2016). International students attending Canadian universities: Their experiences with housing, finances, and other issues. *Canadian Journal of Higher Education, 46*(2), 92–110. doi:10.47678/cjhe.v46i2.184585

Caligiuri, P., DuBois, C. L., Lundby, K., & Sinclair, E. A. (2020). Fostering international students' sense of belonging and perceived social support through a semester-long experiential activity. *Research in Comparative and International Education, 15*(4), 357–370. doi:10.1177/1745499920954311

Caluya, G., Probyn, E., & Vyas, S. (2011). "Affective eduscapes": The case of Indian students within Australian international higher education. *Cambridge Journal of Education, 41*(1), 85–99. doi:10.1080/0305764X.2010.549455

Campbell, J., & Li, M. (2008). Asian students' voices: An empirical study of Asian students' learning experiences at a New Zealand university. *Journal of Studies in International Education, 12*(4), 375–396. doi:10.1177/1028315307299422

Canada's International Education Strategy. (2020). *Building on Success: International Education Strategy (2019-2024).* https://www.international.gc.ca/education/strategy-2019-2024-strategie.aspx?lang=eng

Canadian Bureau for International Education (CBIE). (2014). *A world of learning Canada's performance and potential in international education.* The Canadian Bureau for International Education.

Canadian Bureau for International Education. (2018). *Canada's Performance and Potential in International Education 2018.* Retrieved from: https://cbie.ca/media/facts-and-figures/

Canadian Bureau for International Education. (2018). *International students in Canada.* https://cbie.ca/wp-content/uploads/2018/09/International-Students-in-Canada-ENG.pdf

Canadian Bureau for International Education. (2018). *The student's voice: National results of the 2018 CBIE international student survey.* CBIE Research in Brief Number 9. Retrieved December 21, 2021, from https://cbie.ca/wpcontent/uploads/2018/08/Student_Voice_Report-ENG.pdf

Canadian Bureau for International Education. (2020). *Infographic.*https://cbie.ca/infographic

Canadian Bureau for International Education. (2020). *International Students in Canada 2020.* Retrieved from: https://cbie.ca/infographic/

Canadian Bureau for International Education. (2020, February 21). *International students in Canada continue to grow in 2019* [Press release]. https://cbie.ca/international-students-in-canada-continue-to-grow-in-2019/

Canadian Bureau for International Education. (2021). *Canada's performance and potential in international education.* Retrieved from http://www.cbie.ca/about- ie/facts-and-figures/

Canadian Bureau of International Education. (2018, August). *The student's voice: National results of the 2018 CBIE international student survey* (CBIE Research in Brief No. 9). https://cbie.ca/wp-content/uploads/2018/08/Student_Voice_Report-ENG.pdf

Canadian Bureau of International Education. (2021). *The student's voice: National results of the 2018 CBIE international student survey.* https://cbie.ca/survey/

Canadian Federation of Students–Ontario. (2015, July). *The impact of government underfunding on students.* https://cfsontario.ca/wp-content/uploads/2017/07/Factsheet-Underfunding.pdf

Canale, M., & Swain, M. (1980). Theoretical bases of communicative approaches to second language teaching and testing. *Applied Linguistics, 1*(1), 1–47. doi:10.1093/applin/1.1.1

Çankaya, E. M., Dong, X., & Liew, J. (2017). An examination of the relationship between social self-efficacy and personal growth initiative in international context. *International Journal of Intercultural Relations, 61*, 88–96. doi:10.1016/j.ijintrel.2017.10.001

Cantwell, B. (2015). Are international students cash cows? Examining the relationship between new international undergraduate enrollments and institutional revenue at public colleges and universities in the US. *Journal of International Students, 5*(4), 512–525. doi:10.32674/jis.v5i4.412

Carales, V. D., & Nora, A. (2020). Finding place: Cognitive and psychosocial factors impacting Latina/o students' sense of belonging. *Journal of Student Affairs Research and Practice, 57*(4), 355–370. doi:10.1080/19496591.2019.1662795

Carey, K. (2012). The siege of academe. *The Washington Monthly.*

Carroll, J. (2008). Assessment issues for international students and for teachers of international students. *The enhancing series case studies: International learning experience*, 1-13.

CAST. (2018). *Checkpoint 5.1: Use multiple media for communication.* https://udlguidelines.cast.org/action-expression/expression-communication/use-multimedia

Cauvin, J. (1976). Les proverbes comme expression privilégiée de la pensée imageante. *Afrique et langage, 6*, 5-34.

Cazden, C., Hymes, D., & John, V. (Eds.). (1970). *Functions of language in the classroom.* Teachers College Press.

Cebolla-Boado, H., Hu, Y., & Soysal, Y. N. (2018). Why study abroad? Sorting of Chinese students across British universities. *British Journal of Sociology of Education, 39*(3), 365–380. doi:10.1080/01425692.2017.1349649

Ceo-DiFrancesco, D., & Bender-Slack, D. (2016). Collaborative Online International Learning: Students and professors making global connections. In A. K. Moeller (Ed.), *Fostering Connections, Empowering Communities, Celebrating the World Fostering Connections, Empowering Communities, Celebrating the World* (pp. 147–174). Robert M. Terry.

Cetin, M. (2019). Effects of religious participation on social inclusion and existential well-being levels of Muslim refugees and immigrants in Turkey. *The International Journal for the Psychology of Religion, 29*(2), 64–76. doi:10.1080/10508619.2019.1580092

Chabba, S. (2020, May 5). "IELTS marriages" — India's "ideal bride" is proficient in English. *Deutsche Welle.* https://www.dw.com/en/ielts-marriages-indias-ideal-bride-is-proficient-in-english/a-53341947

Chafe, W., & Tannen, D. (1987). The relation between written and spoken language. *Annual Review of Anthropology, 16*(1), 383–407. doi:10.1146/annurev.an.16.100187.002123

Chakraborty, P., Mittal, P., Gupta, M. S., Yadav, S., & Arora, A. (2021). Opinion of students on online education during the COVID-19 pandemic. *Human Behavior and Emerging Technologies, 3*(3), 357–365. doi:10.1002/hbe2.240

Chalmers, D., & Volet, S. (1997). Common misconceptions about students from South-East Asia studying in Australia. *Higher Education Research & Development, 16*(1), 87–99. doi:10.1080/0729436970160107

Chandler, K. (2016). Using breakout rooms in synchronous online tutorials. *Journal of Perspectives in Applied Academic Practice, 4*(3), 16–23. doi:10.14297/jpaap.v4i3.216

Chan, E. (2007). Student experience of a culturally sensitive curriculum: Ethnic identity development amid conflicting stories to live by. *Journal of Curriculum Studies, 39*(2), 177–194. doi:10.1080/00220270600968658

Chang, H. (2013). Individual and Collaborative Autoethnography as Method: A Social Scientist's Perspective. In *Handbook of autoethnography* (pp. 107-123). Springer. doi:10.4324/9781315427812

Chang, C. L., & Wu, S. (2021). Using Online Social Networks to Globalize and Popularize Product Brands in Different Cultural Areas: A Relational Network Model. *Journal of Global Information Management, 29*(6), 1–30. doi:10.4018/JGIM.20211101.oa38

Chang, H. (2008). *Authoethnography as Method.* Left Coast Press.

Chang, H., Ngunjiri, F., & Hernandez, K.-A. C. (2016). *Collaborative autoethnography.* Routledge. doi:10.4324/9781315432137

Chan, S. (1999). The Chinese learner – A question of style. *Education + Training, 41*(6/7), 294–304. doi:10.1108/00400919910285345

Chen, & Zhou, G. (2019). Chinese International Students' Sense of Belonging in North American Postsecondary Institutions: A Critical Literature Review. *Brock Education, 28*(2), 48–63. doi:10.26522/brocked.v28i2.642

Chen, B. (2011). *An emerging trend of Mandarin-speaking international students* [Paper Presentation]. The American Psychological Association Annual Meeting, Washington, DC, United States.

Chen, D.-T. V., Wang, Y.-M., & Lee, W. C. (2016). Challenges confronting beginning researchers in conducting literature reviews. *Studies in Continuing Education, 38*(1), 47–60. doi:10.1080/0158037X.2015.1030335

Chen, G.-M., & Starosta, W. J. (1998). A review of the concept of intercultural awareness. *Human Communication, 2,* 27–54.

Chen, R. T.-H., & Bennett, S. (2012). When Chinese learners meet constructivist pedagogy online. *Higher Education, 64*(5), 677–691. doi:10.100710734-012-9520-9

Chen, Y.-H., & Van Ullen, M. K. (2011). Helping International Students Succeed Academically through Research Process and Plagiarism Workshops. *College & Research Libraries, 72*(3), 209–235. doi:10.5860/crl-117rl

Ching, Y., Renes, L. S., McMurrow, S., Simpson, J., & Strange, T. A. (2017). Challenges facing Chinese international students studying in the United State. *Educational Research Review, 12*(8), 473–482. doi:10.5897/ERR2016.3106

Chirkov, V. I., Safdar, S., de Guzman, D. J., & Playford, K. (2008). Further examining the role motivation to study abroad plays in the adaptation of international students in Canada. *International Journal of Intercultural Relations, 32*(5), 427–440. doi:10.1016/j.ijintrel.2007.12.001

Choi, Y., Crossman, E., & Hou, F. (2021, June 23). *International students as a source of labour supply: Transition to permanent residency.* Statistics Canada. doi:10.25318/36280001202100600002-eng

Chomsky, N. (1965). *Aspects of the theory of syntax.* MIT Press.

Cho, S., Crenshaw, K. W., & McCall, L. (2013). Toward a Field of Intersectionality Studies: Theory, Applications, and Praxis. *Signs (Chicago, Ill.), 38*(4), 785–810. doi:10.1086/669608

Choudaha, R. (2017). Three waves of international student mobility (1999–2020). *Studies in Higher Education, 42*(5), 825–832. doi:10.1080/03075079.2017.1293872

Christian, M. B., Lutz, E. L., Matthias, B., Richard, D. U., Markus, M. L., & Frank, S. (2021). Leadership in a time of crisis: Lessons learned from a pandemic. *Best Practice & Research. Clinical Anaesthesiology, 35*(3), 405–414. doi:10.1016/j.bpa.2020.11.011 PMID:34511228

Chyung, S. Y., & Vachon, M. (2013). An Investigation of the profiles of satisfying and dissatisfying factors in e-learning. *Performance Improvement Quarterly, 26*(2), 117–140. doi:10.1002/piq.21147

Clandinin, D. J. (2013). *Engaging in narrative inquiry.* Left Coast Press.

Clandinin, D. J. (Ed.). (2007). *Handbook of narrative inquiry: Mapping a methodology.* Sage Publications, Inc., doi:10.4135/9781452226552

Clandinin, D. J., & Rosiek, J. (2007). Mapping a landscape of narrative inquiry: Borderland spaces and tensions. In D. J. Clandinin (Ed.), *Handbook of narrative inquiry: Mapping a methodology* (pp. 35–75). Sage. doi:10.4135/9781452226552.n2

Clark, B. R. (1998). *Creating Entrepreneurial Universities: Organizational Pathways of Transformation.* Emerald Group Publishing Limited.

Clayton, M. (2012, January 24). *There is more to emotional intelligence than Daniel Goleman* [Web log post]. Management Pocketbooks. https://www.pocketbook.co.uk/blog/2012/01/24/theres-more-to-emotional-intelligence-than-daniel-goleman/

Clements, D. (2007). Prior knowledge of mechanics amongst first year engineering students. *Teaching Mathematics and Its Applications, 26*(3), 119–123. doi:10.1093/teamat/hrm005

Clements, R. E. (2003). Proverbs. In J. D. G. Dunn & J. W. Rogerson (Eds.), *Eerdemans Commentary on the Bible.* Eerdemans Publishing Company.

Clifford, V. (2010). The international curriculum: (Dis)locating students. In E. Jones (Ed.), *Internationalization and the student voice: Higher education perspectives* (pp. 169–180). Routledge.

Clifford, V. A. (2009). Engaging the Disciplines in Internationalising the Curriculum. *The International Journal for Academic Development, 14*(2), 133–143. doi:10.1080/13601440902970122

CMY. (2021). *The Schools Standing Up to Racism site Schools Standing Up To Racism.* Centre For Multicultural Youth. cmy.net.au

Cohen, L. (1999). *Philosophical perspectives in education.* Retrieved June 14, 2005 from http://oregonstate.edu/instruct/ed416/pp3.html

Cojocariu, V.-M., Lazar, I., Nedeff, V., & Lazar, G. (2014). SWOT ANALYSIS of e-learning educational services from the perspective of their beneficiaries. *Procedia: Social and Behavioral Sciences, 116,* 1999–2003. doi:10.1016/j.sbspro.2014.01.510

Colpaert, J. (2020). Editorial position paper: How virtual is your research? *Computer Assisted Language Learning, 33*(7), 653–664. doi:10.1080/09588221.2020.1824059

Connell, R. (2013). The neoliberal cascade and education: An essay on the market agenda and its consequences. *Critical Studies in Education, 54*(2), 99–112. doi:10.1080/17508487.2013.776990

Connelly, F. M., & Clandinin, D. J. (1990). Stories of experience and narrative inquiry. *Educational Researcher, 19*(5), 2–14. doi:10.3102/0013189X019005002

Conway, R., & Walker, P. (2017). Curriculum, learning, teaching and assessment adjustments. In P. Foreman & M. Arthur-Kelly. Inclusion in action (5th ed., pp.134-196). Cengage.

Cook-Gumperz, J. (1986). Interactional sociolinguistics in the study of schooling. In J. Cook-Gumperz (Ed.), *The social construction of literacy* (pp. 45–68). Cambridge University Press.

Cook-Harvey, C. M., Darling-Hammond, L., Lam, L., Mercer, C., & Roc, M. (2016). *Equity and ESSA: Leveraging educational opportunity through the every student succeeds act.* Learning Policy Institute. Retrieved from https://learningpolicyinstitute.org/product/equity-essa-report

Cooney, A., & Darcy, E. (2020). 'It was fun': Exploring the pedagogical value of collaborative educational games. *Journal of University Teaching & Learning Practice, 17*(3), 1–15. https://ro.uow.edu.au/jutlp/vol17/iss3/4. doi:10.53761/1.17.3.4

Cooper, C., & Yarbrough, S. (2016). Asian-Indian female international students: A photovoice study of health and adaptation to the immigration experience. *The Qualitative Report, 21*(6), 1035–1051. https://nsuworks.nova.edu/tqr/vol21/iss6/3/

Cornell University. (n.d.). Retrieved from https://gradschool.cornell.edu/academic-progress/pathways-to-success/prepare-for-your-career/take-action/teaching-philosophy-statement

Council of Ministers of Education. Canada. (2013). *The role of education agents in Canada's education system.* https://www.cmec.ca/Publications/Lists/Publications/Attachments/326/The-Role-of-Education-Agents-EN.pdf

Coursera. (2012). Retrieved from Coursera: https://www.coursera.org/in

Coxhead, A. (2020). Academic vocabulary. In S. A. Webb (Ed.), *The Routledge handbook of vocabulary studies* (pp. 97–110). Routledge.

Cox, K., & Yamaguchi, S. (2010). Japanese graduate nursing students' perceptions of the teaching performance of an intercultural teacher. *Nursing Education Perspectives, 31*(3), 156–159. PMID:20635619

Crenshaw, J. (2000). Unresolved Issues in the Wisdom Literature. In M. E. Tate, H. W. Ballard, & D. W. Tucker (Eds.), *An Introduction to Wisdom Literature and the Psalms.* Mercer University Press.

Creswell, J. W., & Creswell, J. D. (2018). *Research design: Qualitative, quantitative, and mixed methods approach* (5th ed.). SAGE Publications.

Creswell, J. W., & Plano Clark, V. L. (2018). *Designing and conducting mixed methods research* (3rd ed.). Sage.

Cui, D. (2015). Capital, distinction, and racialized habitus: Immigrant youth in the educational field. *Journal of Youth Studies*, *18*(9), 1154–1169. doi:10.1080/13676261.2015.1020932

Curtin, M. (2017). *World Economic Forum Future of Jobs Report 2015.* https://www.inc.com/melanie-curtin/the-10-top-skills-that-will-land-you-high-paying-jobs-by-2020-according-to-world-economic-forum.html

Curtin, N., Stewart, A. J., & Ostrove, J. M. (2013). Fostering academic self-concept: Advisor support and sense of belonging among international and domestic graduate students. *American Educational Research Journal*, *50*(1), 108–137. doi:10.3102/0002831212446662

D'hondt, F., Eccles, J. S., Van Houtte, M., & Stevens, P. A. J. (2016). Perceived Ethnic Discrimination by Teachers and Ethnic Minority Students' Academic Futility: Can Parents Prepare Their Youth for Better or for Worse? *Journal of Youth and Adolescence*, *45*(6), 1075–1089. doi:10.100710964-016-0428-z PMID:26861710

Dafouz, E., & Camacho-Miñano, M. M. (2016). Exploring the impact of English-medium instruction on university student academic achievement: The case of accounting. *English for Specific Purposes*, *44*, 57–67. doi:10.1016/j.esp.2016.06.001

Dalporto, G. (2021). *Udacity 2020: The Year in Review.* Retrieved from Udacity: https://www.udacity.com/blog/2021/01/udacity-2020-the-year-in-review.html

Danhoff, K. L. (2012). *A survey of graduate social work educators: Teaching perspectives and classroom environments* (Doctoral dissertation). Colorado State University Libraries.

Darby, F., & Lang, J. (2019). *Small teaching online.* John Wiley & Sons.

Davey, B., Elliott, K., & Bora, M. (2019). Negotiating pedagogical challenges in the shift from face-to-face to fully online learning: A case study of collaborative design solutions by learning designers and subject matter experts. *Journal of University Teaching & Learning Practice*, *16*(1), 3. doi:10.53761/1.16.1.3

Dawson, L. L. (1999). When prophecy fails and faith persists: A theoretical overview. *Nova Religio*, *3*(1), 60–82. doi:10.1525/nr.1999.3.1.60

De Lima-Guedes, K. K. (2020). Integrating MOOCs into traditional UK higher education: Lessons learnt from MOOC-blend practitioners. In K. Borthwick & A. Plutino (Eds.), Education 4.0 revolution: Transformative approaches to language teaching and learning, assessment and campus design (pp. 29-36). Research-publishing.net. doi:10.14705/rpnet.2020.42.1084

De Moissac, D., Graham, J., Prada, K., Gueye, N., & Rocque, R. (2020). Mental health status and help-seeking strategies of international students in Canada. *Canadian Journal of Higher Education*, *50*(4), 52–71. doi:10.47678/cjhe.vi0.188815

de Wit, H. (2002). *Internationalization of higher education in the United States of America and Europe: A historical, comparative, and conceptual analysis.* Greenwood Press.

Deardorff, D., Guth, S., Rubin, J., & Church, A. (2017). *Prompts for student reflections in COIL-enhanced modules* [Unpublished manuscript]. Developed for COIL Stevens Initiative Cohort 2. https://docs.google.com/document/d/1Ghe8QtJczuLd0qdWOCl1ZXB1JFKZREIT/edit

Deardorff, D. K. (2006). Identification and assessment of intercultural competence as a student outcome of internationalization. *Journal of Studies in International Education, 10*(3), 241–266. doi:10.1177/1028315306287002

Debdi, O., Paredes-Velasco, M., & Velázquez-Iturbide, J. Á. (2016). Influence of pedagogic approaches and learning styles on motivation and educational efficiency of computer science students. *IEEE Revista Iberoamericana de Tecnologias del Aprendizaje, 11*(3), 213–218. doi:10.1109/RITA.2016.2590638

DeHaan, R. L. (2009). Teaching Creativity and Inventive Problem Solving in Science[Fall]. *CBE Life Sciences Education, 8*(3), 172–181. doi:10.1187/cbe.08-12-0081 PMID:19723812

DeKeyser, R. (Ed.). (2007). *Practice in a second language: Perspectives from applied linguistics and cognitive psychology.* Cambridge University Press. doi:10.1017/CBO9780511667275

Del Campo, C., Cancer, A., Pascual-Ezama, D., & Urquía-Grande, E. (2015). EMI vs. Non-EMI: Preliminary Analysis of the Academic Output within the INTE-R-LICA Project. *Procedia: Social and Behavioral Sciences, 212*, 74–79.

Delgado, R., & Stefancic, J. (Eds.). (2012). *Critical race theory: An introduction.* New York University Press.

DELNA. (n.d.). *Diagnositc English langauge needs assessment.* https://www.auckland.ac.nz/en/students/student-support/delna.html

Deloitte. (2017, November). *Annual Status of Higher Education of States and UTs in India.* https://www2.deloitte.com/content/dam/Deloitte/in/Documents/public-sector/in-ps-ashe-2017-noexp.pdf

Demuyakor, J. (2020). Coronavirus (COVID-19) and online learning in higher institutions of education: A survey of the perceptions of Ghanaian international students in China. *Online Journal of Communication and Media Technologies, 10*(3), 1–9. doi:10.29333/ojcmt/8286

Denyer, D., & Tranfield, D. (2009). Producing a systematic review. In D. Buchanan & A. Bryman (Eds.), *The Sage Handbook of Organizational Research Methods* (pp. 671–689). Sage Publications.

Department of Education, Skills and Employment (2020). *International student data: Monthly summary.* https://internationaleducation.gov.au/research/international-student-data/Documents/MONTHLY%20SUMMARIES/2020/Dec%202020%20MonthlyInfographic.pdf

Department of Education, Skills and Employment. (2020b). *Education export income by country 2019.* Retrieved from https://internationaleducation.gov.au/research/research-snapshots/Documents/RS%20Education%20export%202019.pdf

Department of Education, Skills and Employment. (2021). *End of Year Summary of International Student Data 2020.* Retrieved from https://internationaleducation.gov.au/research/international-student-data/Documents/Monthly%20Summaries/2020/Full%20year%20summary.pdf

Department of Education, Skills and Employment. (2021). *International student data: Monthly summary.* https://internationaleducation.gov.au/research/international-student-data/Documents/MONTHLY%20SUMMARIES/2021/Jul%202021%20MonthlyInfographic.pdf

Derr, K., Hübl, R., & Ahmed, M. Z. (2018). Prior knowledge in mathematics and study success in engineering: Informational value of learner data collected from a web-based pre-course. *European Journal of Engineering Education, 43*(6), 911–926. doi:10.1080/03043797.2018.1462765

Deveson, A. (2003). *Resilience.* Allen & Unwin.

Dhawan, S. (2020). Online learning: A panacea in the time of covid-19 crisis. *Journal of Educational Technology Systems, 49*(1), 5–22. doi:10.1177/0047239520934018

Direito, I., Pereira, A., & de Oliveira Duarte, A. M. (2012). Engineering undergraduates' perceptions of soft skills: Relations with self-efficacy and learning styles. *Procedia: Social and Behavioral Sciences*, *55*, 843–851. doi:10.1016/j.sbspro.2012.09.571

DiStefano, J. J., & Maznevski, M. L. (2000). Creating value with diverse teams in global management. *Organizational Dynamics*, *29*(1), 45–63. doi:10.1016/S0090-2616(00)00012-7

Domingues, J., & Araújo, E. R. (2010). *Hibridismo y Transnacionalidad en contexto Erasmus. El caso de los estudiantes Erasmus en la Universidad de La Coruña.* Paper presented at the X Congreso Español de Sociología, Pamplona.

Donkin, R., & Rasmussen, R. (2021). Student perception and the effectiveness of Kahoot!: A Scoping review in Histology, Anatomy, and Medical Education. *Anatomical Sciences Education*, *14*(5), 572–585. doi:10.1002/ase.2094 PMID:33900041

Donnell, J. A., Aller, B. M., Alley, M., & Kedrowicz, A. A. (2011, June 26–29). *Why industry says that engineering graduates have poor communication skills: What the literature says* [Conference session]. ASEE Annual Conference & Exposition, Vancouver, BC, Canada. https://tinyurl.com/3kbhe7av

Dooly, M., & Vinagre, M. (2021). Research into practice: Virtual exchange in language teaching and learning. *Language Teaching*, 1–15. doi:10.1017/S0261444821000069

Dotterer, A. M., McHale, S. M., & Crouter, A. C. (2009). Sociocultural factors and school engagement among African American youth: The roles of racial discrimination, racial socialization, and ethnic identity. *Applied Developmental Science*, *13*(2), 61–72. https://bit.ly/3vjpSuh. doi:10.1080/10888690902801442 PMID:27134516

Downes, P. (2009, April 13). *Universities Scotland*. Retrieved from https://www.universities-scotland.ac.uk/publications/taking-pride-in-the-job

Downes, S. (2011). *Welcome to CCK11*. Retrieved 10 1, 2021, from Connectivism and Connective Knowledge 2011: http://cck11.mooc.ca/

Downes, S. (2012). *Creating the Connectivist Course*. Retrieved 08 15, 2019, from Knowledge, Learning, Community: https://www.downes.ca/cgi-bin/page.cgi?post=57750

Duarte, A. & Riedl, K. (2021). 'Virtually' the same learning outcomes. A case study of a virtual client briefed communication project across borders, *Icono 14, 19*(2), 155-177. doi:10.7195/ri14.v19i2.1724

Duarte, A. (2013). *A Atração Da Educação: O Impacto do Estereótipo Nacional na Intenção de Escolha do Destino de Estudo no Contexto do Ensino Superior Europeu: O Caso de Portugal* (Doctoral dissertation). http://hdl.handle.net/1822/29965

Duncan, C. (2020, May 4). New research shows international students keeping study dreams alive, for now. *IDP Connect*. https://www.idp-connect.com/newspage/international-student-crossroads-demand-for-on-campus-education-amidst-covid-19-apac/

Duran, A., Dahl, L. S., Stipeck, C., & Mayhew, M. J. (2020). A Critical Quantitative Analysis of Students' Sense of Belonging: Perspectives on Race, Generation Status, and Collegiate Environments. *Journal of College Student Development*, *61*(2), 133–153. doi:10.1353/csd.2020.0014

Dwivedi, Y., Hughes, D., Coombs, C., Constantiou, I., Duan, Y., Edwards, J. S., Gupta, B., Lal, B., Misra, S., Prashant, P., Raman, R., Rana, N. P., Sharma, S. K., & Upadhyay, N. (2020). Impact of COVID-19 pandemic on information management research and practice: Transforming education, work and life. *International Journal of Information Management*, *55*, 102211. Advance online publication. doi:10.1016/j.ijinfomgt.2020.102211

Dwyer, M. (2017). *These Canadian universities have the most international students.* https://www.macleans.ca/education/which-canadian-universities-have-the-most-international-students/

Dyrberg, N. R., Treusch, A. H., & Wiegand, C. (2017). Virtual laboratories in science education: Students' motivation and experiences in two tertiary biology courses. *Journal of Biological Education, 51*(4), 358–374. doi:10.1080/00219 266.2016.1257498

Dziuban, C. D., Wang, M. C., & Cook, I. J. (2004). *Dr. Fox rocks: Student perceptions of excellent and poor college teaching* [Unpublished manuscript]. University of Central.

Eaton, S., & Christensen Hughes, J. (2022). *Academic Integrity in Canada : An Enduring and Essential Challenge.* Springer International Publishing AG. doi:10.1007/978-3-030-83255-1

Eckersley, R. (2008). Values and vision: Youth and the failure of modern western culture. *Youth Studies Australia, 27,* 10–19.

Economist. (2021). *Full-time MBA Ranking 2021.* http://whichmba.economist.com/ranking/full-time-mba

Eder, J., Smith, W. W., & Pitts, R. E. (2010). Exploring factors influencing student study abroad destination choice. *Journal of Teaching in Travel & Tourism, 10*(3), 232–250. doi:10.1080/15313220.2010.503534

edX. (2012). Retrieved from edX: https://www.edx.org/

El Masri, A., Choubak, M., & Litchmore, R. (2015, Nov. 5). *The Global Competition for International Students as Future Immigrants: The role of Ontario universities in translating government policy into institutional practice.* Higher Education Quality Council of Ontario. https://heqco.ca/wp-content/uploads/2020/03/Global-Competition-for-IS-ENG.pdf

Elliott, C. J., & Reynolds, M. (2014). Participative pedagogies, group work and the international classroom: An account of students' and tutors' experiences. *Studies in Higher Education, 39*(2), 307–320. doi:10.1080/03075079.2012.709492

Ellis, C., & Bochner, A. (2000). Autoethnography, personal narrative, reflexivity: Researcher as subject. In N. K. Denzin & Y. S. Lincoln (Eds.), Handbook of qualitative research (pp. 733–768). Sage.

Ellis, C. (2004). *The ethnographic I: A methodological novel about autoethnography.* AltaMira Press.

Ellis, C., Adams, T. E., & Bochner, A. P. (2011). Autoethnography: An overview. *Historical Social Research. Historische Sozialforschung, 36*(4), 273–290. https://www.jstor.org/stable/23032294

Ellis, C., & Bochner, A. (2000). Autoethnography, personal narrative, reflexivity: Researcher as subject. In N. K. Denzin & Y. S. Lincoln (Eds.), *Handbook of qualitative research* (2nd ed., pp. 733–768). Sage Publications, Inc.

Elshami, W., Taha, H. M., Abuzaid, M., Saravanan, C., Kawas, A. S., & Abdalla, E. M. (2021). Satisfaction with online learning in the new normal: Perspective of students and faculty at medical and health sciences colleges. *Medical Education Online, 26*(1), 1920090. doi:10.1080/10872981.2021.1920090 PMID:33974523

Erb, S., & Drysdale, M. T. (2017). Learning attributes, academic self-efficacy and sense of belonging amongst mature students at a Canadian university. *Studies in the Education of Adults, 49*(1), 62–74. doi:10.1080/02660830.2017.1283754

Evans, N. W., & Andrade, M. S. (2015). Understanding challenges, providing support: ESL readers and writers in higher education. In N. W. Evans, N. J. Anderson & W. Eggington (Eds.), ESL readers and writers in higher education: Understanding challenges, providing support (pp. 3-17). Routledge.

Evans, S., & Morrison, B. (2011). Meeting the challenges of English-medium higher education: The first-year experience in Hong Kong. *English for Specific Purposes, 30*(3), 198–208. doi:10.1016/j.esp.2011.01.001

Fabio, A. D., & Kenny, M. E. (2019). Resources for enhancing employee and organizational well-being beyond personality traits: The promise of emotional intelligence and positive relational management. *Personality and Individual Differences*, *151*, 1–11. doi:10.1016/j.paid.2019.02.022

Fairclough, N., & Wodak, R. (1997). Critical discourse analysis. In T. van Dijk (Ed.), *Discourse studies: A multidisciplinary introduction* (Vol. 2, pp. 258–284). SAGE.

Fantini, A. E. (2012). Language: An essential component of Intercultural Communicative Competence. In J. Jackson (Ed.), *The handbook of language and intercultural communication* (pp. 273-288). Routledge. https://docuri.com/download/the-handbook-of-language-and-intercultural-communication_59c1e904f581710b286cfba3_pdf#page=274

Fantini, A. E. (2000). A central concern: Developing intercultural competence. In A. E. Fantini (Ed.), *Addressing International Education Training & Service* (pp. 25–42). School for International Training.

Fantini, A. E. (2019). *Intercultural communicative competence in educational exchange: a multinational perspective.* Routledge. doi:10.4324/9781351251747-2

Farrell, L., Bourgeois-Law, G., Regehr, G., & Ajjawi, R. (2015). Autoethnography: Introducing 'I' into medical education research. *Medical Education*, *49*(10), 974–982. doi:10.1111/medu.12761 PMID:26383069

Fass-Holmes, B. (2018). International Students Reported for Academic Integrity Violations: Demographics, Retention, and Graduation. *Journal of International Students*, *7*(3), 644–669. doi:10.32674/jis.v7i3.292

Fatemi, G., & Saito, E. (2020). Unintentional plagiarism and academic integrity: The challenges and needs of postgraduate international students in Australia. *Journal of Further and Higher Education*, *44*(10), 1305–1319. doi:10.1080/0309877X.2019.1683521

Fayol, H. (1917). *Administration industrielle et générale; prévoyance, organisation, commandement, coordination, controle.* H. Dunod et E. Pinat.

Fell, E. V., & Lukianova, N. A. (2015). British universities: International students' alleged lack of critical thinking. *Procedia: Social and Behavioral Sciences*, *215*, 2–8. doi:10.1016/j.sbspro.2015.11.565

Fernández-Berrocal, P., & Extremera, N. (2016). Ability Emotional Intelligence, Depression, and Well-Being. *Emotion Review*, *8*(4), 311–315. doi:10.1177/1754073916650494

Figel, J. (2006, April 3). *International competitiveness in higher education—A European perspective* [Conference session]. AHUA Conference, Oxford, UK.

Finardi, K. R. (2014). The slaughter of Kachru's five sacred cows in Brazil: Affordances of the use of English as an international language. *Studies in English Language Teaching*, *2*(4), 401–411. doi:10.22158elt.v2n4p401

Finardi, K. R. (2019). *English in the South.* Editora da Universidade Estadual de Londrina.

Finn, S. (2020). Academic freedom and the choice of teaching methods. *Teaching in Higher Education*, *25*(1), 116–123. doi:10.1080/13562517.2019.1672149

Firang, D. (2020). The impact of COVID-19 pandemic on international students in Canada. *International Social Work*, *63*(6), 820–824. doi:10.1177/0020872820940030

Firang, D., & Mensah, J. (2022). Exploring the Effects of the COVID-19 Pandemic on International Students and Universities in Canada. *Journal of International Students*, *12*(1), 1–18. doi:10.32674/jis.v12i1.2881ojed.org/jis

Flavell, J. H. (1979). Metacognition and cognitive monitoring: A new area of cognitive–developmental inquiry. *The American Psychologist*, *34*(10), 906–911. doi:10.1037/0003-066X.34.10.906

Fleck, E., & Kakouris, A. (2019, September). *Implementing Experiential Teaching Innovations to Encourage Entrepreneurial Activity* [Paper presentation]. Pre-Conference Workshop, the 14th European Conference on Innovation and Entrepreneurship (ECIE 2019), University of Peloponnese, Kalamata, Greece. https://www.academic-conferences.org/conferences/ecie/ecie-workshops/

Flick, U. (2014). Mapping the field. In U. Flick (Ed.), *The SAGE handbook of qualitative data analysis* (pp. 3–18). SAGE. doi:10.4135/9781446282243.n1

Flowerdew, J., & Miller, L. (1995). On the notion of culture in L2 lectures. *TESOL Quarterly, 29*(2), 345–373. doi:10.2307/3587628

Foltýnek, T., & Glendinning, I. (2015). Impact of Policies for Plagiarism in Higher Education across Europe: Results of the Project. *Acta Universitatis Agriculturae et Silviculturae Mendelianae Brunensis, 63*(1), 207–216. doi:10.11118/actaun201563010207

Fook, J. (2015). Reflective practice and critical reflection. In J. Lishman (Ed.), *Handbook for practice learning in social work and social care: Knowledge and theory* (3rd ed., pp. 440–454). Jessica Kingsley Publishers.

Forbes-Mewett, H., & Sawyer, A. (2016). International students and mental health. *Journal of International Students, 6*(3), 661–677. doi:10.32674/jis.v6i3.348

Foster, D. K., & Stapleton, M. D. (2012). Understanding Chinese students' learning needs in Western business classrooms. *International Journal on Teaching and Learning in Higher Education, 24*(3), 301–313.

Foster, M., & Anderson, L. (2015). Editorial: Exploring Internationalisation of the Curriculum to Enhance the Student Experience. *Journal of Perspectives in Applied Academic Practice., 3*(3), 1–2. doi:10.14297/jpaap.v3i3.206

Fox, G. (2018, February 21). *Words to live by*. Retrieved from http://www.nybooks.com/daily/2018/02/21/words-to-live-by/

Freimuth, H. (2013). *Cultural bias on the IELTS examination: A critical realist investigation* (Doctoral dissertation, Rhodes University). SEALS Digital Commons. http://hdl.handle.net/10962/d1012088

Freire, P. (1970). *Pedagogy of the Oppressed*. Continuum.

Freire, P. (1973). *Education for Critical Consciousness*. Continuum.

Freire, P. (1998). *Teachers as cultural workers: Letters to those who dare teach*. Westview Press.

Frenette, M., Choi, Y., & Doreleyers, A. (2020). International student enrolment in post-secondary education programs prior to COVID-19. *Economic Insights*, 105. https://www150.statcan.gc.ca/n1/pub/11-626-x/11-626-x2020003-eng.htm

Frenette, M., Choi, Y., & Doreleyers, A. (2020). *International student enrolment in postsecondary education programs prior to COVID-19*. Statistics Canada. https://www150.statcan.gc.ca/n1/pub/11-626-x/11-626-x2020003-eng.htm

Freyha, A. (1974). *A Dictionary of Modern Lebanese Proverbs*. Librairie du Liban.

Friesen, J. (2019, October 9). In Cape Breton, a dramatic rise in international students has transformed a school and a community. *The Globe and Mail.* https://www.theglobeandmail.com/canada/article-how-the-world-came-to-cape-breton-university/

Fteiha, M., & Awwad, N. (2020). Emotional intelligence and its relationship with stress coping style. *Health Psychology Open, 7*(2). Advance online publication. doi:10.1177/2055102920970416 PMID:33224513

Future Learn. (2012). Retrieved from Future Learn: https://www.futurelearn.com/

FutureLearn. (2020). *Understanding language: Learning and teaching*. University of Southampton & British Council. https://www.futurelearn.com/courses/understanding-language

Gameel, B. G., & Wilkins, K. G. (2019). When it comes to MOOCs, where you are from makes a difference. *Computers & Education*, *136*, 49–60. doi:10.1016/j.compedu.2019.02.014

Gantt, H. L. (1916). *Industrial Leadership*. Yale University Press.

García, H. A., Garza, T., & Yeaton-Hromada, K. (2019). Do we belong? A conceptual model for international students' sense of belonging in community colleges. *Journal of International Students*, *9*(2), 460–487. doi:10.32674/jis.v9i2.669

Garrett, B. M., & Cutting, R. (2012). Using social media to promote international student partnerships. *Nurse Education in Practice*, *12*(6), 340–345. doi:10.1016/j.nepr.2012.04.003 PMID:22595660

Gatwiri, G. (2015). The influence of language difficulties on the wellbeing of international students: An interpretive phenomenological analysis. *Inquiries Journal/Student Pulse*, *7*(5). http://www.inquiriesjournal.com/a?id=1042

Gatwiri, K., & Ife, J. (2021). Teaching about vulnerability and love in social work: Lessons and reflections from two academics. *Social Work Education*, 1–16. doi:10.1080/02615479.2021.1972962

Gay, G. (2010). *Culturally responsive teaching: Theory, research, and practice*. Teachers College Press.

Gay, G. (2013). Teaching to and through cultural diversity. *Curriculum Inquiry*, *43*(1), 48–70. doi:10.1111/curi.12002

Gay, G. (2015). The what, why, and how of culturally responsive teaching: International mandates, challenges, and opportunities. *Multicultural Education Review*, *7*(3), 123–139. doi:10.1080/2005615X.2015.1072079

Gay, G. (2018). *Culturally responsive teaching: Theory, practice, and research*. Teachers College Press.

Gearing, L. (2015). *Coventry University Group education strategy 2015-2021*. Coventry University Higher Education Corporation.

Gee, J. P. (2011). Discourse analysis: What makes it critical? In R. Rogers (Ed.), *An introduction to critical discourse analysis in education* (2nd ed., pp. 23–45). Lawrence Erlbaum Associates.

Gehrke, I., & Abermann, G. (2016). *The Multiculural Classroom-A Guaranteed Intercultural Learning Space*. Academic Press.

Gibbs, R. W. Jr. (1995). Idiomaticity and human cognition. In M. Everaert, E.-J. van der Linden, A. Schenk, & R. Schreuder (Eds.), *Idioms: Structural and psychological perspectives* (pp. 97–116). Lawrence Erlbaum Associates.

Gibson, C. B., & Zellmer-Bruhn, M. E. (2001). Metaphors and meaning: An intercultural analysis of the concept of teamwork. *Administrative Quarterly Science*, *46*(2), 274–306. doi:10.2307/2667088

Gillen-O'Neel, C. (2021). Sense of belonging and student engagement: A daily study of first-and continuing-generation college students. *Research in Higher Education*, *62*(1), 45–71. doi:10.100711162-019-09570-y

Gillett-Swan, J. (2017). The challenges of online learning supporting and engaging the isolated learner. *Journal of Learning Design*, *10*(1), 20–30. doi:10.5204/jld.v9i3.293

Giroux, H. (1992). *Border crossings: Cultural workers and the politics of education*. Rutledge.

Giroux, H. A. (2010). Bare pedagogy and the scourge of neoliberalism: Rethinking higher education as a democratic public sphere. *The Educational Forum*, *74*(3), 184–196. doi:10.1080/00131725.2010.483897

Given, L. M. (Ed.). (2008). *The SAGE encyclopedia of qualitative research methods*. SAGE. doi:10.4135/9781412963909

Glass, C. R. (2018). International students' sense of belonging-locality, relationships, and power. *Peer Review: Emerging Trends and Key Debates in Undergraduate Education, 20*(1), 27–30.

Glass, C. R., Kociolek, E., Wongtrirat, R., Lynch, R. J., & Cong, S. (2015). Uneven Experiences: The Impact of Student-Faculty Interactions on International Students' Sense of Belonging. *Journal of International Students, 5*(4), 353–367. doi:10.32674/jis.v5i4.400

Gleason, N. (2020). Strategic leadership for diversity and inclusion in higher education. In S. S. Sanger & N. W. Gleason (Eds.), Diversity and inclusion in global higher education (pp. 285-304). Palgrave Macmillan. doi:10.1007/978-981-15-1628-3_11

Global Affairs Canada. (2020). *Assessing the economic impact of international students in Canada.* International Education Division. Retrieved February 23, 2022, from https://www.international.gc.ca/education/report-rapport/impact-2017/sec-3.aspx?lang=eng

Goldring, L., Berinstein, C., & Bernhard, J. K. (2009). Institutionalizing precarious migratory status in Canada. *Citizenship Studies, 13*(3), 239–265. doi:10.1080/13621020902850643

Goleman, D. (2006). *Emotional intelligence: Why it can matter more than IQ* (10th ed.). Bantam.

Goleman, D. (2011). *HBR's 10 must reads on leadership.* Harvard Business Review Press.

Goleman, D., & Boyatzis, R. (2008). Social intelligence and the biology of leadership. *Harvard Business Review, 86*(9), 74–81. http://files-au.clickdimensions.com/aisnsweduau-akudz/files/inteligencia-social-y-biologia-de-un-lider.pdf PMID:18777666

Goleman, D., Boyatzis, R., & McKee, A. (2001). Primal leadership: The hidden driver of great performance. *Harvard Business Review, 79*(11), 42–53. https://hbr.org/2001/12/primal-leadership-the-hidden-driver-of-great-performance

Goodson, I., Biesta, J. G., Tedder, M., & Adair, N. (2010). *Narrative Learning.* Routledge. doi:10.4324/9780203856888

Gopal, A. (2016). Visa and immigration trends: A comparative examination of international student mobility in Canada, Australia, the United Kingdom, and the United States. *Strategic Enrollment Management Quarterly, 4*(3), 130–141. doi:10.1002em3.20091

Gore, J., Ladwig, J., Elsworth, W., Ellis, H., Parkes, R., & Griffiths, T. (2009). *Quality assessment: Linking assessment tasks and teaching outcomes in the social sciences.* Australian Learning and Teaching Council. https://ltr.edu.au/vufind/Record/365398

Government of Canada. (2019a). *Student direct stream: About the process.*https://www.canada.ca/en/immigration-refugees-citizenship/services/study-canada/study-permit/student-direct-stream.html

Government of Canada. (2019b). *Building on success: International educational strategy 2019-2024.* https://www.international.gc.ca/education/assets/pdfs/ies-sei/Building-on-Success-International-Education-Strategy-2019-2024.pdf

Government of Canada. (2021). *Study permit: Get the right documents.* https://www.canada.ca/en/immigration-refugees-citizenship/services/study-canada/study-permit/get-documents.html

Government of Punjab. (2020). *Punjab economic survey 2019-20.*https://www.esopb.gov.in/static/PDF/EconomicSurvey-2019-20.pdf

Grabke, S. V. R. (2013). *Institutional strategies and factors that contribute to the engagement of recent immigrant adult students in Ontario post-secondary education* [Unpublished dissertation]. York University.

Gravett, K., & Winstone, N. E. (2020). Making connections: Authenticity and alienation within students' relationships in higher education. *Higher Education Research & Development*, 1–15.

Gray, K., Chang, S., & Kennedy, G. (2010). Use of social web technologies by international and domestic undergraduate students: Implications for internationalizing learning and teaching in Australian universities. *Technology, Pedagogy and Education*, *19*(1), 31–46. doi:10.1080/14759390903579208

Grayson, J. P. (2008). The experiences and outcomes of domestic and international students at four Canadian universities. *Higher Education Research & Development*, *27*(3), 215–230. doi:10.1080/07294360802183788

Greatbatch, D., & Lewis, P. (2007). *Generic Employability Skills II*. Retrieved from http://www.swslim.org.uk/ges/documents/GES_II-FULL_REPORT_06.03.07.pdf

Grix, J. (2002). Introducing students to the generic terminology of social research. *Politics*, *22*(3), 175–186. doi:10.1111/1467-9256.00173

Grubb, W. N., & Lazerson, M. (2009). *The education gospel*. Harvard University Press.

Gudiño Paredes, S., de Jesús Jasso Peña, F., & de La Fuente Alcazar, J. (2021). Remote proctored exams: Integrity assurance in online education? *Distance Education*, *42*(2), 200–218. doi:10.1080/01587919.2021.1910495

Guimarães, F. F., & Finardi, K. R. (2021). Global citizenship education (GCE) in internationalization: COIL as alternative Thirdspace. *Globalisation, Societies and Education*, *19*(5), 641–657. doi:10.1080/14767724.2021.1875808

Gumperz, J., & Hymes, D. (Eds.). (1986). *Directions in sociolinguistics* (2nd ed.). Blackwell.

Gunnarsson, J., Kulesza, W. J., & Pettersson, A. (2014). Teaching international students how to avoid plagiarism: Librarians and faculty in collaboration. *Journal of Academic Librarianship*, *40*(3–4), 413–417. doi:10.1016/j.acalib.2014.04.006

Guo, Y., & Guo, S. (2017). Internationalization of Canadian Higher Education: Discrepancies between Policies and International Student Experiences. *Studies in Higher Education*, *42*(5), 851–868. doi:10.1080/03075079.2017.1293874

Guo, S., & Chase, M. (2011). Internationalisation of Higher Education: Integrating International Students into Canadian Academic Environment. *Teaching in Higher Education*, *16*(3), 305–318. doi:10.1080/13562517.2010.546524

Guo, S., & Jamal, Z. (2012). *Cultural diversity and inclusive teaching*. Society for Teaching and Learning in Higher Education.

Gupta, S., Taneja, S., & Kumar, N. (2015). Redefining the Classroom: Integration of open and classroom learning in higher education. In Macro-level learning through massive open online courses (MOOCs): Strategies and predictions for the future (pp. 168-182). IGI Global.

Gu, Q. (2010). Variations in Beliefs and Practices: Teaching English in Crosscultural Contexts. *Language and Intercultural Communication*, *10*(1), 32–53. doi:10.1080/14708470903377357

Gutiérrez, B. F., Glimäng, M. R., O'Dowd, R., & Sauro, S. (2021). *Mentoring handbook for virtual exchange teachers. Strategies to help students achieve successful synchronous and asynchronous online intercultural communication*. Stevens Initiative. https://www.stevensinitiative.org/resource/mentoring-handbook-for-virtual-exchange-teachers/

Guyotte, K. W., & Sochacka, N. W. (2016). Is This Research? Productive Tensions in Living the (Collaborative) Autoethnographic Process. *International Journal of Qualitative Methods*, *15*(1). doi:10.1177/1609406916631758

Hackett, R. D., & Kline, T. (1998). Editorial: Industrial-organizational psychology and emerging needs of the Canadian workplace: Traversing the next millennium. *Canadian Psychology*, *39*(1–2), 1–2. doi:10.1037/h0092483

Hall, D., & Buzwell, S. (2013). The problem of free-riding in group projects: Looking beyond social loafing as reason for non-contribution. *Active Learning in Higher Education, 14*(1), 37–49. doi:10.1177/1469787412467123

Hall, S. (2013). Introduction. In S. Hall (Ed.), *Representation: Cultural representations and signifying practices* (pp. 1–11). Sage.

Handa, N., & Power, C. (2005). Land and discover! A case study investigating the cultural context of plagiarism. *Journal of University Teaching & Learning Practice, 2*(3), 64–84. doi:10.53761/1.2.3.8

Han, H. S., Vomvoridi-Ivanović, E., Jacobs, J., Karanxha, Z., Lypka, A., Topdemir, C., & Feldman, A. (2014). Culturally responsive pedagogy in higher education: A collaborative self-study. *Studying Teacher Education, 10*(3), 290–312. do i:10.1080/17425964.2014.958072

Hannon, J., & D'Netto, B. (2007). Cultural diversity online: Student engagement with learning technologies. *International Journal of Educational Management, 21*(5), 418–432. doi:10.1108/09513540710760192

Harman, G. (2004). New directions in internationalizing higher education: Australia's development as an exporter of higher education services. *Higher Education Policy, 17*(1), 101–120. doi:10.1057/palgrave.hep.8300044

Harman, G. (2005). Internationalization of Australian higher education: A critical review of literature and research. In P. Ninnes & M. Hellstén (Eds.), *Internationalizing higher education: Critical explorations of pedagogy and policy* (Vol. 16, pp. 119–140). Springer Netherlands. doi:10.1007/1-4020-3784-8_7

Harmey, S. (2021). Responses to Educating Students at Risk During the COVID-19 Pandemic Special Issue Editorial for Journal of Education for Students Placed at Risk. *Journal of Education for Students Placed at Risk, 26*(2), 87–90. doi:10.1080/10824669.2021.1906252

Harris, A., Marlowe, J., & Nyuon, N. (2015). Rejecting Ahmed's 'melancholy migrant': South Sudanese Australians in higher education. *Studies in Higher Education, 40*(7), 1226–1238. doi:10.1080/03075079.2014.881346

Harrison, M. (2011). Supporting the T and the E in STEM: 2004–2010. *Design and Technology Education: An International Journal, 16*(1), 17–25. https://eric.ed.gov/?id=EJ916493

Harvey, D. (2005). *A brief history of neoliberalism.* Oxford University Press. doi:10.1093/oso/9780199283262.001.0001

Harvey, D., Ling, C., & Shehab, R. (2010). Comparison of student's learning style in STEM disciplines.*IIE Annual Conference Proceedings*, 1-6.

Harvey, L., Moon, S., & Geall, V. (1997). *Graduates' Work: Organizational change and students' attributes.* Centre for Research into Quality. doi:10.1177/095042229701100504

Harwell, D. (2020). Mass school closures in the wake of the coronavirus are driving a new wave of student surveillance. *The Washington Post.* https://www.washingtonpost.com/technology/2020/04/01/online-proctoring-college-exams-coronavirus/

Hassan, A., & Maharoff, M. (2014). The understanding of curriculum philosophy among trainee teachers in regards to soft skills embedment. *International Education Studies, 7*(12), 84. doi:10.5539/ies.v7n12p84

Hatoss, A., O'Neill, S., & Eacersall, D. (2012). Career choices: Linguistic and educational socialization of Sudanese-background high-school students in Australia. *Linguistics and Education, 23*(1), 16-30. doi:10.1016/j.linged.2011.10.003

Haugh, M. (2016). Complaints and troubles talk about the English language skills of international students in Australian universities. *Higher Education Research & Development, 35*(4), 727–740. doi:10.1080/07294360.2015.1137878

Haynes, A. S. (2019). Reaching Diverse Learners by Offering Different Course Delivery Methods. In R. Jeffries (Ed.), *Diversity, Equity, and Inclusivity in Contemporary Higher Education* (pp. 34–55). IGI Global. doi:10.4018/978-1-5225-5724-1.ch003

He, D. (2017). How to cope with foreign language speaking anxiety effectively? The case of university students in China. *Electronic Journal of Foreign Language Teaching, 14*(2), 159-174. https://e-flt.nus.edu.sg/wp-content/uploads/2020/09/he.pdf

Healey, M., Flint, A., & Harrington, K. (2014). *Engagement through partnership: Students as partners in learning and teaching in higher education.* HEA.

Hechanova-Alampay, R., Beehr, T. A., Christiansen, N. D., & Van Horn, R. (2002). Adjustment and strain among domestic and international student sojourners: A longitudinal study. *School Psychology International, 23*(4), 458–474. doi:10.1177/0143034302234007

He, D. (2013). What makes learners anxious while speaking English: A comparative study of the perceptions held by university students and teachers in China. *Educational Studies, 39*(3), 338–350. doi:10.1080/03055698.2013.764819

Helm, F. (2013). A dialogic model for telecollaboration. *Bellaterra Journal of Teaching & Learning Language & Literature, 6*(2), 28–48. doi:10.5565/rev/jtl3.522

Helms, R. M., Brajkovic, L., & Struthers, S. (2017). *Mapping internationalization on U.S. campuses: 2017 edition.* https://cbie.ca/wp-content/uploads/2018/08/Student_Voice_Report-ENG.pdf

Hénard, F., Diamond, L., & Roseveare, D. (2012). Approaches to internationalisation and their implications for strategic management and institutional practice. *IMHE Institutional Management in Higher Education, 11*(12), 2013.

Hendrickson, B., Rosen, D., & Aune, R. K. (2011). An analysis of friendship networks, social connectedness, homesickness, and satisfaction levels of international students. *International Journal of Intercultural Relations, 35*(3), 281–295. doi:10.1016/j.ijintrel.2010.08.001

Heng, T. (2017). Voices of Chinese International Students in USA Colleges: "I want to tell them that …. *Studies in Higher Education, 42*(5), 833–850. doi:10.1080/03075079.2017.1293873

Heng, T. T. (2018a). Coping strategies of international Chinese undergraduates in response to academic challenges in U.S. colleges. *Teachers College Record, 120*(Feb), 1–42. doi:10.1177/016146811812000202

Heng, T. T. (2018b). Different is not deficient: Contradicting stereotypes of Chinese international students in US higher education. *Studies in Higher Education, 43*(1), 22–36. doi:10.1080/03075079.2016.1152466

Heng, T. T. (2021). Socioculturally attuned understanding of and engagement with Chinese international undergraduates. *Journal of Diversity in Higher Education.* Advance online publication. doi:10.1037/dhe0000240

Henze, J., & Zhu, J. (2012). Current research on Chinese students studying abroad. *Research in Comparative and International Education, 7*(1), 90–104. doi:10.2304/rcie.2012.7.1.90

Heringer, R. (2020). From Enrolment Rates to Collaborative Knowledge Production: A Critique to the Internationalization of Higher Education in Canada. *Higher Education for the Future, 7*(2), 169–186. doi:10.1177/2347631120930838

He, Y., & Banhan, H. C. (2011). International student academic performance: Some statistical evidence and its implications. *American Journal of Business Education, 2*(5), 89–100. doi:10.19030/ajbe.v2i5.4073

Hiles, D., Ermk, I., & Chrz, V. (2017). Narrative inquiry. In C. Willig & W. S. Rogers (Eds.), *The SAGE Handbook of Qualitative Research in Psychology* (pp. 157–175). Sage. doi:10.4135/9781526405555.n10

Hindustan Times. (2018, July 31). *Parents sending kids abroad for studies due to drug menace: Punjab CM*. https://www.hindustantimes.com/punjab/parents-sending-kids-abroad-for-studies-due-to-drug-menace-punjab-cm/story-UoRAI4JuMegM81ni7mo02K.html

Hinton, T. (2020). *Number of Chinese student enrolments in Australia from 2010 to 2019, by education sector (in 1,000s)*. Retrieved from https://www.statista.com/statistics/430276/number-of-chinese-students-in-australia-by-education-sector/

Hirst, G., Susan, M., Peter, H., Philip, E., & Diane, H. (1994). Repairing conversational misunderstandings and non-understandings. *Speech Communication, 15*(3-4), 213–229. doi:10.1016/0167-6393(94)90073-6

Hoang, T. V. Y., & Rojas-Lizana, I. (2015). Promotional discourse in the websites of two Australian universities: A discourse analytic approach. *Cogent Education, 2*(1), 1011488. Advance online publication. doi:10.1080/2331186X.2015.1011488

Hodges, C., Moore, S., Lockee, B., Trust, T., & Bond, A. (2020, March 27). The difference between emergency remote teaching and online learning. *EDUCAUSE Review*. https://er.educause.edu/articles/2020/3/the-difference-between-emergency-remote-teaching-and-online-learning

Hofstede, G. (2001). *Culture's consequences: Comparing values, behaviours, institutions and organizations across nations*. Sage.

Hoft, N. L. (1995). *International technical communication: How to export information about high technology*. Wiley.

Holm, G., & Zilliacus, H. (2009). Multicultural education and intercultural education: Is there a difference. *Dialogs on diversity and global education*, 11-28.

Hopkins, C. D., Raymond, M. A., & Carlson, L. (2011). Educating students to give them a sustainable competitive advantage. *Journal of Marketing Education, 33*(3), 337–347. doi:10.1177/0273475311420241

Houshmand, S., Spanierman, L. B., & Tafarodi, R. W. (2014). Excluded and avoided: Racial microaggressions targeting Asian international students in Canada. *Cultural Diversity & Ethnic Minority Psychology, 20*(3), 377–388. doi:10.1037/a0035404 PMID:25045949

Hsieh, M. H. (2007). Challenges for international students in higher education: One student's narrated story of invisibility and struggle. *College Student Journal, 41*(2), 379–391.

Huang, J. Y. (2005). Challenges of academic listening in English: Reports by Chinese students. *College Student Journal, 39*(3), 553–569.

Huang, J., & Rinaldo, V. (2009). Factors affecting Chinese graduate students' cross-cultural learning. *International Journal of Applied Educational Studies, 4*(1), 1–13.

Huang, R., Turner, R., & Chen, Q. (2014). Chinese international students' perspective and strategies in preparing for their future employability. *Journal of Vocational Education and Training, 66*(2), 175–193. doi:10.1080/13636820.2014.894933

Huang, Y. (2012). Transitioning challenges faced by Chinese graduate students. *Adult Learning, 23*(3), 138–147. doi:10.1177/1045159512452861

Hui, L. (2005). Chinese cultural schema of education: Implications for communication between Chinese students and Australian educators. *Issues in Educational Research, 15*(1), 17–36.

Hune-Brown, N. (2021, September/October). The shadowy business of international education. *The Walrus*. https://thewalrus.ca/the-shadowy-business-of-international-education/

Huo, X. Y. (2020). *Higher education internationalization and English language instruction: Intersectionality of race and language in Canadian universities*. Springer. doi:10.1007/978-3-030-60599-5

Hurley, P. (2020). *Coronavirus and international students*. Mitchell Institute, Victoria University.

Husain, M. Y., Mokhtar, S. B., Ahmad, A. A., & Mustapha, R. (2010). Importance of employability skills from employers' perspective. *Procedia: Social and Behavioral Sciences*, *7*, 430–438. doi:10.1016/j.sbspro.2010.10.059

Hutchinson, L., & McAlister-Shields, L. (2020). Culturally responsive teaching: Its application in higher education environments. *Education Sciences*, *10*(124), 124. Advance online publication. doi:10.3390/educsci10050124

Hutchinson, M., & Dorsett, P. (2012). What does the literature say about resilience in refugee people? Implications for practice. *Journal of Social Inclusion*, *2*(3), 55–78. doi:10.36251/josi.55

Hymes, D. (1980). *Language in education: Ethnolinguistic essays*. Center for Applied Linguistics.

Hymes, D. H. (1972). On Communicative Competence. In J. B. Pride & J. Holmes (Eds.), *Sociolinguistics: Selected Readings* (pp. 269–293). Penguin.

Hymes, D. H. (1974). *Foundations in sociolinguistics: An ethnographic approach*. University of Pennsylvania Press.

Ibbotson, M. (2009). *Professional English in use—Engineering with answers: Technical English for professionals*. Cambridge University Press.

IELTS. (2019). *Test taker performance 2019.*https://www.ielts.org/for-researchers/test-statistics/test-taker-performance

i-graduate International Insight. (2017). *Data regarding the 2016 international student barometer autumn wave*. i-graduate International Insight.

Immigration, Refugees and Citizenship Canada. (2020). *Canada—Study permit holders with a valid permit on December 31st by province/territory of intended destination and study level, 2000–2020* [Data set]. https://www.cic.gc.ca/opendata-donneesouvertes/data/IRCC_M_TRStudy_0008_E.xls

Immigration, Refugees and Citizenship Canada. (2020). *Facilitative measures to support international students affected by the COVID-19 pandemic*. https://www.canada.ca/en/immigration-refugees-citizenship/news/2020/08/facilitative-measures-to-support-international-students-affected-by-the-covid-19-pandemic.html

Institute of International Education. (2014). *Project Atlas/international students in the United States*. https://www.iie.org/Services/Project-Atlas/United-States/International-Students-In-US

Institute of International Education. (2021). *Open doors 2021*. https://opendoorsdata.org/data/international-students/enrollment-trends/

International Center for Academic Integrity. (2020). *Facts and statistics.*https://academicintegrity.org/resources/facts-and-statistics

International Consultants for Education and Fairs. (2020, May 6). New insights on how international students are planning for the coming academic year. *ICEF Monitor*. https://tinyurl.com/yc5sgry7

Islam, S. M. R. (2020). Achievements and challenges in Bangladesh education. *The Financial Express*. https://www.thefinancialexpress.com.bd/views/achievements-and-challenges-in-bangladesh-education-1577975979

Islam, M. S., & Stamp, K. (2020). A reflection on future directions: Global international and intercultural competencies in higher education. *Research in Comparative and International Education*, *15*(1), 69–75. doi:10.1177/1745499920901951

Jackman, J. A., Gentile, D. A., Cho, N.-J., & Park, Y. (2021). Addressing the digital skills gap for future education. *Nature Human Behaviour*, *5*(5), 542–545. doi:10.103841562-021-01074-z PMID:33707657

Jackson, J., & Oguro, S. (2017). Introduction: Enhancing and extending study abroad learning through intercultural interventions. In Intercultural interventions in study abroad (pp. 1-17). Routledge.

Jackson, D. (2014). Testing a model of undergraduate competence in employability skills and its implications for stakeholders. *Journal of Education and Work*, *27*(2), 220–242. doi:10.1080/13639080.2012.718750

Jackson, J., & Chen, X. (2018). Discussion-based pedagogy through the eyes of Chinese international exchange students. *Pedagogies*, *13*(4), 289–307. doi:10.1080/1554480X.2017.1411263

Jacobsen, J. (2019). Diversity and difference in the online environment. *Journal of Teaching in Social Work*, *39*(4-5), 387–401. doi:10.1080/08841233.2019.1654589

Jamieson, M. (2020). Keeping a learning community and academic integrity intact after a mid-term shift to online learning in chemical engineering design during the COVID-19 pandemic. *Journal of Chemical Education*, *97*(9), 2768–2772. doi:10.1021/acs.jchemed.0c00785

Jia, C., Hew, K. F., Bai, S., & Huang, W. (2020). Adaptation of a conventional flipped course to an online flipped format during the Covid-19 pandemic: Student learning performance and engagement. *Journal of Research on Technology in Education*, 1–21. doi:10.1080/15391523.2020.1847220

Jin, L., & Cortazzi, M. (1997). Expectations and questions in intercultural classrooms. *Intercultural Communication Studies*, *7*(2), 37–62. https://www-s3-live.kent.edu/s3fs-root/s3fs-public/file/04-Lixian-Jin-Martin-Cortazzi.pdf

Johnson, R. L., Coleman, R. A., Batten, N. H., Hallsworth, D., & Spencer, E. E. (2020). The quiet crisis of PhDs and COVID-19: Reaching the financial tipping point. doi:10.21203/rs.3.rs-36330/v2

Johnson, D. W., Johnson, R. T., & Smith, K. A. (2014). The power of cooperative learning for university classes: The interrelationships among theory, research, and practice. *Journal on Excellence in College Teaching*, *25*(4).

Jolly, B. C., & MacDonald, M. M. (1989). Education for experience: The role of practical experience in undergraduate and general clinical training. *Medical Education*, *23*(2), 189–195. doi:10.1111/j.1365-2923.1989.tb00885.x PMID:2716558

Jones, S. H. (2005). Autoethnography: Making the Personal Political. In Denzin & Lincoln (Eds.), Handbook of Qualitative Research (3rd ed.). Thousand Oaks, CA: Sage.

Joyce, A., Earnest, J., de Mori, G., & Silvagni, G. (2010). The experiences of students from refugee backgrounds at universities in Australia: Reflections on the social, emotional and practical challenges. *Journal of Refugee Studies*, *23*(1), 82–97. doi:10.1093/jrs/feq001

Kahlon, B. (2021). *Report on the realities for international students*. One Voice Canada. https://onevoicecanada.org/wp-content/uploads/2021/05/The-Realities-of-International-Students-Evidenced-Challenges_Full-Report-2.pdf

Kahn, H. E., & Agnew, M. (2017). Global learning through difference: Considerations for teaching, learning, and the internationalization of Higher Education. *Journal of Studies in International Education*, *21*(1), 52–64. doi:10.1177/1028315315622022

Kahn, M. (1990). Paradigm lost: The importance of practical work in school science from a developing country perspective. *Studies in Science Education*, *18*(1), 127–136. doi:10.1080/03057269008559984

Kainth, S. (2016, December 30). *IELTS score for sale in India: SBS Punjabi investigates*. SBS Punjabi Radio. https://www.sbs.com.au/language/english/audio/ielts-score-for-sale-in-india-sbs-punjabi-investigates

Kamberelis, G., & Dimitriadis, G. (2005). Into the fray: A practiced and practical set of analytical strata. In G. Kamberelis & G. Dimitriadis (Eds.), *On qualitative inquiry* (pp. 13–23). Teachers College Press.

Kamens, D. H. (2015). A maturing global testing regime meets the world economy: Test scores and economic growth, 1960–2012. *Comparative Education Review*, *59*(3), 420–446. doi:10.1086/681989

Kang, P. (2020). Towards Sustainable Internationalization in Post-COVID Higher Education: Voices from Non-Native English-Speaking International Students in Canada. *Migration and Language Education*, *1*(2), 60–73. doi:10.29140/mle.v1n2.383

Karasavvidis, I., & Kollias, V. (2014). Technology integration in the most favorable conditions: findings from a professional development training program. In C. Karagiannidis (Ed.), *Research on e-learning and ICT in education* (pp. 197–224). Springer.

Karkar-Esperat, T. M. (2018). International Graduate Students' Challenges and Learning Experiences in Online Classes. *Journal of International Students*, *8*(4), 1722–1735. doi:10.32674/jis.v8i4.227

Karram, G. L. (2013). International students as lucrative markets or vulnerable populations: A critical discourse analysis of national and institutional events in four nations. *Comparative and International Education*, *42*(1), 6. Advance online publication. doi:10.5206/cie-eci.v42i1.9223

Kasper, G. (2009). Locating cognition in second language interaction and learning: Inside the skull or in public view? *IRAL – International Review of Applied Linguistics in Language Teaching*, *47*(1), 11–36. doi:10.1515/iral.2009.002

Katre, A. (2020). Creative Economy Teaching and Learning–A Collaborative Online International Learning Case. *International Education Studies*, *13*(7), 145. doi:10.5539/ies.v13n7p145

Kealey, D. J. (1990). *Cross-Cultural Effectiveness: A Study of Canadian Technical Advisors Overseas*. Canadian International Development Agency.

Keddie, A. (2010). Pursuing justice for refugee students: Addressing issues of cultural (mis)recognition. *International Journal of Inclusive Education*, *16*(12), 1295–1310. doi:10.1080/13603116.2011.560687

Keegan, D. (1995). *Distance Education Technology for the New Millennium Compressed Video Teaching. ZIFF Papiere 101*. ERIC.

Kehm, B. M., Larsen, M. R., & Sommersel, H. B. (2019). Student dropout from universities in Europe: A review of empirical literature. *Hungarian Educational Research Journal*, *9*(2), 147–164. doi:10.1556/063.9.2019.1.18

Kelly, P. (2000). Internationalizing the Curriculum: For Profit or Planet. In S. Inayatullah & J. Gidley (Eds.), *The University in Transformation: Global Perspectives on the Futures of the University*. Bergin and Harvey.

Kelly, P., & Moogan, Y. (2012). Culture shock and higher education performance: Implications for teaching. *Higher Education Quarterly*, 24–46.

Kemmis, S., & McTaggart, R. (2005). Participatory action research: Communicative action and the public sphere. In N. Denzin & Y. Lincoln (Eds.), Handbook of qualitative research. Sage.

Kennedy, K., Henderson, H., & Marsh, M. (2022). *Becoming a teacher* (7th ed.). Pearson.

Kéri, A. (2021). Online teaching methods and student satisfaction during a pandemic. *Journal of Educational and Pedagogical Sciences*, *15*(4), 373–379.

Keung, N. (2018, December 8). More than 400 students in India told to retake language tests after Niagara College flags concerns. *The Star*. https://www.thestar.com/news/canada/2018/12/08/400-students-in-india-told-to-retake-language-tests-after-niagara-college-flags-concerns.html

Keung, N., & Teotonio, I. (2020, April 8). "Billions of dollars are at risk." Colleges and universities scramble to protect international student sector amid COVID-19 pandemic. *The Star*. https://tinyurl.com/yay5ewp9

Khalil, S. (2019). *International students' perspectives of building communities in online learning environments* (Publication No. 27663440) [Doctoral dissertation, New Mexico University]. ProQuest Dissertations and Theses Global.

Khanal, J., & Gaulee, U. (2019). Challenges of international students from pre-departure to post-study: A literature review. *Journal of International Students*, *9*(2), 560–581. doi:10.32674/jis.v9i2.673

Khan, S., Haleem, A., & Khan, M. I. (2020). Enablers to implement circular initiatives in the supply chain: A Grey DEMATEL Method. *Global Business Review*. Advance online publication. doi:10.1177/0972150920929484

Khawaja, N. G., & Stallman, H. M. (2011). Understanding the coping strategies of international students: A qualitative approach. *Australian Journal of Guidance & Counselling*, *21*(2), 203–224. doi:10.1375/ajgc.21.2.203

Khawaja, N. G., White, K. M., Schweitzer, R., & Greenslade, J. (2008). Difficulties and coping strategies of Sudanese refugees: A qualitative approach. *Transcultural Psychiatry*, *45*(3), 489–512. doi:10.1177/1363461508094678 PMID:18799645

Kilburn, M., Radu, B. M., & Henckell, M. (2019). Conceptual and Theoretical Frameworks for CRT Pedagogy. In L. Kyei-Blankson, J. Blankson, & E. Ntuli (Eds.), *Care and culturally responsive pedagogy in online settings* (pp. 1–21). IGI Global.

Kim, B., Ying, W., Pushpanadham, K., Yamada, T., Lee, T., & Fadzil, M. (2015). *MOOCs and Educational Challenges around Asia and Europe* (B. Kim, Ed.). KNOU Press. Retrieved from http://asemlllhub.org/fileadmin/www.asem.au.dk/publications/MOOCs_and_Educational_Challenges_around_Asia_and_Europe_FINAL.pdf

Kim, E. (2011). Conceptions, critiques and challenges in multicultural education reform the U.S. *KEDI Journal of Educational Policy*, *8*, 201–218.

Kim, Y. (2007). Difficulties in quality doctoral academic advising: Experiences of Korean students. *Journal of Research in International Education*, *6*(2), 171–193. doi:10.1177/1475240907078613

Kim, Y. K., Edens, D., Iorio, M. F., Curtis, C. J., & Romero, E. (2015). Cognitive skills development among international students at research universities in the United States. *Journal of International Students*, *5*(4), 526–540.

King, C., & So, K. K. (2014). Creating a virtual learning community to engage international students. *Journal of Hospitality & Tourism Education*, *26*(3), 136–146. doi:10.1080/10963758.2014.936255

Kinsella, K. (1997). Creating an enabling learning environment for non-native speakers of English. In A. I. Morey & M. K. Kitano (Eds.), *Multicultural course transformation in higher education: A broader truth* (pp. 104–125). Allyn and Bacon.

Kiramba, L. K., & Oloo, J. A. (2019). "It's OK. She doesn't even speak English": Narratives of language, culture, and identity negotiation by immigrant high school students. *Urban Education*. Advance online publication. doi:10.1177/0042085919873696

Klassen, R. (2001). *The international university curriculum: Challenges in English-medium Engineering education* [Doctoral dissertation]. Delft University of Technology.

Klees, S. J. (2016). Human capital and rates of return: Brilliant ideas or ideological dead ends? *Comparative Education Review*, *60*(4), 644–672. doi:10.1086/688063

Knapp, A. (2011). When comprehension is crucial: Using English as a medium of instruction at a German university. *English in Europe today: Sociocultural and educational perspectives*, 51-70.

Knight, J. (1999). Internationalisation of higher education. In H. de Wit & J. Knight (Eds.), Quality and internationalisation in higher education (pp. 13−28). Organisation for Economic Co-operation and Development (OECD). doi:10.1787/9789264173361-en

Knight, J. (2015). Internationalization: A decade of changes and challenges. *International Higher Education: A Quarterly Publication*, 50. doi:10.6017/ihe.2008.50.8001

Knight, J. (1997). A shared vision? Stakeholders' perspectives on the internationalization of higher education in Canada. *Journal of Studies in International Education*, *44*(1), 27–31. doi:10.1177/102831539700100105

Knight, J. (2003). Updated internationalization definition. *Industry and Higher Education*, *33*, 2–3. doi:10.6017/ihe.2003.33.7391

Knight, J., & Liu, Q. (2019). International program and provider mobility in higher education: Research trends, challenges and issues. *Comparative and International Education*, *48*(1). Advance online publication. doi:10.5206/cie-eci.v48i1.9335

Kobayashi, A. (Ed.). (2019). *International encyclopedia of human geography* (2nd ed.). Elsevier.

Kohls, L. R. (1979). *Survival Kit for Overseas Living*. Intercultural Network/SYSTRAN Publications.

Kong, F., Gong, X., Sajjad, S., Yang, K., & Zhao, J. (2019). How is emotional intelligence linked to life satisfaction? The mediating role of social support, positive affect and negative affect. *Journal of Happiness Studies*, *20*(8), 2733–2745. Advance online publication. doi:10.100710902-018-00069-4

Koul, R., & Fisher, D. (2005). Cultural background and students' perceptions of science classroom learning environment and teacher interpersonal behaviour in Jammu, India. *Learning Environments Research*, *8*, 195–211.

Krasnof, B. (2016). *Culturally responsive teaching: A guide to evidence-based practices for teaching all students equitably*. Region X Equity Assistance Center at Education Northwest.

Kulturel-Konak, S., D'Allegro, M. L., & Dickinson, S. (2011). Review of gender differences in learning styles: Suggestions for STEM education. *Contemporary Issues in Education Research*, *4*(3), 9–18. https://doi.org/10.19030/cier.v4i3.4116

Kumaravadivelu, B. (2006). Dangerous liaison, globalization, empire and TESOL. In J. Edge (Ed.), *Relocating TESOL in an age of empire* (pp. 1–26). Palgrave Macmillan.

Kumar, R. (2020). Assessing higher education in the COVID-19 era. *Brock Education Journal*, *29*(2), 37–41. doi:10.26522/brocked.v29i2.841

Kumi Yeboah, A., Dogbey, J., & Yuan, G. (2020). Cultural Diversity in Online Education: An Exploration of Instructors' Perceptions and Challenges. *Teachers College Record*, *122*(7).

Kumi-Yeboah, A., Sallar, A. W., Kiramba, L. K., & Kim, Y. (2020). Exploring the use of digital technologies from the perspective of diverse learners in online learning environments. *Online Learning*, *24*(4), 42–63. doi:10.24059/olj.v24i4.2323

Kwao, A., Torto, G., Ackah-Jnr, F. R., & John, A. (2021). Speak English, Don't Speak Vernacular. Language Culture and Practice, and Policy Implications in Schools. *Advances in Social Sciences Research Journal*, *8*(5), 617–629. doi:10.14738/assrj.85.10202

Labov, W. (1972). *Language in the inner city*. University of Pennsylvania Press.

Ladson-Billings, G. (2014). Culturally Relevant Pedagogy 2.0: A.k.a. the Remix. *Harvard Educational Review*, *84*(1), 74–84. doi:10.17763/haer.84.1.p2rj131485484751

Ladson-Billings, G. (2021). I'm here for the hard re-set: Post pandemic pedagogy to preserve our culture. *Equity & Excellence in Education, 54*(1), 68–78. doi:10.1080/10665684.2020.1863883

LaFleche, G., Keung, N., & Teotonio, I. (2019, September 28). The test said they were good enough to get in, but they were failing in class. How Niagara College tackled an international student crisis. *The Toronto Star.* https://www.niaga-rafallsreview.ca/news/niagara-region/2019/09/28/they-passed-the-admissions-test-but-they-were-failing-in-class-how-niagara-college-tackled-an-international-student-crisis.html

Lai, A. Y., Lee, L., Wang, M. P., Feng, Y., Lai, T. T., Ho, L. M., Lam, V. S., Ip, M. S., & Lam, T. H. (2020). Mental Health Impacts of the COVID-19 Pandemic on International University Students, Related Stressors, and Coping Strategies. *Frontiers in Psychiatry, 11*, 584240. doi:10.3389/fpsyt.2020.584240 PMID:33329126

Lane, C. (2021, August 6). *How has online learning impacted international students?*https://www.topuniversities.com/student-info/studying-abroad-articles/how-has-online-learning-impacted-international-students

Langdridge, D. (2007). *Phenomenological psychology: Theory, research and method.* Pearson Education.

Larke, P. (2013). Culturally responsive teaching in higher education: What professors need to know. In S. Mayo & P. Larke (Eds.), *Integrating multiculturalism into the curriculum* (pp. 38–50). Peter Lang.

Larsen, M. A. (2015). Internationalization in Canadian higher education: A case study of the gap between official discourses and on-the-ground realities. *Canadian Journal of Higher Education, 45*(4), 101–122. doi:10.47678/cjhe.v45i4.184907

Lauand, L. J. (1995, December). *Anthropology and Education: Two Speeches - Memory & Education / Proverbs and the Sense of Concrete. Part I – Memory and Education* [Paper presentation]. Graduation Ceremony at Faculdade de Educação da Universidade de São Paulo, Brazil. http://hottopos.com/harvard1/memory.htm

Lauand, L. J. (1998, April). *Anthropology and Education: Two Speeches – Memory & Education / Proverbs and the Sense of Concrete. Part II – Proverbs and the Sense of the Concrete: the Basis of the Arab Education* [Paper presentation]. Universidad Autónoma de Madrid, Spain. http://hottopos.com/harvard1/memory.htm

Lauring, J. (2011). Intercultural organizational communication: The social organizing of interaction in international encounters. *The Journal of Business Communication*, 231-255.

Lawson, C. (2012). *Student voices: Enhancing the experience of international students in Australia.* Australian Education International.

Le Ha, P., & Li, B. (2012). Silence as right, choice, resistance and strategy among Chinese 'Me Generation' students: Implications for pedagogy. *Discourse, 35*(2), 233–248. 306.2012.745733 doi:10.1080/01596

Le, A. T., LaCost, B. Y., & Wismer, M. (2016). International Female Graduate Students' Experience at a Midwestern University: Sense of Belonging and Identity Development. *Journal of International Students, 6*(1), 128–152. doi:10.32674/jis.v6i1.485

Leask, B. (2009). Using formal and informal curricula to improve interactions between home and international students. *Journal of Studies in International Education, 13*(2), 205–221.

Leask, B. (2015). *Internationalizing the Curriculum.* Routledge. doi:10.4324/9781315716954

Leask, B., & Carroll, J. (2011). Moving beyond 'wishing and hoping': Internationalisation and student experiences of inclusion and engagement. *Higher Education Research & Development, 30*(5), 647–659. doi:10.1080/07294360.2011.598454

Lee, A., Poch, R., Shaw, M., & Williams, R. (2012). *Engaging Diversity in Undergraduate Classrooms: A Pedagogy for Developing Intercultural Competence*. John Wiley & Sons.

Lee, D. S. (1997). What Teachers Can Do To Relieve Problems Identified by International Students. *New Directions for Teaching and Learning, 70*(70), 93–100. doi:10.1002/tl.7011

Lee, O. (2003). Equity for linguistically and culturally diverse students in science education: A research agenda. *Teachers College Record, 105*(3), 465–489. doi:10.1111/1467-9620.00247

Lees, D. (2002). *Information for Academic Staff on Employability*. http://www. palatine.ac.uk/ files/emp/1233.pdf

Lee, S. J., & Nuatomue, J. N. (2021). Students' Perceived Difficulty and Satisfaction in Face-to-Face vs. Online Sections of a Technology-Intensive Course. *International Journal of Distance Education Technologies, 19*(3), 1–13. doi:10.4018/IJDET.2021070101

Lee, S., & Wu, C.-H. (2021). Determinants of Consumption Behaviors of Korean Pop Culture in Taiwan. *International Journal of Asian Business and Information Management, 12*(3), 1–22. doi:10.4018/IJABIM.20210701.oa28

Lee, W. O. (1996). The cultural context for Chinese learners: conceptions of learning in the Confucian tradition. In D. Watkins & J. Biggs (Eds.), *The Chinese learner: Cultural, psychological and contextual influences* (pp. 25–41). The Comparative Education Research Centre, Faculty of Education, University of Hong Kong.

Lepori, B., & Kyvik, S. (2010). The research mission of universities of applied sciences and the future configuration of higher education systems in Europe. *Higher Education Policy, 23*(3), 295–316.

Leung, K., Ang, S., & Tan, M. L. (2014). Intercultural competence. *Annual Review of Organizational Psychology and Organizational Behavior, 1*(1), 489–519. doi:10.1146/annurev-orgpsych-031413-091229

Levinsohn, R. K. (2007). Cultural differences and learning styles of Chinese and European trades student. Institute for Learning Styles Journal, 1.

Lewington, J. (2019, November 4). Why universities are trying to recruit overseas students from as many places as possible. *Maclean's*. https://www.macleans.ca/education/why-universities-are-trying-to-diversify-where-overseas-students-come-from/

Lewin, K. (1946). Action research and minority problems. *The Journal of Social Issues, 2*(4), 34–46. doi:10.1111/j.1540-4560.1946.tb02295.x

Lewis, R. D. (1996). When Cultures Collide: Leading across cultures. Nicholas Brealey International.

Lewis, T., & O'Dowd, R. (2016). *Online intercultural exchange*. Routledge.

Liao, X. (2020). Developing domestic students' intercultural competence – a case study: Immersion program of Sichuan University, China. In M. Carmo (Ed.), *Proceedings of the International Conference Education and New Developments–END 2020* (pp. 203-207). InScience Press. 10.36315/2020end044

Licorish, S. A., Owen, H. E., Daniel, B., & George, J. L. (2018). Students' perception of Kahoot!'s influence on teaching and learning. *Research and Practice in Technology Enhanced Learning, 13*(1), 1–23. doi:10.118641039-018-0078-8 PMID:30595732

Li, J., & Zhang, Z. (2015). An Intercontinental inquiry on multicultural education: Canadian and Hong Kong university students connected through a Web 2.0 learning environment. *Intercultural Education, 26*(6), 562–583. doi:10.1080/14 675986.2015.1109773

Li, L., Shen, W., & Xie, A. (2021). Why students leave Chinese elite universities for doctoral studies abroad: Institutional habitus, career script and college graduates' decision to study abroad. *International Journal of Educational Development, 84*, 102408. Advance online publication. doi:10.1016/j.ijedudev.2021.102408

Li, M., Baker, T., & Marshall, K. (2002). Mismatched expectations: A case study of Asian students in New Zealand. *New Zealand Journal of Applied Business Research, 1*(1), 137–156.

Lin, J.-C. G., & Yi, J. K. (1997). Asian international students' adjustment: Issues and program suggestions. *College Student Journal, 31*(4), 473–479.

Lin, S., & Scherz, S. (2014). Challenges facing Asian international graduate students in the US: Pedagogical considerations in higher education. *Journal of International Students, 4*(1), 16–33. doi:10.32674/jis.v4i1.494

Liu, D. F. (2016). Strategies to promote Chinese international students' school performance: Resolving the challenges in American higher education. *Asian-Pacific Journal of Second and Foreign Language Education, 1*(8).

Liu, J. (2016). Internationalization of higher education: Experiences of intercultural adaptation of international students in Canada. *Antistasis, 6*(2), 1-11. https://journals.lib.unb.ca/index.php/antistasis/article/view/25433

Liu, D., & Lei, L. (2020). Technical Vocabulary. In S. A. Webb (Ed.), *The Routledge handbook of vocabulary studies* (pp. 111–124). Routledge.

Liu, J. (2001). *Asian Students' Classroom Communication Patterns in American Classrooms.* Greenwood Publishing Group.

Liu, X., Liu, S., Lee, S. H., & Magjuka, R. J. (2010). Cultural differences in online learning: International student perceptions. *Journal of Educational Technology & Society, 13*(3), 177–188.

Liu, Y., & Shirley, T. (2021). Without crossing a border: Exploring the impact of shifting study abroad online on students' learning and intercultural competence development during the COVID-19 pandemic. *Online Learning, 25*(1), 182–194. doi:10.24059/olj.v25i1.2471

Li, W., Gillies, R., He, M., Wu, C., Liu, S., Gong, Z., & Sun, H. (2021). Barriers and facilitators to online medical and nursing education during the COVID-19 pandemic: Perspectives from international students from low-and middle-income countries and their teaching staff. *Human Resources for Health, 19*(1), 1–14. doi:10.118612960-021-00609-9 PMID:33980228

Li, X. (2016). Ontario, Canada and Hawaii, USA: Who makes stronger vertical equity efforts? *International Studies in Educational Administration, 44*(1), 71–84.

Lock, D. (2013). *Project Management* (10th ed.). Gower.

Lockee, B. B. (2021). Online education in the post-COVID era. *Nature Electronics*, 5-6.

Lomer, S., & Mittelmeier, J. (2021). Mapping the research on pedagogies with international students in the UK: A systematic literature review. *Teaching in Higher Education,* ●●●, 1–21. doi:10.1080/13562517.2021.1872532

Lopez, L. (2001). *Moglie e buoi... Escursione di uno storico nel mondo dei proverbi.* Rivista Abruzzese.

Luecke, J. (2011). Working with Transgender Children and Their Classmates in Pre-Adolescence. *Just Be Supportive. Journal of LGBT Youth, 8*(2), 116–156. doi:10.1080/19361653.2011.544941

Luthans, F., Youssef, C. M., & Avolio, B. J. (2007). *Psychological capital: Developing the human competitive edge.* Oxford University Press.

Lu, Y., Chui, H., Zhu, R., Zhao, H., Zhang, Y., Liao, J., & Miller, M. J. (2018). What does "good adjustment" mean for Chinese international students? A qualitative investigation. *The Counseling Psychologist*, *46*(8), 979–1009. doi:10.1177/0011000018824283

Lu, Y., & Hou, F. (2019). Student transitions: Earnings of former international students in Canada's labour market. In A. H. Kim & M. Kwak (Eds.), *Outward and upward mobilities: International students in Canada, their families, and structuring institutions* (pp. 219–245). University of Toronto Press. doi:10.3138/9781487530563-014

Lyons, M. (2013). *Books. A Living History*. Thames & Hudson.

Macedo, D. (2019). Rupturing the yoke of colonialism in foreign language education: An introduction. In D. Macedo (Ed.), *Decolonizing foreign language education: The misteaching of English and other colonial languages* (pp. 1–49). Routledge. doi:10.4324/9780429453113-1

Macgregor, A., & Folinazzo, G. (2018). Best practices in teaching international students in higher education: Issues and strategies. *TESOL Journal*, *9*(2), 299–329. doi:10.1002/tesj.324

Machine Learning. (2012). Retrieved 2019, from Coursera: https://www.coursera.org/learn/machine-learning

Mackenzie, I. (2014). *English as a lingua franca: Theorizing and teaching English*. Routledge.

MacLeod, P. D., & Eaton, S. E. (2020). The Paradox of Faculty Attitudes toward Student Violations of Academic Integrity. *Journal of Academic Ethics*, *18*(4), 347–362. doi:10.100710805-020-09363-4

Macrander, A. (2016). An international solution to a national crisis: Trends in student mobility to the United States post 2008. *International Journal of Educational Research*, *8*(2), 1–20. doi:10.1016/j.ijer.2016.12.003

Mada, R. D., & Anharudin, A. (2019). How online learning evaluation (Kahoot) affecting students' achievement and motivation (Case Study on it Students). *International Journal for Educational and Vocational Studies*, *1*(5), 422–427. doi:10.29103/ijevs.v1i5.1494

Madden-Dent, T., Wood, D., & Roskina, K. (2019). An inventory of international student services at 200 US universities and colleges: Descriptive data of pre-departure and post-arrival supports. *Journal of International Students*, *9*(4), 993–1008. doi:10.32674/jis.v9i4.346

Maganello, F., Pozzi, F., Passarelli, M., Persico, D., & Dagnino, F. M. (2021). A Dashboard to Monitor Self-Regulated Learning Behaviours in Online Professional Development. *International Journal of Distance Education Technologies*, *19*(1), 18–34. doi:10.4018/IJDET.2021010102

Mahmoud, M. A., Oppong, E., Twimasie, D., Husseini, M. M., Kastner, A. N. A., & Oppong, M. (2020). Culture and country choice of international students: Evidence from Ghana. *Journal of Marketing for Higher Education*, *30*(1), 105–124. doi:10.1080/08841241.2019.1688444

Mahmud, Z., Amat, S., Rahman, S., & Ishak, N. M. (2010). Challenges for international students in Malaysia: Culture, climate and care. *Procedia: Social and Behavioral Sciences*, *7*, 289–293. doi:10.1016/j.sbspro.2010.10.040

Mairean, C., Turliuc, M. N., & Arghire, D. (2019). The relationship between trait gratitude and psychological wellbeing in university students: The mediating role of affective state and the moderating role of state gratitude. *Journal of Happiness Studies*, *20*(5), 1357–1377. doi:10.100710902-018-9998-7

Malaklolunthu, S., & Selan, P. S. (2011). Adjustment problems among international students in Malaysian private higher education institutions. *Procedia: Social and Behavioral Sciences*, *15*, 833–837. doi:10.1016/j.sbspro.2011.03.194

Maloshonok, N., & Terentev, E. (2017). The mismatch between student educational expectations and realities: Prevalence, causes, and consequences. *European Journal of Higher Education*, *7*(4), 356–372. doi:10.1080/21568235.2017.1348238

Malterud, K., Siersma, V. D., & Guassora, A. D. (2016). Sample size in qualitative interview studies: Guided by information power. *Qualitative Health Research*, *26*(13), 1753–1760. doi:10.1177/1049732315617444 PMID:26613970

Mann, S., & Walsh, S. (2017). *Reflective practice in English language teaching: Research-based principles and practices.* Routledge. doi:10.4324/9781315733395

Mansouri, F., & Jenkins, L. (2010). Schools as Sites of Race Relations and Intercultural Tension. *The Australian Journal of Teacher Education*, *35*(7). Advance online publication. doi:10.14221/ajte.2010v35n7.8

Marginson, S. (2004). National and global competition in higher education. *Australian Educational Researcher*, *31*(2), 1–28. doi:10.1007/BF03249517

Marginson, S. (2014). Student self-formation in international education. *Journal of Studies in International Education*, *18*(1), 6–22.

Marginson, S., & Sawir, E. (2011). *Ideas for intercultural education.* Palgrave Macmillan.

Markova, T., Glazkova, I., & Zaborova, E. (2017). Quality Issues of Online Distance Learning. *Procedia: Social and Behavioral Sciences*, *237*, 685–691. doi:10.1016/j.sbspro.2017.02.043

Marks, R. B., Sibley, S. D., & Arbaugh, J. B. (2005). A structural equation model of predictors for effective online learning. *Journal of Management Education*, *29*(4), 531–563. doi:10.1177/1052562904271199

Marom, L. (2017). Eastern/Western conceptions of the "Good Teacher" and the construction of difference in teacher education. *Asia-Pacific Journal of Teacher Education*, *45*(6), 1–17. doi:10.1080/1359866X.2017.1399982

Marom, L. (2021). Outsiders-insiders-in between: Punjabi international students in Canada navigating identity amid intraethnic tensions. *Globalisation, Societies and Education*, ●●●, 1–15. doi:10.1080/14767724.2021.1882291

Marou, H. I. (1948). *Histoire de l'Education dans l'Antiquité.* Editions du Seuil.

Marshall, S., Zhou, M., Gervan, T., & Wiebe, S. (2012). Sense of belonging and first-year academic literacy. *Canadian Journal of Higher Education*, *43*(3), 116–142. doi:10.47678/cjhe.v42i3.2044

Martinez, M. E. (2006). What is metacognition? *Phi Delta Kappan*, *87*(9), 696–699. doi:10.1177/003172170608700916

Martin, F. (2020). *Chinese International Students' Wellbeing in Australia: The Road to Recovery.* The University of Melbourne. Retrieved from http://hdl.handle.net/11343/240399

Martín-Sómer, M., Moreira, J., & Casado, C. (2021). Use of Kahoot! to keep students' motivation during online classes in the lockdown period caused by Covid 19. *Education for Chemical Engineers*, *36*, 154–159. doi:10.1016/j.ece.2021.05.005

Massachusetts Institute of Technology. (2002). Retrieved from MIT Open Courseware: https://ocw.mit.edu/index.htm

Massey, J., & Burrow, J. (2012). Coming to Canada to study: Factors that influence student's decisions to participate in international exchange. *Journal of Student Affairs Research and Practice*, *49*(1), 83–100. doi:10.1515/jsarp-2012-6177

Mathews, J. (2007). Predicting international students' academic success... may not always be enough: Assessing Turkey's foreign study scholarship program. *Higher Education*, *53*(5), 645–673. doi:10.100710734-005-2290-x

Matias, C., Popovic, A., & Lebel, A. (2021, August 18). *Projected financial impact of the COVID-19 pandemic on Canadian universities for the 2020/21 academic year* (Statistics Canada catalogue no. 81-595-M). https://www150.statcan.gc.ca/n1/en/pub/81-595-m/81-595-m2021002-eng.pdf?st=ZjCI26HC

Mauranen, A. (2018). Second language acquisition, world Englishes, and English as a lingua franca (ELF). *World Englishes*, *37*(1), 106–119. doi:10.1111/weng.12306

Mawr, E. B. (1885). *Analogous proverbs in Ten Languages.* Paternoster.

Maxwell, A., Curtis, G. J., & Vardanega, L. (2008). Does culture influence understanding and perceived seriousness of plagiarism? *International Journal for Educational Integrity*, *4*(2), 25–40. doi:10.21913/IJEI.v4i2.412

Mayer, J. D., Salovey, P., Caruso, D. R., & Cherkasskiy, L. (2011). Emotional intelligence. In R. J. Sternberg & S. B. Kaufman (Eds.), *The Cambridge handbook of intelligence* (pp. 528–549). Cambridge University Press. doi:10.1017/CBO9780511977244.027

May, S., & Hornberger, N. H. (Eds.). (2017). *Encyclopedia of language and education.* Springer.

Mazzarol, T., & Soutar, G. (2002). *The global market for higher education: Sustainable competitive strategies for the new millennium.* Edward Elgar Publishing.

Mazzarol, T., & Soutar, G. N. (2002). "Push-pull" factors influencing international student destination choice. *International Journal of Educational Management*, *16*(2), 82–90. doi:10.1108/09513540210418403

McAlister-Shields, L., Hutchison, L., & Jones, B. E. (2019). Teaching Through Culture: The Case for Culturally Responsive Teaching in American Higher Education Institutions. In R. Jeffries (Ed.), *Diversity, Equity, and Inclusivity in Contemporary Higher Education* (pp. 88–107). IGI Global. doi:10.4018/978-1-5225-5724-1.ch006

McAllister, L., Whiteford, G., Hill, B., Thomas, N., & Fitzgerald, M. (2006). Reflection in intercultural learning: Examining the international experience through a critical incident approach. *Reflective Practice*, *7*(3), 367–381. doi:10.1080/14623940600837624

McBrien, J. L., Cheng, R., & Jones, P. (2009). Virtual spaces: Employing a synchronous online classroom to facilitate student engagement in online learning. *The International Review of Research in Open and Distributed Learning*, *10*(3). Advance online publication. doi:10.19173/irrodl.v10i3.605

McGowan, U. (2008). International students: A conceptual framework for dealing with unintentional plagiarism. In T. Roberts (Ed.), *Student plagiarism in an online world: Problems and solutions* (pp. 92–107). IGI Global. doi:10.4018/978-1-59904-801-7.ch007

McGregor, A., & Hunter, W. (2021). Internationalization in Ontario colleges: Patterns and policies. *Journal of Educational Informatics*, *2*(1), 1–32. https://orcid.org/0000-0001-7346-4277. doi:10.51357/jei.v2i1.134

McInerney, P. (2009). Toward a critical pedagogy of engagement for alienated youth: Insights from Freire and school-based research. *Critical Studies in Education*, *50*(1), 23–35. doi:10.1080/17508480802526637

McKenzie, A. (2018). Academic Integrity across the Canadian Landscape. *Canadian Perspectives on Academic Integrity*, *1*(2), 40–45.

McKeown, J. S., Bista, K., & Chan, R. Y. (2021). COVID-19 and higher education: Challenges and successes during the global pandemic. In J. S. McKeown, K. Bista, & R. Y. Chan (Eds.), *Global higher education during COVID-19: Policy, society, and technology* (pp. 1–8). STAR Scholars.

Mckinney, S. (2014). The relationship of child poverty to school education. *Improving Schools*, *17*(3), 203–216. doi:10.1177/1365480214553742

McKinnon, S. (2013). A mismatch of expectations? An exploration of international students' perceptions of employability skills and work-related learning. In J. Ryan (Ed.), *Cross-cultural teaching and learning for home and international students: Internationalisation of pedagogy and curriculum in higher education* (pp. 211–224). Routledge.

McLean, S., & Attardi, S. M. (2018). Sage or guide? Student perceptions of the role of the instructor in a flipped classroom. In Active learning in higher education (pp. 1–13). doi:10.1177/1469787418793725

McLoughlin, C. (2001). Inclusivity and alignment: Principles of pedagogy, task and assessment design for effective cross-cultural online learning. *Distance Education*, *22*(1), 7–29. doi:10.1080/0158791010220102

McMahon, B. (2007). Educational administrators' conceptions of whiteness, anti-racism and social justice. *Journal of Educational Administration*, *45*(6), 684–696. doi:10.1108/09578230710829874

McPhee, S., & Pickren, G. (2017). Blended learning with international students: A multiliteracies approach. *Journal of Geography in Higher Education*, *41*(3), 418–433. doi:10.1080/03098265.2017.1331208

McWilliam, E., & Dawson, S. (2008). Teaching for creativity: Towards sustainable and replicable pedagogical practice. *Higher Education*, *56*(6), 633–643. doi:10.100710734-008-9115-7

Mehra, A. (2019, December 1). Why mini-Punjabs sprout in distant lands. *The Hindu*. https://www.thehindu.com/opinion/open-page/why-mini-punjabs-sprout-in-distant-lands/article30124230.ece

Mieder, W. (2008). "Proverbs Speak Louder than Words". Folk Wisdom in Art, Culture, Folklore, History, Literature, and Mass Media. Peter Lang. doi:10.3726/978-1-4539-0386-5

Mieder, W. (1983). *Proverbs Are Never Out of Season: Popular Wisdom in the Modern Age*. Oxford University Press.

Mieder, W. (2003). *Proverbs and Social Sciences: An Annotated International Bibliography*. Schneider Verlag Hohengehren.

Migration Advisory Committee. (2018). *Impact of international students in the UK*. https://assets.publishing.service.gov.uk/government/uploads/system/uploads/attachment_data/file/739089/Impact_intl_students_report_published_v1.1.pdf

Miller, J., Mitchell, J., & Brown, J. (2005). African refugees with interrupted schooling in the high education, inequality and society. *British Journal of Sociology of Education*, *25*(4), 457–471. doi:10.1080/0142569042000236952

Miller, R. A., Vaccaro, A., Kimball, E. W., & Forester, R. (2020). "'It's dude culture": Students with minoritized identities of sexuality and/or gender navigating STEM majors'. *Journal of Diversity in Higher Education*. Advance online publication. doi:10.1037/dhe0000171

Mills, C. W. (1959). The promise. In *The Sociological Imagination* (pp. 3–24). Oxford University Press.

Mills, C., & Keddie, A. (2012). 'Fixing' student deficit in contexts of diversity: Another cautionary tale for pre-service teacher education. *International Journal of Pedagogies & Learning*, *7*(1), 9–19. doi:10.5172/ijpl.2012.7.1.9

Minocha, S., Shiel, C., & Hristov, D. (2019). International academic staff in UK higher education: Campus internationalisation and innovation in academic practice. *Journal of Further and Higher Education*, *43*(7), 942–958. doi:10.1080/0309877X.2018.1429582

Mirel, B., & Spilka, R. (Eds.). (2002). *Reshaping technical communication: New directions and challenges for the 21st century*. Routledge. doi:10.4324/9781410603739

Mitchell, C., Del Fabbro, L., & Shaw, J. (2017). The acculturation, language and learning experiences of international nursing students: Implications for nursing education. *Nurse Education Today*, *56*, 16–22. doi:10.1016/j.nedt.2017.05.019 PMID:28623678

Mittelmeier, J., Rienties, B., Tempelaar, D., Hillaire, G., & Whitelock, D. (2018). The influence of internationalised versus local content on online intercultural collaboration in groups: A randomised control trial study in a statistics course. *Computers & Education*, 82–95.

Mohamed, A., Yousef, F., Schroeder, U., Wosnitza, M., & Jakobs, H. (2014). MOOCs. A Review of the State-of-the-Art. *CSEDU 2014-6th International Conference on Computer Supported Education.*

Moorhouse, B. L., Li, Y., & Walsh, S. (2021). E-classroom interactional competencies: Mediating and assisting language learning during synchronous online lessons. *RELC Journal*. Advance online publication. doi:10.1177/0033688220985274

Morais, A. M. (2002). Basil Bernstein at the micro level of the classroom. *British Journal of Sociology of Education*, *23*(4), 559–569. doi:10.1080/0142569022000038413

Mori, S. C. (2000). Addressing the mental health concerns of international students. *Journal of Counseling and Development*, *78*(2), 137–144. doi:10.1002/j.1556-6676.2000.tb02571.x

Mpinganjira, M. (2009). Comparative analysis of factors influencing the decision to study abroad. *African Journal of Business Management*, *3*(8), 358–365.

Muhridza, N. H. M., Rosli, N. A. M., Sirri, A., & Samad, A. A. (2018). Using game-based technology, KAHOOT! for classroom engagement. *LSP International Journal*, *5*(2), 37–48. doi:10.11113/lspi.v5n2.77

Mupenzi, A. (2018). *Narratives of displacement, resilience and education: Experiences of African students with a refugee background in Australian tertiary education* (Thesis). Western Sydney University.

Murray, L. K. (2020). *How to Lead With Emotional Intelligence in the Time of COVID-19.* https://publichealth.jhu.edu/2020/how-to-lead-with-emotional-intelligence-in-the-time-of-covid-19

Mwonga, C. (2005). *Multicultural education: new path toward democracy.* Merrill.

Nafari, J., Arab, A., & Ghaffari, S. (2017). Through the looking glass: Analysis of factors influencing Iranian student's study abroad motivations and destination choice. *SAGE Open*, *7*(2), 1–19. doi:10.1177/2158244017716711

Naidoo, L. (2010). Engaging the refugee community of Greater Western Sydney. *Issues in Educational Research*, *20*(1), 47–56.

Naidoo, L. (2011). School-university-community partnerships. In *Crossing borders: African refugees, teachers and schools* (pp. 73–90). Common Ground Publishing.

Naidoo, L., Wilkinson, J., Langat, K., Adoniou, M., Cunneen, R., & Bolger, D. (2014). *Supporting school-university pathways for refugee students' access and participation in tertiary education: an implementation guide for universities.* University of Western Sydney.

Naidoo, L., Wilkinson, J., Langat, K., Adoniou, M., Cunneen, R., & Bolger, D. (2015). *Case study report: Supporting school-university pathways for refugee students' access and participation in tertiary education.* University of Western Sydney.

Nan, C. (2018). Implications of interrelationship among four language skills for high school English teaching. *Journal of Language Teaching and Research*, *9*(2), 418–423. doi:10.17507/jltr.0902.26

Nathan, M. J., & Sawyer, R. K. (2014). Foundations of the learning sciences. In R. K. Sawyer (Ed.), *The Cambridge handbook of the learning sciences* (2nd ed., pp. 21–43). Cambridge University Press. doi:10.1017/CBO9781139519526.004

National Academies of Sciences, Engineering, and Medicine. (2018). *English learners in STEM subjects: Transforming classrooms, schools, and lives.* National Academies Press.

Nation, I. S. P. (2006). How big a vocabulary is needed for reading and listening? *Canadian Modern Language Review, 63*(1), 59–82.

Neff, K. D. (2020a). Guided Self-Compassion Meditations. *Self-Compassion.* https://self-compassion.org/the-three-elements-of-self-compassion-2/

Neff, K. D. (2020b). Commentary on Muris and Otgaar (2020): Let the empirical evidence speak on the Self-Compassion Scale. *Mindfulness, 11*(8), 1900–1909. Advance online publication. doi:10.100712671-020-01411-9

Neff, K. D., Bluth, K., Tóth-Király, I., Davidson, O., Knox, M. C., Williamson, Z., & Costigan, A. (2020). Development and validation of the Self-Compassion Scale for Youth. *Journal of Personality Assessment.* Advance online publication. doi:10.1080/00223891.2020.1729774 PMID:32125190

Neri, F., & Ville, S. (2008). Social capital renewal and the academic performance of international students in Australia. *Journal of Socio-Economics, 37*(4), 1515–1538. doi:10.1016/j.socec.2007.03.010

Newsome, L. K., & Cooper, P. (2016). International students' cultural and social experiences in a British university: "Such a hard life [it] is here. *Journal of International Students, 6*(1), 195–215. doi:10.32674/jis.v6i1.488

Nguyen, O. T. K., & Balakrishnan, V. D. (2020). International students in Australia - during and after COVID-19. *Higher Education Research & Development, 39*(7), 1372–1376. doi:10.1080/07294360.2020.1825346

Nicholls, S. (2018). Influences of international student choice of study destination: Evidence from the United States. *Journal of International Students, 8*(2), 597–622. doi:10.32674/jis.v8i2.94

Nipperess, S., & Williams, C. (2019). *Critical multicultural practice in social work: New perspectives and practices.* Allen & Unwin.

Nonis, S. A., & Hudson, G. I. (1999). The second course in business statistics and it's role in undergraduate marketing education. *Journal of Marketing Education, 21*(3), 232–241. doi:10.1177/0273475399213008

Novak, J., Armstrong, D., & Browne, B. (2014). *Leading for educational lives: Inviting and sustaining imaginative acts of hope in a connected world.* Sense Publishers. doi:10.1007/978-94-6209-554-0

Nowell, L. S., Norris, J. M., White, D. E., & Moules, N. J. (2017). Thematic Analysis:Striving to Meet the Trustworthiness Criteria. *International Journal of Qualitative Methods, 16*(1), 1609406917733847. doi:10.1177/1609406917733847

NSW Department of Education. (n.d.). *Multicultural Plan 2019-22.* Retrieved May 8th, 2021, from https://library.westernsydney.edu.au/main/guides/referencing-citation/i%3aCite

NSW Education Standards Authority (NESA). (2018). *Australian Professional Teaching Standards for Teachers.* Author.

NSW Government. (2021). *Multicultural Education Policy.* Policy Library. Retrieved May 8th, 2021, from https://policies.education.nsw.gov.au/policy-library/policies/multicultural-education-policy

O'Brien, R. (2018). *COIL at Coventry University.* Coventry University Higher Education Corporation.

O'Donnell, K. R. (2015). *Six hard and six soft skills to look for when hiring your next marketing employee.* Retrieved from www.marketingprofs.com/articles/2015/28393

O'dowd, R. (2017). Virtual exchange and internationalising the classroom. *Training. Language and Culture, 1*(4), 8–24. doi:10.29366/2017tlc.1.4.1

O'Dowd, R. (2020). A transnational model of virtual exchange for global citizenship education. *Language Teaching, 53*(4), 477–490. doi:10.1017/S0261444819000077

O'Dowd, R. (2021). Virtual exchange: Moving forward into the next decade. *Computer Assisted Language Learning*, *34*(3), 209–224. doi:10.1080/09588221.2021.1902201

O'Dowd, R., & Dooly, M. (2021). Exploring teachers' professional development through participation in virtual exchange. *ReCALL*, *34*(1), 21–36. doi:10.1017/S0958344021000215

O'Neil, C. A. (2013). *Developing online learning environments in nursing education*. Springer Publishing Company.

O'Sullivan, M., & Guo, L. (2010). Critical thinking and Chinese international students: An East-West dialogue. *Journal of Contemporary Issues in Education*, *5*(2), 53–73.

Octaberlina, L., & Muslimin, A. (2020). EFL students perspective towards online learning barriers and alternatives using Moodle/Google Classroom during COVID-19 pandemic. *International Journal of Education*, *9*(6), 1–9. doi:10.5430/ijhe.v9n6p1

OCUFA. (2020, November). *OCUFA 2020 study: COVID-19 and the impact on university life and education*. https://ocufa.on.ca/assets/OCUFA-2020-Faculty-Student-Survey-opt.pdf

Oded, B., & Walters, J. (2001). Deeper processing for better EFL reading comprehension. *System*, *29*(3), 357–370. doi:10.1016/S0346-251X(01)00023-9

OECD. (2008). *Education at a Glance 2007: OECD Indicators*. OECD.

Okwuosa, A. (2021, February 24). What it's like for international students graduating during COVID-19. *TVO Current Stories*. https://www.tvo.org/article/what-its-like-for-international-students-graduating-during-covid-19?utm_source=cpc&utm_medium=google&utm_campaign=cov&utm_content=&gclid=CjwKCAjw9MuCBhBUEiwAbDZ-7uBum58fEZ4lHCd91sCrEHXcIUkvDGI3Dn7NRo75l0wCGHX6ZeHCuxoCCdQQAvD_BwE

Olliff, L., & Couch, J. (2005). Pathways and pitfalls: The journey of refugee young people in and around the education system in Greater Dandenong, Victoria. *Youth Studies Australia*, *24*(3), 42–46.

Oloo, J. A., & Kiramba, L. K. (2019). *A narrative inquiry into experiences of Indigenous teachers during and after teacher preparation*. Race Ethnicity and Education. https://digitalcommons.unl.edu/teachlearnfacpub/342/ doi:10.1080/13613324.2019.1604507

Oloo, J. A., & Relland, M. (2021). "I think of my classroom as a place of healing": Experiences of indigenous students in a community-based master of education program in Saskatchewan. *Canadian Journal of Educational Administration and Policy*, (197), 94–107. doi:10.7202/1083335ar

Olssen, M., & Peters, M. A. (2005). Neoliberalism, higher education and the knowledge economy: From the free market to knowledge capitalism. *Journal of Education Policy*, *20*(3), 313–345. doi:10.1080/02680930500108718

One Voice Canada. (2021). *About Us*. https://onevoicecanada.org/about-us-2/

Onsando, G. (2014). Refugee immigrants: Addressing social exclusion by promoting agency in the Australian VET sector. *2013 Postgraduate Research Papers: A Compendium*, 76-96.

Onsando, G., & Billett, S. (2009). African students from refugee backgrounds in Australian TAFE institutes: A case for transformative learning goals and processes. *International Journal of Training Research*, *7*(2), 80–94. doi:10.5172/ijtr.7.2.80

Openo, J. (2020). Education's response to the COVID-19 pandemic reveals online education's three enduring challenges. *Canadian Journal of Learning and Technology*, *46*(2), 1–12. doi:10.21432/cjlt27981

Orellana, M. (2016). *Immigrant children in transcultural spaces: Language, learning, and love*. Routledge.

Orlov, G., McKee, D., Berry, J., Boyle, A., DiCiccio, T., Ransom, T., Rees-Jones, A., & Stoye, J. (2021). Learning during the COVID-19 pandemic: It is not who you teach, but how you teach. *Economics Letters, 202*, 109812. doi:10.1016/j.econlet.2021.109812

Ornstein, A. C., Pajak, E. F., & Ornstein, S. B. (2011). *Contemporary Issues in Curriculum* (5th ed.). Allyn & Bacon.

Orsini-Jones, M., & Cerveró-Carrascosa, A. (2019). BMELTET – Blending MOOCs into English language teacher education with telecollaboration. In A. Plutino, K. Borthwick & E. Corradini (Eds.), New educational landscapes: Innovative perspectives in language learning and technology (pp. 47-53). Research-publishing.net. doi:10.14705/rpnet.2019.36.955

Orsini-Jones, M., Cerveró-Carrascosa, A., & Zou, B. (2020). The trouble with telecollaboration in BMELTET. In K. Frederiksen, S. Larsen, L. Bradley & S. Thouësny (Eds.), CALL for widening participation: Short papers from EURO-CALL 2020 (pp. 259-265). Research-publishing.net. doi:10.14705/rpnet.2020.48.1198

Orsini-Jones, M., Conde, B., Borthwick, K., Zou, B., & Ma, W. (2018). *BMELTT: Blending MOOCs for English language teacher training.* ELT Research Papers 18.02, British Council.

Orsini-Jones, M., & Lee, F. (2018). *Intercultural communicative competence for global citizenship: Identifying rules of engagement in telecollaboration.* Palgrave MacMillan. doi:10.1057/978-1-137-58103-7

Orsini-Jones, M., Wang, X., & Zhao, J. (2015). Study skills for Masters' level 'through the looking glass' of Chinese students on the MA in English language teaching at Coventry University. Case study. In P. Kneale (Ed.), *Masters level teaching, learning and assessment: Issues in design and delivery* (pp. 97–100). Palgrave MacMillan.

Owens, L. W., Miller, J. J., & Grise-Owens, E. (2014). Activating a teaching philosophy in social work education: Articulation, implementation, and evaluation. *Journal of Teaching in Social Work, 34*(3), 332–345. doi:10.1080/08841233.2014.907597

Paige, R. M., & Goode, M. L. (2009). Intercultural competence in international education administration- cultural mentoring: International education professionals and the development of intercultural competence. In D. Deardorff (Ed.), *The SAGE handbook of intercultural competence* (pp. 333–349). SAGE Publications.

Panel on Research Ethics. (2018). *TCPS 2 (2018)—Chapter 5: Privacy and confidentiality.* https://ethics.gc.ca/eng/tcps2-eptc2_2018_chapter5-chapitre5.html#d

Pan, J.-Y., Wong, D. F. K., Joubert, L., & Chan, C. L. W. (2008). The Protective Function of Meaning of Life on Life Satisfaction Among Chinese Students in Australia and Hong Kong: A cross-cultural comparative study. *Journal of American College Health, 57*(2), 221–231. doi:10.3200/JACH.57.2.221-232 PMID:18809539

Parliament of Australia (APH). (2016). *Refugee resettlement to Australia: What are the facts?*https://www.aph.gov.au/About_Parliament/Parliamentary_Departments/Parliamentary_Library/pubs/rp/rp1617/RefugeeResettlement

Patton, M. Q. (2002). *Qualitative research and evaluation methods* (3rd ed.). Sage Publications.

Paul, J., & Jefferson, F. (2019). A comparative analysis of student performance in an online vs. face-to-face environmental science course from 2009 to 2016. *Frontiers of Computer Science, 1*, 7.

Pecorari, D. (2003). Good and original: Plagiarism and patchwriting in academic second-language writing. *Journal of Second Language Writing, 12*(4), 317–345. doi:10.1016/j.jslw.2003.08.004

Peeters, E., Nelissen, J., De Cuyper, N., Forrier, A., Verbruggen, M., & De Witte, H. (2019). Employability capital: A conceptual framework tested through expert analysis. *Journal of Career Development, 46*(2), 79–93. doi:10.1177/0894845317731865

Peltier, J. W., Drago, W., & Schibrowsky, J. A. (2003). Virtual communities and the assessment of online marketing education. *Journal of Marketing Education, 25*(3), 260–276. doi:10.1177/0273475303257762

Peltier, J. W., Schibrowsky, J. A., & Drago, W. (2007). The interdependence of the factors influencing the perceived quality of the online learning experience: A causal model. *Journal of Marketing Education, 29*(2), 140–153. doi:10.1177/0273475307302016

Pezenka, I., Rußmann, U., Schwarzbauer, T., & Bernhard, J. (2020). 100% Distance Learning von heute auf morgen – eine Umfrage unter Studierenden an der FHWien der WKW im April 2020. *FNMA Magazin*, 38–41.

Pham, T., Tomlinson, M., & Thompson, C. (2019). Forms of capital and agency as mediations in negotiating employability of international graduate migrants. *Globalisation, Societies and Education, 17*(3), 394–405. doi:10.1080/14767 724.2019.1583091

Phan, A. N. Q. (2021). Sojourning as a wife, a mother and a daughter: A critical autoethnography of a Vietnamese doctoral student in New Zealand. *Journal of Gender Studies*. Advance online publication. doi:10.1080/09589236.2021.198853

Phang, S. L. (2013). *Factors influencing international students' study destination decision abroad.* University of Gothenburg.

Phillips, A. (1999). *Darwin's Worms*. Faber & Faber.

Phutela, D. (2015). The importance of non-verbal communication. *The IUP Journal of Soft Skills, 9*(4), 43.

Pimpa, N. (2011). Engaging international business students in the online environment. *International Journal of Management Education, 9*(3), 77–89. doi:10.3794/ijme.93.323

Pintrich, P. R., & Schrauben, B. (1992). Students' motivational beliefs and their cognitive engagement in classroom academic tasks. *Student Perceptions in the Classroom, 7*, 149–183.

Pitan, O. S., & Adedeji, S. O. (2012). *Skills Mismatch among University Graduates in the Nigeria Labor Market.* Online Submission.

Plewa, C., Galán-Muros, V., & Davey, T. (2015). Engaging business in curriculum design and delivery: A higher education institution perspective. *Higher Education, 70*(1), 35–53. doi:10.100710734-014-9822-1

Plump, C. M., & LaRosa, J. (2017). Using Kahoot! in the classroom to create engagement and active learning: A game-based technology solution for e-learning novices. *Management Teaching Review, 2*(2), 151–158. doi:10.1177/2379298116689783

Podder, S. K., & Samanta, D. (2022). Green Computing Practice in ICT-Based Methods: Innovation in Web-Based Learning and Teaching Technologies. *International Journal of Web-Based Learning and Teaching Technologies, 17*(4), 1–20. doi:10.4018/IJWLTT.285568

Pokhrel, S., & Chhetri, R. (2021). A literature review on impact of COVID-19 pandemic on teaching and learning. *Higher Education for the Future, 8*(1), 133–141.

Polat, S. (2009). Öğretmen adaylarının çokkültürlü eğitime yönelik kişilik özellikleri[Probationary teachers' level of inclination to multicultural education]. *International Online Journal of Educational Sciences, 1*, 154–164.

Portelli, J. P., & Konecny, C. P. (2013). Neoliberalism, Subversion and Democracy in Education. *Encounters on Education, 14*, 87–97. doi:10.24908/eoe-ese-rse.v14i0.5044

Portelli, J. P., & Sharma, M. (2014). Uprooting and settling in: The invisible strength of deficit thinking. *LEARNing Landscapes, 8*(1), 251–267. doi:10.36510/learnland.v8i1.684

Porter, L. (2007). *Student behaviour: Theory and practice for teachers* (3rd ed.). Allen & Unwin.

Prasetyo, Y. E. (2017). From Storytelling to Social Change: The Power of Story in the Community Building. *SSRN Electronic Journal*. doi:10.2139/ssrn.3094947

Precision Consult. (2007). *Graduate Employment Skills*. Business Industry and Higher Education Collaboration Council.

Protogerou, C., & Flisher, A. (2012). *Bullying in schools*. https://bit.ly/3oNUKk7

Pulcini, V., & Campagna, S. (2015). Controversy in Italian higher education. *English-medium instruction in European higher education, 4*, 65.

Qadeer, T., Javed, M. K., Manzoor, A., Wu, M., & Zaman, S. I. (2021). The experience of international students and institutional recommendations: A comparison between the students from the developing and developed regions. *Frontiers in Psychology, 12*, 667230. doi:10.3389/fpsyg.2021.667230 PMID:34484030

Qian, K., & Bax, S. (2017). *Beyond the language classroom: researching MOOCs and other innovations*. Research-publishing.net.

Qiang, Z. (2003). Internationalization of higher education: Towards a conceptual framework. *Policy Futures in Education, 1*(2), 248–270. doi:10.2304/pfie.2003.1.2.5

Quezada, R. L., Talbot, C., & Quezada-Parker, K. B. (2020). From bricks and mortar to remote teaching: A teacher education programme's response to COVID-19. *Journal of Education for Teaching, 46*(4), 1–12. doi:10.1080/02607476.2020.1801330

Radcliff, J., Aaron, D., Sterle, J. G., von Keyserlingk, M., Irlbeck, N., Maquivar, M., Wulster-Radcliffe, M., & Jones, C. (2020). Moving online: Roadmap and long-term forecast. *Animal Frontiers, 10*(3), 36-45. doi:10.1093/af/vfaa027

Rahman, K. (2013). Belonging and learning to belong in school: The implications of the hidden curriculum for indigenous students. *Discourse (Abingdon, England), 34*(5), 660–672. doi:10.1080/01596306.2013.728362

Rajendram, S., Larson, E., & Sinclair, J. (2019). International graduate students' perspectives on high-stakes English tests and the language demands of Higher Education. *Language and Literature, 21*(4), 68–92.

Ramos, D. B., Monteverde Martins Ramos, I., Gasparini, I., & Harada Teixeira de Oliveira, E. (2021). A New Learning Path Model for E-Learning Systems. *International Journal of Distance Education Technologies, 19*(2), 34–54. doi:10.4018/IJDET.20210401.oa2

Rao, P. (2017). Learning challenges and preferred pedagogies of international students: A perspective from the United States. *International Journal of Educational Management, 31*(7), 1000–1016. doi:10.1108/

Rao, N., Yeh, C. S. H., Hosein, A., & Kinchin, I. (2018). Academics' international teaching journeys: An introduction. In A. Hosein, N. Rao, C. S. H. Yeh, & I. M. Kinchin (Eds.), *Academics' International Teaching Journeys: Personal Narratives of Transitions in Higher Education* (pp. 1–12). Bloomsbury Publishing.

Rao, P. (2017). Learning challenges and preferred pedagogies of international students. *International Journal of Educational Management, 31*(7), 1000–1016. doi:10.1108/IJEM-01-2016-0001

Rashed, H. (2017). *The relationship between federal citizenship and immigration policies and the internationalization of higher education in Canada* (Doctoral dissertation, University of Western Ontario). Scholarship@Western. https://ir.lib.uwo.ca/etd/4676

Raymond, M. A., Carlson, L., & Hopkins, C. D. (2006). Do perceptions of hiring criteria differ for sales managers and sales representatives? Implications for marketing education. *Journal of Marketing Education, 28*(1), 43–55. doi:10.1177/0273475305284640

Read, T., & Barcena, E. (2019). A Role for Inclusive MOOCs in Societal Change. EADTU.

Reave, L. (2004). Technical communication instruction in engineering schools: A survey of top-ranked U.S. and Canadian programs. *Journal of Business and Technical Communication, 18*(4), 452–490. doi:10.1177/1050651904267068

Rebek, J. L. (2019). *Mindful leader development of undergraduate students* [Unpublished doctoral dissertation]. Lakehead University: Knowledge Commons.

Redden, E. (2017, June 14). The state of campus internationalization. *Insider Higher Ed.* https://www.insidehighered.com/news/2017/06/14/survey-more-1100-us-colleges-looks-state-internationalization-efforts

Redfern, K. (2016). An empirical investigation of the incidence of negative psychological symptoms among Chinese international students at an Australian university. *Australian Journal of Psychology, 68*(4), 281–289. doi:10.1111/ajpy.12106

Refugee Council of Australia (RCoA). (2017). *New refugee statistics highlight need for greater Australian support for Africa.* https://www.refugeecouncil.org.au/media/new-refugee-statistics-highlight-need-greater-australian-support-africa/

Refugee Council of Australia (RCoA). (2018). *Recent changes in Australian refugee policy.* https://www.refugeecouncil.org.au/publications/recent-changes-australian-refugee-policy/

Research Centre for Global Learning (GLEA). (n.d.). *Focus of our research.* Coventry University. https://www.coventry.ac.uk/research/areas-of-research/global-learning/global-learning-education-without-boundaries/

Rice, T. S. (2021). Retrieved 10 01, 2021, from Intercultural Communication Competence: https://socialsci.libretexts.org/@go/page/55556

Richards, H. V., Brown, A. F., & Forde, T. B. (2007). Addressing diversity in schools: Culturally responsive pedagogy. *Teaching Exceptional Children, 39*(3), 64–68. doi:10.1177/004005990703900310

Riché, P. (1978). *Education and culture in the Barbarian West: From the Sixth through the Eighth Century.* University of South Carolina Press.

Rider, J. (2019). E-relationships: Using computer-mediated discourse analysis to build ethics of care in digital spaces. In L. Kyei-Blankson, J. Blankson, & E. Ntuli (Eds.), *Care and culturally responsive pedagogy in online settings* (pp. 192–212). IGI Global.

Riemer, M. J. (2007). Communication skills for the 21st century engineer. *Global Journal of Engineering Education, 11*(1), 89–100. http://www.wiete.com.au/journals/GJEE/Publish/vol11no1/Riemer.pdf

Riessman, C. K. (2008). Narrative methods for the human sciences. *Sage (Atlanta, Ga.).*

Rinehart, E., & Cong, Y. (2011). Chinese international students' experience of studying online in New Zealand. *Waikato Journal of Education, 16*(1), 93–105.

Robertson, M., Line, M., Jones, S., & Thomas, S. (2000). International students, learning environments and perceptions: A case study using the Delphi technique. *Higher Education Research & Development, 19*(1), 89–102. doi:10.1080/07294360050020499

Robertson, R. (1995). Glocalization: Time-space and homogeneity-heterogenity. In M. Featherstone, S. Lash, & R. Robertson (Eds.), *Global Modernities* (pp. 25–44). Sage. doi:10.4135/9781446250563.n2

Roberts, P., & Dunworth, K. (2012). Staff and student perceptions of support services for international students in higher education: A case study. *Journal of Higher Education Policy and Management, 34*(5), 517–528. doi:10.1080/136008 0X.2012.716000

Robinson-Pant, A., & Magyar, A. (2018). The recruitment agent in internationalized higher education: Commercial broker and cultural mediator. *Journal of Studies in International Education, 22*(3), 225–241. doi:10.1177/1028315318762485

Rocci, A., & de Saussure, L. (2016). *Verbal communication* (Vol. 3). Walter de Gruyter GmbH & Co KG. doi:10.1515/9783110255478

Rodrigues-Manzanares, M. A. (2012). *Portraits of the activity systems of postsecondary international students in online learning: from tensions to transformations in activity* (Master thesis). Memorial University of Newfoundland. https://research.library.mun.ca/

Rogers, E. M., Hart, W. B., & Miike, Y. (2002). *Edward T. Hall and The History of Intercultural Communication: The United States and Japan.* Keio Communication Review.

Rogers, R. (2011). Becoming discourse analysts: Constructing meanings and identities. *Critical Inquiry in Language Studies, 8*(1), 72–104. doi:10.1080/15427587.2011.545768

Römgens, I., Scoupe, R., & Beausaert, S. (2020). Unraveling the concept of employability, bringing together research on employability in higher education and the workplace. *Studies in Higher Education, 45*(12), 2588–2603. doi:10.1080/03075079.2019.1623770

Ross, S. (2020, May 11). McGill and Concordia universities plan to move most classes online for fall term. *CTV News.* https://tinyurl.com/yb8sprsy

Roy, S. R. (2019). Educating Chinese, Japanese, and Korean international students: Recommendations to American professors. *Journal of International Students, 3*(1), 10.

Roy, V. (2019, February 23). Foreign dreams make IELTS coaching Rs 1,100-cr industry. *The Tribune.* https://www.tribuneindia.com/news/archive/foreign-dreams-make-ielts-coaching-rs-1-100-cr-industry-733521

Roy, R., & Uekusa, S. (2020). Collaborative autoethnography: "Self-reflection" as a timely alternative research approach during the global pandemic. *Qualitative Research Journal, 20*(4), 383–392. doi:10.1108/QRJ-06-2020-0054

Rubdy, R. (2015). Unequal Englishes, the native speaker, and decolonization in TESOL. In R. Tupas (Ed.), *Unequal Englishes* (pp. 42–58). Palgrave Macmillan. doi:10.1057/9781137461223_3

Rubin, J., & Guth, S. (2015). Collaborative online international learning: An emerging format for internationalizing curricula. In *Globally Networked Teaching in the Humanities*. Theories and Practices.

Ruffle, J. (1995). The Teaching of Amenemope and its Connection with the Book of Proverbs. In R. B. Zuck (Ed.), *Learning from Sages: Studies on the Book of Proverbs* (pp. 293–331). Baker Books.

Russell, G. (2020). Reflecting on a way of being: Anchor principles of cultural competence. In J. Frawley J., G. Russell, & J. Sherwood (Eds), Cultural competence and the higher education sector (pp. 31-42). Springer.

Ryan, J. (2010). 'The Chinese learner': Misconceptions and realities. *International education and the Chinese learner*, 37-56.

Ryan, J., & Viete, R. (2009). Respectful interactions: Learning with international students in the English-speaking academy. *Teaching in Higher Education, 14*(3), 303–314. doi:10.1080/13562510902898866

Rychly, L., & Graves, E. (2012). Teacher characteristics for culturally responsive pedagogy. *Multicultural Perspectives, 14*(1), 44–49. doi:10.1080/15210960.2012.646853

Saab, M. M., Hegarty, J., Murphy, D., & Landers, M. (2021). Incorporating virtual reality in nurse education: A qualitative study of nursing students' perspectives. *Nurse Education Today*, *105*, 105045. doi:10.1016/j.nedt.2021.105045 PMID:34245956

Sabouripour, F., Roslan, S., Ghiami, Z., & Memon, M. A. (2021). Mediating role of self-efficacy in the relationship between optimism, psychological well-being, and resilience among Iranian students. *Frontiers in Psychology*, *12*, 675645. Advance online publication. doi:10.3389/fpsyg.2021.675645 PMID:34194372

Sá, C. M., & Sabzalieva, E. (2018). The politics of the great brain race: Public policy and international student recruitment in Australia, Canada, England and the USA. *Higher Education*, *75*(2), 231–253. doi:10.100710734-017-0133-1

Sacks, H. (1984). Notes on methodology. In J. M. Atkinson & J. Heritage (Eds.), *Structures of Social Action: Studies in Conversation Analysis*. Cambridge University Press.

Sadler, R., & Dooly, M. (2016). Twelve years of telecollaboration: What we have learnt. *ELT Journal*, *70*(4), 401–413. doi:10.1093/elt/ccw041

Sadykova, G. (2014). Mediating knowledge through peer-to-peer interaction in a multicultural online learning environment: A case of international students in the US. *The International Review of Research in Open and Distributed Learning*, *15*(3). Advance online publication. doi:10.19173/irrodl.v15i3.1629

Saebø, A. B., McCammon, L. A., & O'Farrell, L. (2007). Creative Teaching—Teaching Creativity. *Caribbean Quarterly*, *53*(1-2), 205–215. doi:10.1080/00086495.2007.11672318

Sageev, P., & Romanowski, C. J. (2001). A message from recent engineering graduates in the workplace: Results of a survey on technical communication skills. *Journal of Engineering Education*, *90*(4), 685–693. doi:10.1002/j.2168-9830.2001.tb00660.x

Saha, L. J. (2014). Australia. In P. A. J. Stevens & A. G. Dworkin (Eds.), *The palgrave handbook of race and ethnic inequalities in education* (pp. 39–69). Palgrave Macmillan. doi:10.1057/9781137317803_3

Sakamoto, I., Chin, M., & Young, M. (2010). "Canadian experience," employment challenges, and skilled immigrants: A close look through "tacit knowledge.". *Canadian Social Work*, *12*, 145–151. https://tspace.library.utoronto.ca/handle/1807/94782

Salamone, F. A. (1976). The arrow and the bird: Proverbs in the solution of Hausa conjugal conflicts. *Journal of Anthropological Research*, *32*(4), 358–371. doi:10.1086/jar.32.4.3630022

Salazar, S. M. (2013). Laying a foundation for artmaking in the 21st century: A description and some dilemmas. *Studies in Art Education*, *54*(3), 246–259. doi:10.1080/00393541.2013.11518897

Salicrú i Lluch, R. (2008). Crossing Boundaries in Late Medieval Mediterranean Iberia: Historical Glimpses of Christian-Islamic Intercultural Dialogue. *International Journal of Euro-Mediterranean Studies*, *1*(1).

Salomão, A. C. B. (2011). The education of teacher educators: Perspectives of collaboration between undergraduate and graduate students in the Project Teletandem Brazil. *Revista Brasileira de Lingüística Aplicada*, *11*, 653–678.

Sandeen, C. (2013). Integrating MOOCs into traditional higher education: The emerging "MOOC 3.0" era. *Change: The Magazine of Higher Learning*, *45*(6), 34–39. doi:10.1080/00091383.2013.842103

Sandelowski, M., Voils, C. I., & Barroso, J. (2006). Defining and designing mixed research synthesis studies. *Research in the Schools*, *13*(1), 29–40. PMID:20098638

Sanger, C. S. (2020). Diversity, inclusion, and context in Asian higher education. In S. S. Sanger & N. W. Gleason (Eds.), *Diversity and inclusion in global higher education* (pp. 1-30). Palgrave Macmillan. doi:10.1007/978-981-15-1628-3_1

Sawir, E. (2005). Language difficulties of international students in Australia: The effects of prior learning experience. *International Education Journal, 6*(5), 567–580. https://files.eric.ed.gov/fulltext/EJ855010.pdf

Sawir, E. (2005). Language Difficulties of International Students in Australia: The Effects of Prior Learning Experience. *International Education Journal, 6*(5), 56780.

Sawir, E., Marginson, S., Deumert, A., Nyland, C., & Ramia, G. (2008). Loneliness and international students: An Australian study. *Journal of Studies in International Education, 12*(2), 148–180.

Sawyer, R. K. (2017). Teaching creativity in art and design studio classes: A systematic literature review. *Educational Research Review, 22*, 99–113. doi:10.1016/j.edurev.2017.07.002

Scales, P. C., Roehlkepartain, E. C., Neal, M., Kielsmeier, J. C., & Benson, P. L. (2006). Reducing academic achievement gaps: The role of community service and service-learning. *Journal of Experiential Education, 29*(1), 38–60. doi:10.1177/105382590602900105

Scarlat, C. (2007). Teaching decision-making process through proverb cases: 12 Romanian proverbs. In *Proceedings of the Eighth International Conference on Operational & Quantitative Management(ICOQM-8): "Emerging Perspectives of Decision Making in a New Globalized World: Theory, Practice and Future Directions"* (pp. 400-406). Academic Press.

Scarlat, C. (2013). Project Management Skills. Lecture notes. 2008 – 2014. Mikkeli University of Applied Sciences.

Scarlat, C. (2014). Proverbele: sinteză a experienţei de viaţă şi lecţiilor învăţate din managementul proiectelor [Proverbs: a synthesis of life-experience and lessons learnt on project management. In Managementul Proiectelor [Project Management] (pp. 135-160). Ed. Printech.

Scarlat, C. (2016). Project Management. Lecture notes. 2013 – 2016. Karel de Grote University College.

Scarlat, C. (2020). Communication Revolutions that Marked the History of Education. Proverbs in Education – Theses and Paradoxes. In M. Carmo (Ed.), *Proceedings of the International Conference Education and New Developments–END 2020* (pp. 266-270). InScience Press.

Scarlat, C. (2021). Today's Higher Education at a Crossroads. The Critical Point and Paradigm Shift in the Educator's Role. In M. Carmo (Ed.), Education Applications & Developments, Advances in Education and Educational Trends Series (pp. 265-277). InScience Press.

Scarlat, C., & Afendras, E. (2007, October). *Precursors to 21ˢᵗ Century 'Global' Business Management: Proverbial expressions from the Balkans* [Paper presentation]. Twelfth Annual AUSACE International Conference: "Communication at the Crossroad of Globalization", Dubai, UAE.

Scarlat, C., & Afendras, E. (2008, November). *Proverb Culture in Balkans – Communication Bridge between the Arabic Wisdom and Western Modern Management* [Paper presentation]. Thirteenth Annual AUSACE International Conference "Best Communication Practices in an Interconnected World", Richmond, VA, United States.

Scarlat, C., & Kasim, A. (2008, December). *Bridging the gap between Asian and European cultures through common proverb metaphors – in order to facilitate the business communication and international business* [Paper presentation]. The International Conference on International Studies (ICIS): "The Asia Pacific Region: Contemporary Trends and Challenges", Kuala Lumpur, Malaysia.

Scarlat, C., & Pavan, E. (2011). Is It the Same Old Story? It Is the Modern Business Management! In C. Jayachandran & S. Seshadri (Eds.), *Proceedings of the Twelfth International Conference of the Society for Global Business & Economic Development SGBED 2011: "Building Capabilities for Sustainable Global Business: Balancing Corporate Success & Social Good"* (pp. 830-839). Academic Press.

Scarlat, C., & Stănciulescu, G. D. (2021). Covid-19 Pandemic: Threat or Accelerator? The Case of Romanian Book Publishing Industry. In M. Al Haziazi, A. Al Hajri, K. P. Subramanian, & S. Muthuraman (Eds.), Co-creating the Post COVID-19 World: Exploring Sustainable Paths (pp. 83-98). Arab Open University.

Scarlat, C., & Taatila, V. (2009, February). *Transcending the geographical borders through business management and entrepreneurship metaphors: Romanian and Finnish proverbs* [Paper presentation]. The Third International Conference on "Transcending Horizons through Innovative Practices", Indore, India.

Scarlat, C., Panduru, D. A., & Stănciulescu, G. D. (2021). COVID-19 Pandemic: Threat, Opportunity or Accelerator? From Strategy Accelerator to Digital Acceleration. In *Proceedings of the 38th IBIMA (International Business Information Management Association) International Conference*. IBIMA Publishing. https://www.ibimapublishing.com

Scarlat, C. (2008a). Entrepreneurship and management in Romanians' proverbs. *UPB Scientific Bulletin, Series D, 70*(1), 13–22.

Scarlat, C. (2008b). Learning Business, Management, and Entrepreneurship by Proverb Cases: 21 Romanian Proverbs. *SPACE Journal Advances in Higher Education, 1*(1), 77–88.

Scarlat, C. (2015). *Cartea cu proverbe de management* [The Book with Management Proverbs]. Ed. Printech.

Scarlat, C. (2019). *O sută de proverbe ale Românilor pentru 100 de ani de management modern* [One hundred Romanians' proverbs for 100 years of modern management]. Ed. Niculescu.

Scarlat, C., & Albuquerque, A. (2009). Business, management and entrepreneurship in Romanian and Portuguese proverbs. *SPACE Journal Advances in Higher Education, 2*(1), 121–134.

Scarlat, C., & Petrişor, A.-I. (2021). Old Proverbs for a Future Sustainable Development: An environmental management perspective. *Present Environment and Sustainable Development Journal, 15*(1), 93–107. doi:10.15551/pesd2021151008

Schlee, R. P., & Harich, K. R. (2010). Knowledge and skill requirements for marketing jobs in the 21st century. *Journal of Marketing Education, 32*(3), 341–352. doi:10.1177/0273475310380881

Schmitt, D. (2005). Writing in the international classroom. In Teaching international students: Improving learning for all. London: Routledge.

Schmitt, N. (2010). *Researching vocabulary: A vocabulary research manual*. Palgrave Macmillan.

Schön, D. (1983). *The reflective practitioner: How practitioners think in practice*. Basic books.

Schönwetter, D. J., Sokal, L., Friesen, M., & Taylor, K. L. (2002). Teaching philosophies reconsidered: A conceptual model for the development and evaluation of teaching philosophy statements. *The International Journal for Academic Development, 7*(1), 83–97. doi:10.1080/13601440210156501

Schoorman, D., & Bogotch, I. (2010). Moving beyond 'diversity' to 'social justice': The challenge to reconceptualise multicultural education. *Intercultural Education, 21*(1), 79–85. doi:10.1080/14675980903491916

Schulz, B. (2008). The importance of soft skills: Education beyond academic knowledge. *NAWA Journal of Language and Communication*, 146-154.

Schutz, A., & Sandy, M. G. (2015). Friendship and the public stage: Revisiting Hannah Arendt's resistance to "political education". *Educational Theory*, *65*(1), 21–38. doi:10.1111/edth.12093

Scott, C., Safdar, S., Trilokekar, R., & El Masri, A. (2015). International students as "ideal immigrants" in Canada: A disconnect between policy makers' assumptions and the lived experiences of international students. *Comparative and International Education*, *43*(3), 5. Advance online publication. doi:10.5206/cie-eci.v43i3.9261

Scott, J. D., & Frontczak, N. T. (1996). Ad executives grade new grads: The final exam that counts. *Journal of Advertising Research*, *36*(2), 40–47.

Sellar, S., & Gale, T. (2011). Globalisation and student equity in higher education. *Cambridge Journal of Education*, *41*(1), 1–4. doi:10.1080/0305764X.2011.549652

Sert, N. (2008). The language of instruction dilemma in the Turkish context. *System*, *36*(2), 156–171. doi:10.1016/j.system.2007.11.006

Shadowen, N. L., Williamson, A. A., Guerra, N. G., Ammigan, R., & Drexler, M. L. (2019). Prevalence and correlates of depressive symptoms among international students: Implications for university support offices. *Journal of International Students*, *9*(1), 129–149. doi:10.32674/jis.v9i1.277

Shah, D. (2012). *The MOOC Juggernaut: One Year Later.* Retrieved from Class Central: https://www.classcentral.com/report/growth-of-moocs/

Shah, D. (2013). *The MOOC Juggernaut: Year 2.* Retrieved from Class Central: https://www.classcentral.com/report/the-mooc-juggernaut-year-2/

Shah, D. (2015). *By The Numbers: MOOCS in 2015.* Retrieved from Class Central: https://www.classcentral.com/report/moocs-2015-stats/

Shah, D. (2016). *By The Numbers: MOOCS in 2016.* Retrieved from Class Central: https://www.classcentral.com/report/mooc-stats-2016/

Shah, D. (2017). *By The Numbers: MOOCS in 2017.* Retrieved from Class Central: https://www.classcentral.com/report/mooc-stats-2017/

Shah, D. (2018). *By The Numbers: MOOCs in 2018.* Retrieved 08 15, 2019, from Class Central: https://www.classcentral.com/report/mooc-stats-2018/

Shah, D. (2019). *By The Numbers: MOOCs in 2019.* Retrieved from Class Central: https://www.classcentral.com/report/mooc-stats-2019/

Shah, D. (2020). *By The Numbers: MOOCs in 2020.* Retrieved from Class Central: https://www.classcentral.com/report/mooc-stats-2020/

Shah, D. (2014). *Online Courses Raise Their Game: A Review of MOOC Stats and Trends in 2014.* Retrieved from Class Central.

Shah, S. (2008). Leading multi-ethnic schools: Adjustments in concepts and practices for engaging with diversity. *British Journal of Sociology of Education*, *29*(5), 532–536. doi:10.1080/01425690802263684

Shakespeare-Finch, J., & Wickham, K. (2010). Adaptation of Sudanese refugees in an Australian context: Investigating helps and hindrances. *International Migration (Geneva, Switzerland)*, *48*(1), 23–46. doi:10.1111/j.1468-2435.2009.00561.x

Shao, K., Yu, W., & Ji, Z. (2013). An exploration of Chinese EFL students' emotional intelligence and foreign language anxiety. *Modern Language Journal*, *97*(4), 917–929. doi:10.1111/j.1540-4781.2013.12042.x

Shapiro, S., & MacDonald, M. T. (2017). From deficit to asset: Locating discursive resistance in a refugee-background student's written and oral narrative. *Journal of Language, Identity, and Education, 16*(2), 80–93. doi:10.1080/153484 58.2016.1277725

Sharma, S. (2005). Multicultural education: Teachers perceptions and preparation. *Journal of College Teaching and Learning, 2*(5). Advance online publication. doi:10.19030/tlc.v2i5.1825

Sharma, S., & Bumb, A. (2021). The Challenge Faced in Technology-Driven Classes during COVID-19. *International Journal of Distance Education Technologies, 19*(1), 66–88. doi:10.4018/IJDET.20210101.oa2

Shaw, L. (1995). *Humanistic and social aspects of teaching.* Retrieved June 14, 2005 from http://edweb.sdsu.edu/LShaw/ f95syll/ philos/phbehav.html

Shea, P., Fredericksen, E., Pickett, A., & Pelz, W. (2004). Faculty development, student satisfaction and reported learning in the SUNY Learning Network. In T. Duffy & J. Kirkley (Eds.), *Learner centered theory and practice in distance education* (pp. 343–377). Lawrence Erlbaum.

Shea, P., Sau Li, C., & Pickett, A. (2006). A study of teaching presence and student sense of learning community in fully online and web-enhanced college courses. *The Internet and Higher Education, 9*(3), 175–190. doi:10.1016/j. iheduc.2006.06.005

Sherry, M., Thomas, P., & Chui, W. H. (2010). International students: A vulnerable student population. *Higher Education, 60*(1), 33–46. doi:10.100710734-009-9284-z

Sidhu, R. (2006). *Universities and globalization: To market, to market.* Lawrence Erlbaum Associates Publishers. doi:10.4324/9781410617217

Siemens, G. (2003). *Connectivism by Siemens.* Retrieved from http://www.ceebl.manchester.ac.uk/events/archive/aligningcollaborativelearning/Siemens.pdf

Sikes, P., & Goodson, I. F. (2017). What have you got when you've got a life story? In I. F. Goodson, A. Antikainen, P. J. Sikes, & M. Andrews (Eds.), *International handbook on narrative and life history* (pp. 60–71). Routledge.

Sillitoe, J., Webb, J., & Zhang, M. C. (2005). Postgraduate research: The benefits for institutions, supervisors and students of working across and between cultures. In J. Carroll & J. Ryan (Eds.), Teaching international students: Improving learning for all (pp. 130-136). Routledge.

Singh, J. K. N. (2020). Academic Failure: Unspoken Experiences by International Postgraduate Students in a Malaysian University. *IAFOR Journal of Education: Studies in Education, 8*(4), 79-94. https://eric.ed.gov/?id=EJ1279427

Singh, J. K. N. (2021b). Online learning and best teaching practices in COVID-19 environment: A case study in Australia. *SEAMEO Journal, 2,* 47-53. https://www.seameo.org/img/Publications/SEAMES/SEAMEO%20Journal%202020%20 %20V2%20Special%20Issue.pdf

Singh, J. K. N. (2017). Human capital or talent development? A paradigm shift by Malaysian higher education. In H. de Wit, J. Gacel-Ávila, E. Jones, & N. Jooste (Eds.), *The globalization of internationalization: Emerging voices and perspectives.* Routledge.

Singh, J. K. N. (2021a). Academic resilience among international students: Lived experiences of postgraduate international students in Malaysia. *Asia Pacific Education Review, 22*(1), 129–138. doi:10.100712564-020-09657-7

Singh, J. K. N., & Chowdhury, H. (2021). Early-career international academics' learning and teaching experiences during COVID-19 in Australia: A collaborative autoethnography. *Journal of University Teaching & Learning Practice, 18*(5), 1–17. doi:10.53761/1.18.5.12

Singh, J. K. N., & Jack, G. (2018). The benefits of overseas study for international postgraduate students in Malaysia. *Higher Education*, *75*(4), 607–624. doi:10.100710734-017-0159-4

Singh, J. K. N., Jacob, J., Nagpal, S., & Inglis, S. (2021). Undergraduate international students' challenges in a flipped classroom environment: An Australian perspective. *Innovations in Education and Teaching International*, 1–12. Advance online publication. doi:10.1080/14703297.2021.1948888

Singh, J. K. N., & Jamil, H. (2021). International education and meaningful contributions to society: Exploration of postgraduate international students' perspectives studying in a Malaysian research university. *International Journal of Educational Development*, *81*, 102331. Advance online publication. doi:10.1016/j.ijedudev.2020.102331

Singh, J. K. N., Nagpal, S., Inglis, S., & Jacob-John, J. (2019). International students' experiences in a flipped class-room environment: An Australian perspective. *International Journal of Educational Management*, *33*(6), 1303–1315. doi:10.1108/IJEM-11-2018-0362

Slack, J. D., Miller, D. J., & Doak, J. (1993). The technical communicator as author: Meaning, power, authority. *Journal of Business and Technical Communication*, *7*(1), 12–36. doi:10.1177/1050651993007001002

Sleeman, J., Lang, C., & Dakich, E. (2019). International students' transition to university: Connection and disconnection in online group work interactions. *Student Success*, *10*(2), 35–45. doi:10.5204sj.v10i2.1300

Sleeter, C. E. (2011). *The academic and social value of ethnic studies. A research review*. NEA. https://files.eric.ed.gov/fulltext/ED521869.pdf

Smith, C. (2016). Promoting international student success. In American Association of Collegiate Registrars and Admissions Officers (Ed.), The AACRAO international guide: A resource for international education professionals (pp. 105-115). American Association of Collegiate Registrars and Admissions Officers.

Smith, C. (2020). International Students and Their Academic Experiences: Student Satisfaction, Student Success Challenges, and Promising Teaching Practices. In Rethinking Education Across Borders (pp. 271–287). Springer. doi:10.1007/978-981-15-2399-1_16

Smith, C. A., Zhou, G., Potter, M., & Wang, D. (2019). Connecting best practices for teaching linguistically and cultur-ally diverse international students with international student satisfaction and student perceptions of student learning. *Advances in Global Education and Research*, *3*, 252-265. https://scholar.uwindsor.ca/educationpub/24

Smith, C. A., Zhou, G., Potter, M., & Wang, D. (2019a). Connecting Best Practices for Teaching Linguistically and Culturally Diverse International Students with International Student Satisfaction and Student Perceptions of Student Learning. *Advances in Global Education and Research*, *3*, 252-265. https://scholar.uwindsor.ca/educationpub/24/

Smith, C., Zhou, G., Potter, M., & Wang, D. (2019). Connecting best practices for teaching linguistically and culturally diverse international students with international student satisfaction and student perceptions of student learning. *Advances in Global Education and Research, 3*, 252-265.

Smith, C., Zhou, G., Potter, M., & Wang, D. (2019). Connecting Best Practices for Teaching Linguistically and Cultur-ally Diverse International Students with International Student Satisfaction and Student Perceptions of Student Learning. *Advances in Global Education and Research, 3*, 252-265. https://scholar.uwindsor.ca/educationpub/24

Smith, C., Zhou, G., Potter, M., Wang, D., Menezes, F., & Kaur, G. (2021). Connecting best practices for teaching inter-national students with student satisfaction: A review of STEM and non-STEM student perspectives. In V. Tavares (Ed.), Multidisciplinary perspectives on international student experience in Canadian higher education (pp. 63-80). IGI Global.

Smith, A. C., Zhou, G., Potter, M., & Wang, D. (2019). Connecting best practices for teaching linguistically and culturally diverse international students with international student satisfaction and student perceptions of student learning. *Advances in Global Education and Research*, *3*, 252–265.

Smith, B. (2017). Narrative inquiry and autoethnography. In M. L. Silk, D. L. Andrews, & H. Thorpe (Eds.), *Routledge Handbook of Physical Cultural Studies* (pp. 505–515). Routledge. doi:10.4324/9781315745664-51

Smith, C. (2016). International Student Success. *Strategic Enrolment Quarterly*, *4*(2), 61–73. doi:10.1002em3.20084

Smith, C. (2020). International students and their academic experiences: Student satisfaction, student success challenges, and promising teaching practices. In U. Galuee, S. Sharma, & K. Bista (Eds.), *Rethinking education across borders: Emerging issues and critical insight on globally mobile students* (pp. 271–287). Springer Nature.

Smith, C., Zhou, G., Potter, M., & Ammar, F. (2021). Engaging diverse international students: Promising online teaching practices. In J. Christensen Hughes, J. Mighty, & D. Stockley (Eds.), *Taking stock 2.0: Transforming and learning in higher education*. Society for Teaching and Learning in Higher Education.

Smith, C., Zhou, G., Potter, M., Wang, D., Pecoraro, M., & Paulino, R. (2019). Variability by individual student characteristics of student satisfaction with promising international student teaching practices. *Literacy Information and Computer Education Journal*, *10*(2), 3160–3169.

Smith-Carrier, T. (2020, October 20). Low funding for universities puts students at risk for cycles of poverty, especially in the wake of COVID-19. *Academic Matters*. https://academicmatters.ca/low-funding-for-universities-puts-students-at-risk-for-cycles-of-poverty-especially-in-the-wake-of-covid-19/

Smothers, T. (2000). Biblical Wisdom in its Ancient Middle Eastern Context. In M. E. Tate, H. W. Ballard, & D. W. Tucker (Eds.), *An Introduction to Wisdom Literature and the Psalms*. Mercer University Press.

Song, B., Zhao, Y., & Zhu, J. (2021). COVID-19-related Traumatic Effects and Psychological Reactions among International Students. *Journal of Epidemiology and Global Health*, *11*(1), 117–123. doi:10.2991/jegh.k.201016.001 PMID:33605116

Song, L., Singleton, E. S., Hill, J. R., & Koh, M. H. (2004). Improving online learning: Student perceptions of useful and challenging characteristics. *The Internet and Higher Education*, *7*(1), 59–70. doi:10.1016/j.iheduc.2003.11.003

Song-Turner, H. (2008). Plagiarism: Academic Dishonesty or 'Blind Spot' of Multicultural Education? *Australian Universities Review*, *50*(2), 38–50.

Song, X. (2019). "Chinese students syndrome" in Australia: Colonial modernity and the possibilities of alternative framing. *Higher Education*, *79*(4), 605–618. doi:10.100710734-019-00426-z

Song, X., & Cadman, K. (2013). Education With(out) Distinction: Beyond Graduate Attributes for Chinese International Students. *Higher Education Research & Development*, *32*(2), 258–271. doi:10.1080/07294360.2012.673573

South Asian Mental Health Alliance. (2021). *About Us*. http://samhaa.org/about

Sovic, S., & Blythman, M. (2013). *International Students Negotiating Higher Education: Critical perspectives*. Routledge.

Sowa, P. A. (2002). How valuable are student exchange programs? *New Directions for Higher Education*, *2002*(117), 63–70. doi:10.1002/he.49

Sperber, D., & Wilson, D. (1986). *Relevance: Communication and Cognition*. Blackwell.

Spry, T. (2001). Performing Autoethnography: An Embodied Methodological Praxis. *Qualitative Inquiry*, *7*(6), 706–732. doi:10.1177/107780040100700605

Stahlke Wall, S. (2016). Toward a moderate autoethnography. *International Journal of Qualitative Methods*, *15*(1), 1–9. doi:10.1177/1609406916674966

Stallings, D. (2002). Measuring success in the virtual university. *Journal of Academic Librarianship*, *28*(1-2), 47–53. doi:10.1016/S0099-1333(01)00300-7

Stanchevici, D., & Siczek, M. (2019). Performance, interaction, and satisfaction of graduate EAP students in a face-to-face and an online class: A comparative analysis. *TESL Canada Journal*, *36*(3), 132–153. doi:10.18806/tesl.v36i3.1324

Stanford University. (2011). Retrieved from Stanford Engineering Everywhere: https://see.stanford.edu

Starke-Meyerring, D., & Wilson, M. (2008). Learning environments for a globally networked world: emerging visions. Designing globally networked environments: Visionary partnerships, policies, and pedagogies.

Statistics Canada. (2016). *Census profile Surrey and BC*.https://www.statcan.gc.ca/eng/start

Statistics Canada. (2020, November 25). International students accounted for all of the growth in postsecondary enrolments in 2018/2019. *The Daily*. https://www150.statcan.gc.ca/n1/daily-quotidien/201125/dq201125e-eng.htm

Statistics Canada. (2021). *Distribution of International Student Enrolments, by Level of Tertiary Education*. Statistics Canada. https://www150.statcan.gc.ca/

Statistics Canada. (2021a). *Post-secondary enrolments, by international standard classification of education, institution type, classification of instructional programs, STEM and BHASE groupings, status of student in Canada, age group and gender* (Table 37-10-0163-01). doi:10.25318/3710016301-eng

Statistics Canada. (2021b). *Canadian and international tuition fees by level of study* (Table 37-10-0045-01). doi:10.25318/3710004501-eng

Stein, S. (2018). National Exceptionalism in the "EduCanada" Brand: Unpacking the Ethics of Internationalization Marketing in Canada. *Discourse (Abingdon, England)*, *39*(3), 461–477. doi:10.1080/01596306.2016.1276884

Stevens Initiative. (2021). *2021 Survey of the Virtual Exchange Field Report*. The Aspen Institute.

Stier, J. (2004). Taking a critical stance toward internationalization ideologies in higher education: Idealism, instrumentalism and educationalism. *Globalisation, Societies and Education*, *2*(1), 83–97. doi:10.1080/14767720420000177069

Stoesz, B., & Eaton, S. E. (2020). Academic Integrity Policies of Publicly Funded Universities in Western Canada. *Educational Policy*, *00*(0), 1–20. doi:10.1177/0895904820983032

Stoesz, B., Eaton, S. E., Miron, J. B., & Thacker, E. (2019). Academic Integrity and Contract Cheating Policy Analysis of Colleges in Ontario, Canada. *International Journal for Educational Integrity*, *15*(1), 1–18. doi:10.100740979-019-0042-4

Sutherland-Smith, W. (2008). *Plagiarism, the internet and student learning: Improving academic integrity*. Routledge. doi:10.4324/9780203928370

Svensson, L., & Wihlborg, M. (2010). Internationalising the Content of Higher Education: The Need for a Curriculum Perspective. *Higher Education*, *60*(6), 595–613. doi:10.100710734-010-9318-6

Tang, R. (Ed.). (2012). *Academic writing in a second or foreign language: Issues and challenges facing ESL/EFL academic writers in higher education contexts*. Continuum.

Tannen, D. (1981). Health to Our Mouths: Formulaic Expressions in Turkish and Greek. In F. Coulmas (Ed.), *Conversational Routine* (pp. 37–54). Mouton. doi:10.1515/9783110809145.37

Tanner, D., & Tanner, L. N. (1990). *History of the school curriculum*. Macmillan Publisher Co.

Tao, Y., & Hu, R. J. (2013). Challenges and problems of overseas Chinese students socializing into international academic settings. In *Proceedings of the 2013 Conference on Education Technology and Management Science*. Atlantis Press.

Taras, V., Caprar, D., Rottig, D., Sarala, R. M., Zakaria, N., Zhao, F., Jiménez, A., Wankel, C., Lei, W. S., Minor, M. S., Bryla, P., Ordeñana, X., Bode, A., Schuster, A., Vaiginiene, E., Froese, F. J., Bathula, H., Yajnik, N., Baldegger, R., & Huang, V. Z. (2013). A global classroom evaluating the effectiveness of global virtual collaboration as a teaching tool in management education. *Academy of Management Learning & Education, 12*(3), 414–435. Advance online publication. doi:10.5465/amle.2012.0195

Taskoh, A. K. (2020). Internationalization in Canadian higher education institutions: Ontario. *Higher Education for the Future, 7*(2), 97–117. doi:10.1177/2347631120930538

Tate, M. E., Ballard, H. W., & Tucker, D. W. (Eds.). (2000). *An Introduction to Wisdom Literature and the Psalms*. Mercer University Press.

Tatzl, D. (2011). English-medium masters' programmes at an Austrian university of applied sciences: Attitudes, experiences and challenges. *Journal of English for Academic Purposes, 10*(4), 252–270. doi:10.1016/j.jeap.2011.08.003

Taylor, E., Gillborn, D., & Ladson-Billings, G. (2009). *Foundations of critical race theory in education*. Routledge.

Taylor, F. W. (1911). *The Principles of Scientific Management*. Harper and Brothers.

Taylor, S. (2008). Schooling and settlement of refugee young people in Queensland: '…The challenges are massive'. *Social Alternatives, 27*(3), 58–65. https://bit.ly/3hWSTIt

Te Wiata, I. (2001). A big ask: To what extent can universities develop useful generic skills? In C. K. F. Bevan (Ed.), *Knowledge Demands for the New Economy* (pp. 290–297). Australian Academic Press.

Telles, J. A. (2015). Learning foreign languages in teletandem: Resources and strategies. *Documentação de Estudos em Lingüística Teórica e Aplicada, 31*(3), 603–632. doi:10.1590/0102-4450226475643730772

Terry, L., Naylor, R., Nguyen, N., & Rizzo, A. (2016). *Not yet there: an investigation into the access and participation of students from humanitarian refugee background in the Australian Higher ducation System*. Centre for the Study of Higher Education, The University of Melbourne.

The Higher Education Academy. (2014). *Addressing plagiarism*. https://www.aqa.ac.nz/sites/all/files/addressing_plagiarism.pdf

Thompson, B., Bagby, J. H., Sulak, T. N., Sheets, J., & Trepinski, T. M. (2017). The Cultural Elements of Academic Honesty. *Journal of International Students, 7*(1), 136–153. doi:10.32674/jis.v7i1.249

Tinto, V. (1993). Building community. *Liberal Education, 79*(4), 16–21. PMID:10124451

Tinto, V. (1993). *Leaving college: Rethinking the causes and cures of student attrition*. University of Chicago Press.

Tobbell, J., & O'Donnell, V. L. (2013). Transition to postgraduate study: Postgraduate ecological systems and identity. *Cambridge Journal of Education, 43*(1), 123–138. doi:10.1080/0305764X.2012.749215

Todd, D. (2019a, December). An inside look at Indian students in Canada. *The Vancouver Sun.* https://vancouversun.com/news/staff-blogs/an-inside-look-at-indian-students-in-canada

Todd, D. (2019b, September 3). Over-reliance on students from India and China sparks Ottawa reaction. *The Vancouver Sun.* https://vancouversun.com/opinion/columnists/douglas-todd-feds-to-address-over-reliance-on-students-from-india-and-chinaSun

Tracy, B. (2017, October 30). Why emotional intelligence is indispensable for leaders [Web log post]. *Forbes*. https://www.forbes.com/sites/forbescoachescouncil/2017/10/30/why-emotional-intelligence-is-indispensable-for-leaders/amp/

Tran, L. T. (2009). Making visible 'hidden' intentions and potential choices: International students in intercultural communication. *Language and Intercultural Communication*, *9*(4), 271–284. doi:10.1080/14708470902807693

Tran, L. T. (2020). Teaching and engaging international students: People-to-people connections and people-to-people empathy. *Journal of International Students*, *10*(3), xii–xvii. https://doi.org/10.32674/jis.v10i3.2005

Tran, T., & Thao, T. (2016). 'I'm not like that, why treat me the same way?' The impact of stereotyping international students on their learning, employability, and connectedness with the workplace. *Australian Educational Researcher*, *43*(2), 203–220. doi:10.100713384-015-0198-8

Traoré, R. L. (2004). Colonialism continued: African students in an urban high school in America. *Journal of Black Studies*, *34*(3), 348–369. doi:10.1177/0021934703258986

Treasury, H. M. (2000). *Productivity in the UK: The evidence and the Government's approach*. UK Treasury.

Trilokekar, R., Safdar, S., El Masri, A., & Scott, C. (2014). *International education, labour market and future citizens: prospects and challenges for Ontario*. Unpublished Report, Ontario Human Capital Research.

Trilokekar, R. D., Thomson, K., & El Masri, A. (2019). *Open borders, closed minds: The experiences of international students in the Ontario labour market. In Internationalization and Employability in Higher Education*. Routledge. doi:10.4324/9781351254885-8

Trilokekar, R., & El Masri, A. (2019). "International students are … golden": Canada's changing policy contexts, approaches, and national peculiarities in attracting international students and future immigrants. In A. H. Kim & M. Kwak (Eds.), *Outward and upward mobilities: International students in Canada, their families, and structuring institutions* (pp. 25–55). University of Toronto Press., doi:10.3138/9781487530563-005

Trilokekar, R., & Kukar, P. (2011). Disorienting Experiences During Study Abroad: Reflections of Pre-service Teacher Candidates. *Teaching and Teacher Education*, *27*(7), 1141–1150. doi:10.1016/j.tate.2011.06.002

Trullas, I., Simo, P., Fusalba, O. R., Fito, A., & Sallan, J. M. (2018). Student-perceived organizational support and perceived employability in the marketing of higher education. *Journal of Marketing for Higher Education*, *28*(2), 1–16. doi:10.1080/08841241.2018.1488334

Tsai, J. L., Ying, Y., & Lee, P. A. (2000). The meaning of "being Chinese" and "being American": Variation among Chinese American young adults. *Journal of Cross-Cultural Psychology*, *31*(3), 302–332.

Tsai, S. C. (2016). Perceptions of East Asian Students in Canadian Graduate Schools: What They May Indicate about a Chinese Model of Education. In C. P. Chou & J. Spangler (Eds.), *Chinese education models in a global age* (pp. 217–230). Springer. doi:10.1007/978-981-10-0330-1_16

Tseng, H. W., & Walsh, E. J. Jr. (2016). Blended vs. traditional course delivery: Comparing students' motivation, learning outcomes, and preferences. *Quarterly Review of Distance Education*, *17*(1).

Tucker, W. D. (2000). Literary Forms in the Wisdom Literature. In M. E. Tate, H. W. Ballard, & D. W. Tucker (Eds.), *An Introduction to Wisdom Literature and the Psalms*. Mercer University Press.

Turner, Y. (2006). Chinese students in a UK business school: Hearing the student voice in reflective teaching and learning practice. *Higher Education Quarterly*, *60*(1), 27–51.

Turner, Y. (2009). "Knowing me, knowing you," is there nothing we can do? Pedagogic challenges in using group work to create an intercultural learning space. *Journal of Studies in International Education, 13*(2), 240–255. doi:10.1177/1028315308329789

Tusasiirwe, S., Kansiime, P., Eyaa, S., Namisango, F., & Bulamu, N. (2021). Living and revitalizing Ubuntu: Challenges of passing on Ubuntu values to the younger generation and attempted strategies to overcome them. In *Understanding ubuntu for enhancing intercultural communications* (pp. 85–101). IGI Global. doi:10.4018/978-1-7998-7947-3.ch008

Tweed, R. G., & Lehman, D. R. (2002). Learning considered within a cultural context: Confucian and Socratic approaches. *The American Psychologist, 57*(2), 89–99.

Tymon, A. (2013). The student perspective on employability. *Studies in Higher Education, 38*(6), 841–856. doi:10.10 80/03075079.2011.604408

Udacity. (2011). Retrieved from Udacity: https://www.udacity.com/

UNESCO. (2011). *WSIS Knowledge Commons.* Retrieved from http://www.wsiscommunity.org/pg/groups/14358/open-educational-resources-oer/

UNESCO. (2020). *Education: From disruption to recovery.* Retrieved from https://en.unesco.org/covid19/educationresponse

Universities Canada. (2017). *Canada's global moment: Students from around the world choose Canada.* https://www.univcan.ca/media-room/media-releases/canadas-global-moment-students-around-world-choose-canada/

Uptin, J., Wright, J., & Harwood, V. (2016). Finding education: Stories of how young former refugees constituted strategic identities in order to access school. *Race, Ethnicity and Education, 19*(3), 598–617. doi:10.1080/13613324.2014.885428

Valentine, D., & Cheney, R. S. (2001). Intercultural business communication, international students, and experiential learning. *Business Communication Quarterly, 64*(4), 90–104. doi:10.1177/108056990106400410

Van Dijk, T. A. (2015). Critical discourse analysis. In D. Tannen, H. E. Hamilton, & D. Schiffrin (Eds.), *The handbook of discourse analysis.* Wiley. doi:10.1002/9781118584194.ch22

Vanada, D. I. (2016). An equitable balance: Designing quality thinking systems in art education. *International Journal of Education & the Arts, 17*(11).

Vanderklippe, N. (2019, March 1). In a shift on Canadian campuses driven by Trump policies, Indian students now outnumber Chinese. *The Globe and Mail.* https://www.theglobeandmail.com/world/article-in-a-shift-on-canadian-campuses-driven-by-trump-policies-indian/

Vandeville, G. (2020). *The biggest resource we have is each other.* https://www.utoronto.ca/news/biggest-resource-we-have-each-other-how-u-t-s international-students-are-coping-covid-19

VeLure Roholt, R., & Fisher, C. (2013). Expect the unexpected: International short-term study course pedagogies and practices. *Journal of Social Work Education, 49*(1), 48–65. doi:10.1080/10437797.2013.755416

Veryaeva, K., & Solovyeva, O. (2021). The Influence of Gamification and Platform Affordances on User Engagement in Online Learning. *International Journal of Distance Education Technologies, 19*(1), 1–17. doi:10.4018/IJDET.2021010101

Vincent-Lancrin, S., Urgel, J., Kar, S., & Jacobin, G. (2019). *Measuring innovation in education 2019: What has changed in the classroom?* Educational Research and Innovation, OECD Publishing. doi:10.1787/9789264311671-en

Visser, J. (2008). Constructive Interaction with Change: Implications for Learners and the Environment in which They Learn. In J. V. Visser-Valfrey (Ed.), *Learners in a Changing Learning Landscape: Reflection from a Dialogue on New Roles and Expectations* (Vol. 12, pp. 11–35). Springer. doi:10.1007/978-1-4020-8299-3_2

Vygotsky, L. (1978). *Mind in society* (M. Cole, Trans.). Harvard University Press.

Wachsmuth, D., & Kilfoil, P. (2021). Two logics of regionalism: The development of a regional imaginary in the Toronto–Waterloo Innovation Corridor. *Regional Studies*, *55*(1), 63–76. doi:10.1080/00343404.2020.1817362

Wadhwa, R. (2016). Students on move: Understanding decision-making process and destination choice of Indian students. *Higher Education for the Future, 3*(1), 54-75. https://journals.sagepub.co/doi/10.1177/2347631115610221

Waller, V., Farquharson, K., & Dempsey, D. (2015). *Qualitative social research: Contemporary methods for the digital age*. Sage Publications.

Wall, F. E. (1943). The importance of technical writing in chemical education. *Journal of Chemical Education*, *20*(12), 580–586. doi:10.1021/ed020p580

Walton, J. (2010). Examining a transformative approach to communication education: A teacher-research study. *College Student Journal*, *44*(1), 157–177.

Wang, Y. (2003). *The contextual knowledge of language and culture in education: Exploring the American university experiences of Chinese graduate students*. https://aquila.usm.edu/theses_dissertations/2631/

Wang, A. I., & Tahir, R. (2020). The effect of using Kahoot! for learning–A literature review. *Computers & Education*, *149*, 1–22. doi:10.1016/j.compedu.2020.103818

Wang, C. C., Andre, K., & Greenwood, K. M. (2015). Chinese students studying at Australian universities with specific reference to nursing students: A narrative literature review. *Nurse Education Today*, *35*(4), 609–619. doi:10.1016/j.nedt.2014.12.005 PMID:25537169

Wang, C. M., & Reeves, T. C. (2007). Synchronous online learning experiences: The perspectives of international students from Taiwan. *Educational Media International*, *44*(4), 339–356. https://doi.org/10.1080/09523980701680821

Wang, F. (2009). Student experiences of English language training: A comparison of teaching in UK and Chinese contexts. *English Language Teaching*, *2*(3), 237–242. doi:10.5539/elt.v2n3p237

Wang, H. (2006). Teaching Asian students online: What matters and why? *PAACE Journal of Lifelong Learning*, *15*, 69–84.

Wang, X. W., Riaz, M., Haider, S., Alam, K. M., & Yang, M. (2021). Information Sharing on Social Media by Multicultural Individuals: Experiential, Motivational, and Network Factors. *Journal of Global Information Management*, *29*(6), 1–25. doi:10.4018/JGIM.20211101.oa22

Watkins, M. (2018). Culture, hybridity and globalisation: Rethinking multicultural education in schools. In Understanding Sociological Theory for Educational Practices (pp. 159-175). Cambridge University Press.

Watkins, M. (2011). Complexity reduction, regularities and rules: Grappling with cultural diversity in schooling. *Continuum*, *25*(6), 841–856. doi:10.1080/10304312.2011.617876

Webb, J., Schirato, T., & Danaher, G. (2002). Understanding bourdieu. *Sage (Atlanta, Ga.)*.

Webster, L., & Mertova, P. (2007). *Using narrative inquiry as a research method*. Routledge. doi:10.4324/9780203946268

Weekes, T., Phelan, L., Macfarlane, S., Pinson, J., & Francis, V. (2011). Supporting successful learning for refugee students: The Classroom Connect project. *Issues in Educational Research*, *21*(3), 310–329.

Weigand, E. (1999). Misunderstanding: The standard case. *Journal of Pragmatics*, *31*(6), 763–785. doi:10.1016/S0378-2166(98)00068-X

Wei, L., & Mayouf, M. A. (2009). The effects of the social status of the elderly in Libya on the way they institutionally interact and communicate with younger physicians. *Journal of Pragmatics*, *41*(1), 136–146. doi:10.1016/j.pragma.2008.09.001

Weiner, M. F. (1976). Don't waste a crisis—Your patient's or your own. *Medical Economics*, *53*(5), 227.

Weis, L., & Dolby, N. (Eds.). (2011). *Social class and education: Global perspectives*. Routledge.

Weligamage, S. S. (2009). *Graduates' employability skills: Evidence from literature review*. University of Kelaniya.

Wells, K. (2011). *Narrative inquiry*. Oxford University Press. doi:10.1093/acprof:oso/9780195385793.001.0001

Wenger, E. (1998). *Communities of practice: learning, meaning, and identity*. Cambridge University Press. doi:10.1017/CBO9780511803932

Wickramasinghe, V., & Perera, L. (2010). Graduates', university lecturers' and employers' perceptions towards employability skills. *Education + Training*, *52*(3), 226–244. doi:10.1108/00400911011037355

Wilkins, J. L. M. (2000). Preparing for the 21st Century: The status of quantitative literacy in the United States. *School Science and Mathematics*, *100*(8), 405–418. doi:10.1111/j.1949-8594.2000.tb17329.x

Willems, P. P., & Gonzalez-DeHass, A. R. (2012). School−community partnerships: Using authentic contexts to academically motivate students. *School Community Journal*, *22*(2), 9–30. https://www.adi.org/journal/2012fw/Willems-DeHassFall2012.pdf

Wilson, L. O. (1990). *Curriculum course packets ED 721 & 726* (Unpublished). School Curriculum-Hidden Curriculum-Messages, Students, Schools, Political, Example, and Public.

Wimpenny, K., & Orsini-Jones, M. (2020). Innovation in collaborative online international learning: A holistic blend. In D. Burgos (Ed.), Radical Solutions in eLearning (pp. 1-25). Springer. doi:10.1007/978-981-15-4952-6_1

Windle, J., & Miller, J. (2013). Migration integration: The reception of refugee-background students in Australian schools. In L. Bartlett & A. Ghaffar-Kucher (Eds.), *Refugees, immigrants, and education in the global south: Lives in motion* (pp. 196–209). Routledge.

Wit, H. D. (2020). Internationalization of higher education: The need for a more ethical and qualitative approach. *Journal of International Students*, *10*(1), 1–4.

Wong, J., Hian, B. T. C., Haldmann, A., & Agrawal, A. (2020, May 11). *Interviews with international students in Canada about the Covid-19 situation*. The World University Rankings. https://www.timeshighereducation.com/student/blogs/interviews-international-students-canada-about-covid-19-situation#

Wong, C. A., Eccles, J. S., & Sameroff, A. (2004). The influence of ethnic discrimination and ethnic identification on African American adolescents' school and socioemotional adjustment. *Journal of Personality*, *71*(6), 1197–1232. doi:10.1111/1467-6494.7106012 PMID:14633063

Woodley, X., Hernandez, C., Parra, J., & Negash, B. (2017). Celebrating difference: Best practice in culturally responsive teaching online. *TechTrends*, *6*(5), 470–478. https://doi.org/10.1007/s11528-017-0207-z

Woo, Y., & Reeves, T. C. (2007). Meaningful interaction in web-based learning: A social constructivist interpretation. *The Internet and Higher Education*, *10*(1), 15–25. doi:10.1016/j.iheduc.2006.10.005

Wright, S. (2008). Demanding knowledge–marketing and consumption. In D. Epstein, R. Boden, R. Deem, F. Rizvi, & S. Wright (Eds.), *Geographies of knowledge, geometries of power: Framing the future of higher education* (pp. 181–189). Routledge.

Wu, H., Garza, E., & Guzman, N. (2015). International student's challenge and adjustment to college. *Education Research International, 2015*, 1–9. Advance online publication. doi:10.1155/2015/202753

Wu, Q. (2014). Motivations and decision-making processes of mainland Chinese students for undertaking master's programs abroad. *Journal of Studies in International Education, 18*(5), 426–444. doi:10.1177/1028315313519823

Xiang, B. (2017). *Classroom engagement and participation among Chinese international graduate students: A case study*. Academic Press.

Xiao, H., & Petraki, E. (2007). An investigation of Chinese students' difficulties in intercultural communication and its role in ELT. *Journal of Intercultural Communication, 13*(6), 1–17.

Xiao, Y., & Watso, M. (2019). Guidance on conducting a Systematic Literature Review. *Journal of Planning Education and Research, 39*(1), 93–112. https://doi.org/10.1177%2F0739456X17723971

Xu, S., & Connelly, F. M. (2009). Narrative inquiry for teacher education and development: Focus on English as a foreign language in China. *Teaching and Teacher Education, 25*(2), 219–227. .tate.2008.10.006 doi:10.1016/j

Xue, M. (2013). Effects of group work on English communicative competence of Chinese international graduates in United States institutions of higher education. *Qualitative Report, 18*, 14.

Xu, M. (1991). The impact of English-language proficiency on international graduate students' perceived academic difficulty. *Research in Higher Education, 32*(5), 557–570. doi:10.1007/BF00992628

Xu, S. (2021). Processes and effects of test preparation for writing tasks in a high-stakes admission test in China: Implications for test takers. *Studies in Educational Evaluation, 70*, 101015. Advance online publication. doi:10.1016/j.stueduc.2021.101015

Yang, W., & Jing, X. (2021). Chinese Graduate Students at a Canadian University: Their Academic Challenges and Coping Strategies. In Multidisciplinary Perspectives on International Student Experience in Canadian Higher Education (pp. 120-136). IGI Global.

Yang, M., Webster, B., & Prosser, M. (2011). Travelling a thousand miles: Hong Kong Chinese students' study abroad experience. *International Journal of Intercultural Relations, 35*(1), 69–78. doi:10.1016/j.ijintrel.2010.09.010

Yao, C. W. (2015). *Sense of belonging in international students: Making the case against integration to US institutions of higher education*. Academic Press.

Yao, C. W. (2016). Better English is the Better Mind: Influence of Language Skills on Sense of Belonging in Chinese International Students. *The Journal of College and University Student Housing, 43*(1).

Yeh, C. J., & Inose, M. (2003). International students' reported English fluency, social support satisfaction, and social connectedness as predictors of acculturative stress. *Counselling Psychology Quarterly, 16*(1), 15–28. doi:10.1080/0951507031000114058

Yi, S. (2018). Why am I here? A self-study of an international art education student lost in transition. *International Journal of Education through Art, 14*(2), 197-210. doi:10.1386/eta.14.2.197_1

Yong, E., & Ashman, P. J. (2019). Integration of the structured development of communication skills within a chemical engineering curriculum at the University of Adelaide. *Education for Chemical Engineers, 27*, 20–27. doi:10.1016/j.ece.2018.12.002

Yorke, M. (2004). *Employability in higher education: what it is - what it is not*. Retrieved 13 July, 2018. https://www.skillsyouneed.com/general/graduate-employability-skills.html

Yorke, M. (2006). Employability in higher education: what it is – what it is not. Learning and Employability. Series 1. The Higher Education Academy

Zalat, M. M. (2021). The experiences, challenges, and acceptance of e-learning as a tool for teaching during the COVID-19 pandemic among university medical staff. *PLoS One*, *16*(3), e0248758.

Zamudio, M., Russell, C., Rios, F., & Bridgeman, J. L. (2011). *Critical race theory matters: Education and ideology.* Routledge. doi:10.4324/9780203842713

Zhang, H., Chen, K., Chen, C., & Schlegel, R. (2019). Personal aspirations, person-environment fit, meaning in work, and meaning in life: A moderated mediation model. *Journal of Happiness Studies*, *20*(5), 1481–1497. doi:10.100710902-018-0005-0

Zhang, J., & Pearlman, A. M. G. (2018). Expanding access to international education through technology-enhanced collaborative online international learning (COIL) courses. *International Journal of Technology in Teaching and Learning*, *1*(14), 1–11. doi:10.37120/ijttl.2018.14.1.01

Zhang, X., & Zhou, M. (2019). Interventions to promote learners' intercultural competence: A meta-analysis. *International Journal of Intercultural Relations*, *71*, 31–47. doi:10.1016/j.ijintrel.2019.04.006

Zhang, Y. L. (2013). Power distance in online learning: Experience of Chinese learners in U.S. higher education. *The International Review of Research in Open and Distributed Learning*, *14*(4). https://doi.org/10.19173/irrodl.v14i4.1557

Zhang, Y. S. D., & Noels, K. (2021). The frequency and importance of accurate heritage name pronunciation for post-secondary international students in Canada. *Journal of International Students*, *11*(3), 608–627. doi:10.32674/jis.v11i3.2232

Zhang, Z., & Zhou, G. (2010). Understanding Chinese international students at a Canadian university: Perspectives, expectations, and experiences. *Comparative and International Education*, *39*(3), 5. Advance online publication. doi:10.5206/cie-eci.v39i3.9162

Zhao, N., & McDougall, D. (2008). Cultural Influences on Chinese Students' Asynchronous Online Learning in a Canadian University. *Journal of Distance Education*, *22*(2), 59–79.

Zheng, X. (2010). Re-interpreting Silence: Chinese International Students' Verbal Participation in US Universities. *International Journal of Learning*, *17*(5), 451–464. doi:10.18848/1447-9494/CGP/v17i05/47068

Zhou, G., & Zhang, Z. (2014). A Study of the First Year International Students at a Canadian University: Challenges and Experiences with Social Integration. *Comparative and International Education/Éducation Comparée et Internationale*, *43*(2), 7.

Zhou, G., Liu, T., & Rideout, G. (2017). A study of Chinese international students enrolled in the Master of Education program at a Canadian university: Experiences, challenges, and expectations. *International Journal of Chinese Education*, *6*(2), 210–235. doi:10.1163/22125868-12340081

Zhou, G., Yu, Z., Rideout, G., & Smith, C. (2021). Why don't they participate in class?: A study of Chinese students' classroom participation in an international master of education program. In V. Tavares (Ed.), *Multidisciplinary perspectives on international student experience in Canadian higher education* (pp. 81–101). IGI Global. doi:10.4018/978-1-7998-5030-4.ch005

Zhou, J. (2015, May). International students' motivation to pursue and complete a Ph.D. in the U.S. *Higher Education*, *69*(5), 719–733. doi:10.100710734-014-9802-5

Zhou, Y. (2021). How Chinese Multinational Corporations Solve Cross-cultural Conflicts in Internationalization - A Case Study of SAIC's Merging of Ssangyong Motor. *Advances in Social Sciences Research Journal, 8*(5), 137–156. doi:10.14738/assrj.85.10181

Zhou, Y., Jindal-Snape, D., Topping, K., & Todman, J. (2008). Theoretical models of culture shock and adaptation in international students in higher education. *Studies in Higher Education, 33*(1), 63–75. doi:10.1080/03075070701794833

Zhu, M., Sabir, N., Bonk, C. J., Sari, A., Xu, S., & Kim, M. (2021). Addressing learner cultural diversity in MOOC design and delivery: Strategies and practices of experts. *Turkish Online Journal of Distance Education*, 1-25. doi:10.17718/tojde.906468

Zhu, W., & Flaitz, J. (2005). Using focus group methodology to understand international students' academic language needs: A comparison of perspectives. *Teaching English as a Second or Foreign Language, 8*(4), 1–11. http://tesl-ej.org/ej32/a3.html

Zimmerman, B. (2002). Becoming a self-regulated learner: An overview. *Theory into Practice, 41*(2), 64–70.

Zobel, J. & Hamilton, M. (2002). Managing student plagiarism in large academic departments. *Australian Universities Review, 45*.

About the Contributors

Clayton Smith is Professor at the University of Windsor in the Faculty of Education where he teaches at both the undergraduate and graduate levels. Over the course of his career, Dr. Smith has amassed significant knowledge and expertise in the areas of enrolment management, internationalization of higher education, and student success.

George Zhou has a PhD in science education from the University of Alberta. He is full professor in the Faculty of Education, University of Windsor, Canada. He taught at the City University of New York before he moved to Windsor. His research covers science education, teacher education, educational technology, comparative, and international education.

* * *

George Kofi Amoako, BSc (Hons, KNUST), MBA (Marketing, UG), Ph.D. (LondonMet), is an Associate Professor at the Department of Marketing at Ghana Communication Technology University in Accra Ghana, an academic and a practicing Chartered Marketer (CIM_UK) with a specialization in, Sustainability, Branding, CSR and Strategic Marketing. He was educated in Kwame Nkrumah University of Science and Technology in Kumasi Ghana and at the University of Ghana and the London School of Marketing (UK). He has considerable research, teaching, consulting and practice experience in the application of Marketing Theory and principles to everyday marketing challenges and management and Organizational issues. He is a Chartered Marketer with The Chartered Institute of Marketing-UK. He has consulted for Public Sector and Private organizations both in Ghana and UK. George has published extensively in internationally peer-reviewed academic journals and presented many papers at international conferences.

Gideon Boadu completed a PhD in Education at the University of Newcastle, Australia. Gideon has teaching and research interests in history education, teacher education and teacher professional development. He applies constructivist epistemology to teaching, with focus on the nexus between teacher reasoning, classroom practice, and curriculum mandates. Gideon is currently a Lecturer in the School of Education at Excelsia College, Sydney.

Abraham Cerveró-Carrascosa was awarded his International PhD at the Universitat de València. He is the leader of the TEFL modules for undergraduate and postgraduate teacher education at Florida Universitària in València, Spain. He is a former secondary school teacher and Erasmus coordinator and was a member of the official body of CLIL examiners in València. He has contributed to numerous national and international conferences and published work on multilingual policies, collaborative online international learning (COIL) and active methods in Higher Education.

Víctor del Corte Lora obtained a Diploma in Business Administration, a Master in Market Research and Marketing and his PhD in Business Administration and Marketing from the Universitat Jaume I of Castellón. He is a member of the AERT Research Group focusing his research on SNA, Innovation, Creativity and Industrial Clusters. His work has been published in journals such as Entrepreneurship and Regional Development. In addition to it, he has presented his work in congresses of Business Administration and Marketing such as, ACEDE, ERSA or AEMARK.

Alexandre Duarte, with a PhD in Communication Sciences from University of Minho, a Master degree in Communication & Image and a Bachelor in Marketing & Advertising by IADE, is the Ruler of several classes in Universidade Católica Portuguesa and in IADE/Universidade Europeia, visiting Professor in other Universities, researcher of the R&D Unit CECS from Universidade do Minho, and Course Coordinator of OFICINA de PORTFOLIO™. Throughout his career, Alexandre had the opportunity to work for several multinational advertising agencies, in Portugal and Brazil, such as TBWA, Saatchi & Saatchi, Ogilvy, W/Portugal, W/Brazil, Lowe&Partners, or BrandiaCentral as a Senior Creative Copywriter. Author of many seminars on communication, regularly participates in different conferences and lectures in both business and academic contexts. It is the former Communications Director of the Portuguese Federation of Krav Maga, Text Editor of the Surf Magazine SOUP and occasionally collaborates with many other academic and professional media. Between 2012 and 2014, was the Tutor of the EUROBEST Young Marketers Academy and in the beginning of 2014, was appointed CEO of RESTART, an Institute of Creativity, Arts and New Technologies. In 2018 was invited to teach in the Communication Sciences Master of UNIVERSIDADE CATÓLICA PORTUGUESA, where now Coordinates the Post-Graduation Courses in Advertising&Creativity and Service Design and, in 2019 was re-elected member of the Directors Board of EDCOM - European Institute for Commercial Communications Education.

Sarah Eyaa is a motivated and self-driven academic with a passion to research, share knowledge with students and support them through the learning process so that they can succeed academically and personally. She holds tertiary qualifications in the business and management, with over 18 years' experience in academic management, research, teaching, and curriculum development in a range of management, marketing, and business-related courses at tertiary level in Australia and Uganda.

Kyria Rebeca Finardi is a Senior Lecturer in the Department of Languages, Culture and Education (DLCE) and a researcher in the post-graduate programs of Education (PPGE) and Linguistics (PPGEL) at the Federal University of Espirito Santo (UFES). She has a Productivity (PQ) scholarship from Cnpq. At the undergraduate level, her teaching focuses on pre-service English language teacher education and at the post-graduate level it focuses on aspects related to languages in the production of knowledge, language policies in higher education, the use of technology in education and internationalization. She has an extensive list of publications including the books English in Brazil and English in the South. She was the President of the Brazilian Association of Applied Linguistics (ALAB) 2018-2019, is the co-founder and co-coordinator of the Ibero-America Association of Applied Linguistics (AIALA) and is the vice-president of the International Association of Applied Linguistics (AILA).

Samarth Gupta is a third year student of B.Tech. CSE. His research interests include machine learning and image classification.

Shikha Gupta is an Associate Professor, Computer Science, S.S. College of Business Studies, University of Delhi. In her rich experience that spans almost two and a half decades, she worked as a software analyst in her early career and later involved herself in teaching and research. Her present research interests include quantum-inspired computing and deep learning.

Xiangying Huo, holds a Ph.D. in Language, Culture, and Teaching (Education) from York University. She is an assistant professor and English language specialist at the University of Toronto. She has presented widely on ESL/EFL policy and pedagogy, writing studies, internationalization in higher education, intercultural and cross-cultural teaching and learning, anti-racism education, and World Englishes. She is the author of *Higher Education Internationalization and English Language Instruction: Intersectionality of Race and Language in Canadian Universities* (2020, Springer).

Phoebe EunKyung Kang is a doctoral candidate in Educational Leadership and Policy Program in OISE, University of Toronto. Her collaborative program is in Comparative International Development and Education from which she co-founded the East Asia Interest Group. Her research interests lie with internationalization in higher education, international students' equity and policy analysis in higher education contexts. She has recent publications in Migration and Language Education Journal and Journal of International Students and is a recent recipient of the Canadian Congress 2021 Graduate Merit Award.

Peninah Kansiime has been practicing social work for over thirteen years. Currently, she lectures social work at Excelsia College in Sydney, Australia. Peninah has an International Master's degree in Social Work and Human Rights from Gothenburg University in Sweden, and a Master of Philosophy in Public Mental Health from Stellenbosch University, South Africa. She completed her Bachelors degree in Social Work and Social Administration at Makerere University, Kampala. She has completed her doctoral degree in Social Work at the University of Newcastle, Australia. She has both domestic and international practice in the areas of child protection, gender-based violence, social administration, forced migration, HIV/AIDS, and disability with a range of individuals from diverse cultural backgrounds. Peninah uses a holistic and critical approach to social work and aims at helping students become critically reflective practitioners.

Clinton Kewley is an International Student Services Coordinator in the Faculty of Education, Brock University. His interests lie in equity, diversity, and inclusion with a specific emphasis on international students.

Elaine Khoo, Ph.D., is an Associate Professor (Teaching Stream) at the University of Toronto Scarborough (UTSC). She founded the English Language Development (ELD) support program in 2006 to proactively address diverse language development needs in ways that counter the deficit narrative on students with low English language proficiency. As the coordinator of the program, she has incorporated her research interests that include positive pedagogy in higher education, internationalization, technology-supported language learning, inclusive practices in academic integrity, language learning motivation, second language writing, and vocabulary studies into ELD programs to empower students to gain accelerated progress in academic reading, writing, and oral communication.

Rahul Kumar is an Assistant Professor in the Faculty of Education. His scholarship spans the areas of international education, quality in and of education, technology, and higher education.

Thu Le has been working as a lecturer for ten years at the Faculty of Foreign Languages, Ho Chi Minh University of Technology and Education before becoming a full-time Phd student in Educational Studies in the University of Windsor, Canada. Her research interests lie in technology-enhanced teaching and learning, online learning, TESOL and internationalization of higher education.

Lilach Marom is a department chair and a faculty member in the Department of Educational Studies at Kwantlen Polytechnic University. Her research is focused on questions of diversity, equity, and social justice in education and aims to highlight structural and institutional barriers to the diversification of teacher education and the teaching profession. Lilach has worked as an educator in multiple locations and countries (Israel, the United States, and Canada) with culturally and racially diverse populations. Her research has appeared in publications such as, Review of Education, Pedagogy, and Cultural Studies (2017), Teaching and Teacher Education (2019/2020), Race Ethnicity and Education (2019), Critical Studies is Education (2019), and Globalisation, Societies and Education (2021). Lilach's current project explores the experiences of international students in Canadian higher education.

Alfred Mupenzi is the Senior Project Support Officer for the Refugee, New and Emerging Communities (NEC) program and teaches Culture, Subjectivity and Schooling in the School of Education at Western Sydney University. Dr Mupenzi finished his Doctor of Philosophy (PhD) in Education at Western Sydney University in 2018. He also trained in Uganda as a high school teacher at Makerere University where he finished his Masters of Arts in Public Administration and Management. Dr Mupenzi's areas of specialisation are in equity, diversity and social justice education. He has published several peer reviewed articles on educational resilience the most recent being "Reflections on COVID-19 and impacts on equitable participation: the case of culturally and linguistically diverse migrant and/or refugee (CALDM/R) students in Australian higher education".

Jasvir Kaur Nachatar Singh is an award-winning Senior Lecturer at the Department of Management, Sport and Tourism, La Trobe Business School, La Trobe University, Australia. Dr Singh's research expertise is in higher education with a particular interest in exploring international students' lived experiences of academic success, employability, career aspirations and learning experiences in a blended learning environment. Dr Singh also explores lived experiences of international academics with leadership positions.

James Alan Oloo, PhD, is an Assistant Professor of Educational Administration, Policy, and Leadership at the Faculty of Education, University of Windsor, Canada.

Marina Orsini-Jones is Associate Head of School Global Engagement and Course Director for the MA in English Language Teaching and Applied Linguistics in the School of Humanities at Coventry University. Marina has published work on intercultural communicative competence, e-learning innovation, language awareness, CALL, digital literacies and e-portfolio-supported personal development planning. She has delivered numerous papers (including plenaries) at national and international conferences and has been invited to run pedagogical innovation workshops by various HEIs. She is currently investigating the features of Intercultural Communicative Competence (ICC) in Computer Mediated Communication (CMC). Recent publications include: Intercultural Communicative Competence for Global Citizenship with Fiona Lee in 2018 and a British Council ELT research report in 2019 on the re-purposing of existing MOOCs for teacher education in collaboration with Zou, Ma, Conde and Borthwick: https://www.teachingenglish.org.uk/article/b-meltt-blending-moocs-english-language-teacher-training. Marina is currently (2021) working on a British Council Funded research project on Virtual Exchange with Hanoi University of Science and Technology: ViVEXELT (Viet Nam Virtual Exchange for English Language Teaching).

Khanh Pham is a passionate and professional EFL lecturer at undergraduate level in Vietnam. Currently, he is working for the Faculty of Foreign Languages at HCMUTE, which is one of the most prestigious universities in the country. He holds his MA in TESOL from the University of Southern Queensland (Australia). His philosophy is to create a collaborative studying environment for his students that is encouraging and relevant to their learning needs. His research interests include educational technologies, teacher training, and translation and interpreting teaching.

Jody-Lynn Rebek is Assistant Professor at Algoma University, in the School of Business and Economics (Sault Ste. Marie, ON), and is also a serial social entrepreneur launching WaterWise, Hearterra, and has operated Vive Strategy Consulting for more than a decade. She is an interdisciplinary researcher who uses action research and a variety of qualitative and quantitative methodologies to engage individuals, teams, and communities in positive change. Her research topics centre around culture, management, governance, learning, strategy, and leadership development to promote and better understand wellbeing, inclusivity, team and human motivation and performance, creativity, and entrepreneurship.

Eunjung Riauka is an international education professional who is dedicated to helping students and higher education institutions better understand, engage with, global issues through international mobility programs and experiential learning. Leveraging over 10 years of experience in higher education in the field of international mobility programs, recruitment, partnership development & agreements, admissions (domestic/international), and assessment of transfer credits. Highly motivated and have a great interest in developing a strategic plan and direction in advancing internationalization agenda and positive student experience in post-secondary institutions.

Shannon Said is a social work researcher and practitioner, working with Pacific, Maori and culturally diverse people groups over the past ten years. He has held various positions as a researcher at Western Sydney University, The University of Sydney, Australian Catholic University and others in the areas of music and other cultures, support programs for disadvantaged and minority university student groups, and music therapy as an alternative for young people from trauma backgrounds. Shannon has more recently has worked as a Youth Access Practitioner at headspace and Youth Development Worker at Bridging the Gap.

Cezar Scarlat is a Professor within Department of Entrepreneurship & Management and PhD Supervisor within Doctoral School of Entrepreneurship, Business Engineering & Management at University "Politehnica" of Bucharest (UPB), Romania. He is teaching Technology Entrepreneurship, Business development and strategy, Project Management, Marketing as well as related courses at universities in Romania and abroad (Finland, Portugal, Belgium) – as visiting/exchange professor. Director of the

Center for Business Excellence from UPB for almost two decades (1991-2009) and currently running private consulting firm, he also acquired project management expertise by participation in over forty international programmes or projects. The author has two master degrees: Electronics engineering from UPB, and International business from Academy for Economic Studies from Bucharest. He got his PhD degree in management and industrial engineering at UPB. International exposure and experience by post-graduate studies in Romania and abroad (USA, Canada, France, Italy); research and study tours in Europe and North America. His list of publications counts: about forty books, book chapters and manuals; more than two hundred published articles and scientific reports on technology entrepreneurship, entrepreneurial education, management and administration, project management, business development, marketing, and related areas. Membership in numerous international bodies as well as member of scientific/editorial boards of many international journals – among them: Industrial Management & Data Systems (IMDS); Expert Systems with Applications (ESWA); Advances in Business Related Scientific Research Journal (ABSRJ).

Hanshu Wang is a researcher majored in digital education, she also interested in comparative education.

Meng Xiao holds an Ed.D. and M.Ed. degree in Social Justice Education. The Ed.D. focused on a collaborative specialization in Comparative, International and Development Education and the M.Ed. on a collaborative specialization in Environmental Studies at the University of Toronto. Meng was a research assistant in the Canada-China Partnership Grant Project, which explored the interactions between teachers in Canada and China as they learned about each other. The diverse coursework in her doctoral program, along with the preliminary research for her study has provided her with a substantial level of interdisciplinary familiarity with cross-cultural understanding of Chinese and Canadian education. This Ed.D. research aims to support Chinese international students' engagement in and out of the classroom in Canadian graduate schools.

Rakha Zabin is a full-time Ph.D. student in the Joint Ph.D. in Educational Studies Program at Brock University, Canada. Her research interest and experience lie in the areas of internationalization of higher education, institutional policy, educational administration, and leadership.

Syed Zaidi lives in Windsor, Ontario and works as an instructor for St. Clair College for Applied Arts and Technology. His educational curriculum vitae includes Bachelor of Arts in Political Science and Economics and Master of Arts in English Literature. Not only does he have an extensive teaching background in multiple international locations, but also he has proclivity for writing, reading and listening educational podcasts. He has also Master's degree in Education (Second Language Acquisition) from University of Windsor, Canada. Currently he is involved in a school project from the scratch in Windsor.

Hangyu Zhang is a researcher interested in English communication, TESOL, and applied linguistics. She has obtained two master's degrees in English Language and Literature and TESOL respectively.

468

Index

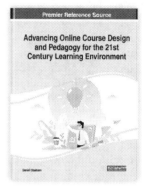

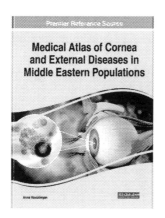

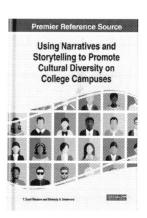

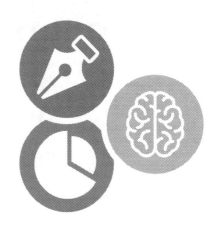

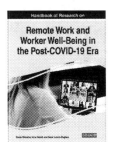
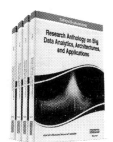
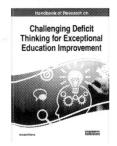